PISA 2009 Results: Overcoming Social Background

EQUITY IN LEARNING OPPORTUNITIES AND OUTCOMES

(VOLUME II)

OECD

This work is published on the responsibility of the Secretary-General of the OECD. The opinions expressed and arguments employed herein do not necessarily reflect the official views of the Organisation or of the governments of its member countries.

Please cite this publication as:

OECD (2010), PISA 2009 Results: Overcoming Social Background – Equity in Learning Opportunities and Outcomes (Volume II)
http://dx.doi.org/10.1787/9789264091504-en

ISBN 978-92-64-09146-7 (print)
ISBN 978-92-64-09150-4 (PDF)

The statistical data for Israel are supplied by and under the responsibility of the relevant Israeli authorities. The use of such data by the OECD is without prejudice to the status of the Golan Heights, East Jerusalem and Israeli settlements in the West Bank under the terms of international law.

Photo credits:
Getty Images © Ariel Skelley
Getty Images © Geostock
Getty Images © Jack Hollingsworth
Stocklib Image Bank © Yuri Arcurs

Foreword

One of the ultimate goals of policy makers is to enable citizens to take advantage of a globalised world economy. This is leading them to focus on the improvement of education policies, ensuring the quality of service provision, a more equitable distribution of learning opportunities and stronger incentives for greater efficiency in schooling.

Such policies hinge on reliable information on how well education systems prepare students for life. Most countries monitor students' learning and the performance of schools. But in a global economy, the yardstick for success is no longer improvement by national standards alone, but how education systems perform internationally. The OECD has taken up that challenge by developing PISA, the Programme for International Student Assessment, which evaluates the quality, equity and efficiency of school systems in some 70 countries that, together, make up nine-tenths of the world economy. PISA represents a commitment by governments to monitor the outcomes of education systems regularly within an internationally agreed framework and it provides a basis for international collaboration in defining and implementing educational policies.

The results from the PISA 2009 assessment reveal wide differences in educational outcomes, both within and across countries. The education systems that have been able to secure strong and equitable learning outcomes, and to mobilise rapid improvements, show others what is possible to achieve. Naturally, GDP per capita influences educational success, but this only explains 6% of the differences in average student performance. The other 94% reflect the potential for public policy to make a difference. The stunning success of Shanghai-China, which tops every league table in this assessment by a clear margin, shows what can be achieved with moderate economic resources in a diverse social context. In mathematics, more than a quarter of Shanghai-China's 15-year-olds can conceptualise, generalise, and creatively use information based on their own investigations and modelling of complex problem situations. They can apply insight and understanding and develop new approaches and strategies when addressing novel situations. In the OECD area, just 3% of students reach this level of performance.

While better educational outcomes are a strong predictor of economic growth, wealth and spending on education alone are no guarantee for better educational outcomes. Overall, PISA shows that an image of a world divided neatly into rich and well-educated countries and poor and badly-educated countries is out of date.

This finding represents both a warning and an opportunity. It is a warning to advanced economies that they cannot take for granted that they will forever have "human capital" superior to that in other parts of the world. At a time of intensified global competition, they will need to work hard to maintain a knowledge and skill base that keeps up with changing demands.

PISA underlines, in particular, the need for many advanced countries to tackle educational underperformance so that as many members of their future workforces as possible are equipped with at least the baseline competencies that enable them to participate in social and economic development. Otherwise, the high social and economic cost of poor educational performance in advanced economies risks becoming a significant drag on economic development. At the same time, the findings show that poor skills are not an inevitable consequence of low national income – an important outcome for countries that need to achieve more with less.

But PISA also shows that there is no reason for despair. Countries from a variety of starting points have shown the potential to raise the quality of educational outcomes substantially. Korea's average performance was already high in 2000, but Korean policy makers were concerned that only a narrow elite achieved levels of excellence in PISA. Within less than a decade, Korea was able to double the share of students demonstrating excellence in reading literacy. A major overhaul of Poland's school system helped to dramatically reduce performance variability among

schools, reduce the share of poorly performing students and raise overall performance by the equivalent of more than half a school year. Germany was jolted into action when PISA 2000 revealed a below-average performance and large social disparities in results, and has been able to make progress on both fronts. Israel, Italy and Portugal have moved closer to the OECD average and Brazil, Chile, Mexico and Turkey are among the countries with impressive gains from very low levels of performance.

But the greatest value of PISA lies in inspiring national efforts to help students to learn better, teachers to teach better, and school systems to become more effective.

A closer look at high-performing and rapidly improving education systems shows that these systems have many commonalities that transcend differences in their history, culture and economic evolution.

First, while most nations declare their commitment to education, the test comes when these commitments are weighed against others. How do they pay teachers compared to the way they pay other highly-skilled workers? How are education credentials weighed against other qualifications when people are being considered for jobs? Would you want your child to be a teacher? How much attention do the media pay to schools and schooling? Which matters more, a community's standing in the sports leagues or its standing in the student academic achievement league tables? Are parents more likely to encourage their children to study longer and harder or to spend more time with their friends or in sports activities?

In the most successful education systems, the political and social leaders have persuaded their citizens to make the choices needed to show that they value education more than other things. But placing a high value on education will get a country only so far if the teachers, parents and citizens of that country believe that only some subset of the nation's children can or need to achieve world class standards. This report shows clearly that education systems built around the belief that students have different pre-ordained professional destinies to be met with different expectations in different school types tend to be fraught with large social disparities. In contrast, the best-performing education systems embrace the diversity in students' capacities, interests and social background with individualised approaches to learning.

Second, high-performing education systems stand out with clear and ambitious standards that are shared across the system, focus on the acquisition of complex, higher-order thinking skills, and are aligned with high stakes gateways and instructional systems. In these education systems, everyone knows what is required to get a given qualification, in terms both of the content studied and the level of performance that has to be demonstrated to earn it. Students cannot go on to the next stage of their life – be it work or further education – unless they show that they are qualified to do so. They know what they have to do to realise their dream and they put in the work that is needed to achieve it.

Third, the quality of an education system cannot exceed the quality of its teachers and principals, since student learning is ultimately the product of what goes on in classrooms. Corporations, professional partnerships and national governments all know that they have to pay attention to how the pool from which they recruit is established; how they recruit; the kind of initial training their recruits receive before they present themselves for employment; how they mentor new recruits and induct them into their service; what kind of continuing training they get; how their compensation is structured; how they reward their best performers and how they improve the performance of those who are struggling; and how they provide opportunities for the best performers to acquire more status and responsibility. Many of the world's best-performing education systems have moved from bureaucratic "command and control" environments towards school systems in which the people at the frontline have much more control of the way resources are used, people are deployed, the work is organised and the way in which the work gets done. They provide considerable discretion to school heads and school faculties in determining how resources are allocated, a factor which the report shows to be closely related to school performance when combined with effective accountability systems. And they provide an environment in which teachers work together to frame what they believe to be good practice, conduct field-based research to confirm or disprove the approaches they develop, and then assess their colleagues by the degree to which they use practices proven effective in their classrooms.

Last but not least, the most impressive outcome of world-class education systems is perhaps that they deliver high-quality learning consistently across the entire education system, such that every student benefits from excellent learning opportunities. To achieve this, they invest educational resources where they can make the greatest difference, they attract the most talented teachers into the most challenging classrooms, and they establish effective spending choices that prioritise the quality of teachers.

These are, of course, not independently conceived and executed policies. They need to be aligned across all aspects of the system, they need to be coherent over sustained periods of time, and they need to be consistently implemented. The path of reform can be fraught with political and practical obstacles. Moving away from administrative and bureaucratic control toward professional norms of control can be counterproductive if a nation does not yet have teachers and schools with the capacity to implement these policies and practices. Pushing authority down to lower levels can be as problematic if there is not agreement on what the students need to know and should be able to do. Recruiting high-quality teachers is not of much use if those who are recruited are so frustrated by what they perceive to be a mindless system of initial teacher education that they will not participate in it and turn to another profession. Thus a country's success in making these transitions depends greatly on the degree to which it is successful in creating and executing plans that, at any given time, produce the maximum coherence in the system.

These are daunting challenges and thus devising effective education policies will become ever more difficult as schools need to prepare students to deal with more rapid change than ever before, for jobs that have not yet been created, to use technologies that have not yet been invented and to solve economic and social challenges that we do not yet know will arise. But those school systems that do well today, as well as those that have shown rapid improvement, demonstrate that it can be done. The world is indifferent to tradition and past reputations, unforgiving of frailty and complacency and ignorant of custom or practice. Success will go to those individuals and countries that are swift to adapt, slow to complain and open to change. The task of governments will be to ensure that countries rise to this challenge. The OECD will continue to support their efforts.

***

This report is the product of a collaborative effort between the countries participating in PISA, the experts and institutions working within the framework of the PISA Consortium, and the OECD Secretariat. The report was drafted by Andreas Schleicher, Francesca Borgonovi, Michael Davidson, Miyako Ikeda, Maciej Jakubowski, Guillermo Montt, Sophie Vayssettes and Pablo Zoido of the OECD Directorate for Education, with advice as well as analytical and editorial support from Marilyn Achiron, Simone Bloem, Marika Boiron, Henry Braun, Nihad Bunar, Niccolina Clements, Jude Cosgrove, John Cresswell, Aletta Grisay, Donald Hirsch, David Kaplan, Henry Levin, Juliette Mendelovitz, Christian Monseur, Soojin Park, Pasi Reinikainen, Mebrak Tareke, Elisabeth Villoutreix and Allan Wigfield. Volume II also draws on the analytic work undertaken by Jaap Scheerens and Douglas Willms in the context of PISA 2000. Administrative support was provided by Juliet Evans and Diana Morales.

The PISA assessment instruments and the data underlying the report were prepared by the PISA Consortium, under the direction of Raymond Adams at the Australian Council for Educational Research (ACER) and Henk Moelands from the Dutch National Institute for Educational Measurement (CITO). The expert group that guided the preparation of the reading assessment framework and instruments was chaired by Irwin Kirsch.

The development of the report was steered by the PISA Governing Board, which is chaired by Lorna Bertrand (United Kingdom), with Beno Csapo (Hungary), Daniel McGrath (United States) and Ryo Watanabe (Japan) as vice chairs. Annex C of the volumes lists the members of the various PISA bodies, as well as the individual experts and consultants who have contributed to this report and to PISA in general.

Angel Gurría
OECD Secretary-General

Table of Contents

This book has...

StatLinkS

**A service that delivers Excel® files
from the printed page!**

Look for the *StatLinks* at the bottom left-hand corner of the tables or graphs in this book.
To download the matching Excel® spreadsheet, just type the link into your Internet browser,
starting with the *http://dx.doi.org* prefix.
If you're reading the PDF e-book edition, and your PC is connected to the Internet, simply
click on the link. You'll find *StatLinks* appearing in more OECD books.

BOXES

FIGURES

Executive Summary

The best performing school systems manage to provide high-quality education to all students.
Canada, Finland, Japan, Korea and the partner economies Hong Kong-China and Shanghai-China all perform well above the OECD mean performance and students tend to perform well regardless of their own background or the school they attend. They not only have large proportions of students performing at the highest levels of reading proficiency, but also relatively few students at the lower proficiency levels.

Disadvantaged students may have access to more teachers, but not necessarily to the best teachers.
With the exception of Turkey, Slovenia, Israel and the United States, where socio-economically disadvantaged schools also tend to be deprived in terms of basic resources, such as larger student-staff ratios, OECD countries place at least an equal, if not a larger, number of teachers into socio-economically disadvantaged schools as those who are placed in advantaged schools. But despite this fact, disadvantaged schools still report great difficulties in attracting qualified teachers. In other words, in disadvantaged schools, quantity of resources does not necessarily translate into quality of resources since, in general, more advantaged students attend schools that have a higher proportion of full-time teachers who have an advanced university degree. Findings from PISA suggest that, in terms of teacher resources, many students face the double liability of coming from a disadvantaged background and attending a school with lower quality resources. Many countries also show a strong relationship between the socio-economic background of students and their success at school and, in some of these countries, these disparities are magnified by large variations in the schools' socio-economic backgrounds, that is, in the backgrounds of the students' peers.

Home background influences educational success, and schooling often appears to reinforce its effects. Although poor performance in school does not automatically follow from a disadvantaged socio-economic background, the socio-economic background of students and schools does appear to have a powerful influence on performance.
Socio-economic disadvantage has many facets and cannot be ameliorated by education policy alone, much less in the short term. The educational attainment of parents can only gradually improve, and average family wealth depends on the long-term economic development of a country and on a culture that promotes individual savings. However, even if socio-economic background itself is hard to change, PISA shows that some countries succeed in reducing its impact on learning outcomes.

While most of the students who perform poorly in PISA are from socio-economically disadvantaged backgrounds, some peers from similar backgrounds excel in PISA, demonstrating that overcoming socio-economic barriers to achievement is possible. Resilient students come from the bottom quarter of the distribution of socio-economic background in their country and score in the top quarter among students from all countries with similar socio-economic background. In Finland, Japan, Turkey, Canada and Portugal and the partner country Singapore, between 39% and 48% of disadvantaged students are resilient. In Korea and in partner economy Macao-China 50% and 56% of disadvantaged students can be considered resilient, and this percentage is 72% and 76% in partner economies Hong Kong-China and Shanghai-China, respectively.

Across OECD countries, a student from a more socio-economically advantaged background (among the top one seventh) outperforms a student from an average background by 38 score points, or about one year's worth of education, in reading. In New Zealand, France and the partner countries and economies Bulgaria and Dubai (UAE), this one point difference in socio-economic background is associated with a performance difference of more than 50 score points. On average across OECD countries, 14% of the differences in student reading performance within each country is associated with differences in students' socio-economic background. In Hungary and the partner countries Peru, Bulgaria and Uruguay, more than 20% of the differences in student performance is associated with differences in background.

Regardless of their own socio-economic background, students attending schools with a socio-economically advantaged intake tend to perform better than those attending schools with more disadvantaged peers.
In the majority of OECD countries, the effect of the school's economic, social and cultural status on students' performance far outweighs the effects of the individual student's socio-economic background. And the magnitude of the differences is striking. In Japan, the Czech Republic, Germany, Belgium and Israel and the partner countries Trinidad and Tobago and Liechtenstein, the performance gap between two students with similar socio-economic backgrounds, one of whom attends a school with an average socio-economic background and the another attending a school with an advantaged socio-economic background (among the top 16% in the country), is equivalent to more than 50 score points, on average, or more than a year's worth of education.

Across OECD countries, first-generation students – those who were born outside the country of assessment and who also have foreign-born parents – score, on average, 52 score points below students without an immigrant background
In New Zealand, Canada and Switzerland, 20% to 25% of students are from an immigrant background while the proportions are even higher in Liechtenstein (30%), Hong Kong-China (39%), Luxembourg (40%) and Qatar (46%). In Macao-China and Dubai (UAE), that percentage is at least 70%. There is no positive association between the size of the immigrant student population and average performance at the country or economy level, and there is also no relationship between the proportion of students with an immigrant background and the performance gaps between native and immigrant students. These findings contradict the assumption that high levels of immigration will inevitably lower the mean performance of school systems.

Students in urban schools perform better than students in other schools, even after accounting for differences in socio-economic background.
In Turkey, the Slovak Republic, Chile, Mexico and Italy, as well as the partner countries Peru, Tunisia, Albania, Argentina and Romania, the performance gap between students in urban schools and those in rural schools is more than 45 score points after accounting for differences in socio-economic background. This is more than one year of education across OECD countries. That gap is 80 score points or more – or two years of schooling – in Hungary and in the partner countries Bulgaria, Kyrgyzstan and Panama. However, this pattern is not observed in Belgium, Finland, Germany, Greece, Iceland, Ireland, Israel, the Netherlands, Poland, Sweden, the United Kingdom and the United States.

On average across the OECD, 17% of students come from single-parent families and they score five score points lower than students from other types of families after accounting for socio-economic background.
Among OECD countries, the gap is particularly large in the United States where, after accounting for socio-economic background, the performance difference between students from single-parent families and those from other types of families stands at 23 score points. In Ireland, Poland and Mexico, the gap is 13 score points and in Belgium, Japan and Luxembourg it is 10 score points, double the average among OECD countries. Among partner countries and economies students from single-parent families score 10 points lower than peers from other types of families after accounting for socio-economic background.

Parents' engagement with their children's reading life has a positive impact on their children's reading performance. Students whose parents reported that they had read a book with their child "every day or almost every day" or "once or twice a week" during the first year of primary school performed higher in PISA 2009 than students whose parents reported that they had done this "never or almost never" or "once or twice a month". On average across the 14 countries that had collected information on this question, the difference is 25 score points, but it ranges from 4 score points in the partner country Lithuania to 63 score points in New Zealand. Also, 15-year-olds whose parents discuss political or social issues once a week or more score 28 score points higher than those whose parents do not, or who talk about these issues less often. The performance advantage was largest in Italy, at 42 score points, and smallest in the partner economy Macao-China, and it is observed across all countries.

The following table summarises the key data of this volume. For each country, it shows the average score of 15-year-olds in reading and seven equity measures from PISA: *i)* and *ii)* two measures focusing on those that achieve the baseline level of proficiency in PISA: the proportion of boys and girls who score below Level 2; *iii)* a measure of those who overcome socio-economic disadvantaged and do best given their weak prospects, the proportion of resilient students; *iv)* and *v)* two measures of the relationship between student background and performance: the percentage of variation in student performance explained by the student's socio-economic background and the slope of the socio-economic gradient, the average gap in performance between students from different socio-economic backgrounds; and *vi)* and *vii)* two measures of equality in the distribution of educational resources, namely the quality and quantity of teachers. For the first five measures, cells shaded in light blue indicate values of quality or equity above the OECD average. Cells shaded in dark blue indicate values of equity below the OECD average. Cells shaded in medium blue indicate values that are not statistically different from the OECD average. In the last two columns, cells shaded in light blue indicate that disadvantaged schools are more likely to have more or better resources. Cells shaded in dark blue that advantaged schools are more likely to have more or better resources. Cells shaded in medium blue indicate values where disadvantaged and advantaged schools are equally likely to have more or better resources. In these two last columns, estimates in bold indicate that they are statistically different from the OECD average.

■ Table II.A ■
SUMMARY OF PISA MEASURES OF EDUCATIONAL EQUITY

Higher quality or equity than OECD average

Lower quality or equity than OECD average

At OECD average (no statistically significant difference)

Disadvantaged schools are more likely to have more or better resources, in **bold** if relationship is statistically different from the OECD average

Advantaged schools are more likely to have more or better resources, in **bold** if relationship is statistically different from the OECD average

Within country correlation is not statistically significant

	Mean reading score	Percentage of boys below proficiency Level 2	Percentage of girls below proficiency Level 2	Percentage of resilient students	Percentage of variance in student performance explained by students' socio-economic background	Slope of the socio-economic gradient	Correlation between the socio-economic background of schools and the percentage of teachers with university-level (ISCED 5A) among all full-time teachers	Correlation between socio-economic background of schools and the student/teacher ratio
OECD average	493	25	13	8	14	38	0.15	-0.15
Korea	539	10	4	14	11	32	-0.03	0.30
Finland	536	17	5	11	8	31	-0.01	0.08
Canada	524	18	7	10	9	32	0.03	0.09
New Zealand	521	21	8	9	17	52	0.07	0.11
Japan	520	18	8	11	9	40	0.20	**0.38**
Australia	515	20	9	8	13	46	0.02	-0.07
Netherlands	508	16	9	8	13	37	**0.62**	**0.38**
Belgium	506	21	13	8	19	47	**0.58**	**0.66**
Norway	503	21	8	6	9	36	0.15	0.19
Estonia	501	21	9	9	8	29	0.00	**0.43**
Switzerland	501	21	11	8	14	40	0.24	0.06
Poland	500	25	10	9	15	39	-0.05	0.01
Iceland	500	25	10	7	6	27	**0.30**	**0.40**
United States	500	24	16	7	17	42	0.10	**-0.17**
Sweden	497	23	9	6	13	43	-0.04	0.12
Germany	497	25	15	6	18	44	-0.02	**0.28**
Ireland	496	23	10	7	13	39	-0.08	**0.49**
France	496	27	15	8	17	51	w	w
Denmark	495	21	12	6	15	36	0.16	**0.27**
United Kingdom	494	26	15	6	14	44	-0.03	-0.10
Hungary	494	23	12	6	26	48	0.07	0.02
Portugal	489	26	12	10	17	30	0.04	**0.39**
Italy	486	30	15	8	12	32	0.13	**0.50**
Slovenia	483	29	10	6	14	39	**0.55**	**-0.25**
Greece	483	35	19	7	12	34	0.24	0.25
Spain	481	27	17	9	14	29	m	**0.45**
Czech Republic	478	31	15	5	12	46	**0.37**	0.08
Slovak Republic	477	29	12	5	15	41	**-0.21**	0.00
Israel	474	38	22	6	13	43	0.20	**-0.20**
Luxembourg	472	34	21	5	18	40	**0.39**	**0.28**
Austria	470	33	21	5	17	48	**0.64**	-0.07
Turkey	464	32	18	10	19	29	0.04	**-0.26**
Chile	449	38	29	6	19	31	**0.25**	-0.05
Mexico	425	42	32	7	14	25	-0.04	0.03
Shanghai-China	556	11	5	19	12	27	**0.32**	**-0.13**
Hong Kong-China	533	13	7	18	5	17	0.12	0.02
Singapore	526	17	9	12	15	47	**0.22**	**-0.14**
Liechtenstein	499	18	10	9	8	26	**0.57**	**0.70**
Chinese Taipei	495	26	13	10	12	36	0.29	-0.07
Macao-China	487	22	11	13	2	12	**-0.18**	**0.17**
Latvia	484	31	13	8	10	29	0.19	**0.38**
Croatia	476	28	11	7	11	32	**0.28**	0.32
Lithuania	468	35	14	5	14	33	0.19	0.21
Dubai (UAE)	459	41	23	3	14	51	-0.01	**-0.27**
Russian Federation	459	34	19	5	11	37	0.31	**0.29**
Serbia	442	40	22	4	10	27	0.06	0.11
Bulgaria	429	50	31	2	20	51	0.17	0.21
Uruguay	426	50	36	4	21	37	0.08	0.13
Romania	424	50	33	2	14	36	0.11	-0.02
Thailand	421	50	30	7	13	22	0.16	-0.02
Trinidad and Tobago	416	56	36	5	10	38	**0.56**	**0.38**
Colombia	413	52	50	6	17	28	-0.08	**-0.14**
Brazil	412	57	45	6	13	28	0.03	**-0.20**
Montenegro	408	59	37	2	10	31	**0.38**	**0.33**
Jordan	405	63	43	3	8	24	-0.02	0.06
Tunisia	404	60	51	7	8	19	0.20	-0.02
Indonesia	402	63	44	6	8	17	0.16	**-0.16**
Argentina	398	59	48	3	20	40	0.22	-0.02
Kazakhstan	390	62	46	1	12	38	**0.34**	**0.44**
Albania	385	68	46	3	11	31	**0.38**	0.15
Qatar	372	73	58	1	4	25	-0.07	0.11
Panama	371	70	60	2	18	31	-0.13	0.03
Peru	370	69	62	1	27	41	**0.48**	-0.02
Azerbaijan	362	72	62	1	7	21	**0.44**	0.23
Kyrgyzstan	314	87	76	0	15	40	**0.35**	0.27

Countries are ranked in descending order of the mean score in reading, separately for OECD and partner countries and economies.
Source: OECD, *PISA 2009 Database*, Tables I.2.2., II.1.1., II.2.3., II.3.2 and II.3.3.
StatLink ▄▄▓▄ http://dx.doi.org/10.1787/888932343684

Introduction to PISA

THE PISA SURVEYS

Are students well prepared to meet the challenges of the future? Can they analyse, reason and communicate their ideas effectively? Have they found the kinds of interests they can pursue throughout their lives as productive members of the economy and society? The OECD Programme for International Student Assessment (PISA) seeks to answer these questions through its triennial surveys of key competencies of 15-year-old students in OECD member countries and partner countries/economies. Together, the group of countries participating in PISA represents nearly 90% of the world economy.[1]

PISA assesses the extent to which students near the end of compulsory education have acquired some of the knowledge and skills that are essential for full participation in modern societies, with a focus on reading, mathematics and science.

PISA has now completed its fourth round of surveys. Following the detailed assessment of each of PISA's three main subjects – reading, mathematics and science – in 2000, 2003 and 2006, the 2009 survey marks the beginning of a new round with a return to a focus on reading, but in ways that reflect the extent to which reading has changed since 2000, including the prevalence of digital texts.

PISA 2009 offers the most comprehensive and rigorous international measurement of student reading skills to date. It assesses not only reading knowledge and skills, but also students' attitudes and their learning strategies in reading. PISA 2009 updates the assessment of student performance in mathematics and science as well.

The assessment focuses on young people's ability to use their knowledge and skills to meet real-life challenges. This orientation reflects a change in the goals and objectives of curricula themselves, which are increasingly concerned with what students can do with what they learn at school and not merely with whether they have mastered specific curricular content. PISA's unique features include its:

- Policy orientation, which connects data on student learning outcomes with data on students' characteristics and on key factors shaping their learning in and out of school in order to draw attention to differences in performance patterns and identify the characteristics of students, schools and education systems that have high performance standards.

- Innovative concept of "literacy", which refers to the capacity of students to apply knowledge and skills in key subject areas and to analyse, reason and communicate effectively as they pose, interpret and solve problems in a variety of situations.

- Relevance to lifelong learning, which does not limit PISA to assessing students' competencies in school subjects, but also asks them to report on their own motivations to learn, their beliefs about themselves and their learning strategies.

- Regularity, which enables countries to monitor their progress in meeting key learning objectives.

- Breadth of geographical coverage and collaborative nature, which, in PISA 2009, encompasses the 34 OECD member countries and 41 partner countries and economies.[2]

The relevance of the knowledge and skills measured by PISA is confirmed studies tracking young people in the years after they have been assessed by PISA. Longitudinal studies in Australia, Canada and Switzerland display a strong relationship between performance in reading on the PISA 2000 assessment at age 15 and future educational attainment and success in the labour-market (see Volume I Chapter 2).[3]

The frameworks for assessing reading, mathematics and science in 2009 are described in detail in *PISA 2009 Assessment Framework: Key competencies in reading, mathematics and science* (OECD, 2009).

Decisions about the scope and nature of the PISA assessments and the background information to be collected are made by leading experts in participating countries. Governments guide these decisions based on shared, policy-driven interests. Considerable efforts and resources are devoted to achieving cultural and linguistic breadth and balance in the assessment materials. Stringent quality-assurance mechanisms are applied in designing the test, in translation, sampling and data collection. As a result, PISA findings are valid and highly reliable.

Policy makers around the world use PISA findings to gauge the knowledge and skills of students in their own country in comparison with those in the other countries. PISA reveals what is possible in education by showing what students in the highest performing countries can do in reading, mathematics and science. PISA is also used to gauge the pace of educational progress, by allowing policy makers to assess to what extent performance changes observed nationally are in line with performance changes observed elsewhere. In a growing number of countries, PISA is also used to set policy targets against measurable goals achieved by other systems, and to initiate research and peer-learning designed to identify policy levers and to reform trajectories for improving education. While PISA cannot identify cause-and-effect relationships between inputs, processes and educational outcomes, it can highlight the key features in which education systems are similar and different, sharing those findings with educators, policy makers and the general public.

THE FIRST REPORT FROM THE 2009 ASSESSMENT

This volume is the second of six volumes that provide the first international report on results from the PISA 2009 assessment.

This volume starts by closely examining the performance variation shown in Volume I, *What Students Know and Can Do*, particularly the extent to which the overall variation in student performance relates to differences in the results achieved by different schools. The volume then looks at how factors such as socio-economic background and immigrant status affect student and school performance, and the role that education policy can play in moderating the impact of these factors.

The other volumes cover the following issues:

- Volume I, *What Students Know and Can Do: Student Performance in Reading, Mathematics and Science*, summarises the performance of students in PISA 2009, starting with a focus on reading, and then reporting on mathematics and science performance. It provides the results in the context of how performance is defined, measured and reported, and then examines what students are able do in reading. After a summary of reading performance, it examines the ways in which this performance varies on subscales representing three aspects of reading. It then breaks down results by different formats of reading texts and considers gender differences in reading, both generally and for different reading aspects and text formats. Any comparison of the outcomes of education systems needs to take into consideration countries' social and economic circumstances and the resources they devote to education. To address this, the volume also interprets the results within countries' economic and social contexts. The chapter concludes with a description of student results in mathematics and science.

- Volume III, *Learning to Learn: Student Engagement, Strategies and Practices,* explores the information gathered on students' levels of engagement in reading activities and attitudes towards reading and learning. It describes 15-year-olds' motivations, engagement and strategies to learn.

- Volume IV, *What Makes a School Successful? Resources, Policies and Practices,* explores the relationships between student-, school- and system-level characteristics, and educational quality and equity. It explores what schools and school policies can do to raise overall student performance and, at the same time, moderate the impact of socio-economic background on student performance, with the aim of promoting a more equitable distribution of learning opportunities.

- Volume V, *Learning Trends: Changes in Student Performance Since* 2000, provides an overview of trends in student performance in reading, mathematics and science from PISA 2000 to PISA 2009. It shows educational outcomes over time and tracks changes in factors related to student and school performance, such as student background and school characteristics and practices.

- Volume VI, *Students On Line: Reading and Using Digital Information*, (OECD, forthcoming) explains how PISA measures and reports student performance in digital reading and analyses what students in the 20 countries participating in this assessment are able to do.

Box II.A **Key features of PISA 2009**

Content

- The main focus of PISA 2009 was reading. The survey also updated performance assessments in mathematics and science. PISA considers students' knowledge in these areas not in isolation, but in relation to their ability to reflect on their knowledge and experience and to apply them to real-world issues. The emphasis is on mastering processes, understanding concepts and functioning in various contexts within each assessment area.

- For the first time, the PISA 2009 survey also assessed 15-year-old students' ability to read, understand and apply digital texts.

Methods

- Around 470 000 students completed the assessment in 2009, representing about 26 million 15-year-olds in the schools of the 65 participating countries and economies. Some 50 000 students took part in a second round of this assessment in 2010, representing about 2 million 15-year-olds from 10 additional partner countries and economies.

- Each participating student spent two hours carrying out pencil-and-paper tasks in reading, mathematics and science. In 20 countries, students were given additional questions via computer to assess their capacity to read digital texts.

- The assessment included tasks requiring students to construct their own answers as well as multiple-choice questions. The latter were typically organised in units based on a written passage or graphic, much like the kind of texts or figures that students might encounter in real life.

- Students also answered a questionnaire that took about 30 minutes to complete. This questionnaire focused on their background, learning habits, attitudes towards reading, and their involvement and motivation.

- School principals completed a questionnaire about their school that included demographic characteristics and an assessment of the quality of the learning environment at school.

Outcomes

PISA 2009 results provide:

- a profile of knowledge and skills among 15-year-olds in 2009, consisting of a detailed profile for reading and an update for mathematics and science;

- contextual indicators relating performance results to student and school characteristics;

- an assessment of students' engagement in reading activities, and their knowledge and use of different learning strategies;

- a knowledge base for policy research and analysis; and

- trend data on changes in student knowledge and skills in reading, mathematics, science, changes in student attitudes and socio-economic indicators, and in the impact of some indicators on performance results.

Future assessments

- The PISA 2012 survey will return to mathematics as the major assessment area, PISA 2015 will focus on science. Thereafter, PISA will turn to another cycle beginning with reading again.

- Future tests will place greater emphasis on assessing students' capacity to read and understand digital texts and solve problems presented in a digital format, reflecting the importance of information and computer technologies in modern societies.

All data tables referred to in the analysis are included at the end of the respective volume. A Reader's Guide is also provided in each volume to aid in interpreting the tables and figures accompanying the report.

Technical annexes that describe the construction of the questionnaire indices, sampling issues, quality-assurance procedures and the process followed for developing the assessment instruments, and information about reliability of coding are posted on the OECD PISA website (*www.pisa.oecd.org*). Many of the issues covered in the technical annexes will be elaborated in greater detail in the *PISA 2009 Technical Report* (OECD, forthcoming).

THE PISA STUDENT POPULATION

In order to ensure the comparability of the results across countries, PISA devoted a great deal of attention to assessing comparable target populations. Differences between countries in the nature and extent of pre-primary education and care, in the age of entry to formal schooling, and in the structure of the education system do not allow school grade levels to be defined so that they are internationally comparable. Valid international comparisons of educational performance, therefore, need to define their populations with reference to a target age. PISA covers students who are aged between 15 years 3 months and 16 years 2 months at the time of the assessment and who have completed at least six years of formal schooling, regardless of the type of institution in which they are enrolled, whether they are in full-time or part-time education, whether they attend academic or vocational programmes, and whether they attend public or private schools or foreign schools within the country. (For an operational definition of this target population, see the *PISA 2009 Technical Report* [OECD, forthcoming].) The use of this age in PISA, across countries and over time, allows the performance of students to be compared in a consistent manner before they complete compulsory education.

As a result, this report can make statements about the knowledge and skills of individuals born in the same year who are still at school at 15 years of age, despite having had different educational experiences, both in and outside school.

Stringent technical standards were established to define the national target populations and to identify permissible exclusions from this definition (for more information, see the PISA website *www.pisa.oecd.org*). The overall exclusion rate within a country was required to be below 5% to ensure that, under reasonable assumptions, any distortions in national mean scores would remain within plus or minus 5 score points, *i.e.* typically within the order of magnitude of two standard errors of sampling (see Annex A2). Exclusion could take place either through the schools that participated or the students who participated within schools. There are several reasons why a school or a student could be excluded from PISA. Schools might be excluded because they are situated in remote regions and are inaccessible or because they are very small, or because of organisational or operational factors that precluded participation. Students might be excluded because of intellectual disability or limited proficiency in the language of the test.

In 29 out of the 65 countries participating in PISA 2009, the percentage of school-level exclusions amounted to less than 1%; it was less than 5% in all countries. When the exclusion of students who met the internationally established exclusion criteria is also taken into account, the exclusion rates increase slightly. However, the overall exclusion rate remains below 2% in 32 participating countries, below 5% in 60 participating countries, and below 7% in all countries except Luxembourg (7.2%) and Denmark (8.6%). In 15 out of 34 OECD countries, the percentage of school-level exclusions amounted to less than 1% and was less than 5% in all countries. When student exclusions within schools are also taken into account, there were nine OECD countries below 2% and 25 countries below 5%. Restrictions on the level of exclusions in PISA 2009 are described in Annex A2.

The specific sample design and size for each country aimed to maximise sampling efficiency for student-level estimates. In OECD countries, sample sizes ranged from 4 410 students in Iceland to 38 250 students in Mexico. Countries with large samples have often implemented PISA both at national and regional/state levels (*e.g.* Australia, Belgium, Canada, Italy, Mexico, Spain, Switzerland and the United Kingdom). This selection of samples was monitored internationally and adhered to rigorous standards for the participation rate, both among schools selected by the international contractor and among students within these schools, to ensure that the PISA results reflect the skills of the 15-year-old students in participating countries. Countries were also required to administer the test to students in identical ways to ensure that students receive the same information prior to and during the test (for details, see Annex A4).

■ Figure II.A ■
A map of PISA countries and economies

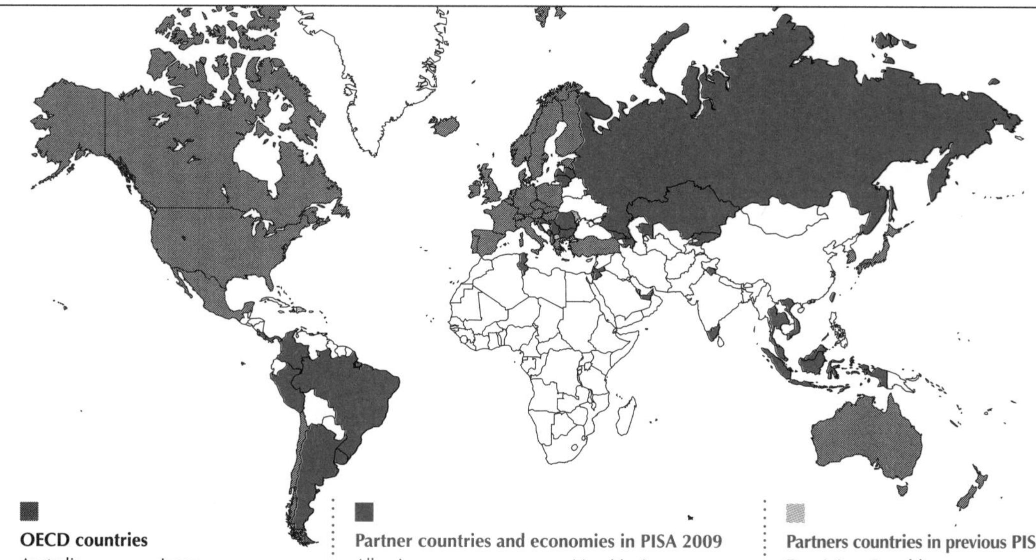

OECD countries

Australia	Japan
Austria	Korea
Belgium	Luxembourg
Canada	Mexico
Chile	Netherlands
Czech Republic	New Zealand
Denmark	Norway
Estonia	Poland
Finland	Portugal
France	Slovak Republic
Germany	Slovenia
Greece	Spain
Hungary	Sweden
Iceland	Switzerland
Ireland	Turkey
Israel	United Kingdom
Italy	United States

Partner countries and economies in PISA 2009

Albania	Mauritius*
Argentina	Miranda-Venezuela*
Azerbaijan	Montenegro
Brazil	Netherlands-Antilles*
Bulgaria	Panama
Colombia	Peru
Costa Rica*	Qatar
Croatia	Romania
Georgia*	Russian Federation
Himachal Pradesh-India*	Serbia
Hong Kong-China	Shanghai-China
Indonesia	Singapore
Jordan	Tamil Nadu-India*
Kazakhstan	Chinese Taipei
Kyrgyzstan	Thailand
Latvia	Trinidad and Tobago
Liechtenstein	Tunisia
Lithuania	Uruguay
Macao-China	United Arab Emirates*
Malaysia*	Viet Nam*
Malta*	

Partners countries in previous PISA surveys

Dominican Republic
Macedonia
Moldova

_____

* These partner countries and economies carried out
the assessment in 2010 instead of 2009.

Notes

1. The GDP of the countries that participated in PISA 2009 represents 86% of the 2007 world GDP. Some of the entities represented in this report are referred to as partner economies. This is because they are not strictly national entities.

2. Thirty-one partner countries and economies originally participated in the PISA 2009 assessment and ten additional partner countries and economies took part in a second round of the assessment.

3. Marks, G.N (2007); Bertschy, K., Cattaneo, M.A. and Wolter, S.C. (2009); OECD (2010).

Reader's Guide

Data underlying the figures

The data referred to in this volume are presented in Annex B and, in greater detail, on the PISA website (*www.pisa.oecd.org*).

Five symbols are used to denote missing data:

a   The category does not apply in the country concerned. Data are therefore missing.

c   There are too few observations or no observation to provide reliable estimates (*i.e.* there are fewer than 30 students or less than five schools with valid data).

m   Data are not available. These data were not submitted by the country or were collected but subsequently removed from the publication for technical reasons.

w   Data have been withdrawn or have not been collected at the request of the country concerned.

x   Data are included in another category or column of the table.

Country coverage

This publication features data on 65 countries and economies, including all 34 OECD countries and 31 partner countries and economies (see Figure IV.A). The data from another ten partner countries were collected one year later and will be published in 2011.

The statistical data for Israel are supplied by and under the responsibility of the relevant Israeli authorities. The use of such data by the OECD is without prejudice to the status of the Golan Heights, East Jerusalem and Israeli settlements in the West Bank under the terms of international law.

Calculating international averages

An OECD average was calculated for most indicators presented in this report. The OECD average corresponds to the arithmetic mean of the respective country estimates.

Readers should, therefore, keep in mind that the term "OECD average" refers to the OECD countries included in the respective comparisons.

Rounding figures

Because of rounding, some figures in tables may not exactly add up to the totals. Totals, differences and averages are always calculated on the basis of exact numbers and are rounded only after calculation.

All standard errors in this publication have been rounded to one or two decimal places. Where the value 0.00 is shown, this does not imply that the standard error is zero, but that it is smaller than 0.005.

Reporting student data

The report uses "15-year-olds" as shorthand for the PISA target population. PISA covers students who are aged between 15 years 3 months and 16 years 2 months at the time of assessment and who have completed at least 6 years of formal schooling, regardless of the type of institution in which they are enrolled and of whether they are in full-time or part-time education, of whether they attend academic or vocational programmes, and of whether they attend public or private schools or foreign schools within the country.

Reporting school data

The principals of the schools in which students were assessed provided information on their schools' characteristics by completing a school questionnaire. Where responses from school principals are presented in this publication, they are weighted so that they are proportionate to the number of 15-year-olds enrolled in the school.

Focusing on statistically significant differences

This volume discusses only statistically significant differences or changes. These are denoted in darker colours in figures and in bold font in tables. See Annex A3 for further information.

Abbreviations used in this report

ESCS PISA index of economic, social and cultural status

GDP Gross domestic product

ISCED International Standard Classification of Education

PPP Purchasing power parity

S.D. Standard deviation

S.E. Standard error

Further documentation

For further information on the PISA assessment instruments and the methods used in PISA, see the *PISA 2009 Technical Report* (OECD, forthcoming) and the PISA website (*www.pisa.oecd.org*).

This report uses the OECD's StatLinks service. Below each table and chart is a url leading to a corresponding Excel workbook containing the underlying data. These urls are stable and will remain unchanged over time. In addition, readers of the e-books will be able to click directly on these links and the workbook will open in a separate window, if their Internet browser is open and running.

1

Moderating the Impact of Socio-Economic Background on Educational Outcomes

This chapter focuses on the magnitude of differences in student performance across countries, as well as between and within schools. It also describes the extent to which these differences relate to the socio-economic background of students and schools.

Providing equal educational opportunities is a major goal for policy makers. PISA shows that school systems differ not only in their average performance but also in how equitably they distribute educational opportunities among students, regardless of family and socio-economic background. PISA collected data on a broad set of family background characteristics, including the socio-economic background of the students' parents, home possessions, immigrant status, home language, family structure and school location. While Volume I, *What Students Know and Can Do*, focuses on the performance of students and countries, this volume focuses on equity-related issues and analyses how differences in background characteristics relate to differences in student performance in reading.

The evidence emerging from a growing body of international studies shows that educational equity is not only an issue of fairness but also an economic issue. A recent OECD study of economic growth projections, for example, estimated the current net value of educational reforms that would bring everyone in a country to a baseline level of performance in PISA. The results suggest that bringing the lowest-performing students in the OECD area – many of whom are socio-economically disadvantaged – at least up to 400 score points on the PISA scale, which corresponds roughly to the lower boundary of the PISA baseline Level 2 of proficiency, could imply an aggregate gain of national income in the order of USD 200 trillion over the lifetime of the generation born in 2010. Of course, the estimated benefits vary from one country to the next, and the projections are full of the uncertainties associated with these kinds of exercises. Yet, the estimated benefits of raising quality and equity in educational outcomes are likely large and beyond any conceivable cost of improvement (OECD, 2010a).

This volume explores equity in education from three perspectives:

First, it examines *equality in learning outcomes* by examining the distribution of student performance on the PISA assessment. Are there large performance gaps among groups of students or schools? Where are these differences more marked – at the top or at the bottom end of the performance distribution? What proportion of students is falling behind the PISA baseline Level 2 of proficiency?

Second, it examines *equity in the distribution of learning resources*, namely the extent to which students and schools have access to similar educational resources, both in quantity and quality, regardless of schools' socio-economic background.

Third, and most important, it looks at *equity in the distribution of learning opportunities* by analysing the impact of the family and the socio-economic background of students and schools on learning outcomes (Box II.1.2 provides details on the variables used to measure family and socio-economic background). In an equitable school system, that impact is small; that is, the educational success of students is largely independent of their own family or socio-economic background or the average background of the other students in their schools. In contrast, if that impact is large – that is, if the success of students depends to a great extent on their family background or the socio-economic background of the school in which they are enrolled – then educational opportunities are distributed inequitably.

An analysis of performance gaps and how performance varies across identifiable groups of students, among schools or across school systems, provides valuable policy insights related to the quality and distribution of educational opportunities. In addition, identifying the characteristics of those students, schools and education systems that perform well despite socio-economic disadvantages can help policy makers design effective policies to overcome inequalities in learning (OECD, 2010b).

Volume IV, *What Makes a School Successful?*, furthers the analysis by reviewing how the socio-economic background of students and schools is interrelated with educational resources, policies and practices to influence learning outcomes, and how policies and practices can mediate the impact of socio-economic background on educational success.

Previous analyses have shown that the relationship between the socio-economic background of students and schools and learning outcomes generally does not vary markedly across the subject areas of reading, mathematics and science that are measured by PISA. This volume thus limits the analysis to reading, which was the focus of the PISA 2009 assessment. The analysis builds on work from earlier PISA assessments (OECD, 2001; OECD, 2004; Willms, 2006; OECD, 2007a; Willms, 2010).

INTERPRETING GAPS AND DISPERSION IN STUDENT PERFORMANCE

This volume focuses on differences in student performance. How large are these differences and where do they come from? Much of the variation in students' capacity to understand, use, reflect on and engage with written texts can be traced to differences between within countries and among schools and students within countries. Across the OECD, 11% of all variation in student reading performance can be attributed to differences across countries, while 34% arises from differences among schools and the remaining 55% can be attributed to differences among individual students. Across all countries and economies participating in PISA, which include some countries and economies that are more heterogeneous than OECD member countries, cross-country differences represent 25% of the overall performance variation, school differences account for 30% of the overall variation and student differences account for the remaining 45%.[1] These percentages do not suggest that the performance differences among countries are small, but rather that the performance variation within countries is often very large.

Figure II.1.1 depicts equality in learning outcomes through the performance variation in each country, highlighting student performance at the 10th, 25th, 50th, 75th and 90th percentiles of the performance distribution. These percentiles correspond, respectively, to the score points below which 90%, 75%, 50%, 25% and 10% of students perform. The difference between two adjacent percentiles appears within each section of the bar.

For example, as shown in Volume 1, *What Students Know and Can Do* (and Figure II.1.4 in this chapter), the differences in mean performance between the top performing OECD school systems, Korea and Finland, and the OECD average is 46 and 42 score points on the PISA reading scale, respectively. But in these two countries, as Figure II.1.1 shows, 25% of students score below 490 and 481 score points, respectively, and half of all students score below 545 and 542, respectively. Thus, in Korea there is at least a difference of 54 score points, and in Finland of 62 score points, between those scoring in the bottom quarter and those scoring in the top half of the within-country distribution of student performance. On average across OECD countries, the performance gaps between the median student (the point on the performance distribution where half of all students score above and the other half scores below) and the weakest 10% and 25% of readers are 130 and 67 score points, respectively (Table II.1.1). Box II.1.1 explains how these and other gaps described in this chapter may be interpreted.

Box II.1.1 **Interpreting differences in PISA scores: How large a gap?**

What is meant by a difference of, say, 46 or 42 points between the scores of two different groups of students?

In PISA 2009, as described in Volume I, *What Students Know and Can Do*, student performance in reading is described through seven levels of proficiency (Levels 1b, 1a, 2, 3, 4, 5 and 6). A difference of about 73 score points represents one proficiency level on the PISA reading scale. This can be considered a comparatively large difference in student performance. For example, as described in the *PISA 2009 Assessment Framework* (OECD, 2009), students proficient at Level 3 on the overall reading literacy scale are capable of completing moderately complex reading tasks, such as locating multiple pieces of information, making links between different parts of a text, and relating the text to familiar knowledge. Meanwhile, students proficient at Level 2 on the reading literacy scale are able to locate information that meets several conditions, to make comparisons or contrasts around a single feature, to work out what a well-defined part of a text means, even when the information is not prominent, and to make connections between the text and personal experience.

For the 32 OECD countries in which a sizeable number of 15-year-olds in the PISA samples were enrolled in at least two different grade levels, the difference between students in the two grades implies that one school year corresponds to an average of 39 score points on the PISA reading scale (see Table A1.2).

The difference in performance on the reading scale between the countries with the highest and lowest mean performance is 242 score points, and the performance gap between the countries with the 5th highest and the 5th lowest mean performance is 154 score points.

In relation to the overall distribution of students in the PISA reading scale, 100 points represent one standard deviation; this means that two-thirds of the OECD student population have scores within 100 points of the OECD mean.

■ Figure II.I.1 ■
Variation of reading performance within countries
Percentiles on the reading scale

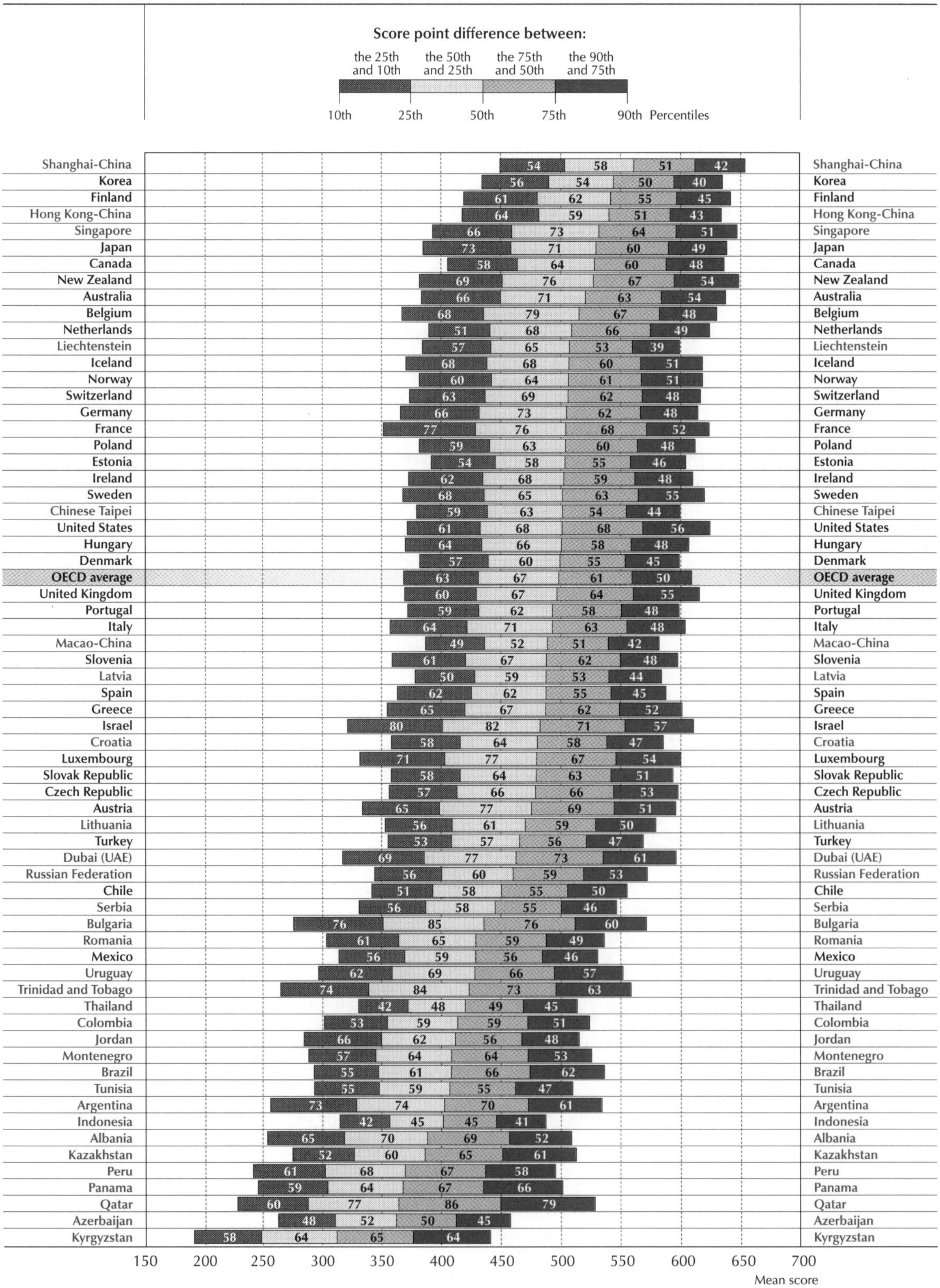

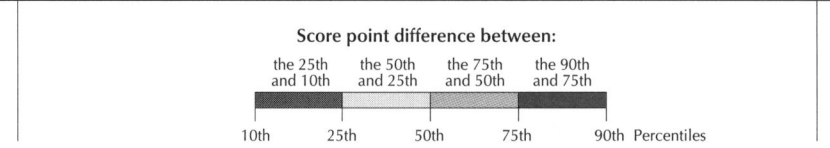

Score point difference between:

the 25th and 10th	the 50th and 25th	the 75th and 50th	the 90th and 75th

10th   25th   50th   75th   90th Percentiles

Country	25th–10th	50th–25th	75th–50th	90th–75th
Shanghai-China	54	58	51	42
Korea	56	54	50	40
Finland	61	62	55	45
Hong Kong-China	64	59	51	43
Singapore	66	73	64	51
Japan	73	71	60	49
Canada	58	64	60	48
New Zealand	69	76	67	54
Australia	66	71	63	54
Belgium	68	79	67	48
Netherlands	51	68	66	49
Liechtenstein	57	65	53	39
Iceland	68	68	60	51
Norway	60	64	61	51
Switzerland	63	69	62	48
Germany	66	73	62	48
France	77	76	68	52
Poland	59	63	60	48
Estonia	54	58	55	46
Ireland	62	68	59	48
Sweden	68	65	63	55
Chinese Taipei	59	63	54	44
United States	61	68	68	56
Hungary	64	66	58	48
Denmark	57	60	55	45
OECD average	63	67	61	50
United Kingdom	60	67	64	55
Portugal	59	62	58	48
Italy	64	71	63	48
Macao-China	49	52	51	42
Slovenia	61	67	62	48
Latvia	50	59	53	44
Spain	62	62	55	45
Greece	65	67	62	52
Israel	80	82	71	57
Croatia	58	64	58	47
Luxembourg	71	77	67	54
Slovak Republic	58	64	63	51
Czech Republic	57	66	66	53
Austria	65	77	69	51
Lithuania	56	61	59	50
Turkey	53	57	56	47
Dubai (UAE)	69	77	73	61
Russian Federation	56	60	59	53
Chile	51	58	55	50
Serbia	56	58	55	46
Bulgaria	76	85	76	60
Romania	61	65	59	49
Mexico	56	59	56	46
Uruguay	62	69	66	57
Trinidad and Tobago	74	84	73	63
Thailand	42	48	49	45
Colombia	53	59	59	51
Jordan	66	62	56	48
Montenegro	57	64	64	53
Brazil	55	61	66	62
Tunisia	55	59	55	47
Argentina	73	74	70	61
Indonesia	42	45	45	41
Albania	65	70	69	52
Kazakhstan	52	60	65	61
Peru	61	68	67	58
Panama	59	64	67	66
Qatar	60	77	86	79
Azerbaijan	48	52	50	45
Kyrgyzstan	58	64	65	64

150   200   250   300   350   400   450   500   550   600   650   700

Mean score

Countries are ranked in ascending order of median performance (50th percentile) in reading.
Source: OECD, *PISA 2009 Database*, Table II.1.1.
StatLink ᗧᗩᓮ http://dx.doi.org/10.1787/888932343551

FAMILY AND SOCIO-ECONOMIC BACKGROUND

One of the central themes examined in this volume is the relationship between differences in family and socio-economic background and differences in student performance. National and international evidence has shown that student family background and performance can be closely associated for various reasons (for a pioneering national study, see Coleman *et al.,* 1966 and for international evidence see OECD, 2001; OECD, 2004; and OECD, 2007a). PISA 2009 provides further insights into these relationships.

Box II.1.2 **Summarising student and school background characteristics**

This volume examines a number of different background characteristics of students and schools:

Background refers to various characteristics of each student's family and community, including: *i)* their socio-economic background (as captured by the *PISA index of social, economic and cultural status*); *ii)* their immigrant status: whether the student or parents were born in another country (captured by the student's immigrant status: first- or second-generation immigrant or native); *iii)* their home language*:* whether students usually speak the language of assessment at home or not (captured by a variable indicating whether it is the assessment language or another language, which could still be an official language of the country or economy); *iv)* their family structure: whether students usually live with one parent or more (captured by a variable indicating whether the family structure is single-parent or other); and *v)* their school location or home background in its community context (captured by a variable indicating whether the student attends a school located in a village, hamlet or rural area of fewer than 3 000 people, a small town of 3 000 to about 15 000 people, a town of 15 000 to about 100 000 people, a city of 100 000 to about one million people, or a large city with over one million people).

Socio-economic background refers to a combination of characteristics of a student's family that describes its social, economic and cultural status. Socio-economic background is measured by the *PISA index of economic, social and cultural status* (ESCS). This index captures a range of aspects of a student's family and home background that combines information on parents' education and occupations and home possessions. The index was derived from the following variables: the international socio-economic index of occupational status of the father or mother, whichever is higher; the level of education of the father or mother, whichever is higher, converted into years of schooling; and the *index of home possessions,* obtained by asking students whether they had a desk at which they studied at home, a room of their own, a quiet place to study, educational software, a link to the Internet, their own calculator, classic literature, books of poetry, works of art (*e.g.* paintings), books to help them with their school work, a dictionary, a dishwasher, a DVD player or VCR, three other country-specific items and the number of cellular phones, televisions, computers, cars and books at home. The rationale for choosing these variables is that socio-economic background is usually seen as being determined by occupational status, education and wealth. As no direct measure of parental income or wealth was available from PISA (except for those countries that undertook the PISA Parent Questionnaire), access to relevant household items was used as a proxy.

At the individual level, the analysis in this volume considers the relationship between each student's socio-economic background and his or her individual reading performance as assessed in PISA 2009. At the school level, it considers the relationship between the average socio-economic background of 15-year-old students in the school and the reading scores of 15-year-old students attending that school. At the country level, too, the socio-economic background of students, both overall and in terms of the distribution, can be related to reading performance.

The values of the *PISA index of economic, social and cultural status* have been standardised to a mean of zero for the population of students in OECD countries, with each country given equal weight. A one-point difference on the scale of the index represents a difference of one standard deviation on the distribution of this measure. This means that a score of -1.0 on this scale indicates that a student has a combination of socio-economic attributes that makes the student more advantaged than about one in six students in the average OECD country, and more disadvantaged than five-sixths of students. Having a score above +1.0 means being more advantaged than five-sixths of the students.

Some of the connections between family background and performance are well understood, while there is less of a consensus on others.[2] In general, more highly educated parents may decide to invest more of their time and energy into educating their children or they may choose to guide their daily interactions with their children in ways that help them succeed at school. Parents with more prestigious occupations may become role models for their children.[3] The possibility of ultimately having one of these occupations, which are generally associated with better education, can be an incentive for children to devote more effort to their performance at school. Certain household possessions, such as a quiet place to study or a desk, may also provide an advantage for children. Wealthier families will generally be able either to provide more educational resources at home or to choose schools that will supply them with these resources. Family home background may also be related to student performance through the community context. If a school is located in a city, students may enjoy additional resources nearby, such as public libraries and museums, which support learning and may be less accessible to students attending a rural school. However, not all students enjoy these advantages and many of them have to struggle with individual challenges, such as an immigrant background, speaking a different language at home than the one spoken at school or having only one parent to turn to for support and assistance.

For a school system, a weak relationship between the family and socio-economic background of students and performance is an indication of an equitable distribution of educational opportunities. In such a school system, where the student comes from, his or her family background and the school the student attends are weak predictors of reading performance.

In PISA, family background is measured by a broad set of student characteristics, including the country of birth, the language commonly used at home, family structure and a range of measures that capture the social, economic and cultural status of the student's family. Box II.1.2 briefly describes the indicators used to measure different dimensions of the background characteristics of students and schools.

One of the most commonly analysed family background characteristics is the socio-economic status of the student's family. Socio-economic background is a narrower concept than family background and is summarised in the *PISA index of social, economic and cultural status*. This index is calculated by taking into consideration the parents' education and occupations and an array of household possessions. The index is standardised to have a mean of zero and a standard deviation of one across countries in the OECD area. Throughout the volume, a student's socio-economic background refers to the student's score on this index. A school's socio-economic background refers to the average socio-economic index of the students attending that school. The average socio-economic index of the students in the country is referred to as the socio-economic profile of the education system. A low score on the index relates to a socio-economically disadvantaged background; a high score on the index relates to a socio-economically advantaged background.

SOCIO-ECONOMIC BACKGROUND, UNDERLYING SOCIAL AND ECONOMIC INEQUALITY AND MEAN PERFORMANCE AT THE LEVEL OF THE EDUCATION SYSTEM

Comparing the distribution of educational opportunities across countries is a challenging task. An education system's outcomes depend not only on past and current educational resources, policies and practices, but also on a country's broader economic, social and institutional characteristics. Analysing how learning opportunities are related to certain economic, demographic and social factors can provide a framework for interpreting this volume's results. Given that reading performance varies according to student background, by taking into account the differences in the socio-economic background of students in a country and how students perform as related to their backgrounds, these analyses can shed new light on issues relating to both educational quality and equity.

To what extent, then, are country differences in PISA simply a product of the aggregated differences in young people's backgrounds? The remaining chapters in this volume provide a detailed analysis that tackles this question from different perspectives.

Figure II.1.2 shows the relationship between the average level of students' socio-economic background in each country (on the horizontal axis) and the average reading scores of 15-year-old students in PISA (on the vertical axis). The top-right corner shows those countries that are socio-economically advantaged when compared with a typical OECD country and that perform well relative to the OECD average; the top-left corner shows those that are socio-economically disadvantaged but still perform well; the lower-left corner shows those that are disadvantaged and perform poorly; and the lower-right corner shows those that are advantaged and perform poorly.

■ Figure II.1.2 ■
Reading performance and socio-economic profile

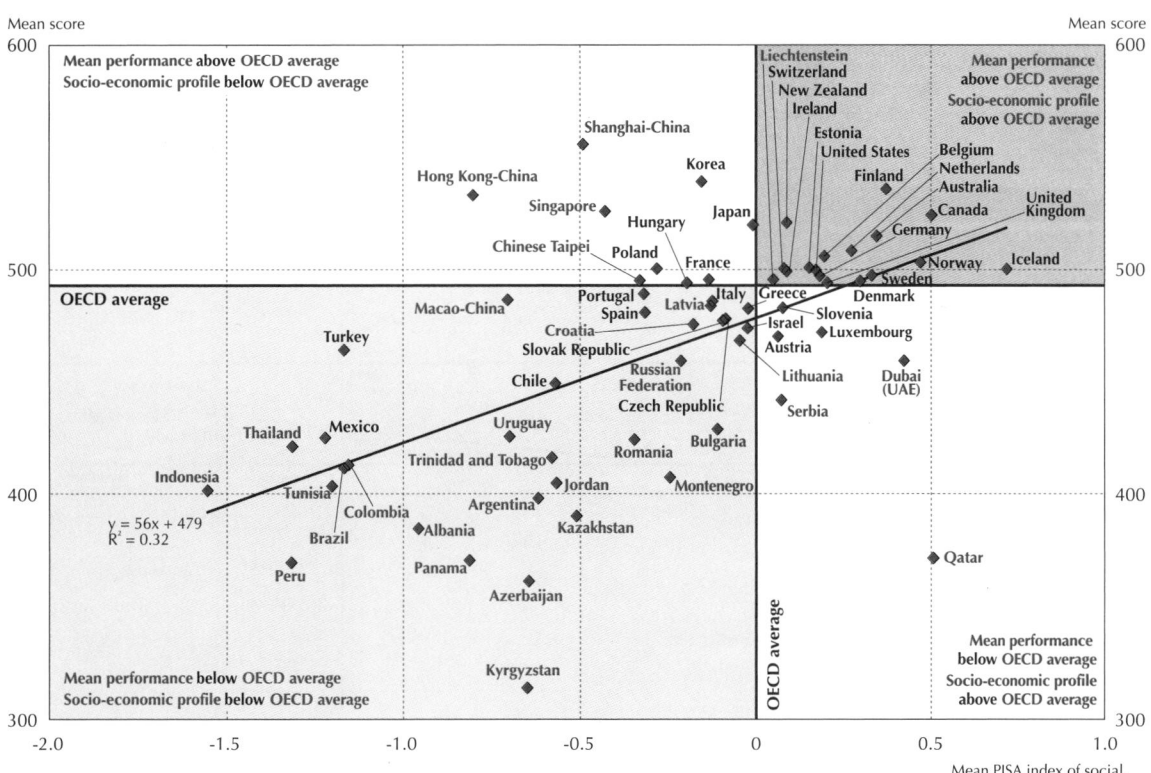

Source: OECD, *PISA 2009 Database,* Table II.1.1.
StatLink http://dx.doi.org/10.1787/888932343551

Figure II.1.2 shows that, in general, countries with more socio-economically advantaged students perform better. However, there are many exceptions. Indeed, the mean index of socio-economic background is almost identical for the country with the lowest mean reading performance, Kyrgyzstan, and the economy with the highest mean reading performance, Shanghai-China. The same pattern is apparent among OECD countries. Austria, the Czech Republic, Greece, Ireland, Israel, Japan, New Zealand, the Slovak Republic, Slovenia and Switzerland all share a similar average socio-economic background among their students, with an average close to the OECD average (between −0.09 and +0.09 with the OECD average at 0). The mean performance, however, ranges from 470 to 521 points among this small group of countries with similar socio-economic profiles.

Figure II.1.3 shows the relationship between a common measure of income inequality, the Gini coefficient,[4] and equity in the distribution of learning opportunities. As described in more detail in subsequent chapters, equity in the distribution of learning opportunities is measured by the percentage of variation in student performance that can be explained by differences in the socio-economic background of students. Each dot places a school system along these two dimensions. The measures have been inverted so that countries with low levels of income inequality and a loose relationship between student performance and socio-economic background are in the top right corner (low Gini coefficient and low explained variance as compared to the OECD average).

The results in Figure II.1.3 suggest that equity in the distribution of learning opportunities is only weakly associated with a country's underlying income inequality. In fact, the evidence suggests that, in general, cross-national differences in inequalities of performance are associated more closely with the characteristics of the education system than with underlying social inequalities or measures of economic development (Marks, 2005). While many studies show strong evidence that the educational attainment of an individual is closely related to that of his or her parents, some of these studies conclude that income inequality is more closely associated with the policies and institutions that govern the labour markets than the distribution of cognitive skills (Devroye and Freeman, 2001; Blau and Kahn, 2005; Carbonaro, 2006; Hanushek and Woessmann, 2008).

■ Figure II.1.3 ■
Income inequality in the population and strength of the relationship between socio-economic background and performance

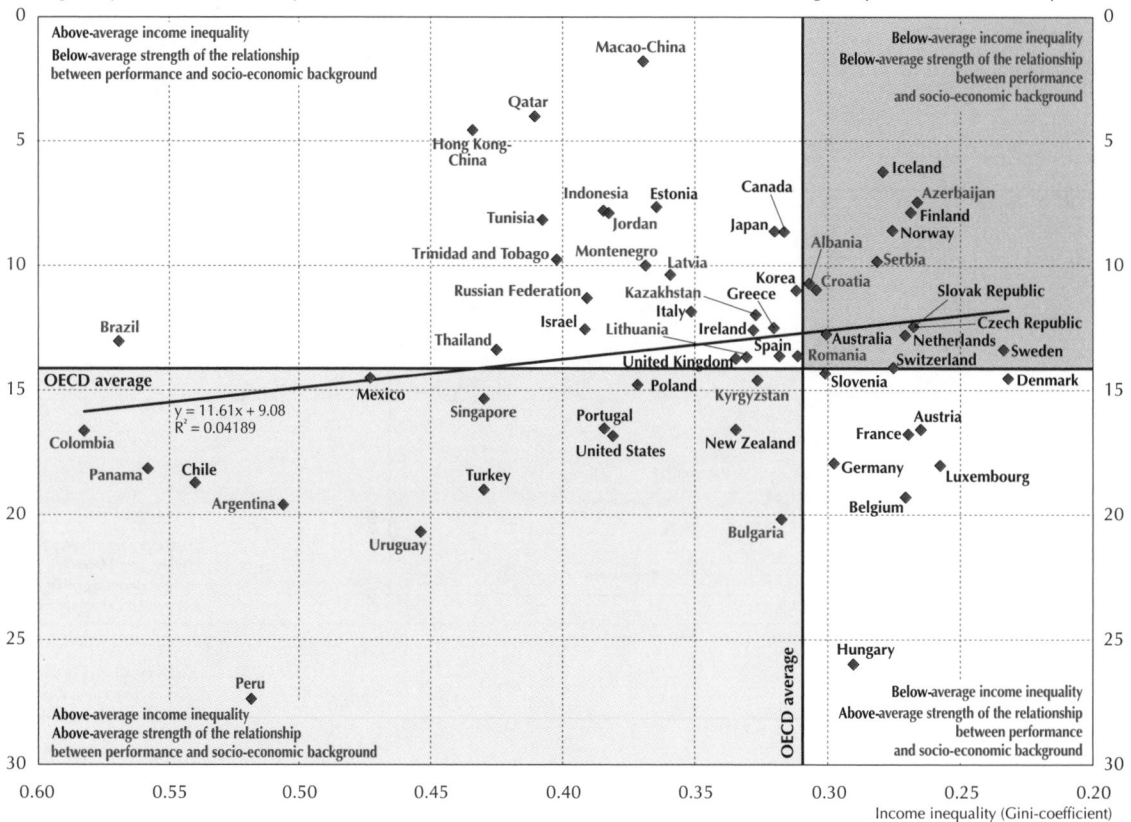

Note: The Gini coefficient measures the extent to which the distribution of income among individuals or households within an economy deviates from a perfectly equal distribution. The Gini index measures the area between the Lorenz curve and the hypothetical line of absolute equality, expressed as a proportion of the maximum area under the line. A Gini index of zero represents perfect equality and 1, perfect inequality.
Source: OECD, *PISA 2009 Database*, Table II.1.1.
StatLink ⎙ᒲᓰᔆᒷ http://dx.doi.org/10.1787/888932343551

The weak relationship shown in Figure II.1.3 suggests that countries with similar levels of income inequality distribute learning opportunities very differently. This finding is important as it shows that equity in educational opportunities can be achieved even where income is distributed highly inequitably. For example, in Iceland and Hungary, two OECD countries with a Gini coefficient of around 0.29, close to the OECD average of 0.31, the proportion of the variation in student reading performance explained by the variation in students' socio-economic background is 6% and 26%, respectively. A wide range of countries sits between these two extremes. Finland and Norway appear with Iceland in the top-right corner with below-average impact of socio-economic background on performance and below-average underlying inequality. Austria, Belgium, France, Germany and Luxembourg join Hungary in the bottom-right quadrant with above-average impact of socio-economic background and below-average underlying inequalities. Estonia, Greece, Israel, Italy and Japan appear in the top-left quadrant, with above-average underlying inequalities and a below-average impact of socio-economic background; while Chile, New Zealand, Portugal, the United States and Turkey appear in the bottom-left quadrant, where income inequalities are large and the impact of socio-economic background on learning outcomes is also large. The same pattern is seen among the partner countries and economies, whether at a Gini coefficient above or below the OECD average (Table II.1.2).

That educational equity can be achieved in diverse socio-economic contexts is also apparent when analysing the relationship between how students of varying socio-economic backgrounds are distributed in a society and other measures of the relationship between students' socio-economic background and performance. The inter-percentile

range in socio-economic background is a simple measure of dispersion, indicating the difference in socio-economic background between students at the 95th and 5th percentile of the distribution. Larger inter-percentile ranges indicate a wider distribution of socio-economic background. The average difference in student reading performance associated with a one unit increase in the *PISA index of economic, social and cultural status*, known as the slope of the socio-economic gradient (see Chapter 3 of this volume), is another common measure of the relationship between these two variables and provides another measure of educational equity in PISA.

In general, countries characterised by wide socio-economic disparities are not necessarily those in which the relationship between socio-economic background and performance is more marked. Again, this is an important finding as it suggests that equity in educational opportunities can be achieved even when the socio-economic background of students varies widely. In fact, across OECD countries, the slope of the socio-economic gradient is 30 score points or less in Mexico, Iceland, Estonia, Turkey, Spain and Portugal, but the inter-percentile range in socio-economic background goes from over 4.0 score points in Mexico and Turkey to 2.9 or less in Estonia and Iceland. Among the partner countries and economies, the patterns are similar, with large differences in the slopes despite similar socio-economic disparities. This is observed both among countries with large inter-percentile ranges (*e.g.* Peru and Colombia, with slopes of 41 and 28, respectively, and an inter-percentile range of around 4.2) and with inter-percentile ranges close to that of the OECD average (*e.g.* Azerbaijan and Kyrgyzstan, both with slopes of 21 and 40 and an inter-percentile range of around 3.1) (Table II.1.2).

Furthermore, country differences in the level and distribution of students' socio-economic background explain only a small part of the PISA 2009 differences on the quality and equity of school systems. Among OECD countries, Poland, Hungary, Korea and France are characterised by more socio-economically disadvantaged backgrounds than countries at the OECD average, yet mean performance in reading is at or above the OECD average. Among the partner countries and economies, the same is true in Hong Kong-China, Shanghai-China, Singapore and Chinese Taipei (see Figure II.1.2). Chapters 3 and 6 revisit this issue in greater detail.

LOOKING AHEAD

Figure II.1.4 introduces a broad range of indicators on equity that are discussed in this volume. Countries are ranked by their mean performance in reading. For each school system, each cell reports the value of a particular indicator. If the country performs above the OECD average in the respective indicator of equity, the cell is highlighted in light blue. If the opposite is true, then the cell is highlighted in dark blue. If the system performs close to the OECD average, the cell is coloured in blue. In the last two columns, it is the direction of the relationship that matters. Those systems in which the relationship is more favourable for socio-economically disadvantaged schools are highlighted in light blue; and, if the relationship is stronger than on average across OECD countries, the value is marked in bold. If the relationship is more favourable for advantaged schools, then the cell is highlighted in dark blue; and, if the relationship is stronger than on average across OECD countries, then it is marked in bold. For example, a positive relationship between a school's socio-economic background and student-teacher ratios suggests that socio-economically advantaged schools have more students per teacher and, conversely, socio-economically disadvantaged schools have more favourable student-teacher ratios. Since that implies that disadvantaged schools have more teacher resources at their disposal, the corresponding cells are marked in light blue.

Figure II.1.4 highlights that equity in education has many facets. The performance of education systems and the share of poorly performing students, marked here as those who do not reach the PISA baseline Level 2 of reading proficiency, are closely related (Chapter 2).

Even in countries with educational opportunities that are distributed highly inequitably, according to the PISA indicators, there are students from disadvantaged backgrounds who show high levels of performance. These students can be considered resilient, and they are more prevalent in those education systems that PISA indicators show to be more equitable (Chapter 3).

The relationship between socio-economic background and performance is a key measure of how equitably a school system distributes educational opportunities. The socio-economic gradient (Chapter 3) captures this relationship. While Chapter 4 is devoted to the analysis of performance differences between students with and without an immigrant background, the between and within school socio-economic gradients are explored in Chapter 5.

■ Figure II.1.4 ■
Summary of PISA measures of educational equity

▢ Higher quality or equity than OECD average	▢	Disadvantaged schools are more likely to have more or better resources, in **bold** if relationship is statistically different from the OECD average
▢ Lower quality or equity than OECD average	▢	Advantaged schools are more likely to have more or better resources, in **bold** if relationship is statistically different from the OECD average
▢ At OECD average (no statistically significant difference)	▢	Within country correlation is not statistically significant

	Mean reading score	Percentage of boys below proficiency Level 2	Percentage of girls below proficiency Level 2	Percentage of resilient students	Percentage of variance in student performance explained by students' socio-economic background	Slope of the socio-economic gradient	Correlation between the socio-economic background of schools and the percentage of teachers with university-level (ISCED 5A) among all full-time teachers	Correlation between socio-economic background of schools and the student/teacher ratio
OECD average	493	25	13	8	14	38	0.15	-0.15
Korea	539	10	4	14	11	32	-0.03	0.30
Finland	536	17	5	11	8	31	-0.01	0.08
Canada	524	18	7	10	9	32	0.03	0.09
New Zealand	521	21	8	9	17	52	0.07	0.11
Japan	520	18	8	11	9	40	0.20	0.38
Australia	515	20	9	8	13	46	0.02	-0.07
Netherlands	508	16	9	8	13	37	**0.62**	**0.38**
Belgium	506	21	13	8	19	47	**0.58**	**0.66**
Norway	503	21	8	6	9	36	0.15	0.19
Estonia	501	21	9	9	8	29	0.00	**0.43**
Switzerland	501	21	11	8	14	40	0.24	0.06
Poland	500	25	10	9	15	39	-0.05	0.01
Iceland	500	25	10	7	6	27	**0.30**	**0.40**
United States	500	24	16	7	17	42	0.10	**-0.17**
Sweden	497	23	9	6	13	43	-0.04	0.12
Germany	497	25	15	6	18	44	-0.02	**0.28**
Ireland	496	23	10	7	13	39	-0.08	**0.49**
France	496	27	15	8	17	51	w	w
Denmark	495	21	12	6	15	36	0.16	**0.27**
United Kingdom	494	26	15	6	14	44	-0.03	-0.10
Hungary	494	23	12	6	26	48	0.07	0.02
Portugal	489	26	12	10	17	30	0.04	**0.39**
Italy	486	30	15	8	12	32	0.13	**0.50**
Slovenia	483	29	10	6	14	39	**0.55**	**-0.25**
Greece	483	35	19	7	12	34	0.24	0.25
Spain	481	27	17	9	14	29	m	**0.45**
Czech Republic	478	31	15	5	12	46	**0.37**	0.08
Slovak Republic	477	29	12	5	15	41	**-0.21**	0.00
Israel	474	38	22	6	13	43	0.20	**-0.20**
Luxembourg	472	34	21	5	18	40	**0.39**	**0.28**
Austria	470	33	21	5	17	48	**0.64**	-0.07
Turkey	464	32	18	10	19	29	0.04	**-0.26**
Chile	449	38	29	6	19	31	0.25	-0.05
Mexico	425	42	32	7	14	25	-0.04	0.03
Shanghai-China	556	11	5	19	12	27	**0.32**	**-0.13**
Hong Kong-China	533	13	7	18	5	17	0.12	0.02
Singapore	526	17	9	12	15	47	**0.22**	**-0.14**
Liechtenstein	499	18	10	9	8	26	**0.57**	**0.70**
Chinese Taipei	495	26	13	10	12	36	0.29	-0.07
Macao-China	487	22	11	13	2	12	**-0.18**	**0.17**
Latvia	484	31	13	8	10	29	0.19	**0.38**
Croatia	476	28	11	7	11	32	**0.28**	0.32
Lithuania	468	35	14	5	14	33	0.19	0.21
Dubai (UAE)	459	41	23	3	14	51	-0.01	**-0.27**
Russian Federation	459	34	19	5	11	37	0.31	**0.29**
Serbia	442	40	22	4	10	27	0.06	0.11
Bulgaria	429	50	31	2	20	51	0.17	0.21
Uruguay	426	50	36	4	21	37	0.08	0.13
Romania	424	50	33	2	14	36	0.11	-0.02
Thailand	421	50	30	7	13	22	0.16	-0.02
Trinidad and Tobago	416	56	36	5	10	38	**0.56**	**0.38**
Colombia	413	52	50	6	17	28	-0.08	**-0.14**
Brazil	412	57	45	6	13	28	0.03	**-0.20**
Montenegro	408	59	37	2	10	31	**0.38**	**0.33**
Jordan	405	63	43	3	8	24	-0.02	0.06
Tunisia	404	60	51	7	8	19	0.20	-0.02
Indonesia	402	63	44	6	8	17	0.16	**-0.16**
Argentina	398	59	48	3	20	40	0.22	-0.02
Kazakhstan	390	62	46	1	12	38	**0.34**	**0.44**
Albania	385	68	46	3	11	31	**0.38**	0.15
Qatar	372	73	58	1	4	25	-0.07	0.11
Panama	371	70	60	2	18	31	-0.13	0.03
Peru	370	69	62	1	27	41	**0.48**	-0.02
Azerbaijan	362	72	62	1	7	21	**0.44**	0.23
Kyrgyzstan	314	87	76	0	15	40	**0.35**	0.27

Countries are ranked in descending order of the mean score in reading, separately for OECD and partner countries and economies.
Source: OECD, *PISA 2009 Database*, Tables I.2.2., II.1.1., II.2.3., II.3.2 and II.3.3.
StatLink ᵃᶜᵉ http://dx.doi.org/10.1787/888932343551

Notes

1. These results are based on the variance decomposition of a null three-level hierarchical model (student, school, country) on the first plausible value of performance in reading.

2. For a review of this literature see Levin and Belfield (2002).

3. The classic work on this literature is Kohn (1969).

4. The Gini coefficient measures the extent to which the distribution of income among individuals or households within an economy deviates from a perfectly equal distribution. The Gini coefficient measures the area between the Lorenz curve and the hypothetical line of absolute equality, expressed as a percentage of the maximum area under the line. A Gini coefficient of zero represents perfect equality; a Gini coefficient of one represents perfect inequality.

2

Three Perspectives on Educational Equity and Equality

In discussing equity and equality in education, this chapter examines how differences in student performance are distributed across countries and schools, and the extent to which students and schools with different socio-economic backgrounds have access to similar educational resources, both in quantity and quality. It also discusses the impact of students' family background and school location on learning outcomes.

This chapter explores equity and equality in education from three perspectives: first, it examines differences in the distribution of learning outcomes among students and schools; then it studies the extent to which students and schools with different socio-economic backgrounds have access to similar educational resources, both in terms of quantity and quality; and finally, it looks at the impact of students' family background and school location on learning outcomes. This chapter provides a broad perspective of two themes that are further developed in Chapters 3, 4 and 5: Chapter 3 concentrates on how student performance is related to students' socio-economic background; Chapter 4 focuses on the relationship between student performance and immigrant status and the language spoken at home; and Chapter 5 examines how students' performance is related to their schools' socio-economic intake. Chapter 6 discusses the policy implications of this volume's findings.

EQUALITY IN LEARNING OUTCOMES

An analysis of how the learning outcomes are distributed throughout a school system provides valuable policy insights for stakeholders interested in education. Equality in learning outcomes can be understood as the difference between high- and low-performing students. It can also be understood to mean that all students perform at a baseline level of proficiency. In the former approach, the difference between the low- and high-performing students identifies the performance disadvantage of low-performing students relative to their high-performing peers. By contrast, the absolute proportion of students who fall below a baseline level of performance can signal those students who have not acquired the fundamental knowledge or mastered the basic skills that will enable them to progress further in education and beyond. Both these relative and absolute measures of equality in learning outcomes provide insight into the extent to which a school system fails to provide all students with equal and adequate levels of knowledge and skills.

Relative performance gaps within countries

At the top end of the performance distribution, students with more ability, effort and/or opportunities to learn achieve high scores on the PISA assessment of reading, pulling ahead from the middle of the performance distribution. A similar situation occurs at the bottom of the scale: low-performing students, whether due to low levels of ability, effort and/or opportunities to learn fall behind the middle of the distribution. A relatively large gap at the bottom implies that there is a large difference in reading performance between a country's low performers and the middle of the distribution. In countries with large performance gaps at the bottom, the low-performing students are at a double disadvantage: not only do they perform less well than their peers; they are also more likely to lack the most basic reading skills. International comparisons are another useful benchmark as they help policy makers develop a deeper understanding of performance gaps within countries by providing examples of countries where the gaps are narrower (see Chapter 1 and Figure II.1.1).

The score point differences across percentiles of the performance distribution are good measures of performance gaps within countries. The 10th percentile is the score reached by 9 out of 10 students, but not reached by the lowest performing 10%. The 50th percentile, also known as the median score, is defined as the score that half of the students in the country do not reach and the other half exceed. Therefore, the median student is the student in the middle of the performance distribution for each system. The difference in score points between the median and the 10th percentile is a measure of the achievement gap at the bottom end of the distribution.[1] Similarly, the gap between the median and the 90th percentile (the score exceeded by only 1 in 10 students) is a measure of the achievement gap at the top.

Figure II.2.1 compares these two measures of performance gaps across the whole distribution of student performance within each country. The figure shows the gap at the top end of the distribution on the vertical axis and the gap at the bottom end in the horizontal axis. The dots represent each education system, and their position indicates how they fare along these two dimensions. A diagonal line divides the figure into two halves. Dots in the top half, above the diagonal, represent systems where the gap at the top end is larger than the gap at the bottom end of the student performance distribution.

Figure II.2.1 shows that the gap at the bottom end of the performance distribution is, in general, wider than the gap at the top end (except in six partner countries). The distinction hints at the source of variation in student performance within each country. The gap at the top end of the scale is also a good within-country benchmark to gauge the size of the gap at the bottom end. In general, school systems with low mean performance have wider performance gaps, particularly at the top of the performance distribution.[2]

■ Figure II.2.1 ■
Performance differences among the highest- and lowest-achieving students
Gaps at the top and bottom end of the distribution of reading performance

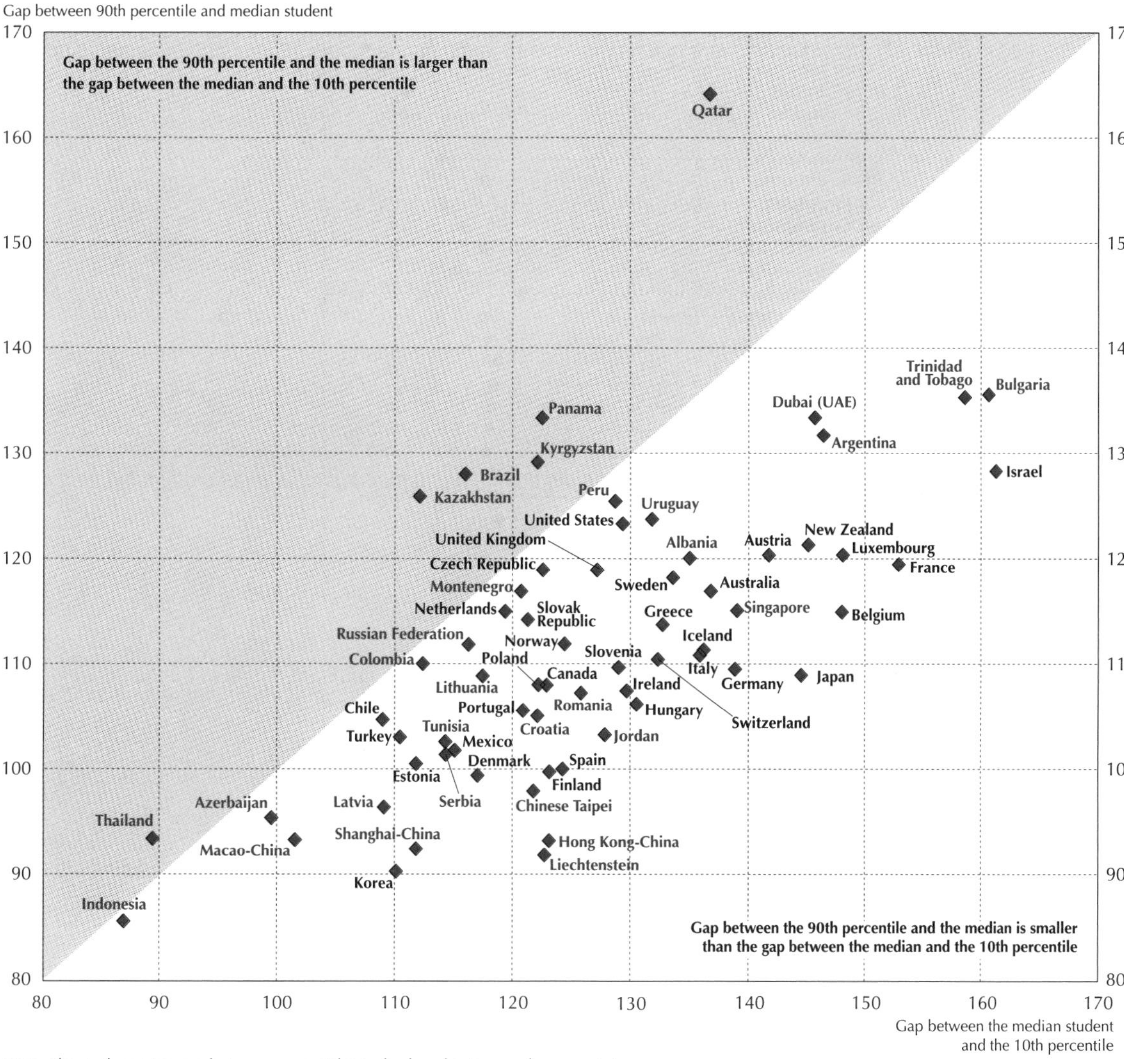

Gap between 90th percentile and median student

Gap between the 90th percentile and the median is larger than the gap between the median and the 10th percentile

Qatar

Trinidad and Tobago
Bulgaria

Dubai (UAE)

Panama
Argentina

Kyrgyzstan
Israel

Brazil
Kazakhstan
Peru
Uruguay

United States
New Zealand

United Kingdom
Albania
Austria
Luxembourg

Czech Republic
France

Montenegro
Sweden
Australia

Netherlands
Slovak Republic
Greece
Singapore
Belgium

Russian Federation
Norway
Iceland

Colombia
Poland
Slovenia
Italy
Japan

Canada
Ireland
Germany

Lithuania
Romania
Hungary

Chile
Portugal
Croatia
Switzerland

Turkey
Tunisia
Mexico
Jordan

Estonia
Denmark
Spain

Finland

Azerbaijan
Latvia
Serbia
Chinese Taipei

Thailand
Shanghai-China
Hong Kong-China

Macao-China
Liechtenstein

Korea

Indonesia

Gap between the 90th percentile and the median is smaller than the gap between the median and the 10th percentile

Gap between the median student and the 10th percentile

Note: The performance gap between percentiles is displayed in terms of score points.
Source: OECD, *PISA 2009 Database,* Table II.1.1.
StatLink ᵐˢˡ http://dx.doi.org/10.1787/888932343570

Figure II.2.1 also highlights large differences between the gaps at the top and bottom ends of the distribution for some countries. Among OECD countries, for example, Japan, Germany, Slovenia, Switzerland, Italy, Iceland and Norway all share similar gaps at the top end of the distribution of about 111 score points, the OECD average. However, the gaps at the bottom end of the distribution within this group of countries range from 124 in Norway to 144 score points in Japan (Table II.1.1). Also, Austria, Luxembourg, New Zealand, the United States and Israel show similar gaps at the top of the distribution, all with gaps of 120 score points or more. Yet, in the United States, the gap at the bottom is very similar to the gap at the top at 129 score points, whereas in Israel, the gap at the bottom is 161 score points and at the top is 128 score points; in Austria, Luxembourg and New Zealand, the gap at the bottom is in the range of 142 to 148 score points. The same patterns are evident among the partner countries and economies, where, for example, Argentina, Bulgaria, Dubai (UAE) and Trinidad and Tobago have large gaps at the bottom, both in absolute terms and relative to the gaps at the top end of their performance distributions. A similar picture emerges if other percentiles are used to analyse performance distribution, or if this analysis is carried out with data from previous PISA assessments. These findings mirror the results from other international assessments (Brown and Micklewright, 2004).

■ Figure II.2.2 ■
Percentage of students below proficiency Level 2 and at Level 3 or above

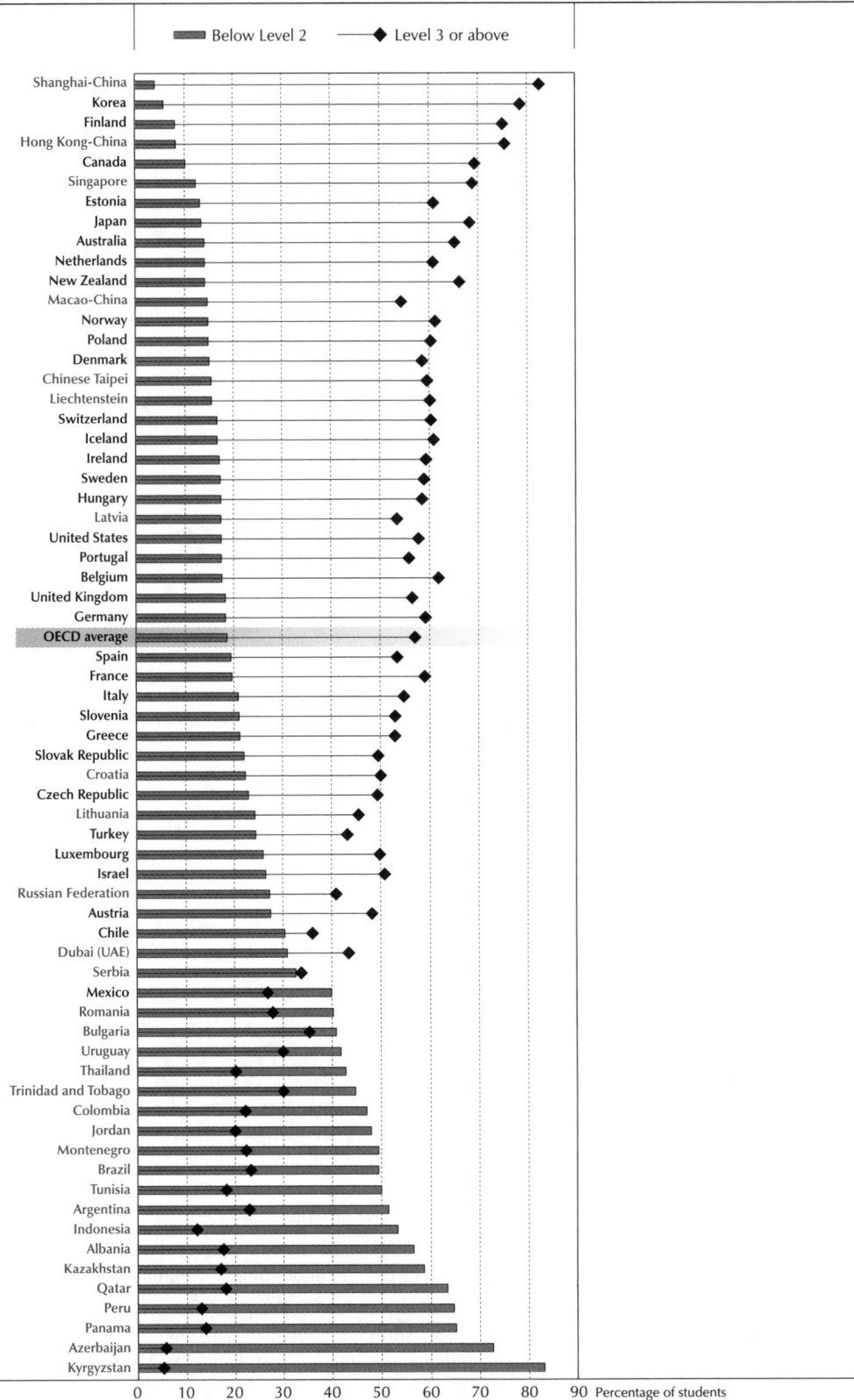

Countries are ranked in ascending order of percentage of students below proficiency Level 2.
Source: OECD, *PISA 2009 Database*, Table I.2.1.
StatLink ⬛ꤹ⬛ http://dx.doi.org/10.1787/888932343570

Share of the students failing to reach a baseline level of proficiency

As discussed in Volume I, *What Students Know and Can Do*, PISA assesses reading performance along seven levels of proficiency, of which Level 2 is judged the baseline level at which students begin to demonstrate the reading literacy competencies that will enable them to participate effectively and productively in life. Students proficient at Level 2 are capable of tasks such as locating information that meets several criteria, comparing or contrasting against a single feature in the text, working out what a well-defined part of a text means, even when the information is not prominent and making connections between the text and personal experience. Students performing below Level 2 may have learned to read, but they struggle with using reading for learning. From an equity perspective, this is a critical group of students. These students are disadvantaged by their performance, particularly from an international perspective, as they move beyond education and into increasingly globalised labour markets.

Students scoring below reading proficiency Level 2 are a particularly vulnerable group. Their limited abilities put their future educational and work-related careers at risk. Longitudinal studies confirm this. In Canada, for example, of the 9% of students who scored below Level 2 in reading in PISA 2000, two-thirds of them had not progressed to post-secondary education and only 10% of them had reached university. In contrast, the majority of students proficient at Level 2, but no higher, had moved to post-secondary education, and only 7% of those proficient at Level 5 had not pursued any form of post-secondary education (OECD, 2010c). Evidence from Australia, Switzerland and Uruguay shows similar results and emphasises the direct or indirect positive relationship between performance in PISA and acquiring more education, attending and successfully completing more intellectually challenging vocational schools or acquiring tertiary education (Marks, 2007; Bertschy *et al.,* 2009; Boado and Fernández, 2010).

Level 2 on the PISA reading scale is thus a useful benchmark for many countries as it assists them in identifying the population that is at greater risk of leaving school early or not achieving its full potential. Figure II.2.2 shows the percentage of students across countries who do not reach Level 2. In some countries with a high proportion of students proficient at Level 2, a different benchmark might be more meaningful. For example, students who perform at Level 3 or above are those who perform well above the baseline requirements.

Figure II.2.2 shows marked differences across countries in the percentage of students who do not reach proficiency Level 2.[3] On average across the OECD, 19% of students are not proficient at Level 2. In Korea, Finland and Canada, among OECD countries, 10% or less of students do not reach this basic level of competency. In contrast, in Austria, Israel and Luxembourg, more than a quarter of students do not reach Level 2, and in Chile and Mexico, 30% and 40% of students, respectively, do not reach this level. In Mexico and Turkey, the proportion of students not enrolled at school by the age of 15 is around 35% while it is below 10% in all other OECD countries (Table A2.1). If these students who are not enrolled in school were assessed by PISA, the proportion of students who do not reach Level 2 in the PISA assessment would most likely be higher. In 19 out of the 31 partner countries and economies, 40% or more of students do not reach Level 2 (Table II.2.1). In 21 out of 31 partner countries and economies, the proportion of 15-year-olds not enrolled at school by the age of 15 is larger than the OECD average, and in 16 countries it is more than double the average, reaching more than 20% in 5 cases.

EQUITY IN THE DISTRIBUTION OF EDUCATIONAL RESOURCES

A potential source of inequities in learning opportunities lies in the distribution of resources across students and schools. In a school system characterised by an equitable distribution of educational resources, the quality or quantity of school resources would not be related to a school's average socio-economic background as all schools would benefit from similar resources. Therefore, if there is a positive relationship between the socio-economic background of schools and the quantity or quality of resources, more advantaged schools benefit from more or better resources. A negative relationship implies that more or better resources are devoted to disadvantaged schools. No relationship implies that resources are distributed similarly among schools attended by socio-economically advantaged and disadvantaged students.

Figure II.2.3 shows the relationship between the socio-economic background of schools – the average *PISA index of economic, social and cultural status* of the students in the school – and a host of school characteristics, such as the student-teacher ratio, the proportion of full-time teachers, the *index of teacher shortage,* and the *index of quality of educational resources*. Relationships in which students that attend disadvantaged schools where the principal reports more quantity and/or better quality resources are coloured light blue; those relationships where students that attend disadvantaged schools have less or lower-quality resources are coloured dark blue. If the relationship in a school system is stronger than the OECD average, it appears in bold. For those systems where there is no apparent association, the cell is coloured in blue.

■ Figure II.2.3 ■

Relationship between school average socio-economic background and school resources

	Disadvantaged schools are more likely to have more or better resources, in **bold** if relationship is statistically different from the OECD average
	Advantaged schools are more likely to have more or better resources, in **bold** if relationship is statistically different from the OECD average
	Within country correlation is not statistically significant

		Simple correlation between the school mean socio-economic background and:					
		Percentage of full-time teachers	Percentage of certified teachers among all full-time teachers	Percentage of teachers with university-level (ISCED 5A) among all full-time teachers	Index of quality of school's educational resources	Computer/student ratio	Student/teacher ratio[1]
OECD	Australia	**-0.21**	**-0.05**	0.02	**0.31**	0.01	-0.07
	Austria	-0.13	**0.21**	**0.64**	0.03	-0.05	-0.07
	Belgium	**-0.18**	0.05	**0.58**	0.02	**-0.23**	**0.66**
	Canada	0.01	**0.14**	0.03	0.18	-0.05	0.09
	Chile	-0.04	-0.01	**0.25**	**0.35**	**0.32**	-0.05
	Czech Republic	**-0.32**	**0.29**	**0.37**	0.00	0.15	0.08
	Denmark	0.01	-0.17	0.16	0.04	-0.08	**0.27**
	Estonia	0.14	0.00	0.00	0.10	-0.09	**0.43**
	Finland	**0.17**	-0.01	-0.01	0.13	-0.01	0.08
	France	c	c	c	c	c	c
	Germany	-0.15	-0.02	-0.02	0.06	-0.18	**0.28**
	Greece	-0.11	0.06	0.24	0.16	-0.12	0.25
	Hungary	**-0.33**	0.07	0.07	0.11	**-0.20**	0.02
	Iceland	**0.20**	**0.39**	**0.30**	0.06	**-0.41**	**0.40**
	Ireland	0.12	-0.10	-0.08	0.16	-0.03	**0.49**
	Israel	-0.08	-0.06	0.20	0.25	0.08	**-0.20**
	Italy	-0.06	**0.16**	0.13	0.15	**-0.19**	**0.50**
	Japan	-0.14	0.04	0.20	0.17	**-0.34**	**0.38**
	Korea	-0.14	0.00	-0.03	-0.04	**-0.53**	0.30
	Luxembourg	**-0.16**	**-0.01**	**0.39**	0.13	-0.13	**0.28**
	Mexico	-0.09	**-0.13**	-0.04	**0.59**	0.14	0.03
	Netherlands	**-0.34**	-0.12	**0.62**	0.06	-0.16	**0.38**
	New Zealand	-0.04	0.08	0.07	0.16	-0.02	0.11
	Norway	-0.05	0.04	0.15	0.14	-0.02	0.19
	Poland	-0.02	0.03	-0.05	0.06	-0.16	0.01
	Portugal	**0.14**	-0.05	0.04	0.24	-0.02	**0.39**
	Slovak Republic	-0.09	**0.28**	**-0.21**	-0.05	-0.06	0.00
	Slovenia	**0.46**	**0.32**	**0.55**	0.13	**-0.21**	**-0.25**
	Spain	**-0.29**	c	c	0.10	-0.16	**0.45**
	Sweden	0.05	0.01	-0.04	0.26	0.13	0.12
	Switzerland	-0.11	-0.07	0.24	0.10	0.03	0.06
	Turkey	0.12	-0.04	0.04	0.04	-0.06	**-0.26**
	United Kingdom	**-0.36**	0.05	-0.03	0.00	0.01	-0.10
	United States	**-0.42**	-0.24	0.10	0.22	0.06	**-0.17**
	OECD average	-0.07	0.04	0.15	0.13	-0.08	0.15
Partners	Albania	**-0.25**	0.00	**0.38**	**0.44**	**0.24**	0.15
	Argentina	0.13	0.13	0.22	**0.51**	**0.21**	-0.02
	Azerbaijan	0.05	-0.06	**0.44**	0.19	0.17	0.23
	Brazil	-0.03	0.10	0.03	**0.52**	**0.25**	**-0.20**
	Bulgaria	-0.08	0.17	0.17	0.09	-0.17	0.21
	Colombia	**-0.24**	**-0.16**	-0.08	**0.53**	**0.19**	-0.14
	Croatia	0.09	0.02	**0.28**	0.09	0.17	0.32
	Dubai (UAE)	**0.32**	**0.61**	-0.01	**0.34**	**0.47**	**-0.27**
	Hong Kong-China	-0.19	-0.06	0.12	0.06	0.04	0.02
	Indonesia	**0.24**	**0.27**	0.16	**0.44**	0.14	**-0.16**
	Jordan	-0.04	0.00	-0.02	0.26	0.05	0.06
	Kazakhstan	**0.23**	0.04	**0.34**	0.21	-0.12	**0.44**
	Kyrgyzstan	**0.17**	0.08	**0.35**	0.27	**0.13**	0.27
	Latvia	**0.19**	-0.03	0.19	0.14	0.00	**0.38**
	Liechtenstein	-0.15	0.02	**0.57**	**-0.91**	**0.79**	**0.70**
	Lithuania	**0.21**	0.09	0.19	-0.02	**-0.49**	0.21
	Macao-China	**0.11**	0.05	**0.05**	0.26	**0.22**	**0.17**
	Montenegro	0.07	**0.32**	**0.38**	-0.11	-0.19	**0.33**
	Panama	**-0.51**	**-0.47**	-0.13	**0.68**	**0.38**	0.03
	Peru	-0.21	0.08	**0.48**	**0.53**	**0.46**	-0.02
	Qatar	0.03	-0.04	-0.07	**0.23**	**0.19**	**0.11**
	Romania	0.05	0.10	0.11	0.20	-0.07	-0.02
	Russian Federation	**0.18**	0.08	**0.31**	**0.26**	0.02	**0.29**
	Serbia	0.10	0.06	0.06	-0.01	0.00	0.11
	Shanghai-China	**0.14**	0.13	**0.32**	0.16	-0.10	**-0.13**
	Singapore	-0.13	0.00	**0.22**	**0.10**	**-0.18**	**-0.14**
	Chinese Taipei	0.12	**0.34**	0.29	0.19	-0.04	-0.07
	Thailand	0.07	0.06	0.16	**0.39**	0.00	-0.02
	Trinidad and Tobago	**-0.19**	**0.09**	**0.56**	0.12	0.08	**0.38**
	Tunisia	-0.06	0.00	0.20	0.13	0.15	-0.02
	Uruguay	-0.01	**0.27**	0.08	**0.33**	**0.30**	0.13

1. In contrast to the other columns, negative correlations indicate more favourable characteristics for advantaged students.
Source: OECD, *PISA 2009 Database*, Table II.2.2.
StatLink ᵐˢᵖ http://dx.doi.org/10.1787/888932343570

As Figure II.2.3 shows, in 16 OECD countries, the student-teacher ratio relates positively to the socio-economic background of schools. In these countries, more disadvantaged schools tend to have more teachers in comparison with the number of students, which signals that around half of OECD countries try to allocate more teachers into socio-economically disadvantaged schools, presumably with the objective of moderating that disadvantage. This relationship is particularly pronounced in Belgium, Italy, Ireland, Spain, Estonia, Iceland, Portugal, Japan, the Netherlands and Korea. Among OECD countries, only in Turkey, Slovenia, Israel and the United States are socio-economically disadvantaged schools characterised by higher student-teacher ratios; that is, in these countries disadvantaged schools tend to be worse off in terms of the availability of teachers (Table II.2.2).

Figure II.2.3 also shows the relationship between the average socio-economic background of schools and the proportion of full-time teachers on the school staff, as well as the proportion of full-time teachers with advanced university-level qualifications. In the majority of OECD countries, disadvantaged schools tend to have higher proportions of full-time teachers. However, when taking into account the proportion of those full-time teachers who have an advanced university degree, it is the students attending more advantaged schools who tend to enjoy a higher proportion of high-quality, full-time teachers. These results suggest that students attending socio-economically disadvantaged schools are not at an educational disadvantage in terms of the number of teachers available. They are, however, at a disadvantage in terms of the quality of teachers available to instruct them.

Together, the preceding findings suggest that ensuring an equitable distribution of resources is still a major challenge for many countries, if not in terms of the quantity of resources, then in terms of their quality. Volume IV, *What Makes a School Successful?*, takes this analysis further by examining the interrelationship between socio-economic background and resources, policies and practices in greater detail.

EQUITY IN LEARNING REGARDLESS OF STUDENT BACKGROUND

In a system characterised by an equitable distribution of educational opportunities, students' performance is independent of their background. This includes several dimensions, such as the socio-economic status of the students' family, their family structure and the geographic location of the school. In this system, the relationship between academic achievement and student background is weak as all students enjoy the same opportunities to achieve their potential and their outcomes represent their efforts, abilities and ambitions fairly. In contrast, in a system characterised by a strong relationship between background and performance, some students, characterised by their socio-economic disadvantage, their family structure or the school location, are less likely to fulfil their academic potential because they do not enjoy the same opportunities.

This section introduces elements of family and community background that have been measured by PISA and studies their interrelationship. It also reviews how student performance relates to these variables and discusses the extent to which that relationship varies among countries. Weaker relationships between background characteristics and reading performance in some countries compared to others signal that inequalities in educational opportunity are not inevitable.

Family and socio-economic background

Data gathered through PISA allow researchers to examine the extent to which socio-economic background relates to successful student and school performance, and thus to assess how equitably educational opportunities are distributed. Where students and schools consistently perform well, regardless of their socio-economic status, educational opportunities can be considered to be distributed more equitably; where student and school performance strongly depends on socio-economic status, large inequalities in the distribution of educational opportunities persist and the potential of students remains unfulfilled.

To assess the impact of socio-economic background on student performance, PISA collected detailed information from students on various aspects relating to the economic, social and cultural status of their families. More specifically, PISA includes information on the education level and occupational status of students' fathers and mothers and their access to cultural and educational resources at home. Box II.1.2 and Annex A1 give details on the construction of these indices. The relationship between socio-economic background and performance does not necessarily reflect inequalities that occur within the boundaries of the school; inequities also hinge on societal arrangements for family healthcare, income maintenance, housing and childcare, to name just a few factors. Indeed, some of these factors, or their interaction with socio-economic background, may have as much or a greater impact on performance than schools. While PISA did not collect information about these factors, it is worth keeping them in mind when interpreting the results reported here.

■ Figure II.2.4 ■
Percentage of variance in reading performance explained by various aspects of family background

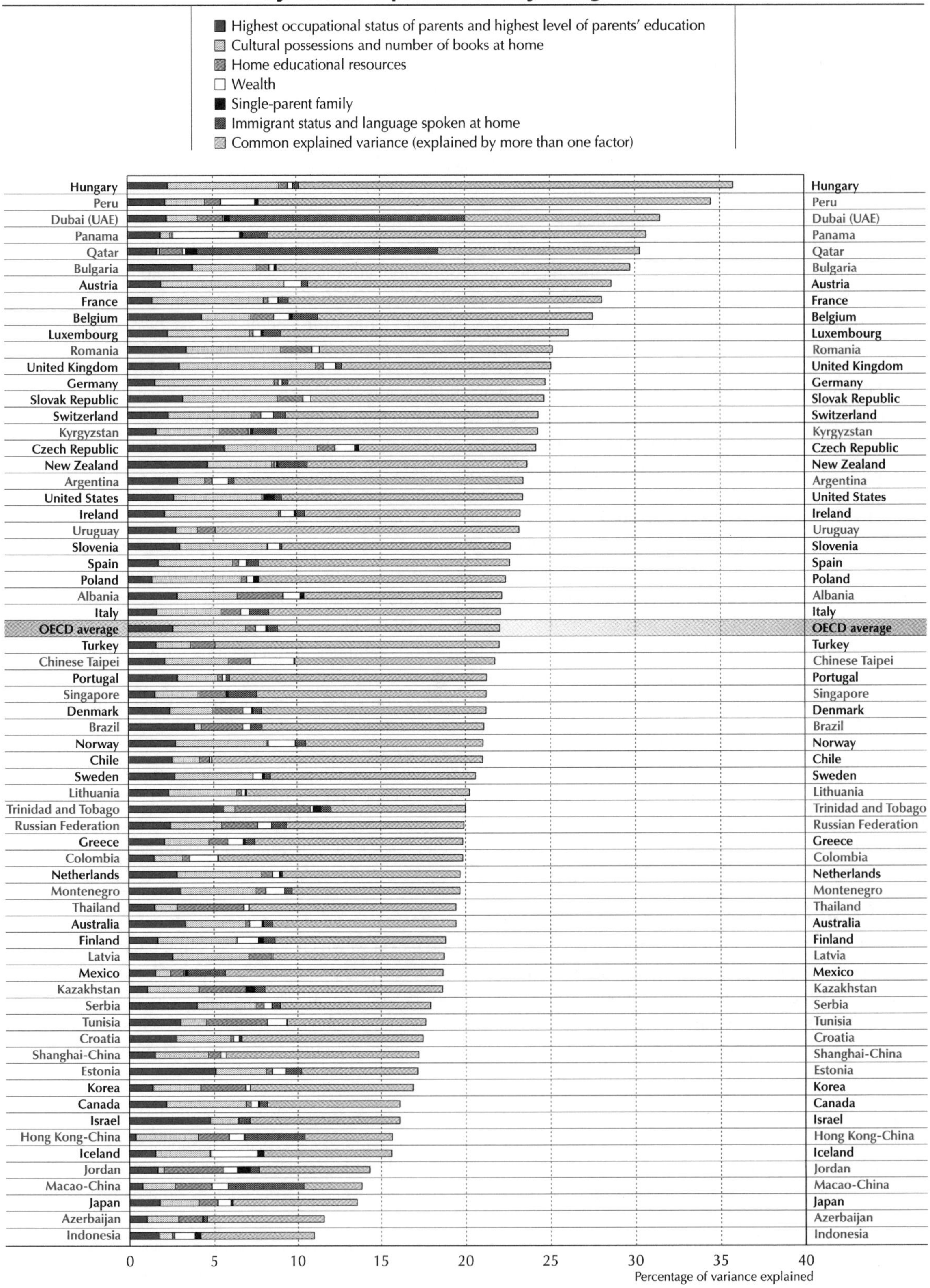

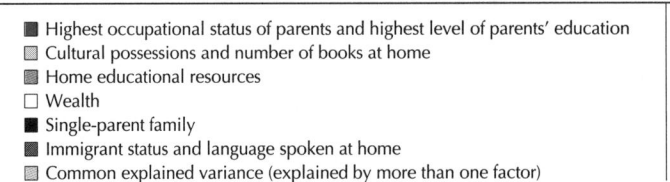

■ Highest occupational status of parents and highest level of parents' education
☐ Cultural possessions and number of books at home
■ Home educational resources
☐ Wealth
■ Single-parent family
■ Immigrant status and language spoken at home
☐ Common explained variance (explained by more than one factor)

Countries are ranked in descending order of the sum of common explained variance and variance explained by each component.
Source: OECD, *PISA 2009 Database*, Table II.2.4.

StatLink ⟐ http://dx.doi.org/10.1787/888932343570

Previous PISA assessments showed that in many countries, poor performance in school did not automatically follow from a disadvantaged home background. This finding has important implications for policy makers. Skills in reading are the basis for lifelong learning and enhance future opportunities for employment and earnings. As a consequence, countries in which the relationship between socio-economic background and reading performance is strong do not fully capitalise on the potential of students from disadvantaged backgrounds. Human capital may thus be wasted and intergenerational mobility from a lower to a higher socio-economic status may be limited. Poorer performing students will almost certainly be those least likely to obtain employment that offers the promise of economic and social mobility. This is a loss not just for individuals, but also for societies that are increasingly dependent on the contributions of all of their members for economic growth (OECD, 2010a).

Figure II.2.4 summarises, for each country, the degree to which various components of home and family background are associated with reading performance. The figure provides a first broad view of this issue, which is further developed in subsequent chapters of this volume. The components analysed here are: parents' occupational status; parents' level of education converted into years of schooling; cultural possessions; family structure; students' immigrant status; and the language spoken at home. Since these components tend to be associated with each other – for example, a student whose parents are better educated is also likely to have parents in higher-status occupations – the graph displays the influence of these features together and shows the variance in student performance explained by each feature once the influence of the others has been accounted for. The final segment in Figure II.2.4 shows the variance explained jointly by all factors (Table II.2.4).

Home and family background exerts a powerful influence on student performance across countries. For example, across OECD countries, differences in students' family background characteristics explain up to 22% of differences in student performance. Figure II.2.4 shows that, in general, these background characteristics explain reading performance jointly; that is, the different background characteristics are related to each other, such that the variance in reading performance explained by more than one factor jointly is 13% across the OECD countries. However, countries differ widely in the proportion of the variation in student performance explained by these factors. The percentage of explained variance ranges from 14% in Japan to 36% in Hungary, it is less than 18% in Iceland, Israel, Canada, Korea and Estonia, and more than 26% in Austria, France, Belgium and Luxembourg. The same is true among the partner countries and economies, with comparative little variance explained in Azerbaijan, Indonesia, Macao-China, Jordan, Hong Kong-China, Croatia, Shanghai-China and Serbia and a large portion of variance explained in Peru, Bulgaria, Dubai (UAE), Panama, Qatar and Romania (Table II.2.4). In some countries, many 15-year-olds have already left school and are thus not assessed by PISA (Table A2.1). Because these students are likely to be disadvantaged and to perform poorly, the variation in the performance of 15-year-olds in these countries may be grossly underestimated by the variation in the performance of enrolled students.

Since various aspects of socio-economic background tend to be closely interrelated, most of the remainder of the report summarises them in a single index, the *PISA index of the economic, social and cultural status* of students. The index was constructed such that roughly two-thirds of the OECD student population are between the values of -1 and 1, with an average score of 0 (*i.e.* the mean for the combined student population from the participating OECD countries is set to 0 and the standard deviation is set to 1).

Socio-economic background is only one aspect of a student's background. Other factors include family structure, school location (related to home background in terms of community context), immigrant status and home language (relative to the language of assessment in PISA). The rest of this chapter discusses the relationship between student performance and family structure and school location. Chapters 3 and 5 take a deeper and more thorough look at the relationship between socio-economic background and student performance at both the student- and school-level. Chapter 4 focuses specifically on immigration and the language spoken at home with regard to reading performance.

Family structure

The family is usually the first place where students can be encouraged to learn and family differences may influence learning beyond what occurs in the classroom. For example, parents may read to their young children, assist them with homework and, in some countries, actively participate and help out in schools. For older students, a supportive family can provide encouragement and meet with teachers or school administrators to keep track of their children's progress in school. Students with less supportive family backgrounds may therefore benefit from targeted support within the school system.[4]

Across countries, a large number of students live in families with one parent. Among OECD countries, 17% of the 15-year-old population covered by the PISA 2009 assessments were students from single-parent families. This proportion was 15% in PISA 2000. Many of these students share a socio-economically disadvantaged background. On average across the OECD, the average socio-economic background of students from single-parent families is -0.2, significantly below the average socio-economic background of 0.1 that corresponds to students living in other types of families (Table II.2.5).

Figure II.2.5 shows the average performance of students living in a single-parent household compared to other students (mixed and two-parent family structures), before and after accounting for socio-economic background. Across the OECD area, the performance gap between students from single-parent families and students from other types of families is 18 score points, before taking into account socio-economic background, which is roughly equivalent to half a year of schooling. In general, accounting for socio-economic background reduces, and in some cases eliminates, the gap. The reduction shows that family structure is related to socio-economic background and the separate impact of each of these variables on student performance cannot be disentangled easily using PISA. The fact that, in many countries and even after accounting for students' socio-economic status, differences in reading performance by family structure remain signals that there is an independent relationship between family structure and educational opportunities.

On average, after accounting for background, students from single-parent families score five points lower than students from other types of families. As Figure II.2.5 shows, across OECD countries, the gap is particularly large in the United States, where, after accounting for socio-economic background the difference stands at 23 score points. In Mexico, Ireland and Poland, it is 13 score points, and in Japan, Luxembourg and Belgium it is 10 score points, double the average size of the gap in OECD countries (Table II.2.5). In contrast, 25% of students in Chile come from single-parent families and they perform on a par with their peers from other family structures. In the United Kingdom, which has a similar proportion of single-parent family students as Chile, the same is true only after accounting for socio-economic background. In Austria, Slovenia, Portugal and Switzerland, about 15% of students live in single-parent households and there is no marked difference in performance between them and students from other family structures. In Estonia, students from single-parent families actually perform better after accounting for socio-economic background. Among the partner countries and economies, 28% of students in Trinidad and Tobago come from single-parent families, and they score 28 points lower than their peers from other types of families, after accounting for socio-economic background. The performance gap is 61 score points in Qatar and affects 12% of students. In Jordan, the proportion of students from single-parent families is similar to that of Qatar and the gap is 38 score points, while in Tunisia and Dubai (UAE) the gap is 25 points.

Evidence that students in single-parent families perform poorly might seem to be discouraging. The variation in the differences across countries, however, suggests that the disadvantage associated with single-parent families is not inevitable. Public policy in general, and educational policies in particular, can narrow the gaps by making it easier for single parents to support and foster their children's education (Pong, Dronkers and Hampden-Thompson, 2004). School systems and individual schools can consider, for example, how and what kinds of parental engagement are to be encouraged among single parents who have limited time to devote to school activities. Obviously, education policies need to be examined in conjunction with other policies, such as those relating to welfare and childcare.

School location and variation in performance across geographical areas

In some countries, student performance and the socio-economic or organisational profile of school systems also vary considerably according to where schools are located. To capture variation among school systems and regions within countries, some countries have undertaken the PISA surveys at regional levels (*e.g.* Belgium, Finland, Italy, Spain and the United Kingdom). Results at the regional levels for these countries are presented in Annex B2 of this volume.

An analysis of regional differences adds a useful perspective. Compared with an international perspective, regions within a country are likely to share many cultural, social and economic characteristics. A regional analysis thus yields insights for policy makers that are less influenced by cross-country differences. PISA countries that gather data at the regional level have the unique opportunity to foster greater co-operation and collaboration across educational authorities and some do so actively (Bussière *et al.*, 2007).

■ Figure II.2.5 ■
Reading performance difference between students from single-parent families and those from other types of families
Differences in performance before and after accounting for socio-economic background

☐ ■ Differences in peformance between students from single-parent familes and other types of families, **before** accounting for socio-economic background

☐ ■ Differences in peformance between students from single-parent familes and other types of families, **after** accounting for socio-economic background

Percentage of students from a single-parent family

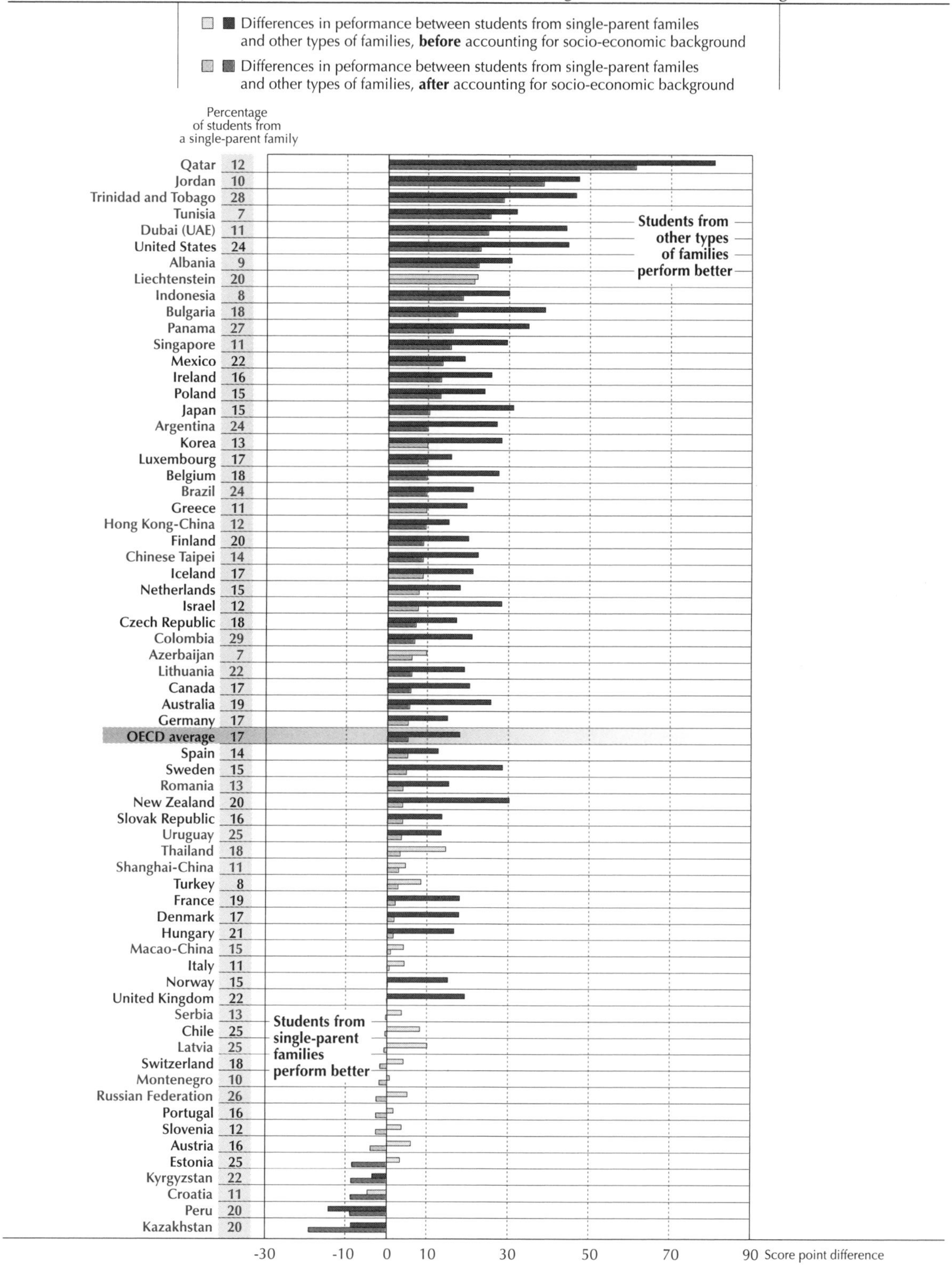

Note: Score point differences that are statistically significant are marked in a darker tone.
Countries are ranked in descending order of the score point differences between students from single-parent families and other types of families after accounting for socio-economic background.
Source: OECD, *PISA 2009 Database,* Table II.2.5.
StatLink ⧉ http://dx.doi.org/10.1787/888932343570

■ Figure II.2.6 ■
Reading performance, by school location
Mean scores after accounting for socio-economic background

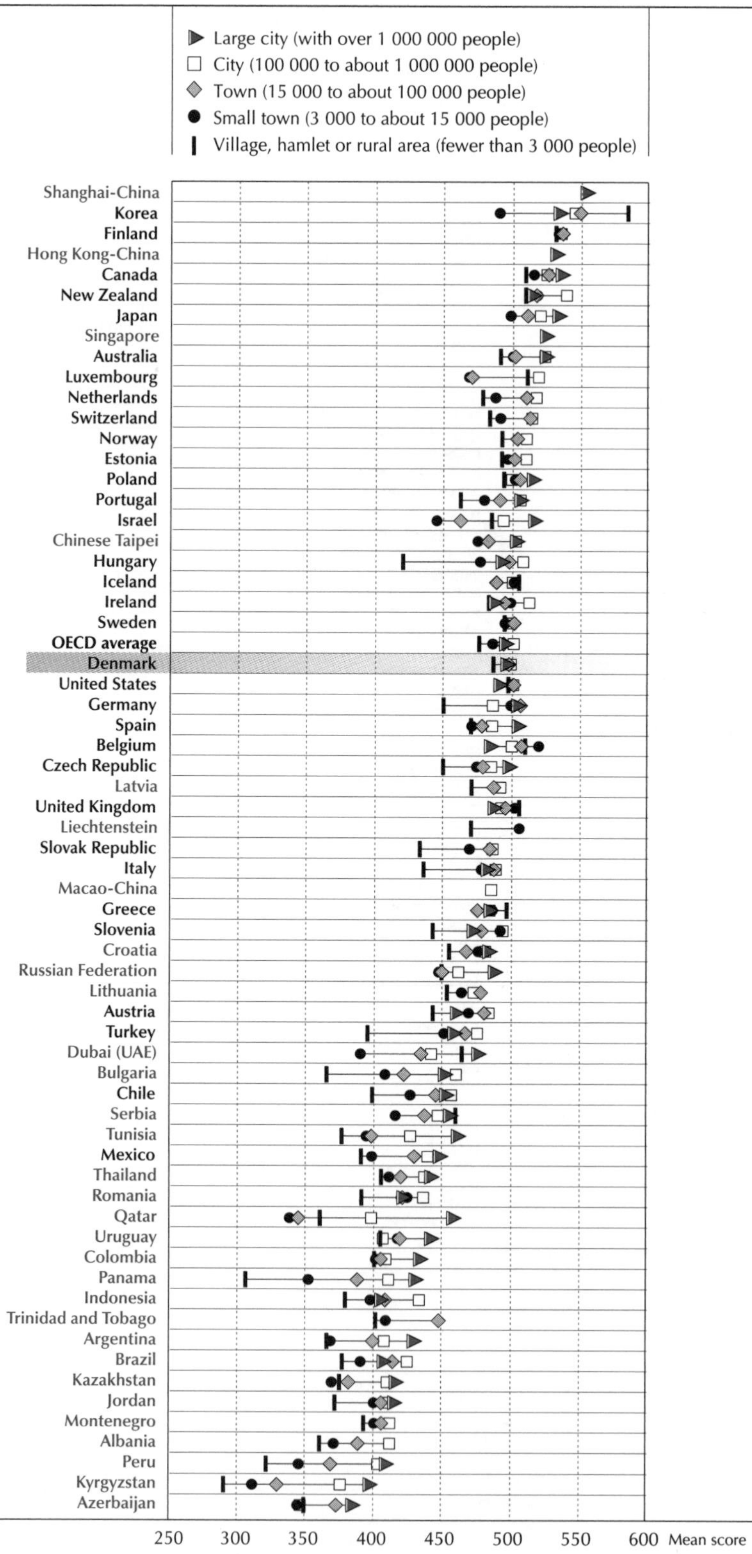

▷ Large city (with over 1 000 000 people)
□ City (100 000 to about 1 000 000 people)
◇ Town (15 000 to about 100 000 people)
● Small town (3 000 to about 15 000 people)
| Village, hamlet or rural area (fewer than 3 000 people)

Shanghai-China
Korea
Finland
Hong Kong-China
Canada
New Zealand
Japan
Singapore
Australia
Luxembourg
Netherlands
Switzerland
Norway
Estonia
Poland
Portugal
Israel
Chinese Taipei
Hungary
Iceland
Ireland
Sweden
OECD average
Denmark
United States
Germany
Spain
Belgium
Czech Republic
Latvia
United Kingdom
Liechtenstein
Slovak Republic
Italy
Macao-China
Greece
Slovenia
Croatia
Russian Federation
Lithuania
Austria
Turkey
Dubai (UAE)
Bulgaria
Chile
Serbia
Tunisia
Mexico
Thailand
Romania
Qatar
Uruguay
Colombia
Panama
Indonesia
Trinidad and Tobago
Argentina
Brazil
Kazakhstan
Jordan
Montenegro
Albania
Peru
Kyrgyzstan
Azerbaijan

250   300   350   400   450   500   550   600   Mean score

Countries are ranked in descending order of the average performance of students in cities (cities and large cities). For Liechtenstein and Trinidad and Tobago where this is not possible, the average of remaining categories was used.
Source: OECD, *PISA 2009 Database*, Table II.2.6.
StatLink ᵐˢᵖ http://dx.doi.org/10.1787/888932343570

Another way to analyse geographical performance variation is by school location. Schools are located in communities of different sizes. A large community or a densely populated area can make more educational resources available for students. Isolated communities might need targeted support or specific educational policies to ensure that students attending these schools reach their full potential. Sometimes the differences in performance by school location are the result of the different socio-economic context of these locations. Countries vary widely in the densities, characteristics and distributions of populations across different types of communities (Table II.2.6) and these differences need to be borne in mind when interpreting a cross-country analysis of how students in these different communities perform.

On average across the OECD, students in city schools perform better than students in other schools, even after accounting for differences in socio-economic background. As Figure II.2.6 shows, in the OECD area, students in city schools outperform students in rural schools by 40 score points, or the equivalent of one year of education. This general pattern is not observed, however, after accounting for socio-economic background, in Korea, Belgium, the United Kingdom, Greece, Iceland, the United States, Finland, Sweden, Poland, Israel, Ireland, the Netherlands and Germany. Where the pattern is evident, the size of the gaps differs across countries, which probably reflects differences in the resources and learning opportunities available in rural, urban and suburban areas, as well as differences in population density, distribution of labour markets, and the extent to which urban and suburban areas are sought and populated by different individuals that may indirectly impact learning outcomes. For example, in Turkey, the Slovak Republic, Chile, Mexico and Italy as well as the partner countries Peru, Tunisia, Albania, Argentina and Romania, the performance gap between students in city schools and those in rural schools is more than 45 score points, after accounting for students' socio-economic background. This gap is 80 score points or more – or the equivalent of two years of schooling – in Hungary and in the partner countries Bulgaria, Kyrgyzstan and Panama (Table II.2.6).

Figure II.2.6 can also be used to compare the performance of large cities across countries. In the OECD countries Canada, Japan, Korea, Poland and Australia, large cities - those with more than one million inhabitants - perform best, above 530 score points on average, before accounting for socio-economic background. The performance of students attending large-city schools, after accounting for their socio-economic background, is close to 536 score points in Korea, Japan and Canada, whereas in Australia it is 526 score points and in Poland 517 score points. In Luxembourg and Finland, the average performance of schools in their largest communities, cities with 100 000 to 1 000 000 inhabitants, is also high at 564 and 543 score points, respectively, while, after accounting for socio-economic background, it is 520 score points in Luxembourg and 537 score points in Finland. Among the partner countries and economies, students in cities with more than 1 000 000 people in Hong Kong-China and Shanghai-China perform at 534 and 556 score points, respectively, before and after accounting for students' socio-economic background.

Comparing performance before and after accounting for socio-economic background shows the extent to which differences in student performance by school location are related to differences in socio-economic background between school locations within countries. A large difference in adjusted and unadjusted performance, as is the case with Poland, is evidence of the large gap in socio-economic background between urban and rural areas. In the case of Poland, this difference in the average socio-economic background of urban and rural students is close to one standard deviation, so differences in performance reflect, in part, differences in the social background of students living in urban and rural areas. They may also reflect differences in the distribution of other educational factors that may be associated with socio-economic disparities that have an impact on student performance (Table II.2.6).

Many of the analyses presented in this chapter highlight the existence of inequities and inequality in educational outcomes, in the distribution of educational resources, and in learning outcomes inasmuch as they are associated with students' background characteristics. This chapter also highlights the fact that inequities and inequality vary substantially across countries, signalling that they are by no means inevitable, although some countries succeed better than others in reducing educational inequities.

Notes

1. Although PISA describes a wide range of student performance, the variance in student performance in countries with very low average performance may be underestimated because it is more difficult to distinguish between very low and extremely low levels of performance.

2. The Pearson correlation between the gap at the top and bottom ends of the distribution is 0.64 and statistically significant across all countries and economies that participated in the PISA 2009 assessment. The same correlation is stronger and statistically significant if the group is restricted to OECD countries (0.71) or partner countries and economies (0.69). Spearman correlations are very similar (0.65, 0.69 and 0.68, respectively). The correlation between the gap at the top end of the distribution and the mean performance is negative and statistically significant, but smaller at 0.40. The same is true if the median is used instead of the mean performance. However, the Spearman correlation is smaller, 0.31, and not statistically significant. This suggests that the relationship might be driven by a particular country. Comparing only OECD countries, the correlation between the gap at the top and the mean performance, whether Pearson or Spearman, is negative, weak (-0.10) and not statistically significant, while among partner countries and economies it is negative, strong (-0.51) and statistically significant. There is no statistically significant correlation between the gap at the bottom end of the distribution and mean or median performance, however it is measured, across systems. Across all countries or just for OECD countries, the correlations are small and positive (around 0.10), while across the partner countries and economies the correlations are very small and negative (around -0.01).

3. The percentage of students below Level 2 are calculated on the basis of students with valid information on the *PISA index of economic, social and cultural status.* As a result, estimates differ slightly from those presented in Volume I, *What Students Know and Can Do.*

4. The literature on the relationship between family structure and performance is vast, and parental engagement is only one of the aspects analysed in this literature. The literature has focused on the economic situation and, particularly, the stress levels of the family stemming from the transition from one type of family to another and from precarious economic situations. See, for example, Buchmann and Hannum (2001) for a cross-national look at this relationship; McLanahan and Sandefur (1994) for the consequences for students; Raley, Frisco and Wildsmith (2005) for a study of status and stress by comparing single-parent households to cohabitation; and Jeynes (2005) for a discussion about parental involvement in single-parent households. For classic studies on the differences in the use of language by social class, including parent-child interactions and language quality and richness, see Brice (1983). Also, see Volume IV, *What Makes a School Successful?,* for differences in the types and level of parental involvement in school across selected PISA countries.

3

Learning Outcomes and Socio-Economic Background

This chapter examines the relationship between student performance and different aspects of socio-economic background. It also discusses the extent to which countries have been able to moderate the impact of socio-economic background on learning outcomes. The chapter defines and uses the socio-economic gradient extensively, which summarises many of the aspects of educational equity that can be analysed by PISA.

While education has expanded over recent decades, inequalities in educational outcomes and in educational and social mobility persist in many countries (OECD, 2010d; OECD, 2010e). The long-term social and financial costs of educational inequalities can be high, as those without the competencies to participate in society fully may not realise their potential and they are likely to generate higher costs for health, income support, child welfare and security (Levin, 2009; Belfield and Levin, 2007). Given that education is a powerful determining factor of life chances, overall, equity in education can improve equity in economic and social outcomes. This is because depending on the equity levels of an education system, education can either reinforce economic advantages across generations or help improve social and economic mobility from one generation to another (OECD, 2010e; OECD, 2010f).

STUDENTS' SOCIO-ECONOMIC AND CULTURAL STATUS AND PERFORMANCE

Analyses of the impact of students' socio-economic background and their performance in school have usually provided discouraging conclusions, particularly at the national level. For example, using longitudinal methods, researchers who have tracked children's vocabulary development have found that growth trajectories for children from differing socio-economic backgrounds begin to diverge early on, and that when children enter school the impact of socio-economic background on both cognitive skills and behaviour is already well established (Willms, 2002). In addition, during the primary and middle-school years, children whose parents have low incomes, have low education levels, are unemployed or working in low-prestige occupations are less likely to do well in academic pursuits than children growing up in more socio-economically advantaged households. They are also less likely to be engaged in curricular and extra-curricular school activities than their more advantaged peers (Datcher, 1982; Voelkl, 1995; Finn and Rock, 1997; Johnson et al., 2001).

The international comparative evidence from PISA offers a more encouraging outlook on educational equity. Although the relationship between student's background and school performance points to inequities in all countries, the strength of this relationship varies across school systems. Thus, by comparing the relationship between student performance and different aspects of socio-economic background it is possible to identify school systems that successfully reduce the strong relationship between background and performance.

Furthermore, PISA results show that some countries simultaneously demonstrate both high average performance and a relatively moderate relationship between student background and performance, suggesting that equity and performance are by no means opposing or impossible policy objectives. These successful school systems are analysed in more detail in Volume IV, *What Makes a School Successful?*, as they set important benchmarks and policy orientations of what can be achieved in terms of quality and equity in learning outcomes.

Understanding the relationship between students' socio-economic background and performance helps analyse the distribution of educational opportunities. From a school-policy perspective, the relationship indicates how equitably the benefits of education – due to the schools themselves or to other social interactions and policies – are shared among students from different socio-economic backgrounds, as seen in student performance. More generally, these analyses also show how economic, social and cultural status is distributed among the population. Moreover, the relationship between students' performance and their socio-economic background points to how well education systems succeed in providing quality education for all students.

THE SOCIO-ECONOMIC GRADIENT: AN APPROACH TO EQUITY IN PISA

Within a single construct, the socio-economic gradient summarises many of the aspects of educational equity that can be analysed by PISA.[1] Throughout this volume, the term socio-economic gradient is used to refer to the overall relationship between socio-economic background and performance. More specifically, it refers to the relationship between student performance and the *PISA index of economic, social and cultural status* (see Box II.1.2 for a description of the index). Figure II.3.1 shows the socio-economic gradient for the PISA 2009 assessment. It shows how well students with different socio-economic backgrounds perform on the PISA reading scale for the combined OECD area (Box II.3.1). Summary statistics on different aspects of this relationship for individual countries are shown in Figure II.3.2.

■ Figure II.3.1 ■
Socio-economic background and reading performance in the OECD area

——————— Socio-economic gradient line
for the OECD area as a whole

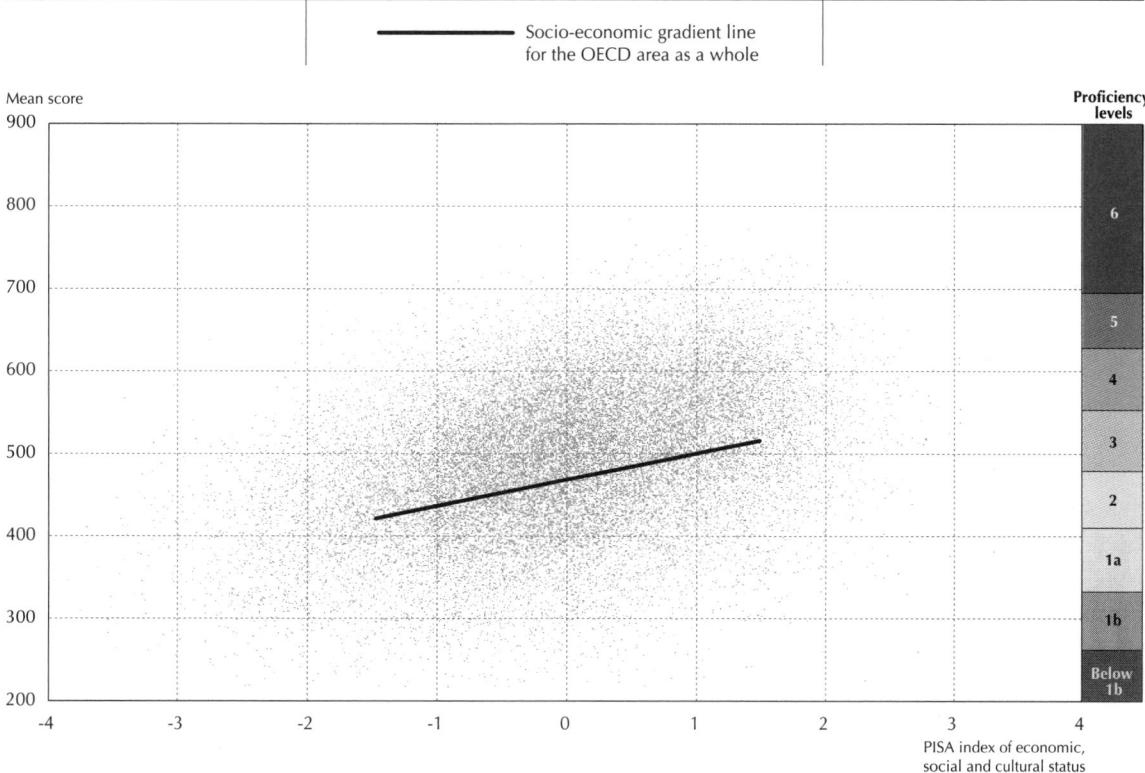

Note: Each dot represents an OECD student picked at random out of 10 OECD students.
Source: OECD, *PISA 2009 Database*.
StatLink ⬛⬛⬛ http://dx.doi.org/10.1787/888932343589

Box II.3.1 **How to read Figure II.3.1**

Each dot on this graph represents one in ten 15-year-old students drawn randomly from the combined OECD area. Figure II.3.1 plots their performance in reading against their economic, social and cultural status.

The vertical axis shows student scores on the reading scale, for which the mean was set in PISA 2000 at 500. About two-thirds of the dots fall between 400 and 600. The different shaded areas show the seven proficiency levels in reading.

The horizontal axis shows values on the *PISA index of economic, social and cultural status*. This has been constructed to have a mean of 0 and a standard deviation of 1 in the OECD area, so that about two-thirds of students are between +1 and –1.[2]

The dark line is the gradient line. It summarises the socio-economic gradient, by showing the average association between reading performance and socio-economic background across students in OECD countries.

Since the aim of the figure is not to compare education systems but to highlight a relationship throughout the combined OECD area, each student in that area contributes equally to this picture – *i.e.* larger countries, with more students in the PISA population, such as Japan, Mexico and the United States –, influence the international gradient line more than smaller countries, such as Iceland or Luxembourg.

Figure II.3.1 highlights three recurrent findings regarding the socio-economic background of students and their reading performance:

- Students with more socio-economically advantaged backgrounds generally perform better. This finding is shown by the upward slope of the gradient line. Across the OECD countries, this advantage averages to 38 score points in reading for each increase of one standard deviation in socio-economic background (*i.e.* one point in the index shown on the horizontal axis), which is roughly equivalent to a year's worth of schooling, on average across OECD countries.

- A given difference in socio-economic background is associated with a difference in student reading performance that is roughly the same throughout the distribution – *i.e.* the marginal benefit of a greater socio-economic advantage neither diminishes nor rises by a substantial amount as this advantage grows. This is shown by the fact that the socio-economic gradient line is nearly straight.

- The relationship between student performance and the *PISA index of economic, social and cultural status* is far from deterministic. Many disadvantaged students, shown on the left of the figure, score well above what is predicted by the gradient line; in this sense they are "resilient". Meanwhile, a sizeable proportion of students from privileged home backgrounds perform below what those backgrounds would suggest. In fact, for any group of students with similar backgrounds, there is a considerable range in performance.

The relationship between socio-economic background and performance, as depicted in Figure II.3.1, has five features worth considering from an international comparative perspective: the strength of the gradient and the slope, length, height and linearity of the gradient line. Figure II.3.2 presents each of these dimensions for each country and economy that participated in the PISA 2009 assessment. Each of the five dimensions is considered separately below. The study of these dimensions of the relationship between socio-economic status and reading performance sheds light on which countries succeed in moderating the relationship between background and performance.

The *strength* of the gradient measures the *strength* of the association between student performance and background: that is, it measures the proportion of the variation in student performance that is accounted for by socio-economic background.[3] Expressed as a percentage, it ranges from 0 to 100. If this number is low, relatively little of the variation in student performance is associated with students' socio-economic background; if it is high, a large part of the performance variation can be attributed to socio-economic background. This can be seen for the combined OECD area in Figure II.3.1 by how well the line fits the dispersion of the dots: the closer the dots are to the line, the more the variance is explained by socio-economic background, and the better the socio-economic and cultural status of a student can predict his or her achievement.

Figure II.3.2 shows the strength of the gradient for individual countries. On average across OECD countries, 14% of the variation in student performance in reading within each country is associated with the *PISA index of economic, social and cultural status*. In some OECD countries, the strength of the gradient is relatively weak. For example, less than 10% of the variance in student performance is explained in Estonia, Finland, Norway, Japan and Canada, and it is weakest in Iceland, at less than 7%. The relationship is strongest in Hungary, at 26%, and relatively strong, 18% or more, in Belgium, Turkey, Chile and Luxembourg. Among the partner countries and economies, the strength of the gradient is as high as 27% in Peru and more than 20% in Uruguay and Bulgaria. It is less than 10% in Macao-China, Qatar, Hong Kong-China, Azerbaijan, Indonesia, Jordan, Tunisia, Liechtenstein, Trinidad and Tobago and Serbia. For some of these countries, however, these numbers do not necessarily provide evidence of equity in education in general, because the proportion of students who are not at school at age 15, and so are not assessed by PISA, may be large (see Table A2.1). These students who are not assessed by PISA are more likely to perform poorly and come from socio-economically disadvantaged backgrounds. As a result, equity estimates are probably overestimated for educational systems with low enrolment rates.[4]

The *slope* of the gradient line measures the steepness of the average relationship between reading performance and socio-economic background. The slope shows how much students' performance changes, on average, with a change of one unit on the index of socio-economic status. In Figure II.3.1, the slope of the gradient is shown by the inclination of the gradient line: the sharper the inclination, or the closer it is to a vertical line, the greater the impact of economic, social and cultural status on student performance, suggesting greater inequity; gentler gradients indicate a lower impact of socio-economic background on student performance, *i.e.* more equity. On average across OECD countries, the slope of the gradient is 38 score points (Figure II.3.2, Table II.3.2).

■ Figure II.3.2 ■

Measures of the relationship between socio-economic background and reading performance

		Strength of the gradient[1]	Slope of the gradient[1]	Mean performance in reading	Mean socio-economic background	Height of the gradient	Length of the gradient	Linearity of the gradient[2]
		Percentage of variance in student performance explained by student socio-economic background	Score point difference associated with one unit increase in the PISA index of economic, social and cultural status	Average student performance	Average students' PISA index of economic, social and cultural status	Predicted performance for a student with a socio-economic background equal to zero, the OECD average	Range of socio-economic index points for the middle 90% of students (difference between the 95th and 5th percentiles)	Score point difference associated with one unit increase in the PISA index of economic, social and cultural status squared
OECD	Australia	12.7	46	515	0.34	502	2.38	-2.58
	Austria	16.6	48	470	0.06	468	2.73	-1.29
	Belgium	19.3	47	506	0.20	499	2.93	1.87
	Canada	8.6	32	524	0.50	510	2.63	2.79
	Chile	18.7	31	449	-0.57	468	3.73	3.53
	Czech Republic	12.4	46	478	-0.09	483	2.30	-1.98
	Denmark	14.5	36	495	0.30	485	2.81	-2.67
	Estonia	7.6	29	501	0.15	497	2.53	1.61
	Finland	7.8	31	536	0.37	525	2.45	-3.60
	France	16.7	51	496	-0.13	505	2.74	-1.50
	Germany	17.9	44	497	0.18	493	2.94	-2.95
	Greece	12.5	34	483	-0.02	484	3.21	-0.29
	Hungary	26.0	48	494	-0.20	504	3.14	-4.71
	Iceland	6.2	27	500	0.72	483	2.88	-4.85
	Ireland	12.6	39	496	0.05	496	2.72	-3.50
	Israel	12.5	43	474	-0.02	480	2.75	2.14
	Italy	11.8	32	486	-0.12	490	3.32	-3.09
	Japan	8.6	40	520	-0.01	522	2.32	-4.91
	Korea	11.0	32	539	-0.15	544	2.71	-0.06
	Luxembourg	18.0	40	472	0.19	466	3.63	-0.13
	Mexico	14.5	25	425	-1.22	456	4.18	0.23
	Netherlands	12.8	37	508	0.27	499	2.66	4.55
	New Zealand	16.6	52	521	0.09	519	2.53	-0.15
	Norway	8.6	36	503	0.47	487	2.36	-5.03
	Poland	14.8	39	500	-0.28	512	2.86	-3.10
	Portugal	16.5	30	489	-0.32	499	3.79	-0.03
	Slovak Republic	14.6	41	477	-0.09	482	2.70	-5.48
	Slovenia	14.3	39	483	0.07	481	2.78	-0.75
	Spain	13.6	29	481	-0.31	491	3.58	-0.58
	Sweden	13.4	43	497	0.33	485	2.57	-2.45
	Switzerland	14.1	40	501	0.08	498	2.90	-0.57
	Turkey	19.0	29	464	-1.16	499	4.02	-0.27
	United Kingdom	13.7	44	494	0.20	488	2.52	0.84
	United States	16.8	42	500	0.17	493	3.01	6.61
	OECD average	14.0	38	493	0.00	494	2.92	-0.95
Partners	Albania	10.7	31	385	-0.95	416	3.44	2.71
	Argentina	19.6	40	398	-0.62	424	3.90	5.01
	Azerbaijan	7.4	21	362	-0.64	376	3.18	2.26
	Brazil	13.0	28	412	-1.16	445	3.94	6.51
	Bulgaria	20.2	51	429	-0.11	437	3.08	-2.79
	Colombia	16.6	28	413	-1.15	445	4.15	3.23
	Croatia	11.0	32	476	-0.18	482	3.04	-1.88
	Dubai (UAE)	14.2	51	459	0.42	439	2.61	-1.35
	Hong Kong-China	4.5	17	533	-0.80	548	3.42	-3.22
	Indonesia	7.8	17	402	-1.55	428	3.55	2.74
	Jordan	7.9	24	405	-0.57	420	3.30	0.31
	Kazakhstan	12.0	38	390	-0.51	410	2.66	-0.65
	Kyrgyzstan	14.6	40	314	-0.65	341	3.02	7.02
	Latvia	10.3	29	484	-0.13	488	2.75	0.28
	Liechtenstein	8.4	26	499	0.09	497	2.93	-4.38
	Lithuania	13.6	33	468	-0.05	471	2.99	0.39
	Macao-China	1.8	12	487	-0.70	495	2.92	-0.92
	Montenegro	10.0	31	408	-0.24	416	3.09	-1.62
	Panama	18.1	31	371	-0.81	402	4.23	8.20
	Peru	27.4	41	370	-1.31	424	4.18	0.45
	Qatar	4.0	25	372	0.51	360	3.00	-0.97
	Romania	13.6	36	424	-0.34	437	2.93	-0.67
	Russian Federation	11.3	37	459	-0.21	468	2.51	0.23
	Serbia	9.8	27	442	0.07	440	3.17	0.63
	Shanghai-China	12.3	27	556	-0.49	569	3.35	0.79
	Singapore	15.3	47	526	-0.43	547	2.57	2.71
	Chinese Taipei	11.8	36	495	-0.33	507	2.74	1.37
	Thailand	13.3	22	421	-1.31	450	3.72	4.41
	Trinidad and Tobago	9.7	38	416	-0.58	441	3.11	6.87
	Tunisia	8.1	19	404	-1.20	426	4.18	2.38
	Uruguay	20.7	37	426	-0.70	453	4.00	1.15

1. In these columns values that are statistically significantly different from the OECD average are indicated in bold.
2. Values that are statistically significant are indicated in bold.
Source: OECD, *PISA 2009 Database*, Table II.3.2.
StatLink ᴍ꜒꜖ᴘ http://dx.doi.org/10.1787/888932343589

This means that students' scores on the reading scale are, on average in the OECD countries, 38 score points higher for each extra unit on the *PISA index of economic, social and cultural status*. This can be interpreted as showing that a student just within the top 15 percent of the population by socio-economic background would be predicted to score about 38 points higher than an average student or one proficiency level higher than a student just within the bottom 15 percent of the population.

As Figure II.3.2 shows, among OECD countries, the slope of the gradient is relatively gentle in Iceland, Estonia, Spain and Portugal, all with slopes of 30 score points or less. This is also the case in Turkey and Mexico; but in both of these countries, large numbers of students have already left the school system by the time they are 15. By contrast, the slope of the gradient is steep in New Zealand, France, Austria, Hungary, Belgium, Australia and the Czech Republic at over 45 score points. Among the partner countries and economies, the slope of the gradient ranges from more than 45 score points in Bulgaria, Dubai (UAE) and Singapore to less than 20 score points in Macao-China, Indonesia, Hong Kong-China and Tunisia. Where the number of students who no longer attend school in these countries and economies by the time they are 15 is large, these figures cannot necessarily be interpreted as providing evidence of an equitable distribution of educational opportunities and outcomes.

The slope and the strength of the gradient measure different aspects of the relationship between socio-economic background and performance. Figure II.3.2 illustrates both the strength and the slope of the gradient side by side for all countries and economies. For example, in Austria and Hungary, the slope of the gradient is 48 score points, a relatively steep relationship; but in Austria, differences in socio-economic background explain 17% of the variation in student performance, while in Hungary, socio-economic background explains more than 26% of that variation. This means that in Austria, disadvantaged students are more likely to perform beyond expectations and in Hungary fewer disadvantaged students perform at the level of their advantaged peers. The same occurs among countries with gentler gradients. For example, both Chile and Finland have a gradient slope of 31 score points. In Chile, the strength of the gradient is more than 19% while in Finland it is only 8%. This disparity indicates that while the average performance difference between advantaged and disadvantaged students in Finland and Chile is similar, the likelihood of disadvantaged students performing at levels similar to those of their advantaged peers is much lower in Chile than in Finland.

Where the slope of the gradient is steep and the gradient is strong, the challenges are greatest because this combination implies that students and schools are unlikely to "escape" the close relationship between socio-economic background and learning outcomes. In these countries, this strong relationship also produces marked differences in performance between students from advantaged and disadvantaged backgrounds. Where the slope is steep and the gradient weak, the relationship between socio-economic background and learning outcomes is an average tendency with many students performing above or below what is expected by this general trend.

The *height* of the gradient line[5] measures performance after accounting for socio-economic background. It indicates the performance of a student with a background equal to the average across OECD countries, which has been standardised to a value of 0. In Figure II.3.1, the height of the gradient line is shown by the performance level at which the gradient line crosses the vertical axis depicted at a socio-economic background score of zero. This can be applied to each country individually. The height of the gradient line for individual countries is given in Figure II.3.2.

The height of the gradient line provides an indication of what students' mean performance in an education system would be if the average economic, social and cultural background of its student population were identical to the OECD average. The average performance of students depends on the education system and the overall social, economic and political institutions that influence student performance. This includes, but is not restricted to, government institutions that improve children's material conditions, like housing, nutrition and health care. Thus, these comparisons are limited because differences in these conditions across countries are not taken into account. Figure II.3.5 highlights the difference between the country mean score, as predicted by the socio-economic distribution and the actual mean performance score.

The *length* of the gradient line measures socio-economic differences in the student population. The longer the gradient, the wider the potential disparities between advantaged and disadvantaged students. In countries with large socio-economic disparities among households, even a gentle gradient can indicate large differences in the extent to which socio-economic background affects student outcomes when advantaged and disadvantaged students are compared. Longer gradients imply greater challenges for public policy, since schools and school systems face a socio-economically more heterogeneous student population in these countries.

Figure II.3.1 shows the length of the gradient line. The line is drawn from the 5th percentile to the 95th percentile of the *PISA index of economic, social and cultural status* among the OECD students. It depicts the range of socio-economic scores for the middle-performing 90% of students. Figure II.3.2 shows that some education systems need to cater to students from a wider range of socio-economic backgrounds than others. Across the OECD area, the length of the gradient ranges from less than 2.5 standard deviations on *the PISA index of social, economic and cultural status* in the Czech Republic, Japan, Norway, Australia and Finland to more than 3.5 standard deviations in Mexico, Turkey, Portugal, Chile, Luxembourg and Spain. Among partner countries and economies, the length of the gradient is never less than 2.5 standard deviations, yet is is more than 3.5 standard deviations in Uruguay, Brazil, Argentina, Thailand and Indonesia and more than 4.0 in Panama, Peru, Tunisia and Colombia (Table II.3.2).

The *linearity* of the gradient line measures the extent to which the performance difference associated with an advantaged background remains constant across levels of socio-economic background. In Figure II.3.1, the gradient line is almost straight. Figure II.3.2 presents the index of curvilinearity, in which a positive value indicates that the socio-economic gradient becomes steeper for more advantaged socio-economic students. In other words, as socio-economic background increases, there is an increase in the extent to which inequalities in socio-economic background translate into performance differences. A negative value indicates the flattening off of the gradient at higher levels of socio-economic background: as socio-economic background becomes more advantaged, there is a decline in the extent to which inequalities in socio-economic background translate into performance differences.

As Figure II.3.2 shows, the gradient line for many countries is roughly linear. Although the OECD average in the index of curvilinearity is -1 and statistically significant, it can be considered as practically linear. In some countries, however, the gradients are steep at low levels of economic, social and cultural status, and tend to level off at higher status levels, signalling that there is progressively less associated advantage in student performance at higher levels of socio-economic background. This phenomenon is moderate in the Slovak Republic, Norway, Japan, Iceland and Hungary, and is also visible in Finland, Ireland, Poland, Italy, Denmark and Sweden and in the partner economy Hong Kong-China. However, in another group of countries, most notably in the United States and the Netherlands but also in Chile and Canada and the partner countries and economies Panama, Kyrgyzstan, Trinidad and Tobago, Brazil, Argentina, Thailand, Colombia, Indonesia and Tunisia, the gradients are relatively gentle at low levels of socio-economic background, becoming steeper at higher levels (Table II.3.2). In these countries, the greater the socio-economic advantage, the greater the marginal increase observed in student performance, and among students from socio-economically less advantaged backgrounds, there are small differences in performance.

The finding that across countries gradients tend to be roughly linear, or only modestly curved, across the range of economic, social and cultural status, has an important policy implication. Many socio-economic policies are aimed at providing more resources to the most disadvantaged students, either through taxation or by targeting benefits and socio-economic programmes for certain groups. The results from PISA suggest that, in many countries, it is not easy to establish a particular level of economic, social and cultural status below which performance declines sharply. If such a status is taken as a surrogate for parents' decisions and actions aimed at providing a richer environment for their children (such as taking an interest in their school work) then these findings suggest that there is room for improvement at all levels of the socio-economic continuum. But difficulty in determining such a level of socio-economic disadvantage does not imply that differentiated student support is unwarranted. As discussed in Chapter 6, education policy can also take the form of performance-targeted policies. In this respect, and from an equity perspective, it is useful to identify students not proficient at Level 2 on the PISA reading scale (see Chapter 1 of this volume), as the future education, occupation and social careers of these students are at risk.

A COMPARATIVE PERSPECTIVE ON SOCIO-ECONOMIC GRADIENTS

Countries differ not just in their overall performance, but also in the extent to which they are able to moderate the association between socio-economic background and performance. PISA suggests that maximising overall performance and securing similar levels of performance among students from different socio-economic backgrounds can be achieved simultaneously. These results suggest that quality and equity need not be considered as competing policy objectives.

Figure II.3.3 contrasts average performance in reading (on the vertical axis) with the strength of the relationship between socio-economic background and reading performance used as an indicator of equity in the distribution of learning opportunities (on the horizontal axis). Figure II.3.4 provides a similar perspective, but with the slope of the socio-economic gradient on the horizontal axis.

■ Figure II.3.3 ■
Strength of the socio-economic gradient and reading performance

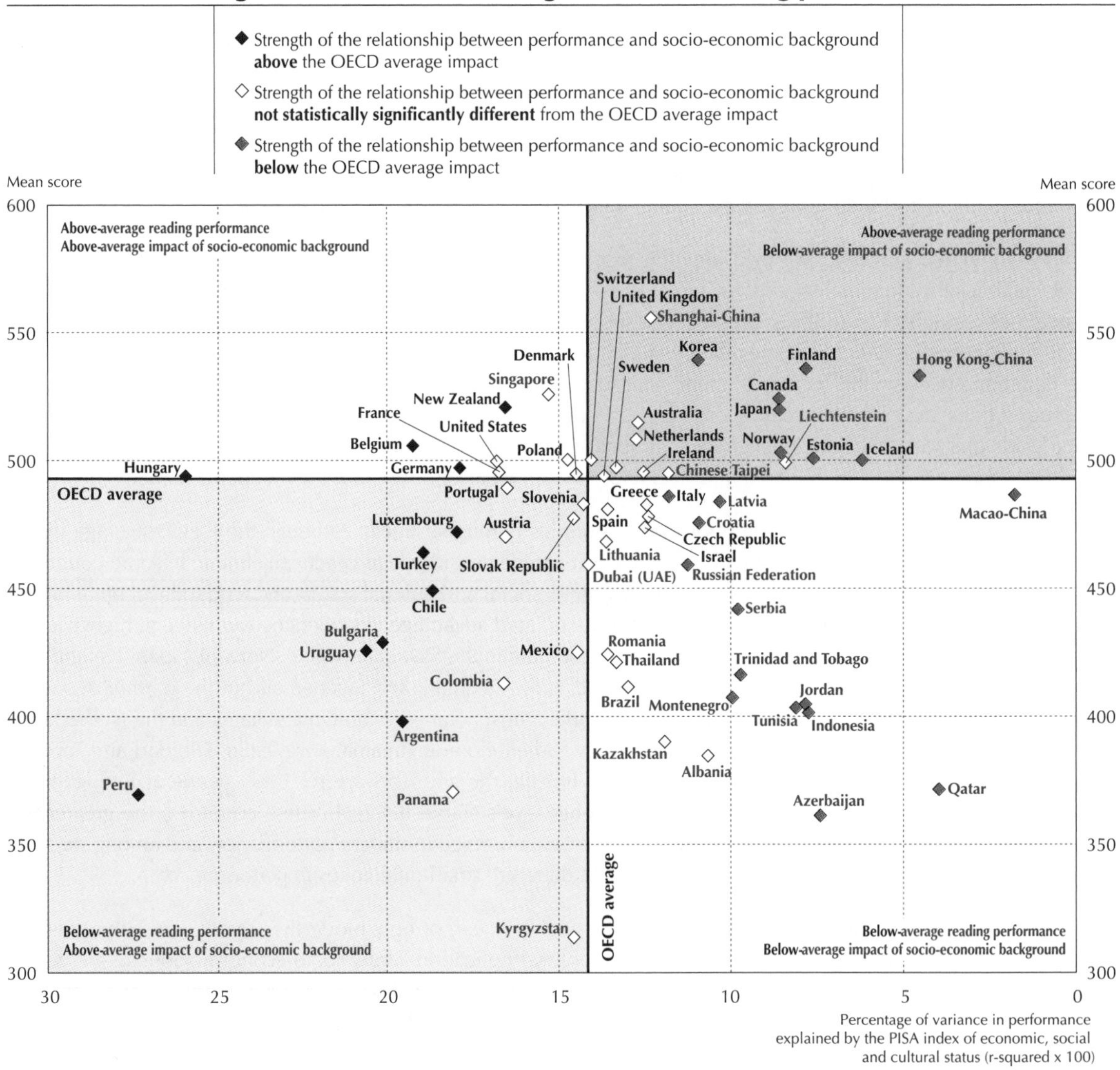

◆ Strength of the relationship between performance and socio-economic background
above the OECD average impact

◇ Strength of the relationship between performance and socio-economic background
not statistically significantly different from the OECD average impact

◆ Strength of the relationship between performance and socio-economic background
below the OECD average impact

Source: OECD, *PISA 2009 Database*, Table II.3.2.
StatLink http://dx.doi.org/10.1787/888932343589

In the upper-right quadrant of both Figures II.3.3 and II.3.4 appear Canada, Finland and Korea, among OECD countries together with the partner economy Hong Kong-China. Japan is also in this quadrant in Figure II.3.3, as is the partner economy Shanghai-China in Figure II.3.4. These countries display high student performance in reading and, at the same time, a below-average impact of economic, social and cultural status on student performance. With mean performance closer to the OECD average, Estonia and Iceland also appear among the countries with relatively gentle and weak relationships between socio-economic background and performance, while in Norway the relationship is also weak but the slope of the gradient is close to the OECD average. These school systems can be considered worthwhile cases for analysis inasmuch as they succeed in having both high levels of equity and high levels of performance. Volume IV, *What Makes a School Successful?,* delves into the organisational characteristics of these successful school systems.

In contrast, the lower-left quadrant of Figure II.3.3 displays the OECD countries Chile, Turkey and Luxembourg together with the partner countries Peru, Argentina, Uruguay and Bulgaria with below-average student performance in reading and an above-average strength in the relationship between socio-economic background and performance. Of this group, only Bulgaria remains in Figure II.3.4 and it is joined by Austria, Israel and the Czech Republic, among OECD countries, and the partner economy Dubai (UAE). In these countries, educational policy faces the greatest challenge of raising the average performance and providing more equal educational opportunities for disadvantaged students.

Only New Zealand and Belgium show high average performance and large socio-economic inequalities. Figure II.3.3 shows no other countries with above-average performance levels and a comparatively strong relationship between performance and socio-economic background. Germany and Hungary both show a greater-than-average strength of the socio-economic gradient and a mean performance very close to the OECD average. When the slope, instead of the strength, of the gradient is used, as Figure II.3.4 shows, these OECD countries are joined by Australia and the partner country Singapore among those with steeper-than-average socio-economic gradients and above-average performance. France, Sweden and the United Kingdom all have steeper-than-average socio-economic gradients and a mean performance around the OECD average.

In the lower-right quadrant of Figures II.3.3 and II.3.4, the partner countries and economies Azerbaijan, Qatar, Indonesia, Tunisia, Jordan, Montenegro, Serbia and Croatia show below-average performance and below-average impact of socio-economic background on performance (this group also includes Trinidad and Tobago and the Russian Federation, but only in Figure II.3.3, and Lithuania, Thailand, Colombia, Brazil and Albania, but only in Figure II.3.4).

■ Figure II.3.4 ■
Slope of the socio-economic gradient and reading performance

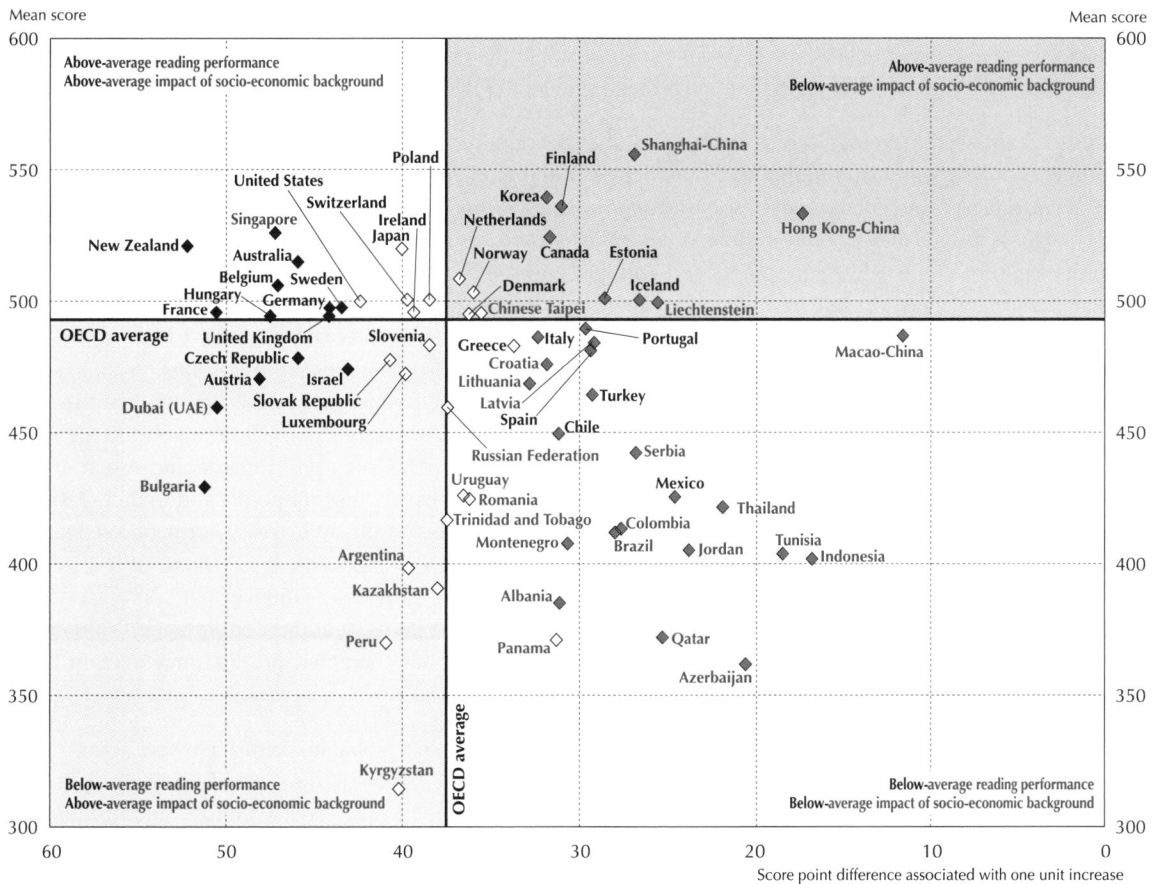

Source: OECD, *PISA 2009 Database*, Table II.3.2.
StatLink ⬛ℝ⬛ http://dx.doi.org/10.1787/888932343589

Italy and the partner countries and economies Latvia and Macao-China also show weaker-than-average gradients, but their mean performance is 10 points or less below the OECD average. In the lower-right quadrant of Figure II.3.4, among OECD countries, Italy is joined by Chile, Mexico, Spain, Portugal and Turkey as countries with gentler-than-average slopes and lower-than-average performance, although Portugal and Italy are less than 10 score points below the OECD average. Although some of these countries show that below-average performance in reading is associated with an average impact of socio-economic background, in some cases only a portion of 15-year-olds in these countries are enrolled in school (see Table A2.1). Since PISA only surveys 15-year-olds that are in school, the impact of socio-economic background on the reading performance of 15-year-olds may be underestimated where enrolment rates are low.

Comparing the relationship between socio-economic background and student performance, it is important to take into account the marked differences in the distribution of socio-economic characteristics between countries. Figure II.3.2 presents each country or economy's mean socio-economic score. Among OECD countries, students in Mexico and Turkey have a mean socio-economic background of more than one standard deviation below the average OECD student. In Chile, the average student has a socio-economic index that lies more than half a standard deviation below the OECD average, and in Spain and Portugal, mean socio-economic background is about 0.3 of a standard deviation below the OECD average.

Among the partner countries and economies, the mean socio-economic background across students is generally below the OECD average. In Indonesia, Peru, Thailand, Tunisia, Brazil and Colombia the mean socio-economic background is more than one standard deviation below the OECD average. As discussed above, in some of these countries, large numbers of students, particularly students who are disadvantaged and perform poorly, are no longer in the school system. This will have an impact on the inferences drawn from the PISA data on the issue of equity.

The socio-economically disadvantaged background of the average student in Hong Kong-China (0.8 of a standard deviation below the OECD average) Shanghai-China and Singapore (0.5 below the average) makes their high performance all the more impressive. At the same time, the socio-economically disadvantaged background of the average student in other countries and economies helps explain their observed below-average performance, where students have fewer home advantages than the average student in OECD countries.

Figure II.3.5 shows the average scores before and after accounting for countries' socio-economic profile. This hypothetical adjustment, also referred to as the height of the gradient line, assumes that all countries have the same average *PISA index of economic, socio-economic and cultural status,* equal to that of the OECD average. This change in the socio-economic profile of countries would result, for example, in an increase in Turkey's performance from 464 to 499 score points and Portugal's from 489 to 499 score points, higher than the OECD average performance. With such an adjustment, Spain and Italy would move from a below-average unadjusted score to an adjusted score around the OECD average. Similarly, the partner economy Macao-China would also improve its score to a level above the OECD average. The adjustment also improves scores for Mexico by 30 score points and reduces Iceland's mean performance from 500 to 483 score points. Among the partner countries and economies, the adjustment raises the performance score by more than 25 score points in Thailand, Kyrgyzstan, Uruguay, Indonesia and Argentina; more than 30 score points in Brazil, Colombia, Panama and Albania; and more than 50 score points in Peru. The score for Dubai (UAE) decreases by 21 score points and that of Qatar by 12 score points. These differences between the observed performance and the adjusted performance reflect the extent to which performance differences are driven by the average socio-economic background of the student population. The fact that adjusted scores still differ across countries provides evidence that socio-economic differences across countries explain only part of the differences in systems' reading performance (Volume IV, *What Makes a School Successful?,* delves deeper into the organisational characteristics that may explain these differences across school systems).

Such an adjustment is obviously entirely hypothetical: countries operate in a global marketplace where actual rather than adjusted performance in cognitive skills and abilities – and non-cognitive skills beyond PISA's measure – is all that counts. Also, the adjustment does not take into consideration the complex social, cultural and institutional context of each educational system. However, in the same way that comparisons of school quality focus on the added value that schools provide, accounting for the socio-economic intake of schools when interpreting results, those who use cross-country comparisons need to bear in mind the economic, social and educational differences among countries.

■ Figure II.3.5 ■

Countries' mean reading performance, observed and after accounting for socio-economic profile

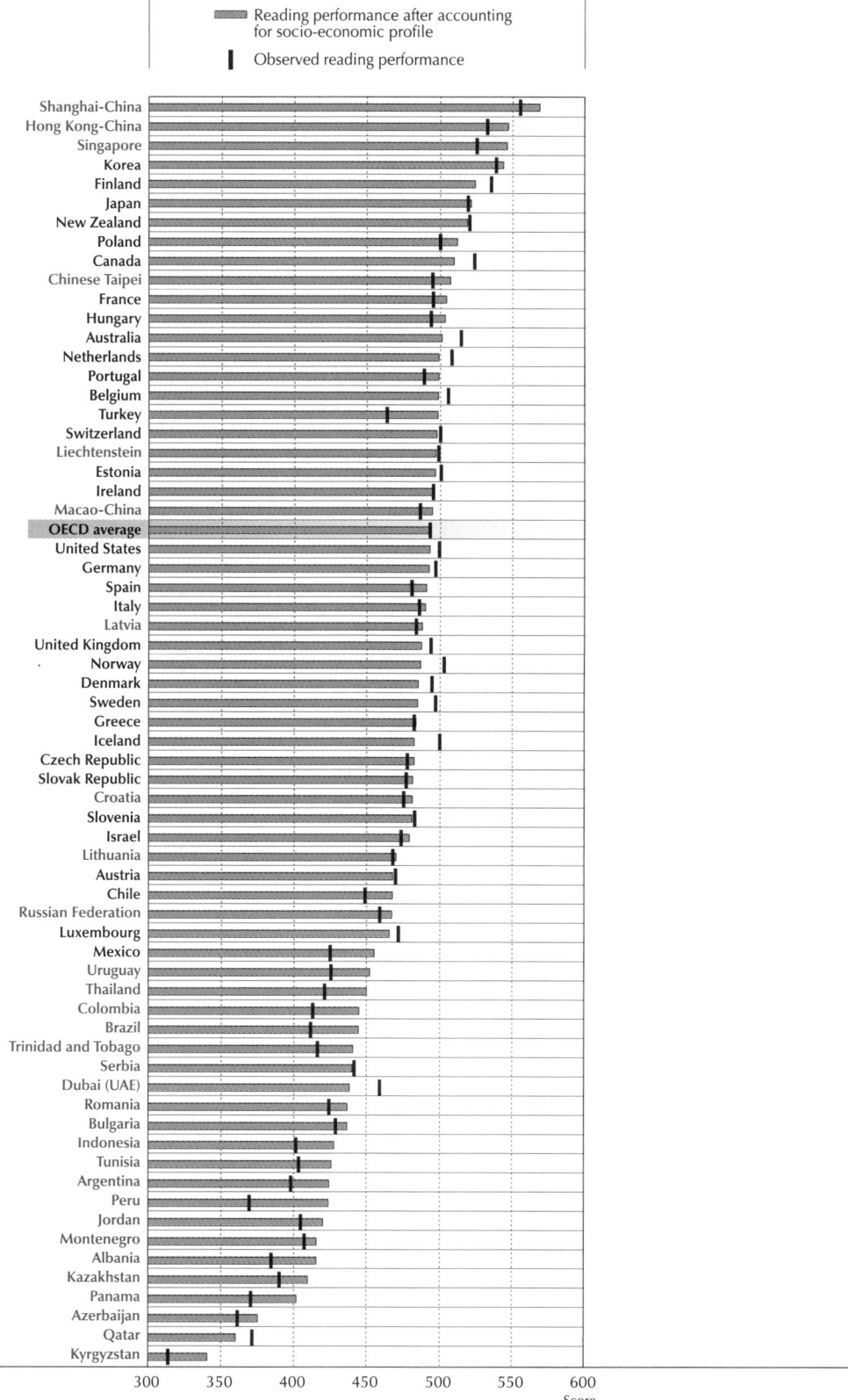

Countries are ranked in descending order of the reading performance after accounting for socio-economic profile.
Source: OECD, *PISA 2009 Database*, Table II.3.2.
StatLink ᴀ ᴍ ᴤ ᴘ http://dx.doi.org/10.1787/888932343589

The heterogeneity in socio-economic characteristics within each system should also be considered. Figure II.3.2 reports the socio-economic range in which 90% of the students can be found (the length of the gradient). In fact, many of the countries with below-average socio-economic backgrounds, most notably Mexico, Turkey and the partner countries Peru, Tunisia, Colombia, Brazil, Thailand and Indonesia, also show significant heterogeneity in the socio-economic backgrounds of 15-year-olds.

Socio-economic gradients with similar slopes will have a much larger impact on the performance gap in countries whose student populations are highly heterogeneous than in countries that have more socio-economically homogeneous student populations. For example, in Norway and Uruguay, a given socio-economic difference is associated with a similar difference in performance. However, since the distribution of socio-economic characteristics is much more heterogeneous in Uruguay than in Norway, the performance gap among students in the top and bottom quarters of the *PISA index of economic, social and cultural status* is much larger in Uruguay than in Norway.

For countries whose average socio-economic background is relatively disadvantaged, and which have a large dispersion of socio-economic characteristics, it is particularly difficult to meet the needs of disadvantaged students: not only are there many disadvantaged students, but many disadvantaged students show very low levels of socio-economic background. For example, in Mexico, Turkey and the partner countries Brazil and Colombia, more than half of all students come from a socio-economic background below that of the least-advantaged 15% of students in the OECD countries (as indicated by one standard deviation below the OECD average), while in Indonesia, Peru and Thailand, more than 60% of students do so. In contrast, in Norway, Australia, Iceland, Canada and Finland, less than 5% of students have a socio-economic background below that of the least advantaged 15% of students in the OECD countries (Table II.3.2).

STUDENT RESILIENCE IN PISA: THE PROPORTION OF DISADVANTAGED STUDENTS WHO SUCCEED IN PISA

While many of the students who perform poorly in PISA are from socio-economically disadvantaged backgrounds, a large number of disadvantaged students excel in PISA (OECD, 2010b). These students and their school systems show that overcoming socio-economic barriers to achievement is possible.

Resilient students are those who come from a disadvantaged socio-economic background and perform much higher than would be predicted by their background. To identify these students, first, the relationship between performance and socio-economic background across all students participating in the PISA 2009 assessment is established. Then the actual performance of each disadvantaged student is compared with the performance predicted by the average relationship among students from similar socio-economic backgrounds across countries. This difference is defined as the student's residual performance. A disadvantaged student is classified as resilient if his or her residual performance is found to be amongst the top quarter of students' residual performance from all countries.[6] While the prevalence of resilience is not the same across educational systems, it is possible to identify substantial numbers of resilient students in practically all OECD countries.

Figure II.3.6 shows that on average across the OECD, 31% of disadvantaged students are resilient. The figure shows that more than half of all disadvantaged students in Korea can be considered resilient. In the partner economies Shanghai-China and Hong Kong-China, the percentage of disadvantaged students that are resilient students is higher than 70% and in Macao-China it is 50%. This percentage is also higher than 35% in Finland, Japan, Turkey, Canada, Portugal, Poland, New Zealand, Spain and in the partner countries and economies Singapore, Chinese Taipei and Liechtenstein.

The analyses of this chapter provide an overview of how socio-economic background is related to reading performance. Although this relationship is present in all countries and economies, countries vary in the strength, steepness and length of the socio-economic gradient, with different proportions of disadvantaged students overcoming the odds and succeeding in school. These cross-country differences in the socio-economic gradient pose different policy challenges for countries. These are discussed in greater detail in the policy implications section of this volume.

■ Figure II.3.6 ■
Percentage of resilient students among disadvantaged students

Shanghai-China	
Hong Kong-China	
Korea	
Macao-China	
Singapore	
Finland	
Japan	
Turkey	
Canada	
Portugal	
Chinese Taipei	
Poland	
New Zealand	
Spain	
Liechtenstein	
Estonia	
Netherlands	
Italy	
Switzerland	
Latvia	
Australia	
OECD average	
France	
Belgium	
Ireland	
Iceland	
Mexico	
United States	
Greece	
Thailand	
Croatia	
Tunisia	
Norway	
Hungary	
Sweden	
Slovenia	
Indonesia	
Denmark	
Chile	
United Kingdom	
Israel	
Colombia	
Germany	
Brazil	
Czech Republic	
Slovak Republic	
Luxembourg	
Lithuania	
Austria	
Russian Federation	
Trinidad and Tobago	
Uruguay	
Serbia	
Jordan	
Albania	
Argentina	
Dubai (UAE)	
Romania	
Bulgaria	
Panama	
Montenegro	
Kazakhstan	
Peru	
Azerbaijan	
Qatar	
Kyrgyzstan	

0   10   20   30   40   50   60   70   80
Percentage of resilient students

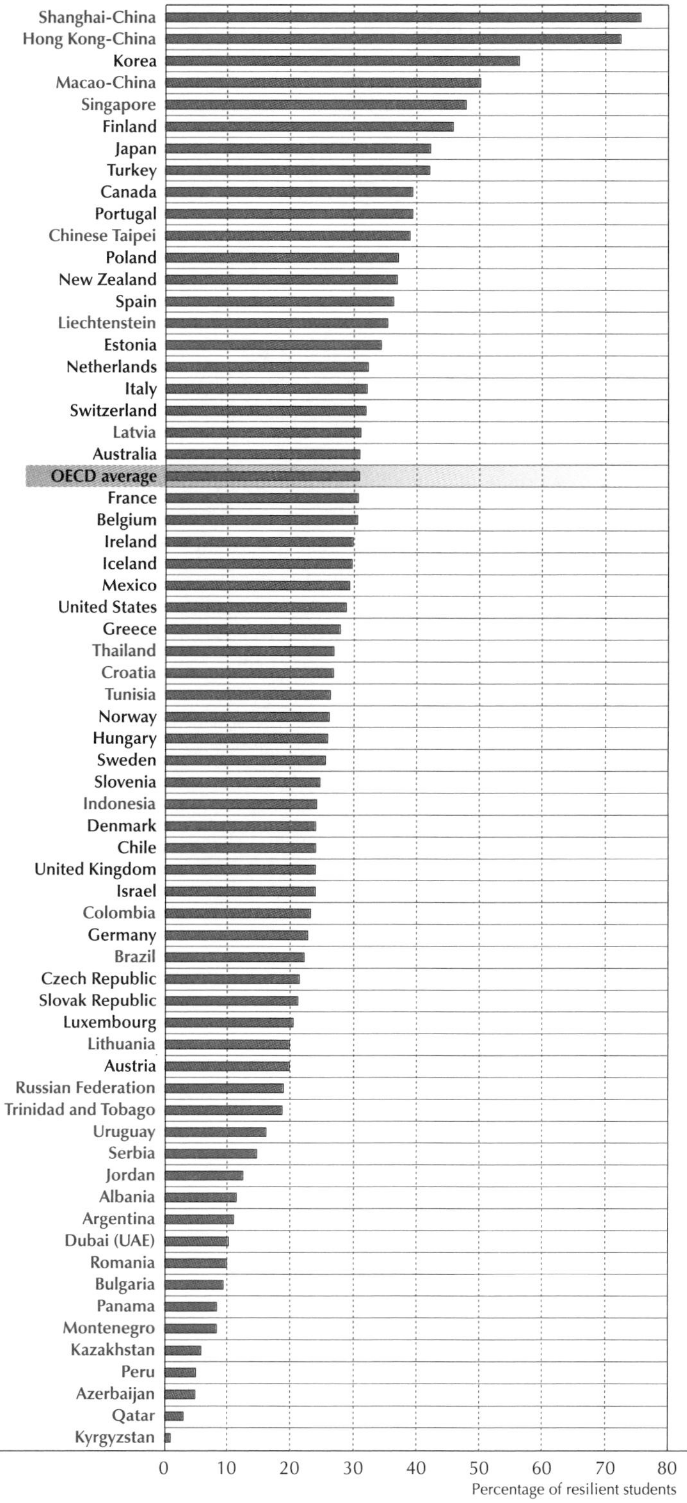

Note: A student is classified as resilient if he or she is in the bottom quarter of the PISA index of economic, social and cultural status (ESCS) in the country of assessment and performs in the top quarter across students from all countries after accounting for socio-economic background. The share of resilient students among all students has been multiplied by 4 so that the percentage values presented here reflect the proportion of resilient students among disadvantaged students (those in the bottom quarter of the PISA index of social, economic and cultural status).
Source: OECD, *PISA 2009 Database*, Table II.3.3.
StatLink ᵃᵐˢᵖ http://dx.doi.org/10.1787/888932343589

Notes

1. The socio-economic gradient has become a fixture of the PISA analysis of equity in education systems (OECD, 2001, 2004, and 2007b). The first application of socio-economic gradients to PISA data was developed by Douglas Willms for the last chapter of the PISA 2000 international report (Chapter 8).

2. While this is true for the OECD as a whole, it will not be so for each member country individually.

3. More formally, it is the R^2 of a regression with reading performance as the dependent variable and the *PISA index of economic, social and cultural status* as predictor. Hauser (2010) argues for using a different measure to evaluate the relationship between socio-economic background and performance that is related to the explained variance used here, the error variance.

4. It is also possible that the measures of socio-economic background are weaker approximations to socio-economic status in these countries and therefore the observed relationship with performance is weaker and/or the slope is gentler.

5. As shown in Figure II.3.2 and Table II.3.2, the unadjusted mean score for the OECD average is 493 score points, and the height of the gradient line is 494, eventhough the OECD average *PISA index of economic, social and cultural status* is 0.0. The discrepancy between the unadjusted mean score and the height of the gradient line is due to rounding error. In strict terms, the OECD average *PISA index of economic, social and cultural status* is 0.0013 producing a small difference between the unadjusted OECD average (493.45) and the OECD average height of the gradient line (493.88).

6. For an internationally comparable definition of resilient students, students were defined as disadvantaged and non-disadvantaged within each country relative to distribution of socio-economic background in this country. Disadvantaged students are those with a PISA index of socio-economic background in the bottom quarter of the distribution within their country. Performance level categories were defined in an internationally comparable fashion as follows. Performance thresholds were calculated by regressing student performance on their socio-economic background, more precisely, on the *PISA index of economic, social and cultural status* (with its square term to allow for non-linearities). Student performance levels were then defined by dividing regression residuals into equal quarters. In other words, students were divided into groups of successful (top quarter), low-performers (bottom quarter) and the rest, by looking at their performance in comparison with peers sharing similar socio-economic background across countries. The analysis was conducted on the pooled sample of students from all countries, so performance was compared among students from all countries (weighting countries equally). Students were defined as resilient or internationally successful disadvantaged students, if they were disadvantaged students who performed in the top quarter of students from all countries after accounting for their socio-economic background. Similarly, a disadvantaged student whose performance after accounting for socio-economic background lies in the lowest quarter was defined as a disadvantaged low achiever. Shares of students in these two groups were then compared across countries to study where disadvantaged students were more likely to be among top performing students sharing a similar socio-economic background from all countries.

4

Learning Outcomes of Students with an Immigrant Background

On average, more than 10% of 15-year-old students across OECD countries are foreign-born or have foreign-born parents. This chapter compares the reading performance of students with an immigrant background with the performance of students without an immigrant background in the same country, and with the performance of students in other countries. It examines performance differences among first- and second-generation immigrants; and between those students who speak a different language at home than the one in which they were assessed, and those who speak the same language at home. Performance in reading is also analysed according to immigrant students' country or region of origin.

STUDENTS WITH AN IMMIGRANT BACKGROUND

Immigrant populations in OECD countries have grown significantly in recent decades. Between 1990 and 2000 alone, the number of people living outside their country of birth nearly doubled worldwide, to 175 million (OECD, 2006). As discussed in Volume V, *Learning Trends,* the proportion of students with an immigrant background also increased in OECD countries, with some countries observing changes of more than five percentage points in their student immigrant population between 2000 and 2009. This growing proportion of students with an immigrant background poses challenges to education systems. Larger immigrant student populations increase the diversity of the student body and school systems need to engage with this diversity to secure high-quality instruction for all students. PISA offers a unique opportunity to identify school systems that are effective in capitalising on the potential of students with an immigrant background.

PISA distinguishes between three types of student immigrant status: *i)* students without an immigrant background, also referred to as native students, are students who were born in the country where they were assessed by PISA or who had at least one parent born in the country;[1] *ii)* second-generation students are students who were born in the country of assessment but whose parents are foreign-born; and *iii)* first-generation students are foreign-born students whose parents are also foreign-born.[2] Students with an immigrant background thus include students who are first- or second- generation immigrants.

THE SIZE OF THE IMMIGRANT-BACKGROUND STUDENT POPULATION AND MEAN PERFORMANCE OF THE SYSTEM

Figure II.4.1 shows the proportion of 15-year-old students who have an immigrant background. The grey bar represents the percentage of first-generation students and the blue bar represents the percentage of second-generation students. Across OECD countries, 10% of the students assessed by PISA have an immigrant background. This group represents 40% of students in Luxembourg. In New Zealand, Canada and Switzerland, students with an immigrant background represent around 24% of students. In Israel, the United States, Australia, Germany and Austria, students with an immigrant background represent between 15% and 20% of the student population, and in Belgium, France, the Netherlands, Sweden and the United Kingdom, between 10% and 15%. Among the partner countries and economies, students with an immigrant background represent around 70% of the student population in Dubai (UAE) and Macao-China. They also represent a sizeable percentage of the student population in Qatar, Hong Kong-China and Liechtenstein (between 30% and 50%). In Singapore, Jordan, the Russian Federation, Kazakhstan and Croatia, the percentage is between 10% and 15% (Table II.4.1).

Both within and across countries, students with an immigrant background constitute a heterogeneous group. They differ in their country of origin, language and culture, and bring a wide range of skills, knowledge and motivations to their schools. Although a significant subgroup of migrants is highly skilled, that is not true for many others who are socio-economically disadvantaged (OECD, 2010f). Such a disadvantage, along with cultural and ethnic differences, can create divisions and inequities between the host society and newcomers. These problems go well beyond how migration flows can be channelled and managed; they require consideration of how immigrants can be integrated into host societies in ways that are acceptable to both the immigrants and the populations in the receiving countries.

Education and training are key to integrating immigrants into labour markets and society. They can help overcome language barriers and facilitate the transmission of the norms and values that provide a basis for social cohesion. PISA offers a crucial perspective on this discussion by assessing the performance of 15-year-old students with an immigrant background. The performance disadvantages of these students pose major challenges to education systems; in some countries, the disadvantage is as high, or even higher, among second-generation immigrants than among first-generation immigrants.

The performance of foreign-born students is influenced at least in part by their educational experience in another country and can therefore be only partially attributed to the host country's education system. The educational disadvantage in the country of origin can be magnified in the host country even though, in absolute terms, the students' educational performance might have improved. Foreign-born students may be academically disadvantaged either because they are immigrants entering a new education system or because they need to learn a new language in a home environment that may not facilitate this learning. Comparing within subgroups of the immigrant student population (*i.e.* by first- or second-generation immigrant status, by year of arrival or by language spoken at home), PISA sheds light on the sources of the disadvantages faced by students with an immigrant background.

■ Figure II.4.1 ■
Percentage of students with an immigrant background

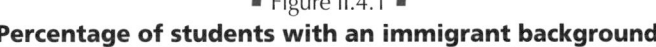

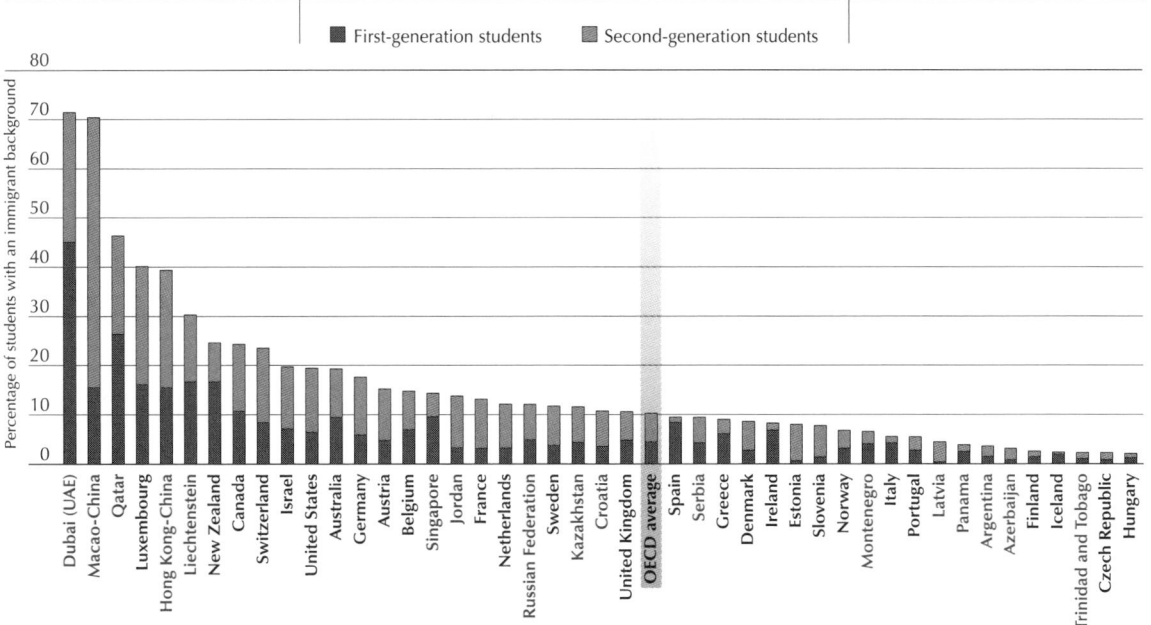

Countries are ranked in descending order of the percentage of students with an immigrant background (first- or second-generation students).
Source: OECD, *PISA 2009 Database*, Table II.4.1.
StatLink ⟨graphic⟩ http://dx.doi.org/10.1787/888932343608

When interpreting performance gaps between native students and those with an immigrant background, it is important to account for differences among countries in terms of the national origin(s) and socio-economic, educational and linguistic backgrounds of their immigrant populations. The composition of immigrant populations is shaped by immigration policies and practices, and the criteria used to decide who will be admitted into a country vary considerably across countries. While some countries tend to admit relatively large numbers of immigrants each year, often with a low degree of selectivity, other countries have much lower or more selective migrant inflows. In addition, the extent to which the social, educational and occupational status of potential immigrants is taken into account in immigration and naturalisation decisions differs across countries. The composition of past migration flows tends to persist because of network effects that facilitate migration from the same countries of origin. In addition, some migration flows may not be easily restricted because of international treaties (*i.e.* free circulation agreements and the Convention Relating to the Status of Refugees) or because of generally recognised human rights (*i.e.* the right of immigrants or citizens to live with their families). As a result, immigrant populations have more skilled or socio-economically advantaged backgrounds in some countries than in others. Among OECD countries:

▪ Australia, Canada and New Zealand are countries with immigration policies that favour the better qualified (OECD, 2005).

▪ The United States has a migration system that tends to favour family migration, both of immediate family, as in other countries, and also of parents, siblings and adult children.

▪ In the 1960s and 1970s, European countries such as Austria, Denmark, Germany, Luxembourg, Norway, Sweden and Switzerland recruited temporary immigrant workers, many of whom then settled permanently. Immigration has increased again over the past ten years, except in Germany. In Austria, Germany and Switzerland, and to a lesser extent in Sweden, immigrants are less likely to have an upper secondary education and more likely to have a tertiary degree (OECD, 2005). As a result, migrants tend to be of two types – the low-skilled and the highly qualified.

▪ France and the United Kingdom draw many immigrants from former colonies who have often already mastered the language of the host country.

▪ Finland, Greece, Ireland, Italy, Portugal and Spain, among other countries, have recently experienced a sharp growth in migration inflows. In Spain, for example, the pace of immigration increased more than tenfold between 1998 and 2004 (OECD, 2010f).

A new OECD review of migrant education, *Closing the Gap for Immigrant Students: Policies, Practice and Performance* (OECD, 2010g), highlights the diversity of immigrant populations across and within OECD countries and the challenges this diversity presents for developing effective education policy. The review finds that the most effective policies to address the needs of at-risk immigrant students are not of the "one size fits all" kind. Policies that adopt a holistic approach, considering education policy along with other types of policy interventions, are critically important at all levels (schools, communities, and municipal, regional and national governments). The review also acknowledges that in this field of education policy, finding the right balance between universal and targeted interventions is particularly challenging.

■ Figure II.4.2 ■

Students' reading performance, by percentage of students with an immigrant background

Mean score

Mean score

[Scatter plot showing mean reading score (vertical axis, 300–600) versus percentage of students with an immigrant background (horizontal axis categories: Below 1%, Between 1% and 5%, Between 5% and 15%, Between 15% and 30%, More than 30%).

Below 1%:
- Shanghai-China (~583)
- Korea (~540)
- Japan (~520)
- Poland (~500)
- Chinese Taipei (~495)
- Slovak Republic (~477)
- Turkey (~464)
- Chile (~449)
- Uruguay, Bulgaria, Romania, Thailand (~426)
- Colombia, Brazil (~413)
- Tunisia, Indonesia (~402)
- Albania (~385)
- Peru (~370)

Between 1% and 5%:
- Finland (~536)
- Singapore (~526)
- Iceland (~500)
- Hungary (~494)
- Latvia (~484)
- Czech Republic (~478)
- Lithuania (~468)
- Serbia (~442)
- Mexico (~425)
- Trinidad and Tobago (~416)
- Argentina (~398)
- Panama (~371)
- Azerbaijan (~362)
- Kyrgyzstan (~314)

Between 5% and 15%:
- Netherlands, Belgium, Estonia, Norway (~506–503)
- France, Sweden, Denmark, Ireland, United Kingdom (~500–494)
- Portugal, Italy, Slovenia, Greece, Spain (~489–481)
- Croatia (~476)
- Russian Federation (~459)
- Montenegro, Jordan (~408)
- Kazakhstan (~390)

Between 15% and 30%:
- Canada (~524)
- New Zealand (~521)
- Australia (~515)
- Switzerland, United States, Germany (~501–497)
- Israel (~474)
- Austria (~470)

More than 30%:
- Hong Kong-China (~533)
- Liechtenstein (~499)
- Macao-China (~487)
- Luxembourg (~472)
- Dubai (UAE) (~459)
- Qatar (~372)]*

Below 1% | Between 1% and 5% | Between 5% and 15% | Between 15% and 30% | More than 30%

Percentage of students with an immigrant background

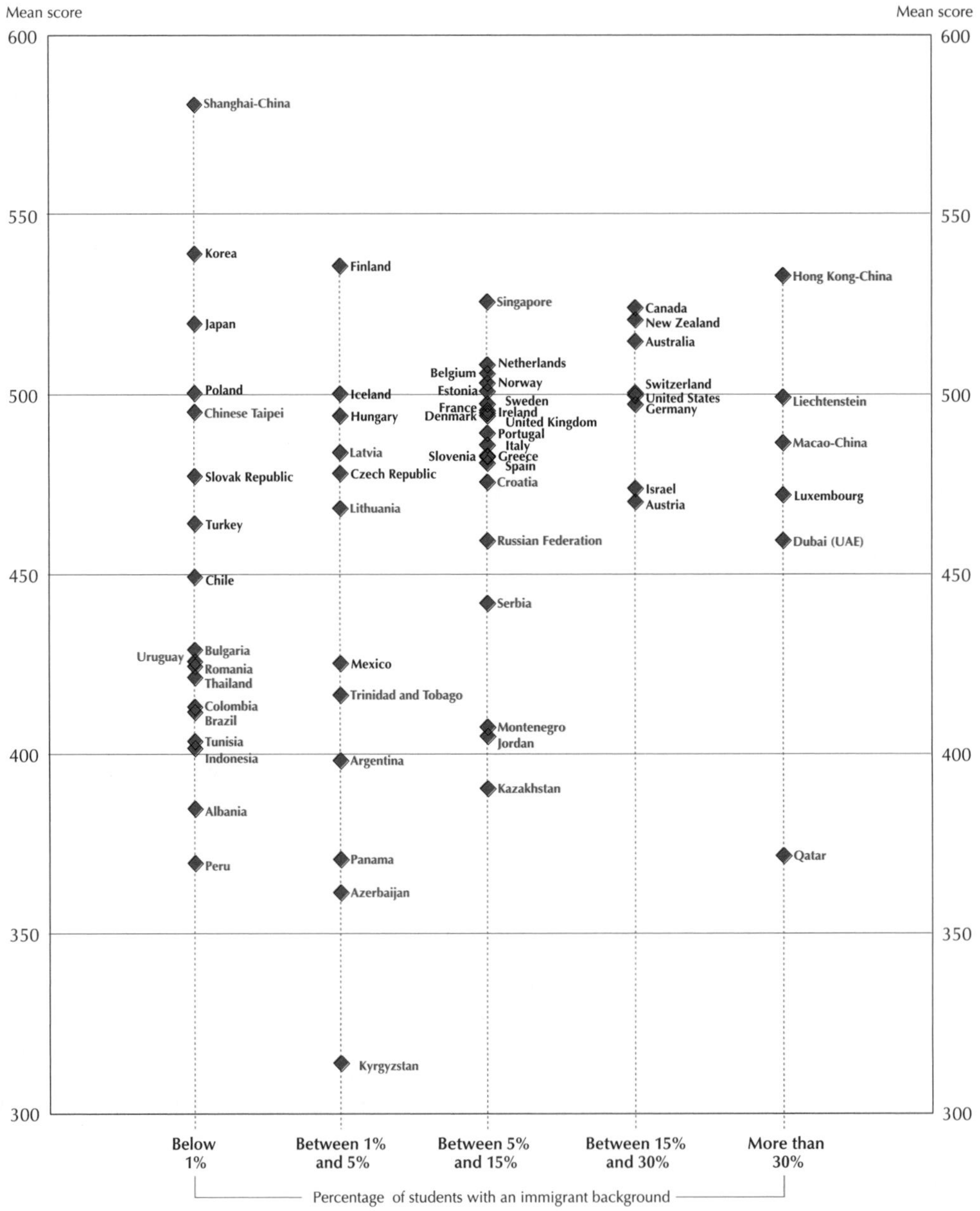

Source: OECD, *PISA 2009 Database*, Table II.4.1.

StatLink ᨆᨅᨋ http://dx.doi.org/10.1787/888932343608

Figure II.4.2 groups countries and economies by the proportion of immigrant students in their student populations and shows the mean performance in reading for all students. The figure shows that there is no relationship between a country's or economy's mean performance and the proportion of students with an immigrant background. There is also no relationship between mean performance and the size of the performance gap between native students and those with an immigrant background, as Figure II.4.3 shows.[3] These findings contradict the assumption that high immigration levels will inevitably result in a decline in the performance of an education system.

This chapter compares the performance of students with an immigrant background to both the performance of other students in the same country without an immigrant background and the performance of immigrant students in other countries. It also describes performance differences among first- and second-generation immigrants. Following a review of the extent to which such performance differences can be attributable to socio-economic and linguistic factors, the chapter concludes with an analysis of the extent to which students with an immigrant background face inferior or superior schooling conditions in their host countries relative to their native peers.

■ Figure II.4.3 ■

Performance difference between students with and without an immigrant background, by percentage of students with an immigrant background

Score point difference between students with and students without an immigrant background

Score point difference between students with and students without an immigrant background

Students WITHOUT an immigrant background perform better

- Colombia ◆ (~103)
- Brazil ◆ (~98)
- Mexico ◆ (~98)
- Iceland ◆ (~81)
- Italy ◆ (~73)
- Finland ◆ (~70)
- Belgium, Sweden, Denmark, France ◆ (~65)
- Austria ◆ (~67)
- Greece, Spain ◆ (~58)
- Germany ◆ (~56)
- Norway ◆ (~53)
- Luxembourg ◆ (~52)
- Slovenia, Netherlands ◆ (~47)
- Switzerland ◆ (~48)
- Argentina ◆ (~40)
- Estonia ◆ (~35)
- Panama ◇ (~31)
- Liechtenstein ◆ (~30)
- Czech Republic ◇, Lithuania ◆ (~23)
- Portugal, Ireland ◆ (~27), Russian Federation (~25), United Kingdom ◆ (~23)
- United States ◆ (~23)
- Croatia ◆ (~18)
- Latvia ◇ (~10)
- New Zealand ◆ (~13)
- Canada ◇ (~8)
- Israel ◇ (~5)
- Hong Kong-China ◇ (~6)
- Trinidad and Tobago ◇, Azerbaijan ◇ (~0)
- Singapore ◇ (~-1)
- Kazakhstan ◇, Montenegro ◇ (~-5)
- Macao-China ◆ (~-7)
- Hungary ◇ (~-11)
- Jordan ◆, Serbia ◆ (~-12)
- Australia ◆ (~-19)
- Kyrgyzstan ◆ (~-32)

Students WITH an immigrant background perform better

| Below 1% | Between 1% and 5% | Between 5% and 15% | Between 15% and 30% | More than 30% |

Percentage of students with an immigrant background

Note: Score point differences that are statistically significant are marked in a darker tone.
Source: OECD, *PISA 2009 Database*, Table II.4.1.

StatLink http://dx.doi.org/10.1787/888932343608

PERFORMANCE GAPS ACROSS IMMIGRANT STATUS

Figure II.4.4 shows the average performance of students according to their immigrant status for those countries with significant shares of 15-year-olds with an immigrant background,[4] with countries sorted by the average performance of all students. The figure highlights three main findings. First, students without an immigrant background tend to outperform students with an immigrant background in most countries and economies. The exceptions are Australia for both first- and second-generation students, and Israel and Hungary where second-generation students outperform students without an immigrant background. Second, the size of the performance gap among these groups of students varies markedly across countries. Third, second-generation students tend to outperform first-generation students.

■ Figure II.4.4 ■
Reading performance, by immigrant status

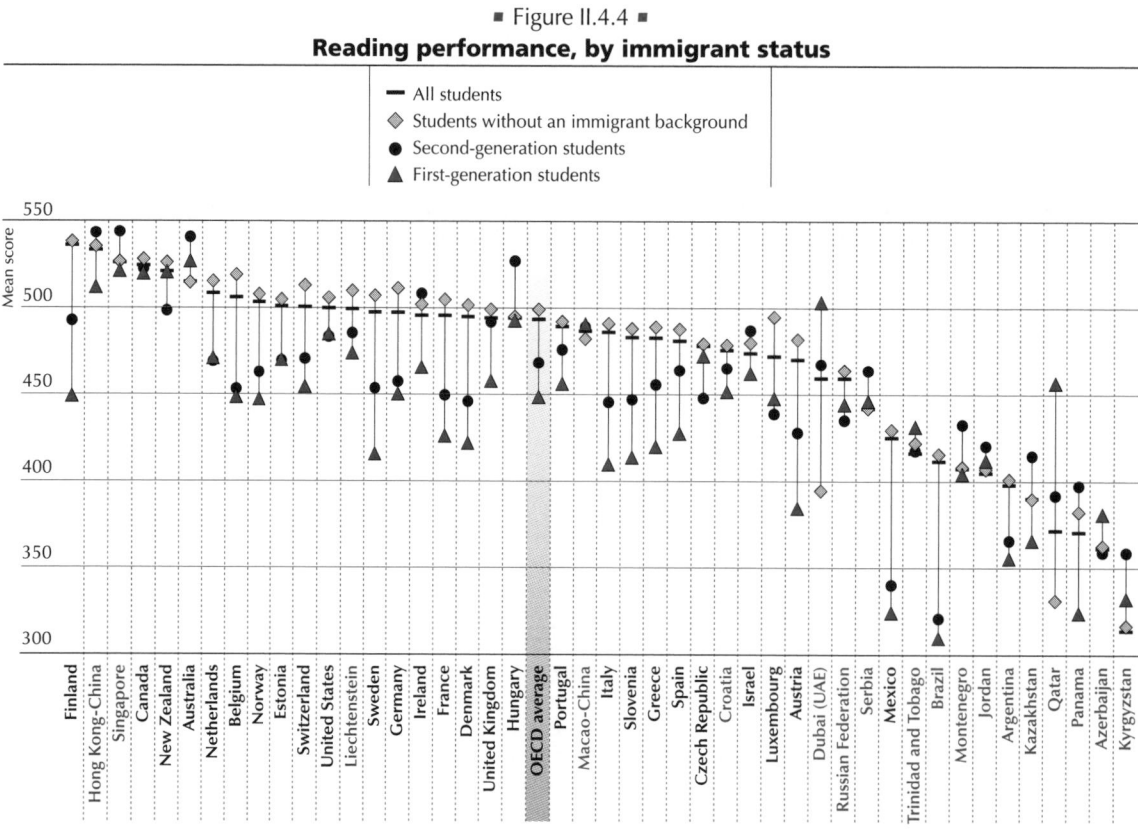

Countries are ranked in descending order of the mean score of all students.
Source: OECD, *PISA 2009 Database*, Table II.4.1.
StatLink ᕫᖒᔚᒲ http://dx.doi.org/10.1787/888932343608

Among OECD countries, first-generation students lag 52 score points, on average, behind students without an immigrant background, a difference that exceeds the equivalent of one school year's progress (see Table A1.2 and Box II.1.1).

Moreover, in many OECD countries, first-generation immigrant students are at a significantly greater risk of being poor performers. In Mexico, Austria, Denmark, Sweden, Finland, Italy, Iceland, Belgium, Spain, Norway, France, Greece and Slovenia, first-generation immigrant students are at least twice as likely to perform among the bottom quarter of students when compared to students without an immigrant background. The same is true in the partner countries Brazil and Panama (Table II.4.1).

While the educational experience abroad can help to explain the performance gap for first-generation immigrants, second-generation students were born in the country and therefore benefited from the education system of the host country from the beginning of their schooling trajectories. Despite this, second-generation students also lag behind those without an immigrant background by an average of 33 score points across OECD countries (Table II.4.1).

In general, students with an immigrant background are socio-economically disadvantaged, and this explains part of the performance disadvantage among these students. On average across OECD countries, students with an immigrant background tend to have a socio-economic background that is 0.4 of a standard deviation lower than that of their non-immigrant peers. This relationship is particularly strong in Luxembourg, the Netherlands, Iceland, Denmark, Austria, Germany and the United States. Only in Australia, the Czech Republic, Estonia, Hungary, Ireland, New Zealand and Portugal is there no observed difference in the socio-economic background of students by immigrant status (Table II.4.1).

The large gaps in performance and socio-economic background suggest that schools and societies face major challenges in realising the potential of students with an immigrant background. However, as Figure II.4.4 shows, in some education systems the gaps are barely noticeable or very narrow, while in others they are significantly above these averages. For example, in Australia, second-generation students, who account for 10% of the student population, outperform students without an immigrant background by 26 score points.[5] In Canada, where almost 25% of students have an immigrant background, these students perform as well as students without an immigrant background. Similarly, no statistically significant differences are observed for the Czech Republic, for second-generation students in Israel, Ireland, Portugal and the United Kingdom, and for first-generation students in Hungary and New Zealand, among OECD countries.

In general, a part of these differences persist even after accounting for socio-economic factors. Figure II.4.5 shows the size of the performance gap between students with and without an immigrant background before and after accounting for socio-economic status. In Luxembourg, for example, accounting for the socio-economic status of students reduces the performance disadvantage of students with an immigrant background from 52 to 19 score points and, on average across OECD countries, the gap is reduced from 43 to 27 score points.

■ Figure II.4.5 ■

Reading performance by immigrant status, before and after accounting for socio-economic background

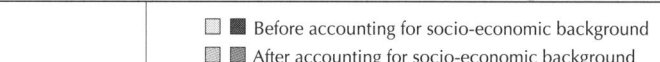

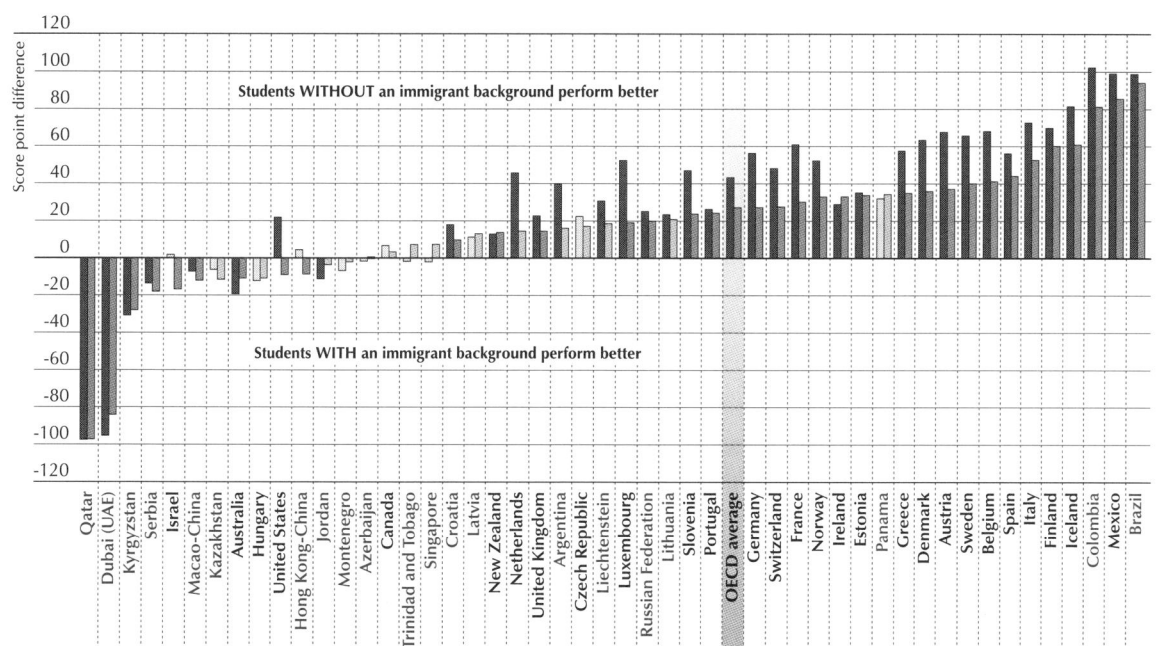

Note: Score point differences that are statistically significant are shown in a darker tone.
Countries are ranked in descending order of score point differences after accounting for the economic, social and cultural status of students.
Source: OECD, *PISA 2009 Database,* Table II.4.1.
StatLink ⟨ms⟩ http://dx.doi.org/10.1787/888932343608

The narrowing of the gap after accounting for the socio-economic status of students tends to be similar across countries. The rank order of countries in terms of the performance gap between immigrant and native students remains fairly stable before and after accounting for socio-economic context. This reduction shows the extent to which performance differences between students of different immigrant status reflects their lower socio-economic background and not necessarily their immigrant background. The fact that the gap is still apparent after accounting for socio-economic background, however, indicates that students from an immigrant background face educational challenges that can be attributed directly to their immigrant background, placing them at a particular disadvantage.

Without longitudinal data it is not possible to directly assess to what extent the observed disadvantages of students with an immigrant background are reduced over successive generations. However, it is possible to compare the performance of second-generation students, who were born in the country of assessment and have thereby benefited from participating in the same formal education system as their native peers for the same number of years, with that of first-generation students, who usually started their education in another country.

On average across OECD countries, second-generation students outperform first-generation students by 18 score points in reading. The relative advantage of second-generation students compared with first-generation students exceeds 40 score points in Finland, Austria and Ireland (Figure II.4.4) and is larger than 30 score points in Sweden, Spain, Italy, Greece, the United Kingdom and Slovenia. These large gaps highlight the disadvantage of first-generation students and possibly the different backgrounds across immigrant cohorts (Table II.4.1). However, they could also signal positive educational and social mobility across generations.

Cross-country comparisons of performance gaps between first- and second-generation immigrant students need to be treated with caution, since they may in some cases reflect the characteristics of families participating in different waves of immigration more strongly than the success of integration policies. New Zealand is a case in point. First-generation students perform as well as students without an immigrant background while second-generation students lag behind the former group of students by 22 score points (Table II.4.1). This result signals that there may be important differences in the characteristics of the cohorts of students with an immigrant background. Even students from the same countries of origin, however, show considerable differences in their performance across the different host countries (OECD, 2006f).

Despite the gaps, some students with an immigrant background succeed in school in a number of countries. Across OECD countries, an average of 5% of first- and second-generation students perform at Level 5 or 6 and can be considered top performers in PISA; the same is true for 8% of students without an immigrant background. In Australia, New Zealand and Canada, more than 10% of first- and second-generation students are top performers in PISA. Moreover, in these countries, a similar or higher percentage of students with immigrant background reach proficiency Level 5 or above when compared to students with no immigrant background. In Belgium, Finland, Sweden, Germany, France and the Netherlands, the percentage of PISA top performers among students without an immigrant background is at least five percentage points higher than among first- and second-generation students (the same is true in Austria, Canada, Iceland, Italy, Luxembourg, New Zealand, Norway, the United Kingdom and the United States for first-generation students when compared to students with no immigrant background) (Table II.4.2).

Figure II.4.6 shows the percentage of students with an immigrant background who reach at least proficiency Level 3. Among OECD countries with at least 5% of students with an immigrant background, at least half of first-generation students reach Level 3 in Canada, Australia, New Zealand and the United States and at least half of second-generation students do so in Canada, Australia, Ireland, the United Kingdom, New Zealand, Israel and Finland. On the other hand, less than one in three first-generation students reaches Level 3 in Austria, Slovenia, Italy, Denmark, Spain, Greece, Sweden and France. The same is true among second-generation students in Austria (Table II.4.2).

In many countries students with an immigrant background perform poorly. Figure II.4.7 shows the proportion of students not reaching baseline proficiency Level 2 by immigrant status. This is the level at which students begin to demonstrate the reading literacy competencies that will enable them to participate effectively and productively in life (see Chapter 2 in Volume I, *What Students Know and Can Do*). Across the OECD, 17% of students without an immigrant background do not reach this level; the same is true for 27% of second-generation students and for 36% of first-generation students (Table II.4.2).

■ Figure II.4.6 ■
Percentage of students at proficiency Level 3 or above, by immigrant status

◇ Students without an immigrant background
● Second-generation students
▲ First-generation students

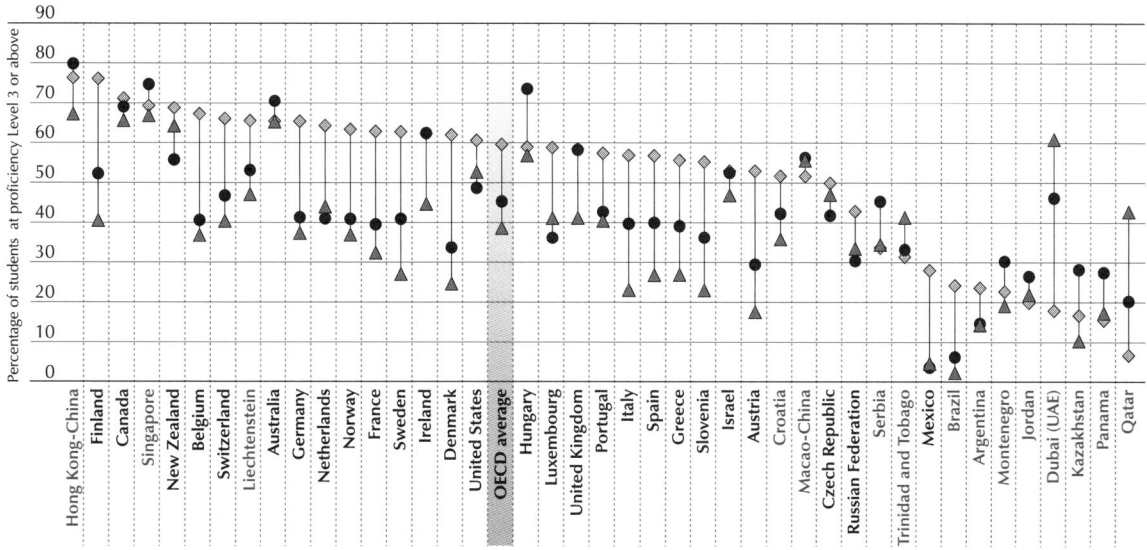

Countries are ranked in descending order of the percentage of students without an immigrant background at proficiency Level 3 or above.
Source: OECD, *PISA 2009 Database,* Table II.4.2.
StatLink ▒▒▒ http://dx.doi.org/10.1787/888932343608

■ Figure II.4.7 ■
Percentage of students below proficiency Level 2, by immigrant status

◇ Students without an immigrant background
● Second-generation students
▲ First-generation students

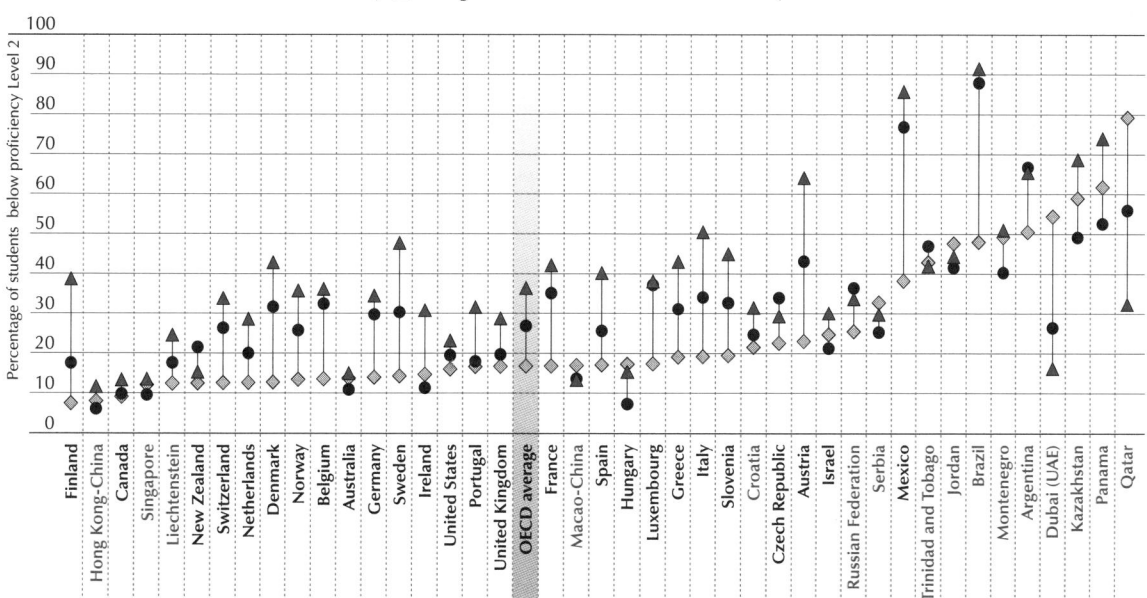

Countries are ranked in ascending order of the percentage of students without an immigrant background below proficiency Level 2.
Source: OECD, *PISA 2009 Database,* Table II.4.2.
StatLink ▒▒▒ http://dx.doi.org/10.1787/888932343608

Even in some countries with good reading performance overall and large proportions of students with an immigrant background, the proportion of poorly performing students with an immigrant background is relatively high. For example, among the OECD countries with more than 10% of students with an immigrant background, the percentage of first-generation students who do not reach Level 2 ranges from 13% and 15% in Australia and Canada, respectively, to 64%, 48% and 42% in Austria, Sweden and France, respectively. In other countries, like Italy, Greece or Denmark, the percentage of students with an immigrant background who do not reach Level 2 is also high, but the percentage of students with an immigrant background is less than 10%. Moreover, in Austria, the percentage of students who do not attain proficiency Level 2 is 42 percentage points higher for first-generation students when compared to students without an immigrant background (Table II.4.2).

FIRST-GENERATION STUDENTS AND AGE OF ARRIVAL

PISA asked first-generation students how old they were when they arrived in the country of assessment. Using this information, it is possible to distinguish between first-generation students who arrived: *i)* when they were five years old or younger, that is before the typical starting age of primary school in many school systems; *ii)* when they were between six and 12 years old, that is before the typical starting age of secondary school in many school systems; and *iii)* when they were older than 12 years. Given that PISA surveyed 15 years-olds, the third group has participated in the education system of the host country for a maximum of three years, the second group for no more than nine years and the first group for their entire school career.

■ Figure II.4.8 ■
Performance differences among first-generation students, by age of arrival

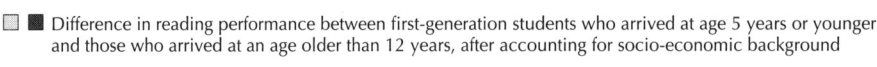
Difference in reading performance between first-generation students who arrived at age 5 years or younger and those who arrived at an age older than 12 years, after accounting for socio-economic background

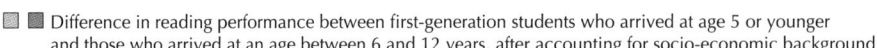
Difference in reading performance between first-generation students who arrived at age 5 or younger and those who arrived at an age between 6 and 12 years, after accounting for socio-economic background

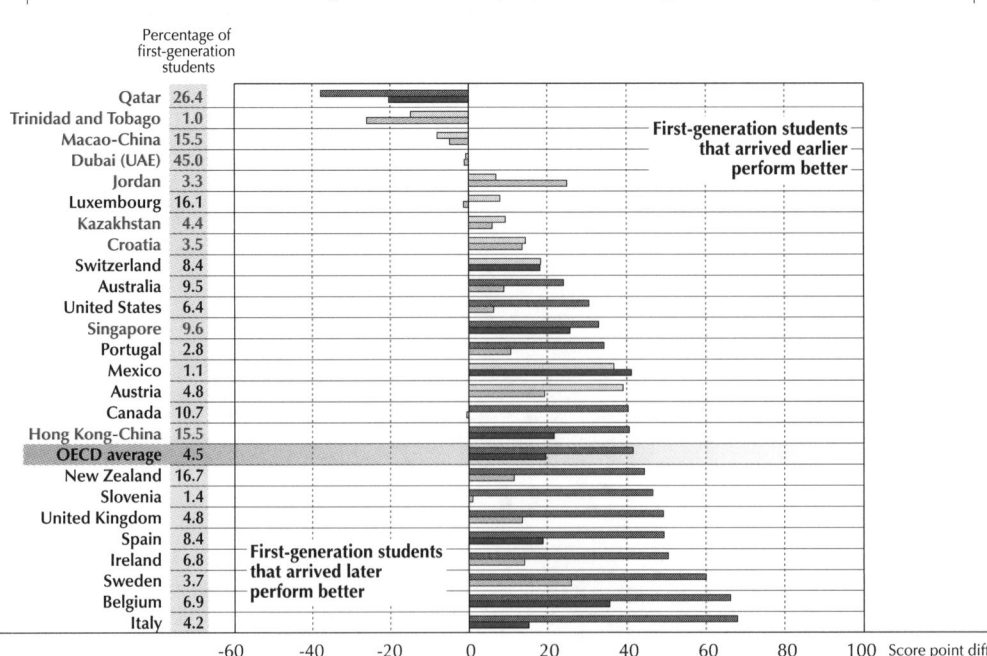

Note: Score point differences that are statistically significant are marked in a darker tone.
Countries are ranked in ascending order of score point differences between first-generation students who arrived at age 5 years or younger and those who arrived at an age older than 12 years.
Source: OECD, *PISA 2009 Database,* Tables II.4.1 and II.4.3.
StatLink ⌧⌧⌧ http://dx.doi.org/10.1787/888932343608

Figure II.4.8 plots the performance differences between those who arrived when they were younger than five and those who arrived when they were between six and 12 years of age and the performance difference between those who arrived when they were younger than five and those who arrived when they were older than 12, after accounting for socio-economic background. For reference, the figure also reports the proportion of first-generation students in these countries and economies. Countries are sorted by the gap between first-generation students who arrived when they were younger than five and those who arrived when they were older than 12, after accounting for socio-economic background.

Figure II.4.8 shows that, in general, first-generation students who arrived in the host country at a younger age outperform those who arrived when they were older. On average across OECD countries, first-generation students who arrived when they were 5-years-old or younger score 42 points higher than first-generation students that arrived after they were 12-years-old. The size of the gaps, however, varies considerably across countries and across groups. For example, after accounting for socio-economic background in Italy and Belgium, the gap between those who arrived when they were 5 or younger and those who arrived when they were older than 12 is greater than 65 score points, while the gap between those who arrived when they were 5 or younger and those who arrived when they were between six and 12 years of age is 36 score points in Belgium and 15 score points in Italy. This suggests that where the education system of the host country had a longer opportunity to shape the learning outcomes of immigrant students, it was able to improve student performance. In contrast, there is no gap between those who arrived when they were younger than five and those who arrived when they were older than 12 in the OECD countries Sweden, the United States, Portugal, Austria, Luxembourg, Switzerland and Mexico, after accounting for socio-economic background (Table II.4.3).

IMMIGRANT STATUS AND HOME LANGUAGE

A different country of birth for the student or the students' parents is not the only attribute shared by students with an immigrant background: in many countries, a large share of students with an immigrant background speak a language at home other than the language they use at school and in which they were assessed by PISA. In PISA it is possible to distinguish between those students whose language at home is the same as the language of assessment and those students whose language at home is different. Across countries, it is common for students with an immigrant background not to speak the language of assessment at home. Students with an immigrant background are more likely to speak a language different than that of the assessement at home in the United States, Sweden, Austria, Norway, Denmark, Australia, New Zealand, Germany and Iceland (Table II.4.4).

Figure II.4.9 shows the percentage of students in each country who fall into each of the four groups regarding immigrant status and the language spoken at home. Countries are ranked by the proportion of students with an immigrant background who do not speak the language of assessment at home. The figure highlights the relationship between these two dimensions and the diversity across countries on these issues. For example, on average across OECD countries 6% of students have an immigrant background and do not speak the language of assessment at home. In Luxembourg, 28% of students have an immigrant background and do not speak the language of assessment at home and 9% have an immigrant background but do speak the language of assessment at home. In Switzerland, New Zealand, Canada, the United States, Austria, Germany and Australia, between 8% and 13% of students have an immigrant background and do not speak the language of assessment at home.

Students with an immigrant background whose language at home is different from the language of assessment face considerable obstacles to succeeding in school. In general, they do not perform as well as students without an immigrant background, as Figure II.4.10 shows. However, the size of the performance gap across countries varies considerably, and accounting for socio-economic background does not eliminate all of these differences.

As Figure II.4.10 shows, on average across OECD countries, students without an immigrant background outperform students with an immigrant background who do not speak the language of assessment at home by 57 score points, but this is reduced to 35 score points after accounting for the students' socio-economic status. In some countries, however, the gaps are quite substantial, even after accounting for socio-economic status. For example, in Italy, Ireland, Spain and Greece, the gap after accounting for socio-economic status remains at 50 or more score points; and in all of these countries, students with an immigrant background who speak a language at home that is different from the language of assessment represent more than 3% of all students. In Belgium, Sweden and Norway this performance difference is at 40 score points or above and the percentage of students with an immigrant background who do not speak the language of assessment at home is greater than 5%.

■ Figure II.4.9 ■
Percentage of students, by immigrant status and language spoken at home

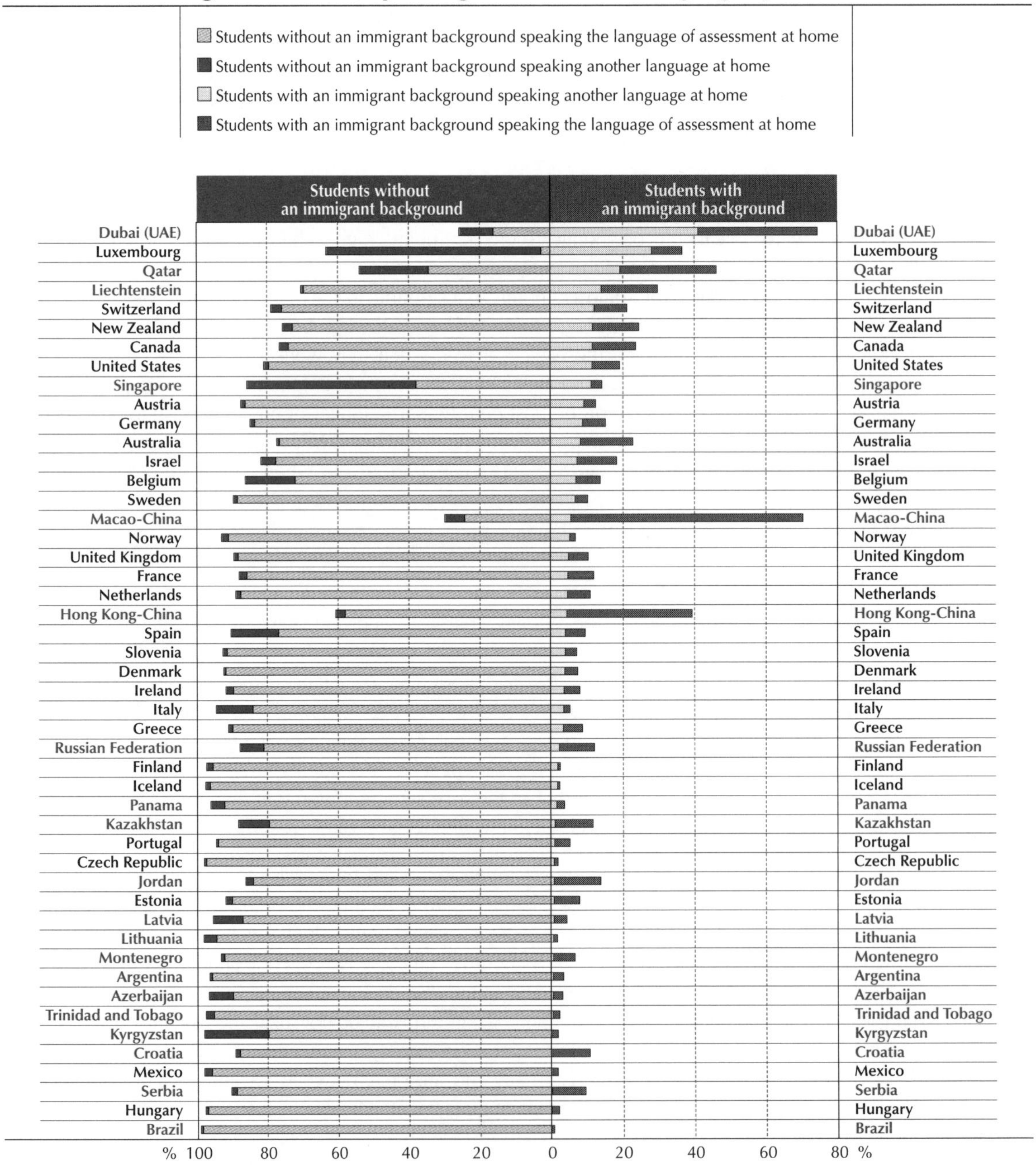

▨ Students without an immigrant background speaking the language of assessment at home

■ Students without an immigrant background speaking another language at home

☐ Students with an immigrant background speaking another language at home

■ Students with an immigrant background speaking the language of assessment at home

	Students without an immigrant background	Students with an immigrant background	
Dubai (UAE)			Dubai (UAE)
Luxembourg			Luxembourg
Qatar			Qatar
Liechtenstein			Liechtenstein
Switzerland			Switzerland
New Zealand			New Zealand
Canada			Canada
United States			United States
Singapore			Singapore
Austria			Austria
Germany			Germany
Australia			Australia
Israel			Israel
Belgium			Belgium
Sweden			Sweden
Macao-China			Macao-China
Norway			Norway
United Kingdom			United Kingdom
France			France
Netherlands			Netherlands
Hong Kong-China			Hong Kong-China
Spain			Spain
Slovenia			Slovenia
Denmark			Denmark
Ireland			Ireland
Italy			Italy
Greece			Greece
Russian Federation			Russian Federation
Finland			Finland
Iceland			Iceland
Panama			Panama
Kazakhstan			Kazakhstan
Portugal			Portugal
Czech Republic			Czech Republic
Jordan			Jordan
Estonia			Estonia
Latvia			Latvia
Lithuania			Lithuania
Montenegro			Montenegro
Argentina			Argentina
Azerbaijan			Azerbaijan
Trinidad and Tobago			Trinidad and Tobago
Kyrgyzstan			Kyrgyzstan
Croatia			Croatia
Mexico			Mexico
Serbia			Serbia
Hungary			Hungary
Brazil			Brazil

% 100   80   60   40   20   0   20   40   60   80 %

Countries are ranked in descending order of the percentage of immigrant students who speak a language at home that is different from the language of assessment.
Source: OECD, *PISA 2009 Database,* Table II.4.4.
StatLink ⬛ http://dx.doi.org/10.1787/888932343608

Among the OECD countries with at least 5% of students with an immigrant background that do not speak the language of assessment at home, the performance difference between them and students without an immigrant background is not apparent in Canada and Australia (Table II.4.4). Despite the varying linguistic, cultural, economic and social backgrounds of immigrant students, these disparities suggest that the relative performance levels of students with an immigrant background cannot be attributed solely to the composition of immigrant populations, the language they speak at home, or their educational and socio-economic backgrounds.

■ Figure II.4.10 ■
Immigrant status, language spoken at home and reading performance
Performance differences between students with an immigrant background whose language at home is different from the language of assessment and students without an immigrant background

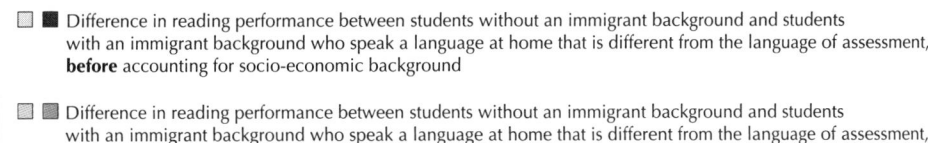

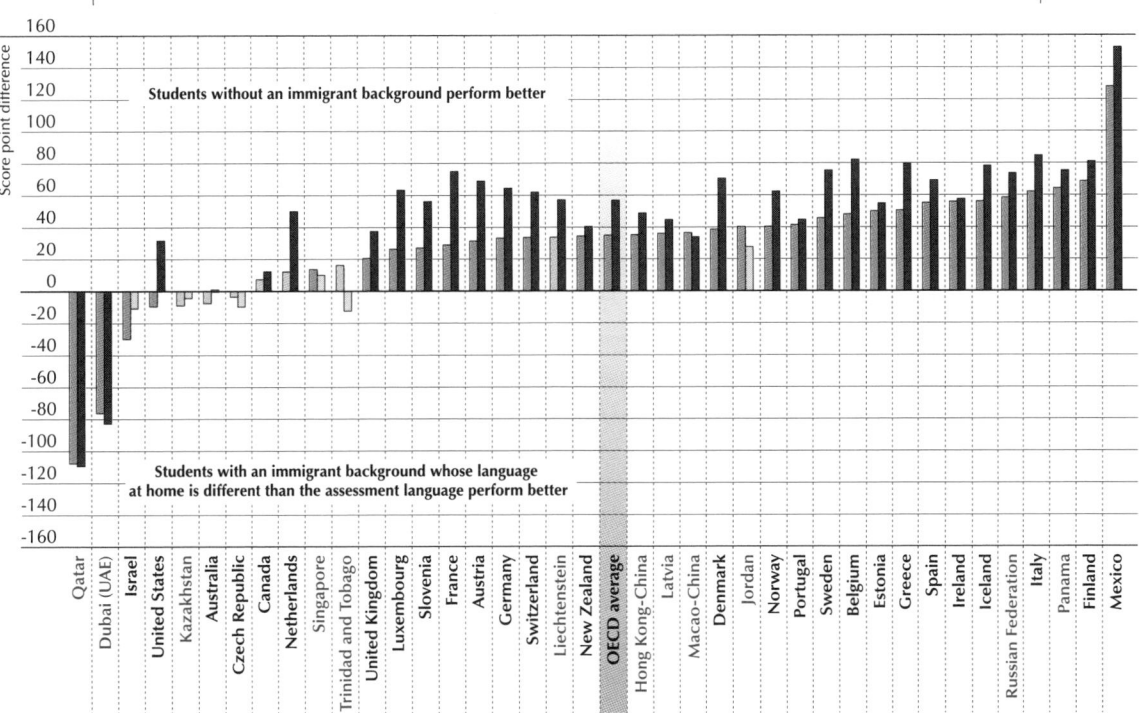

Note: Score point differences that are statistically significant are marked in a darker tone.
Countries are ranked in ascending order of score point differences between students without an immigrant background and students with an immigrant background who speak a language at home that is different from the language of a assessment, after accounting for the economic, social and cultural status of students.
Source: OECD, *PISA 2009 Database*, Table II.4.4.
StatLink ⫶ http://dx.doi.org/10.1787/888932343608

PERFORMANCE, IMMIGRANT STATUS AND COUNTRY OF ORIGIN

The relative performance of students with an immigrant background cannot be attributed solely to their country of origin. Figures II.4.11 and II.4.12 show the performance of students with an immigrant background from the OECD and other countries across a number of host countries, before and after accounting for the socio-economic background of the students or the host country. These figures highlight how performance varies for students with the same country of origin across different host countries. They also show how students from different countries of origin fare within the same host country.

Figure II.4.11 shows, for example, that students with an immigrant background from Turkey perform 69 points lower in Austria than in the Netherlands, even after accounting for their socio-economic status. In Luxembourg, students with an immigrant background from Portugal perform 65 score points below students with an immigrant background from France, after accounting for their own socio-economic status. Students with an immigrant background from Germany perform 44 score points higher in Switzerland than in Luxembourg, while students with an immigrant background from Portugal in Switzerland outperform students with a similar background in Luxembourg by 65 score points (Table II.4.5).

The performance of students with an immigrant background from countries and regions outside the OECD are represented in Figure II.4.12. Students from China perform well above the OECD average (above 560 score points) in Australia and New Zealand. Students with an immigrant background from South Africa also perform above the OECD average in Australia and New Zealand, even after accounting for socio-economic background. Students with an immigrant background from Pakistan perform above the OECD average in the United Kingdom but well below it in Denmark, even after accounting for socio-economic background (Table II.4.5).

■ Figure II.4.11 ■

Reading performance in host countries by students with an immigrant background from OECD countries

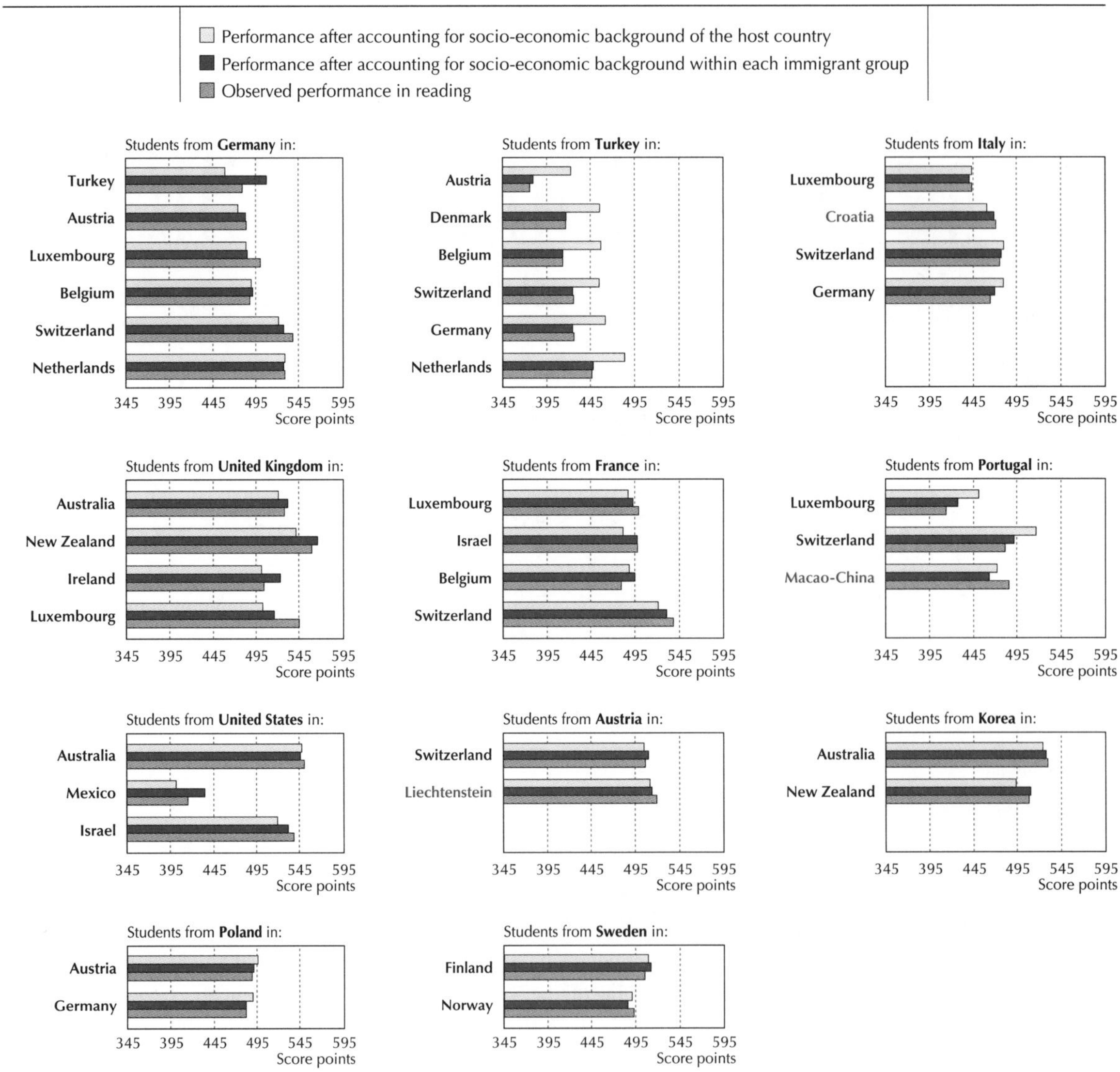

☐ Performance after accounting for socio-economic background of the host country
■ Performance after accounting for socio-economic background within each immigrant group
▨ Observed performance in reading

Students from **Germany** in:

Students from **Turkey** in:

Students from **Italy** in:

Students from **United Kingdom** in:

Students from **France** in:

Students from **Portugal** in:

Students from **United States** in:

Students from **Austria** in:

Students from **Korea** in:

Students from **Poland** in:

Students from **Sweden** in:

Source: OECD, *PISA 2009 Database,* Table II.4.5.
StatLink ⫘ http://dx.doi.org/10.1787/888932343608

These performance differences only account for the socio-economic background of students. It is possible that these differences in the performance of students from the same country of origin in different host countries reflect the selection processes determining how immigrant families choose their country of residence. These selection processes are also determined in part by the immigration policies of different countries and must be kept in mind when analysing these and the other results presented in this chapter.

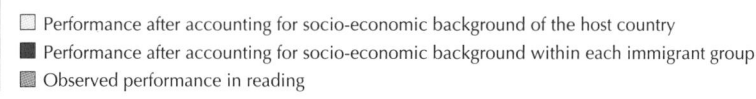

■ Figure II.4.12 ■
Reading performance in host countries by students with an immigrant background from non-OECD countries

☐ Performance after accounting for socio-economic background of the host country
■ Performance after accounting for socio-economic background within each immigrant group
▨ Observed performance in reading

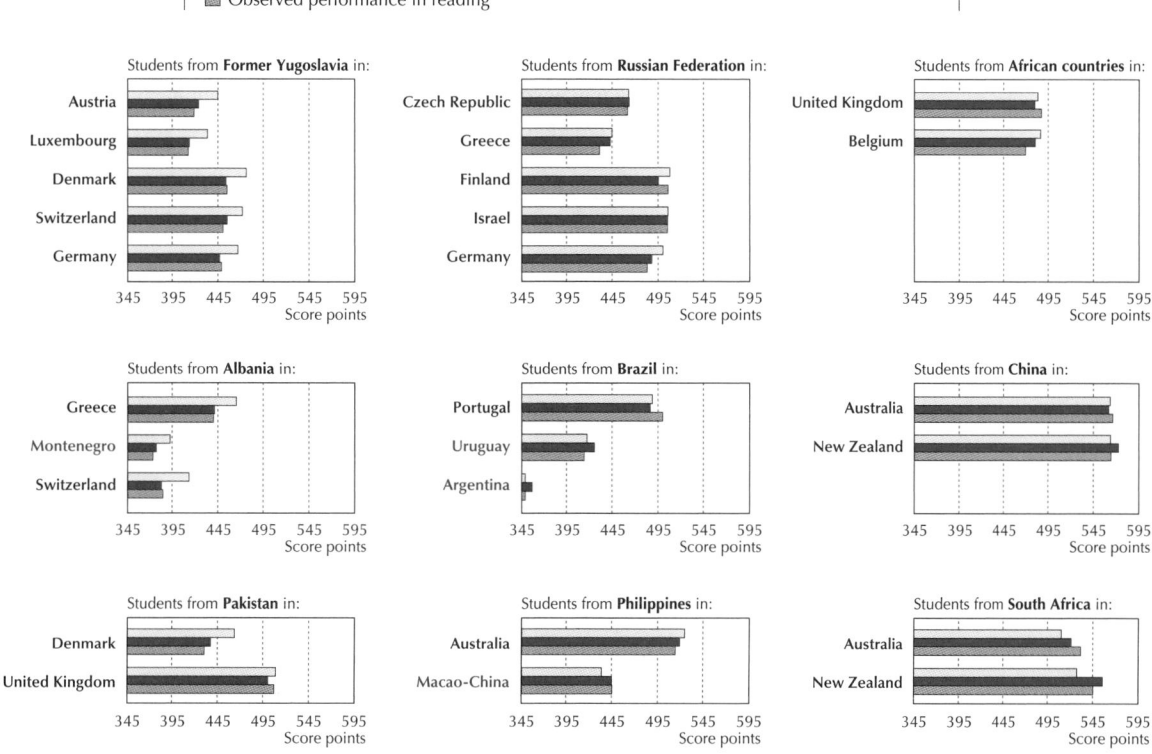

Source: OECD, *PISA 2009 Database,* Table II.4.5.
StatLink ⏴⏵ http://dx.doi.org/10.1787/888932343608

IMMIGRANT STATUS AND SCHOOL RESOURCES

To explore to what extent differences in schooling conditions in host countries might contribute to observed outcomes, Figure II.4.13 examines differences between the characteristics of schools attended by immigrant and native students. The most consistent feature is that students with an immigrant background attend schools with a more disadvantaged socio-economic intake. On average across the OECD, students with an immigrant background attend schools with an average *PISA index of economic, social and cultural status* of -0.26, while students without an immigrant background attend, on average, schools with an index value of 0.04 (Table II.4.6). That is, students with an immigrant background tend to face the double challenge of coming from a disadvantaged background themselves and going to a school with a more disadvantaged profile - both of which chapters of this volume show to be negatively related to student performance. These differences in the composition of schools attended by students with and without an immigrant background are particularly pronounced in the Netherlands, Denmark and Greece, where the difference is higher than two-thirds of a student-level standard deviation in the OECD area. In contrast, in the OECD countries the United Kingdom, Norway, Estonia, Ireland, Portugal, the Czech Republic, New Zealand, Australia, Canada and Finland, students with and without an immigrant background attend schools with a similar socio-economic composition.

By contrast, differences in the quality of resources for education between schools attended by students with and without an immigrant background tend to be small, on average across the OECD area (Figure II.4.13). In Mexico, Belgium, Germany, Iceland, Luxembourg and Switzerland, however, students with an immigrant background attend schools in which principals more frequently report that the low quality of educational resources hinders learning.

■ Figure II.4.13 ■

Characteristics of schools attended by students with and without an immigrant background

	School characteristics are MORE favourable for students with an immigrant background by:	School characteristics are LESS favourable for students with an immigrant background by:
	at least 0.50 index points	
	between 0.20 and 0.49 index points	
	up to 0.19 index points	

	Percentage of students with an immigrant background	Percentage of students in schools that have more than 25% students with an immigrant background	School average PISA index of economic, social and cultural status[1]	Quality of educational resources[1]	Student/teacher ratio[1]	Teacher shortage[1]
OECD						
Australia	19	38				
Austria	15	21				
Belgium	15	19				
Canada	24	37				
Chile	1	0	c	c	c	c
Czech Republic	2	0				
Denmark	9	7				
Estonia	8	12				
Finland	3	0				
France	13	17	w	w	w	w
Germany	18	27				
Greece	9	8				
Hungary	2	0				
Iceland	2	1				
Ireland	8	5				
Israel	20	33				
Italy	6	3				
Japan	0	0	c	c	c	c
Korea	0	0	c	c	c	c
Luxembourg	40	72				
Mexico	2	1				
Netherlands	12	12				
New Zealand	25	38				
Norway	7	3				
Poland	0	0	c	c	c	c
Portugal	5	2				
Slovak Republic	1	0	c	c	c	c
Slovenia	8	7				
Spain	9	10				
Sweden	12	12				
Switzerland	24	40				
Turkey	1	0	c	c	c	c
United Kingdom	11	13				
United States	19	31				
OECD average	10	14				
Partners						
Albania	1	0	c	c	c	c
Argentina	4	1				
Azerbaijan	3	2				
Brazil	1	0				
Bulgaria	1	0	c	c	c	c
Colombia	0	0				
Croatia	11	8				
Dubai (UAE)	71	82				
Hong Kong-China	39	81				
Indonesia	0	0	c	c	c	c
Jordan	14	20				
Kazakhstan	12	13				
Kyrgyzstan	2	0				
Latvia	4	4				
Liechtenstein	30	59				
Lithuania	2	1				
Macao-China	70	100				
Montenegro	7	4				
Panama	4	4				
Peru	0	0	c	c	c	c
Qatar	46	68				
Romania	0	0	c	c	c	c
Russian Federation	12	8				
Serbia	9	6				
Shanghai-China	1	0	c	c	c	c
Singapore	14	10				
Chinese Taipei	0	0	c	c	c	c
Thailand	0	0	c	c	c	c
Trinidad and Tobago	2	1				
Tunisia	0	0	c	c	c	c
Uruguay	1	0	c	c	c	c

Note: Only significant differences between students with and without immigrant background are reported in this figure.
1. Scores were standardised within each country sample to make an index which has 0 as the country mean and 1 as the standard deviation within the country.
Source: OECD, *PISA 2009 Database*, Table II.4.6.
StatLink ⟐⟐ http://dx.doi.org/10.1787/888932343608

In most countries, schools attended by students with and without an immigrant background tend to be comparable in terms of human resources. Among OECD countries, only in Iceland, the United Kingdom, Israel, Portugal, Spain, the Netherlands, Denmark, Austria and Ireland is the are student-teacher ratio higher in schools attended by students without an immigrant background, while the opposite is true in Slovenia, New Zealand and the United States (Figure II.4.13). Only in Canada, Australia and Luxembourg do principals of schools attended by students with an immigrant background report more often than principals of schools attended by native students that a shortage of teachers hinders learning in their schools, while the opposite is true only in Iceland, Belgium and Germany.

In short, while differences in the socio-economic background of schools in many countries make it difficult to provide equity in learning opportunities for students with an immigrant background, inequality in the distribution of resources does not seem to mediate the performance gaps between students with and without an immigrant background except in a small number of countries.

The analyses described in this chapter show that performance gaps between students with and without an immigrant background exist in most countries. These differences in performance are rarely solely the result of the socio-economic background or language of students, signalling that there is an independent relationship between the immigration status of students and their performance. The analyses that compare performance among immigrant students who arrived at a younger age show that some countries help these students improve their performance if their education system had a long enough opportunity to shape learning outcomes. The analysis comparing first- and second-generation immigrants underscore the fact that eliminating performance differences between students with and without an immigrant background takes time; but the fact that some countries succeed in reducing this gap more than others offers reasons to be optimistic about the possibility to ameliorate the disadvantages associated with an immigrant background.

Notes

1. This implies that students who were born abroad but who had at least one parent born in the country of assessment are also classified as students without an immigrant background.

2. If information on only one of the parents is missing, it is assumed that the other parent has the same immigrant background as the one whose information is missing. If the information on the country of birth of the student is missing, the variable is coded as missing.

3. For OECD countries, there is no association (the cross country correlation is equal to -.02, $p = 0.921$) and for all countries the association is slightly negative (the cross country correlation is equal to $r = -.35$ and $p = 0.045$). That is, when all countries are considered, the performance gap tends to be smaller in countries with higher proportions of immigrants.

4. For the purpose of this analysis, these are the countries in which at least 30 students from five schools have an immigrant background.

5. The same is true in Hungary but the margin is smaller and these students are a much smaller proportion of the population, less than 1%. Also in this case, this advantage does not translate to all students with an immigrant background unlike in Australia.

5

School Systems
and the Impact of
Socio-Economic Background

This chapter analyses the impact of the socio-economic background of schools on reading performance. The socio-economic gradient used extensively in Chapter 3 is used here to describe how students' socio-economic background is related to their performance within the same school, and how a school's average level of performance is related to the socio-economic composition of its student intake.

THE RELATIONSHIP BETWEEN PERFORMANCE AND SOCIO-ECONOMIC BACKGROUND

Socio-economic disadvantages have many facets and cannot be ameliorated by education policy alone, much less in the short term. The educational attainment of parents can only improve gradually, and average family wealth depends on the long-term economic development of a country and on a culture that promotes individual savings. However, even if socio-economic background itself is hard to change, previous chapters have shown that some countries succeed in mediating its impact on learning outcomes. So, to what extent can schools and school policies moderate the impact of socio-economic disadvantages on student performance?

This chapter extends the examination of the relationship between socio-economic background and student performance, as measured by the socio-economic gradient discussed in Chapter 3, to a closer analysis of patterns in each country, including how the socio-economic composition of schools affects these patterns. To this end, the gradient for a country is broken down into two parts: a within-school gradient and a between-school gradient. The within-school gradient describes how students' socio-economic background is related to their performance within a common school environment. The between-school gradient describes how schools' average level of performance is related to the average economic, social and cultural status of their student intake.[1]

PERFORMANCE DIFFERENCES WITHIN AND BETWEEN SCHOOLS

As discussed in Volume IV, *What Makes a School Successful?*, the ways in which students are allocated to schools can result in large gaps and marked variations in performance between schools. There may also be large variations in performance among schools due to the socio-economic and cultural characteristics of the communities that are served or to geographical differences, such as differences between regions, provinces or states in federal systems, or between rural and urban areas. Differences can also be attributed to the organisation of the schooling systems and to characteristics that are more difficult to quantify, such as differences in the quality or the effectiveness of instruction that those schools provide. Variation in performance also occurs within schools. Students attending the same school may display different abilities or effort, or may be exposed to different learning opportunities.

Figure II.5.1 shows the extent to which the reading performance of 15-year-olds varies between and within schools in each country. Countries are sorted according to the total variance in student performance as a percentage of the average variance across OECD countries (a figure that appears next to the country names). Countries at the bottom end of the figure have a student variance well above the OECD average. For example, the total variance in Israel is 44% higher than that observed on average across OECD countries. In the figure, the total length of both the dark blue and the light blue bars indicates this observed total variation in reading performance.[2] In countries where a sizable proportion of 15-year-olds are not at school, the variance in student performance is likely to be underestimated (Table A2.1). This effect may explain, at least partially, the list of countries that appears at the top of this figure.

The darker segment of the bar in Figure II.5.1 represents the performance variation that can be attributed to differences in student results in different schools (between-school variation); the light bar represents the part of the performance variation that can be attributed to the range of student results that cannot be attributed to differences between schools and can thus be attributed to differences in the performance of students within schools (within-school variation).[3] The vertical lines in Figure II.5.1 mark the OECD averages of the percentage of the total variance in student performance that can be attributed to either differences among schools or differences among students within schools.

In Belgium, for example, where the overall variance is 20% above the OECD average, the proportion of the total variance that is attributed to between-school differences is higher than the OECD average, but the within-school variance is lower than the OECD average. The same holds for Germany, Italy, Austria, Greece and Japan, among OECD countries with higher total variance than the OECD average and higher variance between schools, but lower within school variance than the OECD average. In contrast, in Sweden, New Zealand, Iceland, Australia, Ireland, the United Kingdom and Switzerland, the above-average total variation is driven by large performance differences within schools. In Israel, the United States and Luxembourg, both the between- and within-school variations contribute to a total variance in student performance that is above the OECD average.

The proportion of the variance in student performance that occurs between schools can be interpreted as a measure of vertical or academic inclusion (Monseur and Crahay, 2008; Willms, 2010).[4] Table II.5.1 provides an index of

■ Figure II.5.1 ■
Variation in reading performance between and within schools
Expressed as a percentage of the variance in student performance across OECD countries

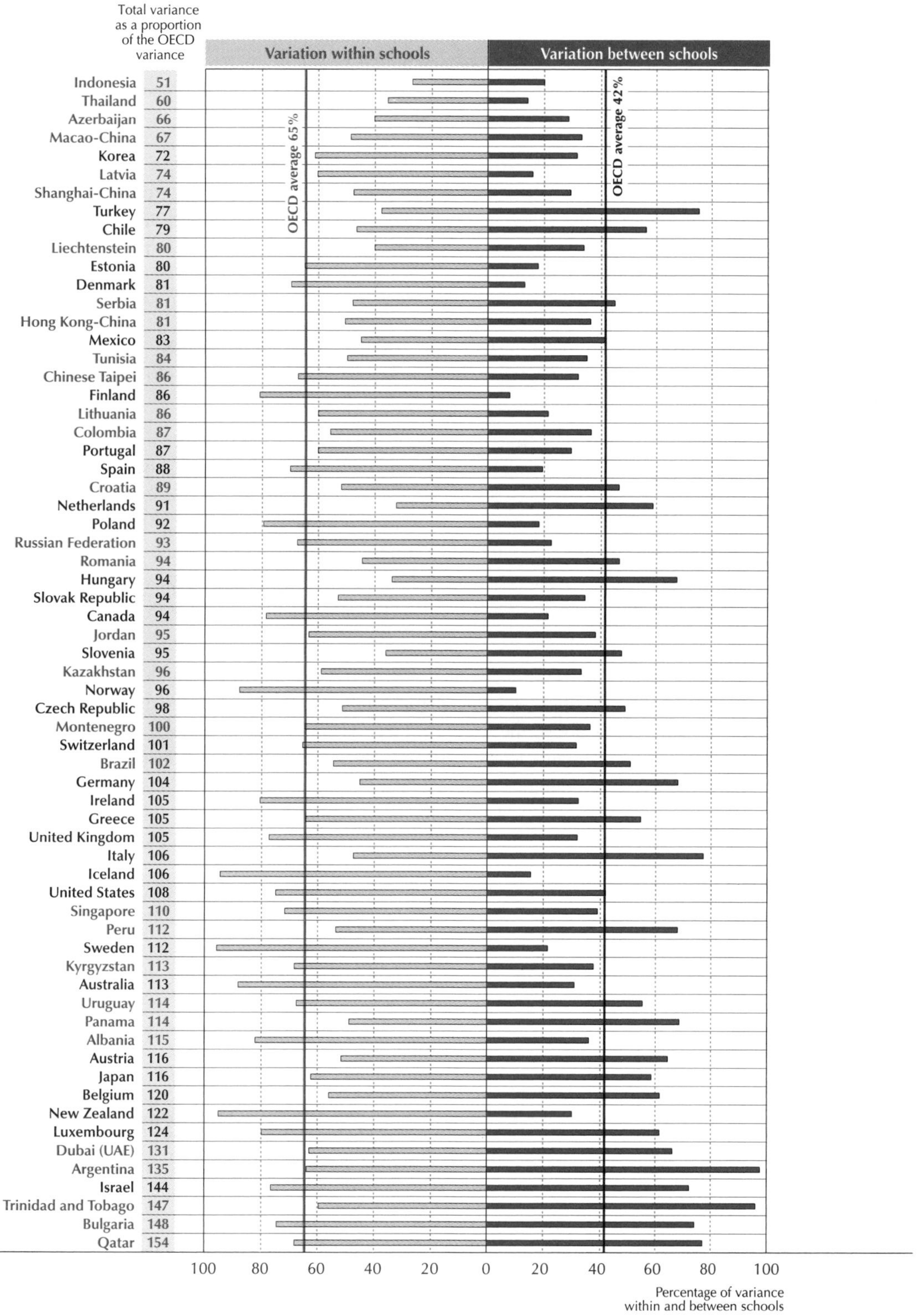

	Total variance as a proportion of the OECD variance	Variation within schools	Variation between schools
Indonesia	51		
Thailand	60		
Azerbaijan	66		
Macao-China	67		
Korea	72		
Latvia	74		
Shanghai-China	74		
Turkey	77		
Chile	79		
Liechtenstein	80		
Estonia	80		
Denmark	81		
Serbia	81		
Hong Kong-China	81		
Mexico	83		
Tunisia	84		
Chinese Taipei	86		
Finland	86		
Lithuania	86		
Colombia	87		
Portugal	87		
Spain	88		
Croatia	89		
Netherlands	91		
Poland	92		
Russian Federation	93		
Romania	94		
Hungary	94		
Slovak Republic	94		
Canada	94		
Jordan	95		
Slovenia	95		
Kazakhstan	96		
Norway	96		
Czech Republic	98		
Montenegro	100		
Switzerland	101		
Brazil	102		
Germany	104		
Ireland	105		
Greece	105		
United Kingdom	105		
Italy	106		
Iceland	106		
United States	108		
Singapore	110		
Peru	112		
Sweden	112		
Kyrgyzstan	113		
Australia	113		
Uruguay	114		
Panama	114		
Albania	115		
Austria	116		
Japan	116		
Belgium	120		
New Zealand	122		
Luxembourg	124		
Dubai (UAE)	131		
Argentina	135		
Israel	144		
Trinidad and Tobago	147		
Bulgaria	148		
Qatar	154		

OECD average 65%

OECD average 42%

100 80 60 40 20 0 20 40 60 80 100

Percentage of variance
within and between schools

Countries are ranked in ascending order of the total variance as a proportion of the overall variance in student performance across the OECD.
Source: OECD, *PISA 2009 Database*, Table II.5.1.
StatLink http://dx.doi.org/10.1787/888932343627

inclusion. Where there is substantial variation in performance among schools but less variation among students within schools, these students tend to be grouped systematically in schools in which most students have relatively similar abilities. This may reflect school choices made by families according to geographic location and/or policies on school enrolment or on allocating students to different curricula in the form of tracking or streaming (see Volume IV, *What Makes a School Successful?,* for a more detailed analysis on the relationship between school policies and practices and equity). Where performance variation is concentrated within schools (*i.e.* high academic inclusion), educational policies that targed individual schools are likely to miss out on many low-performing students. These, and other policy implications related with the distribution of performance between and within schools are discussed in more detail in the policy implication section of this volume.

DIFFERENCES IN THE SOCIO-ECONOMIC BACKGROUND OF STUDENTS AND SCHOOLS

Socio-economic background and student performance vary greatly within countries across schools and students. On average across OECD countries, the difference between the 25th percentile and the 75th percentile in the *PISA index of social, economic and cultural status* of students amounts to 1.29 units on that index. The dispersion of schools' socio-economic backgrounds can be calculated in a similar way. The gap between the 25th and 75th percentile of the socio-economic background of schools is about half that of students (0.65 units).

Figures II.5.2 and II.5.3[5] show that the range between these two percentiles, both between individuals and between schools, varies greatly from one country to another (Table II.5.2). Longer bars indicate more diverse background of students and schools within the school system.

The proportion of the variation in socio-economic background between schools provides a measure of horizontal or social inclusion (to be distinguished from vertical or academic inclusion as discussed above). Table II.5.2 provides the index of social inclusion for PISA 2009. In a socially inclusive school system, the distribution of socio-economic backgrounds in each school reflects the distribution of socio-economic background in the system, that is, each school accommodates a range of socio-economic profiles among its students similar to the range in the population in general. In contrast, where students with very similar socio-economic backgrounds attend the same schools, the system displays low social inclusion. The extent of social inclusion for each school system may also reflect geographic location, policy, institutions or family choices.

Countries with high social inclusion also tend to show relatively high levels of academic inclusion, whether in reading, mathematics or science.[6] Every OECD country with academic and social inclusion above the OECD average, except Spain, has a mean performance at or above the OECD average (Tables II.5.1 and II.5.2). These countries include Australia, Canada, Denmark, Estonia, Finland, Iceland, Ireland, New Zealand, Norway, Sweden, Switzerland and the United Kingdom. Schools in the OECD countries Chile, Hungary, Mexico, Turkey, Greece, Austria, Belgium and Italy show below-average levels of both academic and social inclusion. This signals a school system in which students of similar socio-economic background and academic performance generally attend the same schools.

PERFORMANCE DIFFERENCES AND THE SOCIO-ECONOMIC BACKGROUND OF STUDENTS AND SCHOOLS

Chapter 3 introduced the socio-economic gradient as a tool to analyse the relationship between socio-economic background and student performance. The following section explores the extent to which differences in performance between schools and among students within schools can be attributed to differences in socio-economic background between and within schools.

Figure II.5.4 shows the proportion of the between- and within-school variance in performance that can be attributed to socio-economic background differences within and between schools. The lighter segment of the bar represents the between-school variation that is explained by schools' socio-economic background; the dark bar represents the within-school variation that is explained by the socio-economic background of students within schools. The sum of both lengths gives an indication of the extent to which socio-economic differences are associated with performance differences. Countries are ranked according to total explained variance.

In many countries, variation in socio-economic background is closely related to variation in performance across and, to a lesser extent, within schools. Across OECD countries, differences in the socio-economic backgrounds of students attending different schools account for 57% of the performance differences between schools. However, this proportion varies considerably across countries. For example, and relative to the overall performance variation in OECD countries, in Finland, Iceland and Norway, differences in the socio-economic background of schools account for less than 30% of the already-small performance differences between schools.

- Figure II.5.2 -
Range of students' socio-economic background
Student variability in the distribution of the PISA index of economic, social and cultural status

Percentiles

25th | 75th

Dubai (UAE)
Czech Republic
Norway
Slovak Republic
Austria
Japan
New Zealand
Australia
Qatar
United Kingdom
Poland
Chinese Taipei
Romania
Singapore
Sweden
Finland
Macao-China
Korea
Canada
Croatia
Israel
Germany
Kazakhstan
Ireland
Trinidad and Tobago
Estonia
Switzerland
Netherlands
Denmark
Russian Federation
OECD average
Iceland
United States
Montenegro
Hungary
Serbia
Slovenia
Liechtenstein
Belgium
Latvia
Bulgaria
Kyrgyzstan
Hong Kong-China
Italy
Albania
Azerbaijan
Greece
Luxembourg
Jordan
Lithuania
Shanghai-China
Indonesia
Spain
Chile
Portugal
Argentina
Peru
Turkey
Brazil
Uruguay
Thailand
Colombia
Mexico
Tunisia
Panama

-2.5   -2.0   -1.5   -1.0   -0.5   0   0.5   1.0   1.5   2.0

PISA index of economic,
social and cultural status

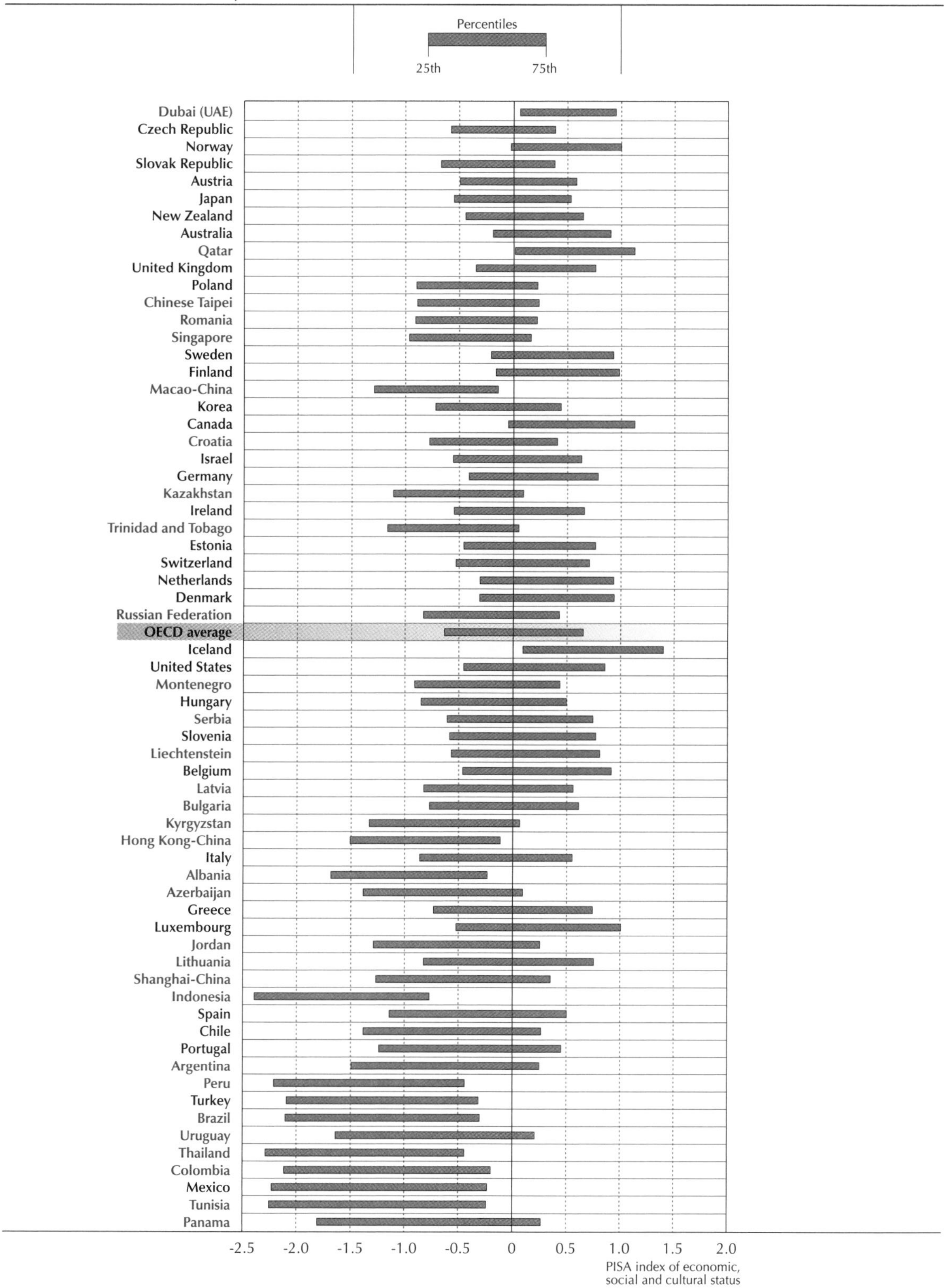

Countries are ranked in ascending order of the interquartile range of the distribution of student-level socio-economic background.
Source: OECD, *PISA 2009 Database,* Table II.5.2.
StatLink ⟶ http://dx.doi.org/10.1787/888932343627

- Figure II.5.3 -
Range of schools' socio-economic background
School variability in the distribution of the students' average PISA index of economic, social and cultural status

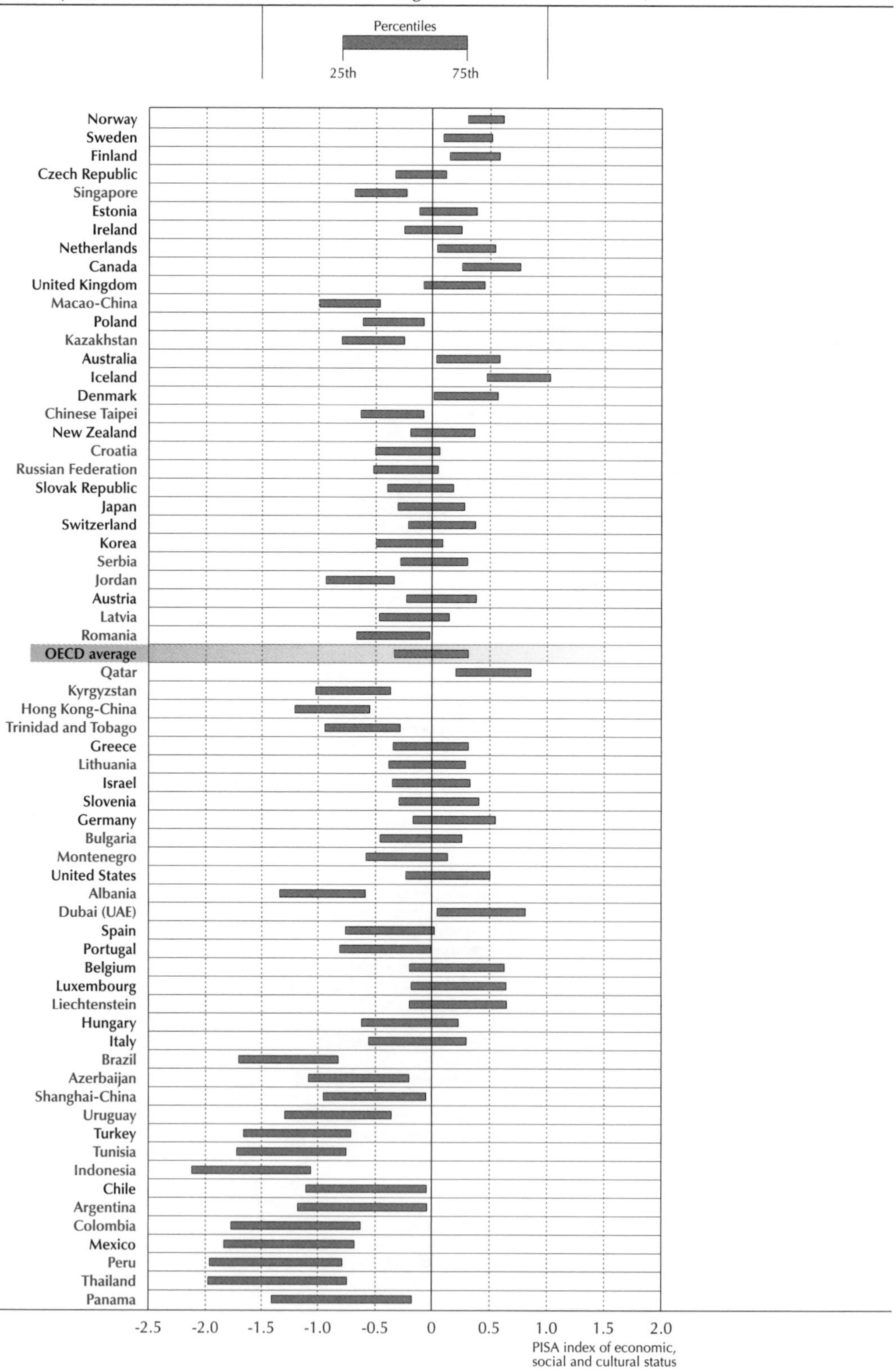

Countries are ranked in ascending order of the interquartile range of the distribution of school-level socio-economic background.
Source: OECD, *PISA 2009 Database*, Table II.5.2.
StatLink ⟨⟨⟨ http://dx.doi.org/10.1787/888932343627

■ Figure II.5.4 ■
Variation in reading performance explained by students' and schools' socio-economic background
Expressed as a percentage of the average variance in student performance in OECD countries

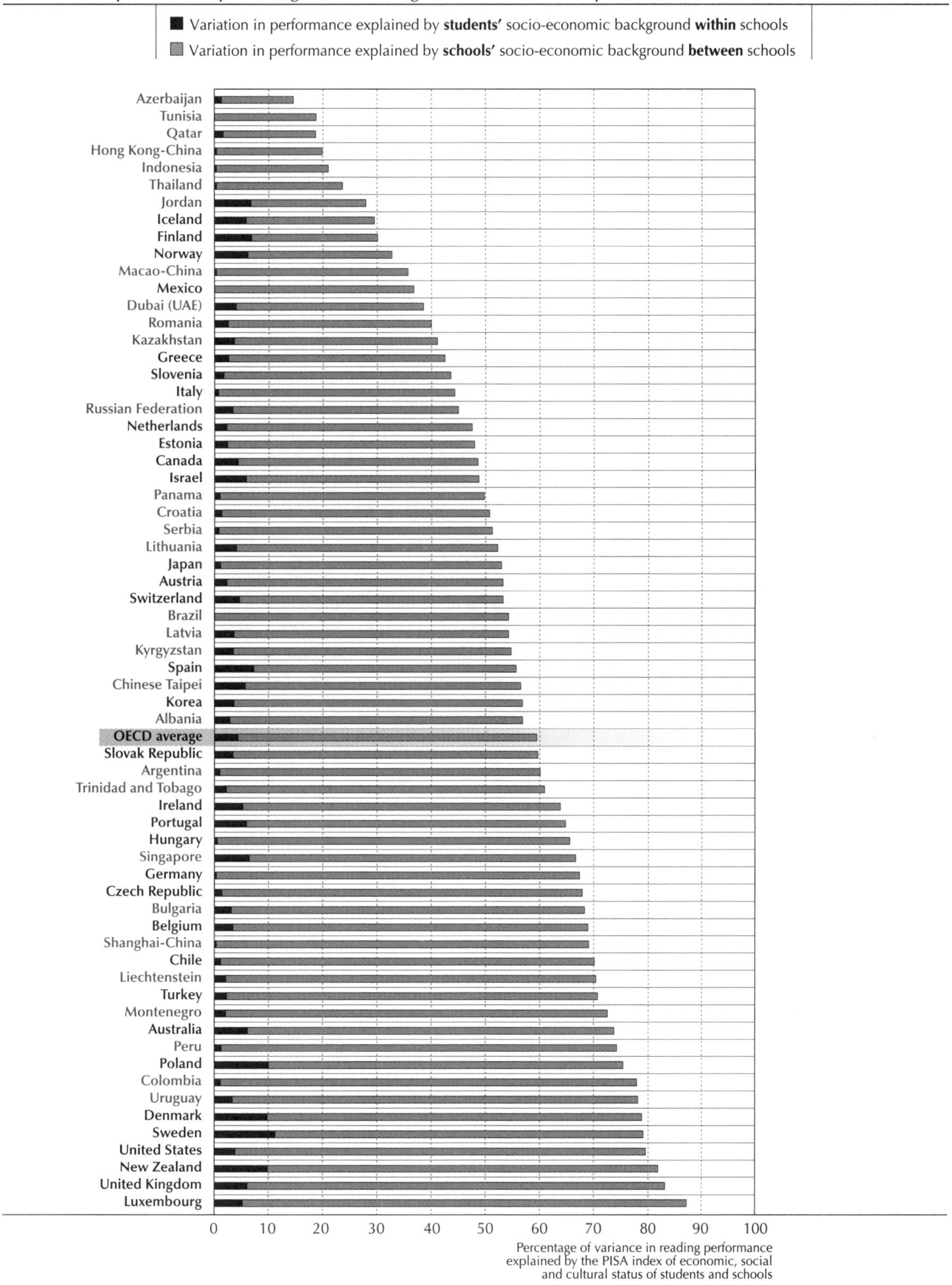

■ Variation in performance explained by **students'** socio-economic background **within** schools
▨ Variation in performance explained by **schools'** socio-economic background **between** schools

Azerbaijan
Tunisia
Qatar
Hong Kong-China
Indonesia
Thailand
Jordan
Iceland
Finland
Norway
Macao-China
Mexico
Dubai (UAE)
Romania
Kazakhstan
Greece
Slovenia
Italy
Russian Federation
Netherlands
Estonia
Canada
Israel
Panama
Croatia
Serbia
Lithuania
Japan
Austria
Switzerland
Brazil
Latvia
Kyrgyzstan
Spain
Chinese Taipei
Korea
Albania
OECD average
Slovak Republic
Argentina
Trinidad and Tobago
Ireland
Portugal
Hungary
Singapore
Germany
Czech Republic
Bulgaria
Belgium
Shanghai-China
Chile
Liechtenstein
Turkey
Montenegro
Australia
Peru
Poland
Colombia
Uruguay
Denmark
Sweden
United States
New Zealand
United Kingdom
Luxembourg

0   10   20   30   40   50   60   70   80   90   100

Percentage of variance in reading performance
explained by the PISA index of economic, social
and cultural status of students and schools

Countries are ranked in ascending order of the percentage of overall variance in reading performance explained by the PISA index of economic, social and cultural status of students and schools.
Source: OECD, *PISA 2009 Database*, Table II.5.2.
StatLink ⌗ http://dx.doi.org/10.1787/888932343627

In the United Kingdom, the United States and New Zealand, the between-school performance variance explained by the socio-economic intake of schools is larger than 70%, and in Luxembourg it exceeds 80%. Among the partner countries and economies, the range is similar. In Azerbaijan, Qatar, Tunisia, Hong Kong-China, Indonesia, Jordan and Thailand, less than 30% of the performance variation between schools is explained by socio-economic background, while in Colombia, Uruguay, Peru and Montenegro, more than 70% is so explained.

In the same way that the strength of the relationship between socio-economic background and performance can be separately examined at the level of schools and students within schools, so too can the slope of the gradient.[7]

Figure II.5.5 displays the between- and within-school slopes of the socio-economic gradient. The length of each bar indicates the difference in scores on the PISA reading scale that is associated with an increment of half a standard deviation on the *PISA index of economic, social and cultural status* for the individual student (grey bar) and for the school's average (blue bar). Differences in the averages of schools' socio-economic backgrounds are, as observed in Figures II.5.2 and II.5.3, smaller than comparable differences between individual students, given that every school's intake includes students from mixed socio-economic backgrounds.[8] A difference of 0.25 in the *PISA index of economic, social and cultural status* is thus a considerably more important gap across schools than among students.

To help interpretation, Figure II.5.5 includes the typical range of the average socio-economic background of schools for each country. Half a student-level standard deviation is the benchmark for measuring performance gaps in the figure because this value describes realistic differences between schools in terms of their socio-economic composition. On average across OECD countries, the difference between the 75th and 25th quartiles of the distribution of the school mean *PISA index of economic, social and cultural status* is 0.65 of a student-level standard deviation (Table II.5.2). Diversity in the socio-economic background of schools ranges from half or less of a standard deviation in Norway, Sweden, Finland, the Czech Republic, Estonia, Ireland, the Netherlands and Canada and the partner country Singapore, to one standard deviation or more in Mexico and Chile and the partner countries Panama, Thailand, Peru, Colombia, Argentina and Indonesia.

In almost all countries, and for all students, the blue bars in Figure II.5.5 indicate that regardless of their own socio-economic background, students attending schools in which the average socio-economic background is advantageous tend to perform better than when they are enrolled in a school with a disadvantaged socio-economic intake. In the majority of the OECD countries, the relationship between the average economic, social and cultural status of students in a school and their performance is steeper than the relationship between the individual student's socio-economic background and their performance in the same school.

The magnitude of the differences in performance associated with the socio-economic composition of the school is striking.[9] In Japan, the Czech Republic, Germany, Belgium and Israel, and the partner countries Trinidad and Tobago and Liechtenstein, the improvement in student performance associated with a school's average economic, social and cultural status is substantial. In these countries, half a unit increase on the *PISA index of economic, social and cultural status* at the school level is equivalent to a difference of more than 50 score points.

To put these numbers in more concrete terms, consider the hypothetical case of two students in any of these countries living in families with an average socio-economic background, as measured by the *PISA index of economic, social and cultural status*. One student attends a socio-economically advantaged school, say where the mean *PISA index of economic, social and cultural status* of the school's intake is one-quarter of a (student-level) standard deviation above the OECD average. Most of this student's peers will come from families that are more affluent. The other student attends a more socio-economically disadvantaged school: the school's mean *PISA index of economic, social and cultural status* is one-quarter of a standard deviation below the OECD average, so that the student comes from a more affluent family than many of his or her peers. The result indicates that the first student would be expected to show, on average across the OECD countries, 32 score point higher reading performance than the second student, and this difference is expected to exceed 50 score points in several countries (blue bar in Figure II.5.5).[10]

Within-school differences in socio-economic background across students display a gentler relationship with performance than the between-school differences. Consider the case of two students in the same country living with families whose different economic, social and cultural status gives them scores on the index that are one-quarter of a student-level standard deviation above, and one-quarter below the mean. If these students attend the same school, with an average socio-economic profile, the predicted performance gap is smaller: on average across OECD countries it stands at 9 score points. It is between 10 and 18 score points in New Zealand, Sweden, Poland, Australia, Finland, Norway, Denmark, Ireland, the United Kingdom, Iceland, the United States, Canada, Spain, Luxembourg and Switzerland, and in the partner countries and economies Singapore, Chinese Taipei and the Russian Federation (grey bar in Figure II.5.5).

■ Figure II.5.5 ■

Slope of the socio-economic gradient between and within schools

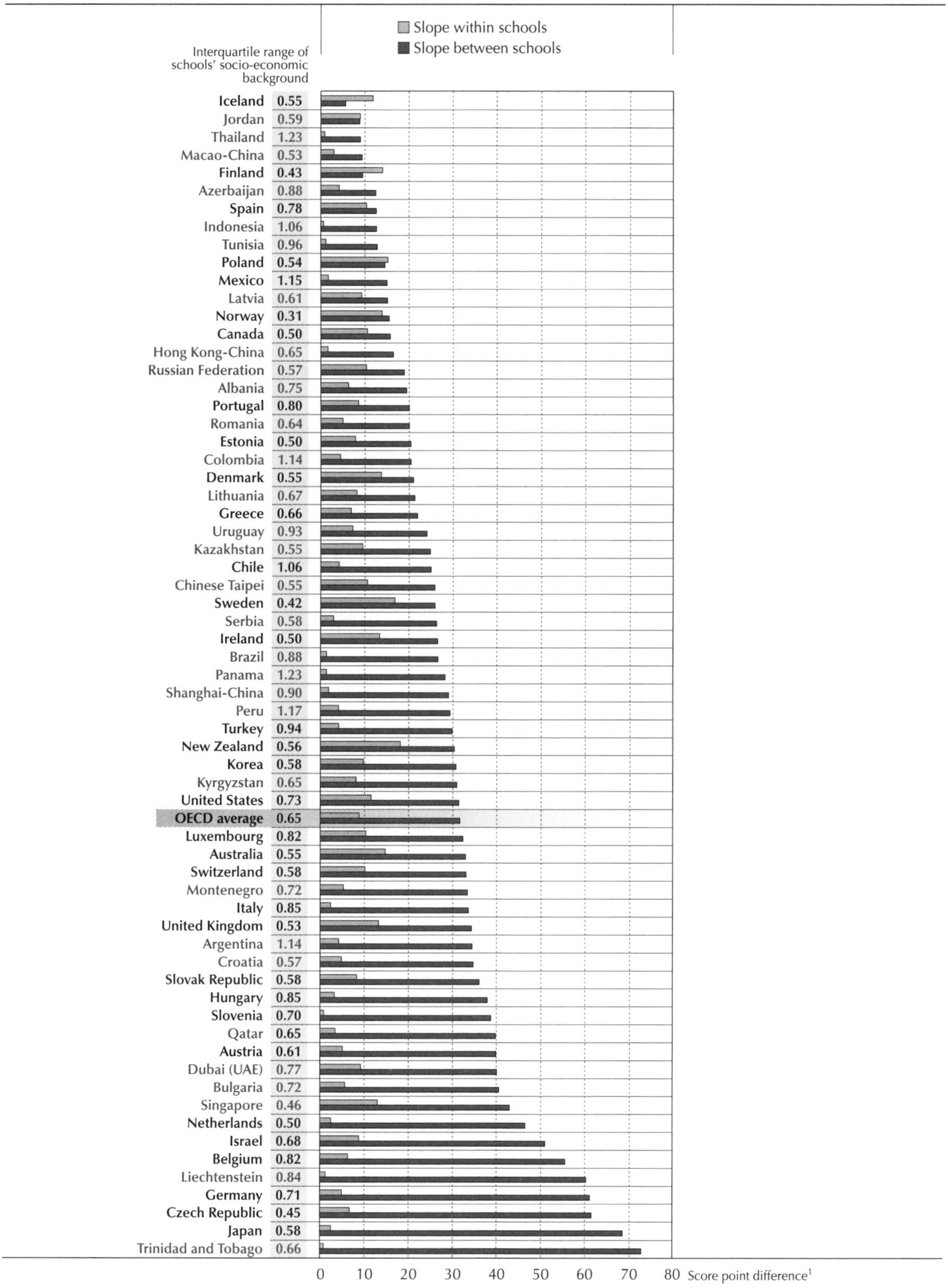

▨ Slope within schools
■ Slope between schools

Interquartile range of schools' socio-economic background	
Iceland	0.55
Jordan	0.59
Thailand	1.23
Macao-China	0.53
Finland	0.43
Azerbaijan	0.88
Spain	0.78
Indonesia	1.06
Tunisia	0.96
Poland	0.54
Mexico	1.15
Latvia	0.61
Norway	0.31
Canada	0.50
Hong Kong-China	0.65
Russian Federation	0.57
Albania	0.75
Portugal	0.80
Romania	0.64
Estonia	0.50
Colombia	1.14
Denmark	0.55
Lithuania	0.67
Greece	0.66
Uruguay	0.93
Kazakhstan	0.55
Chile	1.06
Chinese Taipei	0.55
Sweden	0.42
Serbia	0.58
Ireland	0.50
Brazil	0.88
Panama	1.23
Shanghai-China	0.90
Peru	1.17
Turkey	0.94
New Zealand	0.56
Korea	0.58
Kyrgyzstan	0.65
United States	0.73
OECD average	0.65
Luxembourg	0.82
Australia	0.55
Switzerland	0.58
Montenegro	0.72
Italy	0.85
United Kingdom	0.53
Argentina	1.14
Croatia	0.57
Slovak Republic	0.58
Hungary	0.85
Slovenia	0.70
Qatar	0.65
Austria	0.61
Dubai (UAE)	0.77
Bulgaria	0.72
Singapore	0.46
Netherlands	0.50
Israel	0.68
Belgium	0.82
Liechtenstein	0.84
Germany	0.71
Czech Republic	0.45
Japan	0.58
Trinidad and Tobago	0.66

0   10   20   30   40   50   60   70   80   Score point difference[1]

Note: Data on blue background are values of the interquartile range of the school-level average PISA index of economic, social and cultural status.
Countries are ranked in ascending order of the slope between schools.
1. Score point difference associated with a 0.5 unit increase in the student- or school-level PISA index of economic, social and cultural status.
Source: OECD, *PISA 2009 Database,* Table II.5.2.
StatLink ▨▥▤ http://dx.doi.org/10.1787/888932343627

Some of the contextual effect of socio-economically advantaged schools, the between-school strength and slope of the gradient, can be attributed to peer groups as, for example, talented students work with each other. However, the socio-economic advantage of schools more often implies a better learning environment and access to better educational resources at school. Also, the manner in which students are allocated to schools within a district or region, or classes and programmes within schools, can have implications for the teaching and learning conditions in schools, which are associated with educational outcomes. A number of studies have found that schools with a higher average socio-economic background among their students are likely to have fewer disciplinary problems, better teacher-student relations, higher teacher morale, and a general school climate that is oriented towards higher performance. Often, such schools also have faster-paced curricula. Talented and motivated teachers are more likely to be attracted to schools with a higher socio-economic background and less likely to transfer to another school or to leave the profession. The potential influence of such school characteristics is examined in Volume IV, *What Makes a School Successful?*

External factors that PISA does not examine may also explain socio-economic backgrounds' effect on the learning environment. For example, the parents of a student attending a more socio-economically advantaged school may be more engaged in the student's learning at home - even if their socio-economic background is comparable to that of the parents of a student attending a less privileged school. Since no data on students' earlier achievement are available from PISA, it is not possible to infer students' abilities and motivations. Therefore, neither is it possible to determine whether or to what extent the socio-economic background of students at the school directly determines performance. Factors such as peer interactions indirectly influence performance by contributing to those school features associated with success, such as better classroom atmosphere or more school resources.

Moving all students to schools with a higher socio-economic background is, of course, a practical impossibility. The results shown in Figure II.5.5 should not lead to the conclusion that transferring a group of students from a school with a socio-economically disadvantaged intake to a school with a privileged intake would automatically result in the gains suggested in the figure. The estimated effects shown in these figures describe the distribution of school performance and should not necessarily be interpreted as causal.

In any attempt to develop education policy in the light of the above findings, the nature of the formal and informal selection mechanisms that contribute to between-school socio-economic segregation, and the effect of this segregation on student performance, must be taken into consideration. In some countries, socio-economic segregation may be firmly entrenched, through residential segregation in major cities or by a large urban/rural socio-economic divide. In other countries, the school system tends to stream or track students into programmes with different curricula and teaching practices, often resulting in socio-economic segregation across these tracks or streams. The policy options are either to reduce socio-economic segregation or to mitigate its effects (for further analysis, see Volume IV, *What Makes a School Successful?*).

PREDICTED AND ACTUAL PERFORMANCE OF STUDENTS IN DIFFERENT SOCIO-ECONOMIC CONTEXTS

How does a school's socio-economic composition relate to the performance of students from different socio-economic backgrounds? To answer this question, schools are grouped according to their socio-economic intake relative to the national average. Three categories of schools are identified: socio-economically disadvantaged schools, in which the average socio-economic background of students is below the national average; socio-economically advantaged schools, in which the average socio-economic background of students is above the national average; and socio-economically mixed schools, whose socio-economic intake is around the national average.

Figure II.5.6 shows that while in some school systems most students attend mixed schools, in others a majority of students attend advantaged or disadvantaged schools. The figure also shows that the socio-economic segregation of schools is stronger in certain school systems where there is a lower percentage of mixed schools. Consistent with the index of social inclusion presented in Chapter 3, the figure also shows that disadvantaged students are more likely to attend mixed or advantaged schools in certain school systems. Thus, countries vary markedly in the extent to which disadvantaged students are overrepresented in disadvantaged schools, and also, in the extent to which advantaged students are overrepresented in advantaged schools.

■ Figure II.5.6 ■
Percentage of students in disadvantaged, mixed and advantaged schools, by students' socio-economic background

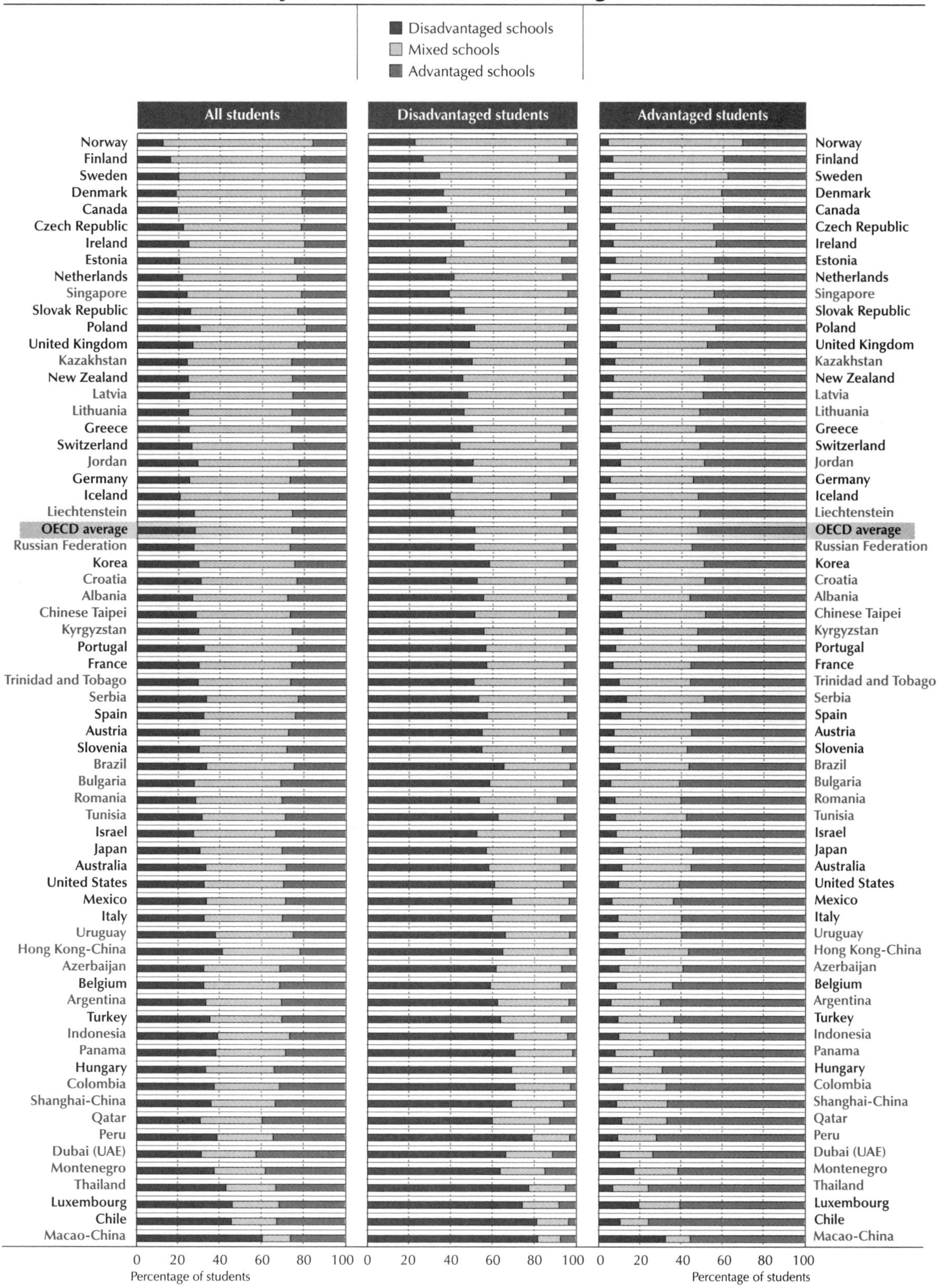

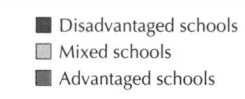

■ Disadvantaged schools
□ Mixed schools
■ Advantaged schools

All students	Disadvantaged students	Advantaged students

Norway
Finland
Sweden
Denmark
Canada
Czech Republic
Ireland
Estonia
Netherlands
Singapore
Slovak Republic
Poland
United Kingdom
Kazakhstan
New Zealand
Latvia
Lithuania
Greece
Switzerland
Jordan
Germany
Iceland
Liechtenstein
OECD average
Russian Federation
Korea
Croatia
Albania
Chinese Taipei
Kyrgyzstan
Portugal
France
Trinidad and Tobago
Serbia
Spain
Austria
Slovenia
Brazil
Bulgaria
Romania
Tunisia
Israel
Japan
Australia
United States
Mexico
Italy
Uruguay
Hong Kong-China
Azerbaijan
Belgium
Argentina
Turkey
Indonesia
Panama
Hungary
Colombia
Shanghai-China
Qatar
Peru
Dubai (UAE)
Montenegro
Thailand
Luxembourg
Chile
Macao-China

0 20 40 60 80 100   0 20 40 60 80 100   0 20 40 60 80 100
Percentage of students   Percentage of students   Percentage of students

Countries are ranked in descending order of the percentage of all students in mixed schools.
Source: OECD, *PISA 2009 Database,* Table II.5.10.
StatLink ᵐˢᵖ http://dx.doi.org/10.1787/888932343627

■ Figure II.5.7 ■

Difference between observed and predicted performance in disadvantaged, mixed and advantaged schools, by students' socio-economic background

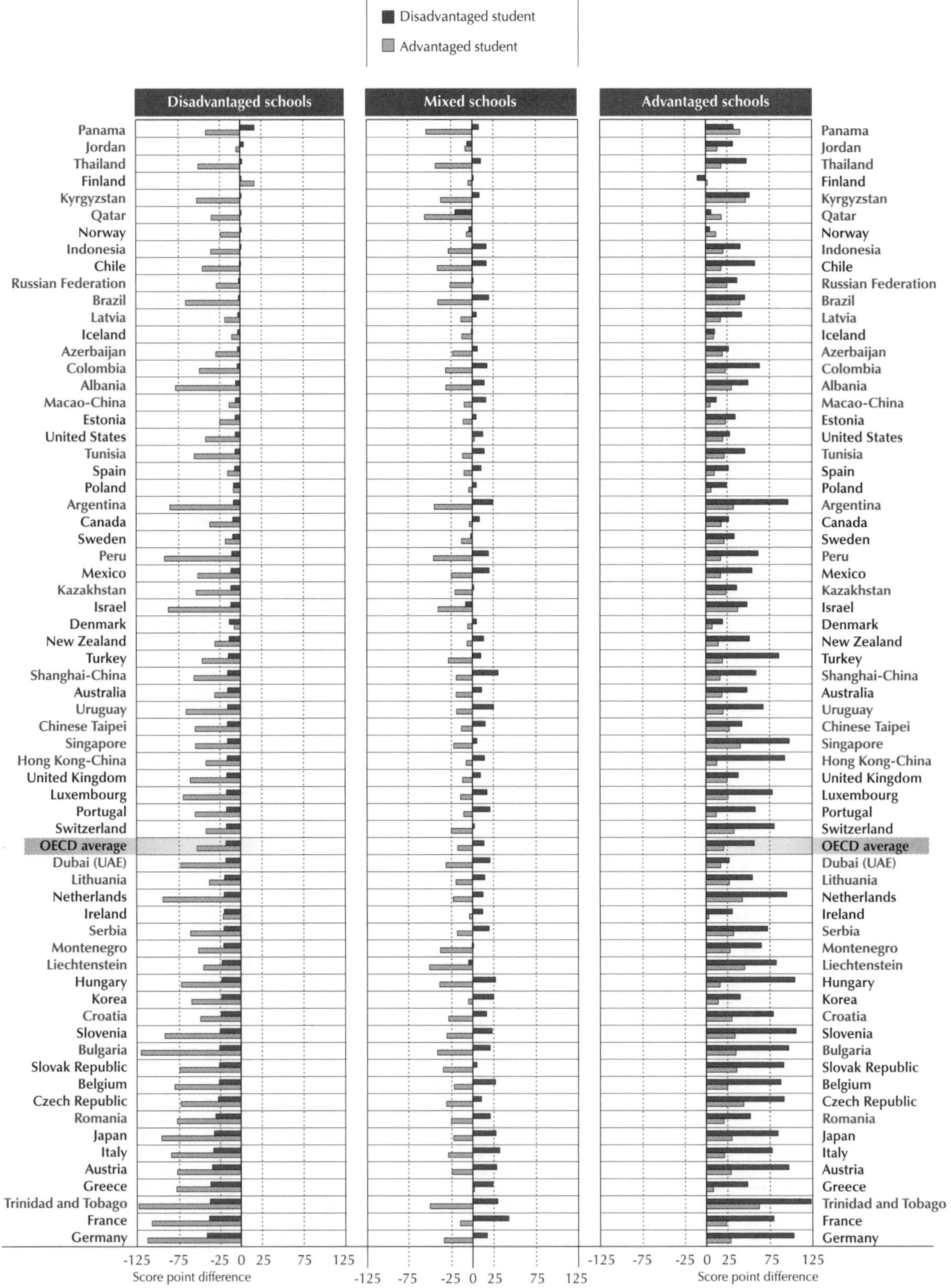

■ Disadvantaged student

■ Advantaged student

Countries are ranked in ascending order of the difference between observed and predicted performance of disadvantaged students in disadvantaged schools.

Source: OECD, *PISA 2009 Database,* Table II.5.10.

StatLink ⌦ http://dx.doi.org/10.1787/888932343627

Figure II.5.7 compares students' actual performance in advantaged, disadvantaged and mixed schools with their predicted performance based on their individual socio-economic background. Schools with a mixture of socio-economic intake perform not statistically significantly differently from the country average; schools with an advantaged socio-economic intake perform above the country average; and schools with a disadvantaged socio-economic intake perform below the country average. In the figure, countries are sorted by the difference in observed and expected performance of disadvantaged students attending disadvantaged schools. The figure highlights that while the differences between observed and expected performance are relatively small in those systems at the top of the figure, in others systems, across the three categories of schools, student performance is closer to what would have been predicted by the students'socio-economic background, regardless of the type of school they attend.

In general, Figure II.5.7 shows that students attending schools with a relatively disadvantaged intake perform at lower levels, on average, than what would be predicted based on the students' own socio-economic background; the opposite is true for those attending schools with more advantaged intakes. For mixed schools, the gap between expected and actual performance is smaller. In some countries, disadvantaged students perform better than expected and advantaged students perform worse than expected, depending on the socio-economic composition of the school they attend (Table II.5.10). Advantaged students perform as expected in mixed schools in the OECD countries Canada, Denmark, Finland, France, Greece, Ireland, Korea, New Zealand, Norway, Poland and the United States.

PERFORMANCE, SOCIO-ECONOMIC BACKGROUND AND THE ROLE OF PARENTS

As part of the PISA 2009 assessment, 14 countries complemented the perspectives of students and school principals with data collected from parents. These data provide important insights into the role that parents can play in raising student performance and moderating the impact of socio-economic background.

Parents' responses show a close relationship between their own involvement and their child's engagement in reading-related activities during the first year of primary school and their reading performance at age 15. For example, students whose parents reported that they had read a book with their child "every day or almost every day" or "once or twice a week" during the first year of primary school performed higher in PISA 2009 than students whose parents reported that they had done this "never or almost never" or "once or twice a month". On average across the 14 countries that had collected information on this question, the difference is 25 score points, but it ranges from four score points in the partner country Lithuania to 63 score points in New Zealand, as Figure II.5.8 shows. Comparing students of similar socio-economic backgrounds, those students with more engaged parents perform better in eight cases. The score point difference is reduced to 14 points, suggesting that, in general, socio-economic background and parental engagement go hand in hand. For example, more educated parents tend to read books with their children more often. Similar results are obtained for other kinds of activities parents were asked about, including "tell stories", "sing songs", "play with alphabet toys", "talk about things you had done", "talk about what you had read", "play word games", "write letters or words" and "read aloud signs and labels" (Table II.5.3).

Parents' engagement in educational activities when students are 15 years old is also related to student performance. For example, students whose parents discuss political or social issues once a week or more score 28 score points higher, on average, than those who do not or who talk about these issues less often. The performance advantage is largest in Italy, at 42 score points, and smallest in the partner economy Macao-China, at 14 score points, but it can be observed across all countries, as Figure II.5.8 shows. In addition, while accounting for socio-economic background reduces the size of the advantage, it is still present in all countries except Hungary. Other activities, such as "discuss books, films or television programmes", "discuss how well your child is doing at school", "eat (the main meal) with your child around the table" or "spend time just talking to your child" show similar but somewhat weaker results. The data also suggest that parents whose children tend to do poorly at school become more involved and engaged with helping out with homework (Figure II.5.8 and Table II.5.4).

PERFORMANCE, SOCIO-ECONOMIC BACKGROUND AND PARTICIPATION IN PRE-PRIMARY EDUCATION

Many of the inequalities that exist within school systems are already present when students enter formal schooling and persist as students progress through school (Entwisle, Alexander and Olson, 1997; Downey, Von Hippel and Broh, 2004). Because inequalities tend to grow when school is out of session, earlier entrance into the school system may reduce educational inequalities. In addition, with earlier entrance into pre-primary education, students are better prepared to enter and succeed in formal schooling.

■ Figure II.5.8 ■
Parents' educational support at home and student performance, before and after accounting for socio-economic background

☐ ■ Before accounting for socio-economic background
☐ ■ After accounting for socio-economic background

Parental support at the beginning of primary school

Score point difference between students whose parents often (weekly or daily) "read books" with the student and those who did not

Lithuania, Hong Kong-China, Macao-China, Croatia, Portugal, Italy, Panama, Chile, Korea, Denmark, Hungary, Qatar, Germany, New Zealand

Score point difference between students whose parents often (weekly or daily) "talk about what they had done" and those who did not

Lithuania, Germany, Denmark, Croatia, Hong Kong-China, Korea, Macao-China, Portugal, Hungary, New Zealand, Chile, Italy, Panama, Qatar

Parental support at age 15

Score point difference between students whose parents often (weekly or daily) "discuss political or social issues" and those who do not

Hungary, Hong Kong-China, Macao-China, Lithuania, Germany, Korea, Croatia, Denmark, Portugal, New Zealand, Panama, Chile, Qatar, Italy

Score point difference between students whose parents often (weekly or daily) "discuss books, films or televisions programmes" and those who do not

Lithuania, Panama, Korea, Macao-China, Hungary, Hong Kong-China, Germany, Croatia, Portugal, Chile, Denmark, New Zealand, Italy, Qatar

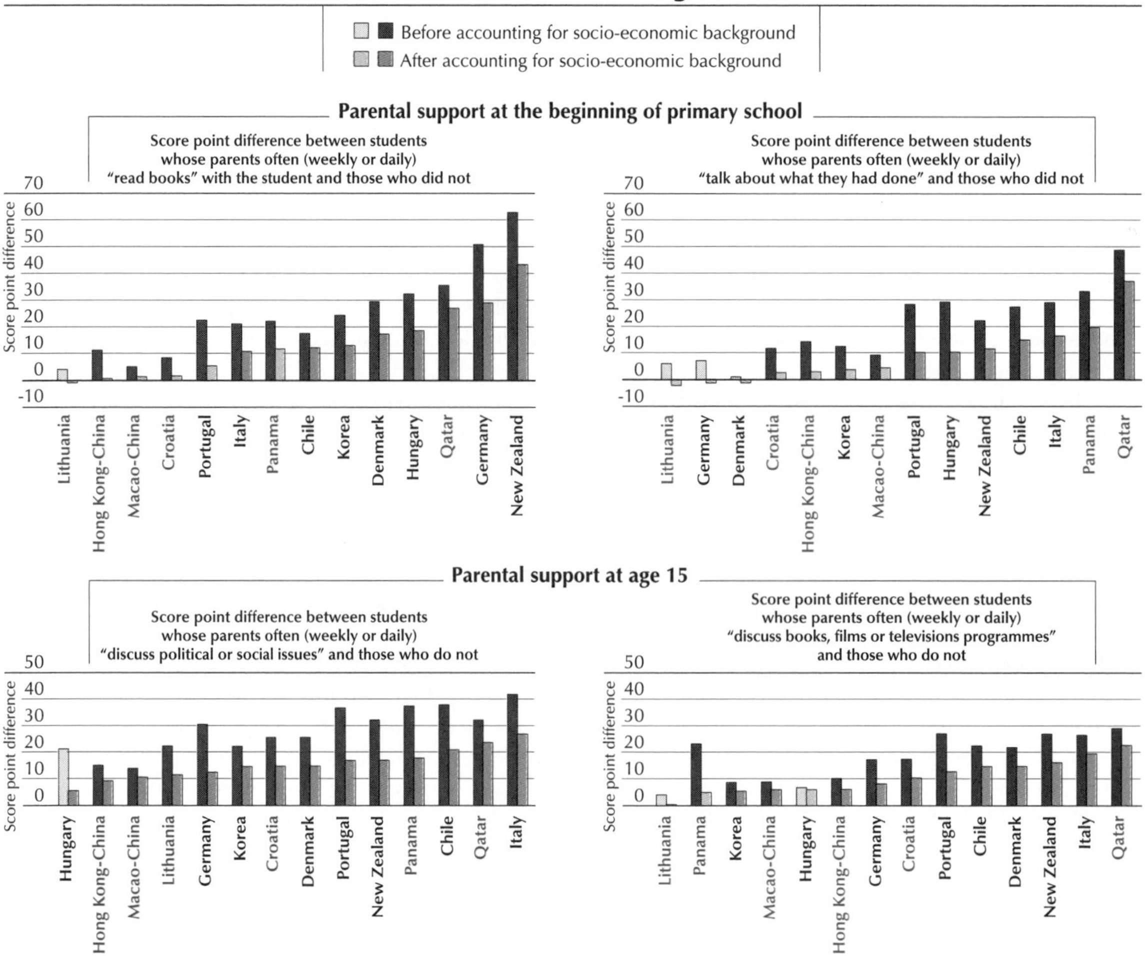

Note: Values that are statistically significant are marked in a darker tone.
Countries are ranked in ascending order of score point differences after accounting for socio-economic background.
Source: OECD, *PISA 2009 Database,* Tables II.5.3 and II.5.4.
StatLink http://dx.doi.org/10.1787/888932343627

On average across OECD countries, 72% of the 15-year-old students assessed by PISA reported that they had attended more than one year of pre-primary education when they were children. According to students' responses, more than one year of pre-primary education is practically universal in Japan, the Netherlands, Hungary, Belgium, Iceland and France, where over 90% of 15-year-olds reported that they had attended pre-primary education for more than one year. More than 90% of students in 27 OECD countries had attended pre-primary education for at least some time, and more than 98% of students in Japan, Hungary, France and the United States reported having done so. Pre-primary education is rare in Turkey, where less than 30% of 15-year-olds attended pre-primary education for any period of time. More than one year of pre-primary education is uncommon in Chile, Ireland, Canada and Poland, where less than 50% of students had attended pre-primary education for that length of time (Table II.5.5).

In the partner countries and economies Liechtenstein, Hong Kong-China and Singapore, more than 90% of students reported that they attended more than one year of pre-primary education. In 10 of the 31 partner countries and economies, more than 90% of students attended pre-primary education for some time. Only in Liechtenstein and Chinese Taipei did more than 98% of students report that they attended pre-primary education for some time. In contrast, in Azerbaijan, Kyrgyzstan and Kazakhstan, less than 45% of students had attended pre-primary education; and in Azerbaijan, Kyrgyzstan, Tunisia, Qatar and Indonesia, less than 25% of students had attended pre-primary education for more than one year.

■ Figure II.5.9 ■

Performance difference between students who had attended pre-primary school for more than one year and those who had not

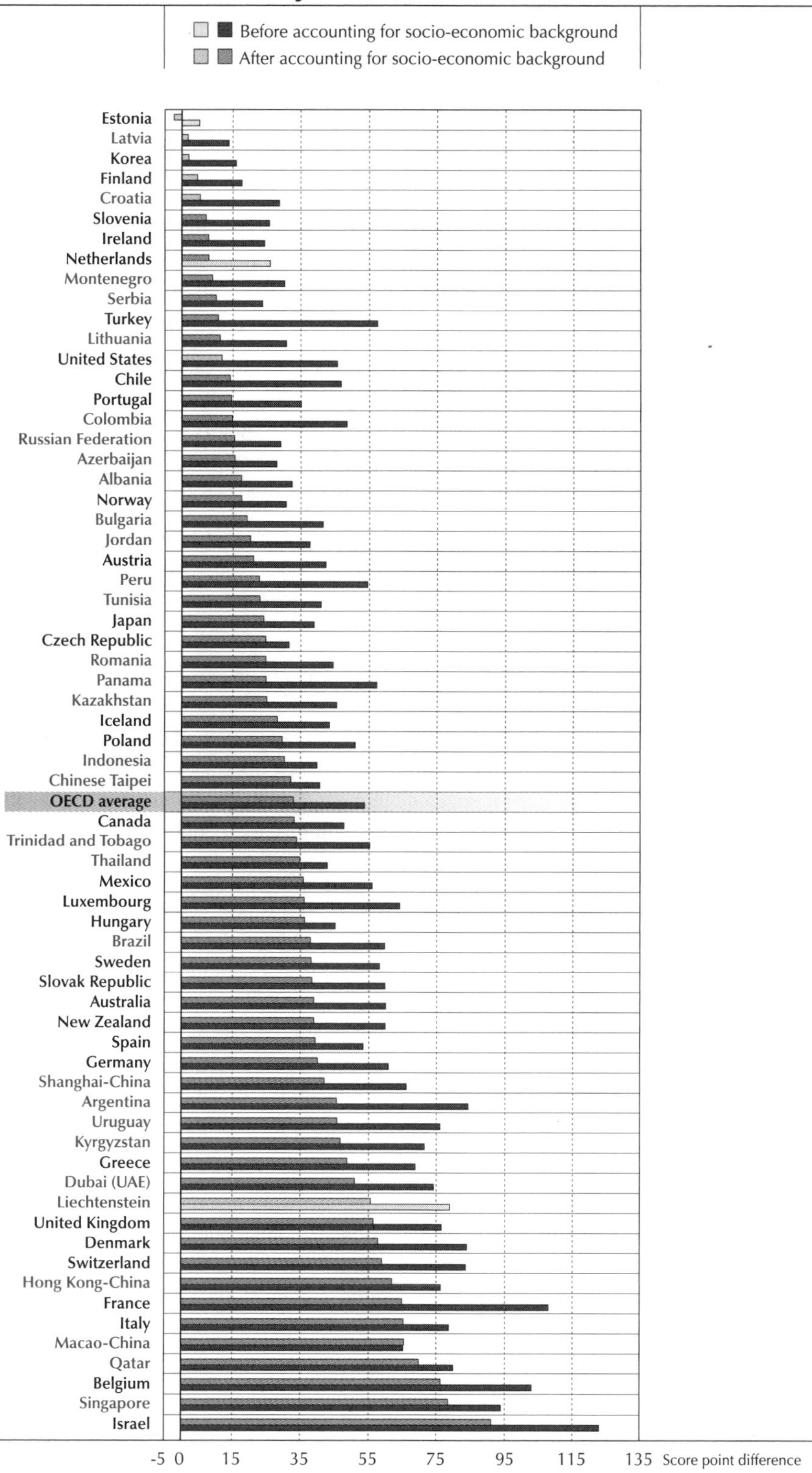

☐ ■ Before accounting for socio-economic background
☐ ■ After accounting for socio-economic background

Estonia
Latvia
Korea
Finland
Croatia
Slovenia
Ireland
Netherlands
Montenegro
Serbia
Turkey
Lithuania
United States
Chile
Portugal
Colombia
Russian Federation
Azerbaijan
Albania
Norway
Bulgaria
Jordan
Austria
Peru
Tunisia
Japan
Czech Republic
Romania
Panama
Kazakhstan
Iceland
Poland
Indonesia
Chinese Taipei
OECD average
Canada
Trinidad and Tobago
Thailand
Mexico
Luxembourg
Hungary
Brazil
Sweden
Slovak Republic
Australia
New Zealand
Spain
Germany
Shanghai-China
Argentina
Uruguay
Kyrgyzstan
Greece
Dubai (UAE)
Liechtenstein
United Kingdom
Denmark
Switzerland
Hong Kong-China
France
Italy
Macao-China
Qatar
Belgium
Singapore
Israel

-5 0   15   35   55   75   95   115   135   Score point difference

Note: Score point differences that are statistically significant are marked in a darker tone.
Countries are ranked in ascending order of the score point difference between students who report having attended pre-primary school (ISCED 0) for more than one year and those without pre-primary school attendance after accounting for socio-economic background.
Source: OECD, *PISA 2009 Database*, Table II.5.5.
StatLink ᴍᔕᶅ http://dx.doi.org/10.1787/888932343627

Figure II.5.9 shows the performance advantage of students who reported attending pre-primary education for more than one year over those who did not, both before and after accounting for students' socio-economic background. In all 34 OECD countries, students who attended pre-primary education for more than one year outperformed students who did not. This finding remains unchanged after socio-economic background is accounted for. On average across OECD countries, the advantage before accounting for socio-economic factors stands at more than 54 score points, and after at 33 score points. In general, this reduction signals that attendance in pre-primary education for more than one year and socio-economic characteristics are somewhat related, yet there is still a strong independent relationship between attending primary school and performance at age 15.

In the OECD countries Israel, France and Belgium, students who reported attending pre-primary education for more than one year perform at least 100 score points higher in reading than students who did not attend pre-primary education. Strong relationships remain in these countries even after students' socio-economic background is accounted for. However, in Estonia, Korea and Finland, and in the partner country Latvia, the difference in reading scores between those who attended and those who did not attend pre-primary education is 20 points or less.

Why does the relationship between performance and pre-primary attendance vary across countries? One hypothesis points to differences in the quality of pre-primary education. This hypothesis is supported by the fact that the relationship between pre-primary attendance and performance tends to be greater in school systems with a longer duration of pre-primary education, smaller pupil-to-teacher ratios in pre-primary education and higher public expenditure per child at the pre-primary level of education (Table II.5.6).

Within countries, does the relationship between pre-primary attendance and performance of 15-year-olds vary significantly across population subgroups? Specifically, do students from socio-economically disadvantaged backgrounds benefit more from pre-primary attendance than students from advantaged backgrounds? Are pre-primary attendance and immigrant status related?

When the relationship between pre-primary attendance and performance in reading at age 15 is compared between different socio-economic backgrounds, there is no significant difference between students from socio-economically disadvantaged and advantaged backgrounds (Table II.5.7). Disadvantaged and advantaged students benefit equally from pre-primary attendance in 31 OECD countries and 25 partner countries and economies. The performance advantage of attending pre-school is greater for socio-economically disadvantaged students in the United States and Lithuania; while in two OECD countries and five partner countries and economies, the advantage is greater for students from higher socio-economic backgrounds.

Part of the variation in the strength of the relationship between pre-primary attendance and the socio-economic background of students may be due to the fact that many other factors apart from pre-primary attendance (*e.g.* education in and out of school that students received between the ages of six and 15) may influence the performance of 15-year-olds. Many studies have concluded that while pre-primary attendance may raise students' cognitive test scores and build a foundation for students to develop further in the course of their study, the gains attributed to attendance in pre-primary education diminish over time, in part because students return to socio-economically advantaged or disadvantaged environments and schools (Barnett, 1995; Lee, 1995). The estimates provided here are limited because they cannot take many of these issues into account. Accounting for the socio-economic background of the student and the school addresses the issue only partially.

When the relationship between pre-primary attendance and performance is compared between students with and without an immigrant background, a significant difference is found in some countries (Table II.5.8). In Finland, Ireland and Canada and the partner country Qatar, the relationship between attendance in pre-primary education and performance is greater for students with an immigrant background than for students without an immigrant background.

The analyses presented in this chapter delve deeper into the relationship between socio-economic background and reading performance. These analyses show not only that the student's own socio-economic background is related to his/her performance, but that the school's composition may be even more important in shaping the learning outcomes of students. Disadvantaged students tend to perform better than expected from their individual socio-economic background when they attend socio-economically advantaged schools and advantaged students tend to perform worse than expected when they attend socio-economically disadvantaged schools. It is telling, moreover, that those school systems with the greatest levels of both academic and social inclusion, that is, those systems in which students of different socio-economic backgrounds and academic performance attend the same schools, are, generally, school systems that also perform above the OECD average.

Notes

1. The decomposition is a function of the between-school slope, the average within-school slope, and η^2, which is the proportion of variation in socio-economic background that is between schools. The statistic η^2 can be considered a measure of segregation by socio-economic background (Willms and Paterson, 1995), which theoretically can range from zero for a completely desegregated system, in which the distribution of socio-economic background is the same in every school, to one for a system in which students within schools are from similar socio-economic backgrounds, but the schools vary in their average socio-economic profile. One can also think of the term $1-\eta^2$ as an index of socio-economic inclusion, which would range from 0 for a segregated schooling system to 1 for a fully desegregated schooling system. The overall slope is related to the within- and between-school slopes through the segregation and inclusion indices: $\beta_t = \eta^2 * \beta_b + (1-\eta^2) * \beta_w$, where β_t is the overall slope, β_b is the between-school slope, and β_w is the average within-school slope. Note that there are two multilevel regression models, the first one is the null model on student performance and the second one includes only the student's socio-economic background.

2. Variation is expressed by statistical variance. This is obtained by squaring the standard deviation referred to in Volume I, *What Students Know and Can Do*. The statistical variance rather than the standard deviation is used for this comparison to allow for the decomposition of the components of variation in student performance. For reasons explained in the *PISA 2009 Technical Report* (OECD, forthcoming) and, most important, because the data in this table only account for students with valid data on their socio-economic background, the variance differs slightly from the square of the standard deviation shown in Volume I. The *PISA 2009 Technical Report* (OECD, forthcoming) also explains why, for some countries, the sum of the between-school and within-school variance components differs slightly from the total variance. The average is calculated over OECD countries.

3. These results are influenced by differences in how schools are defined and organised within countries and by the units that were chosen for sampling purposes. For example, in some countries the schools in the PISA sample were defined as administrative units (even if they spanned several geographically separate institutions, as in Italy); in others, they were defined as those parts of larger educational institutions that serve 15-year-olds; in others, they were defined as physical school buildings; and in others, they were defined from a management perspective (*e.g.* entities having a principal). Annex A2 and the *PISA 2009 Technical Report* (OECD, forthcoming) provides an overview of how schools were defined. Note also that, because of the manner in which students were sampled, the within-school variance includes performance variation between classes as well as between students.

4. More specifically, the index is defined as one minus the variation in student performance that lies between schools as a proportion of the variation that takes place between and within schools.

5. Figure II.5.2 and II.5.3 depict the inter-percentile range between the 5th and 95th percentile.

6. The relationship is strongest for reading. The correlation between the country rankings on social inclusion and academic inclusion is 0.47 for reading and 0.38 for mathematics and science.

7. The within- and between-school slopes of the socio-economic gradient represent, respectively, the gap in the predicted scores of two students within a school separated by a fixed level of socio-economic background, and the gap in the predicted scores of two students with identical socio-economic backgrounds attending different schools where the average background of their fellow-students is separated by the same fixed level. The slopes were estimated with a multilevel model that included the *PISA index of economic, social and cultural status* at the student and school levels.

8. The average socio-economic background of the school is calculated as the average of the students sampled. As such, this is a more accurate measure of socio-economic background than the *PISA index of social, economic and cultural status* at the student level. The within-school estimates, which are based on students' reports, are therefore biased downwards. The bias explains, at least in part, the differences between these two estimates. The magnitude of the difference is so large, however, that it is unlikely that the bias is the sole explanation for this difference.

9. Annex A2 discusses the construction of the primary sampling units and how this may affect different within- and between-school analyses.

10. This example assumes that the socio-economic gradients are linear, which is not the case for some countries, as discussed in Chapter 3 of this volume.

Policy Implications

While all countries participating in PISA 2009 show a relationship between home background and educational outcomes, some countries show that high levels of performance and equity of educational opportunities can be jointly achieved. What can explain these positive outcomes? This chapter discusses policies that target low-performing students or schools, target socio-economically disadvantaged students or schools, and more universally aim to raise educational standards for all students.

PATTERNS IN THE RELATIONSHIP BETWEEN PERFORMANCE AND SOCIO-ECONOMIC BACKGROUND

Home background influences educational success, and schooling often appears to reinforce its effects. Although poor performance in school does not automatically stem from a disadvantaged socio-economic background, the socio-economic background of students and schools does appear to have a powerful influence on learning outcomes.

There are thus considerable obstacles for policies aimed at providing equal learning opportunities for all students, regardless of their socio-economic background. National evidence from countries tends to paint a discouraging picture. In general, schools appear to have had little success in "levelling the playing field" for students. Indeed, either because privileged families are better able to reinforce and enhance the effect of schools, because students from privileged families attend higher-quality schools, or because schools are simply better equipped to nurture and develop young people from privileged backgrounds, it often appears that schools reproduce existing patterns of privilege, rather than create a more equitable distribution of opportunities and outcomes.

The internationally comparable results that emerge from this volume paint a more encouraging picture, with large differences between countries in the extent to which socio-economic background influences learning outcomes, which suggests that high levels of equity are an achievable goal.

With the exception of Israel, Slovenia, Turkey and the United States, where socio-economically disadvantaged schools also tend to be deprived of basic resources, such as favourable student-staff ratios, OECD countries try to place at least an equal, if not a larger, number of teachers in socio-economically disadvantaged schools as they do in advantaged schools. This being said, disadvantaged schools still report great difficulties in attracting qualified teachers. In other words, in disadvantaged schools, a high quantity of resources does not necessarily translate into a high quality of resources. This finding suggests that many students face the double liability of coming from a disadvantaged background and attending a school with lower-quality resources. Many countries also show a strong relationship between the socio-economic background of students and their success at school. In some of these countries, these disparities are magnified by large variations in the schools' socio-economic background – that is, in the backgrounds of the students' peers.

However, many students, many schools, and some countries perform better than expected given their socio-economic backgrounds. Korea, Finland, Canada and Japan, as well as the partner economies Hong Kong-China and Shanghai-China, show high mean performance and a low or, at most, moderate relationship between socio-economic background and student performance (whether measured by the slope or the strength of the socio-economic gradient). These countries combine high average performance with equity and have a large proportion of top-performing students, which demonstrates that excellence and equity can go together.

■ Figure II.B [Part 1/2] ■

Summary of students' and schools' socio-economic background and performance

		Mean performance score in reading	Percentage of students below proficiency level[2] in reading	Average PISA index of economic, social and cultural status (ESCS) (Mean index)	Overall strength of the relationship between student performance and the ESCS[1]	Overall slope of the socio-economic gradient[1,2]	Within-school effects of ESCS	
					Percentage of explained variance in student performance	Score point difference associated with one unit on the ESCS	Student-level score point difference associated with one unit of the student-level ESCS	Explained within-school variance
OECD	Australia	515	14.2	0.34	12.7	**46**	30	6.1
	Austria	470	27.6	0.06	16.6	**48**	10	2.3
	Belgium	506	17.7	0.20	**19.3**	**47**	13	3.4
	Canada	524	10.3	0.50	**8.6**	**32**	21	4.3
	Chile	449	30.6	-0.57	**18.7**	**31**	8	1.1
	Czech Republic	478	23.1	-0.09	12.4	**46**	14	1.4
	Denmark	495	15.2	0.30	14.5	36	28	9.7
	Estonia	501	13.3	0.15	**7.6**	**29**	16	2.3
	Finland	536	8.1	0.37	**7.8**	**31**	28	6.8
	France	496	19.8	-0.13	16.7	**51**	w	w
	Germany	497	18.5	0.18	**17.9**	**44**	10	0.1
	Greece	483	21.3	-0.02	12.5	34	14	2.6
	Hungary	494	17.6	-0.20	**26.0**	**48**	7	0.5
	Iceland	500	16.8	0.72	**6.2**	**27**	24	5.8
	Ireland	496	17.2	0.05	12.6	39	27	5.2
	Israel	474	26.5	-0.02	12.5	**43**	18	5.8
	Italy	486	21.0	-0.12	**11.8**	**32**	5	0.7
	Japan	520	13.6	-0.01	**8.6**	40	5	1.1
	Korea	539	5.8	-0.15	**11.0**	**32**	20	3.6
	Luxembourg	472	26.0	0.19	**18.0**	40	21	5.2
	Mexico	425	40.1	-1.22	14.5	**25**	3	0.0
	Netherlands	508	14.3	0.27	12.8	37	5	2.2
	New Zealand	521	14.3	0.09	**16.6**	**52**	36	9.7
	Norway	503	15.0	0.47	**8.6**	36	28	6.1
	Poland	500	15.0	-0.28	14.8	39	31	9.9
	Portugal	489	17.6	-0.32	16.5	**30**	17	5.9
	Slovak Republic	477	22.2	-0.09	14.6	41	17	3.4
	Slovenia	483	21.2	0.07	14.3	39	2	1.7
	Spain	481	19.6	-0.31	13.6	**29**	21	7.2
	Sweden	497	17.4	0.33	13.4	**43**	34	11.1
	Switzerland	501	16.8	0.08	14.1	40	20	4.6
	Turkey	464	24.5	-1.16	**19.0**	**29**	8	2.2
	United Kingdom	494	18.4	0.20	13.7	**44**	27	6.0
	United States	500	17.6	0.17	16.8	42	23	3.8
	OECD average	493	18.8	0.00	14.0	38	18	4.3
Partners	Albania	385	56.7	-0.95	10.7	**31**	13	2.8
	Argentina	398	51.6	-0.62	**19.6**	40	9	0.9
	Azerbaijan	362	72.8	-0.64	**7.4**	**21**	8	1.3
	Brazil	412	49.6	-1.16	13.0	**28**	3	-0.2
	Bulgaria	429	41.0	-0.11	**20.2**	**51**	11	3.1
	Colombia	413	47.1	-1.15	16.6	**28**	9	1.1
	Croatia	476	22.4	-0.18	**11.0**	**32**	10	1.3
	Dubai (UAE)	459	31.0	0.42	14.2	**51**	19	4.0
	Hong Kong-China	533	8.3	-0.80	**4.5**	**17**	3	0.4
	Indonesia	402	53.4	-1.55	**7.8**	**17**	1	0.1
	Jordan	405	48.0	-0.57	**7.9**	**24**	18	6.7
	Kazakhstan	390	58.7	-0.51	12.0	38	19	3.6
	Kyrgyzstan	314	83.2	-0.65	14.6	40	16	3.5
	Latvia	484	17.6	-0.13	**10.3**	**29**	19	3.6
	Liechtenstein	499	15.7	0.09	8.4	**26**	3	2.1
	Lithuania	468	24.4	-0.05	13.6	**33**	16	4.0
	Macao-China	487	14.9	-0.70	**1.8**	**12**	6	0.3
	Montenegro	408	49.5	-0.24	**10.0**	**31**	11	2.0
	Panama	371	65.3	-0.81	18.1	31	3	1.0
	Peru	370	64.8	-1.31	**27.4**	41	8	1.2
	Qatar	372	63.5	0.51	**4.0**	**25**	7	1.6
	Romania	424	40.4	-0.34	13.6	36	10	2.5
	Russian Federation	459	27.4	-0.21	**11.3**	37	21	3.3
	Serbia	442	32.8	0.07	**9.8**	**27**	6	0.8
	Shanghai-China	556	4.1	-0.49	12.3	**27**	4	0.1
	Singapore	526	12.5	-0.43	15.3	**47**	26	6.4
	Chinese Taipei	495	15.6	-0.33	11.8	36	21	5.6
	Thailand	421	42.9	-1.31	13.3	**22**	2	0.2
	Trinidad and Tobago	416	44.8	-0.58	**9.7**	38	2	2.2
	Tunisia	404	50.2	-1.20	**8.1**	**19**	2	-0.2
	Uruguay	426	41.9	-0.70	**20.7**	37	15	3.3

1. Values that are statistically significantly different from the OECD average are indicated in bold.
2. Single-level bivariate regression of reading performance on the ESCS, the slope is the regression coefficient for the ESCS.
3. The index of academic inclusion is calculated as 100*(1-rho), where rho stands for the intra-class correlation of performance, *i.e.* the variance in student performance between schools, divided by the sum of the variance in student performance between schools and the variance in student performance within schools.
4. The index of social inclusion is calculated as 100*(1-rho), where rho stands for the intra-class correlation of socio-economic background, *i.e.* the variance in the PISA index of social, economic and cultural status of students between schools, divided by the sum of the variance in students' socio-economic background between schools and the variance in students' socio-economic background within schools.
Source: OECD, *PISA 2009 Database*. Tables II.2.1, II.3.1, II.3.2, II.5.1 and II.5.2.
StatLink http://dx.doi.org/10.1787/888932343646

■ Figure II.B [Part 2/2] ■

Summary of students' and schools' socio-economic background and performance

	Student variability in the distribution of ESCS	Between-school effects of ESCS		School variability in the distribution of ESCS		
	Interquartile range of the distribution of the student-level ESCS	School-level score point difference associated with one unit on the school mean ESCS	Explained between-school variance	Interquartile range of the distribution of school mean distribution of ESCS	Academic inclusion index[3]	Social inclusion index[4]
OECD						
Australia	1.09	66	67.6	0.55	73.9	76.4
Austria	1.08	80	50.9	0.61	44.4	69.2
Belgium	1.38	111	65.5	0.82	47.5	69.8
Canada	1.17	32	44.2	0.50	78.3	82.4
Chile	1.64	50	69.0	1.06	45.0	48.6
Czech Republic	0.96	123	66.5	0.45	51.0	75.1
Denmark	1.25	42	69.1	0.55	84.1	83.6
Estonia	1.22	41	45.6	0.50	78.2	81.5
Finland	1.14	19	23.2	0.43	91.3	89.2
France	1.15	w	w	w	w	w
Germany	1.20	122	67.2	0.71	39.8	76.0
Greece	1.48	44	39.8	0.66	53.9	68.0
Hungary	1.34	76	65.0	0.85	33.3	54.2
Iceland	1.31	11	23.6	0.55	85.9	82.8
Ireland	1.21	53	58.5	0.50	71.3	76.7
Israel	1.19	102	42.9	0.68	51.4	76.7
Italy	1.41	67	43.5	0.85	37.9	73.9
Japan	1.08	137	51.9	0.58	51.4	78.2
Korea	1.16	62	53.2	0.58	65.8	74.1
Luxembourg	1.53	65	82.0	0.82	56.4	73.3
Mexico	2.00	30	36.7	1.15	51.9	56.2
Netherlands	1.24	93	45.2	0.50	35.4	76.2
New Zealand	1.09	61	72.1	0.56	75.8	78.9
Norway	1.02	31	26.6	0.31	89.7	91.2
Poland	1.12	29	65.4	0.54	81.2	73.3
Portugal	1.69	40	58.9	0.80	66.9	73.2
Slovak Republic	1.05	72	56.2	0.58	60.4	76.6
Slovenia	1.36	77	41.8	0.70	42.8	75.0
Spain	1.64	25	48.4	0.78	78.2	77.1
Sweden	1.14	52	67.9	0.42	81.5	85.7
Switzerland	1.24	66	48.6	0.58	67.4	85.4
Turkey	1.78	60	68.5	0.94	33.2	63.5
United Kingdom	1.11	69	77.1	0.53	70.7	81.6
United States	1.31	63	75.7	0.73	64.0	70.7
OECD average	1.29	63	55.1	0.65	61.4	74.8
Partners						
Albania	1.45	39	54.0	0.75	69.4	67.7
Argentina	1.74	69	59.1	1.14	39.5	59.8
Azerbaijan	1.48	25	13.2	0.88	58.2	72.0
Brazil	1.80	53	54.2	0.88	51.6	64.7
Bulgaria	1.38	81	65.2	0.72	50.1	57.9
Colombia	1.91	41	76.7	1.14	60.4	60.2
Croatia	1.18	69	49.4	0.57	52.5	77.2
Dubai (UAE)	0.89	80	34.5	0.77	48.7	62.4
Hong Kong-China	1.39	33	19.4	0.65	58.1	69.9
Indonesia	1.62	25	20.8	1.06	56.8	61.3
Jordan	1.54	18	21.2	0.59	62.2	76.4
Kazakhstan	1.20	50	37.4	0.55	63.8	71.7
Kyrgyzstan	1.39	62	51.2	0.65	64.4	72.0
Latvia	1.38	30	50.6	0.61	78.9	75.4
Liechtenstein	1.38	121	68.3	0.84	54.0	88.2
Lithuania	1.58	43	48.2	0.67	73.6	73.7
Macao-China	1.15	19	35.3	0.53	59.2	65.2
Montenegro	1.34	67	70.4	0.72	63.9	77.2
Panama	2.07	57	48.7	1.23	41.5	57.7
Peru	1.77	59	72.9	1.17	44.0	50.7
Qatar	1.11	80	17.0	0.65	46.9	70.6
Romania	1.12	40	37.4	0.64	48.6	65.3
Russian Federation	1.25	38	41.5	0.57	74.8	71.5
Serbia	1.35	53	50.5	0.58	51.3	76.6
Shanghai-China	1.61	58	69.0	0.90	61.6	66.3
Singapore	1.12	86	60.3	0.46	64.7	81.7
Chinese Taipei	1.12	52	50.8	0.55	67.7	80.1
Thailand	1.85	18	23.3	1.23	71.3	48.9
Trinidad and Tobago	1.21	145	58.7	0.66	38.2	77.3
Tunisia	2.01	26	18.7	0.96	58.6	67.2
Uruguay	1.84	48	74.7	0.93	54.8	59.8

1. Values that are statistically significantly different from the OECD average are indicated in bold.
2. Single-level bivariate regression of reading performance on the ESCS, the slope is the regression coefficient for the ESCS.
3. The index of academic inclusion is calculated as 100*(1-rho), where rho stands for the intra-class correlation of performance, *i.e.* the variance in student performance between schools, divided by the sum of the variance in student performance between schools and the variance in student performance within schools.
4. The index of social inclusion is calculated as 100*(1-rho), where rho stands for the intra-class correlation of socio-economic background, *i.e.* the variance in the PISA index of social, economic and cultural status of students between schools, divided by the sum of the variance in students' socio-economic background between schools and the variance in students' socio-economic background within schools.
Source: OECD, *PISA 2009 Database*. Tables II.2.1, II.3.1, II.3.2, II.5.1 and II.5.2.
StatLink ᵃᵛˢᵖ http://dx.doi.org/10.1787/888932343646

What are useful strategies for moderating the impact of social background so that all students can realise their potential? The relationships between background and performance described in this volume are manifested in very different patterns across different countries. Thus, strategies for improvement need to be tailored accordingly. Figure II.B shows the key characteristics of the relationship between students' and schools' socio-economic background and performance across education systems.

For each country, Figures II.C to II.O show the average performance and the socio-economic composition of the student population for each school in the PISA sample. As elsewhere in this volume, the socio-economic composition of a school is measured by the mean *PISA index of economic, social and cultural status* of the students attending this school. Each dot in Figures II.C-II.O represents one school, with the size of the dot proportionate to the number of 15-year-olds enrolled in that school. The patterns show how strongly students are segregated along socio-economic lines, whether because of residential segregation, economic factors or selection within the school system. The figures also display the gradient line between socio-economic background and student performance (black line in Figures II.C-II.O). Finally, the figures present the between-school gradient line (grey line in Figures II.C-II.O) and the average within-school gradient line (blue line in Figures II.C-II.O). Schools above the between-school gradient line (grey line) perform better than predicted by their socio-economic intake. Schools below the between-school gradient line perform worse than expected.

The figures summarise the three levels at which the relationship between student background and performance manifests itself. One is how strong the relationship between socio-economic background and learning outcomes is in a given country, as measured by how much of the variation in student performance can be attributed to variation in socio-economic background. The second shows how much of the variation in average performance among schools can be attributed to variation in the average socio-economic background of the schools' intake. The third reflects the relationship within a given school: how much of the variation in student performance within a given school can be attributed to variation in socio-economic background within that particular school. The amount of socio-economic variability and the overall performance differences within a country are also relevant. Analysing these patterns can assist in designing policies to improve equity in educational opportunities (Willms, 2006). Some options, which can be considered in combination, include:

- ***Targeting low performance, regardless of students' background, either by targeting low-performing schools or low-performing students within schools, depending on the extent to which low performance is concentrated by school****. Where academic inclusion (Figure II.B) is low, interventions may be targeted at low-performing schools; where academic inclusion is high interventions can be directed at low-performing students in each school. Such policies often tend to provide a specialised curriculum or additional instructional resources for particular students based on their levels of academic performance. For example, some school systems provide early prevention programmes that target children who are deemed to be at risk of failure at school when they enter early childhood programmes or schools, while other systems provide late prevention or recovery programmes for children who fail to progress at a normal rate during the first few years of primary school. Some performance-targeted programmes aim to provide a modified curriculum for high-achieving students, such as programmes for gifted students. More generally, policies that involve tracking or streaming of students into different types of programmes could be considered performance-targeted as they strive to match curriculum and instruction to students' academic ability or performance. Grade repetition is also sometimes considered a performance-targeted policy, because the decision to make a student repeat a grade is usually based on school performance. However, in many cases, grade repetition does not entail a modified curriculum or additional instructional resources. Therefore, it does not fit the definition of a performance-targeted policy used here. The focus of performance-targeted policies tends to be at the lower end of the performance scale, regardless of the students' socio-economic background, and their objective is to bring low-performing students up to par with their peers.

- ***Targeting disadvantaged children through a specialised curriculum, additional instructional resources or economic assistance for these students****. A relatively strong social gradient, which accounts for a substantial proportion of performance variation, can indicate the relevance of such policies. Again, policies can be designed either at the school or individual level, depending on the strength of the inter-school social gradient and the extent to which schools are segregated by socio-economic background. An example is the Head Start pre-

school programme in the United States for children from socio-economically disadvantaged backgrounds. Some approaches select students on the basis of a risk factor other than socio-economic background, such as whether the students are recent immigrants, members of an ethnic minority, or living in a low-income community. The important distinction is that these programmes select students based on the families's socio-economic backgrounds rather than on the students' cognitive ability.

- ***While policies targeted at disadvantaged children can aim at their performance in school, they can also be used to provide additional economic resources to these students.*** The emphasis here is on improving the economic circumstances of students from poor families, rather than offering specialised curricula or additional educational resources. Providing free transportation and free lunch programmes for students from poor families is an example. More generally, and in many countries, providing transfer payments to poor families is one of the primary policy levers at the national level. The distinction between these kinds of compensatory policies and socio-economically targeted policies is not always clear-cut. For example, some jurisdictions have compensatory funding formulas that allocate educational funds to schools based on their socio-economic intake. In some sense this is a compensatory policy, but it could also be considered a socio-economically targeted policy since the intention is to provide additional educational resources to students from disadvantaged backgrounds.

- ***More universal policies rely mainly on raising standards for all students.*** These types of policies are likely to be most relevant in countries with weaker gradients and less variation in student performance. They can involve altering the content and pace of the curriculum, improving instructional techniques, introducing full-day schooling, changing the age of entry into school, or increasing the time spent in language classes. Some jurisdictions responded to PISA 2000 results by introducing major school and curricular reforms that included some of these changes. There have been also efforts to increase parents' involvement in schooling in several ways, including greater involvement at home and greater participation in school governance. Many universal policies are directed at changing teacher practices or they aim to increase the accountability of schools and school systems by assessing student performance.

- ***Inclusive policies strive to include marginalised students into mainstream schools and classrooms.*** Inclusive practices often concentrate on including students with disabilities in regular classrooms, rather than segregating them in special classes or schools. This volume considers inclusive policies as those that aim to include any type of student who may be segregated, whether because of his/her disabilities or ethnic or socio-economic background. Some inclusive policies try to reduce between-school socio-economic segregation by redrawing school catchment boundaries, amalgamating schools, or by creating magnet schools in low-income areas.

The following examples illustrate a range of different patterns observed in the PISA 2009 reading data that point to the relevance of such policy options.

A DISPROPORTIONATE NUMBER OF LOW-PERFORMING STUDENTS

As shown in Chapter 2, in some countries, most students are relatively weak in reading. In others, there are relatively large numbers with low proficiency in reading, even though substantial numbers also demonstrate high proficiency. In the partner countries Kyrgyzstan, Azerbaijan, Panama, Peru, Qatar, Kazakhstan, Albania, Indonesia, Argentina, Tunisia, Brazil, Montenegro, Jordan, Colombia, Trinidad and Tobago, Thailand, Uruguay, Romania, Bulgaria, and the OECD country Mexico, the absolute number of poorly-performing students is high, with 40% or more of 15-year-olds performing below Level 2 (Figure II.B). These countries are characterised by students' very low average performance and extremely disadvantaged backgrounds, both when compared to the average background and length of the socio-economic gradient, and particularly when compared to countries that show relatively high levels of excellence and equity in PISA. The slope of the gradient and the proportion of the variance explained often tend to be small. In some of these countries, this can be explained by the limited proportion of 15-year-olds who are enrolled in school and who represent a more homogeneous student group than the entire group of 15-year-olds; in other countries, it can be explained by the fact that the PISA measures of socio-economic background often do not discriminate sufficiently among very poor performing students.

Among these countries, the performance variation between schools is high, but within-school variation is around the average. Social and academic inclusion is low, particularly when compared with countries that show high levels

of performance and equity. Some countries in this group, like Brazil or Mexico, have successfully experimented with compensatory interventions. However, the fairly small proportion of student performance variation that is explained by socio-economic background suggests that poor performance deserves as much attention as poverty. Figure II.C contrasts the profiles of some of these countries.

■ Figure II.C ■
Relationship between school performance and schools' socio-economic background in Peru, Albania, Indonesia and Tunisia

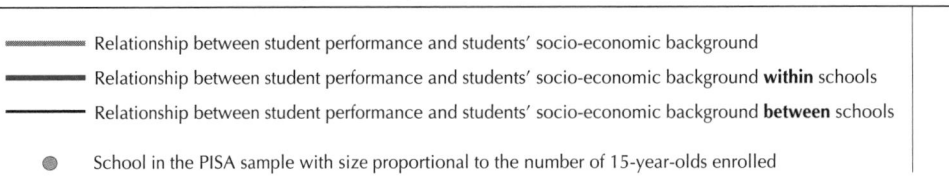

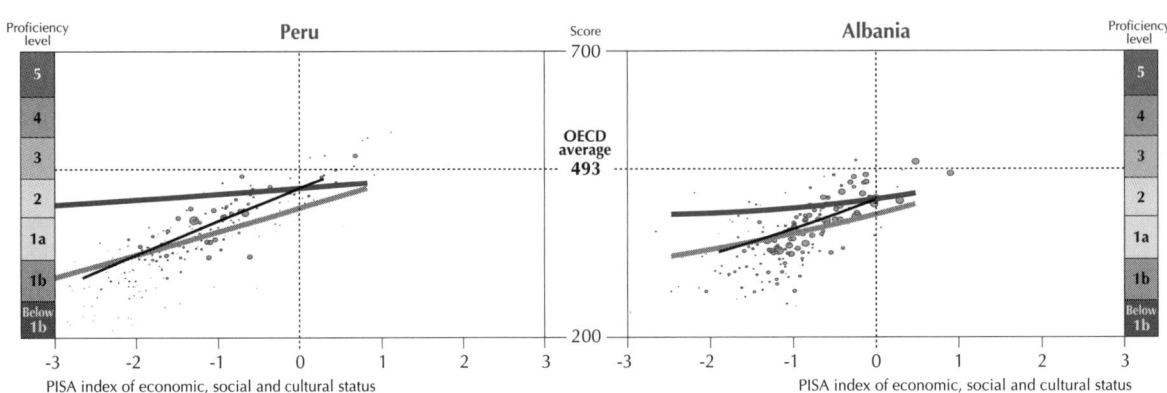

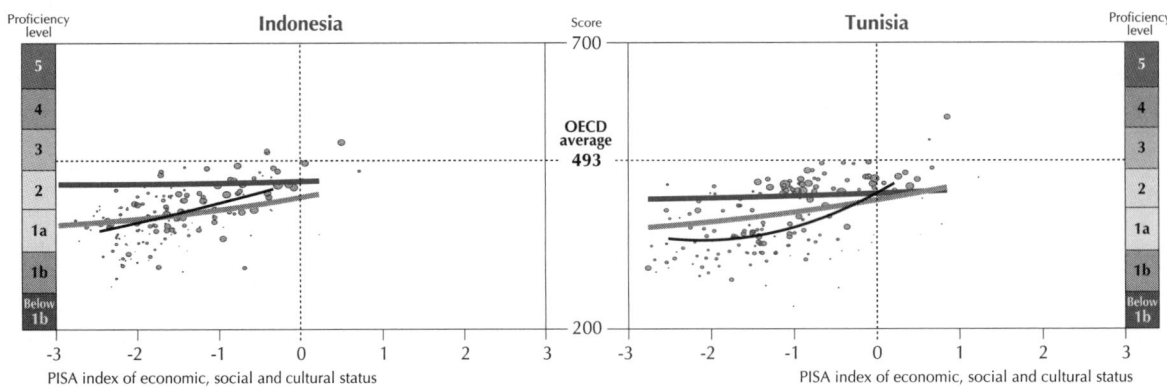

Source: OECD, *PISA 2009 Database*.
StatLink ⬛🔳 http://dx.doi.org/10.1787/888932343646

In another group of countries, the proportion of poor performers is moderate in absolute terms, but the gap between poor performers and other students is large. For example, as shown in Figure II.D, Luxembourg, Israel, Austria and the partner country Dubai (UAE) show between 5% and 8% of students performing at Level 5 or 6 in reading, roughly the OECD average, but more than one-quarter performing below Level 2. These are countries with average socio-economic backgrounds, both in terms of the mean and how socio-economic advantage is distributed, but with mean performance below the OECD average. They are characterised by steep socio-economic gradients and average levels of socio-economic inclusion, particularly between schools.

Such patterns suggest that targeted interventions based on socio-economic background can prove successful, often in combination with performance-targeted interventions, such as additional support for students who struggle with reading, particularly in those systems that show low academic inclusion.

■ Figure II.D ■
Relationship between school performance and schools' socio-economic background in Luxembourg, Israel, Austria and Dubai (UAE)

——— Relationship between student performance and students' socio-economic background

——— Relationship between student performance and students' socio-economic background **within** schools

——— Relationship between student performance and students' socio-economic background **between** schools

● School in the PISA sample with size proportional to the number of 15-year-olds enrolled

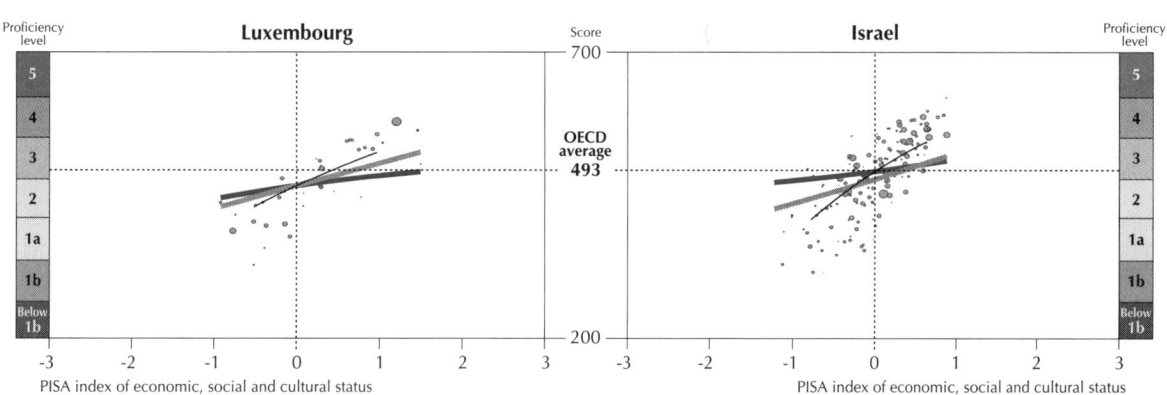

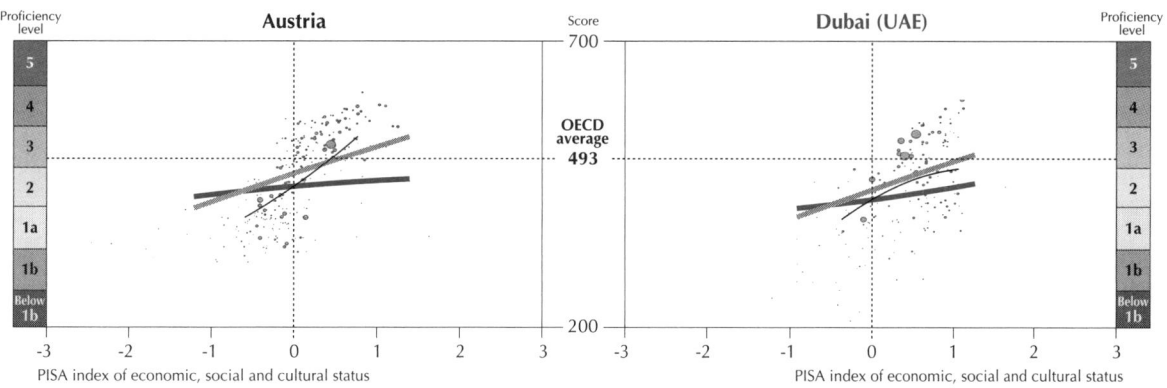

Source: OECD, *PISA 2009 Database.*
StatLink ⟋⟋⟋ http://dx.doi.org/10.1787/888932343646

Other countries that show a comparatively large gap between better and poorer performing students include the United States and Belgium (Figure II.E), where at least 10% of students score at Level 5 or 6 but between 17% and 20% of students score below Level 2. This group of countries has mean performance and socio-economic backgrounds slightly above the OECD average. However, the socio-economic gradients are steep and socio-economic background explains a large part of the observed performance variation between schools. These countries also show lower levels of social inclusion. With steep gradients and low levels of inclusion, interventions that target both performance and socio-economic background can assist low-performing students from disadvantaged backgrounds.

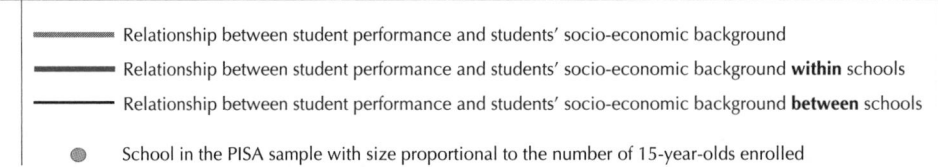

■ Figure II.E ■
Relationship between school performance and schools' socio-economic background in United States and Belgium

——— Relationship between student performance and students' socio-economic background

——— Relationship between student performance and students' socio-economic background **within** schools

——— Relationship between student performance and students' socio-economic background **between** schools

● School in the PISA sample with size proportional to the number of 15-year-olds enrolled

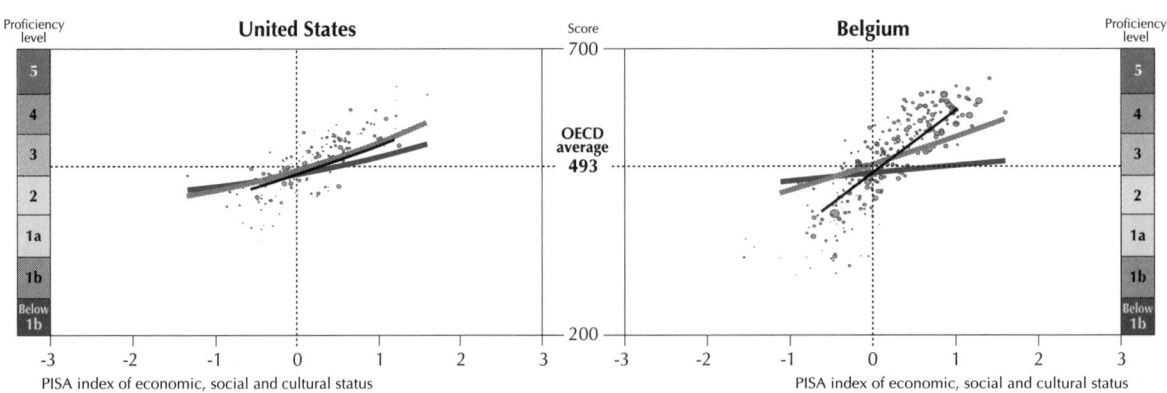

Source: OECD, *PISA 2009 Database*.
StatLink http://dx.doi.org/10.1787/888932343646

DIFFERENT SLOPES AND STRENGTHS OF SOCIO-ECONOMIC GRADIENTS

School administrators often wonder whether efforts to improve student performance should be targeted mainly at those students who perform poorly or those from socio-economically disadvantaged backgrounds. The overall slope of the socio-economic gradient, together with the proportion of performance variation as explained by socio-economic background, are useful indicators for answering this question. As noted above, there is an important distinction between the slope of the social gradient, which refers to the average size of the performance gap associated with a given difference in socio-economic status, and its strength, which is associated with how closely students conform to the predictions of the gradient line.

In countries with relatively shallow gradients, *i.e.* where predicted student performance tends to be similar across socio-economic groups, policies that specifically target students from disadvantaged backgrounds would not, by themselves, address the needs of many of the country's low-performing students.

Gentle slopes and weak-versus-strong gradients

Among the high-performing countries and economies, Shanghai-China, Korea, Finland, Hong Kong-China and Canada all show gentle slopes of the socio-economic gradients, suggesting that even large differences in the socio-economic backgrounds of students are, on average, not associated with large performance differences among students. Among countries and economies in which students perform slightly below or around the OECD average, the same is true for Estonia, Iceland, Portugal, Italy, Spain and the partner countries and economies Liechtenstein, Macao-China and Latvia.

In these countries, a relatively smaller proportion of low-performing students come from disadvantaged backgrounds, and the relationship between school performance and schools' socio-economic intake is weaker. Thus, by themselves, policies that specifically target students from disadvantaged backgrounds would not address the needs of many of the country's lower-performing students. Moreover, if the goal is to ensure that most students achieve some minimum level of performance, socio-economically-targeted policies in these countries would be providing services to a sizeable proportion of students who already perform well.

■ Figure II.F ■

Relationship between school performance and schools' socio-economic background in Shanghai-China, Korea, Finland and Canada

Relationship between student performance and students' socio-economic background
Relationship between student performance and students' socio-economic background **within** schools
Relationship between student performance and students' socio-economic background **between** schools
School in the PISA sample with size proportional to the number of 15-year-olds enrolled

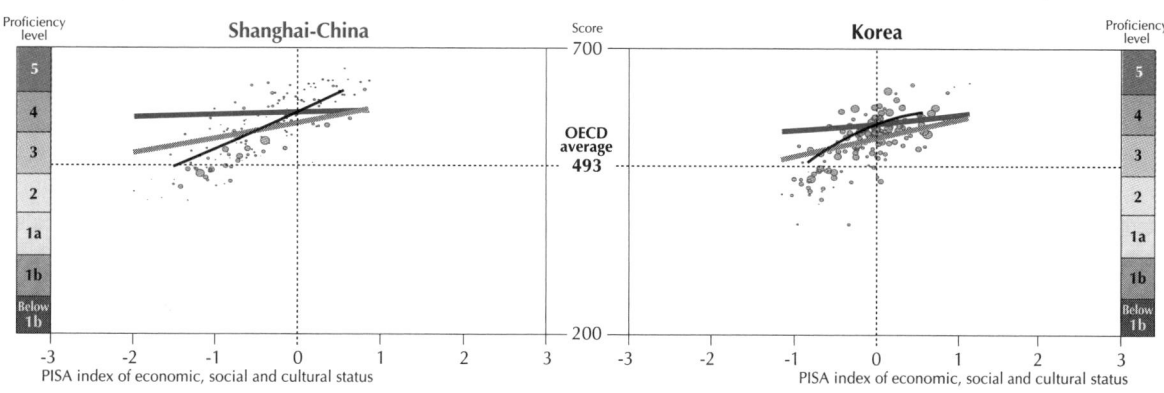

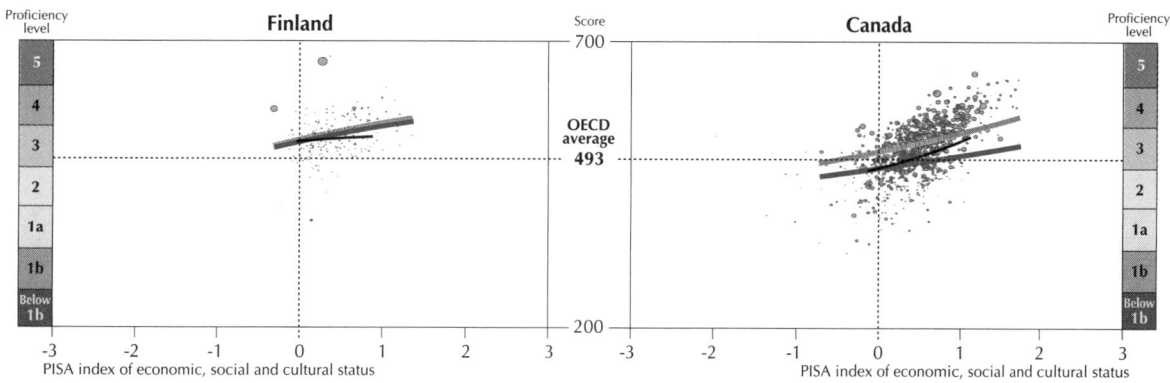

Source: OECD, *PISA 2009 Database*.
StatLink http://dx.doi.org/10.1787/888932343646

■ Figure II.G ■

Relationship between school performance and schools' socio-economic background in Iceland and Estonia

Relationship between student performance and students' socio-economic background
Relationship between student performance and students' socio-economic background **within** schools
Relationship between student performance and students' socio-economic background **between** schools
School in the PISA sample with size proportional to the number of 15-year-olds enrolled

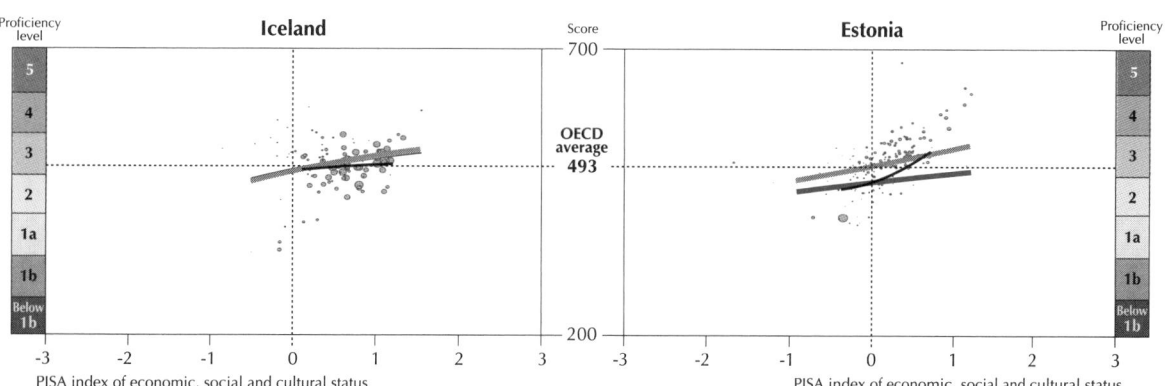

Source: OECD, *PISA 2009 Database*.
StatLink http://dx.doi.org/10.1787/888932343646

Steep slopes and weak-versus-strong gradients

Among the high-performing countries, New Zealand and Australia as well as the partner country Singapore show a steep relationship between socio-economic background and student performance, suggesting that two students from slightly different backgrounds tend to show large performance differences. Among countries in which students perform around the OECD average, the same holds true for Sweden, Germany, France, the United Kingdom and Hungary. In these countries, socio-economically targeted policies would direct more resources towards students who are likely to require these services. An illustration of this can be observed in the comparison of Finland or Canada, on the one hand, and New Zealand or the partner country Singapore, on the other – all countries with similar levels of overall performance. By focusing on actions indicated in the left area of the chart, for example, socio-economically-targeted policies would exclude many schools and students in Canada that show comparatively low performance but have advantaged backgrounds, as shown in the bottom right area of the graph. In contrast, performance-targeted policies would reach most of the lower-performing students and schools. In the partner country Singapore, where the relationship between socio-economic background and student performance is much steeper, socio-economically-targeted interventions are likely to have a much stronger impact, as a much larger proportion of students and schools are located in the lower-left quadrant of the figure.

Countries where the gradient is steep will find that socio-economically-targeted policies are more likely to reach the students who most need help. Socio-economically targeted interventions are of particular relevance in countries that show steep socio-economic gradients and an above-average strength of the relationship between socio-economic background and learning outcomes. Interestingly, there is no such country among the high-performing countries, but Belgium, Germany and Hungary are examples of such countries with performance around the OECD average.

■ Figure II.H ■
Relationship between school performance and schools' socio-economic background in Australia, New Zealand, Germany and Belgium

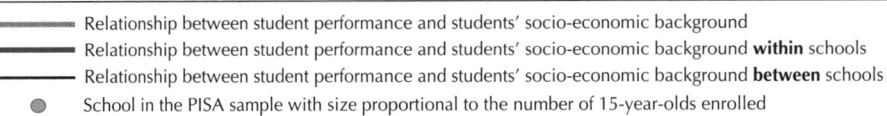

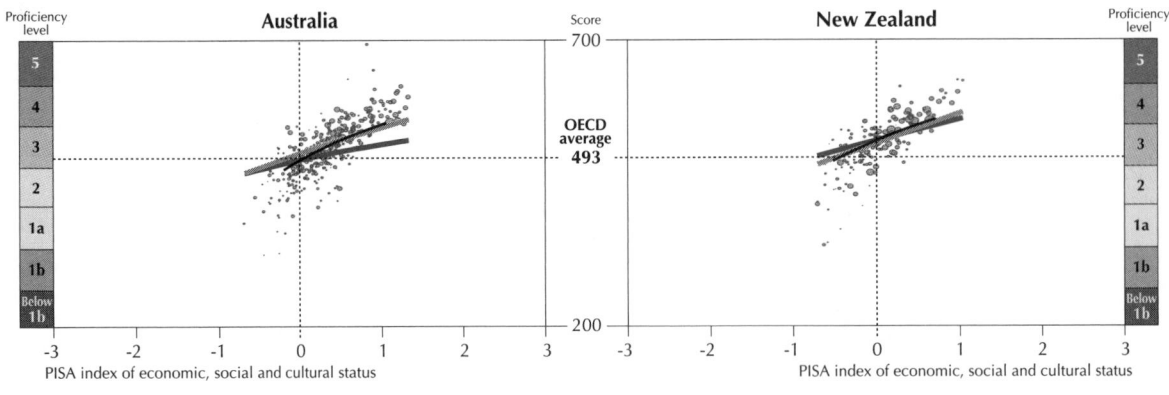

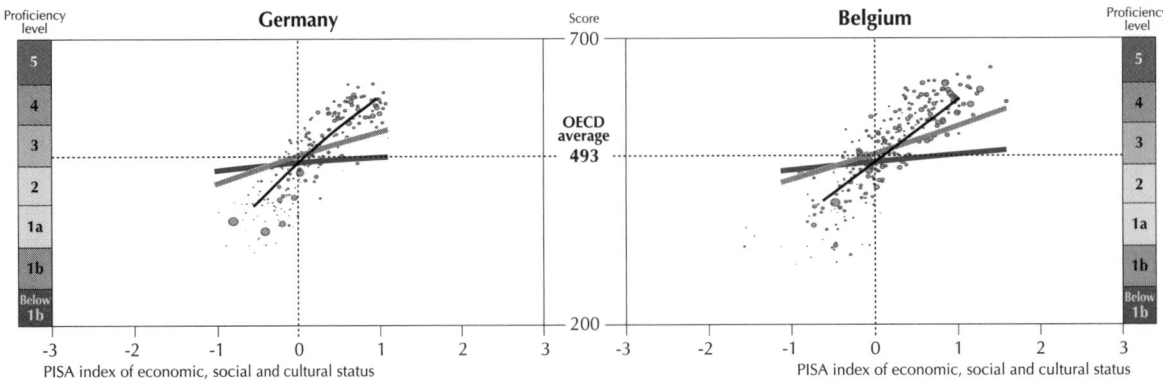

Source: OECD, *PISA 2009 Database*.
StatLink ⫯ http://dx.doi.org/10.1787/888932343646

In contrast, the case for socio-economically-targeted policies can be overstated for countries with steep socio-economic gradients where the variation explained by socio-economic background is only moderate. In these countries, there tends to be a sizeable group of poorly-performing students from more privileged socio-economic backgrounds. Among the high-performing countries, Australia, New Zealand and partner country Singapore have steep gradients but the strength of the relationship is only around the OECD average.

As the vertical cut-off point in Figure II.H shifts to the left – *i.e.* as the picture focuses on more disadvantaged backgrounds – the proportion of schools and students with low levels of performance that is not covered by these policies increases. In these cases, socio-economically-targeted policies are likely to miss a large proportion of students who perform relatively poorly.

Alternatively, compare France and Germany, which show the same level of reading performance. France has a steeper socio-economic gradient than Germany, but there are more exceptions to this pattern than in Germany, where the link between socio-economic background and student performance is stronger (Figure II.B).

Among the low-performing countries, the partner economy Dubai (UAE) (a country with a steeper-than-average gradient, estimated at 51 score points), Mexico and the partner country Thailand (with much lower estimated gradients, at around 22-25 score points) provide an interesting contrast (Figure II.I). The gradient in Dubai (UAE), Mexico or Thailand has an average strength of 13% to 14%. Thus, whereas students in Mexico or Thailand pay a lower penalty than those in Dubai (UAE), on average, for coming from a disadvantaged background, because of the less-steep gradients, Mexico and Thailand may find it more feasible to narrow this gap by targeting disadvantaged students.

■ Figure II.I ■

Relationship between school performance and schools' socio-economic background in Dubai (UAE), Mexico and Thailand

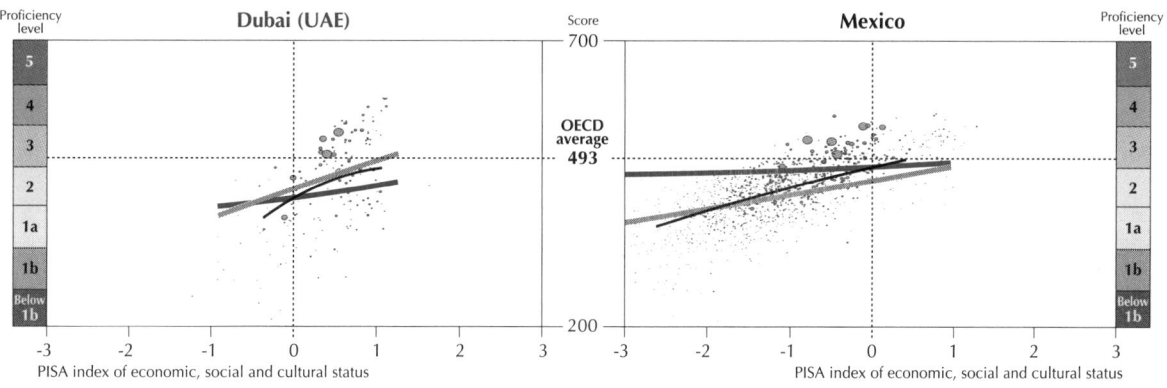

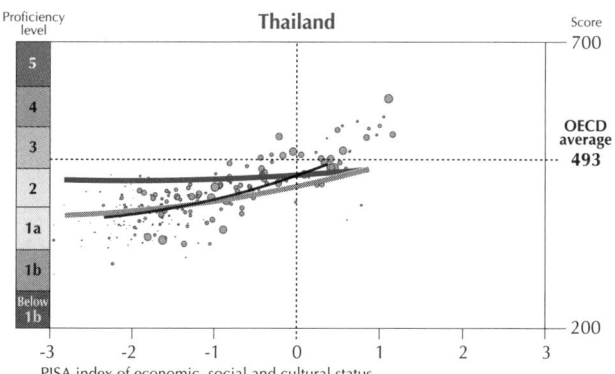

Source: OECD, *PISA 2009 Database*.
StatLink ᵐˢᴾ http://dx.doi.org/10.1787/888932343646

DIFFERENT SOCIO-ECONOMIC PROFILES

It is equally important to understand the degree of socio-economic differences within a country when interpreting the socio-economic gradient. For example, Finland and the partner country Panama have similar socio-economic gradients, but the range of scores on the *PISA index of economic, social and cultural status* (length of the gradient) between the 5th and 95th percentile of students is 4.2 in Panama and 2.5 in Finland (Table II.3.2). In other words, the student population in Panama is far more socio-economically diverse than the student population in Finland. This difference explains why, in Finland, socio-economic background accounts for less-than-average variation in performance, whereas in Panama the performance gap between the bottom and top quarters of the socio-economic distribution is much larger than in Finland (Figure II.J). Among OECD countries, socio-economic diversity, measured in this way, is largest in Mexico, Turkey, Portugal, Chile, Luxembourg and Spain, but many of the partner countries have much greater diversity, including Panama, Peru, Tunisia, Colombia, Uruguay, Brazil, Argentina, and Thailand. In all of these countries, addressing socio-economic diversity is a major challenge and can substantially improve educational performance and equity.

■ Figure II.J ■

Relationship between school performance and schools' socio-economic background in Finland and Panama

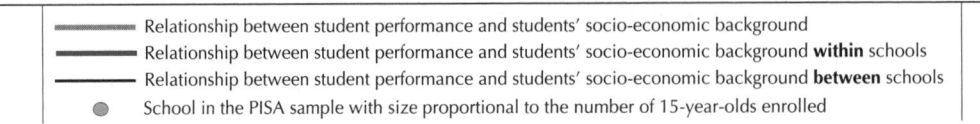

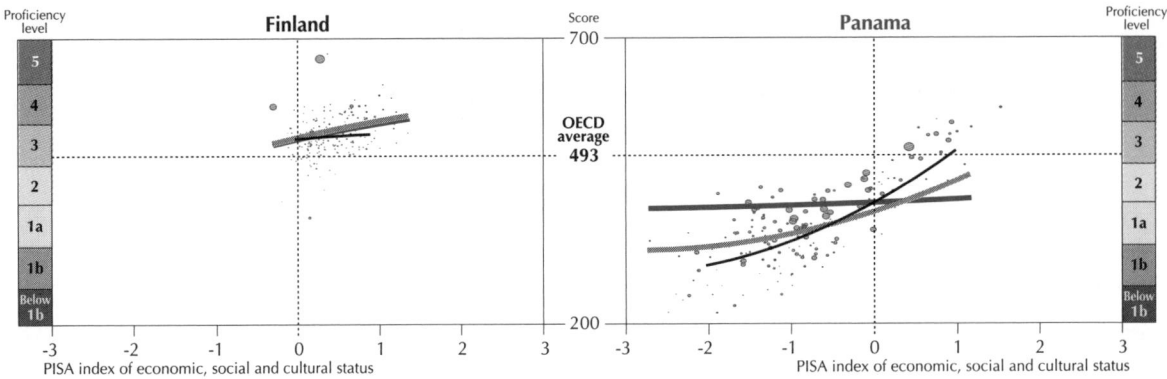

Source: OECD, *PISA 2009 Database*.
StatLink ᵐˢᵖ http://dx.doi.org/10.1787/888932343646

■ Figure II.K ■

Relationship between school performance and schools' socio-economic background in Spain and Mexico

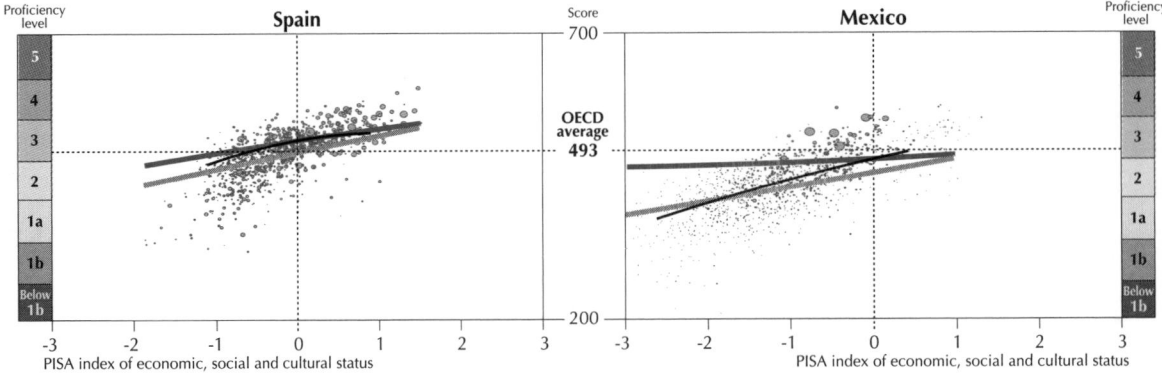

Source: OECD, *PISA 2009 Database*.
StatLink ᵐˢᵖ http://dx.doi.org/10.1787/888932343646

Spain and Mexico offer a similar comparison, although Mexico also has a highly skewed distribution of family background, with a high concentration of socio-economically disadvantaged students. This suggests the need for compensatory policies to help the most disadvantaged students, despite the fact that the slope of the gradient is modest. In Norway or Japan, in contrast, a relatively egalitarian society means that socio-economic differences between students have a relatively small effect on performance, and policies targeting social reform are unlikely to be the most effective way of raising scores.

DIFFERING GRADIENTS ACROSS SCHOOLS

The relationship between a school's socio-economic intake and student performance can vary in several ways. One is the extent to which a student who goes to a school with a more socio-economically advantaged intake can be predicted to perform better in reading. A second is how closely the performance of individual students actually follows this prediction, or the strength of the relationship. Both aspects are most pronounced in the OECD countries Japan, the Czech Republic, Germany, Slovenia, Israel, Belgium, the Netherlands and the partner countries Trinidad and Tobago, Liechtenstein and Singapore (Table II.5.2).

These factors are all important in countries where students' opportunities are strongly affected by differences in schools' intake. In these countries, policies that target socio-economically disadvantaged schools are more likely to succeed in improving performance and equity.

■ Figure II.L ■
Relationship between school performance and schools' socio-economic background in the Czech Republic, Germany, Norway and Poland

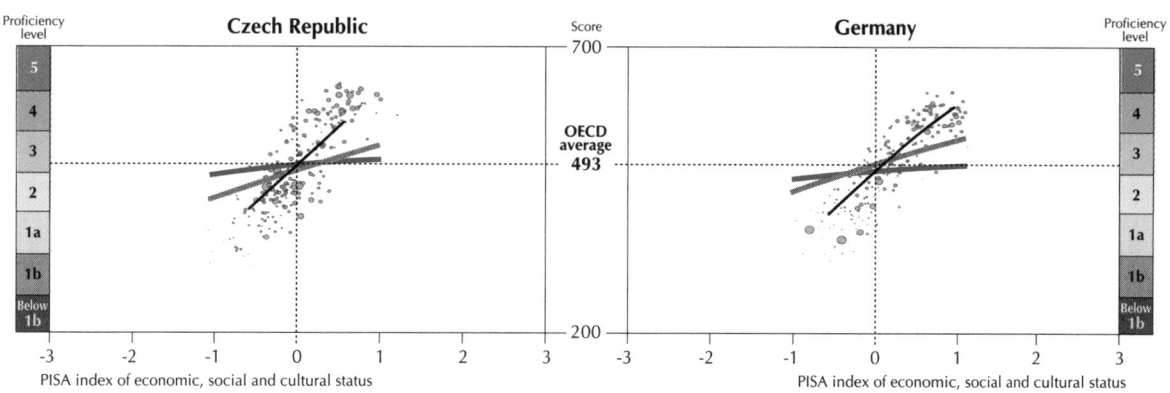

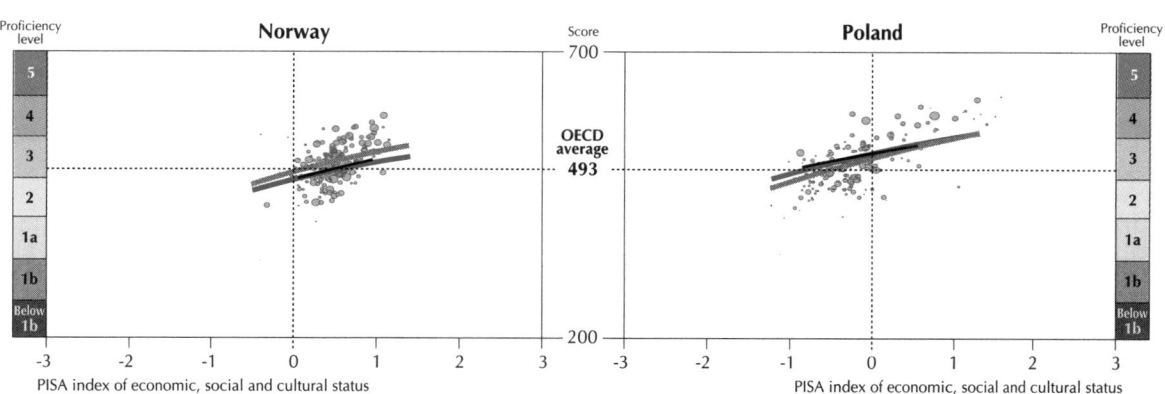

Source: OECD, *PISA 2009 Database*.
StatLink ⟐⟐⟐ http://dx.doi.org/10.1787/888932343646

This point can be illustrated by comparing countries (Figure II.L): Australia and Luxembourg, with between-school gradients around the OECD average; Germany, the Czech Republic and Japan, with comparatively steep between-school gradients; and Spain, Finland, Poland and Norway, with comparatively shallow between-school gradients. In Germany, more than three-quarters of the difference in student performance across schools is accounted for by socio-economic factors, that is, schools tend to fall into two categories: higher-performing schools with a more privileged socio-economic background, and schools with lower performance levels and a more disadvantaged intake. Most important, the variability in the social intake of schools is great, in that there is a large gap in social background between schools with more and less privileged socio-economic backgrounds. In Japan, in contrast, performance disparities by schools' socio-economic background are comparatively large as well, but the overall differences in the socio-economic profiles of schools are much smaller. That explains why, overall, Japan has one of the more equitable education systems while Germany has one of the more inequitable systems. In countries in which a high level of variation is accounted for by between-school socio-economic factors, policies aimed at reducing social segregation can be a priority, as such social disparities among schools tend to reinforce the inequalities of the system.

A similar contrast can be observed among countries with a comparatively gentle socio-economic gradient. For example, in Greece and Portugal, the slope of the socio-economic gradients is relatively gentle, around 40 score points. The dispersion of schools' socio-economic backgrounds is similar and relatively large, close to an inter-quartile range of 0.75. A school's socio-economic background is a much better predictor of performance in Portugal, where the explained variance is close to 60%, than in Greece, where the explained variance is close to 40%. That is, while many schools in Greece perform differently than what would have been predicted based on their background, in Portugal, socio-economic background is closely associated with a school's performance. Policies that target socio-economically disadvantaged schools are thus more likely to succeed in Portugal. In Greece, these policies will miss more low-performing schools that are not necessarily socio-economically disadvantaged.

■ Figure II.M ■

Relationship between school performance and schools' socio-economic background in Greece and Portugal

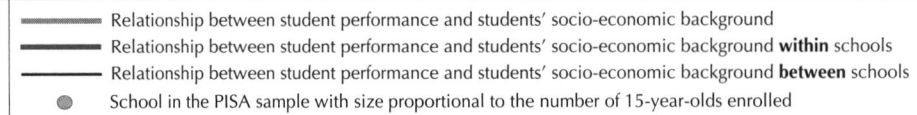

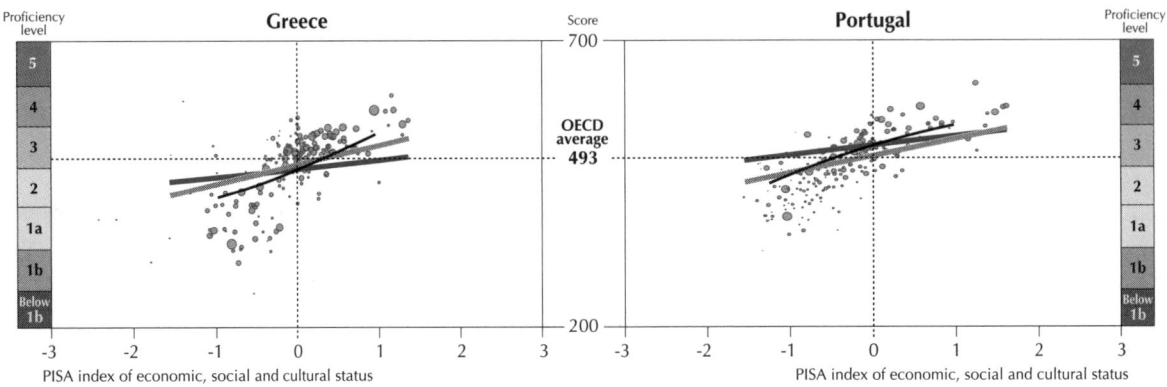

Source: OECD, *PISA 2009 Database*.
StatLink ⌨ http://dx.doi.org/10.1787/888932343646

DIFFERING GRADIENTS WITHIN SCHOOLS

To some extent, school systems that separate students into different schools by ability can expect to have narrower differences in student performance within each school, both overall and relative to socio-economic background. This is also the pattern shown by PISA. However, the social disparities between schools account for more of the differences among these countries than social disparities within schools. Thus, even Norway and New Zealand,

which represent, respectively, one of the least and one of the most unequal countries in terms of between-school gradients, show similar results when analysed according to within-school gradients (Figure II.N). In no country do within-school social differences account for more than 12% of student-level performance variation. Thus, while there may be some instances where socio-economic differences within schools should be addressed, in no country will within-school measures to moderate socio-economic differences succeed on their own in creating more equal student performance.

■ Figure II.N ■

Relationship between school performance and schools' socio-economic background in Norway and New Zealand

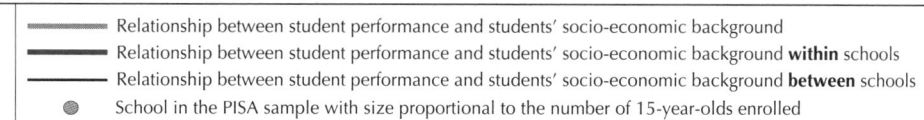

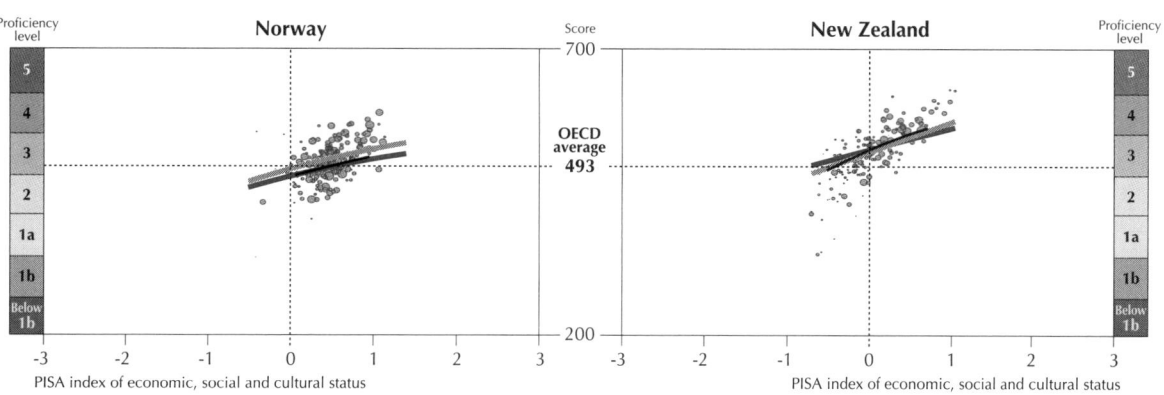

Source: OECD, *PISA 2009 Database*.
StatLink ⟶ http://dx.doi.org/10.1787/888932343646

Figure II.O shows the relationship between school performance and schools' socio-economic background for all OECD countries and partner countries and economies that are not used as examples in previous chapters. Countries and economies that appear in previous figures include the OECD countries Australia (II.H), Belgium (II.E and II.H), Canada (II.F), the Czech Republic (II.L), Estonia (II.G), Finland (II.F and II.J), Germany (II.H and II.L), Greece (II.M), Iceland (II.F), Israel (II.D), Korea (II.F), Luxembourg (II.D), Mexico (II.I and II.K), Norway (II.L and II.N), New Zealand (II.H and II.N), Poland (II.L), Spain (II.K), the United States (II.E) and the partner countries and economies Albania (II.C), Dubai (UAE) (II.D and II.I), Indonesia (II.C), Panama (II.J), Peru (II.C), Shanghai-China (II.F), Thailand (II.I) and Tunisia (II.C).

Volume IV, *What Makes a School Successful?* examines the observed relationships and identifies resources, policies and practices associated with the socio-economic inequalities seen among students, schools and school systems.

The analyses pertaining to school effectiveness presented in this report are based on data describing school offerings at the late-primary or secondary levels. However, an assessment such as PISA shows not only what young people have learned during their previous year at school, or even during their secondary school years, but also provides an indication of students' cumulative learning. A country's results in PISA, or in any assessment for that matter, depend on the quality of care and stimulation provided to children during infancy and their pre-school years, as well as on the opportunities children have to learn, both in school and at home, during their elementary and secondary school years.

Improving quality and equity thus requires a long-term view and a broad perspective. For some countries, this may mean taking measures to safeguard the healthy development of young children or to improve early childhood education. For others, it may mean socio-economic reforms that enable families to provide better care for their children. And in many countries, it may mean greater efforts to increase socio-economic inclusion and improve school offerings.

■ Figure II.O [Part 1/6] ■

Relationship between school performance and schools' socio-economic background

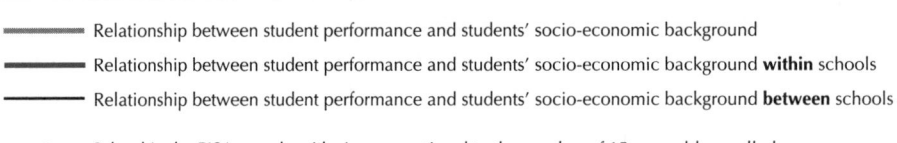

▬▬▬▬▬ Relationship between student performance and students' socio-economic background

▬▬▬▬▬ Relationship between student performance and students' socio-economic background **within** schools

▬▬▬▬▬ Relationship between student performance and students' socio-economic background **between** schools

● School in the PISA sample with size proportional to the number of 15-year-olds enrolled

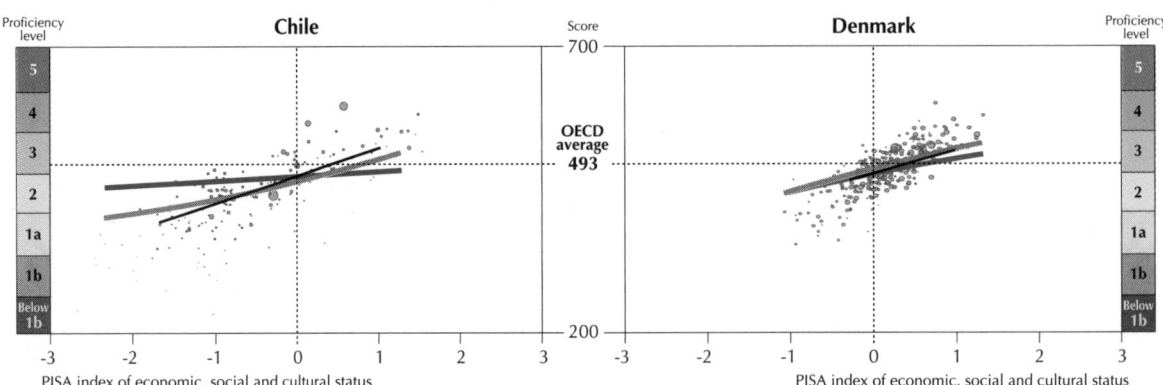

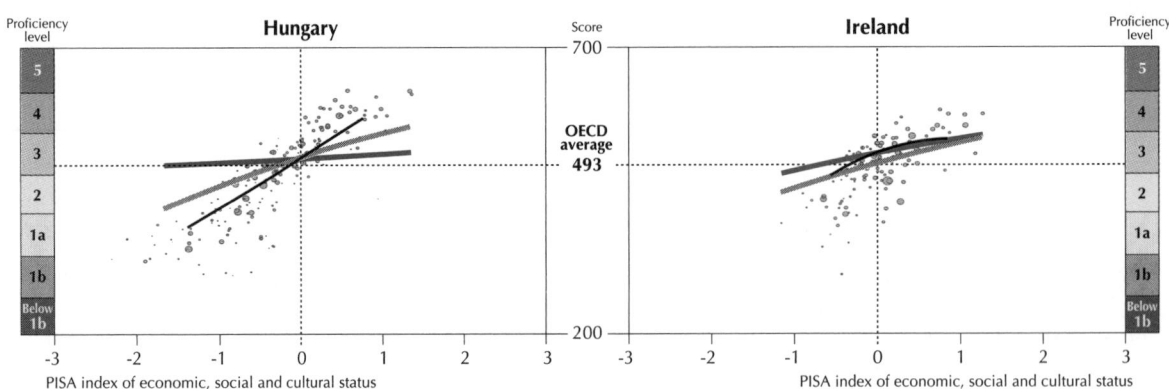

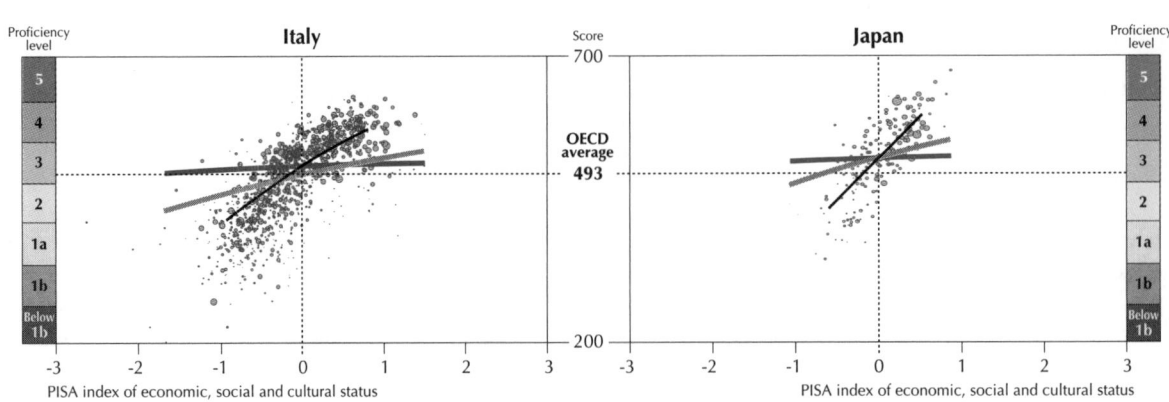

Source: OECD, *PISA 2009 Database.*
StatLink ═══⬛═ http://dx.doi.org/10.1787/888932343646

■ Figure II.O [Part 2/6] ■

Relationship between school performance and schools' socio-economic background

──────── Relationship between student performance and students' socio-economic background

──────── Relationship between student performance and students' socio-economic background **within** schools

──────── Relationship between student performance and students' socio-economic background **between** schools

⬤ School in the PISA sample with size proportional to the number of 15-year-olds enrolled

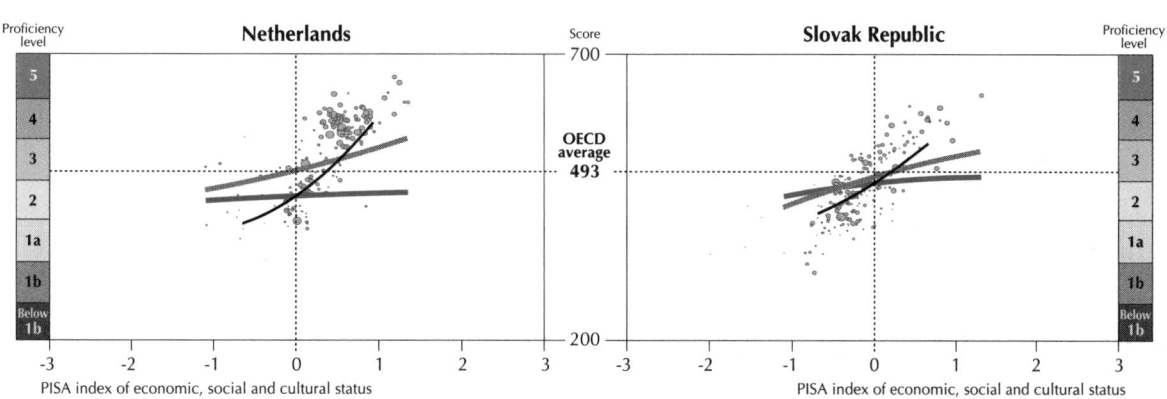

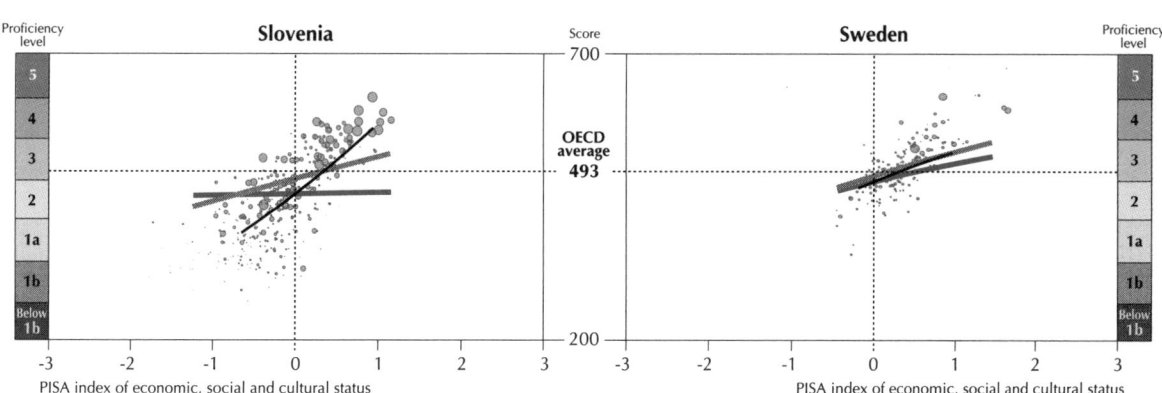

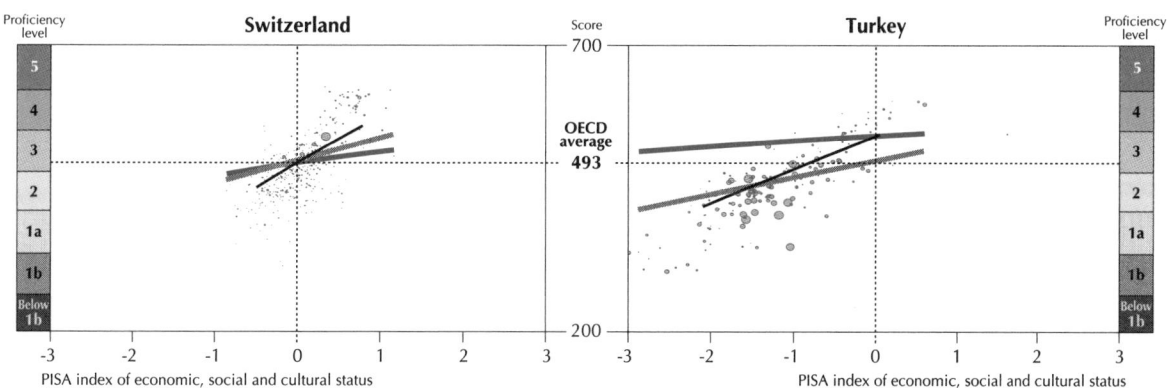

Source: OECD, *PISA 2009 Database.*
StatLink ⍚⍚⍚⍚⍚ http://dx.doi.org/10.1787/888932343646

■ Figure II.O [Part 3/6] ■

Relationship between school performance and schools' socio-economic background

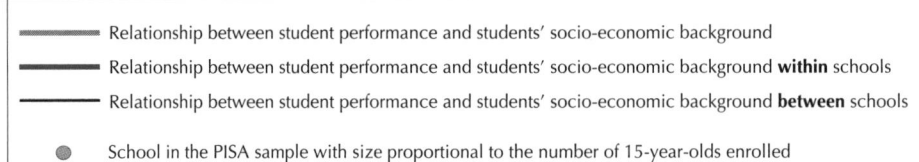

Relationship between student performance and students' socio-economic background

Relationship between student performance and students' socio-economic background **within** schools

Relationship between student performance and students' socio-economic background **between** schools

School in the PISA sample with size proportional to the number of 15-year-olds enrolled

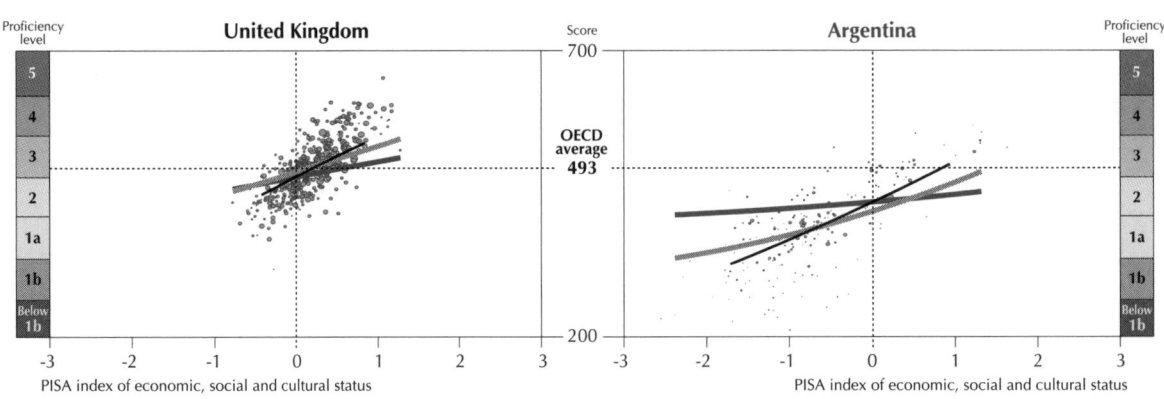

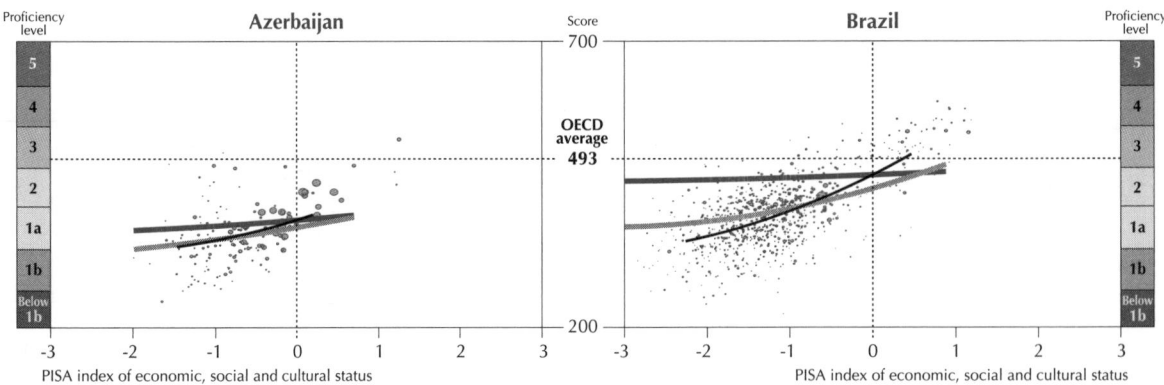

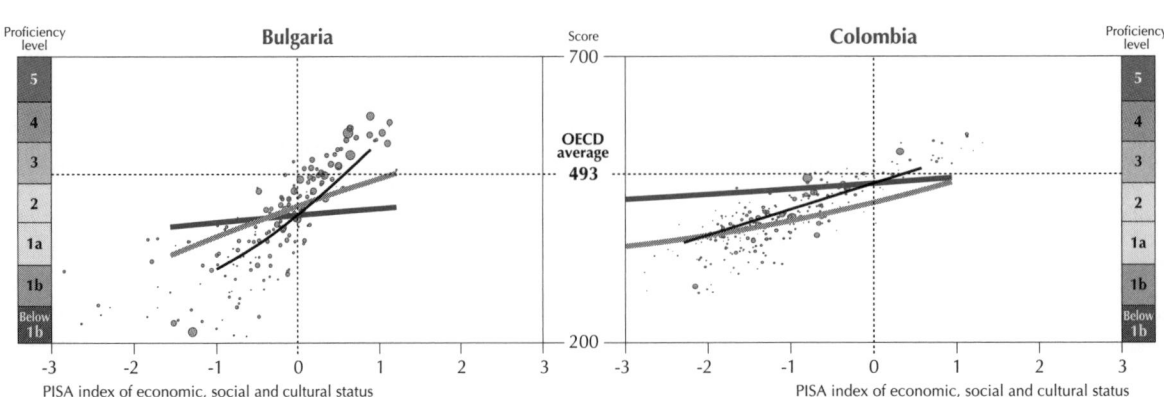

Source: OECD, *PISA 2009 Database*.

StatLink ⫲⫯⧫ http://dx.doi.org/10.1787/888932343646

■ Figure II.O [Part 4/6] ■

Relationship between school performance and schools' socio-economic background

———— Relationship between student performance and students' socio-economic background

———— Relationship between student performance and students' socio-economic background **within** schools

———— Relationship between student performance and students' socio-economic background **between** schools

⬤ School in the PISA sample with size proportional to the number of 15-year-olds enrolled

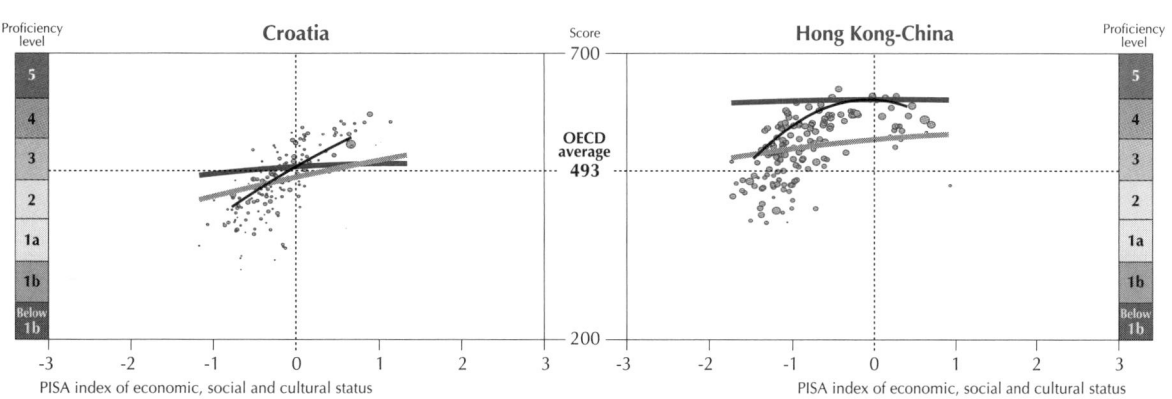

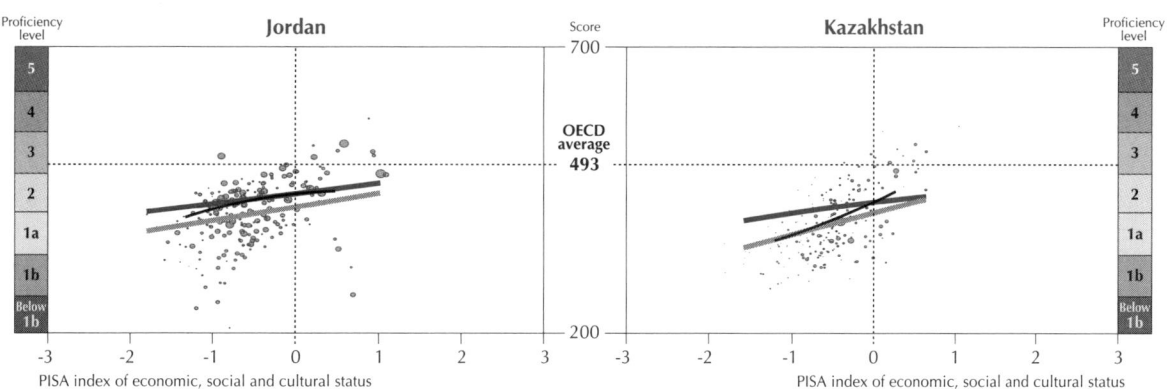

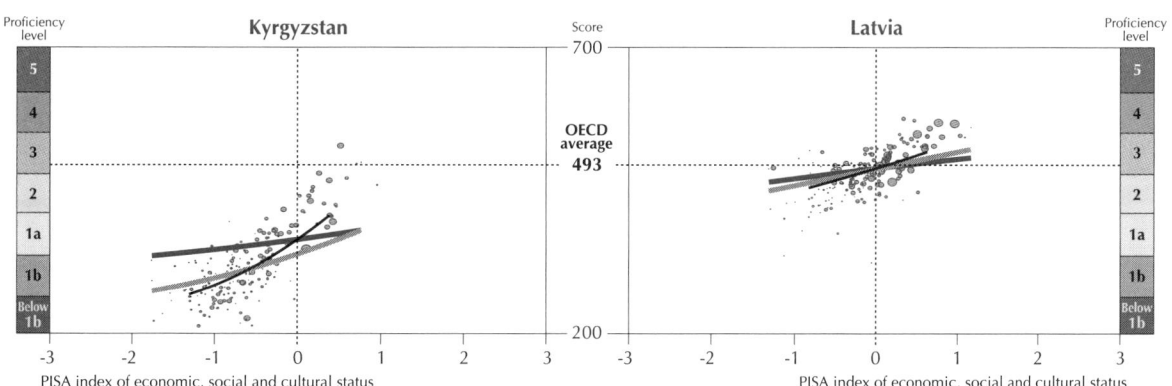

Source: OECD, *PISA 2009 Database.*
StatLink ▒▒ http://dx.doi.org/10.1787/888932343646

■ Figure II.O [Part 5/6] ■
Relationship between school performance and schools' socio-economic background

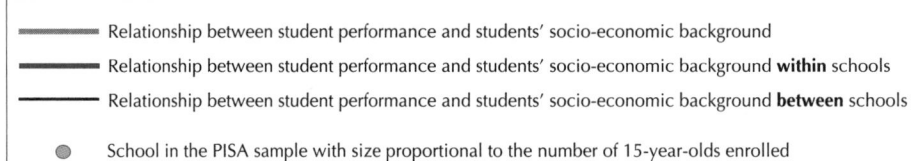

Relationship between student performance and students' socio-economic background

Relationship between student performance and students' socio-economic background **within** schools

Relationship between student performance and students' socio-economic background **between** schools

School in the PISA sample with size proportional to the number of 15-year-olds enrolled

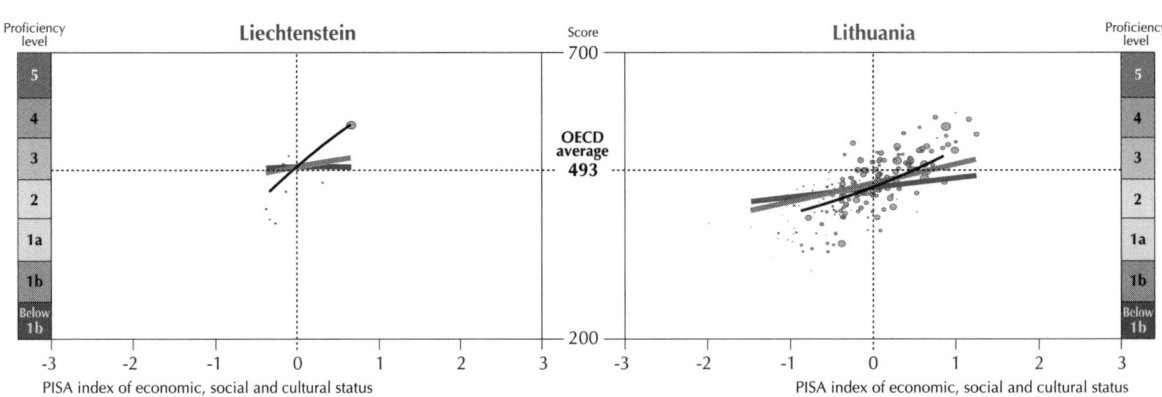

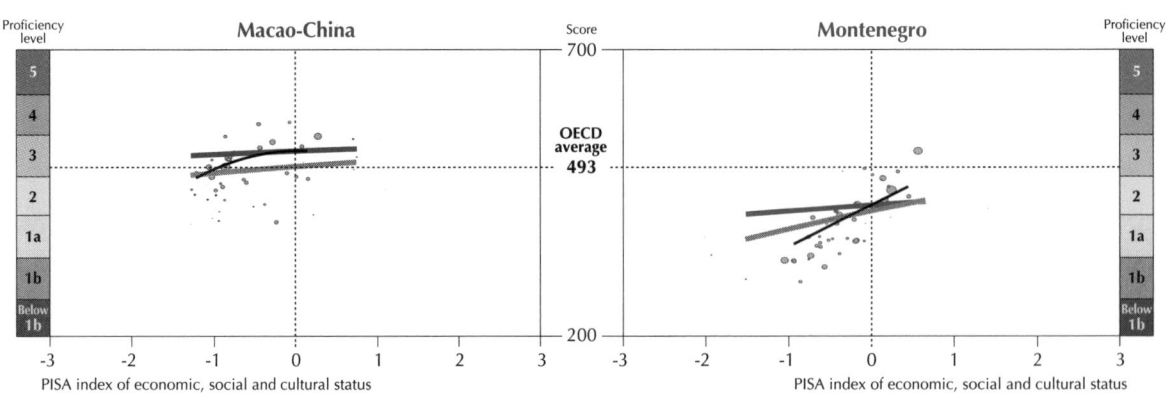

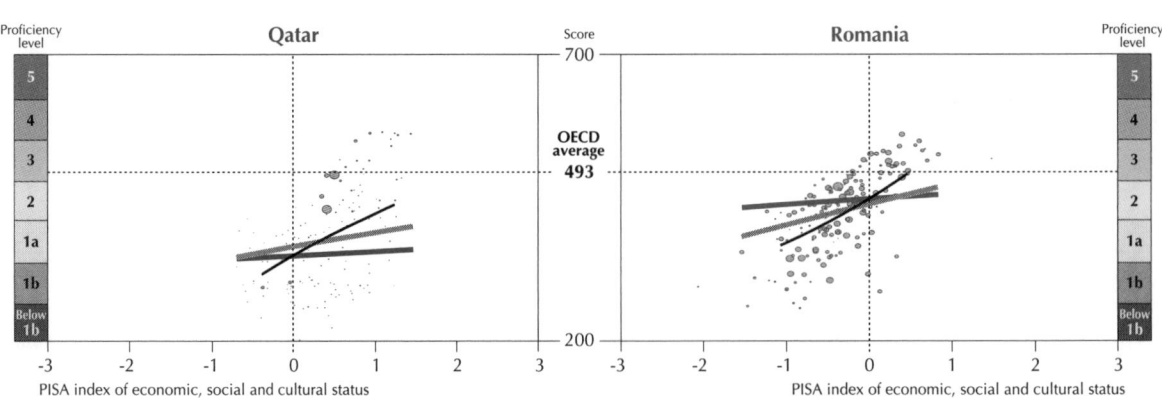

Source: OECD, *PISA 2009 Database.*
StatLink ▨▨ http://dx.doi.org/10.1787/888932343646

■ Figure II.O [Part 6/6] ■
Relationship between school performance and schools' socio-economic background

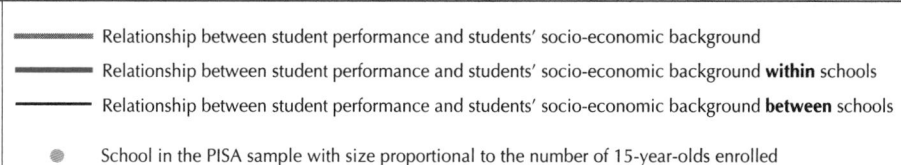

Relationship between student performance and students' socio-economic background

Relationship between student performance and students' socio-economic background **within** schools

Relationship between student performance and students' socio-economic background **between** schools

● School in the PISA sample with size proportional to the number of 15-year-olds enrolled

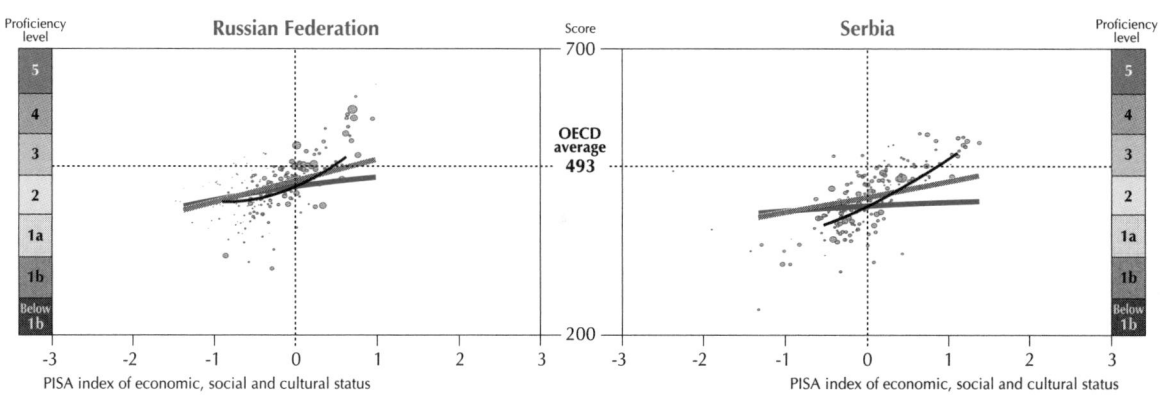

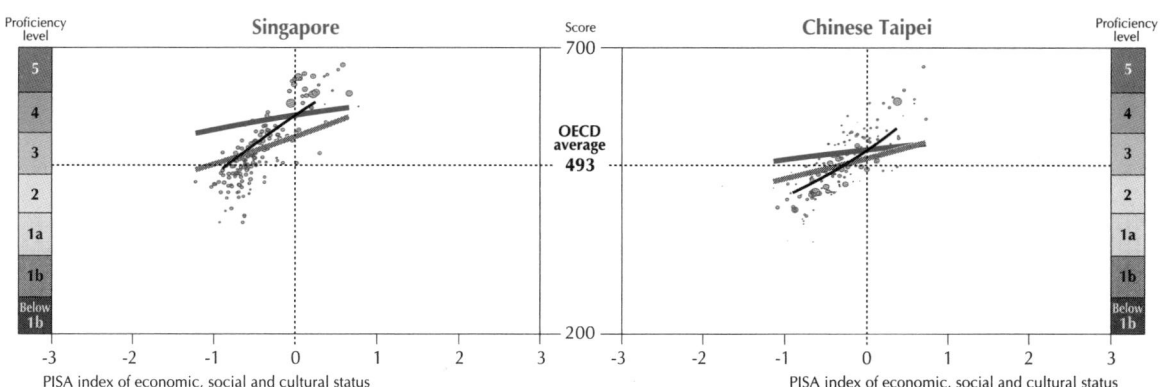

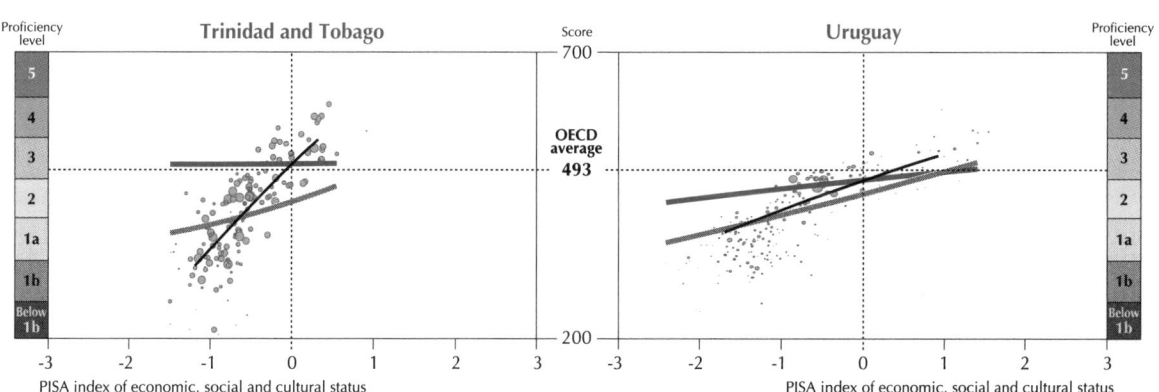

Source: OECD, *PISA 2009 Database*.
StatLink ᴴᴵˢᴾ http://dx.doi.org/10.1787/888932343646

References

Alexander, K.L., D.R. Entwisle and L.S. Olson (2007), "Lasting Consequences of the Summer Learning Gap", *American Sociological Review*, Vol. 72, pp. 167-180.

Belfield C. and H.M. Levin (eds.) (2007), *The Price We Pay: Economic and Social Consequences of Inadequate Education*, Brookings Institution Press, Washington DC.

Bertschy, K., M.A. Cattaneo and S.C. Wolter (2009), "PISA and the Transition into the Labour Market", *Labour*, Vol. 23, No. s1, pp. 111-137.

Blau, F. and L. Kahn (2005), "Do Cognitive Test Scores Explain Higher US Wage Inequality?", *Review of Economics and Statistics*, Vol. 87, No. 1, pp. 184-193.

Boado, M. and T. Fernández (2010), *Trayectorias Académicas y Laborales de los Jóvenes Uruguayos (Academic and Work Trajectories of Young Uruguayans)*, Facultad de Ciencias Sociales, Universidad de la República, Montevideo.

Buchmann, C. and E. Hannum (2001), "Education and Stratification in Developing Countries: A Review of Theories and Research", *Annual Review of Sociology*, Vol. 27, pp. 77-102.

Brown, G. and J. Micklewright (2004), *Using International Surveys of Achievement and Literacy: A view from the Outside*, UNESCO Institute for Statistics, Montreal.

Bussière P., T. Knighton and D. Pennock (2007), *Measuring Up: Canadian Results of the OECD PISA Study: The Performance of Canada's Youth in Science, Reading and Mathematics 2006 First Results for Canadians Aged 15*, Human Resources and Social Development Canada and Council of Ministers of Education Canada, Ottawa.

Carbonaro, W. (2006), "Cross-National Differences in the Skills-Earnings Relationship: The Role of Labor Market Institutions", *Social Forces*, Vol. 84, No. 3, pp. 1819-1842.

Coleman, J.S., *et al.* (1966), *Equality of Educational Opportunity*, U.S. Government Printing Office, Washington DC.

Datcher, L. (1982), "Effects of Community and Family Background on Achievement", *Review of Economics and Statistics*, Vol. 64, No. 1, pp. 32-41.

Devroye, D. and R. Freeman (2001), "Does Inequality in Skills Explain Inequality of Earnings across Advanced Countries?", *National Bureau of Economic Research Working Paper*, No. 8140.

Finn, J. and D.A. Rock (1997), "Academic Success among Students at Risk for School Failure", *Journal of Applied Psychology*, Vol. 82, No. 2, pp. 221-234.

Ganzeboom, H.B.G., P.M. De Graaf and D.J. Treiman (1992), "A Standard International Socio-economic Index of Occupational Status", *Social Science Research*, 21.1, pp. 1-56.

Hanushek, E. and L. Woessmann (2008), "The Role of Cognitive Skills in Economic Development", *Journal of Economic Literature*, Vol. 46, No. 3, pp. 607-668.

Hart B. and T.R. Risley (1995), *Meaningful Differences in the Everyday Experience of Young American Children*, Paul H. Brookes Publishing Co, Baltimore.

Hauser R.M. (2010), "On 'Quality and Equity in Performance of Students and Schools'", mimeo The University of Wisconsin-Madison, downloaded from: *https://edsurveys.rti.org/PISA/*

Heath, S.B. (1983), *Ways with Words: Language, Life, and Work in Communities and Classrooms*, Cambridge University Press, Cambridge.

Heyns, B. (1978), *Summer Learning and the Effects of Schooling*, Academic Press, New York City, New York.

ILO (International Labour Organization) (1990*), International Standard Classification of Occupations*, ISCO-88, Geneva.

Jeynes, W. (2005), "The Effects of Parental Involvement on the Academic Achievement of African American Youth", *Marriage and Family Review*, Vol. 37, No. 3, pp. 99-116.

Johnson, M.K., R. Crosnoe and **G.H. Elder** (2001), "Students' Attachment and Academic Engagement: The Role of Race and Ethnicity", *Sociology of Education*, Vol. 74, No. 3, pp. 318-340.

Kohn, M. (1969), *Class and Conformity: A Study in Values,* Dorsey Press, Homewood, Illinois.

Levin, H.M. (2009) "The Economic Payoff to Investing in Educational Justice", *Educational Researcher*, Vol 38, No. 1, pp. 5-14.

Levin, H.M. and **C.R. Belfield** (2002), "Families as Contractual Partners in Education", *Occasional Paper* No. 14, National Center for the Study of Privatization in Education, Teachers College, Columbia University, New York City, New York.

Marks, G.N. (2005), "Cross-National Differences and Accounting for Social Class Inequalities in Education," *International Sociology*, Vol. 20, No. 4, pp. 483-505.

Marks, G.N. (2007), "Do Schools Matter for Early School Leaving? Individual and School Influences in Australia," *School Effectiveness and School Implementation*, Vol. 18, No. 4, pp. 429-450.

McLanahan, S. and **G. Sandefur** (1994), *Growing Up with a Single Parent: What Hurts, What Helps,* Harvard University Press, Cambridge, Massachusetts.

Monseur, C. and **M. Crahay** (2008), "Composition Académique et Sociale des Établissements, Efficacité et Inégalités Scolaires : une Comparaison Internationale. Analyse Secondaire des Données PISA 2006" ("Schools' Academic and Social Composition, Efficacy and Schooling Inequalities: An International Comparison, Secondary Analysis of PISA 2006 Data"), *Revue Française de Pédagogie*, Vol. 164, pp. 55-65.

OECD (1999), *Classifying Educational Programmes: Manual for ISCED-97 Implementation in OECD Countries*, OECD Publishing.

OECD (2001), *Knowledge and Skills for Life: First Results from PISA 2000*, OECD Publishing.

OECD (2004), *Learning for Tomorrow's World: First Results from PISA 2003*, OECD Publishing.

OECD (2005), *Where Immigrant Students Succeed – A Comparative Review of Performance and Engagement in PISA 2003*, OECD Publishing.

OECD (2007a), *Understanding the Social Outcomes of Learning*, OECD Publishing.

OECD (2008), *Growing Unequal? Income Distribution and Poverty in OECD Countries*, OECD Publishing.

OECD (2007b), *PISA 2006: Science Competencies for Tomorrow's World*, OECD Publishing.

OECD (2009), *PISA 2009 Assessment Framework*, OECD Publishing.

OECD (2010a), *The High Costs of Low Educational Performance*, OECD Publishing.

OECD (2010b), *Against the Odds: Disadvantaged Students who Succeed at School*, OECD Publishing.

OECD (2010c), *Pathways to Success: How Knowledge and Skills at Age 15 Shapes Future Lives in Canada*, OECD Publishing.

OECD (2010d), *Education at a Glance: OECD Indicators 2010*, OECD Publishing.

OECD (2010e), *Economic Policy Reforms: Going for Growth 2010*, OECD Publishing.

OECD (2010f), *International Migration Outlook, 2010*, OECD Publishing.

OECD (2010g), *OECD Reviews of Migrant Education Closing the Gap for Immigrant Students: Policies, Practice and Performance*, OECD Publishing.

Raley, R., M. Frisco and **E. Wildsmith** (2005), "Maternal Cohabitation and Educational Success", *Sociology of Education*, Vol. 78, No. 2, pp. 144-164.

Voelkl, K.E. (1995), "School Warmth, Student Participation, and Achievement", *Journal of Experimental Education*, Vol. 63, No.2, pp. 127-138.

Willms, J.D. (2002), *Vulnerable Children: Findings from Canada's National Longitudinal Survey of Children and Youth*, University of Alberta Press, Edmonton.

Willms, J.D. (2006), *Learning Divides: Ten Policy Questions About the Performance and Equity of Schools and Schooling Systems*, UNESCO Institute for Statistics, Montreal.

Willms, J.D. (2010), "School Composition and Contextual Effects on Student Outcomes", *Teachers College Record*, Vol. 112, No. 4, pp. 1008-1037.

Annex A

TECHNICAL BACKGROUND

All tables in Annex A are available on line

ANNEX A1
CONSTRUCTION OF READING SCALES AND INDICES FROM THE STUDENT, SCHOOL AND PARENT CONTEXT QUESTIONNAIRES

How the PISA 2009 reading assessments were designed, analysed and scaled

The development of the PISA 2009 reading tasks was co-ordinated by an international consortium of educational research institutions contracted by the OECD, under the guidance of a group of reading experts from participating countries. Participating countries contributed stimulus material and questions, which were reviewed, tried out and refined iteratively over the three years leading up to the administration of the assessment in 2009. The development process involved provisions for several rounds of commentary from participating countries, as well as small-scale piloting and a formal field trial in which samples of 15-year-olds from all participating countries took part. The reading expert group recommended the final selection of tasks, which included material submitted by 21 of the participating countries. The selection was made with regard to both their technical quality, assessed on the basis of their performance in the field trial, and their cultural appropriateness and interest level for 15-year-olds, as judged by the participating countries. Another essential criterion for selecting the set of material as a whole was its fit to the framework described in *Volume 1, What Students Know and Can Do*, to maintain the balance across various categories of text, aspect and situation. Finally, it was carefully ensured that the set of questions covered a range of difficulty, allowing good measurement and description of the reading literacy of all 15-year-old students, from the least proficient to the highly able.

More than 130 print reading questions were used in PISA 2009, but each student in the sample only saw a fraction of the total pool because different sets of questions were given to different students. The reading questions selected for inclusion in PISA 2009 were organised into half-hour clusters. These, along with clusters of mathematics and science questions, were assembled into booklets containing four clusters each. Each participating student was then given a two-hour assessment. As reading was the focus of the PISA 2009 assessment, every booklet included at least one cluster of reading material. The clusters were rotated so that each cluster appeared in each of the four possible positions in the booklets, and each pair of clusters appeared in at least one of the 13 booklets that were used.

This design, similar to those used in previous PISA assessments, makes it possible to construct a single scale of reading proficiency, in which each question is associated with a particular point on the scale that indicates its difficulty, whereby each student's performance is associated with a particular point on the same scale that indicates his or her estimated proficiency. A description of the modelling technique used to construct this scale can be found in the *PISA 2009 Technical Report* (OECD, forthcoming).

The relative difficulty of tasks in a test is estimated by considering the proportion of test takers who answer each question correctly. The relative proficiency of students taking a particular test can be estimated by considering the proportion of test questions they answer correctly. A single continuous scale shows the relationship between the difficulty of questions and the proficiency of students. By constructing a scale that shows the difficulty of each question, it is possible to locate the level of reading literacy that the question represents. By showing the proficiency of each student on the same scale, it is possible to describe the level of reading literacy that the student possesses.

The location of student proficiency on this scale is set in relation to the particular group of questions used in the assessment. However, just as the sample of students taking PISA in 2009 is drawn to represent all the 15-year-olds in the participating countries, so the individual questions used in the assessment are designed to represent the definition of reading literacy adequately. Estimates of student proficiency reflect the kinds of tasks they would be expected to perform successfully. This means that students are likely to be able to complete questions successfully at or below the difficulty level associated with their own position on the scale (but they may not always do so). Conversely, they are unlikely to be able to successfully complete questions above the difficulty level associated with their position on the scale (but they may sometimes do so).

The further a student's proficiency is located above a given question, the more likely he or she is to successfully complete the question (and other questions of similar difficulty); the further the student's proficiency is located below a given question, the lower the probability that the student will be able to successfully complete the question, and other questions of similar difficulty.

How reading proficiency levels are defined in PISA 2009

PISA 2009 provides an overall reading literacy scale for the reading texts, drawing on all the questions in the reading assessment, as well as scales for three aspects and two text formats. The metric for the overall reading scale is based on a mean for OECD countries set at 500 in PISA 2000, with a standard deviation of 100. To help interpret what students' scores mean in substantive terms, the scale is divided into levels, based on a set of statistical principles, and then descriptions are generated, based on the tasks that are located within each level, to describe the kinds of skills and knowledge needed to successfully complete those tasks.

For PISA 2009, the range of difficulty of tasks allows for the description of seven levels of reading proficiency: Level 1b is the lowest described level, then Level 1a, Level 2, Level 3 and so on up to Level 6.

Students with a proficiency within the range of Level 1b are likely to be able to successfully complete Level 1b tasks (and others like them), but are unlikely to be able to complete tasks at higher levels. Level 6 reflects tasks that present the greatest challenge in terms of reading skills and knowledge. Students with scores in this range are likely to be able to complete reading tasks located at that level successfully, as well as all the other reading tasks in PISA.

PISA applies a standard methodology for constructing proficiency scales. Based on a student's performance on the tasks in the test, his or her score is generated and located in a specific part of the scale, thus allowing the score to be associated with a defined proficiency level. The level at which the student's score is located is the highest level for which he or she would be expected to answer correctly, most of a random selection of questions within the same level. Thus, for example, in an assessment composed of tasks spread uniformly across Level 3, students with a score located within Level 3 would be expected to complete at least 50% of the tasks successfully. Because a level covers a range of difficulty and proficiency, success rates across the band vary. Students near the bottom of the level would be likely to succeed on just over 50% of the tasks spread uniformly across the level, while students at the top of the level would be likely to succeed on well over 70% of the same tasks.

Figure I.2.12 in Volume I provides details of the nature of reading skills, knowledge and understanding required at each level of the reading scale.

Explanation of indices

This section explains the indices derived from the student, school and parent context questionnaires used in PISA 2009. Parent questionnaire indices are only available for the 14 countries that chose to administer the optional parent questionnaire.

Several PISA measures reflect indices that summarise responses from students, their parents or school representatives (typically principals) to a series of related questions. The questions were selected from a larger pool of questions on the basis of theoretical considerations and previous research. Structural equation modelling was used to confirm the theoretically expected behaviour of the indices and to validate their comparability across countries. For this purpose, a model was estimated separately for each country and collectively for all OECD countries.

For a detailed description of other PISA indices and details on the methods, see the *PISA 2009 Technical Report* (OECD, forthcoming).

There are two types of indices: simple indices and scale indices.

Simple indices are the variables that are constructed through the arithmetic transformation or recoding of one or more items, in exactly the same way across assessments. Here, item responses are used to calculate meaningful variables, such as the recoding of the four-digit ISCO-88 codes into "Highest parents' socio-economic index (HISEI)" or, teacher-student ratio based on information from the school questionnaire.

Scale indices are the variables constructed through the scaling of multiple items. Unless otherwise indicated, the index was scaled using a weighted maximum likelihood estimate (WLE) (Warm, 1985), using a one-parameter item response model (a partial credit model was used in the case of items with more than two categories).

The scaling was done in three stages:

- The item parameters were estimated from equal-sized subsamples of students from each OECD country.

- The estimates were computed for all students and all schools by anchoring the item parameters obtained in the preceding step.

- The indices were then standardised so that the mean of the index value for the OECD student population was 0 and the standard deviation was 1 (countries being given equal weight in the standardisation process).

Sequential codes were assigned to the different response categories of the questions in the sequence in which the latter appeared in the student, school or parent questionnaires. Where indicated in this section, these codes were inverted for the purpose of constructing indices or scales. It is important to note that negative values for an index do not necessarily imply that students responded negatively to the underlying questions. A negative value merely indicates that the respondents answered less positively than all respondents did on average across OECD countries. Likewise, a positive value on an index indicates that the respondents answered more favourably, or more positively, than respondents did, on average, in OECD countries. Terms enclosed in brackets < > in the following descriptions were replaced in the national versions of the student, school and parent questionnaires by the appropriate national equivalent. For example, the term <qualification at ISCED level 5A> was translated in the United States into "Bachelor's degree, post-graduate certificate program, Master's degree program or first professional degree program". Similarly the term <classes in the language of assessment> in Luxembourg was translated into "German classes" or "French classes" depending on whether students received the German or French version of the assessment instruments.

In addition to simple and scaled indices described in this annex, there are a number of variables from the questionnaires that correspond to single items not used to construct indices. These non-recoded variables have prefix of "ST" for the questionnaire items in the student questionnaire, "SC" for the items in the school questionnaire, and "PA" for the items in the parent questionnaire. All the context questionnaires as well as the PISA international database, including all variables, are available through *www.pisa.oecd.org*.

Student-level simple indices

Occupational status of parents

Occupational data for both a student's father and a student's mother were obtained by asking open-ended questions in the student questionnaire (ST9a, ST9b, ST12, ST13a, ST13b and ST16). The responses were coded to four-digit ISCO codes (ILO, 1990) and then mapped to Ganzeboom *et al.*'s SEI index (1992). Higher scores of SEI indicate higher levels of occupational status. The following three indices are obtained:

- Mother's occupational status (BMMJ).

- Father's occupational status (BFMJ).

- The highest occupational level of parents (HISEI) corresponds to the higher SEI score of either parent or to the only available parent's SEI score.

Educational level of parents

The educational level of parents is classified using ISCED (OECD, 1999) based on students' responses in the student questionnaire (ST10, ST11, ST14 and ST15). Please note that the question format for school education in PISA 2009 differs from the one used in PISA 2000, 2003 and 2006 but the method used to compute parental education is the same.

As in PISA 2000, 2003 and 2006, indices were constructed by selecting the highest level for each parent and then assigning them to the following categories: (0) None, (1) ISCED 1 (primary education), (2) ISCED 2 (lower secondary), (3) ISCED Level 3B or 3C (vocational/pre-vocational upper secondary), (4) ISCED 3A (upper secondary) and/or ISCED 4 (non-tertiary post-secondary), (5) ISCED 5B (vocational tertiary), (6) ISCED 5A, 6 (theoretically oriented tertiary and post-graduate). The following three indices with these categories are developed:

- Mother's educational level (MISCED).

- Father's educational level (FISCED).

- Highest educational level of parents (HISCED) corresponds to the higher ISCED level of either parent.

Highest educational level of parents was also converted into the number of years of schooling (PARED). For the conversion of level of education into years of schooling, see Table A1.1.

Immigration and language background

Information on the country of birth of students and their parents (ST17) is collected in a similar manner as in PISA 2000, PISA 2003 and PISA 2006 by using nationally specific ISO coded variables. The ISO codes of the country of birth for students and their parents are available in the PISA international database (COBN_S, COBN_M, and COBN_F).

The index on immigrant background (IMMIG) has the following categories: (1) native students (those students born in the country of assessment, or those with at least one parent born in that country; students who were born abroad with at least one parent born in the country of assessment are also classified as 'native' students), (2) second-generation students (those born in the country of assessment but whose parents were born in another country), and (3) first-generation students (those born outside the country of assessment and whose parents were also born in another country). Students with missing responses for either the student or for both parents, or for all three questions have been given missing values for this variable.

Students indicate the language they usually speak at home. The data are captured in nationally-specific language codes, which were recoded into variable ST19Q01 with the following two values: (1) language at home is the same as the language of assessment, and (2) language at home is a different language than the language of assessment.

Relative grade

Data on the student's grade are obtained both from the student questionnaire (ST01) and from the student tracking form. As with all variables that are on both the tracking form and the questionnaire, inconsistencies between the two sources are reviewed and resolved during data-cleaning. In order to capture between-country variation, the relative grade index (GRADE) indicates whether students are at the modal grade in a country (value of 0), or whether they are below or above the modal grade level (+ x grades, - x grades).

The relationship between the grade and student performance was estimated through a multilevel model accounting for the following background variables: *i)* the **PISA index of economic, social and cultural status**; *ii)* the **PISA index of economic, social and cultural status** squared; *iii)* the school mean of the **PISA index of economic, social and cultural status**; *iv)* an indicator as to whether students were foreign born first-generation students; *v)* the percentage of first-generation students in the school; and *vi)* students' gender.

[Part 1/1]
Table A1.1 Levels of parental education converted into years of schooling

	Did not go to school	Completed ISCED Level 1 (primary education)	Completed ISCED Level 2 (lower secondary education)	Completed ISCED Levels3B or 3C (upper secondary education providing direct access to the labor market or to ISCED 5B programmes)	Completed ISCED Level 3A (upper secondary education providing access to ISCED 5A and 5B programmes) and/or ISCED Level 4 (non-tertiary post-secondary)	Completed ISCED Level 5A (university level tertiary education) or ISCED Level 6 (advanced research programmes)	Completed ISCED Level 5B (non-university tertiary education)
OECD							
Australia	0.0	6.0	10.0	11.0	12.0	15.0	14.0
Austria	0.0	4.0	9.0	12.0	12.5	17.0	15.0
Belgium	0.0	6.0	9.0	12.0	12.0	17.0	14.5
Canada	0.0	6.0	9.0	12.0	12.0	17.0	15.0
Chile	0.0	6.0	8.0	12.0	12.0	17.0	16.0
Czech Republic	0.0	5.0	9.0	11.0	13.0	16.0	16.0
Denmark	0.0	6.0	9.0	12.0	12.0	17.0	15.0
Estonia	0.0	4.0	9.0	12.0	12.0	16.0	15.0
Finland	0.0	6.0	9.0	12.0	12.0	16.5	14.5
France	0.0	5.0	9.0	12.0	12.0	15.0	14.0
Germany	0.0	4.0	10.0	13.0	13.0	18.0	15.0
Greece	0.0	6.0	9.0	11.5	12.0	17.0	15.0
Hungary	0.0	4.0	8.0	10.5	12.0	16.5	13.5
Iceland	0.0	7.0	10.0	13.0	14.0	18.0	16.0
Ireland	0.0	6.0	9.0	12.0	12.0	16.0	14.0
Israel	0.0	6.0	9.0	12.0	12.0	15.0	15.0
Italy	0.0	5.0	8.0	12.0	13.0	17.0	16.0
Japan	0.0	6.0	9.0	12.0	12.0	16.0	14.0
Korea	0.0	6.0	9.0	12.0	12.0	16.0	14.0
Luxembourg	0.0	6.0	9.0	12.0	13.0	17.0	16.0
Mexico	0.0	6.0	9.0	12.0	12.0	16.0	14.0
Netherlands	0.0	6.0	10.0	a	12.0	16.0	a
New Zealand	0.0	5.5	10.0	11.0	12.0	15.0	14.0
Norway	0.0	6.0	9.0	12.0	12.0	16.0	14.0
Poland	0.0	a	8.0	11.0	12.0	16.0	15.0
Portugal	0.0	6.0	9.0	12.0	12.0	17.0	15.0
Scotland	0.0	7.0	11.0	13.0	13.0	16.0	16.0
Slovak Republic	0.0	4.5	8.5	12.0	12.0	17.5	13.5
Slovenia	0.0	4.0	8.0	11.0	12.0	16.0	15.0
Spain	0.0	5.0	8.0	10.0	12.0	16.5	13.0
Sweden	0.0	6.0	9.0	11.5	12.0	15.5	14.0
Switzerland	0.0	6.0	9.0	12.5	12.5	17.5	14.5
Turkey	0.0	5.0	8.0	11.0	11.0	15.0	13.0
United Kingdom	0.0	6.0	9.0	12.0	13.0	16.0	15.0
United States	0.0	6.0	9.0	a	12.0	16.0	14.0
Partners							
Albania	0.0	6.0	9.0	12.0	12.0	16.0	16.0
Argentina	0.0	6.0	10.0	12.0	12.0	17.0	14.5
Azerbaijan	0.0	4.0	9.0	11.0	11.0	17.0	14.0
Brazil	0.0	4.0	8.0	11.0	11.0	16.0	14.5
Bulgaria	0.0	4.0	8.0	12.0	12.0	17.5	15.0
Colombia	0.0	5.0	9.0	11.0	11.0	15.5	14.0
Croatia	0.0	4.0	8.0	11.0	12.0	17.0	15.0
Dubai (UAE)	0.0	5.0	9.0	12.0	12.0	16.0	15.0
Hong Kong- China	0.0	6.0	9.0	11.0	13.0	16.0	14.0
Indonesia	0.0	6.0	9.0	12.0	12.0	15.0	14.0
Jordan	0.0	6.0	10.0	12.0	12.0	16.0	14.5
Kazakhstan	0.0	4.0	9.0	11.5	12.5	15.0	14.0
Kyrgyzstan	0.0	4.0	8.0	11.0	10.0	15.0	13.0
Latvia	0.0	3.0	8.0	11.0	11.0	16.0	16.0
Liechtenstein	0.0	5.0	9.0	11.0	13.0	17.0	14.0
Lithuania	0.0	3.0	8.0	11.0	11.0	16.0	15.0
Macao-China	0.0	6.0	9.0	11.0	12.0	16.0	15.0
Montenegro	0.0	4.0	8.0	11.0	12.0	16.0	15.0
Panama	0.0	6.0	9.0	12.0	12.0	16.0	a
Peru	0.0	6.0	9.0	11.0	11.0	17.0	14.0
Qatar	0.0	6.0	9.0	12.0	12.0	16.0	15.0
Romania	0.0	4.0	8.0	11.5	12.5	16.0	14.0
Russian Federation	0.0	4.0	9.0	11.5	12.0	15.0	a
Serbia	0.0	4.0	8.0	11.0	12.0	17.0	14.5
Shanghai-China	0.0	6.0	9.0	12.0	12.0	16.0	15.0
Singapore	0.0	6.0	8.0	10.5	10.5	12.5	12.5
Chinese Taipei	0.0	6.0	9.0	12.0	12.0	16.0	14.0
Thailand	0.0	6.0	9.0	12.0	12.0	16.0	14.0
Trinidad and Tobago	0.0	5.0	9.0	12.0	12.0	16.0	15.0
Tunisia	0.0	6.0	9.0	12.0	13.0	17.0	16.0
Uruguay	0.0	6.0	9.0	12.0	12.0	17.0	15.0

StatLink ╗╜┻╛ http://dx.doi.org/10.1787/888932343171

[Part 1/1]

Table A1.2 A multilevel model to estimate grade effects in reading, accounting for some background variables

	Grade		Index of economic, social and cultural status		PISA index of economic, social and cultural status squared		School mean PISA index of economic, social and cultural status		First generation students		School percentage of first generation students		Gender – student is a female		Intercept	
	Coef.	S.E.	Coef.	S.E.	Coef.	S.E.	Coef.	S.E.	Coef.	S.E.	Coef.	S.E.	Coef.	S.E.	Coef.	S.E.
OECD																
Australia	33.2	(1.95)	30.0	(1.36)	-3.8	(1.05)	66.4	(1.87)	-7.4	(2.82)	0.1	(0.07)	32.9	(1.91)	466.0	(1.39)
Austria	35.3	(2.18)	11.4	(1.66)	-0.5	(1.00)	89.7	(3.86)	-33.1	(6.11)	1.4	(0.13)	19.9	(2.67)	467.9	(2.45)
Belgium	48.9	(1.98)	10.0	(1.12)	-0.1	(0.63)	79.9	(1.73)	-3.2	(5.18)	0.3	(0.11)	11.3	(1.81)	507.0	(1.70)
Canada	45.0	(2.14)	19.4	(1.52)	1.5	(0.91)	33.9	(2.28)	-13.7	(3.18)	0.3	(0.04)	30.4	(1.60)	483.4	(1.76)
Chile	35.5	(1.55)	8.6	(1.52)	0.3	(0.63)	37.4	(1.61)	c	c	c	c	13.8	(2.33)	478.6	(1.60)
Czech Republic	44.6	(3.39)	13.4	(1.89)	-2.3	(1.47)	111.5	(3.12)	-8.9	(12.29)	0.4	(0.33)	32.3	(2.84)	460.7	(2.39)
Denmark	36.1	(3.02)	27.9	(1.51)	-2.8	(1.10)	35.1	(2.91)	-37.5	(5.97)	0.0	(0.14)	25.5	(2.59)	471.4	(1.95)
Estonia	44.4	(2.74)	14.1	(1.80)	1.6	(1.43)	52.1	(4.52)	-18.7	(14.08)	-3.3	(0.44)	36.7	(2.45)	485.8	(2.02)
Finland	37.3	(3.60)	27.7	(1.66)	-2.5	(1.30)	10.4	(3.28)	-56.0	(13.09)	-0.1	(0.29)	51.5	(2.26)	500.6	(2.02)
France	47.1	(5.14)	12.5	(1.70)	-1.9	(1.12)	81.6	(4.04)	-11.6	(9.24)	0.2	(0.15)	25.9	(2.67)	516.5	(2.35)
Germany	34.4	(1.74)	9.2	(1.23)	-1.6	(0.74)	109.1	(2.16)	-13.2	(4.80)	0.2	(0.12)	27.2	(1.92)	458.0	(1.46)
Greece	22.6	(10.86)	15.9	(1.46)	1.5	(1.07)	41.2	(2.84)	-15.0	(7.82)	0.0	(0.18)	36.2	(2.55)	469.0	(2.04)
Hungary	25.6	(2.19)	8.3	(1.39)	0.9	(0.87)	74.8	(2.09)	2.8	(7.92)	0.0	(0.27)	21.4	(2.22)	494.1	(1.65)
Iceland	c	c	29.8	(2.56)	-5.1	(1.56)	-3.8	(5.12)	-52.2	(11.45)	-1.3	(0.40)	44.9	(2.59)	469.1	(4.23)
Ireland	18.2	(1.99)	29.7	(1.78)	-3.5	(1.44)	43.6	(2.68)	-32.8	(6.52)	-0.1	(0.20)	33.9	(3.62)	474.8	(2.77)
Israel	36.6	(3.85)	19.9	(1.90)	3.4	(1.04)	104.7	(2.10)	-11.0	(6.13)	1.5	(0.08)	29.4	(2.81)	460.1	(2.13)
Italy	36.1	(1.67)	4.5	(0.69)	-1.4	(0.42)	76.4	(1.07)	-29.7	(3.36)	0.2	(0.08)	24.0	(1.29)	491.4	(0.85)
Japan	a	a	4.1	(1.51)	0.1	(1.47)	144.2	(2.40)	c	c	c	c	27.9	(2.43)	508.6	(1.58)
Korea	31.2	(9.77)	12.9	(1.42)	1.9	(1.18)	64.9	(2.24)	a	a	a	a	30.6	(3.21)	537.7	(2.08)
Luxembourg	45.3	(1.95)	16.6	(1.31)	-2.6	(1.08)	62.0	(2.89)	-10.4	(5.11)	-0.2	(0.10)	33.0	(2.22)	435.7	(2.40)
Mexico	32.6	(1.59)	7.5	(0.92)	0.8	(0.34)	27.8	(0.80)	-41.9	(6.36)	-1.8	(0.15)	17.9	(1.03)	473.7	(1.02)
Netherlands	26.6	(2.04)	6.0	(1.52)	-1.2	(1.02)	106.7	(2.32)	-11.6	(5.72)	1.7	(0.14)	15.3	(1.85)	484.5	(2.33)
New Zealand	44.2	(4.15)	38.9	(1.82)	-1.7	(1.44)	56.3	(3.35)	-12.2	(3.84)	0.0	(0.10)	44.8	(2.62)	496.5	(2.44)
Norway	37.6	(18.19)	34.2	(2.00)	-3.4	(1.62)	31.1	(4.32)	-33.4	(7.52)	0.4	(0.25)	48.3	(2.56)	453.2	(2.87)
Poland	73.8	(4.44)	29.4	(1.59)	-1.8	(1.21)	19.4	(2.99)	c	c	c	c	44.2	(2.41)	498.9	(1.89)
Portugal	48.9	(1.71)	12.0	(0.94)	1.0	(0.64)	21.3	(1.33)	-5.3	(5.75)	0.0	(0.23)	22.9	(1.84)	518.6	(1.92)
Slovak Republic	34.2	(3.85)	14.7	(1.44)	-3.2	(0.98)	64.3	(6.30)	c	c	c	c	39.1	(2.58)	483.2	(2.33)
Slovenia	22.8	(3.41)	4.8	(1.28)	0.0	(1.25)	100.2	(2.74)	-23.4	(7.48)	-0.2	(0.24)	27.7	(2.16)	452.4	(1.63)
Spain	61.7	(1.21)	9.8	(0.83)	0.4	(0.64)	22.7	(1.25)	-29.7	(2.86)	0.4	(0.04)	18.0	(1.42)	511.3	(1.07)
Sweden	63.8	(6.69)	31.4	(1.82)	-1.3	(1.04)	49.0	(6.55)	-38.8	(8.53)	0.3	(0.34)	43.2	(2.41)	454.4	(3.62)
Switzerland	45.5	(2.75)	18.2	(1.27)	-1.0	(1.23)	59.5	(2.95)	-25.1	(3.99)	-0.7	(0.11)	27.0	(2.00)	488.8	(1.50)
Turkey	33.7	(1.96)	7.7	(1.50)	0.3	(0.61)	46.3	(1.70)	c	c	c	c	27.9	(1.74)	524.0	(1.59)
United Kingdom	35.9	(6.21)	27.7	(2.01)	-0.3	(1.51)	65.7	(2.49)	-13.6	(8.49)	-0.3	(0.13)	23.1	(2.48)	468.7	(1.73)
United States	36.3	(2.17)	23.5	(1.70)	4.4	(1.15)	50.4	(2.56)	-5.6	(5.57)	0.8	(0.14)	25.4	(2.36)	463.5	(2.01)
Partners																
Albania	11.9	(5.07)	20.8	(3.04)	3.2	(1.35)	43.0	(2.47)	c	c	c	c	56.5	(3.40)	421.5	(3.44)
Argentina	33.6	(2.50)	11.2	(1.96)	0.9	(0.87)	52.6	(2.03)	-27.0	(10.55)	0.5	(0.20)	24.0	(2.38)	439.7	(2.32)
Azerbaijan	13.2	(1.78)	10.5	(1.67)	1.3	(0.90)	36.4	(2.00)	-9.8	(12.34)	-0.3	(0.49)	22.6	(2.16)	390.9	(2.12)
Brazil	36.1	(1.23)	7.7	(1.54)	1.3	(0.57)	38.3	(1.25)	-71.7	(17.16)	-0.9	(0.47)	20.2	(1.63)	445.5	(1.33)
Bulgaria	27.8	(5.08)	15.7	(1.93)	0.2	(1.29)	75.7	(3.99)	c	c	c	c	42.1	(3.51)	423.7	(2.61)
Colombia	33.2	(1.12)	6.9	(2.01)	0.9	(0.72)	39.4	(1.53)	c	c	c	c	3.2	(2.17)	477.7	(1.83)
Croatia	31.8	(2.33)	10.3	(1.36)	-4.0	(0.99)	75.3	(2.01)	-13.0	(5.71)	-0.1	(0.22)	31.4	(2.56)	472.8	(1.69)
Dubai (UAE)	34.6	(1.56)	15.2	(1.52)	3.2	(1.03)	25.9	(3.13)	21.5	(3.25)	1.1	(0.05)	28.2	(3.94)	362.4	(2.92)
Hong Kong-China	33.6	(2.03)	-0.9	(1.70)	-1.0	(0.76)	41.9	(1.64)	23.4	(3.70)	-0.4	(0.06)	21.9	(2.42)	575.8	(1.83)
Indonesia	14.4	(2.00)	4.7	(2.44)	0.9	(0.62)	29.1	(1.83)	c	c	c	c	28.0	(1.48)	430.8	(2.46)
Jordan	47.6	(6.38)	17.7	(1.52)	0.7	(0.81)	26.9	(1.55)	-11.5	(7.50)	-0.2	(0.20)	48.1	(2.73)	415.5	(2.04)
Kazakhstan	22.2	(2.42)	16.2	(2.12)	-1.7	(1.31)	55.7	(2.70)	-12.2	(6.78)	0.0	(0.10)	38.1	(2.23)	411.1	(1.57)
Kyrgyzstan	20.5	(2.92)	18.3	(2.23)	1.7	(1.10)	75.2	(2.03)	-23.4	(21.78)	3.3	(0.50)	46.0	(2.45)	345.7	(1.83)
Latvia	43.8	(3.07)	16.2	(1.89)	-0.8	(1.35)	37.0	(2.77)	c	c	c	c	38.9	(2.36)	479.6	(1.77)
Liechtenstein	23.8	(7.40)	2.1	(4.18)	-5.3	(3.07)	112.5	(12.17)	-12.6	(10.22)	-0.7	(0.44)	20.3	(6.86)	499.8	(8.42)
Lithuania	27.4	(2.87)	18.1	(1.56)	0.2	(1.04)	44.0	(2.45)	c	c	c	c	51.1	(2.34)	447.6	(1.87)
Macao-China	36.7	(1.01)	1.8	(1.61)	-1.1	(0.78)	1.0	(4.75)	16.7	(2.17)	-0.1	(0.23)	14.1	(1.51)	511.0	(3.47)
Montenegro	22.9	(3.44)	12.1	(1.38)	-0.3	(1.05)	64.2	(6.54)	-1.8	(6.69)	-1.2	(0.32)	39.3	(2.63)	409.5	(2.58)
Panama	32.6	(3.41)	7.9	(2.42)	1.2	(0.79)	45.8	(2.60)	-3.4	(10.77)	-1.4	(0.16)	15.8	(4.48)	431.3	(3.22)
Peru	27.5	(1.23)	10.5	(2.05)	0.9	(0.64)	47.2	(1.46)	c	c	c	c	8.3	(2.17)	445.6	(1.59)
Qatar	30.7	(1.70)	5.3	(0.98)	0.4	(0.85)	12.7	(2.91)	31.5	(2.98)	1.7	(0.07)	31.4	(3.71)	302.5	(2.94)
Romania	19.6	(4.19)	10.7	(1.63)	-0.3	(0.79)	63.9	(2.34)	c	c	c	c	13.7	(2.56)	446.4	(1.70)
Russian Federation	31.0	(2.01)	18.2	(1.93)	-1.6	(1.40)	38.8	(3.32)	-9.1	(5.88)	-0.4	(0.22)	38.7	(2.28)	452.9	(1.89)
Serbia	21.3	(4.48)	9.2	(1.25)	-0.8	(0.74)	55.1	(3.42)	1.2	(5.65)	0.3	(0.13)	27.1	(2.22)	425.1	(1.60)
Shanghai-China	21.8	(3.34)	4.6	(1.41)	0.1	(0.85)	57.3	(1.48)	c	c	c	c	29.3	(1.98)	583.5	(2.04)
Singapore	28.9	(2.09)	22.2	(2.19)	-2.8	(1.14)	104.7	(2.86)	0.4	(4.21)	-1.0	(0.13)	24.6	(2.57)	590.2	(2.76)
Chinese Taipei	15.4	(4.12)	15.5	(1.50)	-1.2	(1.05)	82.8	(3.06)	c	c	c	c	36.8	(2.25)	515.6	(2.03)
Thailand	22.1	(2.05)	10.4	(1.54)	2.4	(0.66)	28.8	(1.31)	a	a	a	a	31.3	(1.78)	454.6	(1.67)
Trinidad and Tobago	35.3	(1.60)	-0.6	(2.00)	-0.2	(0.91)	123.2	(3.42)	-9.2	(13.59)	-0.7	(0.28)	40.4	(2.90)	484.9	(2.77)
Tunisia	49.7	(1.57)	3.7	(1.76)	0.7	(0.56)	17.8	(1.25)	c	c	c	c	14.4	(1.84)	449.6	(1.63)
Uruguay	41.4	(1.49)	12.4	(1.58)	0.5	(0.75)	29.7	(1.58)	c	c	c	c	30.1	(2.48)	464.2	(2.29)

StatLink http://dx.doi.org/10.1787/888932343171

Table A1.2 presents the results of the multilevel model. Column 1 in Table A1.2 estimates the score point difference that is associated with one grade level (or school year). This difference can be estimated for the 32 OECD countries in which a sizeable number of 15-year-olds in the PISA samples were enrolled in at least two different grades. The average score point difference between two grades is about 39 score points on the PISA reading scale. This implies that one school year corresponds to an average of 39 score points. Since 15-year-olds cannot be assumed to be distributed at random across the grade levels, adjustments had to be made for the above-mentioned contextual factors that may relate to the assignment of students to the different grade levels. These adjustments are documented in columns 2 to 7 of the table. While it is possible to estimate the typical performance difference among students in two adjacent grades net of the effects of selection and contextual factors, this difference cannot automatically be equated with the progress that students have made over the last school year but should be interpreted as a lower boundary of the progress achieved. This is not only because different students were assessed but also because the content of the PISA assessment was not expressly designed to match what students had learned in the preceding school year but more broadly to assess the cumulative outcome of learning in school up to age 15. For example, if the curriculum of the grades in which 15-year-olds are enrolled mainly includes material other than that assessed by PISA (which, in turn, may have been included in earlier school years) then the observed performance difference will underestimate student progress.

Student-level scale indices

Family wealth

The *index of family wealth* (WEALTH) is based on the students' responses on whether they had the following at home: a room of their own, a link to the Internet, a dishwasher (treated as a country-specific item), a DVD player, and three other country-specific items (some items in ST20); and their responses on the number of cellular phones, televisions, computers, cars and the rooms with a bath or shower (ST21).

Home educational resources

The *index of home educational resources* (HEDRES) is based on the items measuring the existence of educational resources at home including a desk and a quiet place to study, a computer that students can use for schoolwork, educational software, books to help with students' school work, technical reference books and a dictionary (some items in ST20).

Cultural possessions

The *index of cultural possessions* (CULTPOSS) is based on the students' responses to whether they had the following at home: classic literature, books of poetry and works of art (some items in ST20).

Economic, social and cultural status

The *PISA index of economic, social and cultural status* (ESCS) was derived from the following three indices: highest occupational status of parents (HISEI), highest educational level of parents in years of education according to ISCED (PARED), and home possessions (HOMEPOS). The index of home possessions (HOMEPOS) comprises all items on the indices of WEALTH, CULTPOSS and HEDRES, as well as books in the home recoded into a four-level categorical variable (0-10 books, 11-25 or 26-100 books, 101-200 or 201-500 books, more than 500 books).

The *PISA index of economic, social and cultural status* (ESCS) was derived from a principal component analysis of standardised variables (each variable has an OECD mean of 0 and a standard deviation of 1), taking the factor scores for the first principal component as measures of the index of economic, social and cultural status.

Principal component analysis was also performed for each participating country to determine to what extent the components of the index operate in similar ways across countries. The analysis revealed that patterns of factor loading were very similar across countries, with all three components contributing to a similar extent to the index. For the occupational component, the average factor loading was 0.80, ranging from 0.66 to 0.87 across countries. For the educational component, the average factor loading was 0.79, ranging from 0.69 to 0.87 across countries. For the home possession component, the average factor loading was 0.73, ranging from 0.60 to 0.84 across countries. The reliability of the index ranged from 0.41 to 0.81. These results support the cross-national validity of the *PISA index of economic, social and cultural status*.

The imputation of components for students missing data on one component was done on the basis of a regression on the other two variables, with an additional random error component. The final values on the *PISA index of economic, social and cultural status* (ESCS) have an OECD mean of 0 and a standard deviation of 1.

School-level simple indices

School and class size

The *index of school size* (SCHSIZE) was derived by summing up the number of girls and boys at a school (SC06).

Student-teacher ratio

Student-teacher ratio (STRATIO) was obtained by dividing the school size by the total number of teachers. The number of part-time teachers (SC09Q12) was weighted by 0.5 and the number of full-time teachers (SC09Q11) was weighted by 1.0 in the computation of this index.

Availability of computers

The *index of computer availability* (IRATCOMP) was derived from dividing the number of computers available for educational purposes available to students in the modal grade for 15-year-olds (SC10Q02) by the number of students in the modal grade for 15-year-olds (SC10Q01).

The *index of computers connected to the Internet* (COMPWEB) was derived from dividing the number of computers for educational purposes available to students in the modal grade for 15-year-olds that are connected to the web (SC10Q03) by the number of computers for educational purposes available to students in the modal grade for 15-year-olds (SC10Q02).

Quantity of teaching staff at school

The proportion of fully certified teachers (PROPCERT) was computed by dividing the number of fully certified teachers (SC09Q21 plus 0.5*SC09Q22) by the total number of teachers (SC09Q11 plus 0.5*SC09Q12). The proportion of teachers who have an ISCED 5A qualification (PROPQUAL) was calculated by dividing the number of these kind of teachers (SC09Q31 plus 0.5*SC09Q32) by the total number of teachers (SC09Q11 plus 0.5*SC09Q12).

School-level scale indices
School responsibility for resource allocation

School principals were asked to report whether "principals", "teachers", "school governing board", "regional or local education authority", or "national education authority" has a considerable responsibility for the following tasks (SC24): *i)* selecting teachers for hire; *ii)* firing teachers; *iii)* establishing teachers' starting salaries; *iv)* determining teachers' salaries increases; *v)* formulating the school budget; and *vi)* deciding on budget allocations within the school. The *index of school responsibility for resource allocation* (RESPRES) was derived from these six items. The ratio of the number of responsibility that "principals" and/or "teachers" have for these six items to the number of responsibility that "regional or local education authority" and/or "national education authority" have for these six items was computed. Higher values on this index indicate relatively more responsibility for schools than local, regional or national education authority. This index has an OECD mean of 0 and a standard deviation of 1.

School responsibility for curriculum and assessment

School principals were asked to report whether "principals", "teachers", "school governing board", "regional or local education authority", or "national education authority" has a considerable responsibility for the following tasks (SC24): *i)* establishing student assessment policies; *ii)* choosing which textbooks are used; *iii)* determining course content; and *iv)* deciding which courses are offered. The *index of school responsibility for curriculum and assessment* (RESPCURR) was derived from these four items. The ratio of the number of responsibility that "principals" and/or "teachers" have for these four items to the number of responsibility that "regional or local education authority" and/or "national education authority" have for these four items was computed. Higher values on this index indicate relatively more responsibility for schools than local, regional or national education authority. This index has an OECD mean of 0 and a standard deviation of 1.

Teacher shortage

The *index on teacher shortage* (TCSHORT) was derived from four items measuring school principals' perceptions of potential factors hindering instruction at their school (SC11). These factors are a lack of: *i)* qualified science teachers; *ii)* a lack of qualified mathematics teachers; *iii)* qualified <test language> teachers; and *iv)* qualified teachers of other subjects. Higher values on this index indicate school principals' reports of higher teacher shortage at a school.

School's educational resources

The *index on the school's educational resources* (SCMATEDU) was derived from seven items measuring school principals' perceptions of potential factors hindering instruction at their school (SC11). These factors are: *i)* shortage or inadequacy of science laboratory equipment; *ii)* shortage or inadequacy of instructional materials; *iii)* shortage or inadequacy of computers for instruction; *iv)* lack or inadequacy of Internet connectivity; *v)* shortage or inadequacy of computer software for instruction; *vi)* shortage or inadequacy of library materials; and *vii)* shortage or inadequacy of audio-visual resources. As all items were inverted for scaling, higher values on this index indicate better quality of educational resources.

Parent questionnaire scale indices
Parents' current support of their child's reading literacy

The *index of parents' current support of their child's reading literary* (CURSUPP) was derived from parents' reports on the frequency with which they or someone else in their home did the following with their child (PA08): *i)* discuss political or social issues; *ii)* discuss books, films or television programmes; *iii)* discuss how well the child is doing at school; *iv)* go to a bookstore or library with the child; *v)* talk with the child about what he/she is reading; and *vi)* help the child with his/her homework. Higher values on this index indicate greater parental support of child's reading literacy.

Parents' support of their child's reading literacy at the beginning of primary school

This *index of parents' support of their child's reading literacy at the beginning of primary school* (PRESUPP) was derived from parents' reports on the frequency with which they or someone else in their home undertook the following activities with their child when the child attended the first year of primary school (PA03): *i)* read books; *ii)* tell stories; *iii)* sing songs; *iv)* play with alphabet toys; *v)* talk about what parent had read; *vi)* play word games; *vii)* write letters or words; and *viii)* read aloud signs and labels. Higher values on this index indicate greater levels of parents' support.

ANNEX A2
THE PISA TARGET POPULATION, THE PISA SAMPLES AND THE DEFINITION OF SCHOOLS

Definition of the PISA target population

PISA 2009 provides an assessment of the cumulative yield of education and learning at a point at which most young adults are still enrolled in initial education.

A major challenge for an international survey is to ensure that international comparability of national target populations is guaranteed in such a venture.

Differences between countries in the nature and extent of pre-primary education and care, the age of entry into formal schooling and the institutional structure of educational systems do not allow the definition of internationally comparable grade levels of schooling. Consequently, international comparisons of educational performance typically define their populations with reference to a target age group. Some previous international assessments have defined their target population on the basis of the grade level that provides maximum coverage of a particular age cohort. A disadvantage of this approach is that slight variations in the age distribution of students across grade levels often lead to the selection of different target grades in different countries, or between education systems within countries, raising serious questions about the comparability of results across, and at times within, countries. In addition, because not all students of the desired age are usually represented in grade-based samples, there may be a more serious potential bias in the results if the unrepresented students are typically enrolled in the next higher grade in some countries and the next lower grade in others. This would exclude students with potentially higher levels of performance in the former countries and students with potentially lower levels of performance in the latter.

In order to address this problem, PISA uses an age-based definition for its target population, *i.e.* a definition that is not tied to the institutional structures of national education systems. PISA assesses students who were aged between 15 years and 3 (complete) months and 16 years and 2 (complete) months at the beginning of the assessment period, plus or minus a 1 month allowable variation, and who were enrolled in an educational institution with Grade 7 or higher, regardless of the grade levels or type of institution in which they were enrolled, and regardless of whether they were in full-time or part-time education. Educational institutions are generally referred to as schools in this publication, although some educational institutions (in particular, some types of vocational education establishments) may not be termed schools in certain countries. As expected from this definition, the average age of students across OECD countries was 15 years and 9 months. The range in country means was 2 months and 5 days (0.18 years), from the minimum country mean of 15 years and 8 months to the maximum country mean of 15 years and 10 months.

Given this definition of population, PISA makes statements about the knowledge and skills of a group of individuals who were born within a comparable reference period, but who may have undergone different educational experiences both in and outside of schools. In PISA, these knowledge and skills are referred to as the yield of education at an age that is common across countries. Depending on countries' policies on school entry, selection and promotion, these students may be distributed over a narrower or a wider range of grades across different education systems, tracks or streams. It is important to consider these differences when comparing PISA results across countries, as observed differences between students at age 15 may no longer appear as students' educational experiences converge later on.

If a country's scale scores in reading, scientific or mathematical literacy are significantly higher than those in another country, it cannot automatically be inferred that the schools or particular parts of the education system in the first country are more effective than those in the second. However, one can legitimately conclude that the cumulative impact of learning experiences in the first country, starting in early childhood and up to the age of 15, and embracing experiences both in school, home and beyond, have resulted in higher outcomes in the literacy domains that PISA measures.

The PISA target population did not include residents attending schools in a foreign country. It does, however, include foreign nationals attending schools in the country of assessment.

To accommodate countries that desired grade-based results for the purpose of national analyses, PISA 2009 provided a sampling option to supplement age-based sampling with grade-based sampling.

Population coverage

All countries attempted to maximise the coverage of 15-year-olds enrolled in education in their national samples, including students enrolled in special educational institutions. As a result, PISA 2009 reached standards of population coverage that are unprecedented in international surveys of this kind.

The sampling standards used in PISA permitted countries to exclude up to a total of 5% of the relevant population either by excluding schools or by excluding students within schools. All but 5 countries, Denmark (8.17%), Luxembourg (8.15%), Canada (6.00%), Norway (5.93%) and the United States (5.16%), achieved this standard, and in 36 countries and economies, the overall exclusion rate was less than 2%. When language exclusions were accounted for (*i.e.* removed from the overall exclusion rate), the United States no longer had an exclusion rate greater than 5%. For details, see *www.pisa.oecd.org*.

Exclusions within the above limits include:

- *At the school level:* i) schools that were geographically inaccessible or where the administration of the PISA assessment was not considered feasible; and ii) schools that provided teaching only for students in the categories defined under "within-school exclusions", such as schools for the blind. The percentage of 15-year-olds enrolled in such schools had to be less than 2.5% of the nationally desired target population [0.5% maximum for i) and 2% maximum for ii)]. The magnitude, nature and justification of school-level exclusions are documented in the *PISA 2009 Technical Report* (OECD, forthcoming).

- *At the student level:* i) students with an intellectual disability; ii) students with a functional disability; iii) students with limited assessment language proficiency; iv) other – a category defined by the national centres and approved by the international centre; and v) students taught in a language of instruction for the main domain for which no materials were available. Students could not be excluded solely because of low proficiency or common discipline problems. The percentage of 15-year-olds excluded within schools had to be less than 2.5% of the nationally desired target population.

Table A2.1 describes the target population of the countries participating in PISA 2009. Further information on the target population and the implementation of PISA sampling standards can be found in the *PISA 2009 Technical Report* (OECD, forthcoming).

- *Column 1* shows the **total number of 15-year-olds** according to the most recent available information, which in most countries meant the year 2008 as the year before the assessment.

- *Column 2* shows the number of 15-year-olds enrolled in schools in Grade 7 or above (as defined above), which is referred to as the **eligible population**.

- *Column 3* shows the **national desired target population**. Countries were allowed to exclude up to 0.5% of students *a priori* from the eligible population, essentially for practical reasons. The following *a priori* exclusions exceed this limit but were agreed with the PISA Consortium: Canada excluded 1.1% of its population from Territories and Aboriginal reserves; France excluded 1.7% of its students in its *territoires d'outre-mer* and other institutions; Indonesia excluded 4.7% of its students from four provinces because of security reasons; Kyrgyzstan excluded 2.3% of its population in remote, inaccessible schools; and Serbia excluded 2% of its students taught in Serbian in Kosovo.

- *Column 4* shows the **number of students enrolled in schools that were excluded from the national desired target population** either from the sampling frame or later in the field during data collection.

- *Column 5* shows the **size of the national desired target population after subtracting the students enrolled in excluded schools**. This is obtained by subtracting Column 4 from Column 3.

- *Column 6* shows the **percentage of students enrolled in excluded schools**. This is obtained by dividing Column 4 by Column 3 and multiplying by 100.

- *Column 7* shows the **number of students participating in PISA 2009**. Note that in some cases this number does not account for 15-year-olds assessed as part of additional national options.

- *Column 8* shows the **weighted number of participating students**, *i.e.* the number of students in the nationally defined target population that the PISA sample represents.

- Each country attempted to maximise the coverage of PISA's target population within the sampled schools. In the case of each sampled school, all eligible students, namely those 15 years of age, regardless of grade, were first listed. Sampled students who were to be excluded had still to be included in the sampling documentation, and a list drawn up stating the reason for their exclusion. *Column 9* indicates the **total number of excluded students,** which is further described and classified into specific categories in Table A2.2. *Column 10* indicates the **weighted number of excluded students,** *i.e.* the overall number of students in the nationally defined target population represented by the number of students excluded from the sample, which is also described and classified by exclusion categories in Table A2.2. Excluded students were excluded based on five categories: i) students with an intellectual disability – the student has a mental or emotional disability and is cognitively delayed such that he/she cannot perform in the PISA testing situation; ii) students with a functional disability – the student has a moderate to severe permanent physical disability such that he/she cannot perform in the PISA testing situation; iii) students with a limited assessment language proficiency – the student is unable to read or speak any of the languages of the assessment in the country and would be unable to overcome the language barrier in the testing situation (typically a student who has received less than one year of instruction in the languages of the assessment may be excluded); iv) other – a category defined by the national centres and approved by the international centre; and v) students taught in a language of instruction for the main domain for which no materials were available.

- *Column 11* shows the **percentage of students excluded within schools**. This is calculated as the weighted number of excluded students (Column 10), divided by the weighted number of excluded and participating students (Column 8 plus Column 10), then multiplied by 100.

[Part 1/2]

Table A2.1 **PISA target populations and samples**

		Population and sample information						
		Total population of 15-year-olds	Total enrolled population of 15-year-olds at Grade 7 or above	Total in national desired target population	Total school-level exclusions	Total in national desired target population after all school exclusions and before within-school exclusions	School-level exclusion rate (%)	Number of participating students	Weighted number of participating students
		(1)	(2)	(3)	(4)	(5)	(6)	(7)	(8)
OECD	Australia	286 334	269 669	269 669	7 057	262 612	2.62	14 251	240 851
	Austria	99 818	94 192	94 192	115	94 077	0.12	6 590	87 326
	Belgium	126 377	126 335	126 335	2 474	123 861	1.96	8 501	119 140
	Canada	430 791	426 590	422 052	2 370	419 682	0.56	23 207	360 286
	Chile	290 056	265 542	265 463	2 594	262 869	0.98	5 669	247 270
	Czech Republic	122 027	116 153	116 153	1 619	114 534	1.39	6 064	113 951
	Denmark	70 522	68 897	68 897	3 082	65 815	4.47	5 924	60 855
	Estonia	14 248	14 106	14 106	436	13 670	3.09	4 727	12 978
	Finland	66 198	66 198	66 198	1 507	64 691	2.28	5 810	61 463
	France	749 808	732 825	720 187	18 841	701 346	2.62	4 298	677 620
	Germany	852 044	852 044	852 044	7 138	844 906	0.84	4 979	766 993
	Greece	102 229	105 664	105 664	696	104 968	0.66	4 969	93 088
	Hungary	121 155	118 387	118 387	3 322	115 065	2.81	4 605	105 611
	Iceland	4 738	4 738	4 738	20	4 718	0.42	3 646	4 410
	Ireland	56 635	55 464	55 446	276	55 170	0.50	3 937	52 794
	Israel	122 701	112 254	112 254	1 570	110 684	1.40	5 761	103 184
	Italy	586 904	573 542	573 542	2 694	570 848	0.47	30 905	506 733
	Japan	1 211 642	1 189 263	1 189 263	22 955	1 166 308	1.93	6 088	1 113 403
	Korea	717 164	700 226	700 226	2 927	697 299	0.42	4 989	630 030
	Luxembourg	5 864	5 623	5 623	186	5 437	3.31	4 622	5 124
	Mexico	2 151 771	1 425 397	1 425 397	5 825	1 419 572	0.41	38 250	1 305 461
	Netherlands	199 000	198 334	198 334	6 179	192 155	3.12	4 760	183 546
	New Zealand	63 460	60 083	60 083	645	59 438	1.07	4 643	55 129
	Norway	63 352	62 948	62 948	1 400	61 548	2.22	4 660	57 367
	Poland	482 500	473 700	473 700	7 650	466 050	1.61	4 917	448 866
	Portugal	115 669	107 583	107 583	0	107 583	0.00	6 298	96 820
	Slovak Republic	72 826	72 454	72 454	1 803	70 651	2.49	4 555	69 274
	Slovenia	20 314	19 571	19 571	174	19 397	0.89	6 155	18 773
	Spain	433 224	425 336	425 336	3 133	422 203	0.74	25 887	387 054
	Sweden	121 486	121 216	121 216	2 323	118 893	1.92	4 567	113 054
	Switzerland	90 623	89 423	89 423	1 747	87 676	1.95	11 812	80 839
	Turkey	1 336 842	859 172	859 172	8 569	850 603	1.00	4 996	757 298
	United Kingdom	786 626	786 825	786 825	17 593	769 232	2.24	12 179	683 380
	United States	4 103 738	4 210 475	4 210 475	15 199	4 195 276	0.36	5 233	3 373 264
Partners	Albania	55 587	42 767	42 767	372	42 395	0.87	4 596	34 134
	Argentina	688 434	636 713	636 713	2 238	634 475	0.35	4 774	472 106
	Azerbaijan	185 481	184 980	184 980	1 886	183 094	1.02	4 727	105 886
	Brazil	3 292 022	2 654 489	2 654 489	15 571	2 638 918	0.59	20 127	2 080 159
	Bulgaria	80 226	70 688	70 688	1 369	69 319	1.94	4 507	57 833
	Colombia	893 057	582 640	582 640	412	582 228	0.07	7 921	522 388
	Croatia	48 491	46 256	46 256	535	45 721	1.16	4 994	43 065
	Dubai (UAE)	10 564	10 327	10 327	167	10 160	1.62	5 620	9 179
	Hong Kong-China	85 000	78 224	78 224	809	77 415	1.03	4 837	75 548
	Indonesia	4 267 801	3 158 173	3 010 214	10 458	2 999 756	0.35	5 136	2 259 118
	Jordan	117 732	107 254	107 254	0	107 254	0.00	6 486	104 056
	Kazakhstan	281 659	263 206	263 206	7 210	255 996	2.74	5 412	250 657
	Kyrgyzstan	116 795	93 989	91 793	1 149	90 644	1.25	4 986	78 493
	Latvia	28 749	28 149	28 149	943	27 206	3.35	4 502	23 362
	Liechtenstein	399	360	360	5	355	1.39	329	355
	Lithuania	51 822	43 967	43 967	522	43 445	1.19	4 528	40 530
	Macao-China	7 500	5 969	5 969	3	5 966	0.05	5 952	5 978
	Montenegro	8 500	8 493	8 493	10	8 483	0.12	4 825	7 728
	Panama	57 919	43 623	43 623	501	43 122	1.15	3 969	30 510
	Peru	585 567	491 514	490 840	984	489 856	0.20	5 985	427 607
	Qatar	10 974	10 665	10 665	114	10 551	1.07	9 078	9 806
	Romania	152 084	152 084	152 084	679	151 405	0.45	4 776	151 130
	Russian Federation	1 673 085	1 667 460	1 667 460	25 012	1 642 448	1.50	5 308	1 290 047
	Serbia	85 121	75 128	73 628	1 580	72 048	2.15	5 523	70 796
	Shanghai-China	112 000	100 592	100 592	1 287	99 305	1.28	5 115	97 045
	Singapore	54 982	54 212	54 212	633	53 579	1.17	5 283	51 874
	Chinese Taipei	329 249	329 189	329 189	1 778	327 411	0.54	5 831	297 203
	Thailand	949 891	763 679	763 679	8 438	755 241	1.10	6 225	691 916
	Trinidad and Tobago	19 260	17 768	17 768	0	17 768	0.00	4 778	14 938
	Tunisia	153 914	153 914	153 914	0	153 914	0.00	4 955	136 545
	Uruguay	53 801	43 281	43 281	30	43 251	0.07	5 957	33 971

Note: For a full explanation of the details in this table, please refer to the *PISA 2009 Technical Report* (OECD, forthcoming). The figure for total national population of 15-year-olds enrolled in Column 1 may occasionally be larger than the total number of 15-year-olds in Column 2 due to differing data sources. In Greece, Column 1 does not include immigrants but Column 2 does include immigrants.

StatLink ⟐⟐ http://dx.doi.org/10.1787/888932343190

[Part 2/2]

Table A2.1 **PISA target populations and samples**

	Population and sample information				Coverage indices		
	Number of excluded students	Weighted number of excluded students	Within-school exclusion rate (%)	Overall exclusion rate (%)	Coverage index 1: Coverage of national desired population	Coverage index 2: Coverage of national enrolled population	Coverage index 3: Coverage of 15-year-old population
	(9)	(10)	(11)	(12)	(13)	(14)	(15)
OECD							
Australia	313	4 389	1.79	4.36	0.956	0.956	0.841
Austria	45	607	0.69	0.81	0.992	0.992	0.875
Belgium	30	292	0.24	2.20	0.978	0.978	0.943
Canada	1 607	20 837	5.47	6.00	0.940	0.930	0.836
Chile	15	620	0.25	1.22	0.988	0.987	0.852
Czech Republic	24	423	0.37	1.76	0.982	0.982	0.934
Denmark	296	2 448	3.87	8.17	0.918	0.918	0.863
Estonia	32	97	0.74	3.81	0.962	0.962	0.911
Finland	77	717	1.15	3.40	0.966	0.966	0.928
France	1	304	0.04	2.66	0.973	0.957	0.904
Germany	28	3 591	0.47	1.30	0.987	0.987	0.900
Greece	142	2 977	3.10	3.74	0.963	0.963	0.911
Hungary	10	361	0.34	3.14	0.969	0.969	0.872
Iceland	187	189	4.10	4.50	0.955	0.955	0.931
Ireland	136	1 492	2.75	3.23	0.968	0.967	0.932
Israel	86	1 359	1.30	2.68	0.973	0.973	0.841
Italy	561	10 663	2.06	2.52	0.975	0.975	0.863
Japan	0	0	0.00	1.93	0.981	0.981	0.919
Korea	16	1 748	0.28	0.69	0.993	0.993	0.879
Luxembourg	196	270	5.01	8.15	0.919	0.919	0.874
Mexico	52	1 951	0.15	0.56	0.994	0.994	0.607
Netherlands	19	648	0.35	3.46	0.965	0.965	0.922
New Zealand	184	1 793	3.15	4.19	0.958	0.958	0.869
Norway	207	2 260	3.79	5.93	0.941	0.941	0.906
Poland	15	1 230	0.27	1.88	0.981	0.981	0.930
Portugal	115	1 544	1.57	1.57	0.984	0.984	0.837
Slovak Republic	106	1 516	2.14	4.58	0.954	0.954	0.951
Slovenia	43	138	0.73	1.61	0.984	0.984	0.924
Spain	775	12 673	3.17	3.88	0.961	0.961	0.893
Sweden	146	3 360	2.89	4.75	0.953	0.953	0.931
Switzerland	209	940	1.15	3.08	0.969	0.969	0.892
Turkey	11	1 497	0.20	1.19	0.988	0.988	0.566
United Kingdom	318	17 094	2.44	4.62	0.954	0.954	0.869
United States	315	170 542	4.81	5.16	0.948	0.948	0.822
Partners							
Albania	0	0	0.00	0.87	0.991	0.991	0.614
Argentina	14	1 225	0.26	0.61	0.994	0.994	0.686
Azerbaijan	0	0	0.00	1.02	0.990	0.990	0.571
Brazil	24	2 692	0.13	0.72	0.993	0.993	0.632
Bulgaria	0	0	0.00	1.94	0.981	0.981	0.721
Colombia	11	490	0.09	0.16	0.998	0.998	0.585
Croatia	34	273	0.63	1.78	0.982	0.982	0.888
Dubai (UAE)	5	7	0.07	1.69	0.983	0.983	0.869
Hong Kong-China	9	119	0.16	1.19	0.988	0.988	0.889
Indonesia	0	0	0.00	0.35	0.997	0.950	0.529
Jordan	24	443	0.42	0.42	0.996	0.996	0.884
Kazakhstan	82	3 844	1.51	4.21	0.958	0.958	0.890
Kyrgyzstan	86	1 384	1.73	2.96	0.970	0.948	0.672
Latvia	19	102	0.43	3.77	0.962	0.962	0.813
Liechtenstein	0	0	0.00	1.39	0.986	0.986	0.890
Lithuania	74	632	1.53	2.70	0.973	0.973	0.782
Macao-China	0	0	0.00	0.05	0.999	0.999	0.797
Montenegro	0	0	0.00	0.12	0.999	0.999	0.909
Panama	0	0	0.00	1.15	0.989	0.989	0.527
Peru	9	558	0.13	0.33	0.997	0.995	0.730
Qatar	28	28	0.28	1.35	0.986	0.986	0.894
Romania	0	0	0.00	0.45	0.996	0.996	0.994
Russian Federation	59	15 247	1.17	2.65	0.973	0.973	0.771
Serbia	10	133	0.19	2.33	0.977	0.957	0.832
Shanghai-China	7	130	0.13	1.41	0.986	0.986	0.866
Singapore	48	417	0.80	1.96	0.980	0.980	0.943
Chinese Taipei	32	1 662	0.56	1.09	0.989	0.989	0.903
Thailand	6	458	0.07	1.17	0.988	0.988	0.728
Trinidad and Tobago	11	36	0.24	0.24	0.998	0.998	0.776
Tunisia	7	184	0.13	0.13	0.999	0.999	0.887
Uruguay	14	67	0.20	0.26	0.997	0.997	0.631

Note: For a full explanation of the details in this table please refer to the *PISA 2009 Technical Report* (OECD, forthcoming). The figure for total national population of 15-year-olds enrolled in Column 1 may occasionally be larger than the total number of 15-year-olds in Column 2 due to differing data sources. In Greece, Column 1 does not include immigrants but Column 2 does include immigrants.

StatLink ⌐⌐⌐ http://dx.doi.org/10.1787/888932343190

[Part 1/1]

Table A2.2 **Exclusions**

		Student exclusions (unweighted)					Student exclusion (weighted)					
	Number of excluded students with a disability (Code 1)	Number of excluded students with a disability (Code 2)	Number of excluded students because of language (Code 3)	Number of excluded students for other reasons (Code 4)	Number of excluded students because of no materials available in the language of instruction (Code 5)	Total number of excluded students	Weighted number of excluded students with a disability (Code 1)	Weighted number of excluded students with a disability (Code 2)	Weighted number of excluded students because of language (Code 3)	Weighted number of excluded students for other reasons (Code 4)	Number of excluded students because of no materials available in the language of instruction (Code 5)	Total weighted number of excluded students
	(1)	(2)	(3)	(4)	(5)	(6)	(7)	(8)	(9)	(10)	(11)	(12)
OECD												
Australia	24	210	79	0	0	313	272	2 834	1 283	0	0	4 389
Austria	0	26	19	0	0	45	0	317	290	0	0	607
Belgium	3	17	10	0	0	30	26	171	95	0	0	292
Canada	49	1 458	100	0	0	1 607	428	19 082	1 326	0	0	20 837
Chile	5	10	0	0	0	15	177	443	0	0	0	620
Czech Republic	8	7	9	0	0	24	117	144	162	0	0	423
Denmark	13	182	35	66	0	296	165	1 432	196	656	0	2 448
Estonia	3	28	1	0	0	32	8	87	2	0	0	97
Finland	4	48	12	11	2	77	38	447	110	99	23	717
France	1	0	0	0	0	1	304	0	0	0	0	304
Germany	6	20	2	0	0	28	864	2 443	285	0	0	3 591
Greece	7	11	7	117	0	142	172	352	195	2 257	0	2 977
Hungary	0	1	0	9	0	10	0	48	0	313	0	361
Iceland	3	78	64	38	1	187	3	78	65	39	1	189
Ireland	4	72	25	35	0	136	51	783	262	396	0	1 492
Israel	10	69	7	0	0	86	194	1 049	116	0	0	1 359
Italy	45	348	168	0	0	561	748	6 241	3 674	0	0	10 663
Japan	0	0	0	0	0	0	0	0	0	0	0	0
Korea	7	9	0	0	0	16	994	753	0	0	0	1 748
Luxembourg	2	132	62	0	0	196	2	206	62	0	0	270
Mexico	25	25	2	0	0	52	1 010	905	36	0	0	1 951
Netherlands	6	13	0	0	0	19	178	470	0	0	0	648
New Zealand	19	84	78	0	3	184	191	824	749	0	29	1 793
Norway	8	160	39	0	0	207	90	1 756	414	0	0	2 260
Poland	2	13	0	0	0	15	169	1 061	0	0	0	1 230
Portugal	2	100	13	0	0	115	25	1 322	197	0	0	1 544
Slovak Republic	12	37	1	56	0	106	171	558	19	768	0	1 516
Slovenia	6	10	27	0	0	43	40	32	66	0	0	138
Spain	45	441	289	0	0	775	1 007	7 141	4 525	0	0	12 673
Sweden	115	0	31	0	0	146	2 628	0	732	0	0	3 360
Switzerland	11	106	92	0	0	209	64	344	532	0	0	940
Turkey	3	3	5	0	0	11	338	495	665	0	0	1 497
United Kingdom	40	247	31	0	0	318	2 438	13 482	1 174	0	0	17 094
United States	29	236	40	10	0	315	15 367	127 486	21 718	5 971	0	170 542
Partners												
Albania	0	0	0	0	0	0	0	0	0	0	0	0
Argentina	4	10	0	0	0	14	288	937	0	0	0	1 225
Azerbaijan	0	0	0	0	0	0	0	0	0	0	0	0
Brazil	21	3	0	0	0	24	2 495	197	0	0	0	2 692
Bulgaria	0	0	0	0	0	0	0	0	0	0	0	0
Colombia	7	2	2	0	0	11	200	48	242	0	0	490
Croatia	4	30	0	0	0	34	34	239	0	0	0	273
Dubai (UAE)	1	1	3	0	0	5	2	2	3	0	0	7
Hong Kong-China	0	9	0	0	0	9	0	119	0	0	0	119
Indonesia	0	0	0	0	0	0	0	0	0	0	0	0
Jordan	11	7	6	0	0	24	166	149	127	0	0	443
Kazakhstan	10	17	0	0	55	82	429	828	0	0	2 587	3 844
Kyrgyzstan	68	13	5	0	0	86	1 093	211	80	0	0	1 384
Latvia	6	8	5	0	0	19	25	44	33	0	0	102
Liechtenstein	0	0	0	0	0	0	0	0	0	0	0	0
Lithuania	4	69	1	0	0	74	33	590	9	0	0	632
Macao-China	0	0	0	0	0	0	0	0	0	0	0	0
Montenegro	0	0	0	0	0	0	0	0	0	0	0	0
Panama	0	0	0	0	0	0	0	0	0	0	0	0
Peru	4	5	0	0	0	9	245	313	0	0	0	558
Qatar	9	18	1	0	0	28	9	18	1	0	0	28
Romania	0	0	0	0	0	0	0	0	0	0	0	0
Russian Federation	11	47	1	0	0	59	2 081	13 010	157	0	0	15 247
Serbia	4	5	0	0	1	10	66	53	0	0	13	133
Shanghai-China	1	6	0	0	0	7	19	111	0	0	0	130
Singapore	2	22	24	0	0	48	17	217	182	0	0	417
Chinese Taipei	13	19	0	0	0	32	684	977	0	0	0	1 662
Thailand	0	5	1	0	0	6	0	260	198	0	0	458
Trinidad and Tobago	1	10	0	0	0	11	3	33	0	0	0	36
Tunisia	4	1	2	0	0	7	104	21	58	0	0	184
Uruguay	2	9	3	0	0	14	14	34	18	0	0	67

Exclusion codes:
Code 1 Functional disability – student has a moderate to severe permanent physical disability.
Code 2 Intellectual disability – student has a mental or emotional disability and has either been tested as cognitively delayed or is considered in the professional opinion of qualified staff to be cognitively delayed.
Code 3 Limited assessment language proficiency – student is not a native speaker of any of the languages of the assessment in the country and has been resident in the country for less than one year.
Code 4 Other defined by the national centres and approved by the international centre.
Code 5 No materials available in the language of instruction.
Note: For a full explanation of other details in this table, please refer to the *PISA 2009 Technical Report* (OECD, forthcoming).

StatLink ⌐⌐∎⌐ http://dx.doi.org/10.1787/888932343190

- **Column 12** shows the **overall exclusion rate**, which represents the weighted percentage of the national desired target population excluded from PISA either through school-level exclusions or through the exclusion of students within schools. It is calculated as the school-level exclusion rate (Column 6 divided by 100) plus within-school exclusion rate (Column 11 divided by 100) multiplied by 1 minus the school-level exclusion rate (Column 6 divided by 100). This result is then multiplied by 100. Five countries, Denmark, Luxembourg, Canada, Norway and the United States, had exclusion rates higher than 5%. When language exclusions were accounted for (*i.e.* removed from the overall exclusion rate), the United States no longer had an exclusion rate greater than 5%.

- **Column 13** presents an **index of the extent to which the national desired target population is covered by the PISA sample**. Denmark, Luxembourg, Canada, Norway and the United States were the only countries where the coverage is below 95%.

- **Column 14** presents an **index of the extent to which 15-year-olds enrolled in schools are covered by the PISA sample**. The index measures the overall proportion of the national enrolled population that is covered by the non-excluded portion of the student sample. The index takes into account both school-level and student-level exclusions. Values close to 100 indicate that the PISA sample represents the entire education system as defined for PISA 2009. The index is the weighted number of participating students (Column 8) divided by the weighted number of participating and excluded students (Column 8 plus Column 10), times the nationally defined target population (Column 5) divided by the eligible population (Column 2) (times 100).

- **Column 15** presents an **index of the coverage of the 15-year-old population**. This index is the weighted number of participating students (Column 8) divided by the total population of 15-year-old students (Column 1).

This high level of coverage contributes to the comparability of the assessment results. For example, even assuming that the excluded students would have systematically scored worse than those who participated, and that this relationship is moderately strong, an exclusion rate in the order of 5% would likely lead to an overestimation of national mean scores of less than 5 score points (on a scale with an international mean of 500 score points and a standard deviation of 100 score points). This assessment is based on the following calculations: if the correlation between the propensity of exclusions and student performance is 0.3, resulting mean scores would likely be overestimated by 1 score point if the exclusion rate is 1%, by 3 score points if the exclusion rate is 5%, and by 6 score points if the exclusion rate is 10%. If the correlation between the propensity of exclusions and student performance is 0.5, resulting mean scores would be overestimated by 1 score point if the exclusion rate is 1%, by 5 score points if the exclusion rate is 5%, and by 10 score points if the exclusion rate is 10%. For this calculation, a model was employed that assumes a bivariate normal distribution for performance and the propensity to participate. For details, see the *PISA 2009 Technical Report* (OECD, forthcoming).

Sampling procedures and response rates

The accuracy of any survey results depends on the quality of the information on which national samples are based as well as on the sampling procedures. Quality standards, procedures, instruments and verification mechanisms were developed for PISA that ensured that national samples yielded comparable data and that the results could be compared with confidence.

Most PISA samples were designed as two-stage stratified samples (where countries applied different sampling designs, these are documented in the *PISA 2009 Technical Report* [OECD, forthcoming]). The first stage consisted of sampling individual schools in which 15-year-old students could be enrolled. Schools were sampled systematically with probabilities proportional to size, the measure of size being a function of the estimated number of eligible (15-year-old) students enrolled. A minimum of 150 schools were selected in each country (where this number existed), although the requirements for national analyses often required a somewhat larger sample. As the schools were sampled, replacement schools were simultaneously identified, in case a sampled school chose not to participate in PISA 2009.

In the case of Iceland, Liechtenstein, Luxembourg, Macao-China and Qatar, all schools and all eligible students within schools were included in the sample.

Experts from the PISA Consortium performed the sample selection process for most participating countries and monitored it closely in those countries that selected their own samples. The second stage of the selection process sampled students within sampled schools. Once schools were selected, a list of each sampled school's 15-year-old students was prepared. From this list, 35 students were then selected with equal probability (all 15-year-old students were selected if fewer than 35 were enrolled). The number of students to be sampled per school could deviate from 35, but could not be less than 20.

Data-quality standards in PISA required minimum participation rates for schools as well as for students. These standards were established to minimise the potential for response biases. In the case of countries meeting these standards, it was likely that any bias resulting from non-response would be negligible, *i.e.* typically smaller than the sampling error.

A minimum response rate of 85% was required for the schools initially selected. Where the initial response rate of schools was between 65 and 85%, however, an acceptable school response rate could still be achieved through the use of replacement schools. This procedure brought with it a risk of increased response bias. Participating countries were, therefore, encouraged to persuade as many of the schools in the original sample as possible to participate. Schools with a student participation rate between 25% and 50% were not regarded as participating schools, but data from these schools were included in the database and contributed to the various estimations. Data from schools with a student participation rate of less than 25% were excluded from the database.

[Part 1/2]
Table A2.3 **Response rates**

		Initial sample – before school replacement					Final sample – after school replacement		
		Weighted school participation rate before replacement (%)	Weighted number of responding schools (weighted also by enrolment)	Weighted number of schools sampled (responding and non-responding) (weighted also by enrolment)	Number of responding schools (unweighted)	Number of responding and non-responding schools (unweighted)	Weighted school participation rate after replacement (%)	Weighted number of responding schools (weighted also by enrolment)	Weighted number of schools sampled (responding and non-responding) (weighted also by enrolment)
		(1)	(2)	(3)	(4)	(5)	(6)	(7)	(8)
OECD	Australia	97.78	265 659	271 696	342	357	98.85	268 780	271 918
	Austria	93.94	88 551	94 261	280	291	93.94	88 551	94 261
	Belgium	88.76	112 594	126 851	255	292	95.58	121 291	126 899
	Canada	88.04	362 152	411 343	893	1 001	89.64	368 708	411 343
	Chile	94.34	245 583	260 331	189	201	99.04	257 594	260 099
	Czech Republic	83.09	94 696	113 961	226	270	97.40	111 091	114 062
	Denmark	83.94	55 375	65 967	264	325	90.75	59 860	65 964
	Estonia	100.00	13 230	13 230	175	175	100.00	13 230	13 230
	Finland	98.65	62 892	63 751	201	204	100.00	63 748	63 751
	France	94.14	658 769	699 776	166	177	94.14	658 769	699 776
	Germany	98.61	826 579	838 259	223	226	100.00	838 259	838 259
	Greece	98.19	98 710	100 529	181	184	99.40	99 925	100 529
	Hungary	98.21	101 523	103 378	184	190	99.47	103 067	103 618
	Iceland	98.46	4 488	4 558	129	141	98.46	4 488	4 558
	Ireland	87.18	48 821	55 997	139	160	88.44	49 526	55 997
	Israel	92.03	103 141	112 069	170	186	95.40	106 918	112 069
	Italy	94.27	532 432	564 811	1 054	1 108	99.08	559 546	564 768
	Japan	87.77	999 408	1 138 694	171	196	94.99	1 081 662	1 138 694
	Korea	100.00	683 793	683 793	157	157	100.00	683 793	683 793
	Luxembourg	100.00	5 437	5 437	39	39	100.00	5 437	5 437
	Mexico	95.62	1 338 291	1 399 638	1 512	1 560	97.71	1 367 668	1 399 730
	Netherlands	80.40	154 471	192 140	155	194	95.54	183 555	192 118
	New Zealand	84.11	49 917	59 344	148	179	91.00	54 130	59 485
	Norway	89.61	55 484	61 920	183	207	96.53	59 759	61 909
	Poland	88.16	409 513	464 535	159	187	97.70	453 855	464 535
	Portugal	93.61	102 225	109 205	201	216	98.43	107 535	109 251
	Slovak Republic	93.33	67 284	72 092	180	191	99.01	71 388	72 105
	Slovenia	98.36	19 798	20 127	337	352	98.36	19 798	20 127
	Spain	99.53	422 692	424 705	888	892	99.53	422 692	424 705
	Sweden	99.91	120 693	120 802	189	191	99.91	120 693	120 802
	Switzerland	94.25	81 005	85 952	413	429	98.71	84 896	86 006
	Turkey	100.00	849 830	849 830	170	170	100.00	849 830	849 830
	United Kingdom	71.06	523 271	736 341	418	549	87.35	643 027	736 178
	United States	67.83	2 673 852	3 941 908	140	208	77.50	3 065 651	3 955 606
Partners	Albania	97.29	39 168	40 259	177	182	99.37	39 999	40 253
	Argentina	97.18	590 215	607 344	194	199	99.42	603 817	607 344
	Azerbaijan	99.86	168 646	168 890	161	162	100.00	168 890	168 890
	Brazil	93.13	2 435 250	2 614 824	899	976	94.75	2 477 518	2 614 806
	Bulgaria	98.16	56 922	57 991	173	178	99.10	57 823	58 346
	Colombia	90.21	507 649	562 728	260	285	94.90	533 899	562 587
	Croatia	99.19	44 561	44 926	157	159	99.86	44 862	44 926
	Dubai (UAE)	100.00	10 144	10 144	190	190	100.00	10 144	10 144
	Hong Kong-China	69.19	53 800	77 758	108	156	96.75	75 232	77 758
	Indonesia	94.54	2 337 438	2 472 502	172	183	100.00	2 473 528	2 473 528
	Jordan	100.00	105 906	105 906	210	210	100.00	105 906	105 906
	Kazakhstan	100.00	257 427	257 427	199	199	100.00	257 427	257 427
	Kyrgyzstan	98.53	88 412	89 733	171	174	99.47	89 260	89 733
	Latvia	97.46	26 986	27 689	180	185	99.39	27 544	27 713
	Liechtenstein	100.00	356	356	12	12	100.00	356	356
	Lithuania	98.13	41 759	42 555	192	197	99.91	42 526	42 564
	Macao-China	100.00	5 966	5 966	45	45	100.00	5 966	5 966
	Montenegro	100.00	8 527	8 527	52	52	100.00	8 527	8 527
	Panama	82.58	33 384	40 426	180	220	83.76	33 779	40 329
	Peru	100.00	480 640	480 640	240	240	100.00	480 640	480 640
	Qatar	97.30	10 223	10 507	149	154	97.30	10 223	10 507
	Romania	100.00	150 114	150 114	159	159	100.00	150 114	150 114
	Russian Federation	100.00	1 392 765	1 392 765	213	213	100.00	1 392 765	1 392 765
	Serbia	99.21	70 960	71 524	189	191	99.97	71 504	71 524
	Shanghai-China	99.32	98 841	99 514	151	152	100.00	99 514	99 514
	Singapore	96.19	51 552	53 592	168	175	97.88	52 454	53 592
	Chinese Taipei	99.34	322 005	324 141	157	158	100.00	324 141	324 141
	Thailand	98.01	737 225	752 193	225	230	100.00	752 392	752 392
	Trinidad and Tobago	97.21	17 180	17 673	155	160	97.21	17 180	17 673
	Tunisia	100.00	153 198	153 198	165	165	100.00	153 198	153 198
	Uruguay	98.66	42 820	43 400	229	233	98.66	42 820	43 400

StatLink http://dx.doi.org/10.1787/888932343190

[Part 2/2]

Table A2.3 **Response rates**

		Final sample – after school replacement		Final sample – students within schools after school replacement				
		Number of responding schools (unweighted)	Number of responding and non-responding schools (unweighted)	Weighted student participation rate after replacement (%)	Number of students assessed (weighted)	Number of students sampled (assessed and absent) (weighted)	Number of students assessed (unweighted)	Number of students sampled (assessed and absent) (unweighted)
		(9)	(10)	(11)	(12)	(13)	(14)	(15)
OECD	Australia	345	357	86.05	205 234	238 498	14 060	16 903
	Austria	280	291	88.63	72 793	82 135	6 568	7 587
	Belgium	275	292	91.38	104 263	114 097	8 477	9 245
	Canada	908	1 001	79.52	257 905	324 342	22 383	27 603
	Chile	199	201	92.88	227 541	244 995	5 663	6 097
	Czech Republic	260	270	90.75	100 685	110 953	6 049	6 656
	Denmark	285	325	89.29	49 236	55 139	5 924	6 827
	Estonia	175	175	94.06	12 208	12 978	4 727	5 023
	Finland	203	204	92.27	56 709	61 460	5 810	6 309
	France	166	177	87.12	556 054	638 284	4 272	4 900
	Germany	226	226	93.93	720 447	766 993	4 979	5 309
	Greece	183	184	95.95	88 875	92 631	4 957	5 165
	Hungary	187	190	93.25	97 923	105 015	4 605	4 956
	Iceland	129	141	83.91	3 635	4 332	3 635	4 332
	Ireland	141	160	83.81	39 248	46 830	3 896	4 654
	Israel	176	186	89.45	88 480	98 918	5 761	6 440
	Italy	1 095	1 108	92.13	462 655	502 190	30 876	33 390
	Japan	185	196	95.32	1 010 801	1 060 382	6 077	6 377
	Korea	157	157	98.76	622 187	630 030	4 989	5 057
	Luxembourg	39	39	95.57	4 897	5 124	4 622	4 833
	Mexico	1 531	1 560	95.13	1 214 827	1 276 982	38 213	40 125
	Netherlands	185	194	89.78	157 912	175 897	4 747	5 286
	New Zealand	161	179	84.65	42 452	50 149	4 606	5 476
	Norway	197	207	89.92	49 785	55 366	4 660	5 194
	Poland	179	187	85.87	376 767	438 739	4 855	5 674
	Portugal	212	216	87.11	83 094	95 386	6 263	7 169
	Slovak Republic	189	191	93.03	63 854	68 634	4 555	4 898
	Slovenia	337	352	90.92	16 777	18 453	6 135	6 735
	Spain	888	892	89.60	345 122	385 164	25 871	28 280
	Sweden	189	191	92.97	105 026	112 972	4 567	4 912
	Switzerland	425	429	93.58	74 712	79 836	11 810	12 551
	Turkey	170	170	97.85	741 029	757 298	4 996	5 108
	United Kingdom	481	549	86.96	520 121	598 110	12 168	14 046
	United States	160	208	86.99	2 298 889	2 642 598	5 165	5 951
Partners	Albania	181	182	95.39	32 347	33 911	4 596	4 831
	Argentina	198	199	88.25	414 166	469 285	4 762	5 423
	Azerbaijan	162	162	99.14	105 095	106 007	4 691	4 727
	Brazil	926	976	89.04	1 767 872	1 985 479	19 901	22 715
	Bulgaria	176	178	97.34	56 096	57 630	4 499	4 617
	Colombia	274	285	92.83	462 602	498 331	7 910	8 483
	Croatia	158	159	93.76	40 321	43 006	4 994	5 326
	Dubai (UAE)	190	190	90.39	8 297	9 179	5 620	6 218
	Hong Kong-China	151	156	93.19	68 142	73 125	4 837	5 195
	Indonesia	183	183	96.91	2 189 287	2 259 118	5 136	5 313
	Jordan	210	210	95.85	99 734	104 056	6 486	6 777
	Kazakhstan	199	199	98.49	246 872	250 657	5 412	5 489
	Kyrgyzstan	173	174	98.04	76 523	78 054	4 986	5 086
	Latvia	184	185	91.27	21 241	23 273	4 502	4 930
	Liechtenstein	12	12	92.68	329	355	329	355
	Lithuania	196	197	93.36	37 808	40 495	4 528	4 854
	Macao-China	45	45	99.57	5 952	5 978	5 952	5 978
	Montenegro	52	52	95.43	7 375	7 728	4 825	5 062
	Panama	183	220	88.67	22 666	25 562	3 913	4 449
	Peru	240	240	96.35	412 011	427 607	5 985	6 216
	Qatar	149	154	93.63	8 990	9 602	8 990	9 602
	Romania	159	159	99.47	150 331	151 130	4 776	4 803
	Russian Federation	213	213	96.77	1 248 353	1 290 047	5 308	5 502
	Serbia	190	191	95.37	67 496	70 775	5 522	5 804
	Shanghai-China	152	152	98.89	95 966	97 045	5 115	5 175
	Singapore	171	175	91.04	46 224	50 775	5 283	5 809
	Chinese Taipei	158	158	95.30	283 239	297 203	5 831	6 108
	Thailand	230	230	97.37	673 688	691 916	6 225	6 396
	Trinidad and Tobago	155	160	85.92	12 275	14 287	4 731	5 518
	Tunisia	165	165	96.93	132 354	136 545	4 955	5 113
	Uruguay	229	233	87.03	29 193	33 541	5 924	6 815

StatLink ▨▧▤ http://dx.doi.org/10.1787/888932343190

PISA 2009 also required a minimum participation rate of 80% of students within participating schools. This minimum participation rate had to be met at the national level, not necessarily by each participating school. Follow-up sessions were required in schools in which too few students had participated in the original assessment sessions. Student participation rates were calculated over all original schools, and also over all schools, whether original sample or replacement schools, and from the participation of students in both the original assessment and any follow-up sessions. A student who participated in the original or follow-up cognitive sessions was regarded as a participant. Those who attended only the questionnaire session were included in the international database and contributed to the statistics presented in this publication if they provided at least a description of their father's or mother's occupation.

Table A2.3 shows the response rates for students and schools, before and after replacement.

- *Column 1* shows the **weighted participation rate of schools before replacement**. This is obtained by dividing Column 2 by Column 3.

- *Column 2* shows the **weighted number of responding schools before school replacement** (weighted by student enrolment).

- *Column 3* shows the **weighted number of sampled schools before school replacement** (including both responding and non-responding schools, weighted by student enrolment).

- *Column 4* shows the unweighted number **of responding schools before school replacement**.

- *Column 5* shows the unweighted **number of responding and non-responding schools before school replacement**.

- *Column 6* shows the **weighted participation rate of schools after replacement**. This is obtained by dividing Column 7 by Column 8.

- *Column 7* shows the **weighted number of responding schools after school replacement** (weighted by student enrolment).

- *Column 8* shows the **weighted number of schools sampled after school replacement** (including both responding and non-responding schools, weighted by student enrolment).

- *Column 9* shows the unweighted number of responding schools after school replacement.

- *Column 10* shows the unweighted number of responding and non-responding schools after school replacement.

- *Column 11* shows the **weighted student participation rate after replacement**. This is obtained by dividing Column 12 by Column 13.

- *Column 12* shows the **weighted number of students assessed**.

- *Column 13* shows the **weighted number of students sampled** (including both students who were assessed and students who were absent on the day of the assessment).

- *Column 14* shows the **unweighted number of students assessed.** Note that any students in schools with student-response rates less than 50% were not included in these rates (both weighted and unweighted).

- *Column 15* shows the **unweighted number of students sampled** (including both students that were assessed and students who were absent on the day of the assessment). Note that any students in schools where fewer than half of the eligible students were assessed were not included in these rates (neither weighted nor unweighted).

Definition of schools

In some countries, sub-units within schools were sampled instead of schools and this may affect the estimation of the between-school variance components. In Austria, the Czech Republic, Germany, Hungary, Japan, Romania and Slovenia, schools with more than one study programme were split into the units delivering these programmes. In the Netherlands, for schools with both lower and upper secondary programmes, schools were split into units delivering each programme level. In the Flemish Community of Belgium, in the case of multi-campus schools, implantations (campuses) were sampled, whereas in the French Community, in the case of multi-campus schools, the larger administrative units were sampled. In Australia, for schools with more than one campus, the individual campuses were listed for sampling. In Argentina, Croatia and Dubai (UAE), schools that had more than one campus had the locations listed for sampling. In Spain, the schools in the Basque region with multi-linguistic models were split into linguistic models for sampling.

Grade levels

Students assessed in PISA 2009 are at various grade levels. The percentage of students at each grade level is presented by country in Table A2.4a and by gender within each country in Table A2.4b.

[Part 1/1]

Table A2.4a **Percentage of students at each grade level**

		7th grade		8th grade		9th grade		10th grade		11th grade		12th grade	
		%	S.E.	%	S.E.	%	S.E.	%	S.E.	%	S.E.	%	S.E.
OECD	Australia	0.0	(0.0)	0.1	(0.0)	10.4	(0.6)	70.8	(0.6)	18.6	(0.6)	0.1	(0.0)
	Austria	0.7	(0.2)	6.2	(1.0)	42.4	(1.0)	50.7	(1.0)	0.0	(0.0)	0.0	c
	Belgium	0.4	(0.2)	5.5	(0.5)	32.0	(0.6)	60.8	(0.7)	1.2	(0.1)	0.0	(0.0)
	Canada	0.0	(0.0)	1.2	(0.2)	13.6	(0.5)	84.1	(0.5)	1.1	(0.1)	0.0	(0.0)
	Chile	1.0	(0.2)	3.9	(0.5)	20.5	(0.8)	69.4	(1.0)	5.2	(0.3)	0.0	(0.0)
	Czech Republic	0.5	(0.2)	3.8	(0.3)	48.9	(1.0)	46.7	(1.1)	0.0	c	0.0	c
	Denmark	0.1	(0.0)	14.7	(0.6)	83.5	(0.8)	1.7	(0.5)	0.0	c	0.0	c
	Estonia	1.6	(0.3)	24.0	(0.7)	72.4	(0.9)	1.8	(0.3)	0.1	(0.1)	0.0	c
	Finland	0.5	(0.1)	11.8	(0.5)	87.3	(0.5)	0.0	c	0.4	(0.1)	0.0	c
	France	1.3	(0.9)	3.6	(0.7)	34.4	(1.2)	56.6	(1.5)	4.0	(0.7)	0.1	(0.0)
	Germany	1.2	(0.2)	11.0	(0.5)	54.8	(0.8)	32.5	(0.8)	0.4	(0.1)	0.0	c
	Greece	0.4	(0.2)	1.4	(0.5)	5.5	(0.8)	92.7	(1.0)	0.0	c	0.0	c
	Hungary	2.8	(0.6)	7.6	(1.1)	67.1	(1.4)	22.4	(0.9)	0.1	(0.1)	0.0	(0.0)
	Iceland	0.0	c	0.0	c	0.0	c	98.3	(0.1)	1.7	(0.1)	0.0	c
	Ireland	0.1	(0.0)	2.4	(0.3)	59.1	(1.0)	24.0	(1.4)	14.4	(1.1)	0.0	c
	Israel	0.0	c	0.3	(0.1)	17.9	(1.0)	81.3	(1.0)	0.5	(0.2)	0.0	(0.0)
	Italy	0.1	(0.1)	1.4	(0.3)	16.9	(0.4)	78.4	(0.6)	3.2	(0.3)	0.0	c
	Japan	0.0	c	0.0	c	0.0	c	100.0	(0.0)	0.0	c	0.0	c
	Korea	0.0	c	0.0	(0.0)	4.2	(0.9)	95.1	(0.9)	0.7	(0.1)	0.0	c
	Luxembourg	0.6	(0.1)	11.6	(0.2)	51.6	(0.3)	36.0	(0.2)	0.3	(0.0)	0.0	c
	Mexico	1.7	(0.1)	7.4	(0.3)	34.5	(0.8)	55.6	(0.9)	0.7	(0.2)	0.0	(0.0)
	Netherlands	0.2	(0.2)	2.7	(0.3)	46.2	(1.1)	50.5	(1.1)	0.5	(0.1)	0.0	c
	New Zealand	0.0	c	0.0	c	0.0	(0.0)	5.9	(0.4)	88.8	(0.5)	5.3	(0.3)
	Norway	0.0	c	0.0	c	0.5	(0.1)	99.3	(0.2)	0.2	(0.1)	0.0	c
	Poland	1.0	(0.2)	4.5	(0.4)	93.6	(0.6)	0.9	(0.3)	0.0	c	0.0	c
	Portugal	2.3	(0.3)	9.0	(0.8)	27.9	(1.6)	60.4	(2.2)	0.4	(0.1)	0.0	c
	Slovak Republic	1.0	(0.2)	2.6	(0.3)	35.7	(1.4)	56.9	(1.6)	3.8	(0.8)	0.0	(0.0)
	Slovenia	0.0	c	0.1	(0.1)	3.0	(0.7)	90.7	(0.7)	6.2	(0.2)	0.0	c
	Spain	0.1	(0.0)	9.9	(0.4)	26.5	(0.6)	63.4	(0.7)	0.0	(0.0)	0.0	c
	Sweden	0.1	(0.1)	3.2	(0.3)	95.1	(0.6)	1.6	(0.5)	0.0	c	0.0	c
	Switzerland	0.6	(0.1)	15.5	(0.9)	61.7	(1.3)	21.0	(1.1)	1.2	(0.5)	0.0	(0.0)
	Turkey	0.7	(0.1)	3.5	(0.8)	25.2	(1.3)	66.6	(1.5)	3.8	(0.3)	0.2	(0.1)
	United Kingdom	0.0	c	0.0	c	0.0	c	1.2	(0.1)	98.0	(0.1)	0.8	(0.0)
	United States	0.0	c	0.1	(0.1)	10.9	(0.8)	68.5	(1.0)	20.3	(0.7)	0.1	(0.1)
	OECD average	0.8	(0.1)	5.8	(0.1)	37.0	(0.2)	52.9	(0.2)	9.9	(0.1)	0.5	(0.0)
Partners	Albania	0.4	(0.1)	2.2	(0.3)	50.9	(2.0)	46.4	(2.0)	0.1	(0.0)	0.0	c
	Argentina	4.7	(0.9)	12.9	(1.3)	20.4	(1.2)	57.8	(2.1)	4.3	(0.5)	0.0	c
	Azerbaijan	0.6	(0.2)	5.3	(0.5)	49.4	(1.3)	44.3	(1.3)	0.4	(0.1)	0.0	c
	Brazil	6.8	(0.4)	18.0	(0.7)	37.5	(0.8)	35.7	(0.8)	2.1	(0.1)	0.0	c
	Bulgaria	1.5	(0.3)	6.1	(0.6)	88.7	(0.9)	3.8	(0.6)	0.0	c	0.0	c
	Colombia	4.4	(0.5)	10.3	(0.7)	22.1	(0.8)	42.3	(1.0)	21.0	(1.0)	0.0	c
	Croatia	0.0	c	0.2	(0.2)	77.5	(0.4)	22.3	(0.4)	0.0	c	0.0	c
	Dubai (UAE)	1.1	(0.1)	3.4	(0.1)	14.8	(0.4)	56.9	(0.5)	22.9	(0.4)	0.9	(0.1)
	Hong Kong-China	1.7	(0.2)	7.2	(0.5)	25.2	(0.5)	65.9	(0.9)	0.1	(0.0)	0.0	c
	Indonesia	1.5	(0.5)	6.5	(0.8)	46.0	(3.1)	40.5	(3.2)	5.0	(0.8)	0.5	(0.4)
	Jordan	0.1	(0.1)	1.3	(0.2)	7.0	(0.5)	91.6	(0.6)	0.0	c	0.0	c
	Kazakhstan	0.4	(0.1)	6.4	(0.4)	73.3	(1.9)	19.7	(2.0)	0.1	(0.0)	0.0	c
	Kyrgyzstan	0.2	(0.1)	7.9	(0.5)	71.4	(1.3)	19.8	(1.4)	0.7	(0.1)	0.0	c
	Latvia	2.7	(0.5)	15.5	(0.7)	79.4	(0.9)	2.4	(0.3)	0.1	(0.1)	0.0	(0.0)
	Liechtenstein	0.8	(0.5)	17.5	(1.1)	71.3	(0.8)	10.4	(1.0)	0.0	c	0.0	c
	Lithuania	0.5	(0.1)	10.2	(0.9)	80.9	(0.8)	8.4	(0.6)	0.0	(0.0)	0.0	c
	Macao-China	6.7	(0.1)	19.2	(0.2)	34.9	(0.1)	38.7	(0.1)	0.5	(0.1)	0.0	c
	Montenegro	0.0	c	2.5	(1.7)	82.7	(1.5)	14.8	(0.3)	0.0	c	0.0	c
	Panama	2.9	(0.8)	10.6	(1.6)	30.6	(3.3)	49.8	(4.5)	6.1	(1.4)	0.0	c
	Peru	4.0	(0.4)	8.9	(0.6)	17.1	(0.7)	44.6	(1.1)	25.4	(0.8)	0.0	c
	Qatar	1.7	(0.1)	3.6	(0.1)	13.5	(0.2)	62.6	(0.2)	18.2	(0.2)	0.4	(0.1)
	Romania	0.0	c	7.2	(1.0)	88.6	(1.1)	4.3	(0.6)	0.0	c	0.0	c
	Russian Federation	0.9	(0.2)	10.0	(0.7)	60.1	(1.8)	28.1	(1.6)	0.9	(0.2)	0.0	c
	Serbia	0.2	(0.1)	2.1	(0.5)	96.0	(0.6)	1.7	(0.2)	0.0	c	0.0	c
	Shanghai-China	1.0	(0.2)	4.1	(0.4)	37.4	(0.8)	57.1	(0.9)	0.4	(0.2)	0.0	(0.0)
	Singapore	1.0	(0.2)	2.6	(0.2)	34.7	(0.4)	61.6	(0.3)	0.0	c	0.0	(0.0)
	Chinese Taipei	0.0	c	0.1	(0.0)	34.4	(0.9)	65.5	(0.9)	0.0	(0.0)	0.0	c
	Thailand	0.1	(0.0)	0.5	(0.1)	23.2	(1.1)	73.5	(1.1)	2.7	(0.4)	0.0	c
	Trinidad and Tobago	2.1	(0.2)	8.8	(0.4)	25.3	(0.4)	56.1	(0.4)	7.7	(0.3)	0.0	c
	Tunisia	6.4	(0.4)	13.4	(0.6)	23.9	(0.9)	50.9	(1.4)	5.4	(0.4)	0.0	c
	Uruguay	7.1	(0.8)	10.6	(0.6)	21.5	(0.8)	56.2	(1.1)	4.6	(0.4)	0.0	c

StatLink ⬛🔗 http://dx.doi.org/10.1787/888932343190

[Part 1/2]
Table A2.4b **Percentage of students at each grade level, by gender**

		Boys – Grade level											
		7th grade		8th grade		9th grade		10th grade		11th grade		12th grade	
		%	S.E.	%	S.E.	%	S.E.	%	S.E.	%	S.E.	%	S.E.
OECD	Australia	0.0	c	0.1	(0.0)	13.1	(0.9)	69.6	(1.1)	17.1	(0.8)	0.1	(0.0)
	Austria	0.7	(0.2)	7.4	(1.2)	42.6	(1.3)	49.3	(1.3)	0.0	(0.0)	0.0	c
	Belgium	0.6	(0.2)	6.4	(0.7)	34.6	(0.9)	57.3	(1.0)	1.1	(0.2)	0.0	(0.0)
	Canada	0.0	(0.0)	1.4	(0.3)	14.6	(0.6)	82.9	(0.6)	1.1	(0.1)	0.0	(0.0)
	Chile	1.3	(0.3)	4.9	(0.6)	23.2	(1.0)	65.9	(1.3)	4.7	(0.3)	0.0	c
	Czech Republic	0.7	(0.2)	4.5	(0.5)	52.5	(2.2)	42.3	(2.4)	0.0	c	0.0	c
	Denmark	0.1	(0.0)	19.5	(0.9)	79.5	(1.0)	0.8	(0.3)	0.0	c	0.0	c
	Estonia	2.4	(0.5)	27.0	(1.0)	69.6	(1.1)	1.0	(0.3)	0.0	c	0.0	c
	Finland	0.6	(0.2)	14.0	(0.8)	85.2	(0.8)	0.0	c	0.2	(0.1)	0.0	c
	France	1.3	(0.9)	4.0	(0.6)	39.6	(1.5)	51.4	(1.9)	3.6	(0.8)	0.0	(0.0)
	Germany	1.4	(0.3)	13.1	(0.7)	56.1	(1.0)	28.8	(0.9)	0.6	(0.1)	0.0	c
	Greece	0.5	(0.2)	1.9	(0.5)	6.2	(1.2)	91.4	(1.5)	0.0	c	0.0	c
	Hungary	3.2	(0.8)	9.3	(1.3)	68.8	(1.6)	18.7	(0.9)	0.0	(0.0)	0.0	(0.0)
	Iceland	0.0	c	0.0	c	0.0	c	98.7	(0.2)	1.3	(0.2)	0.0	c
	Ireland	0.1	(0.0)	2.8	(0.5)	60.9	(1.3)	22.4	(1.5)	13.8	(1.4)	0.0	c
	Israel	0.0	c	0.5	(0.2)	19.9	(1.1)	78.7	(1.2)	1.0	(0.4)	0.0	c
	Italy	0.1	(0.1)	1.7	(0.4)	20.1	(0.6)	75.7	(0.7)	2.5	(0.3)	0.0	c
	Japan	0.0	c	0.0	c	0.0	c	100.0	(0.0)	0.0	c	0.0	c
	Korea	0.0	c	0.1	(0.1)	4.7	(1.3)	94.5	(1.4)	0.7	(0.2)	0.0	c
	Luxembourg	0.8	(0.2)	12.5	(0.4)	52.4	(0.5)	34.0	(0.4)	0.3	(0.1)	0.0	c
	Mexico	2.0	(0.2)	8.8	(0.5)	37.6	(0.9)	51.0	(0.9)	0.5	(0.2)	0.0	c
	Netherlands	0.4	(0.3)	3.0	(0.4)	48.9	(1.3)	47.3	(1.3)	0.3	(0.1)	0.0	c
	New Zealand	0.0	c	0.0	c	0.0	c	6.9	(0.5)	87.9	(0.6)	5.2	(0.5)
	Norway	0.0	c	0.0	c	0.5	(0.1)	99.2	(0.2)	0.3	(0.2)	0.0	c
	Poland	1.5	(0.3)	6.5	(0.6)	91.6	(0.7)	0.5	(0.2)	0.0	c	0.0	c
	Portugal	3.4	(0.5)	10.5	(0.9)	30.9	(2.0)	54.9	(2.6)	0.4	(0.1)	0.0	c
	Slovak Republic	1.4	(0.3)	3.7	(0.5)	40.1	(1.9)	51.6	(2.1)	3.3	(0.7)	0.0	c
	Slovenia	0.0	c	0.1	(0.1)	4.0	(1.2)	91.1	(1.2)	4.7	(0.4)	0.0	c
	Spain	0.1	(0.0)	12.2	(0.6)	28.7	(0.8)	58.9	(0.9)	0.0	(0.0)	0.0	c
	Sweden	0.0	(0.0)	4.1	(0.4)	94.7	(0.6)	1.1	(0.3)	0.0	c	0.0	c
	Switzerland	0.8	(0.2)	18.0	(1.2)	60.7	(1.8)	19.4	(1.8)	1.0	(0.4)	0.1	(0.1)
	Turkey	1.0	(0.2)	4.0	(0.9)	30.2	(1.4)	61.3	(1.7)	3.2	(0.3)	0.2	(0.1)
	United Kingdom	0.0	c	0.0	c	0.0	c	1.3	(0.2)	98.0	(0.2)	0.7	(0.1)
	United States	0.0	c	0.1	(0.0)	13.2	(1.0)	68.6	(1.4)	17.9	(0.9)	0.1	(0.1)
	OECD average	1.0	(0.1)	7.0	(0.1)	40.8	(0.2)	50.8	(0.2)	9.8	(0.1)	0.7	(0.0)
Partners	Albania	0.5	(0.2)	2.6	(0.4)	54.0	(2.0)	42.9	(2.1)	0.0	(0.0)	0.0	c
	Argentina	5.9	(1.1)	15.4	(1.4)	22.7	(1.5)	52.5	(2.4)	3.5	(0.5)	0.0	c
	Azerbaijan	0.6	(0.2)	4.7	(0.5)	47.8	(1.4)	46.5	(1.5)	0.3	(0.1)	0.0	c
	Brazil	8.4	(0.6)	21.0	(0.9)	37.8	(0.8)	31.1	(0.9)	1.7	(0.2)	0.0	c
	Bulgaria	2.0	(0.4)	7.4	(0.9)	86.9	(1.2)	3.7	(0.6)	0.0	c	0.0	c
	Colombia	5.5	(0.9)	11.5	(0.9)	21.9	(1.1)	42.4	(1.4)	18.7	(1.2)	0.0	c
	Croatia	0.0	c	0.1	(0.1)	79.1	(0.6)	20.7	(0.6)	0.0	c	0.0	c
	Dubai (UAE)	1.6	(0.2)	4.5	(0.3)	16.0	(0.6)	53.6	(0.7)	23.1	(0.6)	1.1	(0.2)
	Hong Kong-China	1.9	(0.3)	7.3	(0.6)	26.6	(0.7)	64.1	(1.0)	0.1	(0.1)	0.0	c
	Indonesia	1.8	(0.7)	8.2	(1.0)	49.3	(3.4)	36.2	(3.6)	4.0	(0.9)	0.5	(0.3)
	Jordan	0.1	(0.1)	1.2	(0.4)	7.5	(0.8)	91.2	(0.9)	0.0	c	0.0	c
	Kazakhstan	0.5	(0.1)	7.1	(0.6)	75.2	(2.2)	17.2	(2.3)	0.1	(0.0)	0.0	c
	Kyrgyzstan	0.2	(0.1)	8.9	(0.7)	72.9	(1.6)	17.4	(1.6)	0.5	(0.2)	0.0	c
	Latvia	3.6	(0.9)	19.9	(1.1)	74.7	(1.4)	1.6	(0.4)	0.1	(0.1)	0.0	(0.0)
	Liechtenstein	1.1	(0.7)	19.7	(1.6)	68.9	(1.2)	10.3	(1.2)	0.0	c	0.0	c
	Lithuania	0.6	(0.2)	12.3	(1.2)	80.0	(1.2)	7.2	(0.7)	0.0	c	0.0	c
	Macao-China	8.9	(0.2)	22.0	(0.2)	34.9	(0.2)	33.6	(0.2)	0.5	(0.1)	0.0	c
	Montenegro	0.0	c	3.0	(2.0)	85.0	(1.8)	12.0	(0.4)	0.0	c	0.0	c
	Panama	3.4	(1.1)	13.6	(2.5)	32.6	(4.4)	45.7	(5.5)	4.7	(1.8)	0.0	c
	Peru	4.9	(0.5)	11.2	(0.8)	18.8	(1.0)	42.3	(1.4)	22.9	(0.9)	0.0	c
	Qatar	1.9	(0.1)	4.3	(0.2)	14.8	(0.3)	60.4	(0.3)	18.2	(0.2)	0.4	(0.1)
	Romania	0.0	c	6.3	(1.1)	89.9	(1.3)	3.9	(0.7)	0.0	c	0.0	c
	Russian Federation	1.4	(0.3)	10.4	(0.9)	61.2	(1.9)	26.3	(1.9)	0.8	(0.2)	0.0	c
	Serbia	0.3	(0.1)	2.7	(0.7)	95.6	(0.8)	1.4	(0.2)	0.0	c	0.0	c
	Shanghai-China	1.2	(0.3)	5.1	(0.6)	38.8	(1.2)	54.7	(1.4)	0.2	(0.1)	0.0	c
	Singapore	0.8	(0.2)	2.9	(0.3)	35.7	(0.6)	60.6	(0.5)	0.0	c	0.0	c
	Chinese Taipei	0.0	c	0.2	(0.1)	35.2	(1.5)	64.7	(1.5)	0.0	c	0.0	c
	Thailand	0.2	(0.1)	0.8	(0.2)	26.3	(1.4)	70.5	(1.4)	2.2	(0.5)	0.0	c
	Trinidad and Tobago	2.7	(0.3)	10.7	(0.5)	28.4	(0.6)	51.0	(0.5)	7.1	(0.4)	0.0	c
	Tunisia	8.9	(0.6)	16.8	(0.9)	24.4	(1.1)	45.3	(1.5)	4.7	(0.5)	0.0	c
	Uruguay	9.1	(1.0)	12.0	(0.8)	24.9	(0.8)	50.4	(1.3)	3.6	(0.4)	0.0	c

StatLink ᵃᵢˢᴾ http://dx.doi.org/10.1787/888932343190

[Part 2/2]

Table A2.4b **Percentage of students at each grade level, by gender**

		Girls – Grade level										
		7th grade		8th grade		9th grade		10th grade		11th grade		12th grade	
		%	S.E.	%	S.E.	%	S.E.	%	S.E.	%	S.E.	%	S.E.
OECD	Australia	0.0	(0.0)	0.1	(0.0)	7.9	(0.5)	72.0	(0.8)	20.0	(0.8)	0.1	(0.0)
	Austria	0.6	(0.4)	5.0	(1.2)	42.2	(1.4)	52.1	(1.5)	0.0	(0.0)	0.0	c
	Belgium	0.3	(0.1)	4.5	(0.5)	29.3	(1.1)	64.5	(1.1)	1.3	(0.2)	0.0	(0.0)
	Canada	0.0	(0.0)	1.0	(0.2)	12.5	(0.5)	85.3	(0.5)	1.1	(0.1)	0.0	(0.0)
	Chile	0.7	(0.1)	2.9	(0.5)	17.7	(0.9)	73.0	(1.1)	5.6	(0.4)	0.0	(0.0)
	Czech Republic	0.3	(0.2)	3.1	(0.4)	44.8	(1.9)	51.8	(1.9)	0.0	c	0.0	c
	Denmark	0.1	(0.0)	10.0	(0.7)	87.3	(0.9)	2.5	(0.8)	0.0	c	0.0	c
	Estonia	0.9	(0.3)	20.8	(0.9)	75.4	(1.1)	2.7	(0.5)	0.2	(0.2)	0.0	c
	Finland	0.4	(0.1)	9.6	(0.6)	89.4	(0.6)	0.0	c	0.6	(0.2)	0.0	c
	France	1.3	(0.9)	3.2	(0.9)	29.4	(1.5)	61.6	(1.7)	4.4	(0.8)	0.1	(0.1)
	Germany	1.1	(0.2)	8.8	(0.6)	53.4	(1.1)	36.4	(1.1)	0.3	(0.1)	0.0	(0.0)
	Greece	0.2	(0.2)	0.9	(0.5)	4.9	(0.7)	94.0	(0.9)	0.0	c	0.0	c
	Hungary	2.3	(0.7)	5.9	(1.1)	65.4	(1.6)	26.2	(1.2)	0.2	(0.1)	0.0	c
	Iceland	0.0	c	0.0	c	0.0	(0.1)	97.9	(0.2)	2.1	(0.2)	0.0	c
	Ireland	0.1	(0.1)	2.0	(0.4)	57.3	(1.5)	25.7	(2.0)	15.1	(1.5)	0.0	c
	Israel	0.0	c	0.1	(0.1)	15.9	(1.0)	83.8	(1.1)	0.2	(0.1)	0.0	(0.0)
	Italy	0.2	(0.1)	1.0	(0.2)	13.5	(0.6)	81.4	(0.7)	3.9	(0.3)	0.0	c
	Japan	0.0	c	0.0	c	0.0	c	100.0	(0.0)	0.0	c	0.0	c
	Korea	0.0	c	0.0	c	3.6	(1.0)	95.6	(1.0)	0.8	(0.1)	0.0	c
	Luxembourg	0.4	(0.1)	10.6	(0.3)	50.8	(0.4)	38.0	(0.3)	0.2	(0.1)	0.0	c
	Mexico	1.5	(0.2)	6.1	(0.4)	31.5	(0.9)	60.1	(1.0)	0.8	(0.3)	0.0	(0.0)
	Netherlands	0.1	(0.1)	2.3	(0.4)	43.4	(1.4)	53.5	(1.3)	0.7	(0.2)	0.0	c
	New Zealand	0.0	c	0.0	c	0.1	(0.1)	4.8	(0.5)	89.8	(0.6)	5.4	(0.5)
	Norway	0.0	c	0.0	c	0.4	(0.1)	99.4	(0.2)	0.1	(0.1)	0.0	c
	Poland	0.6	(0.2)	2.5	(0.3)	95.6	(0.7)	1.3	(0.6)	0.0	c	0.0	c
	Portugal	1.4	(0.2)	7.7	(0.8)	25.1	(1.4)	65.4	(1.9)	0.4	(0.1)	0.0	c
	Slovak Republic	0.7	(0.2)	1.5	(0.3)	31.4	(1.8)	62.1	(2.1)	4.3	(0.9)	0.0	(0.0)
	Slovenia	0.0	c	0.0	c	1.9	(0.7)	90.3	(0.8)	7.8	(0.5)	0.0	c
	Spain	0.1	(0.1)	7.6	(0.4)	24.2	(0.7)	68.0	(0.8)	0.0	(0.0)	0.0	c
	Sweden	0.1	(0.1)	2.3	(0.3)	95.4	(0.7)	2.2	(0.7)	0.0	c	0.0	c
	Switzerland	0.4	(0.1)	12.9	(0.9)	62.6	(1.8)	22.7	(2.0)	1.4	(0.6)	0.0	c
	Turkey	0.4	(0.2)	2.9	(0.8)	19.8	(1.3)	72.3	(1.6)	4.4	(0.4)	0.2	(0.1)
	United Kingdom	0.0	c	0.0	c	0.0	c	1.0	(0.1)	98.1	(0.1)	0.9	(0.1)
	United States	0.0	c	0.2	(0.2)	8.5	(0.7)	68.4	(1.1)	22.8	(1.0)	0.1	(0.1)
	OECD average	0.6	(0.1)	5.0	(0.1)	35.6	(0.2)	55.0	(0.2)	10.2	(0.1)	0.5	(0.0)
Partners	Albania	0.2	(0.1)	1.8	(0.4)	47.6	(2.3)	50.2	(2.3)	0.2	(0.1)	0.0	c
	Argentina	3.6	(0.9)	10.7	(1.5)	18.4	(1.2)	62.3	(2.2)	4.9	(0.6)	0.0	c
	Azerbaijan	0.6	(0.3)	5.8	(0.6)	51.0	(1.5)	42.1	(1.4)	0.4	(0.1)	0.0	c
	Brazil	5.4	(0.4)	15.3	(0.6)	37.1	(0.9)	39.7	(0.9)	2.5	(0.2)	0.0	c
	Bulgaria	0.9	(0.3)	4.6	(0.7)	90.6	(1.0)	3.9	(0.7)	0.0	c	0.0	c
	Colombia	3.3	(0.4)	9.1	(0.8)	22.4	(1.0)	42.2	(1.1)	23.0	(1.1)	0.0	c
	Croatia	0.0	c	0.2	(0.2)	75.8	(0.6)	24.1	(0.5)	0.0	c	0.0	c
	Dubai (UAE)	0.6	(0.1)	2.2	(0.2)	13.5	(0.5)	60.4	(0.6)	22.7	(0.7)	0.6	(0.1)
	Hong Kong-China	1.5	(0.2)	7.1	(0.6)	23.5	(0.6)	67.9	(1.0)	0.0	c	0.0	c
	Indonesia	1.2	(0.3)	4.9	(0.8)	42.7	(3.7)	44.6	(3.8)	6.0	(1.1)	0.6	(0.5)
	Jordan	0.1	(0.0)	1.3	(0.3)	6.5	(0.7)	92.1	(0.9)	0.0	c	0.0	c
	Kazakhstan	0.4	(0.1)	5.7	(0.5)	71.5	(2.0)	22.3	(2.1)	0.2	(0.1)	0.0	c
	Kyrgyzstan	0.1	(0.1)	7.1	(0.6)	69.9	(1.5)	22.0	(1.6)	0.9	(0.2)	0.0	c
	Latvia	1.7	(0.4)	11.2	(0.6)	83.9	(0.8)	3.1	(0.4)	0.1	(0.1)	0.0	c
	Liechtenstein	0.6	(0.6)	15.0	(1.5)	74.0	(1.2)	10.4	(1.6)	0.0	c	0.0	c
	Lithuania	0.3	(0.1)	8.1	(0.8)	81.9	(0.9)	9.6	(0.7)	0.0	(0.0)	0.0	c
	Macao-China	4.4	(0.1)	16.3	(0.2)	34.9	(0.2)	43.9	(0.2)	0.5	(0.1)	0.0	c
	Montenegro	0.0	c	2.0	(1.4)	80.3	(1.3)	17.8	(0.4)	0.0	c	0.0	c
	Panama	2.4	(0.6)	7.7	(1.1)	28.7	(3.0)	53.8	(4.0)	7.5	(1.6)	0.0	c
	Peru	3.2	(0.4)	6.5	(0.6)	15.4	(0.8)	47.0	(1.2)	27.9	(1.2)	0.0	c
	Qatar	1.4	(0.1)	3.0	(0.1)	12.1	(0.2)	64.9	(0.2)	18.1	(0.2)	0.5	(0.1)
	Romania	0.0	c	8.1	(1.5)	87.3	(1.5)	4.7	(0.6)	0.0	c	0.0	c
	Russian Federation	0.5	(0.1)	9.7	(0.8)	59.0	(2.0)	29.8	(1.8)	1.0	(0.2)	0.0	c
	Serbia	0.1	(0.1)	1.4	(0.5)	96.4	(0.6)	2.0	(0.2)	0.0	c	0.0	c
	Shanghai-China	0.8	(0.2)	3.0	(0.4)	36.1	(1.0)	59.5	(1.0)	0.6	(0.2)	0.0	(0.0)
	Singapore	1.2	(0.2)	2.3	(0.3)	33.7	(0.5)	62.7	(0.4)	0.0	c	0.0	(0.0)
	Chinese Taipei	0.0	c	0.0	(0.0)	33.7	(1.5)	66.3	(1.5)	0.0	(0.0)	0.0	c
	Thailand	0.0	c	0.3	(0.1)	20.9	(1.4)	75.8	(1.4)	3.0	(0.4)	0.0	c
	Trinidad and Tobago	1.5	(0.3)	6.9	(0.5)	22.3	(0.6)	61.0	(0.6)	8.3	(0.4)	0.0	c
	Tunisia	4.2	(0.4)	10.3	(0.5)	23.4	(1.0)	56.1	(1.4)	6.0	(0.5)	0.0	c
	Uruguay	5.4	(0.6)	9.4	(0.5)	18.5	(0.9)	61.4	(1.2)	5.4	(0.6)	0.0	c

StatLink ᔞᕑᔤ http://dx.doi.org/10.1787/888932343190

Students in or out of the regular education system in Argentina

The low performance of 15-year-old students in Argentina is, to some extent, influenced by a fairly large proportion of 15-year-olds enrolled in programmes outside the regular education system. Table A2.5 shows the proportion of students inside and outside the regular education system, alongside their performance in PISA 2009.

Table A2.5 **Percentage of students and mean scores in reading, mathematics and science, according to whether students are in or out of the regular education system in Argentina**

| | Percentage of students | | Mean performance | | | | | |
| | | | Reading | | Mathematics | | Science | |
	%	S.E.	Mean	S.E.	Mean	S.E.	Mean	S.E.
Students in the regular educational system[1]	60.9	2.2	439	5.1	421	4.8	439	4.9
Students out of the regular educational system[2]	39.1	2.2	335	8.0	337	6.7	341	8.3

1. Students who are not in grade 10 or 11 and in programme 3, 4, 5, 6, 7 or 8.
2. Students who are in grade 10 or 11 and in programme 3, 4, 5, 6, 7 or 8.
StatLink 🔢📨 http://dx.doi.org/10.1787/888932343190

ANNEX A3
STANDARD ERRORS, SIGNIFICANCE TESTS AND SUB-GROUP COMPARISONS

The statistics in this report represent estimates of national performance based on samples of students, rather than values that could be calculated if every student in every country had answered every question. Consequently, it is important to measure the degree of uncertainty of the estimates. In PISA, each estimate has an associated degree of uncertainty, which is expressed through a standard error. The use of confidence intervals provides a way to make inferences about the population means and proportions in a manner that reflects the uncertainty associated with the sample estimates. From an observed sample statistic and assuming a normal distribution, it can be inferred that the corresponding population result would lie within the confidence interval in 95 out of 100 replications of the measurement on different samples drawn from the same population.

In many cases, readers are primarily interested in whether a given value in a particular country is different from a second value in the same or another country, *e.g.* whether females in a country perform better than males in the same country. In the tables and charts used in this report, differences are labelled as statistically significant when a difference of that size, smaller or larger, would be observed less than 5% of the time, if there were actually no difference in corresponding population values. Similarly, the risk of reporting a correlation as significant if there is, in fact, no correlation between two measures, is contained at 5%.

Throughout the report, significance tests were undertaken to assess the statistical significance of the comparisons made. Except when noted statistical test evaluate whether the estimate is significantly different from zero. In specific cases statistical tests evaluate whether the estimates for individual countries are statistically different from the OECD average.

Gender differences

Gender differences in student performance or other indices were tested for statistical significance. Positive differences indicate higher scores for males while negative differences indicate higher scores for females. Generally, differences marked in bold in the tables in this volume are statistically significant at the 95% confidence level.

Performance differences between the top and bottom quartiles of PISA indices and scales

Differences in average performance between the top and bottom quarters of the PISA indices and scales were tested for statistical significance. Figures marked in bold indicate that performance between the top and bottom quarters of students on the respective index is statistically significantly different at the 95% confidence level.

Change in the performance per unit of the index

For many tables, the difference in student performance per unit of the index shown was calculated. Figures in bold indicate that the differences are statistically significantly different from zero at the 95% confidence level.

Relative risk or increased likelihood

The relative risk is a measure of association between an antecedent factor and an outcome factor. The relative risk is simply the ratio of two risks, *i.e.* the risk of observing the outcome when the antecedent is present and the risk of observing the outcome when the antecedent is not present. Figure A3.1 presents the notation that is used in the following.

■ Figure A3.1 ■
Labels used in a two-way table

p_{11}	p_{12}	$p_{1.}$
p_{21}	p_{22}	$p_{2.}$
$p_{.1}$	$p_{.2}$	$p_{..}$

$p_{..}$ is equal to $\frac{n_{..}}{n_{..}}$, with $n_{..}$ the total number of students and $p_{..}$ is therefore equal to 1, $p_{i.}$, $p_{.j}$ respectively represent the marginal probabilities for each row and for each column. The marginal probabilities are equal to the marginal frequencies divided by the total number of students. Finally, the p_{ij} represent the probabilities for each cell and are equal to the number of observations in a particular cell divided by the total number of observations.

In PISA, the rows represent the antecedent factor with the first row for "having the antecedent" and the second row for "not having the antecedent" and the columns represent the outcome with, the first column for "having the outcome" and the second column for "not having the outcome". The relative risk is then equal to:

$$RR = \frac{(p_{11} / p_{1.})}{(p_{21} / p_{2.})}$$

Figures in bold in the data tables presented in Annex B of this report indicate that the relative risk is statistically significantly different from 1 at the 95% confidence level.

Difference in reading performance between public and private schools

Differences in performance between public and private schools were tested for statistical significance. For this purpose, government-dependent and government-independent private schools were jointly considered as private schools. Positive differences represent higher scores for public schools while negative differences represent higher scores for private schools. Figures in bold in data tables presented in Annex B of this report indicate statistically significant different scores at the 95% confidence level.

Difference in reading performance between native students and students with an immigrant background

Differences in performance between native and non-native students were tested for statistical significance. For this purpose, first-generation and second-generation students were jointly considered as students with an immigrant background. Positive differences represent higher scores for native students, while negative differences represent higher scores for first-generation and second-generation students. Figures in bold in data tables presented in this volume indicate statistically significantly different scores at the 95% confidence level.

Effect sizes

Sometimes it is useful to compare differences in an index between groups, such as males and females, across countries. A problem that may occur in such instances is that the distribution of the index varies across groups or countries. One way to resolve this is to calculate an effect size that accounts for differences in the distributions. An effect size measures the difference between, say, the self-efficacy in reading of male and female students in a given country, relative to the average variation in self-efficacy in reading scores among male and female students in the country.

An effect size also allows a comparison of differences across measures that differ in their metric. For example, it is possible to compare effect sizes between the PISA indices and the PISA test scores, as when, for example, gender differences in performance in reading are compared with the gender differences in several of the indices.

In accordance with common practices, effect sizes less than 0.20 are considered small in this volume, effect sizes in the order of 0.50 are considered medium, and effect sizes greater than 0.80 are considered large. Many comparisons in this report consider differences only if the effect sizes are equal to or greater than 0.20, even if smaller differences are still statistically significant; figures in bold in data tables presented in Annex B of this report indicate values equal to or greater than 0.20. Values smaller than 0.20 but that due to rounding are shown as 0.20 in tables and figures have not been highlighted. Light shading represents the absolute value of effect size is equal or more than 0.2 and less than 0.5; medium shading represents the absolute value of effect size is equal or more than 0.5 and less than 0.8; and dark shading represents the absolute value of effect size is equal or more than 0.8.

The effect size between two subgroups is calculated as:

$$\frac{m_1 - m_2}{\sqrt{\dfrac{\sigma_1^2 + \sigma_2^2}{2}}}, \ i.e.$$

m_1 and m_2 respectively represent the mean values for the subgroups 1 and 2. σ_1^2 and σ_2^2 respectively represent the values of variance for the subgroups 1 and 2. The effect size between the two subgroups 1 and 2 is calculated as dividing the mean difference between the two subgroups $(m_1 - m_2)$, by the square root of the sum of the subgroup's variance $(\sigma_1^2 + \sigma_2^2)$ divided by 2.

Skewness of a distribution

The skewness is a measure of the symmetry of a distribution. In PISA 2009, the skewness for the distribution of socio-economic background was calculated. Negative values for the skewness indicate a longer tail of students from disadvantaged socio-economic background while positive values indicate a longer tail of students from advantaged socio-economic backgrounds.

ANNEX A4
QUALITY ASSURANCE

Quality assurance procedures were implemented in all parts of PISA 2009, as was done for all previous PISA surveys.

The consistent quality and linguistic equivalence of the PISA 2009 assessment instruments were facilitated by providing countries with equivalent source versions of the assessment instruments in English and French, and requiring countries (other than those assessing students in English and French) to prepare and consolidate two independent translations using both source versions. Precise translation and adaptation guidelines were supplied, also including instructions for selecting and training the translators. For each country, the translation and format of the assessment instruments (including test materials, marking guides, questionnaires and manuals) were verified by expert translators appointed by the PISA Consortium before they were used in the PISA 2009 Field Trial and Main Study. These translators' mother tongue was the language of instruction in the country concerned and they were knowledgeable about education systems. For further information on the PISA translation procedures, see the *PISA 2009 Technical Report* (OECD, forthcoming).

The survey was implemented through standardised procedures. The PISA Consortium provided comprehensive manuals that explained the implementation of the survey, including precise instructions for the work of School Co-ordinators and scripts for Test Administrators to use during the assessment sessions. Proposed adaptations to survey procedures, or proposed modifications to the assessment session script, were submitted to the PISA Consortium for approval prior to verification. The PISA Consortium then verified the national translation and adaptation of these manuals.

To establish the credibility of PISA as valid and unbiased, and to encourage uniformity in administering the assessment sessions, Test Administrators in participating countries were selected using the following criteria: it was required that the Test Administrator not be the reading, mathematics or science instructor of any students in the sessions he or she would administer for PISA; it was recommended that the Test Administrator not be a member of the staff of any school where he or she would administer for PISA; and it was considered preferable that the Test Administrator not be a member of the staff of any school in the PISA sample. Participating countries organised an in-person training session for Test Administrators.

Participating countries were required to ensure that: Test Administrators worked with the School Co-ordinator to prepare the assessment session, including updating student tracking forms and identifying excluded students; no extra time was given for the cognitive items (while it was permissible to give extra time for the student questionnaire); no instrument was administered before the two one-hour parts of the cognitive session; Test Administrators recorded the student participation status on the student tracking forms and filled in a Session Report Form; no cognitive instrument was permitted to be photocopied; no cognitive instrument could be viewed by school staff before the assessment session; and Test Administrators returned the material to the National Centre immediately after the assessment sessions.

National Project Managers were encouraged to organise a follow-up session when more than 15% of the PISA sample was not able to attend the original assessment session.

National Quality Monitors from the PISA Consortium visited all National Centres to review data-collection procedures. Finally, School Quality Monitors from the PISA Consortium visited a sample of 15 schools during the assessment. For further information on the field operations, see the *PISA 2009 Technical Report* (OECD, forthcoming).

Marking procedures were designed to ensure consistent and accurate application of the marking guides outlined in the PISA Operations Manuals. National Project Managers were required to submit proposed modifications to these procedures to the Consortium for approval. Reliability studies to analyse the consistency of marking were implemented, these are discussed in more detail below.

Software specially designed for PISA facilitated data entry, detected common errors during data entry, and facilitated the process of data cleaning. Training sessions familiarised National Project Managers with these procedures.

For a description of the quality assurance procedures applied in PISA and in the results, see the *PISA 2009 Technical Report* (OECD, forthcoming).

The results of data adjudication show that the PISA Technical Standards were fully met in all countries and economies that participated in PISA 2009, though for one country, some serious doubts were raised. Analysis of the data for Azerbaijan suggest that the PISA Technical Standards may not have been fully met for the following four main reasons: *i)* the order of difficulty of the clusters is inconsistent with previous experience and the ordering varies across booklets; *ii)* the percentage correct on some items is higher than that of the highest scoring countries; *iii)* the difficulty of the clusters varies widely across booklets; and *iv)* the coding of items in Azerbaijan is at an extremely high level of agreement between independent coders, and was judged, on some items, to be too lenient. However, further investigation of the survey instruments, the procedures for test implementation and coding of student responses at the national level did not provide sufficient evidence of systematic errors or violations of the PISA Technical Standards. Azerbaijan's data are, therefore, included in the PISA 2009 international dataset.

For the PISA 2009 assessment in Austria, a dispute between teacher unions and the education minister has led to the announcement of a boycott of PISA which was withdrawn after the first week of testing. The boycott required the OECD to remove identifiable cases from the dataset. Although the Austrian dataset met the PISA 2009 technical standards after the removal of these cases, the negative atmosphere in regard to educational assessment has affected the conditions under which the assessment was administered and could have adversely affected student motivation to respond to the PISA tasks. The comparability of the 2009 data with data from earlier PISA assessments can therefore not be ensured and data for Austria have therefore been excluded from trend comparisons.

Annex B

TABLES OF RESULTS
All tables in Annex B are available on line

Annex B1: Results for countries and economies

Annex B2: Results for regions within countries

Adjudicated regions
Data for which adherence to the PISA sampling standards and international comparability was internationally adjudicated.

Non-adjudicated regions
Data for which adherence to the PISA sampling standards at subnational levels was assessed by the countries concerned.

In these countries, adherence to the PISA sampling standards and international comparability was internationally adjudicated only for the combined set of all subnational entities.

Note: Unless otherwise specified, all the data contained in the following tables are drawn from the OECD PISA Database.

ANNEX B1
RESULTS FOR COUNTRIES AND ECONOMIES

[Part 1/1]

The PISA index of economic, social and cultural status (ESCS), mean score and variation in reading performance

Table II.1.1 *Mean score and percentiles on the reading scale*

| | | PISA index of economic, social and cultural status | | Mean score | | Percentiles | | | | | | | | | | | | | |
| | | | | | | 5th | | 10th | | 25th | | 50th | | 75th | | 90th | | 95th | |
		Mean index	S.E.	Score	S.E.	Score	S.E.	Score	S.E.	Score	S.E.	Score	S.E.	Score	S.E.	Score	S.E.	Score	S.E.
OECD	Australia	0.34	(0.01)	515	(2.3)	343	(3.8)	384	(3.1)	450	(2.9)	521	(2.4)	584	(2.7)	638	(3.2)	668	(3.9)
	Austria	0.06	(0.02)	470	(2.9)	299	(5.2)	334	(6.1)	399	(4.3)	476	(3.8)	545	(3.3)	596	(3.4)	625	(4.3)
	Belgium	0.20	(0.02)	506	(2.3)	326	(6.1)	368	(4.3)	436	(3.8)	516	(2.9)	583	(2.2)	631	(2.7)	657	(2.9)
	Canada	0.50	(0.01)	524	(1.5)	368	(2.9)	406	(2.7)	464	(1.9)	529	(1.8)	588	(1.7)	637	(1.9)	664	(2.1)
	Chile	-0.57	(0.04)	449	(3.1)	310	(5.1)	342	(5.0)	393	(4.1)	451	(3.4)	506	(3.3)	556	(3.6)	584	(5.1)
	Czech Republic	-0.09	(0.01)	478	(2.9)	325	(4.8)	357	(4.9)	413	(4.2)	479	(3.3)	545	(3.3)	598	(3.2)	627	(3.6)
	Denmark	0.30	(0.02)	495	(2.1)	350	(3.8)	383	(3.7)	440	(2.9)	500	(2.3)	554	(2.8)	599	(3.0)	624	(2.9)
	Estonia	0.15	(0.02)	501	(2.6)	359	(5.3)	392	(4.4)	446	(3.3)	504	(2.9)	559	(2.8)	605	(3.6)	633	(4.1)
	Finland	0.37	(0.02)	536	(2.3)	382	(3.4)	419	(3.6)	481	(2.7)	542	(2.9)	597	(2.2)	642	(2.6)	666	(2.6)
	France	-0.13	(0.03)	496	(3.4)	305	(8.2)	352	(7.0)	429	(4.7)	505	(3.8)	572	(4.0)	624	(3.9)	651	(4.6)
	Germany	0.18	(0.02)	497	(2.7)	333	(4.8)	367	(5.1)	432	(4.5)	505	(3.3)	567	(2.8)	615	(3.3)	640	(3.1)
	Greece	-0.02	(0.03)	483	(4.3)	318	(7.8)	355	(8.0)	420	(6.3)	488	(4.4)	550	(3.1)	601	(3.7)	630	(3.7)
	Hungary	-0.20	(0.03)	494	(3.2)	332	(7.4)	371	(6.9)	435	(4.3)	501	(3.5)	559	(3.6)	607	(3.5)	632	(4.0)
	Iceland	0.72	(0.01)	500	(1.4)	331	(4.9)	371	(4.1)	439	(2.9)	507	(1.8)	567	(2.0)	619	(2.6)	648	(3.9)
	Ireland	0.05	(0.02)	496	(3.0)	330	(7.8)	373	(4.7)	435	(3.9)	503	(3.5)	562	(2.8)	611	(2.8)	638	(3.2)
	Israel	-0.02	(0.03)	474	(3.6)	277	(8.8)	322	(7.8)	401	(4.4)	483	(3.9)	554	(3.4)	611	(4.0)	643	(4.3)
	Italy	-0.12	(0.01)	486	(1.6)	320	(3.7)	358	(2.6)	422	(2.3)	493	(2.0)	556	(1.7)	604	(1.7)	631	(2.1)
	Japan	-0.01	(0.01)	520	(3.5)	339	(9.8)	386	(7.1)	459	(4.8)	530	(3.2)	590	(3.0)	639	(3.6)	667	(4.6)
	Korea	-0.15	(0.03)	539	(3.5)	400	(7.6)	435	(5.9)	490	(4.1)	545	(3.7)	595	(3.4)	635	(3.6)	658	(3.8)
	Luxembourg	0.19	(0.01)	472	(1.3)	288	(3.6)	332	(3.5)	403	(2.4)	480	(1.8)	547	(1.7)	600	(2.0)	630	(3.7)
	Mexico	-1.22	(0.03)	425	(2.0)	281	(3.9)	314	(2.9)	370	(2.4)	429	(2.1)	485	(1.9)	531	(2.2)	557	(2.4)
	Netherlands	0.27	(0.03)	508	(5.1)	365	(4.7)	390	(5.0)	442	(6.1)	510	(7.0)	575	(5.4)	625	(4.6)	650	(4.0)
	New Zealand	0.09	(0.02)	521	(2.4)	344	(5.8)	383	(4.5)	452	(3.1)	528	(3.0)	595	(2.8)	649	(2.7)	678	(3.7)
	Norway	0.47	(0.02)	503	(2.6)	346	(4.5)	382	(4.0)	443	(3.6)	507	(3.0)	568	(2.9)	619	(3.9)	647	(4.4)
	Poland	-0.28	(0.02)	500	(2.6)	346	(5.6)	382	(4.2)	441	(3.4)	504	(2.7)	565	(3.2)	613	(3.3)	640	(3.6)
	Portugal	-0.32	(0.04)	489	(3.1)	338	(4.8)	373	(4.9)	432	(4.4)	493	(3.6)	551	(3.4)	599	(3.5)	624	(3.6)
	Slovak Republic	-0.09	(0.02)	477	(2.5)	324	(6.1)	358	(5.2)	416	(4.1)	480	(3.3)	543	(2.7)	594	(3.3)	621	(4.3)
	Slovenia	0.07	(0.01)	483	(1.0)	326	(2.9)	359	(2.1)	421	(1.9)	488	(1.8)	550	(1.7)	598	(2.9)	623	(3.9)
	Spain	-0.31	(0.03)	481	(2.0)	326	(4.2)	364	(3.5)	426	(3.3)	488	(2.5)	543	(2.0)	588	(2.0)	613	(2.4)
	Sweden	0.33	(0.02)	497	(2.9)	326	(5.3)	368	(5.5)	437	(3.3)	502	(2.8)	565	(3.2)	620	(3.7)	651	(3.9)
	Switzerland	0.08	(0.02)	501	(2.4)	337	(4.1)	374	(4.0)	437	(3.6)	506	(2.6)	569	(3.0)	617	(3.3)	645	(4.4)
	Turkey	-1.16	(0.05)	464	(3.5)	325	(5.1)	356	(4.3)	409	(3.8)	466	(3.6)	522	(4.5)	569	(5.2)	596	(5.4)
	United Kingdom	0.20	(0.02)	494	(2.3)	334	(4.1)	370	(3.1)	430	(2.8)	497	(3.0)	561	(3.2)	616	(2.6)	646	(3.7)
	United States	0.17	(0.04)	500	(3.7)	339	(4.2)	372	(3.9)	433	(4.0)	501	(4.2)	569	(4.6)	625	(5.0)	656	(5.8)
	OECD average	0.00	(0.00)	493	(0.5)	332	(1.0)	369	(0.8)	432	(0.7)	499	(0.6)	560	(0.5)	610	(0.6)	637	(0.7)
Partners	Albania	-0.95	(0.04)	385	(4.0)	212	(6.9)	254	(5.4)	319	(4.9)	389	(4.8)	458	(4.8)	509	(4.9)	538	(5.5)
	Argentina	-0.62	(0.05)	398	(4.6)	209	(11.3)	257	(8.3)	329	(5.8)	403	(5.3)	473	(6.3)	535	(7.1)	568	(6.7)
	Azerbaijan	-0.64	(0.03)	362	(3.3)	235	(5.7)	263	(4.7)	311	(4.3)	363	(3.7)	413	(4.0)	458	(4.4)	485	(6.2)
	Brazil	-1.16	(0.03)	412	(2.7)	262	(3.0)	293	(3.2)	348	(2.7)	409	(3.2)	474	(3.9)	537	(4.2)	572	(4.6)
	Bulgaria	-0.11	(0.04)	429	(6.7)	234	(8.4)	276	(7.8)	351	(8.5)	436	(8.5)	512	(6.5)	572	(7.3)	603	(6.7)
	Colombia	-1.15	(0.05)	413	(3.7)	269	(6.4)	302	(5.2)	355	(4.4)	414	(4.3)	473	(3.9)	524	(4.1)	554	(4.0)
	Croatia	-0.18	(0.02)	476	(2.9)	327	(4.9)	359	(3.6)	416	(4.5)	481	(3.5)	539	(3.1)	586	(3.5)	611	(3.8)
	Dubai (UAE)	0.42	(0.01)	459	(1.1)	277	(3.4)	317	(2.8)	386	(2.4)	463	(1.5)	536	(2.4)	596	(2.7)	628	(3.1)
	Hong Kong-China	-0.80	(0.04)	533	(2.1)	380	(5.5)	418	(4.5)	482	(3.0)	541	(2.3)	592	(2.5)	634	(2.9)	659	(3.1)
	Indonesia	-1.55	(0.06)	402	(3.7)	291	(5.8)	315	(5.0)	357	(4.1)	402	(3.6)	447	(4.6)	487	(5.0)	510	(5.8)
	Jordan	-0.57	(0.03)	405	(3.3)	243	(6.6)	284	(5.0)	350	(4.1)	412	(3.8)	468	(3.5)	515	(3.9)	542	(4.7)
	Kazakhstan	-0.51	(0.03)	390	(3.1)	245	(3.8)	275	(3.8)	327	(3.1)	387	(3.8)	452	(4.2)	513	(5.0)	545	(5.2)
	Kyrgyzstan	-0.65	(0.03)	314	(3.2)	155	(5.6)	190	(4.7)	249	(4.1)	312	(2.9)	377	(4.2)	441	(6.4)	483	(7.5)
	Latvia	-0.13	(0.03)	484	(3.0)	348	(6.3)	379	(4.2)	429	(3.8)	488	(3.7)	541	(3.3)	584	(3.2)	610	(4.3)
	Liechtenstein	0.09	(0.05)	499	(2.8)	355	(12.1)	385	(10.6)	442	(6.5)	508	(5.5)	560	(4.5)	600	(8.4)	626	(11.8)
	Lithuania	-0.05	(0.02)	468	(2.4)	324	(4.5)	353	(4.1)	409	(3.3)	471	(2.5)	530	(3.1)	580	(3.4)	608	(4.1)
	Macao-China	-0.70	(0.01)	487	(0.9)	357	(2.7)	388	(1.8)	437	(1.4)	489	(1.2)	540	(1.4)	582	(1.8)	608	(1.8)
	Montenegro	-0.24	(0.02)	408	(1.7)	254	(4.2)	288	(3.8)	345	(2.6)	409	(2.5)	473	(2.4)	526	(2.7)	558	(4.1)
	Panama	-0.81	(0.08)	371	(6.5)	209	(12.0)	246	(10.0)	304	(7.4)	368	(7.2)	436	(7.7)	502	(9.3)	540	(10.0)
	Peru	-1.31	(0.05)	370	(4.0)	209	(5.0)	241	(3.9)	302	(4.3)	370	(4.2)	437	(5.2)	496	(6.4)	530	(7.0)
	Qatar	0.51	(0.01)	372	(0.8)	196	(2.4)	228	(2.2)	288	(1.4)	365	(1.6)	450	(1.4)	529	(2.1)	573	(2.8)
	Romania	-0.34	(0.03)	424	(4.1)	271	(6.9)	304	(5.7)	365	(6.0)	429	(4.7)	488	(4.7)	537	(4.0)	564	(4.6)
	Russian Federation	-0.21	(0.02)	459	(3.3)	310	(5.8)	344	(5.5)	401	(3.6)	461	(3.3)	519	(3.2)	572	(4.5)	607	(5.6)
	Serbia	0.07	(0.02)	442	(2.4)	299	(4.9)	331	(3.8)	388	(3.2)	446	(2.9)	501	(2.5)	547	(2.7)	572	(3.3)
	Shanghai-China	-0.49	(0.04)	556	(2.4)	417	(5.2)	450	(4.8)	504	(3.5)	562	(2.8)	613	(2.8)	654	(2.7)	679	(3.3)
	Singapore	-0.43	(0.01)	526	(1.1)	357	(3.4)	394	(3.1)	460	(2.0)	532	(2.1)	597	(2.1)	648	(2.8)	676	(2.7)
	Chinese Taipei	-0.33	(0.02)	495	(2.6)	343	(4.6)	380	(3.9)	439	(3.2)	502	(2.7)	555	(2.9)	600	(4.6)	627	(6.3)
	Thailand	-1.31	(0.04)	421	(2.6)	305	(4.9)	331	(3.8)	373	(3.2)	420	(3.0)	469	(2.6)	514	(4.0)	542	(5.5)
	Trinidad and Tobago	-0.58	(0.02)	416	(1.2)	220	(5.8)	265	(3.9)	339	(2.5)	423	(2.0)	496	(2.6)	559	(2.5)	594	(3.0)
	Tunisia	-1.20	(0.05)	404	(2.9)	258	(4.4)	293	(3.8)	348	(3.4)	407	(3.2)	462	(3.4)	510	(4.8)	538	(5.2)
	Uruguay	-0.70	(0.03)	426	(2.6)	257	(5.2)	297	(4.2)	359	(3.4)	428	(3.2)	495	(3.1)	552	(3.3)	584	(4.5)

StatLink ᠊ᡅᡏᡅᡖᡇ http://dx.doi.org/10.1787/888932343285

[Part 1/1]
Strength of the relationship among student performance and socio-economic background and Gini Index

Table II.1.2 *Results based on students' self-reports*

| | Strength of the relationship between student performance and the PISA index of economic, social and cultural status (ESCS)[1] | | Gini Index | Slope of the socio-economic gradient[1,2] | | Length of the projection of the gradient line | | | | | |
	Percentage of explained variance in student performance	S.E.		Score point difference associated with one unit increase in the ESCS	S.E.	5th percentile of the ESCS	S.E.	95th percentile of the ESCS	S.E.	Difference between 95th and 5th percentile of the ES CS	S.E.
OECD											
Australia	12.7	(0.85)	0.30	**46**	(1.8)	-0.87	(0.02)	1.51	(0.01)	2.38	(0.02)
Austria	16.6	(1.39)	0.27	**48**	(2.3)	-1.23	(0.04)	1.49	(0.04)	2.73	(0.06)
Belgium	**19.3**	(1.01)	0.27	**47**	(1.5)	-1.29	(0.03)	1.64	(0.04)	2.93	(0.06)
Canada	8.6	(0.74)	0.32	**32**	(1.4)	-0.88	(0.03)	1.76	(0.02)	2.63	(0.04)
Chile	18.7	(1.56)	0.54	31	(1.5)	-2.37	(0.04)	1.36	(0.04)	3.73	(0.05)
Czech Republic	12.4	(1.09)	0.27	46	(2.3)	-1.17	(0.02)	1.13	(0.02)	2.30	(0.03)
Denmark	14.5	(1.02)	0.23	36	(1.4)	-1.14	(0.02)	1.67	(0.02)	2.81	(0.03)
Estonia	7.6	(1.11)	0.36	29	(2.3)	-1.10	(0.04)	1.43	(0.03)	2.53	(0.04)
Finland	7.8	(0.82)	0.27	31	(1.7)	-0.91	(0.04)	1.54	(0.04)	2.45	(0.05)
France	16.7	(1.97)	0.27	**51**	(2.9)	-1.50	(0.03)	1.25	(0.06)	2.74	(0.06)
Germany	**17.9**	(1.29)	0.30	44	(1.9)	-1.24	(0.04)	1.70	(0.03)	2.94	(0.04)
Greece	12.5	(1.43)	0.32	34	(2.4)	-1.63	(0.04)	1.58	(0.02)	3.21	(0.04)
Hungary	**26.0**	(2.17)	0.29	**48**	(2.2)	-1.71	(0.06)	1.43	(0.03)	3.14	(0.06)
Iceland	**6.2**	(0.81)	0.28	27	(1.8)	-0.83	(0.03)	2.06	(0.02)	2.88	(0.04)
Ireland	12.6	(1.17)	0.33	39	(2.0)	-1.28	(0.03)	1.44	(0.04)	2.72	(0.04)
Israel	12.5	(1.14)	0.39	**43**	(2.4)	-1.53	(0.05)	1.22	(0.03)	2.75	(0.06)
Italy	**11.8**	(0.74)	0.35	32	(1.3)	-1.70	(0.02)	1.62	(0.03)	3.32	(0.04)
Japan	8.6	(0.96)	0.32	40	(2.8)	-1.16	(0.02)	1.16	(0.01)	2.32	(0.02)
Korea	**11.0**	(1.51)	0.31	32	(2.5)	-1.53	(0.03)	1.18	(0.04)	2.71	(0.05)
Luxembourg	18.0	(1.06)	0.26	40	(1.3)	-1.82	(0.03)	1.81	(0.04)	3.63	(0.05)
Mexico	14.5	(0.99)	0.47	25	(1.0)	-3.18	(0.03)	1.00	(0.06)	4.18	(0.06)
Netherlands	12.8	(1.20)	0.27	37	(1.9)	-1.12	(0.09)	1.54	(0.02)	2.66	(0.08)
New Zealand	**16.6**	(1.08)	0.34	52	(1.9)	-1.20	(0.02)	1.33	(0.02)	2.53	(0.03)
Norway	8.6	(0.96)	0.28	36	(2.1)	-0.72	(0.02)	1.64	(0.02)	2.36	(0.03)
Poland	14.8	(1.38)	0.37	39	(1.9)	-1.50	(0.03)	1.35	(0.02)	2.86	(0.03)
Portugal	16.5	(1.60)	0.38	30	(1.6)	-1.98	(0.03)	1.81	(0.03)	3.79	(0.04)
Slovak Republic[3]	14.6	(1.48)	0.26	41	(2.3)	-1.24	(0.03)	1.46	(0.04)	2.70	(0.05)
Slovenia	14.3	(1.06)	0.30	39	(1.5)	-1.25	(0.02)	1.53	(0.02)	2.78	(0.03)
Spain	13.6	(1.30)	0.32	29	(1.5)	-2.04	(0.04)	1.54	(0.03)	3.58	(0.04)
Sweden	13.4	(1.33)	0.23	43	(2.2)	-1.01	(0.04)	1.55	(0.04)	2.57	(0.05)
Switzerland	14.1	(1.38)	0.28	40	(2.1)	-1.38	(0.03)	1.52	(0.03)	2.90	(0.03)
Turkey	**19.0**	(1.91)	0.43	29	(1.5)	-2.99	(0.04)	1.03	(0.07)	4.02	(0.07)
United Kingdom	13.7	(1.03)	0.34	44	(1.9)	-1.05	(0.04)	1.48	(0.02)	2.52	(0.04)
United States	16.8	(1.65)	0.38	42	(2.3)	-1.40	(0.08)	1.61	(0.03)	3.01	(0.08)
OECD average	14.0	(0.22)	0.31	38	(0.3)	-1.44	(0.01)	1.48	(0.01)	2.92	(0.01)
Partners											
Albania	10.7	(1.79)	0.31	**31**	(2.6)	-2.61	(0.05)	0.84	(0.05)	3.44	(0.06)
Argentina	**19.6**	(2.23)	0.51	40	(2.3)	-2.54	(0.06)	1.36	(0.05)	3.90	(0.08)
Azerbaijan	**7.4**	(1.57)	0.27	21	(2.3)	-2.17	(0.03)	1.01	(0.04)	3.18	(0.04)
Brazil	13.0	(1.27)	0.57	28	(1.4)	-3.05	(0.03)	0.89	(0.06)	3.94	(0.06)
Bulgaria	**20.2**	(2.19)	0.32	51	(2.8)	-1.59	(0.09)	1.49	(0.04)	3.08	(0.09)
Colombia	16.6	(1.90)	0.58	28	(1.8)	-3.21	(0.05)	0.95	(0.06)	4.15	(0.07)
Croatia	**11.0**	(1.34)	0.30	32	(2.0)	-1.61	(0.04)	1.43	(0.04)	3.04	(0.06)
Dubai (UAE)	14.2	(0.80)	m	51	(1.4)	-1.11	(0.04)	1.50	(0.02)	2.61	(0.04)
Hong Kong-China[5]	**4.5**	(1.08)	0.43	17	(2.2)	-2.42	(0.04)	1.00	(0.07)	3.42	(0.08)
Indonesia	7.8	(2.23)	0.38	17	(2.4)	-3.11	(0.03)	0.43	(0.06)	3.55	(0.06)
Jordan	**7.9**	(1.35)	0.38	24	(2.1)	-2.23	(0.06)	1.07	(0.04)	3.30	(0.07)
Kazakhstan	12.0	(1.73)	0.33	38	(2.8)	-1.79	(0.06)	0.87	(0.05)	2.66	(0.06)
Kyrgyzstan	14.6	(1.83)	0.33	40	(2.9)	-2.13	(0.02)	0.89	(0.05)	3.02	(0.05)
Latvia	10.3	(1.69)	0.36	29	(2.6)	-1.47	(0.03)	1.29	(0.03)	2.75	(0.03)
Liechtenstein	8.4	(2.89)	m	26	(5.0)	-1.42	(0.13)	1.51	(0.06)	2.93	(0.13)
Lithuania	13.6	(1.44)	0.33	33	(1.9)	-1.52	(0.03)	1.47	(0.01)	2.99	(0.03)
Macao-China[3]	**1.8**	(0.35)	0.37	12	(1.2)	-2.09	(0.02)	0.83	(0.04)	2.92	(0.04)
Montenegro	10.0	(0.84)	0.37	31	(1.4)	-1.74	(0.04)	1.35	(0.03)	3.09	(0.05)
Panama	18.1	(3.86)	0.56	31	(3.6)	-3.08	(0.10)	1.16	(0.11)	4.23	(0.14)
Peru	**27.4**	(2.62)	0.52	41	(2.0)	-3.33	(0.05)	0.85	(0.09)	4.18	(0.10)
Qatar	**4.0**	(0.36)	0.41	25	(1.2)	-1.28	(0.03)	1.73	(0.02)	3.00	(0.03)
Romania	13.6	(2.12)	0.31	36	(2.8)	-1.70	(0.08)	1.23	(0.06)	2.93	(0.09)
Russian Federation	**11.3**	(1.35)	0.39	37	(2.5)	-1.43	(0.03)	1.08	(0.03)	2.51	(0.04)
Serbia	9.8	(1.02)	0.28	27	(1.6)	-1.42	(0.03)	1.75	(0.04)	3.17	(0.05)
Shanghai-China	12.3	(1.77)	m	27	(2.1)	-2.16	(0.03)	1.19	(0.03)	3.35	(0.04)
Singapore[4]	15.3	(1.11)	0.43	47	(1.7)	-1.82	(0.03)	0.75	(0.00)	2.57	(0.03)
Chinese Taipei	**11.8**	(1.34)	m	36	(2.4)	-1.73	(0.05)	1.02	(0.03)	2.74	(0.05)
Thailand	13.3	(1.94)	0.43	22	(1.8)	-2.84	(0.03)	0.88	(0.04)	3.72	(0.05)
Trinidad and Tobago[6]	**9.7**	(0.86)	0.40	38	(1.7)	-2.20	(0.05)	0.92	(0.03)	3.11	(0.06)
Tunisia	8.1	(1.47)	0.41	19	(1.8)	-3.15	(0.06)	1.03	(0.05)	4.18	(0.06)
Uruguay	**20.7**	(1.47)	0.45	37	(1.5)	-2.49	(0.02)	1.51	(0.03)	4.00	(0.03)

Note: The Gini coefficient measures the extent to which the distribution of income among individuals or households within an economy deviates from a perfectly equal distribution. The Gini index measures the area between the Lorenz curve and the hypothetical line of absolute equality, expressed as a percentage of the maximum area under the line. A Gini index of zero represents perfect equality and 1, perfect inequality.
1. In these columns values that are statistically significantly different from the OECD average are indicated in bold.
2. Single-level bivariate regression of reading performance on the ESCS, the slope is the regression coefficient for the ESCS.
3. Gini index from City's Statistics and Census Service (DSEC). Year 2007/2008.
4. Gini index from World Bank 1998.
5. Gini index from World Bank 1996.
6. Gini index from World Bank 1992.
Source: Gini indexes for OECD countries come from the OECD, 2008 publication: *Growing Unequal? Income Distribution and Poverty in OECD Countries* and refer to mid-2000. The OECD average refers to the average of 24 OECD countries. Gini indexes of partner countries and economies come from the World Bank database, as the average index between the years 2000 and 2007.

StatLink ᴍᴤᴸ http://dx.doi.org/10.1787/888932343285

[Part 1/2]
Performance by proficiency level in reading and socio-economic background
Table II.2.1 *Results based on students' self-reports*

		Below Level 1b (less than 262.04 score points)		Level 1b (from 262.04 to less than 334.75 score points)		Level 1a (from 334.75 to less than 407.47 score points)		Level 2 (from 407.47 to less than 480.18 score points)		Level 3 (from 480.18 to less than 552.89 score points)		Level 4 (from 552.89 to less than 625.61 score points)		Level 5 (from 625.61 to less than 698.32 score points)		Level 6 (above 698.32 score points)	
		%	S.E.	%	S.E.	%	S.E.	%	S.E.	%	S.E.	%	S.E.	%	S.E.	%	S.E.
OECD	Australia	1.0	(0.1)	3.3	(0.3)	10.0	(0.4)	20.4	(0.6)	28.5	(0.7)	24.1	(0.7)	10.7	(0.5)	2.1	(0.3)
	Austria	1.9	(0.4)	8.1	(0.8)	17.5	(1.0)	24.1	(1.0)	26.0	(0.9)	17.4	(0.9)	4.5	(0.4)	0.4	(0.1)
	Belgium	1.1	(0.3)	4.7	(0.5)	11.9	(0.6)	20.3	(0.7)	25.8	(0.9)	24.9	(0.7)	10.1	(0.5)	1.1	(0.2)
	Canada	0.4	(0.1)	2.0	(0.2)	7.9	(0.3)	20.2	(0.6)	30.0	(0.7)	26.8	(0.6)	11.0	(0.4)	1.8	(0.2)
	Chile	1.3	(0.2)	7.4	(0.8)	21.9	(1.0)	33.2	(1.1)	25.6	(1.1)	9.3	(0.7)	1.3	(0.2)	0.0	(0.0)
	Czech Republic	0.8	(0.3)	5.5	(0.6)	16.8	(1.1)	27.4	(1.0)	27.0	(1.0)	17.4	(1.0)	4.7	(0.4)	0.4	(0.1)
	Denmark	0.4	(0.1)	3.1	(0.3)	11.7	(0.7)	26.0	(0.9)	33.1	(1.2)	20.9	(1.1)	4.4	(0.4)	0.3	(0.1)
	Estonia	0.3	(0.1)	2.4	(0.4)	10.6	(0.9)	25.6	(1.3)	33.8	(1.0)	21.2	(0.8)	5.4	(0.5)	0.6	(0.2)
	Finland	0.2	(0.1)	1.5	(0.1)	6.4	(0.4)	16.7	(0.6)	30.1	(0.8)	30.6	(0.9)	12.9	(0.7)	1.6	(0.2)
	France	2.3	(0.5)	5.6	(0.5)	11.8	(0.8)	21.1	(1.0)	27.2	(1.0)	22.4	(1.1)	8.5	(0.8)	1.1	(0.3)
	Germany	0.8	(0.2)	4.4	(0.5)	13.3	(0.8)	22.2	(0.9)	28.8	(1.1)	22.8	(0.9)	7.0	(0.6)	0.6	(0.2)
	Greece	1.4	(0.4)	5.6	(0.9)	14.3	(1.1)	25.6	(1.1)	29.3	(1.2)	18.2	(1.0)	5.0	(0.5)	0.6	(0.2)
	Hungary	0.6	(0.2)	4.7	(0.8)	12.3	(1.0)	23.8	(1.2)	31.0	(1.3)	21.6	(1.1)	5.8	(0.7)	0.3	(0.1)
	Iceland	1.1	(0.2)	4.2	(0.4)	11.5	(0.7)	22.2	(0.8)	30.6	(0.9)	21.9	(0.8)	7.5	(0.6)	1.0	(0.2)
	Ireland	1.5	(0.4)	3.9	(0.5)	11.8	(0.7)	23.3	(1.0)	30.6	(0.9)	21.9	(0.9)	6.3	(0.5)	0.7	(0.2)
	Israel	3.9	(0.7)	8.0	(0.7)	14.7	(0.6)	22.5	(1.0)	25.5	(0.9)	18.1	(0.7)	6.4	(0.5)	1.0	(0.2)
	Italy	1.4	(0.2)	5.2	(0.3)	14.4	(0.5)	24.0	(0.5)	28.9	(0.6)	20.2	(0.5)	5.4	(0.3)	0.4	(0.1)
	Japan	1.3	(0.4)	3.4	(0.5)	8.9	(0.7)	18.0	(0.8)	28.0	(0.9)	27.0	(0.9)	11.5	(0.7)	1.9	(0.4)
	Korea	0.2	(0.2)	0.9	(0.3)	4.7	(0.6)	15.4	(1.0)	33.0	(1.2)	32.9	(1.4)	11.9	(1.0)	1.0	(0.2)
	Luxembourg	3.1	(0.3)	7.3	(0.4)	15.7	(0.6)	24.0	(0.7)	27.0	(0.6)	17.3	(0.6)	5.2	(0.4)	0.5	(0.2)
	Mexico	3.2	(0.3)	11.4	(0.5)	25.5	(0.6)	33.0	(0.6)	21.2	(0.6)	5.3	(0.4)	0.4	(0.1)	0.0	(0.0)
	Netherlands	0.1	(0.1)	1.8	(0.3)	12.5	(1.4)	24.7	(1.5)	27.6	(1.2)	23.5	(1.7)	9.1	(1.0)	0.7	(0.2)
	New Zealand	0.9	(0.2)	3.2	(0.4)	10.2	(0.6)	19.3	(0.8)	25.8	(0.8)	24.8	(0.8)	12.9	(0.8)	2.9	(0.4)
	Norway	0.5	(0.1)	3.4	(0.4)	11.0	(0.7)	23.6	(0.8)	30.9	(0.9)	22.1	(1.2)	7.6	(0.9)	0.8	(0.2)
	Poland	0.6	(0.1)	3.1	(0.3)	11.3	(0.7)	24.5	(1.1)	31.0	(1.0)	22.3	(1.0)	6.5	(0.4)	0.7	(0.1)
	Portugal	0.6	(0.1)	4.0	(0.4)	13.0	(1.0)	26.4	(1.1)	31.6	(1.1)	19.6	(0.9)	4.6	(0.5)	0.2	(0.1)
	Slovak Republic	0.8	(0.3)	5.6	(0.6)	15.9	(0.8)	28.1	(1.0)	28.5	(1.1)	16.7	(0.8)	4.2	(0.5)	0.3	(0.1)
	Slovenia	0.8	(0.1)	5.2	(0.3)	15.2	(0.5)	25.6	(0.7)	29.2	(0.9)	19.3	(0.8)	4.3	(0.5)	0.3	(0.1)
	Spain	1.2	(0.2)	4.7	(0.4)	13.6	(0.6)	26.8	(0.8)	32.6	(1.0)	17.7	(0.7)	3.2	(0.3)	0.2	(0.1)
	Sweden	1.5	(0.3)	4.3	(0.4)	11.7	(0.7)	23.5	(1.0)	29.8	(1.0)	20.3	(0.9)	7.7	(0.6)	1.3	(0.3)
	Switzerland	0.7	(0.2)	4.1	(0.4)	12.1	(0.6)	22.7	(0.7)	29.7	(0.8)	22.6	(0.8)	7.4	(0.7)	0.7	(0.2)
	Turkey	0.8	(0.2)	5.6	(0.6)	18.1	(1.0)	32.2	(1.2)	29.1	(1.1)	12.4	(1.1)	1.8	(0.4)	0.0	(0.0)
	United Kingdom	1.0	(0.2)	4.1	(0.4)	13.4	(0.6)	24.9	(0.7)	28.8	(0.8)	19.8	(0.8)	7.0	(0.5)	1.0	(0.2)
	United States	0.6	(0.1)	4.0	(0.4)	13.1	(0.6)	24.4	(0.9)	27.6	(0.8)	20.6	(0.9)	8.4	(0.8)	1.5	(0.4)
	OECD average	1.1	(0.0)	4.6	(0.1)	13.1	(0.1)	24.0	(0.2)	28.9	(0.2)	20.7	(0.2)	6.8	(0.1)	0.8	(0.0)
Partners	Albania	11.3	(0.9)	18.7	(1.3)	26.6	(1.2)	25.6	(1.3)	14.4	(1.2)	3.1	(0.5)	0.2	(0.1)	0.0	c
	Argentina	10.8	(1.1)	15.8	(1.3)	25.0	(1.3)	25.4	(1.2)	16.0	(1.0)	6.0	(0.8)	0.9	(0.2)	0.1	(0.1)
	Azerbaijan	9.7	(1.1)	26.1	(1.1)	36.9	(1.2)	21.5	(1.2)	5.3	(0.8)	0.5	(0.2)	0.0	(0.0)	0.0	c
	Brazil	5.0	(0.4)	16.0	(0.7)	28.6	(0.8)	27.1	(0.8)	15.9	(0.9)	6.1	(0.5)	1.2	(0.2)	0.1	(0.1)
	Bulgaria	8.0	(1.1)	12.9	(1.4)	20.1	(1.4)	23.4	(1.1)	21.8	(1.4)	11.0	(1.1)	2.6	(0.5)	0.2	(0.1)
	Colombia	4.2	(0.7)	13.9	(1.0)	29.0	(1.2)	30.6	(1.1)	17.1	(1.0)	4.6	(0.5)	0.5	(0.2)	0.0	(0.0)
	Croatia	1.0	(0.2)	5.0	(0.4)	16.5	(1.0)	27.4	(1.0)	30.6	(1.2)	16.4	(1.0)	3.1	(0.4)	0.1	(0.1)
	Dubai (UAE)	3.7	(0.2)	9.4	(0.5)	17.9	(0.5)	25.4	(0.7)	23.5	(0.8)	14.8	(0.7)	4.8	(0.5)	0.5	(0.2)
	Hong Kong-China	0.2	(0.1)	1.5	(0.3)	6.6	(0.6)	16.1	(0.8)	31.4	(0.9)	31.8	(0.9)	11.2	(0.7)	1.2	(0.3)
	Indonesia	1.7	(0.4)	14.1	(1.3)	37.6	(1.6)	34.3	(1.4)	11.2	(1.3)	1.0	(0.3)	0.0	c	0.0	c
	Jordan	6.9	(0.6)	13.6	(0.8)	27.6	(1.0)	31.8	(1.0)	16.5	(1.0)	3.4	(0.4)	0.2	(0.1)	0.0	c
	Kazakhstan	7.5	(0.7)	20.4	(1.0)	30.7	(0.9)	24.1	(0.9)	13.1	(0.9)	3.7	(0.5)	0.4	(0.1)	0.0	c
	Kyrgyzstan	29.8	(1.2)	29.7	(0.9)	23.8	(0.9)	11.5	(0.8)	4.2	(0.6)	1.0	(0.3)	0.1	(0.1)	0.0	c
	Latvia	0.4	(0.2)	3.3	(0.6)	13.9	(1.0)	28.8	(1.5)	33.5	(1.2)	17.2	(1.0)	2.9	(0.4)	0.1	c
	Liechtenstein	0.0	c	2.8	(1.2)	12.8	(1.8)	24.0	(2.8)	31.1	(2.8)	24.6	(2.3)	4.2	(1.4)	0.4	c
	Lithuania	0.9	(0.3)	5.5	(0.6)	17.9	(0.9)	30.0	(1.1)	28.6	(0.9)	14.1	(0.8)	2.8	(0.4)	0.1	(0.1)
	Macao-China	0.3	(0.1)	2.6	(0.3)	12.0	(0.4)	30.6	(0.6)	34.8	(0.7)	16.9	(0.5)	2.8	(0.2)	0.1	(0.1)
	Montenegro	5.9	(0.5)	15.8	(0.8)	27.8	(0.8)	28.0	(0.9)	16.8	(0.8)	5.0	(0.5)	0.6	(0.2)	0.0	c
	Panama	13.3	(1.8)	23.1	(1.8)	28.9	(1.8)	20.7	(1.4)	10.1	(1.4)	3.4	(0.7)	0.5	(0.2)	0.0	c
	Peru	14.1	(0.9)	22.0	(1.0)	28.7	(1.1)	22.1	(0.9)	10.1	(0.9)	2.6	(0.5)	0.4	(0.2)	0.0	(0.0)
	Qatar	17.8	(0.3)	22.4	(0.5)	23.2	(0.6)	18.3	(0.4)	11.1	(0.5)	5.4	(0.3)	1.5	(0.2)	0.2	(0.1)
	Romania	4.1	(0.7)	12.7	(1.1)	23.6	(1.2)	31.6	(1.3)	21.2	(1.3)	6.1	(0.7)	0.7	(0.2)	0.0	c
	Russian Federation	1.6	(0.3)	6.8	(0.6)	19.0	(0.8)	31.6	(1.0)	26.8	(0.9)	11.1	(0.7)	2.8	(0.4)	0.3	(0.1)
	Serbia	2.0	(0.4)	8.8	(0.7)	22.1	(0.9)	33.2	(1.0)	25.3	(1.0)	7.9	(0.6)	0.8	(0.2)	0.0	(0.0)
	Shanghai-China	0.1	(0.0)	0.6	(0.1)	3.4	(0.5)	13.3	(0.9)	28.5	(1.2)	34.7	(1.0)	17.0	(1.0)	2.4	(0.4)
	Singapore	0.4	(0.1)	2.7	(0.3)	9.3	(0.5)	18.5	(0.6)	27.6	(0.8)	25.7	(0.7)	13.1	(0.5)	2.6	(0.3)
	Chinese Taipei	0.7	(0.2)	3.5	(0.4)	11.4	(0.6)	24.6	(0.8)	33.5	(1.1)	21.0	(1.0)	4.8	(0.8)	0.4	(0.2)
	Thailand	1.2	(0.3)	9.9	(0.8)	31.7	(1.1)	36.8	(1.2)	16.7	(0.8)	3.3	(0.5)	0.3	(0.2)	0.0	c
	Trinidad and Tobago	9.6	(0.5)	14.2	(0.6)	21.0	(0.8)	25.0	(0.9)	19.0	(0.9)	8.9	(0.5)	2.1	(0.3)	0.2	(0.1)
	Tunisia	5.5	(0.5)	15.0	(0.8)	29.6	(1.1)	31.5	(1.2)	15.1	(1.0)	3.1	(0.5)	0.2	(0.1)	0.0	c
	Uruguay	5.5	(0.6)	12.5	(0.7)	23.9	(0.7)	28.0	(0.7)	20.3	(0.7)	8.1	(0.5)	1.7	(0.3)	0.1	(0.1)

Note: Percentages were computed only for students with information on the PISA index of economic, social and cultural status.
StatLink ⟨ms⟩ http://dx.doi.org/10.1787/888932343285

[Part 2/2]
Performance by proficiency level in reading and socio-economic background
Table II.2.1 *Results based on students' self-reports*

		Percentage of students who are							Average PISA index of economic, social and cultural status							
		Top performers (Level 5 or 6) in reading		Strong performers (Level 4) in reading		Moderate performers (Levels 2 or 3) in reading		Lowest performers (below Level 2) in reading		Top performers (Level 5 or 6) in reading		Strong performers (Level 4) in reading		Moderate performers (Levels 2 or 3) in reading		Lowest performers (below Level 2) in reading	
		%	S.E.	%	S.E.	%	S.E.	%	S.E.	Mean index	S.E.	Mean index	S.E.	Mean index	S.E.	Mean index	S.E.
OECD	Australia	12.8	(0.8)	24.1	(0.7)	48.9	(0.8)	14.2	(0.6)	0.77	(0.02)	0.55	(0.02)	0.24	(0.02)	-0.07	(0.02)
	Austria	4.9	(0.5)	17.4	(0.9)	50.1	(1.4)	27.6	(1.3)	0.64	(0.07)	0.48	(0.04)	0.09	(0.02)	-0.38	(0.04)
	Belgium	11.2	(0.6)	24.9	(0.7)	46.1	(0.8)	17.7	(0.9)	0.84	(0.03)	0.55	(0.03)	0.07	(0.02)	-0.42	(0.04)
	Canada	12.8	(0.5)	26.8	(0.6)	50.2	(0.7)	10.3	(0.5)	0.93	(0.03)	0.65	(0.02)	0.39	(0.02)	0.10	(0.04)
	Chile	1.3	(0.3)	9.3	(0.7)	58.8	(1.3)	30.6	(1.5)	0.85	(0.16)	0.37	(0.06)	-0.47	(0.04)	-1.11	(0.05)
	Czech Republic	5.1	(0.5)	17.4	(1.0)	54.5	(1.2)	23.1	(1.3)	0.47	(0.05)	0.23	(0.02)	-0.10	(0.02)	-0.40	(0.02)
	Denmark	4.7	(0.5)	20.9	(1.1)	59.1	(1.2)	15.2	(0.9)	0.89	(0.06)	0.69	(0.03)	0.24	(0.03)	-0.22	(0.04)
	Estonia	6.1	(0.6)	21.2	(0.8)	59.4	(1.1)	13.3	(1.0)	0.62	(0.06)	0.38	(0.04)	0.09	(0.02)	-0.16	(0.05)
	Finland	14.5	(0.8)	30.6	(0.9)	46.8	(1.1)	8.1	(0.5)	0.70	(0.03)	0.49	(0.03)	0.26	(0.02)	-0.04	(0.06)
	France	9.6	(1.0)	22.4	(1.1)	48.3	(1.5)	19.8	(1.2)	0.46	(0.06)	0.18	(0.04)	-0.20	(0.03)	-0.64	(0.04)
	Germany	7.6	(0.6)	22.8	(0.9)	51.1	(1.3)	18.5	(1.1)	0.82	(0.05)	0.54	(0.04)	0.12	(0.03)	-0.41	(0.04)
	Greece	5.6	(0.5)	18.2	(1.0)	54.9	(1.4)	21.3	(1.8)	0.67	(0.06)	0.36	(0.04)	-0.02	(0.03)	-0.53	(0.05)
	Hungary	6.1	(0.7)	21.6	(1.1)	54.8	(1.2)	17.6	(1.4)	0.73	(0.08)	0.32	(0.04)	-0.26	(0.02)	-0.95	(0.06)
	Iceland	8.5	(0.6)	21.9	(0.8)	52.8	(0.9)	16.8	(0.6)	1.14	(0.06)	0.92	(0.03)	0.67	(0.02)	0.39	(0.04)
	Ireland	7.0	(0.5)	21.9	(0.9)	53.8	(1.1)	17.2	(1.0)	0.54	(0.04)	0.38	(0.04)	-0.02	(0.03)	-0.40	(0.04)
	Israel	7.4	(0.6)	18.1	(0.7)	48.0	(1.2)	26.5	(1.2)	0.54	(0.04)	0.34	(0.04)	-0.05	(0.03)	-0.42	(0.03)
	Italy	5.8	(0.3)	20.2	(0.5)	52.9	(0.7)	21.0	(0.6)	0.51	(0.03)	0.27	(0.02)	-0.15	(0.02)	-0.60	(0.02)
	Japan	13.4	(0.9)	27.0	(0.9)	46.0	(1.1)	13.6	(1.1)	0.33	(0.04)	0.16	(0.02)	-0.12	(0.02)	-0.33	(0.03)
	Korea	12.9	(1.1)	32.9	(1.4)	48.4	(1.7)	5.8	(0.8)	0.26	(0.06)	0.02	(0.04)	-0.31	(0.03)	-0.70	(0.05)
	Luxembourg	5.7	(0.5)	17.3	(0.6)	51.0	(0.8)	26.0	(0.6)	1.03	(0.06)	0.74	(0.04)	0.21	(0.02)	-0.43	(0.03)
	Mexico	0.4	(0.1)	5.3	(0.4)	54.2	(0.9)	40.1	(1.0)	0.23	(0.14)	-0.17	(0.07)	-0.96	(0.03)	-1.72	(0.03)
	Netherlands	9.8	(1.1)	23.5	(1.7)	52.3	(1.5)	14.3	(1.5)	0.84	(0.05)	0.57	(0.04)	0.13	(0.04)	-0.09	(0.04)
	New Zealand	15.7	(0.8)	24.8	(0.8)	45.1	(0.9)	14.3	(0.7)	0.57	(0.03)	0.29	(0.03)	-0.05	(0.02)	-0.42	(0.04)
	Norway	8.4	(0.9)	22.1	(1.2)	54.5	(1.1)	15.0	(0.8)	0.88	(0.04)	0.66	(0.03)	0.42	(0.02)	0.12	(0.04)
	Poland	7.2	(0.6)	22.3	(1.0)	55.5	(1.1)	15.0	(0.8)	0.41	(0.06)	0.07	(0.04)	-0.38	(0.02)	-0.76	(0.04)
	Portugal	4.8	(0.5)	19.6	(0.9)	58.0	(1.2)	17.6	(1.2)	0.75	(0.11)	0.25	(0.06)	-0.41	(0.04)	-0.96	(0.05)
	Slovak Republic	4.5	(0.5)	16.7	(0.8)	56.6	(1.3)	22.2	(1.2)	0.63	(0.10)	0.30	(0.04)	-0.11	(0.02)	-0.51	(0.04)
	Slovenia	4.6	(0.5)	19.3	(0.8)	54.9	(0.9)	21.2	(0.6)	0.70	(0.08)	0.51	(0.04)	0.04	(0.02)	-0.38	(0.02)
	Spain	3.3	(0.3)	17.7	(0.7)	59.4	(0.7)	19.6	(0.9)	0.50	(0.07)	0.21	(0.05)	-0.33	(0.04)	-0.88	(0.04)
	Sweden	9.0	(0.7)	20.3	(0.9)	53.2	(1.0)	17.4	(0.9)	0.82	(0.04)	0.61	(0.04)	0.28	(0.02)	-0.13	(0.04)
	Switzerland	8.1	(0.7)	22.6	(0.8)	52.4	(0.9)	16.8	(0.9)	0.67	(0.07)	0.38	(0.04)	0.01	(0.04)	-0.42	(0.03)
	Turkey	1.9	(0.4)	12.4	(1.1)	61.3	(1.4)	24.5	(1.4)	0.23	(0.17)	-0.30	(0.08)	-1.13	(0.04)	-1.80	(0.06)
	United Kingdom	8.0	(0.5)	19.8	(0.8)	53.7	(0.7)	18.4	(0.8)	0.73	(0.04)	0.52	(0.03)	0.14	(0.02)	-0.20	(0.03)
	United States	9.9	(0.9)	20.6	(0.9)	52.0	(1.1)	17.6	(1.1)	0.89	(0.06)	0.52	(0.05)	0.06	(0.04)	-0.34	(0.04)
	OECD average	7.6	(0.1)	20.7	(0.2)	52.9	(0.2)	18.8	(0.2)	0.66	(0.01)	0.38	(0.01)	-0.05	(0.00)	-0.48	(0.01)
Partners	Albania	0.2	(0.1)	3.1	(0.5)	40.1	(1.7)	56.7	(1.9)	0.00	c	0.03	(0.11)	-0.66	(0.05)	-1.22	(0.04)
	Argentina	1.0	(0.2)	6.0	(0.8)	41.4	(1.6)	51.6	(1.9)	0.00	c	0.46	(0.11)	-0.26	(0.05)	-1.06	(0.04)
	Azerbaijan	0.0	(0.0)	0.5	(0.2)	26.7	(1.6)	72.8	(1.6)	0.00	c	0.03	(0.53)	-0.30	(0.06)	-0.77	(0.03)
	Brazil	1.3	(0.2)	6.1	(0.5)	43.1	(1.0)	49.6	(1.3)	0.66	(0.12)	-0.05	(0.10)	-0.98	(0.04)	-1.51	(0.03)
	Bulgaria	2.8	(0.5)	11.0	(1.1)	45.3	(1.4)	41.0	(2.6)	0.75	(0.10)	0.53	(0.06)	0.08	(0.03)	-0.56	(0.05)
	Colombia	0.6	(0.2)	4.6	(0.5)	47.7	(1.7)	47.1	(1.9)	0.00	c	0.04	(0.12)	-0.86	(0.05)	-1.59	(0.05)
	Croatia	3.2	(0.4)	16.4	(1.0)	57.9	(1.3)	22.4	(1.3)	0.50	(0.10)	0.23	(0.05)	-0.18	(0.03)	-0.57	(0.04)
	Dubai (UAE)	5.3	(0.5)	14.8	(0.7)	48.9	(0.7)	31.0	(0.5)	0.93	(0.04)	0.81	(0.02)	0.48	(0.02)	0.06	(0.02)
	Hong Kong-China	12.4	(0.8)	31.8	(0.9)	47.5	(1.1)	8.3	(0.7)	-0.49	(0.07)	-0.62	(0.05)	-0.94	(0.04)	-1.16	(0.10)
	Indonesia	0.0	c	1.0	(0.3)	45.6	(2.1)	53.4	(2.3)	0.00	c	-0.54	(0.30)	-1.29	(0.08)	-1.79	(0.05)
	Jordan	0.2	(0.1)	3.4	(0.4)	48.3	(1.4)	48.0	(1.6)	0.00	c	0.26	(0.09)	-0.37	(0.04)	-0.83	(0.03)
	Kazakhstan	0.4	(0.1)	3.7	(0.5)	37.2	(1.3)	58.7	(1.5)	0.00	c	0.13	(0.08)	-0.27	(0.03)	-0.71	(0.03)
	Kyrgyzstan	0.1	(0.1)	1.0	(0.3)	15.7	(1.1)	83.2	(1.2)	0.00	c	0.55	(0.12)	-0.01	(0.06)	-0.78	(0.02)
	Latvia	2.9	(0.4)	17.2	(1.0)	62.3	(1.3)	17.6	(1.2)	0.43	(0.08)	0.27	(0.05)	-0.16	(0.03)	-0.50	(0.05)
	Liechtenstein	4.6	(1.4)	24.6	(2.3)	55.1	(3.5)	15.7	(1.8)	0.00	c	0.30	(0.11)	0.07	(0.07)	-0.37	(0.15)
	Lithuania	2.9	(0.4)	14.1	(0.8)	58.6	(1.2)	24.4	(1.2)	0.74	(0.08)	0.50	(0.04)	-0.03	(0.04)	-0.50	(0.04)
	Macao-China	2.9	(0.2)	16.9	(0.5)	65.4	(0.6)	14.9	(0.5)	-0.26	(0.10)	-0.53	(0.04)	-0.74	(0.02)	-0.82	(0.04)
	Montenegro	0.6	(0.2)	5.0	(0.5)	44.9	(1.1)	49.5	(1.0)	0.00	c	0.39	(0.08)	-0.04	(0.04)	-0.51	(0.02)
	Panama	0.5	(0.2)	3.4	(0.7)	30.8	(2.2)	65.3	(2.6)	0.00	c	0.81	(0.12)	-0.30	(0.12)	-1.18	(0.06)
	Peru	0.5	(0.2)	2.6	(0.5)	32.1	(1.4)	64.8	(1.7)	0.00	c	0.32	(0.14)	-0.66	(0.06)	-1.72	(0.04)
	Qatar	1.7	(0.2)	5.4	(0.3)	29.4	(0.5)	63.5	(0.5)	1.17	(0.07)	0.97	(0.03)	0.65	(0.01)	0.38	(0.01)
	Romania	0.7	(0.2)	6.1	(0.7)	52.8	(1.8)	40.4	(2.0)	0.00	c	0.28	(0.09)	-0.17	(0.04)	-0.68	(0.05)
	Russian Federation	3.2	(0.5)	11.1	(0.7)	58.3	(1.1)	27.4	(1.3)	0.52	(0.08)	0.21	(0.05)	-0.19	(0.03)	-0.52	(0.03)
	Serbia	0.8	(0.2)	7.9	(0.6)	58.5	(1.1)	32.8	(1.3)	0.00	c	0.61	(0.07)	0.17	(0.03)	-0.27	(0.03)
	Shanghai-China	19.5	(1.1)	34.7	(1.0)	41.8	(1.2)	4.1	(0.5)	0.06	(0.06)	-0.35	(0.04)	-0.80	(0.04)	-1.14	(0.10)
	Singapore	15.7	(0.5)	25.7	(0.7)	46.1	(0.9)	12.5	(0.5)	0.06	(0.04)	-0.22	(0.03)	-0.58	(0.01)	-0.92	(0.04)
	Chinese Taipei	5.2	(0.8)	21.0	(1.0)	58.2	(1.3)	15.6	(0.9)	0.30	(0.08)	-0.03	(0.03)	-0.38	(0.02)	-0.75	(0.04)
	Thailand	0.3	(0.2)	3.3	(0.5)	53.5	(1.4)	42.9	(1.5)	0.00	c	0.12	(0.14)	-1.12	(0.05)	-1.67	(0.04)
	Trinidad and Tobago	2.3	(0.3)	8.9	(0.5)	44.0	(0.8)	44.8	(0.8)	0.31	(0.12)	-0.03	(0.05)	-0.47	(0.03)	-0.85	(0.03)
	Tunisia	0.2	(0.1)	3.1	(0.5)	46.6	(1.4)	50.2	(1.6)	0.00	c	-0.11	(0.15)	-0.93	(0.06)	-1.52	(0.05)
	Uruguay	1.8	(0.3)	8.1	(0.5)	48.2	(1.0)	41.9	(1.2)	0.72	(0.14)	0.39	(0.09)	-0.48	(0.03)	-1.23	(0.03)

Note: Percentages were computed only for students with information on the PISA index of economic, social and cultural status.
StatLink ⟨⟩ http://dx.doi.org/10.1787/888932343285

[Part 1/1]
Schools' average socio-economic background and resources
Table II.2.2   *Results based on students' self-reports and school principals' reports*

Simple correlation between the schools' average socio-economic background and (values shown as Corr. (S.E.)):

	Index of teacher shortage	Percentage of full-time teachers	Percentage of certified teachers among all full-time teachers	Percentage of teachers with university-level degree (ISCED 5A) among all full-time teachers	Index of school responsibility in resource allocation	Index of school curriculum responsibility	Index of quality of school's educational resources	Student/computer ratio	Student/teacher ratio	School size
OECD										
Australia	-0.28 (0.06)	-0.21 (0.06)	-0.05 (0.02)	0.02 (0.07)	0.54 (0.03)	0.11 (0.06)	0.31 (0.05)	0.01 (0.05)	-0.07 (0.05)	0.29 (0.06)
Austria	-0.01 (0.08)	-0.13 (0.06)	0.21 (0.07)	0.64 (0.03)	-0.02 (0.04)	-0.07 (0.07)	0.03 (0.07)	-0.05 (0.05)	-0.07 (0.04)	0.30 (0.05)
Belgium	-0.17 (0.05)	-0.18 (0.05)	0.15 (0.06)	0.58 (0.06)	0.00 (0.06)	0.05 (0.05)	0.02 (0.06)	-0.23 (0.04)	0.66 (0.03)	0.35 (0.06)
Canada	-0.16 (0.04)	0.01 (0.04)	0.14 (0.04)	0.03 (0.03)	0.32 (0.05)	0.14 (0.06)	0.18 (0.05)	-0.05 (0.03)	0.09 (0.05)	0.16 (0.04)
Chile	-0.06 (0.08)	-0.04 (0.09)	-0.01 (0.15)	0.25 (0.05)	0.39 (0.05)	0.24 (0.08)	0.35 (0.05)	0.32 (0.07)	-0.05 (0.08)	0.21 (0.06)
Czech Republic	-0.34 (0.06)	-0.32 (0.06)	0.29 (0.06)	0.37 (0.04)	-0.05 (0.06)	0.02 (0.05)	0.00 (0.06)	0.15 (0.10)	0.08 (0.07)	0.23 (0.07)
Denmark	-0.23 (0.08)	0.01 (0.06)	-0.17 (0.09)	0.16 (0.08)	0.14 (0.08)	0.15 (0.07)	0.04 (0.07)	-0.08 (0.10)	0.27 (0.06)	0.21 (0.07)
Estonia	-0.05 (0.06)	0.14 (0.06)	0.00 (0.03)	0.00 (0.03)	-0.04 (0.09)	-0.07 (0.07)	0.10 (0.07)	-0.09 (0.06)	0.43 (0.07)	0.52 (0.07)
Finland	0.03 (0.07)	0.17 (0.06)	-0.01 (0.09)	-0.01 (0.09)	0.23 (0.11)	0.01 (0.09)	0.13 (0.08)	-0.01 (0.09)	0.08 (0.07)	0.31 (0.06)
France	w	w	w	w	w	w	w	w	w	w
Germany	-0.09 (0.06)	-0.15 (0.06)	-0.02 (0.05)	-0.02 (0.05)	0.08 (0.05)	-0.20 (0.06)	0.06 (0.07)	-0.18 (0.07)	0.28 (0.04)	0.42 (0.07)
Greece	-0.19 (0.05)	-0.11 (0.09)	0.06 (0.08)	0.24 (0.08)	0.30 (0.06)	0.27 (0.04)	0.16 (0.08)	-0.12 (0.14)	0.25 (0.09)	0.27 (0.07)
Hungary	-0.08 (0.08)	-0.33 (0.06)	0.07 (0.12)	0.07 (0.12)	-0.02 (0.07)	0.13 (0.07)	0.11 (0.08)	-0.20 (0.06)	0.02 (0.06)	0.12 (0.08)
Iceland	-0.37 (0.00)	0.20 (0.01)	0.39 (0.01)	0.30 (0.01)	-0.11 (0.01)	-0.07 (0.01)	0.06 (0.00)	-0.41 (0.00)	0.40 (0.01)	0.37 (0.01)
Ireland	-0.16 (0.07)	0.12 (0.10)	-0.10 (0.13)	-0.08 (0.06)	0.33 (0.09)	-0.07 (0.10)	0.16 (0.10)	-0.03 (0.13)	0.49 (0.08)	0.32 (0.07)
Israel	-0.07 (0.08)	-0.08 (0.08)	-0.06 (0.12)	0.20 (0.06)	0.19 (0.07)	0.05 (0.06)	0.25 (0.07)	0.08 (0.07)	-0.20 (0.08)	0.27 (0.06)
Italy	0.02 (0.04)	-0.06 (0.04)	0.16 (0.05)	0.13 (0.04)	0.09 (0.04)	0.03 (0.03)	0.15 (0.04)	-0.19 (0.04)	0.50 (0.03)	0.21 (0.03)
Japan	-0.04 (0.06)	-0.14 (0.06)	0.04 (0.04)	0.20 (0.05)	0.24 (0.06)	0.05 (0.07)	0.17 (0.04)	-0.34 (0.04)	0.38 (0.04)	0.52 (0.04)
Korea	-0.02 (0.09)	-0.14 (0.11)	0.00 (0.14)	-0.03 (0.12)	0.07 (0.08)	0.19 (0.09)	-0.04 (0.10)	-0.53 (0.12)	0.30 (0.11)	0.27 (0.09)
Luxembourg	-0.33 (0.00)	-0.16 (0.00)	-0.01 (0.00)	0.39 (0.00)	0.01 (0.00)	0.35 (0.00)	0.13 (0.00)	-0.13 (0.01)	0.28 (0.00)	0.05 (0.00)
Mexico	-0.26 (0.04)	-0.09 (0.05)	-0.13 (0.06)	-0.04 (0.05)	0.46 (0.04)	0.26 (0.05)	0.59 (0.03)	0.14 (0.05)	0.03 (0.03)	0.28 (0.03)
Netherlands	0.05 (0.10)	-0.34 (0.08)	-0.12 (0.06)	0.62 (0.06)	0.01 (0.06)	-0.03 (0.06)	0.06 (0.09)	-0.16 (0.10)	0.38 (0.11)	0.42 (0.05)
New Zealand	-0.19 (0.07)	-0.04 (0.07)	0.08 (0.05)	0.07 (0.08)	0.17 (0.06)	-0.01 (0.07)	0.16 (0.06)	-0.02 (0.08)	0.11 (0.06)	0.33 (0.03)
Norway	-0.23 (0.07)	-0.05 (0.08)	0.04 (0.06)	0.15 (0.07)	0.12 (0.08)	-0.03 (0.08)	0.14 (0.08)	-0.02 (0.08)	0.19 (0.08)	0.30 (0.06)
Poland	-0.05 (0.06)	-0.02 (0.05)	0.03 (0.05)	-0.05 (0.06)	0.20 (0.11)	-0.07 (0.07)	0.06 (0.07)	-0.16 (0.06)	0.01 (0.09)	0.33 (0.05)
Portugal	-0.09 (0.07)	0.14 (0.07)	-0.05 (0.10)	0.04 (0.10)	0.13 (0.12)	0.24 (0.05)	0.24 (0.05)	-0.02 (0.17)	0.39 (0.05)	0.40 (0.06)
Slovak Republic	-0.20 (0.08)	-0.09 (0.05)	0.28 (0.05)	-0.21 (0.05)	0.04 (0.09)	-0.10 (0.08)	-0.05 (0.06)	-0.06 (0.06)	0.00 (0.06)	0.18 (0.07)
Slovenia	-0.02 (0.01)	0.46 (0.02)	0.32 (0.01)	0.55 (0.01)	-0.05 (0.01)	-0.13 (0.01)	0.13 (0.01)	-0.21 (0.01)	-0.25 (0.02)	0.51 (0.01)
Spain	-0.02 (0.05)	-0.29 (0.06)	m	m	0.47 (0.04)	0.17 (0.06)	0.10 (0.04)	-0.16 (0.04)	0.45 (0.04)	0.45 (0.05)
Sweden	-0.12 (0.08)	0.05 (0.09)	0.01 (0.07)	-0.04 (0.08)	0.30 (0.06)	-0.04 (0.07)	0.26 (0.08)	0.13 (0.06)	0.12 (0.05)	0.16 (0.08)
Switzerland	-0.16 (0.06)	-0.11 (0.08)	-0.07 (0.06)	0.24 (0.09)	0.09 (0.12)	0.25 (0.07)	0.10 (0.09)	0.03 (0.04)	0.06 (0.10)	0.26 (0.04)
Turkey	0.01 (0.07)	0.12 (0.06)	-0.04 (0.08)	0.04 (0.08)	0.30 (0.13)	0.02 (0.06)	0.04 (0.05)	-0.06 (0.06)	-0.26 (0.06)	-0.07 (0.05)
United Kingdom	-0.15 (0.06)	-0.36 (0.06)	0.05 (0.07)	-0.03 (0.04)	0.16 (0.06)	0.10 (0.05)	0.00 (0.06)	0.01 (0.08)	-0.10 (0.06)	0.14 (0.07)
United States	-0.28 (0.08)	-0.42 (0.10)	-0.24 (0.16)	0.10 (0.07)	0.09 (0.08)	0.20 (0.08)	0.22 (0.09)	0.06 (0.09)	-0.17 (0.09)	-0.02 (0.07)
OECD average	-0.13 (0.01)	-0.07 (0.01)	0.04 (0.01)	0.15 (0.01)	0.16 (0.01)	0.06 (0.01)	0.13 (0.01)	-0.08 (0.01)	0.15 (0.01)	0.28 (0.01)
Partners										
Albania	-0.38 (0.08)	-0.25 (0.07)	0.00 (0.06)	0.38 (0.05)	0.25 (0.05)	0.02 (0.07)	0.44 (0.06)	0.24 (0.06)	0.15 (0.07)	0.46 (0.05)
Argentina	-0.22 (0.07)	0.13 (0.07)	0.13 (0.08)	0.22 (0.14)	0.45 (0.06)	0.23 (0.09)	0.51 (0.06)	0.21 (0.04)	-0.02 (0.05)	0.09 (0.06)
Azerbaijan	-0.10 (0.09)	0.05 (0.10)	-0.06 (0.03)	0.44 (0.11)	-0.07 (0.07)	-0.16 (0.09)	0.19 (0.08)	0.17 (0.09)	0.23 (0.08)	0.66 (0.05)
Brazil	-0.37 (0.04)	-0.03 (0.07)	0.10 (0.09)	0.03 (0.07)	0.64 (0.03)	0.41 (0.04)	0.52 (0.04)	0.25 (0.08)	-0.20 (0.04)	0.12 (0.05)
Bulgaria	0.19 (0.08)	-0.08 (0.06)	0.17 (0.08)	0.17 (0.08)	-0.18 (0.08)	-0.01 (0.08)	0.09 (0.08)	-0.17 (0.09)	0.21 (0.06)	0.51 (0.06)
Colombia	-0.30 (0.06)	-0.24 (0.08)	-0.16 (0.07)	-0.08 (0.07)	0.65 (0.04)	0.24 (0.07)	0.53 (0.05)	0.19 (0.10)	-0.14 (0.09)	0.00 (0.06)
Croatia	-0.19 (0.08)	0.09 (0.06)	0.02 (0.03)	0.28 (0.06)	0.26 (0.12)	0.05 (0.13)	0.09 (0.07)	0.17 (0.10)	0.32 (0.09)	0.17 (0.07)
Dubai (UAE)	-0.20 (0.00)	0.32 (0.00)	0.61 (0.00)	-0.01 (0.00)	0.54 (0.00)	0.55 (0.00)	0.34 (0.00)	0.47 (0.00)	-0.27 (0.00)	0.07 (0.00)
Hong Kong-China	-0.17 (0.07)	-0.19 (0.10)	-0.06 (0.04)	0.12 (0.05)	0.13 (0.08)	0.04 (0.05)	0.06 (0.09)	0.04 (0.06)	0.02 (0.10)	0.12 (0.12)
Indonesia	-0.35 (0.07)	0.24 (0.07)	0.27 (0.08)	0.16 (0.09)	-0.03 (0.08)	0.09 (0.09)	0.44 (0.06)	0.14 (0.09)	-0.16 (0.09)	0.42 (0.07)
Jordan	-0.24 (0.07)	-0.04 (0.09)	0.00 (0.07)	-0.02 (0.07)	0.53 (0.05)	0.32 (0.08)	0.26 (0.09)	0.05 (0.07)	0.06 (0.09)	0.32 (0.07)
Kazakhstan	-0.07 (0.06)	0.23 (0.10)	0.04 (0.07)	0.34 (0.06)	0.17 (0.10)	-0.18 (0.07)	0.21 (0.07)	-0.12 (0.07)	0.44 (0.06)	0.38 (0.07)
Kyrgyzstan	0.07 (0.08)	0.17 (0.07)	0.08 (0.08)	0.35 (0.07)	0.41 (0.11)	-0.09 (0.08)	0.27 (0.10)	0.13 (0.05)	0.27 (0.08)	0.46 (0.07)
Latvia	0.07 (0.07)	0.19 (0.08)	-0.03 (0.09)	0.19 (0.07)	-0.10 (0.06)	0.07 (0.07)	0.14 (0.07)	0.00 (0.09)	0.38 (0.09)	0.60 (0.05)
Liechtenstein	0.58 (0.01)	-0.15 (0.01)	0.02 (0.01)	0.57 (0.01)	0.80 (0.01)	0.77 (0.00)	-0.91 (0.00)	0.79 (0.01)	0.70 (0.01)	0.87 (0.01)
Lithuania	-0.06 (0.08)	0.21 (0.06)	0.09 (0.04)	0.19 (0.03)	-0.20 (0.04)	-0.19 (0.06)	-0.02 (0.06)	-0.49 (0.04)	0.21 (0.09)	0.49 (0.06)
Macao-China	-0.01 (0.00)	0.11 (0.00)	0.05 (0.00)	-0.18 (0.00)	-0.03 (0.00)	0.34 (0.00)	0.26 (0.00)	0.22 (0.00)	0.17 (0.00)	0.04 (0.00)
Montenegro	-0.12 (0.04)	0.07 (0.04)	0.32 (0.02)	0.38 (0.03)	-0.01 (0.02)	-0.05 (0.01)	-0.11 (0.02)	-0.19 (0.02)	0.33 (0.04)	0.37 (0.05)
Panama	-0.24 (0.10)	-0.51 (0.06)	-0.47 (0.13)	-0.13 (0.09)	0.68 (0.04)	0.10 (0.11)	0.68 (0.08)	0.38 (0.10)	0.03 (0.08)	0.15 (0.08)
Peru	-0.35 (0.07)	-0.21 (0.08)	0.08 (0.05)	0.48 (0.06)	0.60 (0.04)	0.19 (0.07)	0.53 (0.08)	0.46 (0.06)	-0.02 (0.07)	0.24 (0.05)
Qatar	0.02 (0.00)	0.03 (0.00)	-0.04 (0.00)	-0.07 (0.00)	0.23 (0.00)	0.35 (0.00)	0.23 (0.00)	0.19 (0.00)	0.11 (0.00)	0.04 (0.00)
Romania	-0.18 (0.06)	0.05 (0.08)	0.10 (0.08)	0.11 (0.11)	-0.01 (0.09)	-0.10 (0.07)	0.20 (0.07)	-0.07 (0.07)	-0.02 (0.09)	0.26 (0.07)
Russian Federation	-0.12 (0.08)	0.18 (0.06)	0.08 (0.05)	0.31 (0.10)	0.04 (0.05)	-0.08 (0.06)	0.26 (0.05)	0.02 (0.07)	0.29 (0.06)	0.58 (0.05)
Serbia	-0.27 (0.04)	0.10 (0.08)	0.06 (0.05)	0.06 (0.05)	-0.04 (0.05)	-0.21 (0.05)	-0.01 (0.06)	0.00 (0.05)	0.11 (0.03)	0.12 (0.05)
Shanghai-China	-0.18 (0.06)	0.14 (0.06)	0.13 (0.09)	0.32 (0.07)	0.03 (0.08)	-0.11 (0.08)	0.16 (0.08)	-0.10 (0.09)	-0.13 (0.05)	-0.04 (0.05)
Singapore	-0.29 (0.01)	-0.13 (0.03)	0.00 (0.02)	0.22 (0.00)	0.52 (0.01)	0.10 (0.02)	0.10 (0.01)	-0.18 (0.01)	-0.14 (0.01)	0.40 (0.03)
Chinese Taipei	-0.17 (0.11)	0.12 (0.06)	0.34 (0.05)	0.29 (0.10)	-0.19 (0.07)	-0.01 (0.08)	0.19 (0.08)	-0.04 (0.11)	-0.07 (0.04)	0.05 (0.07)
Thailand	-0.08 (0.10)	0.07 (0.05)	0.06 (0.05)	0.16 (0.05)	0.07 (0.07)	-0.03 (0.08)	0.39 (0.06)	0.00 (0.07)	-0.02 (0.05)	0.69 (0.03)
Trinidad and Tobago	-0.22 (0.01)	-0.19 (0.01)	0.09 (0.01)	0.56 (0.00)	0.17 (0.00)	0.18 (0.01)	0.12 (0.01)	0.08 (0.01)	0.38 (0.00)	0.18 (0.01)
Tunisia	0.07 (0.08)	-0.06 (0.04)	0.00 (0.02)	0.20 (0.05)	0.04 (0.02)	0.01 (0.08)	0.13 (0.07)	0.15 (0.08)	-0.02 (0.09)	0.42 (0.07)
Uruguay	-0.25 (0.08)	-0.01 (0.06)	0.27 (0.08)	0.08 (0.05)	0.65 (0.04)	0.45 (0.05)	0.33 (0.05)	0.30 (0.05)	0.13 (0.09)	-0.01 (0.03)

Note: Values that are statistically significant are indicated in bold (see Annex A3).
StatLink ⟶ http://dx.doi.org/10.1787/888932343285

[Part 1/2]
Characteristics of schools attended by advantaged and disadvantaged students[1]
Table II.2.3   *Results based on students' self-reports and school principals' reports*

| | Percentage of students with an immigrant background | | | | School average PISA index of economic, social and cultural status | | | | | | Index of quality of educational resources | | | | | |
| | Advantaged students | | Disadvantaged students | | Advantaged students | | Disadvantaged students | | Difference (A-D) | | Advantaged students | | Disadvantaged students | | Difference (A-D) | |
	%	S.E.	%	S.E.	Mean index	S.E.	Mean index	S.E.	Dif.	S.E.	Mean index	S.E.	Mean index	S.E.	Dif.	S.E.
OECD																
Australia	24.3	(1.4)	24.5	(1.7)	0.71	(0.04)	-0.61	(0.05)	**1.32**	(0.06)	0.25	(0.06)	-0.18	(0.07)	**0.42**	(0.07)
Austria	6.2	(0.8)	31.7	(2.3)	0.71	(0.05)	-0.68	(0.07)	**1.39**	(0.09)	-0.04	(0.10)	-0.05	(0.08)	0.01	(0.10)
Belgium	8.5	(1.1)	24.8	(2.2)	0.79	(0.05)	-0.66	(0.05)	**1.45**	(0.08)	0.00	(0.08)	-0.03	(0.08)	0.03	(0.09)
Canada	24.3	(1.5)	27.1	(1.8)	0.60	(0.05)	-0.59	(0.06)	**1.19**	(0.08)	0.12	(0.05)	-0.08	(0.05)	**0.20**	(0.06)
Chile	c	c	c	c	1.04	(0.04)	-0.79	(0.05)	**1.83**	(0.07)	0.31	(0.09)	-0.32	(0.09)	**0.63**	(0.11)
Czech Republic	2.0	(0.4)	3.2	(0.6)	0.68	(0.05)	-0.61	(0.04)	**1.28**	(0.08)	-0.01	(0.08)	-0.02	(0.08)	0.01	(0.08)
Denmark	3.3	(0.4)	18.2	(1.3)	0.59	(0.09)	-0.60	(0.05)	**1.18**	(0.09)	0.06	(0.09)	0.00	(0.07)	0.06	(0.08)
Estonia	7.1	(1.1)	9.0	(1.1)	0.59	(0.08)	-0.58	(0.05)	**1.16**	(0.09)	0.08	(0.07)	-0.05	(0.10)	0.13	(0.09)
Finland	2.4	(0.5)	4.0	(0.8)	0.53	(0.10)	-0.45	(0.05)	**0.98**	(0.09)	0.08	(0.11)	-0.04	(0.08)	0.12	(0.08)
France	6.1	(0.8)	25.1	(2.6)	0.78	(0.10)	-0.67	(0.06)	**1.46**	(0.13)	w	w	w	w	w	w
Germany	7.2	(0.9)	37.0	(1.7)	0.72	(0.06)	-0.68	(0.05)	**1.40**	(0.08)	0.01	(0.10)	-0.05	(0.09)	0.06	(0.10)
Greece	2.5	(0.5)	18.1	(2.1)	0.71	(0.05)	-0.71	(0.07)	**1.42**	(0.05)	0.17	(0.11)	-0.04	(0.09)	0.21	(0.11)
Hungary	1.8	(0.5)	2.0	(0.5)	0.82	(0.07)	-0.89	(0.07)	**1.71**	(0.10)	0.11	(0.11)	-0.07	(0.12)	0.18	(0.14)
Iceland	0.4	(0.2)	5.6	(0.9)	0.52	(0.02)	-0.58	(0.03)	**1.09**	(0.04)	0.03	(0.03)	-0.02	(0.03)	0.05	(0.05)
Ireland	9.4	(1.2)	7.5	(1.1)	0.72	(0.11)	-0.59	(0.06)	**1.31**	(0.13)	0.15	(0.14)	-0.08	(0.10)	0.24	(0.14)
Israel	14.6	(1.3)	26.3	(1.6)	0.65	(0.06)	-0.70	(0.06)	**1.35**	(0.04)	0.13	(0.10)	-0.18	(0.09)	**0.31**	(0.11)
Italy	1.9	(0.2)	9.3	(0.7)	0.74	(0.04)	-0.68	(0.03)	**1.42**	(0.05)	0.12	(0.04)	-0.11	(0.04)	**0.23**	(0.06)
Japan	c	c	c	c	0.60	(0.05)	-0.66	(0.05)	**1.26**	(0.07)	0.11	(0.09)	-0.11	(0.09)	**0.23**	(0.09)
Korea	c	c	c	c	0.68	(0.11)	-0.68	(0.05)	**1.37**	(0.13)	-0.03	(0.11)	0.05	(0.13)	-0.08	(0.14)
Luxembourg	27.7	(1.1)	76.8	(1.3)	0.70	(0.02)	-0.65	(0.02)	**1.35**	(0.03)	0.08	(0.02)	-0.07	(0.02)	**0.15**	(0.03)
Mexico	0.8	(0.1)	2.9	(0.3)	0.90	(0.06)	-0.85	(0.03)	**1.75**	(0.07)	0.56	(0.07)	-0.46	(0.03)	**1.02**	(0.07)
Netherlands	4.4	(0.7)	25.0	(2.9)	0.67	(0.07)	-0.60	(0.10)	**1.27**	(0.12)	0.06	(0.11)	-0.04	(0.08)	0.10	(0.12)
New Zealand	27.0	(1.4)	23.4	(1.9)	0.68	(0.06)	-0.60	(0.05)	**1.28**	(0.08)	0.12	(0.08)	-0.06	(0.08)	**0.19**	(0.08)
Norway	4.1	(0.6)	13.6	(1.4)	0.49	(0.09)	-0.47	(0.07)	**0.96**	(0.10)	0.11	(0.09)	-0.06	(0.08)	0.16	(0.08)
Poland	c	c	c	c	0.74	(0.08)	-0.56	(0.05)	**1.30**	(0.10)	0.06	(0.09)	-0.06	(0.07)	0.13	(0.10)
Portugal	4.8	(0.5)	4.9	(0.8)	0.84	(0.10)	-0.59	(0.05)	**1.44**	(0.12)	0.23	(0.10)	-0.11	(0.08)	**0.34**	(0.09)
Slovak Republic	c	c	c	c	0.67	(0.08)	-0.60	(0.06)	**1.27**	(0.11)	-0.04	(0.10)	0.03	(0.09)	-0.07	(0.09)
Slovenia	2.7	(0.5)	16.2	(1.2)	0.77	(0.02)	-0.68	(0.03)	**1.45**	(0.04)	0.13	(0.03)	-0.04	(0.03)	**0.16**	(0.04)
Spain	4.5	(0.6)	12.2	(1.1)	0.83	(0.09)	-0.63	(0.04)	**1.45**	(0.09)	0.11	(0.08)	-0.04	(0.06)	**0.15**	(0.07)
Sweden	6.4	(0.8)	21.5	(2.2)	0.58	(0.09)	-0.51	(0.07)	**1.10**	(0.11)	0.17	(0.11)	-0.14	(0.09)	**0.32**	(0.11)
Switzerland	17.0	(1.9)	44.1	(1.6)	0.69	(0.08)	-0.53	(0.06)	**1.22**	(0.09)	0.05	(0.10)	-0.07	(0.09)	0.12	(0.11)
Turkey	c	c	c	c	0.81	(0.10)	-0.70	(0.06)	**1.51**	(0.11)	0.00	(0.10)	-0.06	(0.09)	0.06	(0.09)
United Kingdom	9.6	(1.3)	13.1	(2.3)	0.70	(0.07)	-0.59	(0.06)	**1.29**	(0.10)	-0.01	(0.09)	0.02	(0.08)	-0.04	(0.08)
United States	9.4	(1.1)	37.1	(2.8)	0.80	(0.10)	-0.69	(0.07)	**1.50**	(0.12)	0.21	(0.11)	-0.14	(0.11)	**0.35**	(0.14)
OECD average	8.6	(0.2)	20.1	(0.3)	0.71	(0.01)	-0.64	(0.01)	**1.34**	(0.02)	0.11	(0.02)	-0.08	(0.01)	**0.19**	(0.02)
Partners																
Albania	c	c	c	c	0.73	(0.07)	-0.79	(0.07)	**1.52**	(0.07)	0.31	(0.09)	-0.37	(0.09)	**0.68**	(0.11)
Argentina	1.4	(0.5)	5.4	(1.0)	0.97	(0.10)	-0.73	(0.06)	**1.70**	(0.13)	0.50	(0.11)	-0.34	(0.09)	**0.84**	(0.13)
Azerbaijan	3.2	(0.6)	2.7	(1.1)	0.70	(0.08)	-0.72	(0.07)	**1.42**	(0.11)	0.18	(0.13)	-0.13	(0.08)	**0.30**	(0.13)
Brazil	0.6	(0.3)	1.1	(0.4)	0.86	(0.06)	-0.75	(0.03)	**1.61**	(0.07)	0.48	(0.08)	-0.33	(0.03)	**0.81**	(0.08)
Bulgaria	c	c	c	c	0.72	(0.07)	-0.80	(0.09)	**1.53**	(0.13)	0.07	(0.11)	-0.08	(0.08)	0.15	(0.10)
Colombia	0.1	(0.1)	0.8	(0.3)	0.90	(0.09)	-0.77	(0.06)	**1.67**	(0.11)	0.48	(0.10)	-0.40	(0.10)	**0.88**	(0.12)
Croatia	8.2	(0.9)	15.4	(1.3)	0.71	(0.10)	-0.57	(0.06)	**1.29**	(0.12)	0.05	(0.10)	-0.06	(0.09)	0.11	(0.10)
Dubai (UAE)	70.4	(1.2)	57.8	(1.2)	0.67	(0.02)	-0.84	(0.02)	**1.51**	(0.03)	0.11	(0.02)	-0.32	(0.03)	**0.43**	(0.04)
Hong Kong-China	17.8	(1.5)	58.8	(2.3)	0.92	(0.11)	-0.58	(0.04)	**1.50**	(0.12)	0.04	(0.11)	-0.07	(0.11)	0.10	(0.13)
Indonesia	c	c	c	c	0.95	(0.11)	-0.70	(0.06)	**1.66**	(0.13)	0.42	(0.12)	-0.30	(0.10)	**0.72**	(0.14)
Jordan	18.4	(1.4)	9.4	(1.3)	0.75	(0.10)	-0.58	(0.05)	**1.33**	(0.11)	0.22	(0.12)	-0.11	(0.09)	**0.33**	(0.13)
Kazakhstan	9.4	(1.5)	14.1	(1.9)	0.69	(0.09)	-0.72	(0.08)	**1.41**	(0.11)	0.13	(0.11)	-0.17	(0.07)	**0.30**	(0.11)
Kyrgyzstan	2.2	(0.5)	2.1	(0.7)	0.74	(0.09)	-0.66	(0.06)	**1.39**	(0.12)	0.20	(0.13)	-0.12	(0.10)	**0.32**	(0.14)
Latvia	5.3	(0.8)	4.2	(1.0)	0.68	(0.06)	-0.68	(0.08)	**1.36**	(0.12)	0.13	(0.08)	-0.08	(0.10)	0.21	(0.09)
Liechtenstein	27.5	(4.7)	48.0	(5.0)	0.61	(0.08)	-0.54	(0.07)	**1.15**	(0.12)	-0.53	(0.09)	0.56	(0.07)	**-1.09**	(0.13)
Lithuania	1.6	(0.5)	1.8	(0.4)	0.69	(0.06)	-0.66	(0.06)	**1.35**	(0.09)	-0.01	(0.07)	0.04	(0.08)	-0.05	(0.08)
Macao-China	54.9	(1.3)	77.8	(1.2)	0.74	(0.02)	-0.49	(0.01)	**1.23**	(0.03)	0.21	(0.02)	-0.09	(0.02)	**0.30**	(0.03)
Montenegro	8.0	(1.0)	5.8	(0.8)	0.55	(0.02)	-0.62	(0.06)	**1.17**	(0.07)	-0.08	(0.02)	0.06	(0.03)	**-0.15**	(0.04)
Panama	3.4	(0.9)	3.1	(1.0)	1.09	(0.13)	-0.75	(0.04)	**1.84**	(0.16)	0.86	(0.15)	-0.42	(0.08)	**1.28**	(0.15)
Peru	c	c	c	c	0.91	(0.10)	-0.92	(0.05)	**1.83**	(0.13)	0.53	(0.12)	-0.41	(0.12)	**0.93**	(0.17)
Qatar	36.9	(0.9)	42.3	(1.1)	0.61	(0.01)	-0.78	(0.01)	**1.38**	(0.02)	0.13	(0.12)	-0.18	(0.02)	**0.31**	(0.03)
Romania	c	c	c	c	0.69	(0.08)	-0.68	(0.10)	**1.37**	(0.13)	0.17	(0.10)	-0.11	(0.08)	0.27	(0.11)
Russian Federation	9.4	(0.9)	14.5	(1.7)	0.74	(0.07)	-0.68	(0.05)	**1.42**	(0.10)	0.19	(0.07)	-0.14	(0.10)	**0.33**	(0.08)
Serbia	8.0	(0.8)	10.6	(1.0)	0.72	(0.06)	-0.55	(0.05)	**1.26**	(0.07)	-0.04	(0.10)	-0.01	(0.09)	-0.03	(0.09)
Shanghai-China	c	c	c	c	0.80	(0.07)	-0.78	(0.07)	**1.58**	(0.11)	0.13	(0.11)	-0.11	(0.10)	0.24	(0.12)
Singapore	19.2	(1.5)	11.6	(0.9)	0.65	(0.03)	-0.52	(0.02)	**1.17**	(0.03)	0.05	(0.03)	-0.04	(0.03)	**0.10**	(0.03)
Chinese Taipei	c	c	c	c	0.61	(0.09)	-0.59	(0.10)	**1.20**	(0.14)	0.05	(0.09)	-0.18	(0.09)	**0.23**	(0.10)
Thailand	c	c	c	c	1.03	(0.08)	-0.76	(0.04)	**1.79**	(0.10)	0.40	(0.12)	-0.32	(0.07)	**0.72**	(0.13)
Trinidad and Tobago	3.9	(0.6)	2.2	(0.5)	0.75	(0.03)	-0.56	(0.02)	**1.31**	(0.03)	0.09	(0.03)	-0.03	(0.03)	**0.12**	(0.04)
Tunisia	c	c	c	c	0.79	(0.10)	-0.74	(0.07)	**1.53**	(0.12)	0.07	(0.12)	-0.15	(0.09)	**0.23**	(0.11)
Uruguay	c	c	c	c	0.95	(0.07)	-0.67	(0.03)	**1.61**	(0.08)	0.33	(0.07)	-0.20	(0.08)	**0.53**	(0.10)

Note: Values that are statistically significant are indicated in bold (see Annex A3).
1. Advantaged (disadvantaged) students are those on the top (bottom) quarter of the socio-economic background distribution within their own country.
StatLink 🔗 http://dx.doi.org/10.1787/888932343285

[Part 2/2]
Characteristics of schools attended by advantaged and disadvantaged students[1]
Table II.2.3   *Results based on students' self-reports and school principals' reports*

Negative mean index indicates more favourable characteristics

		Student/teacher ratio						Index of teacher shortage					
		Advantaged students		Disadvantaged students		Difference (A-D)		Advantaged students		Disadvantaged students		Difference (A-D)	
		Mean index	S.E.	Mean index	S.E.	Dif.	S.E.	Mean index	S.E.	Mean index	S.E.	Dif.	S.E.
OECD	Australia	-0.14	(0.06)	-0.03	(0.08)	-0.10	(0.07)	-0.23	(0.07)	0.15	(0.07)	**-0.38**	(0.08)
	Austria	-0.11	(0.04)	0.02	(0.08)	**-0.14**	(0.07)	0.04	(0.13)	0.04	(0.11)	0.00	(0.11)
	Belgium	0.56	(0.06)	-0.45	(0.06)	**1.00**	(0.06)	-0.11	(0.08)	0.12	(0.06)	**-0.23**	(0.09)
	Canada	0.03	(0.07)	-0.08	(0.04)	0.11	(0.07)	-0.10	(0.04)	0.10	(0.04)	**-0.19**	(0.04)
	Chile	-0.17	(0.12)	-0.08	(0.11)	-0.08	(0.15)	-0.02	(0.11)	0.08	(0.12)	-0.10	(0.14)
	Czech Republic	0.05	(0.09)	-0.05	(0.07)	0.10	(0.09)	-0.24	(0.07)	0.20	(0.08)	**-0.44**	(0.08)
	Denmark	0.14	(0.07)	-0.17	(0.07)	**0.31**	(0.08)	-0.16	(0.08)	0.11	(0.07)	**-0.27**	(0.08)
	Estonia	0.22	(0.07)	-0.31	(0.10)	**0.53**	(0.09)	-0.01	(0.07)	0.05	(0.09)	-0.06	(0.08)
	Finland	0.02	(0.08)	-0.05	(0.08)	0.08	(0.06)	0.02	(0.07)	0.02	(0.08)	0.00	(0.07)
	France	w	w	w	w	w	w	w	w	w	w	w	w
	Germany	0.18	(0.05)	-0.26	(0.07)	**0.44**	(0.07)	-0.07	(0.10)	0.03	(0.08)	-0.10	(0.12)
	Greece	0.15	(0.10)	-0.20	(0.10)	**0.35**	(0.13)	-0.17	(0.06)	0.10	(0.10)	**-0.27**	(0.08)
	Hungary	-0.01	(0.07)	-0.05	(0.10)	0.04	(0.11)	-0.11	(0.12)	0.05	(0.11)	-0.16	(0.14)
	Iceland	0.21	(0.03)	-0.23	(0.03)	**0.44**	(0.04)	-0.23	(0.03)	0.20	(0.03)	**-0.42**	(0.06)
	Ireland	0.35	(0.09)	-0.31	(0.11)	**0.65**	(0.12)	-0.14	(0.09)	0.10	(0.11)	**-0.25**	(0.11)
	Israel	-0.09	(0.07)	0.19	(0.13)	**-0.28**	(0.14)	-0.02	(0.09)	0.02	(0.10)	-0.03	(0.10)
	Italy	0.38	(0.05)	-0.33	(0.04)	**0.71**	(0.05)	-0.01	(0.05)	-0.03	(0.05)	0.02	(0.06)
	Japan	0.21	(0.09)	-0.27	(0.06)	**0.48**	(0.09)	-0.03	(0.08)	0.03	(0.09)	-0.06	(0.08)
	Korea	0.12	(0.13)	-0.30	(0.08)	**0.42**	(0.14)	-0.03	(0.12)	-0.02	(0.12)	-0.01	(0.13)
	Luxembourg	0.26	(0.02)	-0.12	(0.02)	**0.38**	(0.04)	-0.29	(0.03)	0.16	(0.02)	**-0.45**	(0.04)
	Mexico	-0.01	(0.04)	-0.08	(0.02)	0.07	(0.04)	-0.27	(0.05)	0.17	(0.05)	**-0.44**	(0.07)
	Netherlands	0.31	(0.11)	-0.20	(0.12)	**0.51**	(0.11)	-0.04	(0.13)	-0.03	(0.09)	-0.01	(0.14)
	New Zealand	0.06	(0.06)	-0.08	(0.07)	0.13	(0.08)	-0.13	(0.08)	0.09	(0.08)	**-0.22**	(0.09)
	Norway	0.10	(0.10)	-0.07	(0.07)	0.17	(0.08)	-0.16	(0.10)	0.07	(0.08)	**-0.23**	(0.08)
	Poland	0.02	(0.10)	-0.03	(0.10)	0.05	(0.11)	-0.06	(0.08)	-0.01	(0.08)	-0.05	(0.09)
	Portugal	0.34	(0.08)	-0.19	(0.09)	**0.53**	(0.07)	-0.08	(0.08)	0.05	(0.09)	-0.13	(0.11)
	Slovak Republic	0.00	(0.09)	0.02	(0.10)	-0.02	(0.08)	-0.14	(0.10)	0.12	(0.09)	**-0.26**	(0.11)
	Slovenia	-0.17	(0.02)	0.17	(0.03)	**-0.34**	(0.04)	-0.01	(0.03)	-0.01	(0.03)	0.00	(0.05)
	Spain	0.35	(0.06)	-0.28	(0.04)	**0.64**	(0.07)	-0.02	(0.06)	0.00	(0.05)	-0.02	(0.07)
	Sweden	0.10	(0.08)	-0.08	(0.09)	**0.18**	(0.07)	-0.09	(0.09)	0.07	(0.08)	-0.15	(0.09)
	Switzerland	0.04	(0.16)	-0.04	(0.05)	0.08	(0.14)	-0.10	(0.07)	0.07	(0.07)	**-0.17**	(0.07)
	Turkey	-0.23	(0.07)	0.13	(0.07)	**-0.36**	(0.09)	0.04	(0.11)	0.05	(0.09)	-0.01	(0.11)
	United Kingdom	-0.09	(0.08)	0.03	(0.06)	-0.12	(0.08)	-0.12	(0.07)	0.06	(0.08)	**-0.19**	(0.08)
	United States	-0.15	(0.08)	0.11	(0.12)	-0.26	(0.14)	-0.24	(0.10)	0.20	(0.10)	**-0.44**	(0.11)
	OECD average	0.09	(0.01)	-0.11	(0.01)	**0.20**	(0.02)	-0.10	(0.01)	0.07	(0.01)	**-0.17**	(0.02)
Partners	Albania	0.06	(0.10)	-0.18	(0.08)	**0.23**	(0.11)	-0.23	(0.08)	0.34	(0.12)	**-0.56**	(0.13)
	Argentina	-0.05	(0.05)	-0.03	(0.09)	-0.03	(0.09)	-0.23	(0.10)	0.17	(0.10)	**-0.41**	(0.13)
	Azerbaijan	0.16	(0.12)	-0.14	(0.09)	**0.30**	(0.13)	-0.06	(0.11)	0.06	(0.13)	-0.12	(0.13)
	Brazil	-0.18	(0.06)	0.13	(0.06)	**-0.31**	(0.07)	-0.35	(0.05)	0.25	(0.06)	**-0.60**	(0.06)
	Bulgaria	0.20	(0.08)	-0.20	(0.13)	**0.40**	(0.12)	0.19	(0.15)	-0.13	(0.09)	**0.32**	(0.14)
	Colombia	-0.23	(0.12)	0.00	(0.12)	-0.22	(0.15)	-0.27	(0.10)	0.24	(0.12)	**-0.51**	(0.13)
	Croatia	0.20	(0.11)	-0.20	(0.08)	**0.40**	(0.11)	-0.09	(0.11)	0.11	(0.08)	-0.20	(0.11)
	Dubai (UAE)	-0.29	(0.01)	0.23	(0.03)	**-0.52**	(0.04)	-0.07	(0.02)	0.19	(0.03)	**-0.26**	(0.04)
	Hong Kong-China	-0.04	(0.11)	-0.13	(0.08)	0.09	(0.13)	-0.15	(0.10)	0.12	(0.11)	**-0.26**	(0.12)
	Indonesia	-0.13	(0.11)	0.14	(0.10)	**-0.27**	(0.13)	-0.36	(0.10)	0.22	(0.10)	**-0.57**	(0.12)
	Jordan	0.00	(0.13)	-0.05	(0.08)	0.05	(0.14)	-0.20	(0.10)	0.13	(0.09)	**-0.33**	(0.10)
	Kazakhstan	0.28	(0.10)	-0.35	(0.07)	**0.63**	(0.12)	-0.05	(0.08)	0.04	(0.10)	-0.09	(0.09)
	Kyrgyzstan	0.15	(0.10)	-0.22	(0.05)	**0.38**	(0.11)	0.05	(0.11)	-0.02	(0.10)	0.07	(0.11)
	Latvia	0.17	(0.11)	-0.34	(0.07)	**0.50**	(0.11)	0.01	(0.11)	-0.05	(0.09)	0.06	(0.10)
	Liechtenstein	0.44	(0.09)	-0.40	(0.06)	**0.85**	(0.10)	0.34	(0.10)	-0.31	(0.08)	**0.64**	(0.15)
	Lithuania	0.08	(0.11)	-0.18	(0.06)	**0.26**	(0.11)	-0.06	(0.11)	0.01	(0.07)	-0.07	(0.10)
	Macao-China	0.10	(0.02)	-0.12	(0.02)	**0.22**	(0.03)	-0.02	(0.02)	-0.04	(0.02)	0.02	(0.04)
	Montenegro	0.17	(0.02)	-0.23	(0.05)	**0.41**	(0.06)	-0.09	(0.02)	0.05	(0.05)	**-0.14**	(0.06)
	Panama	0.11	(0.10)	0.00	(0.11)	0.12	(0.13)	-0.28	(0.14)	0.18	(0.12)	**-0.46**	(0.17)
	Peru	-0.07	(0.11)	-0.04	(0.08)	-0.03	(0.13)	-0.33	(0.11)	0.27	(0.10)	**-0.60**	(0.14)
	Qatar	-0.09	(0.01)	-0.19	(0.02)	**0.10**	(0.02)	0.07	(0.02)	0.00	(0.02)	**0.07**	(0.03)
	Romania	-0.03	(0.10)	-0.02	(0.10)	-0.01	(0.14)	-0.11	(0.09)	0.15	(0.10)	**-0.26**	(0.10)
	Russian Federation	0.17	(0.07)	-0.23	(0.07)	**0.40**	(0.07)	-0.07	(0.10)	0.08	(0.10)	-0.15	(0.12)
	Serbia	0.09	(0.06)	-0.02	(0.06)	**0.11**	(0.03)	-0.19	(0.06)	0.16	(0.11)	**-0.35**	(0.08)
	Shanghai-China	-0.17	(0.04)	0.06	(0.09)	**-0.23**	(0.09)	-0.12	(0.10)	0.14	(0.08)	**-0.26**	(0.10)
	Singapore	-0.11	(0.04)	0.06	(0.02)	**-0.17**	(0.04)	-0.19	(0.02)	0.14	(0.02)	**-0.33**	(0.04)
	Chinese Taipei	-0.06	(0.05)	0.07	(0.08)	-0.13	(0.07)	-0.05	(0.11)	0.13	(0.11)	-0.18	(0.12)
	Thailand	-0.08	(0.07)	-0.06	(0.07)	-0.02	(0.10)	-0.11	(0.15)	0.04	(0.09)	-0.15	(0.17)
	Trinidad and Tobago	0.26	(0.03)	-0.27	(0.03)	**0.54**	(0.04)	-0.16	(0.03)	0.10	(0.03)	**-0.25**	(0.04)
	Tunisia	-0.07	(0.09)	-0.06	(0.12)	-0.01	(0.14)	0.00	(0.11)	-0.10	(0.10)	0.10	(0.12)
	Uruguay	0.13	(0.15)	-0.11	(0.07)	0.24	(0.15)	-0.27	(0.07)	0.13	(0.07)	**-0.39**	(0.08)

Note: Values that are statistically significant are indicated in bold (see Annex A3).
1. Advantaged (disadvantaged) students are those on the top (bottom) quarter of the socio-economic background distribution within their own country.
StatLink ᴍ⫶ᴤ᠋ http://dx.doi.org/10.1787/888932343285

[Part 1/2]
Table II.2.4 Relationship between student-level factors and reading performance
Results based on students' self-reports

	Intercept		Score point difference associated with the various factors shown below, after accounting for the other factors																					
	Intercept		Highest occupational status of parents (HISEI)		Highest level of parents' education (in years of schooling)		Index of cultural posessions		Index of home educational resources		Number of books at home		Wealth		Single-parent family		Second-generation student		First-generation student		Language spoken at home is different from the language of assessment	
	Mean score	S.E.	Score dif.	S.E.	Score dif.	S.E.	Score dif.	S.E.	Score dif.	S.E.	Score dif.	S.E.	Score dif.	S.E.	Score dif.	S.E.	Score dif.	S.E.	Score dif.	S.E.	Score dif.	S.E.
OECD																								
Australia	351	(8.93)	**1.1**	(0.07)	**5.5**	(0.65)	**9.4**	(1.09)	**5.6**	(1.37)	**13.8**	(0.91)	**-10.7**	(1.47)	**-8.5**	(2.29)	**21.1**	(4.3)	**7.6**	(3.7)	-6.4	(5.7)
Austria	332	(12.04)	**0.9**	(0.12)	**2.9**	(0.76)	**10.1**	(1.78)	0.9	(1.59)	**21.9**	(1.52)	**-13.0**	(2.32)	-1.4	(4.34)	-1.9	(10.6)	**-37.7**	(11.5)	-16.9	(9.1)
Belgium	416	(7.66)	**1.4**	(0.09)	0.5	(0.49)	**11.6**	(1.39)	**14.3**	(1.45)	**11.3**	(0.90)	**-11.4**	(1.66)	**-11.0**	(3.09)	**-32.9**	(6.2)	**-34.9**	(5.9)	-7.2	(4.0)
Canada	413	(7.41)	**0.9**	(0.06)	**1.4**	(0.46)	**5.6**	(1.00)	**6.1**	(1.19)	**15.8**	(0.69)	**-7.7**	(1.32)	**-7.3**	(2.51)	**11.8**	(3.2)	7.3	(4.1)	**-15.6**	(3.4)
Chile	370	(6.72)	**1.0**	(0.09)	**2.0**	(0.48)	**7.4**	(1.65)	**7.8**	(1.66)	**8.9**	(1.29)	**4.1**	(1.82)	1.4	(2.86)	-11.5	(52.4)	c	c	c	c
Czech Republic	363	(10.84)	**1.9**	(0.13)	**-2.0**	(0.82)	**7.2**	(1.48)	**12.3**	(1.92)	**17.9**	(1.26)	**-13.5**	(2.00)	**-10.5**	(3.64)	8.3	(15.3)	16.6	(21.0)	4.8	(17.0)
Denmark	414	(9.23)	**0.9**	(0.09)	**1.2**	(0.56)	**7.8**	(1.70)	**16.3**	(1.96)	**9.8**	(1.21)	**-6.6**	(1.43)	**-6.9**	(3.25)	**-19.8**	(5.8)	**-29.7**	(8.3)	**-20.9**	(7.0)
Estonia	404	(11.38)	**1.3**	(0.11)	-0.3	(0.87)	**11.0**	(1.98)	**7.2**	(2.12)	**10.2**	(1.36)	**-9.0**	(1.86)	1.4	(2.70)	**-28.1**	(6.3)	**-32.6**	(16.0)	**-17.5**	(8.4)
Finland	417	(9.99)	**0.7**	(0.09)	**2.9**	(0.65)	**13.6**	(1.41)	0.8	(1.37)	**13.6**	(1.14)	**-13.3**	(1.71)	**-11.8**	(3.33)	-9.2	(15.5)	**-36.3**	(18.2)	**-41.2**	(7.6)
France	397	(13.70)	**0.8**	(0.11)	**2.0**	(0.93)	**16.3**	(1.99)	**5.8**	(2.17)	**19.0**	(1.42)	**-10.4**	(3.16)	-6.4	(4.58)	-6.3	(8.0)	**-23.8**	(11.5)	**-28.4**	(8.7)
Germany	372	(10.08)	**0.7**	(0.10)	**3.0**	(0.62)	2.3	(1.68)	**5.5**	(1.72)	**20.0**	(1.39)	**-6.1**	(2.45)	-2.5	(3.80)	-7.7	(6.5)	**-17.8**	(7.5)	**-17.7**	(6.8)
Greece	388	(11.41)	**1.0**	(0.10)	**1.3**	(0.66)	**14.4**	(1.93)	**12.2**	(2.14)	**8.5**	(1.56)	**-12.1**	(2.25)	**-11.6**	(5.28)	-10.6	(9.3)	-12.1	(12.7)	**-37.0**	(12.1)
Hungary	349	(8.34)	**1.1**	(0.11)	**2.4**	(0.78)	**12.5**	(1.45)	**7.3**	(1.86)	**17.5**	(1.28)	**-6.7**	(1.89)	-2.6	(3.49)	20.4	(11.9)	8.4	(9.7)	c	c
Iceland	378	(11.15)	**0.7**	(0.11)	**2.8**	(0.71)	**9.6**	(2.37)	3.1	(2.00)	**14.4**	(1.29)	**-18.8**	(2.00)	**-16.7**	(5.00)	c	c	-23.3	(17.4)	c	c
Ireland	380	(9.71)	**0.9**	(0.09)	**2.2**	(0.76)	**7.2**	(1.70)	3.5	(2.09)	**19.2**	(1.34)	**-11.2**	(2.11)	-7.9	(4.40)	-5.8	(12.4)	**-23.3**	(7.5)	**-21.4**	(9.7)
Israel	315	(14.43)	**1.4**	(0.14)	**5.6**	(1.00)	**8.8**	(2.12)	-1.2	(2.06)	**8.6**	(1.27)	-1.0	(2.13)	1.9	(5.44)	**18.7**	(5.0)	**21.6**	(9.7)	-14.5	(9.8)
Italy	407	(4.93)	**0.9**	(0.06)	0.2	(0.29)	**10.0**	(1.21)	**12.4**	(0.79)	**14.7**	(0.77)	**-9.8**	(1.19)	0.1	(2.29)	-8.9	(6.8)	**-31.2**	(5.2)	**-25.7**	(3.0)
Japan	405	(14.21)	**0.6**	(0.10)	**5.2**	(0.96)	**14.9**	(1.48)	**11.0**	(1.61)	**6.6**	(1.21)	**-12.8**	(2.80)	**-9.6**	(4.01)	c	c	c	c	c	c
Korea	427	(11.73)	**0.7**	(0.11)	**2.3**	(0.64)	2.3	(2.29)	**16.2**	(1.86)	**12.2**	(1.38)	**-5.9**	(2.09)	-2.6	(5.38)	c	c	c	c	c	c
Luxembourg	387	(12.52)	**1.1**	(0.12)	0.8	(0.54)	**4.9**	(2.21)	**5.2**	(2.02)	**18.0**	(1.42)	**-9.4**	(2.26)	-8.9	(4.77)	**-17.3**	(5.6)	**-12.5**	(6.0)	**-22.7**	(6.0)
Mexico	388	(3.77)	**0.7**	(0.06)	**1.7**	(0.27)	-0.8	(0.95)	**8.9**	(1.16)	**8.0**	(0.72)	**2.7**	(1.29)	**-8.9**	(1.84)	**-71.6**	(9.8)	**-68.4**	(7.6)	**-58.3**	(6.6)
Netherlands	404	(12.26)	**1.1**	(0.14)	1.0	(0.63)	**4.2**	(1.60)	**9.3**	(1.74)	**15.4**	(1.46)	**-7.4**	(2.62)	-8.3	(4.83)	-8.3	(10.1)	4.3	(12.0)	-2.3	(11.4)
New Zealand	349	(11.36)	**1.5**	(0.12)	**4.0**	(0.82)	2.8	(1.85)	**5.0**	(2.01)	**17.2**	(1.60)	-4.8	(2.45)	**-8.2**	(4.07)	6.9	(5.9)	**10.4**	(4.5)	**-42.9**	(6.0)
Norway	419	(10.99)	**1.1**	(0.10)	-1.4	(0.84)	**12.7**	(1.61)	3.3	(1.91)	**15.6**	(1.12)	**-13.9**	(1.83)	-6.4	(3.41)	2.3	(8.1)	6.5	(10.6)	**-38.1**	(6.9)
Poland	364	(8.59)	**0.7**	(0.11)	**4.4**	(0.76)	**9.1**	(1.53)	**7.2**	(2.17)	**17.0**	(1.21)	**-8.0**	(1.90)	**-14.1**	(3.59)	c	c	c	c	c	c
Portugal	399	(6.61)	**1.2**	(0.12)	**1.2**	(0.49)	**10.3**	(1.44)	**4.9**	(1.43)	**9.9**	(1.14)	**-5.5**	(1.76)	2.1	(3.85)	-10.8	(7.4)	**-22.6**	(10.3)	-9.9	(9.6)
Slovak Republic	348	(9.46)	**1.4**	(0.12)	-0.2	(0.64)	**9.6**	(1.95)	**14.1**	(1.94)	**18.3**	(1.43)	**-8.1**	(1.96)	-2.5	(4.00)	**61.1**	(22.8)	c	c	c	c
Slovenia	360	(7.80)	**1.1**	(0.11)	**1.9**	(0.71)	**11.8**	(1.66)	2.6	(2.59)	**16.4**	(1.24)	**-9.3**	(1.88)	0.4	(3.71)	-4.8	(7.0)	**-28.7**	(12.0)	1.2	(8.5)
Spain	381	(5.83)	**0.8**	(0.09)	**1.3**	(0.36)	**10.8**	(1.16)	**6.2**	(1.19)	**14.6**	(0.89)	**-8.5**	(1.47)	-4.8	(2.88)	-8.6	(9.5)	**-27.3**	(3.5)	-1.1	(4.0)
Sweden	366	(11.81)	**1.0**	(0.10)	**2.5**	(0.84)	**9.7**	(1.91)	0.7	(2.03)	**15.9**	(1.26)	**-8.8**	(2.08)	**-10.3**	(4.14)	-8.6	(8.5)	**-26.7**	(11.3)	**-19.8**	(8.2)
Switzerland	386	(9.15)	**1.0**	(0.09)	**1.5**	(0.53)	**6.1**	(1.72)	**8.3**	(1.78)	**17.1**	(1.08)	**-12.2**	(1.83)	-3.0	(4.35)	1.8	(4.5)	**-19.9**	(5.6)	**-20.7**	(3.9)
Turkey	395	(7.16)	**0.5**	(0.11)	**2.9**	(0.52)	**6.0**	(1.62)	**10.8**	(1.57)	**9.8**	(1.33)	-1.1	(2.13)	-0.7	(5.27)	c	c	c	c	c	c
United Kingdom	379	(11.96)	**1.1**	(0.08)	0.4	(0.83)	**3.0**	(1.35)	**7.7**	(1.33)	**21.3**	(1.00)	**-10.4**	(1.40)	-3.1	(2.78)	1.7	(6.8)	-5.6	(9.1)	**-27.6**	(6.1)
United States	370	(12.34)	**1.1**	(0.11)	**2.4**	(0.79)	**6.3**	(1.74)	**4.3**	(2.09)	**17.8**	(1.35)	-0.8	(2.12)	**-18.4**	(3.17)	**13.4**	(5.6)	**21.0**	(8.2)	-12.2	(6.2)
OECD average	382	(1.75)	**1.0**	(0.02)	**1.9**	(0.12)	**8.5**	(0.29)	**7.2**	(0.31)	**14.6**	(0.21)	**-8.3**	(0.34)	**-6.1**	(0.67)	**-7.4**	(3.0)	**-7.9**	(2.7)	**-25.0**	(2.2)
Partners																								
Albania	316	(12.95)	**1.1**	(0.12)	-0.6	(0.73)	**11.7**	(2.07)	**18.9**	(2.22)	**14.6**	(2.16)	**-14.6**	(3.97)	**-17.7**	(8.37)	c	c	c	c	c	c
Argentina	330	(8.98)	**1.1**	(0.14)	**1.4**	(0.47)	4.6	(2.66)	**8.3**	(3.00)	**11.9**	(2.00)	**15.0**	(3.28)	-2.2	(4.47)	2.8	(13.5)	8.2	(18.2)	c	c
Azerbaijan	304	(11.99)	**0.2**	(0.10)	**2.8**	(0.74)	2.4	(1.85)	**9.5**	(1.55)	**9.3**	(1.40)	-1.3	(2.22)	-3.0	(7.46)	1.2	(9.5)	9.0	(14.2)	c	c
Brazil	377	(6.73)	**1.3**	(0.10)	0.0	(0.30)	-1.2	(1.59)	**17.9**	(1.39)	**5.9**	(1.30)	**9.2**	(2.12)	-2.4	(2.60)	**-77.5**	(17.0)	**-68.7**	(27.1)	c	c
Bulgaria	304	(12.84)	**1.4**	(0.12)	**3.1**	(0.88)	**21.2**	(2.83)	**11.9**	(2.70)	**11.0**	(1.56)	**-7.8**	(2.63)	**-10.0**	(4.55)	c	c	c	c	c	c
Colombia	386	(8.08)	**0.7**	(0.11)	0.7	(0.45)	**-5.6**	(1.96)	**6.4**	(1.73)	**11.9**	(1.83)	**14.5**	(2.22)	-3.1	(3.25)	c	c	c	c	c	c
Croatia	411	(9.95)	**1.1**	(0.10)	-0.1	(0.59)	**16.1**	(1.69)	**4.5**	(1.85)	**8.7**	(1.26)	**-6.4**	(1.63)	5.8	(4.46)	**-9.4**	(4.5)	-7.7	(7.5)	c	c
Dubai (UAE)	268	(10.89)	**0.9**	(0.12)	**5.2**	(0.73)	**9.5**	(1.89)	**18.0**	(2.13)	**9.6**	(1.23)	**3.9**	(1.77)	**-19.0**	(5.29)	**69.3**	(4.9)	**87.6**	(4.2)	**-24.8**	(3.0)
Hong Kong-China	459	(7.59)	**0.3**	(0.12)	**1.4**	(0.51)	1.5	(1.50)	**14.5**	(1.76)	**14.5**	(1.31)	**-11.3**	(1.99)	-5.9	(3.79)	**15.7**	(3.2)	2.9	(4.7)	**-56.3**	(8.5)
Indonesia	375	(8.62)	**0.6**	(0.12)	**2.1**	(0.57)	**-6.7**	(2.05)	2.6	(1.83)	2.3	(1.42)	**7.8**	(1.76)	**-15.6**	(5.17)	c	c	c	c	c	c
Jordan	356	(10.53)	**0.6**	(0.10)	**3.1**	(0.70)	**6.8**	(1.97)	**19.2**	(1.82)	0.1	(1.25)	**-10.0**	(3.14)	**-25.6**	(6.25)	**9.9**	(4.6)	1.3	(7.4)	**-29.2**	(10.8)
Kazakhstan	293	(29.23)	**0.6**	(0.09)	2.4	(1.99)	-1.6	(2.05)	**19.4**	(2.02)	**14.1**	(1.68)	-1.1	(2.52)	**16.4**	(4.37)	**23.6**	(11.3)	-8.5	(6.5)	10.1	(6.4)
Kyrgyzstan	263	(14.09)	**0.7**	(0.10)	0.2	(0.96)	3.0	(2.39)	**13.5**	(1.87)	**17.2**	(1.70)	4.8	(2.67)	**8.8**	(3.74)	**36.3**	(14.3)	17.1	(17.6)	c	c
Latvia	405	(10.92)	**0.9**	(0.12)	0.1	(0.82)	**11.9**	(1.92)	**11.5**	(1.88)	**11.5**	(1.31)	-3.5	(2.10)	-2.0	(2.94)	**-14.2**	(6.8)	c	c	-0.4	(7.6)
Liechtenstein	c	c	c	c	c	c	c	c	c	c	c	c	c	c	c	c	c	c	c	c	c	c
Lithuania	377	(9.87)	**0.8**	(0.08)	**2.3**	(0.73)	**18.9**	(1.86)	**5.7**	(2.03)	**8.8**	(1.24)	**-5.3**	(1.59)	**-6.6**	(2.96)	-10.5	(12.4)	c	c	c	c
Macao-China	436	(6.31)	**0.4**	(0.10)	**1.8**	(0.38)	**12.7**	(1.33)	**13.9**	(1.34)	**4.2**	(0.99)	**-10.5**	(1.44)	-1.5	(2.98)	3.4	(2.7)	0.1	(3.1)	**-52.8**	(2.8)
Montenegro	329	(11.36)	**1.2**	(0.11)	-0.2	(0.78)	**24.6**	(2.04)	**8.2**	(2.72)	**7.9**	(1.35)	**-10.1**	(1.57)	-0.9	(5.52)	**21.6**	(9.5)	2.6	(7.9)	c	c
Panama	387	(17.60)	**0.9**	(0.22)	-0.1	(0.74)	-1.6	(3.18)	4.9	(3.19)	**7.1**	(2.77)	**24.2**	(4.61)	-10.1	(6.42)	**48.1**	(14.4)	-8.8	(26.7)	**-51.0**	(11.9)
Peru	338	(6.70)	**1.0**	(0.12)	**1.9**	(0.43)	**-12.0**	(1.78)	**10.9**	(1.58)	**12.3**	(1.48)	**17.9**	(2.06)	**11.3**	(2.92)	c	c	c	c	c	c
Qatar	271	(8.48)	**1.2**	(0.12)	**1.4**	(0.53)	**6.1**	(1.67)	**19.1**	(1.67)	1.1	(0.99)	**-6.4**	(1.62)	**-32.6**	(4.71)	**53.5**	(3.5)	**103.4**	(3.6)	**-11.0**	(2.7)
Romania	352	(11.62)	**1.1**	(0.10)	**-1.9**	(0.78)	**13.5**	(1.48)	**15.4**	(1.86)	**14.8**	(1.30)	**-7.9**	(2.34)	-3.5	(4.34)	c	c	c	c	c	c
Russian Federation	337	(13.26)	**1.0**	(0.11)	2.1	(1.22)	**8.3**	(1.51)	**15.7**	(1.75)	**11.2**	(1.31)	**-12.2**	(2.02)	-2.0	(2.87)	**-12.3**	(6.0)	-6.6	(6.7)	**-26.5**	(9.0)
Serbia	364	(7.11)	**1.2**	(0.11)	**-1.8**	(0.64)	**14.5**	(1.77)	**6.4**	(1.34)	**9.8**	(0.96)	**-7.0**	(1.43)	-3.3	(3.70)	**20.0**	(6.3)	12.3	(7.6)	c	c
Shanghai-China	455	(8.64)	**0.6**	(0.09)	**2.6**	(0.58)	**12.7**	(1.74)	**8.2**	(1.56)	**9.8**	(1.04)	**-5.1**	(1.70)	-1.7	(3.68)	c	c	c	c	c	c
Singapore	438	(10.10)	**0.9**	(0.11)	**2.2**	(0.93)	**5.9**	(1.57)	**16.1**	(1.79)	**12.5**	(1.28)	-1.2	(2.24)	**-11.3**	(4.81)	**17.2**	(6.6)	-7.5	(5.3)	**-26.8**	(2.9)
Chinese Taipei	387	(9.12)	**0.8**	(0.12)	**3.0**	(0.63)	**11.4**	(1.60)	**12.4**	(1.52)	**11.1**	(1.09)	**-19.4**	(1.80)	-6.1	(3.66)	c	c	c	c	c	c
Thailand	371	(5.89)	**0.6**	(0.11)	**1.6**	(0.42)	-2.0	(1.35)	**18.9**	(1.50)	**7.8**	(1.10)	**-6.2**	(2.02)	-3.2	(3.08)	c	c	c	c	c	c
Trinidad and Tobago	364	(11.24)	**1.8**	(0.13)	-1.2	(0.72)	**10.9**	(2.37)	**29.4**	(2.71)	2.4	(1.57)	**-6.9**	(3.04)	**-16.9**	(4.52)	-7.8	(21.0)	29.5	(21.6)	**-49.4**	(14.9)
Tunisia	344	(7.36)	**1.1**	(0.14)	-0.6	(0.50)	**12.4**	(2.34)	**20.0**	(2.08)	**4.1**	(1.81)	**-11.1**	(2.15)	-7.3	(7.48)	-27.7	(38.2)	c	c	c	c
Uruguay	325	(6.84)	**0.8**	(0.10)	**4.4**	(0.54)	**4.3**	(1.65)	**12.0**	(1.67)	**9.7**	(1.38)	2.2	(2.72)	-2.3	(3.10)	c	c	c	c	c	c

Note: Values that are statistically significant are indicated in bold (see Annex A3).
1. Unique variance is the variance explained by each factor after taking into account the variance explained by the other factors in the model.
StatLink http://dx.doi.org/10.1787/888932343285

[Part 2/2]
Relationship between student-level factors and reading performance
Table II.2.4 *Results based on students' self-reports*

		Explained variance in student performance (unique,[1] common and total)											
		Unique to:										Common explained variance (explained by more than one factor)	Total explained variance
		Highest occupational status of parents (HISEI)	Highest level of parents' education	Index of cultural posessions	Index of home educational resources	Number of books at home	Wealth	Single-parent family	Second-generation students	First-generation students	Language spoken at home is different from the language of assessment		
		%	%	%	%	%	%	%	%	%	%	%	% S.E.
OECD	Australia	2.6	0.7	0.72	0.23	2.95	0.72	0.1	0.5	0.0	0.0	10.9	19.4 (1.13)
	Austria	1.6	0.3	0.66	0.01	6.70	1.01	0.0	0.0	0.3	0.1	17.9	28.6 (1.82)
	Belgium	4.3	0.0	0.92	1.33	2.10	0.91	0.2	0.7	0.7	0.1	16.2	27.5 (1.20)
	Canada	2.0	0.1	0.31	0.29	4.50	0.43	0.1	0.2	0.0	0.2	7.9	16.1 (0.82)
	Chile	2.1	0.5	0.44	0.61	1.17	0.13	0.0	0.0	c	c	16.1	21.3 (1.51)
	Czech Republic	5.6	0.1	0.46	1.06	5.12	1.19	0.2	0.0	0.0	0.0	10.4	24.2 (1.42)
	Denmark	2.3	0.1	0.62	1.85	1.93	0.53	0.1	0.2	0.2	0.1	13.3	21.3 (1.19)
	Estonia	5.1	0.0	0.91	0.33	2.19	0.77	0.0	0.8	0.1	0.1	6.9	17.2 (1.67)
	Finland	1.2	0.5	1.80	0.01	2.97	1.26	0.3	0.0	0.2	0.5	10.1	18.8 (1.10)
	France	1.3	0.1	1.83	0.27	4.84	0.57	0.0	0.0	0.1	0.4	18.5	28.1 (2.03)
	Germany	0.9	0.6	0.05	0.23	7.11	0.23	0.0	0.0	0.1	0.2	15.2	24.7 (1.82)
	Greece	2.0	0.1	1.52	1.15	1.13	0.93	0.1	0.0	0.1	0.5	12.3	19.8 (1.68)
	Hungary	2.1	0.3	1.50	0.49	5.19	0.31	0.0	0.1	0.0	0.3	25.6	35.8 (2.16)
	Iceland	1.1	0.4	0.41	0.06	2.81	2.84	0.4	c	0.1	c	7.6	15.9 (1.21)
	Ireland	1.9	0.3	0.38	0.10	6.44	0.80	0.1	0.0	0.3	0.2	12.8	23.3 (1.55)
	Israel	3.8	1.0	0.51	0.01	1.22	0.01	0.0	0.4	0.2	0.1	8.9	16.1 (1.61)
	Italy	1.6	0.0	0.55	1.21	3.31	0.52	0.0	0.0	0.4	0.8	13.7	22.1 (0.80)
	Japan	0.9	0.9	1.56	1.14	0.75	0.82	0.1	c	c	c	7.4	13.6 (1.30)
	Korea	1.0	0.4	0.06	2.73	2.78	0.28	0.0	c	c	c	9.7	17.0 (1.55)
	Luxembourg	2.3	0.1	0.16	0.19	4.82	0.48	0.1	0.4	0.2	0.5	17.0	26.1 (1.27)
	Mexico	1.1	0.4	0.01	0.74	0.91	0.08	0.2	0.5	0.7	1.1	13.0	18.7 (1.14)
	Netherlands	2.7	0.1	0.18	0.62	4.93	0.41	0.1	0.1	0.0	0.0	10.5	19.7 (1.93)
	New Zealand	4.2	0.5	0.06	0.16	3.81	0.13	0.1	0.0	0.1	1.6	13.0	23.7 (1.43)
	Norway	2.7	0.1	1.38	0.07	4.13	1.57	0.1	0.0	0.0	0.6	10.5	21.1 (1.29)
	Poland	0.7	0.6	0.78	0.33	4.57	0.41	0.3	c	c	c	14.6	22.6 (1.31)
	Portugal	2.7	0.2	0.91	0.28	1.51	0.22	0.0	0.0	0.1	0.0	15.3	21.3 (1.63)
	Slovak Republic	3.2	0.0	0.68	1.50	5.01	0.49	0.0	0.1	c	c	13.8	25.4 (2.03)
	Slovenia	2.9	0.2	1.00	0.03	4.26	0.70	0.0	0.0	0.1	0.0	13.5	22.7 (1.30)
	Spain	1.5	0.2	0.82	0.36	3.64	0.48	0.0	0.0	0.7	0.0	14.9	22.6 (1.34)
	Sweden	2.4	0.3	0.85	0.00	3.89	0.55	0.1	0.0	0.1	0.1	12.2	20.6 (1.61)
	Switzerland	2.2	0.2	0.30	0.57	4.71	0.74	0.0	0.0	0.3	0.4	14.9	24.3 (1.18)
	Turkey	0.5	1.1	0.38	1.45	1.67	0.02	0.0	c	c	c	16.9	22.3 (2.18)
	United Kingdom	3.0	0.0	0.07	0.47	8.11	0.75	0.0	0.0	0.0	0.3	12.3	25.1 (1.37)
	United States	2.4	0.3	0.29	0.11	5.02	0.01	0.6	0.1	0.2	0.1	14.3	23.4 (2.03)
	OECD average	2.3	0.3	0.68	0.59	3.71	0.63	0.1	0.1	0.2	0.3	13.2	22.1 (0.26)
Partners	Albania	2.8	0.0	1.21	2.70	2.42	1.01	0.2	c	c	c	11.7	22.2 (2.19)
	Argentina	2.7	0.3	0.12	0.42	1.51	0.99	0.0	0.0	0.0	0.4	17.1	23.4 (2.27)
	Azerbaijan	0.2	0.8	0.06	1.40	1.83	0.03	0.0	0.0	0.0	0.2	7.0	11.6 (1.81)
	Brazil	3.9	0.0	0.01	2.53	0.39	0.47	0.0	0.4	0.1	0.2	13.1	21.1 (1.57)
	Bulgaria	3.3	0.5	2.16	0.75	1.71	0.31	0.1	c	0.0	c	20.9	31.7 (2.59)
	Colombia	1.4	0.1	0.24	0.38	1.46	1.72	0.0	c	c	0.2	14.6	20.4 (2.24)
	Croatia	2.7	0.0	2.13	0.17	1.16	0.34	0.0	0.1	0.0	0.0	10.8	17.5 (1.55)
	Dubai (UAE)	1.1	1.2	0.54	1.55	1.30	0.09	0.3	4.3	8.3	1.4	11.5	31.5 (1.13)
	Hong Kong-China	0.2	0.2	0.02	1.86	3.67	0.93	0.1	0.6	0.0	2.9	5.2	15.7 (1.66)
	Indonesia	1.0	0.7	0.67	0.10	0.14	1.20	0.4	c	c	c	6.8	11.8 (2.25)
	Jordan	0.9	0.7	0.38	3.52	0.00	0.89	0.8	0.1	0.0	0.4	6.6	14.3 (1.36)
	Kazakhstan	1.0	0.1	0.02	2.87	3.04	0.01	0.5	0.5	0.0	0.1	10.5	18.6 (2.08)
	Kyrgyzstan	1.6	0.0	0.06	1.77	3.71	0.13	0.1	0.2	0.0	1.2	15.4	24.3 (2.44)
	Latvia	2.5	0.0	1.61	1.31	3.01	0.10	0.0	0.1	c	0.0	10.1	18.8 (2.12)
	Liechtenstein	c	c	c	c	c	c	c	c	c	c	c	c c
	Lithuania	2.0	0.3	2.78	0.27	1.35	0.22	0.1	0.0	c	0.2	13.2	20.5 (1.63)
	Macao-China	0.3	0.4	1.57	2.15	0.36	0.99	0.0	0.0	0.0	4.5	3.5	13.9 (0.92)
	Montenegro	3.0	0.0	3.51	0.59	1.05	1.10	0.0	0.1	0.0	0.3	10.0	19.7 (1.32)
	Panama	1.9	0.0	0.02	0.14	0.56	4.06	0.2	0.3	0.0	1.2	22.3	30.7 (4.53)
	Peru	1.8	0.4	0.99	0.97	1.36	2.09	0.2	c	c	c	26.7	36.4 (2.67)
	Qatar	1.6	0.1	0.18	1.34	0.02	0.20	0.7	2.7	11.4	0.2	11.9	30.3 (1.10)
	Romania	3.3	0.2	1.88	1.84	3.81	0.47	0.0	c	c	c	13.7	26.2 (2.10)
	Russian Federation	2.3	0.1	0.78	2.15	2.31	0.84	0.0	0.1	0.0	0.7	10.5	19.9 (1.59)
	Serbia	3.7	0.2	1.77	0.47	1.82	0.48	0.0	0.3	0.1	0.1	8.9	17.9 (1.34)
	Shanghai-China	0.9	0.6	1.44	0.75	1.73	0.32	0.0	c	c	c	11.5	17.7 (1.86)
	Singapore	1.4	0.1	0.27	1.70	2.28	0.01	0.1	0.2	0.1	1.5	13.6	21.3 (1.14)
	Chinese Taipei	1.6	0.6	1.18	1.34	2.61	2.56	0.1	c	c	c	11.9	22.3 (1.74)
	Thailand	1.1	0.4	0.06	4.01	1.28	0.31	0.0	c	c	c	12.3	19.4 (2.16)
	Trinidad and Tobago	5.5	0.1	0.64	4.47	0.09	0.18	0.5	0.0	0.1	0.5	7.9	20.0 (1.22)
	Tunisia	2.9	0.1	1.31	3.70	0.21	1.13	0.0	0.0	c	c	8.3	18.0 (2.08)
	Uruguay	1.1	1.7	0.12	1.05	1.15	0.03	0.0	c	c	c	18.0	23.3 (1.49)

Note: Values that are statistically significant are indicated in bold (see Annex A3).
1. Unique variance is the variance explained by each factor after taking into account the variance explained by the other factors in the model.
StatLink ᘉᏅᓴᐳ http://dx.doi.org/10.1787/888932343285

[Part 1/1]

Percentage of students and reading performance, by family structure

Table II.2.5 *Results based on students' self-reports*

	Students from single-parent families						Students from other types of families						Difference in performance between students from single-parent families and other types of families, before accounting for ESCS		Difference in performance between students from single-parent families and other types of families, after accounting for ESCS		Increased likelihood of students in a single-parent family scoring in the bottom quarter of the reading performance distribution		Effect size for students from single-parent families and other types of families in reading performance	
	Percentage of students		PISA index of economic, social and cultural status (ESCS)		Reading performance		Percentage of students		PISA index of economic, social and cultural status (ESCS)		Reading performance									
	%	S.E.	Mean index	S.E.	Mean score	S.E.	%	S.E.	Mean index	S.E.	Mean score	S.E.	Score dif.	S.E.	Score dif.	S.E.	Ratio	S.E.	Effect size	S.E.
OECD																				
Australia	19.0	(0.5)	0.0	(0.0)	498	(3.0)	81.0	(0.5)	0.4	(0.0)	523	(2.4)	**25**	(2.8)	**5**	(2.6)	**1.34**	(0.05)	**-0.23**	(0.03)
Austria	15.9	(0.6)	-0.1	(0.0)	471	(4.5)	84.1	(0.6)	0.1	(0.0)	477	(3.0)	6	(4.3)	-4	(3.8)	**1.07**	(0.08)	-0.05	(0.04)
Belgium	17.5	(0.5)	-0.1	(0.0)	491	(3.2)	82.5	(0.5)	0.3	(0.0)	519	(2.4)	**27**	(3.3)	**10**	(2.9)	**1.45**	(0.08)	**-0.25**	(0.03)
Canada	16.8	(0.4)	0.2	(0.0)	510	(2.3)	83.2	(0.4)	0.6	(0.0)	530	(1.5)	**20**	(2.4)	**6**	(2.3)	**1.28**	(0.06)	**-0.21**	(0.03)
Chile	25.0	(0.6)	-0.6	(0.0)	452	(3.7)	75.0	(0.6)	-0.5	(0.0)	460	(3.0)	8	(3.3)	0	(2.9)	**1.00**	(0.08)	-0.02	(0.04)
Czech Republic	18.3	(0.7)	-0.3	(0.0)	469	(4.4)	81.7	(0.7)	0.0	(0.0)	486	(2.7)	**17**	(3.6)	**7**	(3.4)	**1.28**	(0.09)	**-0.18**	(0.04)
Denmark	16.9	(0.6)	0.0	(0.0)	482	(3.4)	83.1	(0.6)	0.4	(0.0)	500	(2.2)	**18**	(3.3)	2	(3.0)	**1.23**	(0.09)	**-0.20**	(0.04)
Estonia	25.1	(0.9)	-0.1	(0.0)	501	(3.7)	74.9	(0.9)	0.2	(0.0)	504	(2.7)	3	(3.2)	**-9**	(3.0)	**1.04**	(0.07)	-0.01	(0.04)
Finland	20.4	(0.7)	0.1	(0.0)	522	(3.6)	79.6	(0.7)	0.4	(0.0)	542	(2.3)	**20**	(3.5)	**9**	(3.6)	**1.37**	(0.10)	**-0.22**	(0.04)
France	19.4	(0.8)	-0.4	(0.0)	483	(5.4)	80.6	(0.8)	-0.1	(0.0)	501	(3.5)	**18**	(5.0)	2	(4.7)	**1.25**	(0.09)	**-0.17**	(0.05)
Germany	17.4	(0.6)	0.1	(0.0)	493	(5.2)	82.6	(0.6)	0.2	(0.0)	508	(2.6)	**15**	(4.6)	5	(4.1)	**1.32**	(0.11)	**-0.14**	(0.05)
Greece	10.6	(0.5)	-0.2	(0.1)	470	(7.8)	89.4	(0.5)	0.0	(0.0)	489	(3.9)	**19**	(6.4)	9	(5.7)	**1.29**	(0.15)	**-0.17**	(0.06)
Hungary	21.4	(0.7)	-0.4	(0.0)	485	(4.6)	78.6	(0.7)	-0.1	(0.0)	501	(3.1)	**16**	(4.4)	2	(3.7)	**1.22**	(0.09)	**-0.16**	(0.05)
Iceland	16.9	(0.6)	0.4	(0.0)	485	(4.3)	83.1	(0.6)	0.8	(0.0)	506	(1.6)	**21**	(4.9)	9	(4.7)	**1.34**	(0.10)	**-0.20**	(0.05)
Ireland	15.7	(0.6)	-0.2	(0.0)	478	(5.6)	84.3	(0.6)	0.1	(0.0)	504	(2.9)	**25**	(5.3)	**13**	(5.0)	**1.43**	(0.12)	**-0.26**	(0.05)
Israel	11.7	(0.6)	-0.2	(0.0)	464	(7.1)	88.3	(0.6)	0.0	(0.0)	492	(3.3)	**28**	(6.9)	7	(6.1)	**1.44**	(0.11)	**-0.18**	(0.06)
Italy	11.2	(0.3)	-0.2	(0.0)	484	(2.9)	88.8	(0.3)	-0.1	(0.0)	488	(1.6)	4	(2.8)	1	(2.6)	**1.08**	(0.05)	-0.03	(0.03)
Japan	15.1	(0.5)	-0.4	(0.0)	495	(5.4)	84.9	(0.5)	0.1	(0.0)	526	(3.2)	**31**	(3.9)	**10**	(3.8)	**1.46**	(0.10)	**-0.30**	(0.04)
Korea	12.8	(0.9)	-0.6	(0.0)	516	(7.5)	87.2	(0.9)	-0.1	(0.0)	544	(3.2)	**28**	(6.8)	10	(6.2)	**1.52**	(0.16)	**-0.34**	(0.08)
Luxembourg	16.5	(0.6)	0.1	(0.0)	462	(4.2)	83.5	(0.6)	0.2	(0.0)	477	(1.3)	**16**	(4.4)	**10**	(4.1)	**1.21**	(0.09)	**-0.13**	(0.04)
Mexico	21.5	(0.4)	-1.2	(0.0)	417	(3.0)	78.5	(0.4)	-1.2	(0.0)	435	(1.8)	**19**	(2.3)	**13**	(2.0)	**1.33**	(0.06)	**-0.18**	(0.03)
Netherlands	14.6	(0.8)	0.1	(0.1)	497	(7.0)	85.4	(0.8)	0.3	(0.0)	515	(5.2)	**18**	(5.3)	8	(4.8)	**1.29**	(0.13)	**-0.19**	(0.06)
New Zealand	19.6	(0.7)	-0.2	(0.0)	501	(4.8)	80.4	(0.7)	0.2	(0.0)	531	(2.3)	**30**	(4.9)	4	(4.6)	**1.48**	(0.10)	**-0.25**	(0.05)
Norway	15.2	(0.7)	0.2	(0.0)	493	(4.3)	84.8	(0.7)	0.5	(0.0)	508	(2.4)	**15**	(3.5)	0	(3.7)	**1.13**	(0.08)	**-0.14**	(0.04)
Poland	14.5	(0.6)	-0.5	(0.0)	484	(4.7)	85.5	(0.6)	-0.2	(0.0)	508	(2.5)	**24**	(3.9)	**13**	(3.9)	**1.45**	(0.11)	**-0.24**	(0.04)
Portugal	16.5	(0.6)	-0.4	(0.1)	491	(4.5)	83.5	(0.6)	-0.3	(0.0)	493	(3.1)	2	(4.2)	-3	(3.9)	**0.98**	(0.09)	0.00	(0.05)
Slovak Republic	15.6	(0.6)	-0.2	(0.0)	469	(4.8)	84.4	(0.6)	-0.1	(0.0)	482	(2.5)	**13**	(4.2)	4	(4.1)	**1.24**	(0.08)	**-0.13**	(0.05)
Slovenia	12.2	(0.6)	0.0	(0.0)	486	(3.7)	87.8	(0.6)	0.1	(0.0)	489	(1.3)	4	(4.3)	-3	(3.9)	**1.00**	(0.11)	-0.02	(0.05)
Spain	13.6	(0.4)	-0.5	(0.0)	472	(3.1)	86.4	(0.4)	-0.3	(0.0)	485	(2.1)	**12**	(2.9)	5	(2.8)	**1.20**	(0.07)	**-0.13**	(0.03)
Sweden	15.2	(0.7)	-0.1	(0.0)	477	(4.7)	84.8	(0.7)	0.4	(0.0)	505	(2.9)	**28**	(4.7)	5	(4.4)	**1.36**	(0.10)	**-0.25**	(0.05)
Switzerland	17.7	(0.6)	0.0	(0.0)	499	(3.5)	82.3	(0.6)	0.1	(0.0)	503	(2.6)	4	(3.7)	-2	(4.0)	**1.03**	(0.07)	-0.03	(0.04)
Turkey	7.8	(0.4)	-1.1	(0.1)	468	(6.6)	92.2	(0.4)	-1.1	(0.0)	477	(3.4)	8	(5.6)	3	(5.2)	**1.28**	(0.18)	-0.04	(0.07)
United Kingdom	22.3	(0.5)	-0.1	(0.0)	483	(3.1)	77.7	(0.5)	0.3	(0.0)	502	(2.4)	**19**	(3.0)	0	(2.9)	**1.25**	(0.08)	**-0.18**	(0.03)
United States	24.3	(0.9)	-0.2	(0.0)	470	(4.1)	75.7	(0.9)	0.3	(0.0)	515	(3.8)	**44**	(4.4)	**23**	(3.2)	**1.73**	(0.12)	**-0.43**	(0.04)
OECD average	16.9	(0.1)	-0.2	(0.0)	483	(0.8)	83.1	(0.1)	0.1	(0.0)	501	(0.5)	**18**	(0.7)	**5**	(0.7)	**1.28**	(0.02)	**-0.17**	(0.01)
Partners																				
Albania	8.6	(0.6)	-1.1	(0.1)	364	(7.6)	91.4	(0.6)	-0.9	(0.0)	394	(4.0)	**30**	(7.4)	**22**	(7.6)	**1.49**	(0.16)	**-0.28**	(0.07)
Argentina	24.3	(0.9)	-0.8	(0.1)	385	(6.3)	75.7	(0.9)	-0.5	(0.1)	412	(4.9)	**27**	(5.7)	**10**	(4.6)	**1.32**	(0.10)	**-0.19**	(0.05)
Azerbaijan	7.3	(0.7)	-0.8	(0.1)	354	(7.2)	92.7	(0.7)	-0.6	(0.0)	364	(3.3)	10	(6.6)	6	(6.3)	**1.19**	(0.18)	-0.11	(0.09)
Brazil	23.7	(0.5)	-1.2	(0.0)	407	(3.6)	76.3	(0.5)	-1.1	(0.0)	428	(2.9)	**21**	(2.6)	**9**	(2.6)	**1.15**	(0.06)	**-0.11**	(0.03)
Bulgaria	17.7	(0.8)	-0.3	(0.1)	410	(8.6)	82.3	(0.8)	0.0	(0.0)	449	(5.9)	**39**	(6.1)	**17**	(4.8)	**1.52**	(0.13)	**-0.27**	(0.05)
Colombia	29.3	(1.0)	-1.2	(0.1)	411	(4.0)	70.7	(1.0)	-1.1	(0.1)	432	(3.8)	**21**	(3.5)	**7**	(3.2)	**1.17**	(0.10)	**-0.11**	(0.04)
Croatia	10.8	(0.5)	-0.3	(0.0)	482	(5.4)	89.2	(0.5)	-0.2	(0.0)	477	(2.7)	-5	(4.6)	**-9**	(3.9)	**0.88**	(0.09)	0.06	(0.05)
Dubai (UAE)	11.2	(0.5)	0.2	(0.0)	427	(4.5)	88.8	(0.5)	0.5	(0.0)	471	(1.4)	**44**	(4.9)	**25**	(4.8)	**1.55**	(0.11)	**-0.38**	(0.05)
Hong Kong-China	12.3	(0.5)	-1.0	(0.0)	521	(4.1)	87.7	(0.5)	-0.8	(0.0)	536	(2.1)	**15**	(4.0)	**9**	(3.9)	**1.23**	(0.09)	**-0.16**	(0.05)
Indonesia	7.9	(0.6)	-1.6	(0.1)	386	(6.4)	92.1	(0.6)	-1.5	(0.1)	416	(4.2)	**30**	(5.7)	**18**	(4.6)	**1.50**	(0.16)	**-0.30**	(0.07)
Jordan	10.3	(0.5)	-0.7	(0.1)	370	(5.7)	89.7	(0.5)	-0.5	(0.0)	418	(3.5)	**47**	(5.9)	**38**	(5.8)	**1.88**	(0.14)	**-0.47**	(0.06)
Kazakhstan	19.6	(0.7)	-0.7	(0.0)	401	(5.0)	80.4	(0.7)	-0.5	(0.0)	392	(3.2)	**-9**	(4.4)	**-19**	(4.3)	**0.91**	(0.09)	**0.12**	(0.05)
Kyrgyzstan	22.2	(0.8)	-0.6	(0.0)	324	(4.0)	77.8	(0.8)	-0.6	(0.0)	320	(3.7)	**-4**	(4.0)	**-9**	(3.4)	**0.87**	(0.06)	**0.09**	(0.04)
Latvia	25.3	(0.9)	-0.3	(0.0)	480	(3.9)	74.7	(0.9)	-0.1	(0.0)	490	(3.0)	10	(3.4)	-1	(3.0)	**1.04**	(0.09)	-0.06	(0.04)
Liechtenstein	19.6	(2.0)	0.1	(0.1)	481	(9.3)	80.4	(2.0)	0.1	(0.1)	503	(4.2)	22	(12.1)	21	(11.3)	**1.13**	(0.28)	-0.27	(0.15)
Lithuania	21.7	(0.7)	-0.3	(0.0)	455	(3.5)	78.3	(0.7)	0.0	(0.0)	474	(2.4)	**19**	(3.1)	**6**	(2.6)	**1.37**	(0.08)	**-0.20**	(0.03)
Macao-China	14.9	(0.5)	-0.9	(0.0)	485	(2.7)	85.1	(0.5)	-0.7	(0.0)	489	(1.0)	4	(3.0)	1	(3.0)	**1.09**	(0.07)	-0.04	(0.04)
Montenegro	10.1	(0.5)	-0.3	(0.1)	411	(4.8)	89.9	(0.5)	-0.2	(0.0)	412	(1.7)	1	(4.8)	-2	(4.4)	**1.01**	(0.11)	0.01	(0.05)
Panama	27.5	(1.2)	-0.8	(0.1)	368	(7.5)	72.5	(1.2)	-0.7	(0.1)	402	(6.3)	**35**	(7.3)	**16**	(6.0)	**1.20**	(0.14)	**-0.18**	(0.08)
Peru	19.7	(0.6)	-1.2	(0.1)	383	(5.2)	80.3	(0.6)	-1.3	(0.0)	369	(3.9)	**-14**	(3.7)	**-9**	(3.0)	**0.79**	(0.06)	**0.15**	(0.04)
Qatar	12.2	(0.4)	0.3	(0.0)	320	(3.6)	87.8	(0.4)	0.6	(0.0)	401	(1.2)	**81**	(4.0)	**61**	(4.0)	**2.08**	(0.09)	**-0.62**	(0.04)
Romania	12.6	(0.5)	-0.5	(0.1)	416	(6.0)	87.4	(0.5)	-0.3	(0.0)	431	(4.1)	**15**	(5.2)	4	(4.3)	**1.15**	(0.10)	**-0.13**	(0.06)
Russian Federation	25.6	(0.7)	-0.3	(0.0)	458	(3.8)	74.4	(0.7)	-0.2	(0.0)	463	(3.8)	5	(3.5)	-3	(3.0)	**1.11**	(0.06)	-0.04	(0.04)
Serbia	12.8	(0.5)	0.0	(0.0)	442	(4.0)	87.2	(0.5)	0.1	(0.0)	446	(2.2)	4	(3.8)	0	(3.7)	**1.11**	(0.09)	-0.03	(0.04)
Shanghai-China	10.6	(0.4)	-0.5	(0.1)	553	(5.0)	89.4	(0.4)	-0.5	(0.0)	558	(2.2)	4	(4.4)	3	(4.2)	**1.10**	(0.09)	-0.05	(0.05)
Singapore	11.2	(0.4)	-0.6	(0.0)	503	(4.5)	88.8	(0.4)	-0.4	(0.0)	532	(1.2)	**29**	(4.8)	**15**	(4.6)	**1.47**	(0.10)	**-0.27**	(0.05)
Chinese Taipei	13.6	(0.5)	-0.6	(0.0)	478	(4.9)	86.4	(0.5)	-0.3	(0.0)	501	(2.6)	**22**	(4.6)	**9**	(4.0)	**1.43**	(0.11)	**-0.22**	(0.05)
Thailand	17.9	(0.8)	-1.3	(0.1)	422	(3.6)	82.1	(0.8)	-1.3	(0.0)	436	(2.9)	14	(3.5)	3	(2.8)	**1.01**	(0.11)	-0.07	(0.04)
Trinidad and Tobago	28.4	(0.7)	-0.7	(0.0)	399	(3.5)	71.6	(0.7)	-0.5	(0.0)	446	(1.9)	**46**	(4.4)	**28**	(4.3)	**1.40**	(0.09)	**-0.31**	(0.04)
Tunisia	7.1	(0.5)	-1.2	(0.1)	383	(8.7)	92.9	(0.5)	-1.2	(0.1)	415	(3.2)	**32**	(8.5)	**25**	(8.2)	**1.49**	(0.18)	**-0.28**	(0.09)
Uruguay	25.4	(0.7)	-0.8	(0.0)	422	(3.3)	74.6	(0.7)	-0.6	(0.0)	435	(2.8)	**13**	(3.3)	3	(3.0)	**1.15**	(0.08)	**-0.10**	(0.03)

Note: Values that are statistically significant are indicated in bold (see Annex A3).

StatLink http://dx.doi.org/10.1787/888932343285

[Part 1/3]
Reading performance and socio-economic background, by school location
Table II.2.6   *Results based on students' self-reports and school principals' reports*

		Percentage of students									Average performance in reading									
		Students attending schools located in a village, hamlet or rural area (fewer than 3 000 people)		Students attending schools located in a small town (3 000 to about 15 000 people)		Students attending schools located in a town (15 000 to about 100 000 people)		Students attending schools located in a city (100 000 to about 1 000 000 people)		Students attending schools located in a large city (with over 1 000 000 people)		Students attending schools located in a village, hamlet or rural area (fewer than 3 000 people)		Students attending schools located in a small town (3 000 to about 15 000 people)		Students attending schools located in a town (15 000 to about 100 000 people)		Students attending schools located in a city (100 000 to about 1 000 000 people)		Students attending schools located in a large city (with over 1 000 000 people)	
		%	S.E.	%	S.E.	%	S.E.	%	S.E.	%	S.E.	Mean score	S.E.	Mean score	S.E.	Mean score	S.E.	Mean score	S.E.	Mean score	S.E.
OECD	Australia	4.0	(0.8)	12.0	(1.9)	18.8	(2.1)	25.9	(2.2)	39.3	(2.6)	477	(6.3)	492	(4.6)	497	(4.8)	530	(4.6)	531	(4.7)
	Austria	11.2	(2.3)	36.9	(3.8)	20.6	(3.5)	13.2	(2.0)	18.0	(1.7)	440	(15.4)	467	(7.8)	486	(9.6)	492	(13.6)	461	(9.0)
	Belgium	3.5	(1.2)	22.9	(2.3)	50.8	(3.3)	12.9	(2.1)	9.9	(1.8)	522	(28.4)	523	(6.7)	507	(4.6)	499	(12.9)	490	(15.9)
	Canada	7.6	(0.8)	16.1	(1.5)	26.5	(2.1)	32.8	(2.3)	16.8	(1.9)	503	(3.6)	511	(2.8)	528	(3.2)	529	(3.0)	541	(5.9)
	Chile	1.5	(0.5)	7.9	(2.2)	27.9	(3.9)	41.5	(4.0)	21.2	(3.2)	366	(14.3)	405	(10.1)	443	(7.1)	463	(5.8)	461	(9.8)
	Czech Republic	11.6	(1.7)	25.1	(3.0)	44.4	(3.0)	9.7	(2.1)	9.2	(1.2)	440	(8.1)	470	(7.3)	482	(4.9)	491	(17.6)	517	(8.3)
	Denmark	22.5	(2.7)	27.5	(3.3)	35.1	(3.0)	10.6	(1.9)	4.3	(0.8)	482	(4.2)	500	(5.0)	503	(3.7)	498	(6.6)	489	(9.3)
	Estonia	26.4	(1.9)	26.0	(2.5)	21.3	(2.4)	26.3	(1.6)	c	c	486	(4.4)	498	(4.9)	503	(6.8)	519	(5.3)	c	c
	Finland	11.2	(1.9)	26.7	(2.9)	36.4	(3.0)	25.8	(3.1)	c	c	525	(7.2)	532	(4.3)	538	(3.3)	543	(5.2)	c	c
	France	w	w	w	w	w	w	w	w	w	w	w	w	w	w	w	w	w	w	w	w
	Germany	2.9	(0.8)	22.8	(3.1)	50.6	(3.3)	17.4	(2.7)	6.3	(1.2)	437	(26.9)	498	(7.7)	510	(5.5)	484	(13.1)	510	(13.4)
	Greece	5.9	(1.7)	25.2	(2.8)	43.3	(3.2)	11.8	(2.1)	13.8	(2.3)	472	(20.9)	483	(6.2)	479	(9.2)	493	(13.8)	493	(10.7)
	Hungary	3.2	(1.1)	17.2	(3.1)	38.4	(4.3)	22.5	(2.9)	18.8	(2.1)	381	(18.0)	458	(15.0)	499	(7.5)	515	(9.3)	514	(10.2)
	Iceland	22.9	(0.2)	22.3	(0.2)	25.1	(0.2)	29.7	(0.2)	c	c	494	(2.9)	505	(3.4)	491	(2.9)	508	(2.7)	c	c
	Ireland	21.6	(3.8)	36.0	(4.3)	16.9	(3.0)	13.7	(3.0)	11.9	(2.8)	478	(10.4)	496	(5.7)	500	(9.7)	526	(10.8)	491	(12.6)
	Israel	12.7	(2.4)	12.9	(2.6)	29.4	(3.2)	36.1	(3.7)	8.9	(2.3)	489	(12.6)	442	(14.7)	462	(8.8)	496	(7.8)	528	(12.8)
	Italy	1.4	(0.4)	15.8	(1.5)	51.4	(2.0)	23.0	(1.7)	8.4	(1.2)	422	(14.4)	473	(7.6)	488	(3.0)	495	(5.2)	493	(11.9)
	Japan	c	c	2.0	(1.0)	28.8	(2.9)	47.2	(3.4)	22.1	(2.9)	c	c	487	(13.6)	508	(9.2)	523	(5.1)	541	(12.0)
	Korea	0.9	(0.6)	6.2	(2.3)	7.0	(2.1)	40.5	(2.8)	45.4	(2.2)	615	(19.9)	478	(16.9)	550	(13.5)	547	(5.0)	537	(4.4)
	Luxembourg	0.5	(0.1)	31.5	(0.1)	64.9	(0.1)	3.1	(0.0)	c	c	514	(14.6)	459	(2.0)	474	(1.5)	564	(6.9)	c	c
	Mexico	16.1	(1.3)	16.9	(1.4)	21.3	(1.6)	27.2	(1.5)	18.5	(1.4)	374	(7.1)	391	(4.5)	430	(4.3)	449	(3.1)	462	(5.2)
	Netherlands	0.8	(0.6)	17.4	(3.3)	54.1	(3.9)	27.6	(3.4)	c	c	483	(40.0)	486	(10.7)	512	(7.8)	521	(10.8)	c	c
	New Zealand	4.5	(0.8)	16.0	(2.0)	23.9	(2.8)	25.9	(2.4)	29.6	(2.7)	495	(5.1)	512	(6.6)	514	(6.6)	551	(6.2)	519	(6.2)
	Norway	19.7	(1.9)	36.2	(3.5)	26.4	(3.0)	17.7	(2.8)	c	c	487	(5.2)	503	(3.7)	507	(3.8)	519	(6.5)	c	c
	Poland	33.4	(1.9)	21.7	(2.3)	22.4	(1.8)	19.1	(1.4)	3.3	(1.3)	483	(3.7)	499	(5.3)	514	(5.6)	516	(6.0)	537	(15.4)
	Portugal	8.8	(2.6)	27.4	(3.3)	42.2	(3.6)	16.0	(2.6)	5.6	(1.6)	447	(11.6)	474	(5.8)	492	(4.5)	523	(8.1)	526	(16.0)
	Slovak Republic	10.5	(1.7)	18.4	(3.7)	53.7	(3.7)	17.4	(2.5)	c	c	423	(5.5)	467	(11.8)	487	(4.7)	495	(7.1)	c	c
	Slovenia	2.1	(0.5)	13.0	(0.3)	48.0	(0.4)	25.2	(0.2)	11.6	(0.1)	428	(11.9)	492	(4.1)	477	(1.1)	501	(2.2)	475	(2.9)
	Spain	4.1	(0.8)	26.1	(1.9)	34.2	(2.4)	26.5	(2.0)	9.1	(0.8)	459	(5.1)	464	(3.8)	480	(3.1)	493	(5.2)	516	(5.1)
	Sweden	13.9	(2.6)	26.6	(2.8)	34.3	(3.2)	25.1	(2.6)	c	c	489	(6.3)	489	(5.1)	505	(5.0)	507	(7.6)	c	c
	Switzerland	10.7	(1.9)	48.4	(3.0)	27.2	(3.0)	13.7	(1.9)	c	c	478	(4.0)	490	(5.0)	516	(9.0)	527	(10.1)	c	c
	Turkey	3.0	(0.9)	9.7	(2.0)	28.1	(3.9)	27.9	(3.7)	31.3	(3.2)	360	(13.4)	443	(11.0)	467	(8.4)	481	(8.7)	464	(7.0)
	United Kingdom	6.8	(1.9)	23.1	(2.7)	38.7	(3.9)	20.8	(2.8)	10.5	(2.0)	512	(11.6)	505	(4.4)	497	(4.9)	493	(8.3)	487	(10.4)
	United States	11.9	(1.7)	17.8	(3.2)	31.9	(3.4)	27.1	(3.3)	11.3	(2.2)	491	(9.3)	502	(9.8)	506	(5.0)	504	(10.1)	485	(15.1)
	OECD average	9.9	(0.3)	21.6	(0.5)	34.1	(0.5)	23.1	(0.4)	16.0	(0.4)	467	(2.5)	482	(1.4)	495	(1.1)	509	(1.5)	503	(2.1)
Partners	Albania	25.0	(1.6)	20.0	(2.9)	27.7	(3.3)	27.3	(3.3)	c	c	347	(7.7)	368	(6.2)	394	(8.9)	426	(7.6)	c	c
	Argentina	8.3	(1.9)	16.6	(2.5)	32.5	(4.0)	26.6	(3.4)	15.9	(3.1)	340	(12.1)	359	(10.6)	399	(10.1)	418	(12.4)	447	(11.1)
	Azerbaijan	31.9	(2.9)	17.1	(3.2)	9.6	(2.0)	12.7	(2.6)	28.7	(1.5)	344	(5.5)	342	(10.4)	377	(7.6)	351	(6.3)	395	(5.5)
	Brazil	4.4	(0.8)	14.3	(1.9)	31.4	(2.4)	31.8	(2.6)	18.1	(2.0)	356	(8.9)	379	(6.0)	413	(6.1)	433	(5.5)	418	(7.6)
	Bulgaria	5.2	(1.6)	17.6	(2.5)	38.6	(3.6)	23.3	(2.9)	15.2	(2.0)	328	(18.9)	397	(8.9)	418	(10.9)	474	(13.1)	476	(14.8)
	Colombia	10.9	(2.0)	20.7	(3.8)	20.8	(3.6)	23.0	(3.5)	24.5	(2.3)	382	(9.8)	391	(9.8)	404	(7.0)	417	(9.6)	451	(4.2)
	Croatia	1.2	(0.9)	18.0	(2.5)	44.3	(2.6)	16.6	(1.3)	19.8	(1.1)	445	(20.7)	472	(8.0)	465	(4.5)	488	(7.3)	496	(7.6)
	Dubai (UAE)	1.5	(0.0)	5.0	(0.1)	4.8	(0.1)	32.6	(0.1)	56.1	(0.1)	430	(7.0)	373	(4.1)	416	(5.0)	436	(2.0)	487	(1.7)
	Hong Kong-China	c	c	c	c	c	c	c	c	100.0	(0.0)	c	c	c	c	c	c	c	c	534	(2.1)
	Indonesia	22.2	(3.4)	43.0	(4.2)	14.7	(3.2)	13.2	(3.2)	6.7	(2.2)	376	(6.4)	397	(4.4)	412	(11.1)	442	(8.1)	416	(16.6)
	Jordan	6.1	(1.3)	26.8	(2.7)	26.8	(3.3)	18.6	(3.0)	21.6	(2.5)	363	(14.7)	396	(6.5)	406	(6.5)	413	(8.6)	426	(7.5)
	Kazakhstan	32.7	(3.1)	17.1	(2.9)	10.8	(2.7)	32.0	(2.7)	7.3	(0.3)	367	(4.8)	369	(7.9)	385	(16.2)	419	(6.9)	431	(10.2)
	Kyrgyzstan	52.0	(2.8)	19.9	(2.6)	13.2	(1.6)	10.0	(1.3)	4.9	(1.0)	284	(4.0)	313	(7.7)	338	(12.9)	398	(14.7)	420	(14.1)
	Latvia	32.3	(2.3)	21.8	(2.9)	18.6	(2.1)	27.2	(1.5)	c	c	462	(5.0)	489	(4.5)	490	(7.2)	503	(6.6)	c	c
	Liechtenstein	21.2	(0.4)	78.8	(0.4)	c	c	c	c	c	c	465	(7.0)	509	(3.4)	c	c	c	c	c	c
	Lithuania	23.4	(1.2)	20.7	(2.7)	20.3	(2.5)	35.6	(1.0)	c	c	440	(4.2)	463	(5.9)	480	(7.9)	485	(5.0)	c	c
	Macao-China	c	c	c	c	c	c	100.0	(0.0)	c	c	c	c	c	c	c	c	487	(0.9)	c	c
	Montenegro	1.1	(0.0)	15.3	(0.3)	53.6	(0.9)	30.0	(1.2)	c	c	371	(22.9)	403	(2.3)	405	(1.6)	417	(5.8)	c	c
	Panama	12.8	(3.6)	30.7	(4.7)	23.6	(3.7)	27.1	(4.1)	5.8	(1.9)	295	(15.5)	347	(9.8)	387	(9.0)	426	(16.1)	443	(25.9)
	Peru	17.3	(2.1)	23.5	(3.1)	21.3	(2.6)	28.3	(3.2)	9.3	(2.0)	297	(6.0)	334	(6.4)	368	(5.7)	425	(7.0)	435	(15.5)
	Qatar	3.9	(0.1)	28.5	(0.1)	25.6	(0.1)	32.6	(0.1)	9.4	(0.1)	353	(4.4)	336	(1.6)	346	(1.5)	404	(1.8)	462	(3.3)
	Romania	9.2	(1.6)	15.5	(3.1)	38.3	(4.1)	28.0	(3.9)	9.1	(2.5)	371	(16.2)	419	(8.8)	423	(8.1)	443	(9.5)	438	(21.3)
	Russian Federation	20.1	(2.7)	17.4	(3.2)	16.3	(2.8)	32.7	(2.9)	13.6	(1.4)	436	(7.5)	447	(4.3)	452	(7.4)	468	(6.3)	507	(11.1)
	Serbia	0.4	(0.2)	13.9	(2.9)	37.5	(3.8)	27.0	(2.6)	21.2	(1.4)	432	(19.5)	409	(11.3)	436	(5.2)	449	(5.7)	467	(5.7)
	Shanghai-China	c	c	c	c	c	c	c	c	100.0	(0.0)	c	c	c	c	c	c	c	c	556	(2.4)
	Singapore	c	c	c	c	c	c	c	c	100.0	(0.0)	c	c	c	c	c	c	c	c	527	(1.1)
	Chinese Taipei	c	c	7.1	(1.9)	32.0	(3.6)	36.9	(3.6)	24.0	(2.7)	c	c	468	(11.3)	479	(5.2)	506	(5.8)	510	(8.7)
	Thailand	18.3	(2.3)	19.7	(3.4)	37.1	(3.8)	16.8	(2.7)	8.2	(1.9)	391	(6.2)	407	(4.3)	424	(4.5)	446	(8.4)	464	(9.5)
	Trinidad and Tobago	20.7	(0.2)	42.4	(0.3)	36.9	(0.3)	c	c	c	c	394	(2.8)	410	(2.1)	455	(2.3)	c	c	c	c
	Tunisia	6.2	(1.6)	30.2	(3.6)	44.8	(3.9)	14.9	(3.2)	4.1	(1.7)	365	(13.4)	389	(6.8)	401	(5.1)	437	(11.0)	480	(18.7)
	Uruguay	5.7	(0.9)	12.5	(1.3)	38.3	(2.6)	7.5	(1.8)	36.0	(1.9)	382	(9.6)	407	(6.7)	418	(4.6)	401	(13.7)	457	(4.7)

Note: Values that are statistically significant are indicated in bold (see Annex A3).
StatLink ᴍᴸᴸ http://dx.doi.org/10.1787/888932343285

[Part 2/3]
Reading performance and socio-economic background, by school location

Table II.2.6 *Results based on students' self-reports and school principals' reports*

		PISA index of economic, social and cultural status (ESCS)					Average performance in reading after accounting for ESCS				
		Students attending schools located in a village, hamlet or rural area (fewer than 3 000 people)	Students attending schools located in a small town (3 000 to about 15 000 people)	Students attending schools located in a town (15 000 to about 100 000 people)	Students attending schools located in a city (100 000 to about 1 000 000 people)	Students attending schools located in a large city (with over 1 000 000 people)	Students attending schools located in a village, hamlet or rural area (fewer than 3 000 people)	Students attending schools located in a small town (3 000 to about 15 000 people)	Students attending schools located in a town (15 000 to about 100 000 people)	Students attending schools located in a city (100 000 to about 1 000 000 people)	Students attending schools located in a large city (with over 1 000 000 people)
		Mean index S.E.	Mean index S.E.	Mean index S.E.	Mean index S.E.	Mean index S.E.	Mean score S.E.	Mean score S.E.	Mean score S.E.	Mean score S.E.	Mean score S.E.
OECD	Australia	-0.01 (0.04)	0.11 (0.03)	0.19 (0.03)	0.47 (0.03)	0.44 (0.04)	493 (5.9)	502 (4.3)	503 (3.7)	525 (3.8)	526 (3.8)
	Austria	-0.02 (0.09)	-0.01 (0.04)	0.14 (0.06)	0.20 (0.10)	0.05 (0.07)	444 (12.4)	470 (6.8)	482 (7.6)	485 (10.1)	462 (7.3)
	Belgium	0.43 (0.19)	0.24 (0.05)	0.16 (0.05)	0.14 (0.10)	0.27 (0.15)	511 (20.2)	521 (5.1)	508 (3.4)	501 (9.3)	487 (9.9)
	Canada	0.24 (0.05)	0.32 (0.03)	0.52 (0.03)	0.59 (0.03)	0.60 (0.07)	511 (3.2)	517 (2.5)	528 (2.8)	526 (2.6)	538 (4.5)
	Chile	-1.80 (0.10)	-1.42 (0.11)	-0.72 (0.12)	-0.37 (0.08)	-0.33 (0.13)	400 (14.1)	428 (8.7)	447 (5.1)	458 (4.8)	455 (7.4)
	Czech Republic	-0.34 (0.05)	-0.21 (0.03)	-0.05 (0.02)	0.01 (0.07)	0.29 (0.04)	451 (7.0)	476 (6.4)	480 (4.3)	486 (16.5)	500 (7.0)
	Denmark	0.13 (0.04)	0.36 (0.06)	0.40 (0.04)	0.24 (0.06)	0.04 (0.09)	488 (3.7)	498 (3.8)	499 (3.0)	500 (5.2)	498 (7.3)
	Estonia	-0.15 (0.03)	0.16 (0.03)	0.17 (0.06)	0.43 (0.04)	c c	494 (4.4)	498 (4.6)	503 (5.7)	511 (4.6)	c c
	Finland	0.12 (0.03)	0.27 (0.03)	0.37 (0.03)	0.58 (0.05)	c c	533 (7.7)	535 (4.3)	538 (2.9)	537 (4.4)	c c
	France	w w	w w	w w	w w	w w	w w	w w	w w	w w	w w
	Germany	-0.16 (0.16)	0.12 (0.05)	0.24 (0.04)	0.11 (0.10)	0.27 (0.10)	452 (22.2)	501 (6.2)	508 (4.4)	488 (9.7)	506 (10.1)
	Greece	-0.77 (0.15)	-0.14 (0.06)	0.03 (0.06)	0.18 (0.09)	0.15 (0.11)	498 (17.1)	488 (5.6)	477 (7.5)	486 (11.7)	487 (10.0)
	Hungary	-1.14 (0.15)	-0.66 (0.13)	-0.20 (0.08)	-0.07 (0.07)	0.26 (0.08)	422 (14.2)	478 (10.1)	499 (5.8)	509 (7.1)	495 (8.5)
	Iceland	0.31 (0.03)	0.78 (0.03)	0.75 (0.03)	0.94 (0.02)	c c	506 (3.4)	503 (3.3)	490 (2.8)	502 (2.8)	c c
	Ireland	-0.10 (0.06)	-0.04 (0.04)	0.14 (0.09)	0.31 (0.13)	0.07 (0.16)	484 (9.9)	500 (5.2)	496 (7.1)	514 (8.1)	490 (8.1)
	Israel	0.06 (0.09)	-0.16 (0.11)	-0.09 (0.06)	0.01 (0.05)	0.27 (0.09)	486 (10.7)	446 (12.8)	464 (7.6)	495 (6.6)	518 (11.0)
	Italy	-0.60 (0.07)	-0.34 (0.05)	-0.16 (0.02)	0.04 (0.04)	0.15 (0.09)	437 (14.3)	480 (6.4)	489 (2.7)	490 (4.4)	485 (10.0)
	Japan	c c	-0.33 (0.15)	-0.13 (0.04)	0.02 (0.08)	0.12 (0.05)	c c	500 (10.8)	512 (8.4)	522 (4.5)	536 (10.5)
	Korea	0.84 (0.22)	-0.60 (0.11)	-0.17 (0.10)	-0.15 (0.05)	-0.11 (0.04)	586 (13.6)	492 (16.0)	551 (11.4)	547 (4.3)	536 (3.8)
	Luxembourg	0.23 (0.18)	-0.05 (0.03)	0.23 (0.02)	1.18 (0.05)	c c	512 (16.3)	470 (2.2)	472 (1.6)	520 (7.3)	c c
	Mexico	-2.25 (0.08)	-1.73 (0.05)	-1.25 (0.04)	-0.72 (0.05)	-0.53 (0.07)	392 (6.7)	400 (4.4)	431 (3.9)	441 (2.7)	450 (4.9)
	Netherlands	0.36 (0.15)	0.18 (0.06)	0.27 (0.04)	0.32 (0.08)	c c	480 (33.9)	489 (9.1)	512 (6.9)	519 (8.7)	c c
	New Zealand	-0.23 (0.04)	-0.06 (0.05)	-0.01 (0.05)	0.29 (0.05)	0.12 (0.05)	511 (6.2)	519 (4.8)	519 (5.6)	541 (4.5)	517 (4.5)
	Norway	0.28 (0.03)	0.43 (0.02)	0.53 (0.04)	0.67 (0.05)	c c	494 (5.4)	505 (3.7)	505 (3.2)	512 (5.6)	c c
	Poland	-0.62 (0.04)	-0.41 (0.04)	-0.08 (0.04)	0.12 (0.08)	0.26 (0.18)	495 (3.3)	503 (4.8)	507 (4.8)	501 (4.4)	517 (10.2)
	Portugal	-0.94 (0.10)	-0.57 (0.08)	-0.35 (0.05)	0.30 (0.12)	0.38 (0.23)	464 (9.7)	481 (4.8)	492 (3.9)	507 (6.1)	508 (12.3)
	Slovak Republic	-0.39 (0.06)	-0.20 (0.08)	-0.07 (0.03)	0.11 (0.05)	c c	435 (4.8)	471 (9.2)	486 (4.0)	488 (6.4)	c c
	Slovenia	-0.35 (0.06)	0.04 (0.03)	0.01 (0.02)	0.24 (0.03)	0.10 (0.03)	444 (11.2)	493 (3.9)	480 (1.3)	495 (2.3)	474 (3.1)
	Spain	-0.74 (0.07)	-0.60 (0.05)	-0.29 (0.06)	-0.11 (0.07)	0.01 (0.15)	472 (4.7)	472 (3.4)	480 (3.1)	487 (4.0)	507 (3.6)
	Sweden	0.18 (0.04)	0.18 (0.04)	0.39 (0.04)	0.49 (0.06)	c c	496 (5.2)	496 (4.4)	503 (4.0)	500 (6.0)	c c
	Switzerland	-0.12 (0.07)	0.00 (0.03)	0.14 (0.06)	0.40 (0.08)	c c	485 (3.5)	493 (4.1)	514 (7.7)	516 (8.7)	c c
	Turkey	-2.50 (0.22)	-1.53 (0.16)	-1.19 (0.10)	-1.00 (0.10)	-1.05 (0.09)	397 (12.2)	453 (8.4)	468 (6.6)	477 (6.4)	461 (5.5)
	United Kingdom	0.32 (0.09)	0.24 (0.04)	0.20 (0.04)	0.19 (0.07)	0.14 (0.11)	507 (9.7)	504 (3.2)	497 (4.0)	494 (6.3)	490 (8.2)
	United States	0.00 (0.05)	0.20 (0.09)	0.25 (0.07)	0.22 (0.11)	-0.04 (0.17)	499 (8.1)	500 (6.5)	503 (3.2)	502 (6.3)	493 (9.2)
	OECD average	-0.30 (0.02)	-0.16 (0.01)	0.01 (0.01)	0.19 (0.01)	0.1 (0.02)	477 (2.1)	487 (1.2)	495 (0.9)	502 (1.2)	497 (1.6)
Partners	Albania	-1.60 (0.05)	-1.14 (0.06)	-0.77 (0.06)	-0.41 (0.08)	c c	362 (7.2)	372 (6.5)	390 (8.0)	413 (6.5)	c c
	Argentina	-1.40 (0.14)	-0.91 (0.09)	-0.67 (0.11)	-0.38 (0.11)	-0.18 (0.15)	367 (9.5)	370 (9.1)	401 (7.7)	409 (9.6)	432 (7.7)
	Azerbaijan	-1.13 (0.04)	-0.93 (0.08)	-0.44 (0.07)	-0.47 (0.06)	-0.07 (0.06)	351 (5.5)	346 (10.1)	374 (7.8)	348 (6.0)	387 (5.0)
	Brazil	-2.10 (0.09)	-1.72 (0.05)	-1.29 (0.08)	-0.85 (0.08)	-0.80 (0.06)	378 (8.6)	392 (6.1)	416 (5.3)	426 (4.2)	410 (6.6)
	Bulgaria	-1.02 (0.19)	-0.40 (0.08)	-0.23 (0.06)	0.18 (0.06)	0.41 (0.09)	367 (16.7)	410 (6.1)	423 (9.1)	461 (11.3)	454 (12.3)
	Colombia	-1.99 (0.13)	-1.64 (0.10)	-1.27 (0.11)	-0.89 (0.14)	-0.52 (0.06)	402 (8.2)	403 (8.6)	407 (5.4)	410 (7.1)	436 (3.5)
	Croatia	-0.54 (0.05)	-0.36 (0.06)	-0.31 (0.04)	0.01 (0.06)	0.16 (0.07)	456 (24.4)	477 (6.8)	469 (4.2)	483 (7.0)	486 (6.8)
	Dubai (UAE)	-0.45 (0.08)	-0.01 (0.03)	-0.05 (0.05)	0.25 (0.02)	0.63 (0.01)	466 (7.2)	391 (4.5)	436 (3.2)	443 (2.1)	478 (1.8)
	Hong Kong-China	c c	c c	c c	c c	-0.81 (0.04)	c c	c c	c c	c c	534 (2.0)
	Indonesia	-1.90 (0.10)	-1.71 (0.07)	-1.40 (0.15)	-0.96 (0.16)	-0.87 (0.24)	380 (6.3)	399 (4.1)	410 (10.3)	435 (7.8)	408 (13.8)
	Jordan	-1.01 (0.08)	-0.81 (0.08)	-0.62 (0.07)	-0.44 (0.08)	-0.19 (0.08)	373 (13.8)	402 (6.4)	407 (5.8)	410 (7.5)	417 (6.6)
	Kazakhstan	-0.80 (0.05)	-0.58 (0.05)	-0.44 (0.13)	-0.29 (0.05)	-0.13 (0.12)	376 (4.6)	371 (7.5)	383 (14.0)	411 (5.8)	419 (8.1)
	Kyrgyzstan	-0.95 (0.03)	-0.63 (0.05)	-0.39 (0.07)	0.18 (0.12)	0.14 (0.08)	292 (3.8)	312 (7.3)	331 (11.2)	377 (12.3)	399 (12.6)
	Latvia	-0.50 (0.04)	-0.10 (0.04)	-0.08 (0.06)	0.26 (0.07)	c c	472 (4.7)	489 (4.3)	488 (6.2)	493 (5.5)	c c
	Liechtenstein	-0.22 (0.04)	0.17 (0.05)	c c	c c	c c	472 (7.3)	507 (3.6)	c c	c c	c c
	Lithuania	-0.54 (0.05)	-0.11 (0.05)	-0.01 (0.06)	0.30 (0.04)	c c	455 (4.3)	465 (5.0)	479 (6.7)	474 (4.8)	c c
	Macao-China	c c	c c	c c	-0.70 (0.01)	c c	c c	c c	c c	487 (0.9)	c c
	Montenegro	-1.02 (0.25)	-0.22 (0.03)	-0.31 (0.01)	-0.12 (0.06)	c c	394 (18.1)	402 (2.3)	407 (1.7)	414 (4.5)	c c
	Panama	-1.62 (0.40)	-1.24 (0.13)	-0.94 (0.14)	0.11 (0.17)	-0.12 (0.34)	307 (15.2)	354 (9.6)	389 (9.0)	412 (14.3)	433 (21.9)
	Peru	-2.24 (0.07)	-1.79 (0.08)	-1.40 (0.06)	-0.57 (0.09)	-0.47 (0.17)	323 (5.7)	347 (5.2)	370 (4.6)	405 (5.4)	411 (11.0)
	Qatar	0.01 (0.04)	0.31 (0.02)	0.46 (0.02)	0.75 (0.01)	0.59 (0.02)	362 (4.4)	340 (1.7)	346 (1.5)	399 (1.8)	460 (3.2)
	Romania	-0.97 (0.17)	-0.55 (0.06)	-0.33 (0.05)	-0.19 (0.07)	0.08 (0.10)	392 (13.8)	426 (7.7)	423 (6.9)	438 (8.1)	424 (18.8)
	Russian Federation	-0.70 (0.02)	-0.32 (0.05)	-0.21 (0.04)	-0.07 (0.04)	0.29 (0.06)	451 (3.7)	449 (3.7)	451 (6.6)	463 (5.4)	490 (9.6)
	Serbia	-1.08 (0.63)	-0.26 (0.08)	-0.04 (0.04)	0.11 (0.05)	0.45 (0.04)	461 (29.7)	417 (10.0)	439 (4.8)	448 (5.0)	458 (5.0)
	Shanghai-China	c c	c c	c c	c c	-0.49 (0.04)	c c	c c	c c	c c	556 (1.9)
	Singapore	c c	c c	c c	c c	-0.43 (0.01)	c c	c c	c c	c c	527 (1.1)
	Chinese Taipei	c c	-0.56 (0.07)	-0.48 (0.04)	-0.26 (0.05)	-0.17 (0.06)	c c	476 (9.9)	484 (4.6)	504 (4.8)	505 (7.0)
	Thailand	-2.21 (0.04)	-1.62 (0.10)	-1.15 (0.07)	-0.88 (0.11)	-0.17 (0.17)	407 (6.3)	413 (4.0)	421 (4.0)	438 (7.0)	444 (7.4)
	Trinidad and Tobago	-0.89 (0.03)	-0.58 (0.02)	-0.36 (0.03)	c c	c c	403 (3.0)	410 (2.1)	449 (2.4)	c c	c c
	Tunisia	-2.09 (0.15)	-1.67 (0.10)	-1.06 (0.07)	-0.62 (0.14)	-0.03 (0.26)	378 (12.5)	396 (6.4)	399 (4.5)	428 (10.8)	463 (16.7)
	Uruguay	-1.40 (0.13)	-1.06 (0.08)	-0.79 (0.05)	0.19 (0.18)	-0.32 (0.06)	406 (7.4)	419 (5.6)	421 (3.7)	408 (9.6)	444 (3.6)

Note: Values that are statistically significant are indicated in bold (see Annex A3).
StatLink ᴍ⛷ http://dx.doi.org/10.1787/888932343285

[Part 3/3]

Reading performance and socio-economic background, by school location

Table II.2.6 *Results based on students' self-reports and school principals' reports*

| | BEFORE accounting for the PISA index of economic, social and cultural status of students (ESCS) | | | | | | AFTER accounting for the PISA index of economic, social and cultural status of students (ESCS) | | | | | |
| | Students in small town schools versus rural schools | | Students in town schools versus rural schools | | Students in city or large city schools versus in rural schools | | Students in small town schools versus rural schools | | Students in town schools versus rural schools | | Students in city or large city schools versus in rural schools | |
	Score dif.	S.E.	Score dif.	S.E.	Score dif.	S.E.	Score dif.	S.E.	Score dif.	S.E.	Score dif.	S.E.
OECD												
Australia	15	(7.5)	19	(7.9)	53	(7.2)	10	(7.1)	11	(7.0)	32	(6.6)
Austria	28	(18.0)	47	(19.2)	35	(17.7)	26	(15.1)	39	(15.8)	27	(13.8)
Belgium	1	(29.3)	-15	(29.3)	-27	(30.5)	10	(21.9)	-2	(20.8)	-15	(21.1)
Canada	9	(4.9)	26	(4.8)	30	(4.4)	6	(4.3)	19	(4.3)	18	(3.7)
Chile	38	(17.4)	76	(15.9)	96	(15.1)	30	(14.6)	47	(13.3)	53	(13.4)
Czech Republic	30	(11.6)	42	(9.1)	63	(13.9)	25	(10.1)	29	(7.8)	43	(13.5)
Denmark	18	(6.9)	21	(5.3)	14	(7.2)	11	(5.6)	11	(4.5)	12	(6.0)
Estonia	12	(6.4)	18	(8.1)	33	(6.7)	5	(6.4)	11	(7.6)	20	(6.5)
Finland	7	(8.4)	13	(8.0)	18	(8.9)	2	(8.9)	5	(8.4)	3	(9.4)
France	w	w	w	w	w	w	w	w	w	w	w	w
Germany	61	(28.1)	73	(28.2)	54	(29.2)	50	(23.9)	57	(23.7)	40	(23.4)
Greece	11	(21.9)	7	(23.1)	21	(22.5)	-6	(18.9)	-26	(18.4)	-11	(19.0)
Hungary	77	(25.6)	118	(18.9)	134	(19.0)	53	(17.9)	81	(16.0)	86	(16.6)
Iceland	11	(4.4)	-3	(4.1)	15	(4.3)	0	(4.6)	-13	(4.4)	-4	(4.7)
Ireland	18	(13.0)	23	(14.6)	32	(13.1)	16	(12.1)	13	(12.5)	20	(11.2)
Israel	-47	(20.6)	-28	(15.5)	13	(14.9)	-39	(17.4)	-22	(13.0)	13	(11.8)
Italy	51	(16.7)	65	(15.1)	72	(14.2)	42	(16.2)	53	(14.9)	47	(14.5)
Japan	c	c	c	c	c	c	c	c	c	c	c	c
Korea	-136	(34.2)	-65	(24.1)	-73	(20.1)	-95	(26.1)	-35	(22.2)	-44	(13.8)
Luxembourg	-55	(14.7)	-40	(14.4)	50	(15.7)	-44	(15.7)	-40	(15.6)	c	c
Mexico	17	(8.5)	56	(8.0)	80	(7.5)	10	(8.6)	42	(8.2)	50	(7.5)
Netherlands	3	(43.0)	29	(40.7)	38	(41.5)	8	(38.3)	31	(35.2)	39	(35.1)
New Zealand	17	(7.9)	19	(8.2)	39	(6.6)	10	(7.3)	9	(8.4)	15	(7.4)
Norway	17	(6.3)	20	(6.4)	32	(8.4)	12	(6.1)	13	(6.2)	18	(7.5)
Poland	16	(6.4)	31	(6.7)	36	(7.3)	8	(5.9)	12	(5.8)	9	(6.0)
Portugal	27	(14.0)	44	(13.4)	77	(13.6)	17	(11.6)	30	(11.7)	42	(12.1)
Slovak Republic	44	(13.2)	64	(7.5)	72	(9.8)	37	(10.8)	51	(6.5)	54	(9.2)
Slovenia	64	(12.9)	49	(11.9)	65	(11.9)	53	(12.1)	36	(11.1)	43	(11.5)
Spain	4	(6.5)	21	(5.7)	39	(6.1)	1	(5.7)	9	(5.0)	19	(5.4)
Sweden	0	(8.5)	16	(8.4)	18	(10.4)	0	(7.1)	8	(7.0)	4	(8.8)
Switzerland	12	(6.7)	39	(9.9)	50	(10.9)	8	(5.6)	29	(8.5)	31	(10.2)
Turkey	82	(17.7)	107	(16.2)	112	(14.6)	60	(16.3)	72	(14.2)	70	(13.2)
United Kingdom	-6	(12.1)	-15	(13.9)	-20	(13.2)	-3	(9.1)	-9	(10.7)	-14	(9.9)
United States	10	(13.9)	14	(11.6)	7	(11.7)	1	(10.1)	5	(9.4)	1	(9.4)
OECD average	14	(3.0)	28	(2.8)	40	(2.8)	10	(2.6)	18	(2.4)	23	(2.4)
Partners												
Albania	21	(9.9)	47	(11.7)	79	(10.6)	15	(9.9)	28	(10.9)	49	(9.6)
Argentina	20	(16.6)	59	(16.0)	89	(15.3)	9	(14.4)	37	(12.6)	47	(12.4)
Azerbaijan	-2	(11.5)	33	(9.3)	37	(7.1)	-4	(11.5)	25	(9.8)	20	(6.8)
Brazil	22	(10.8)	56	(11.0)	71	(9.8)	19	(10.4)	38	(10.1)	31	(9.9)
Bulgaria	69	(22.1)	90	(22.4)	146	(23.1)	46	(19.4)	58	(19.4)	94	(22.4)
Colombia	10	(13.6)	22	(11.8)	53	(11.0)	2	(11.9)	12	(10.4)	15	(9.4)
Croatia	27	(21.5)	20	(21.1)	47	(21.4)	21	(24.8)	13	(24.6)	29	(25.1)
Dubai (UAE)	-57	(8.4)	-13	(8.8)	38	(7.2)	-69	(8.7)	-27	(9.5)	-7	(7.5)
Hong Kong-China	c	c	c	c	c	c	c	c	c	c	c	c
Indonesia	21	(8.3)	36	(12.5)	58	(10.4)	19	(8.0)	29	(11.3)	44	(11.1)
Jordan	33	(16.1)	43	(16.3)	57	(15.7)	30	(15.4)	34	(15.3)	41	(14.8)
Kazakhstan	1	(10.3)	18	(16.9)	54	(7.7)	-4	(9.9)	8	(15.1)	36	(7.0)
Kyrgyzstan	29	(9.1)	54	(13.4)	122	(11.2)	22	(8.5)	42	(12.0)	94	(9.6)
Latvia	27	(7.1)	27	(8.6)	41	(8.3)	18	(6.8)	16	(7.4)	21	(7.4)
Liechtenstein	c	c	c	c	c	c	c	c	c	c	c	c
Lithuania	24	(7.3)	41	(9.0)	45	(6.5)	12	(6.9)	27	(8.4)	18	(7.3)
Macao-China	c	c	c	c	c	c	c	c	c	c	c	c
Montenegro	32	(22.6)	35	(23.0)	47	(23.2)	12	(18.2)	14	(18.4)	15	(17.5)
Panama	52	(19.8)	92	(17.6)	134	(19.8)	48	(18.2)	84	(16.9)	82	(17.8)
Peru	37	(9.3)	71	(8.7)	131	(9.5)	27	(8.4)	49	(8.1)	76	(8.5)
Qatar	-17	(4.6)	-7	(4.6)	64	(4.8)	-18	(4.7)	-15	(4.7)	41	(5.0)
Romania	48	(19.2)	52	(18.0)	70	(18.6)	36	(17.7)	28	(15.3)	46	(16.3)
Russian Federation	10	(8.3)	15	(9.0)	43	(9.9)	0	(8.4)	2	(9.7)	16	(10.5)
Serbia	-23	(23.3)	4	(20.0)	25	(20.1)	-39	(29.7)	-21	(29.5)	-9	(30.5)
Shanghai-China	c	c	c	c	c	c	c	c	c	c	c	c
Singapore	c	c	c	c	c	c	c	c	c	c	c	c
Chinese Taipei	c	c	c	c	c	c	c	c	c	c	c	c
Thailand	16	(7.5)	33	(7.7)	61	(8.9)	8	(7.9)	17	(7.8)	29	(8.9)
Trinidad and Tobago	c	c	c	c	c	c	c	c	c	c	c	c
Tunisia	24	(14.8)	36	(15.2)	81	(16.3)	18	(13.4)	23	(14.3)	52	(17.3)
Uruguay	24	(11.7)	35	(9.8)	65	(10.9)	16	(9.6)	17	(7.9)	26	(8.0)

Note: Values that are statistically significant are indicated in bold (see Annex A3).
StatLink ⟐⟐⟐ http://dx.doi.org/10.1787/888932343285

[Part 1/2]

PISA index of economic, social and cultural status and reading performance, by national quarters of this index

Table II.3.1   *Results based on students' self-reports*

| | PISA index of economic, social and cultural status (ESCS) | | | | | | | | | | Performance on the reading scale, by national quarters of this index | | | | | | | |
| | All students | | Bottom quarter | | Second quarter | | Third quarter | | Top quarter | | Bottom quarter | | Second quarter | | Third quarter | | Top quarter | |
	Mean index	S.E.	Mean index	S.E.	Mean index	S.E.	Mean index	S.E.	Mean index	S.E.	Mean score	S.E.	Mean score	S.E.	Mean score	S.E.	Mean score	S.E.
OECD																		
Australia	0.34	(0.01)	-0.63	(0.01)	0.09	(0.00)	0.63	(0.00)	1.29	(0.01)	**471**	(2.7)	504	(2.4)	532	(3.0)	**562**	(3.1)
Austria	0.06	(0.02)	-0.97	(0.02)	-0.22	(0.00)	0.28	(0.00)	1.15	(0.01)	**421**	(4.3)	457	(4.2)	482	(3.8)	**525**	(3.9)
Belgium	0.20	(0.02)	-1.00	(0.02)	-0.13	(0.00)	0.54	(0.00)	1.37	(0.01)	**452**	(3.3)	489	(3.3)	525	(2.5)	**567**	(2.6)
Canada	0.50	(0.02)	-0.59	(0.02)	0.25	(0.00)	0.83	(0.00)	1.52	(0.01)	**495**	(2.3)	514	(1.7)	533	(2.1)	**562**	(2.4)
Chile	-0.57	(0.04)	-2.00	(0.01)	-1.00	(0.01)	-0.22	(0.01)	0.95	(0.02)	**409**	(3.5)	435	(3.6)	457	(3.5)	**501**	(3.5)
Czech Republic	-0.09	(0.01)	-0.95	(0.01)	-0.34	(0.00)	0.11	(0.00)	0.85	(0.01)	**437**	(3.3)	467	(3.7)	490	(3.4)	**521**	(4.1)
Denmark	0.30	(0.02)	-0.83	(0.02)	0.00	(0.01)	0.62	(0.01)	1.39	(0.01)	**455**	(2.7)	486	(3.4)	509	(2.9)	**536**	(2.4)
Estonia	0.15	(0.02)	-0.87	(0.01)	-0.16	(0.01)	0.45	(0.01)	1.19	(0.01)	**476**	(3.6)	490	(3.5)	505	(3.1)	**534**	(3.9)
Finland	0.37	(0.02)	-0.64	(0.01)	0.12	(0.00)	0.69	(0.00)	1.32	(0.01)	**504**	(3.2)	527	(2.7)	548	(2.9)	**565**	(2.8)
France	-0.13	(0.03)	-1.19	(0.02)	-0.42	(0.01)	0.15	(0.01)	0.93	(0.02)	**443**	(5.2)	484	(4.6)	513	(4.4)	**553**	(4.8)
Germany	0.18	(0.02)	-0.93	(0.02)	-0.12	(0.00)	0.42	(0.00)	1.36	(0.01)	**445**	(3.9)	494	(2.9)	515	(3.5)	**550**	(3.3)
Greece	-0.02	(0.03)	-1.28	(0.02)	-0.40	(0.01)	0.32	(0.01)	1.27	(0.01)	**437**	(7.1)	475	(5.2)	493	(3.7)	**528**	(3.4)
Hungary	-0.20	(0.03)	-1.38	(0.03)	-0.56	(0.00)	0.06	(0.01)	1.10	(0.01)	**435**	(5.3)	485	(3.4)	505	(4.1)	**553**	(4.1)
Iceland	0.72	(0.01)	-0.46	(0.02)	0.45	(0.01)	1.10	(0.01)	1.79	(0.01)	**470**	(3.1)	494	(3.3)	513	(3.0)	**530**	(2.8)
Ireland	0.05	(0.03)	-1.01	(0.01)	-0.27	(0.01)	0.31	(0.01)	1.15	(0.02)	**454**	(3.8)	486	(4.0)	511	(3.9)	**539**	(3.5)
Israel	-0.02	(0.03)	-1.20	(0.02)	-0.24	(0.01)	0.33	(0.00)	1.01	(0.01)	**423**	(5.4)	465	(4.0)	501	(3.6)	**526**	(4.1)
Italy	-0.12	(0.01)	-1.41	(0.01)	-0.47	(0.01)	0.18	(0.00)	1.21	(0.01)	**442**	(3.0)	477	(2.0)	500	(2.0)	**526**	(2.1)
Japan	-0.01	(0.01)	-0.93	(0.01)	-0.28	(0.00)	0.24	(0.00)	0.93	(0.01)	**483**	(4.8)	510	(4.8)	536	(4.0)	**558**	(3.5)
Korea	-0.15	(0.03)	-1.22	(0.01)	-0.42	(0.01)	0.14	(0.01)	0.88	(0.02)	**503**	(5.1)	534	(2.8)	548	(3.9)	**572**	(4.6)
Luxembourg	0.19	(0.01)	-1.31	(0.02)	-0.09	(0.01)	0.64	(0.01)	1.51	(0.01)	**411**	(2.7)	460	(3.0)	497	(2.8)	**526**	(3.0)
Mexico	-1.22	(0.03)	-2.83	(0.01)	-1.79	(0.00)	-0.81	(0.01)	0.54	(0.02)	**386**	(2.8)	413	(2.3)	434	(2.2)	**469**	(2.2)
Netherlands	0.27	(0.03)	-0.84	(0.03)	0.01	(0.01)	0.61	(0.00)	1.31	(0.01)	**474**	(5.5)	493	(5.8)	519	(4.7)	**553**	(5.9)
New Zealand	0.09	(0.02)	-0.93	(0.02)	-0.17	(0.01)	0.36	(0.00)	1.08	(0.01)	**475**	(3.9)	508	(3.1)	534	(3.3)	**578**	(3.6)
Norway	0.47	(0.02)	-0.47	(0.01)	0.23	(0.00)	0.73	(0.00)	1.40	(0.01)	**468**	(3.4)	495	(3.3)	517	(2.9)	**536**	(3.9)
Poland	-0.28	(0.02)	-1.29	(0.01)	-0.66	(0.00)	-0.15	(0.00)	0.97	(0.01)	**461**	(3.4)	488	(3.1)	507	(2.9)	**550**	(3.8)
Portugal	-0.32	(0.04)	-1.70	(0.01)	-0.87	(0.01)	-0.05	(0.00)	1.35	(0.03)	**451**	(4.2)	472	(3.4)	499	(3.4)	**537**	(3.7)
Slovak Republic	-0.09	(0.02)	-1.04	(0.02)	-0.44	(0.00)	0.04	(0.01)	1.07	(0.01)	**435**	(5.0)	468	(3.4)	488	(3.3)	**521**	(3.6)
Slovenia	0.07	(0.01)	-1.01	(0.01)	-0.31	(0.01)	0.37	(0.01)	1.25	(0.01)	**444**	(2.6)	468	(2.5)	493	(2.7)	**532**	(2.6)
Spain	-0.31	(0.03)	-1.68	(0.02)	-0.74	(0.01)	0.03	(0.01)	1.14	(0.01)	**443**	(3.3)	468	(2.3)	491	(2.2)	**525**	(3.3)
Sweden	0.33	(0.02)	-0.72	(0.02)	0.08	(0.00)	0.63	(0.01)	1.33	(0.01)	**452**	(4.0)	488	(3.3)	515	(3.3)	**543**	(4.1)
Switzerland	0.08	(0.02)	-1.04	(0.01)	-0.22	(0.00)	0.35	(0.00)	1.22	(0.01)	**457**	(3.9)	492	(2.7)	506	(3.0)	**550**	(3.7)
Turkey	-1.16	(0.05)	-2.63	(0.02)	-1.69	(0.01)	-0.82	(0.01)	0.49	(0.03)	**422**	(3.8)	454	(3.5)	469	(3.9)	**514**	(4.6)
United Kingdom	0.20	(0.02)	-0.80	(0.02)	-0.06	(0.00)	0.47	(0.01)	1.21	(0.01)	**451**	(2.9)	483	(3.1)	508	(2.7)	**544**	(3.2)
United States	0.17	(0.04)	-1.05	(0.02)	-0.11	(0.01)	0.52	(0.01)	1.32	(0.02)	**451**	(3.6)	481	(3.6)	512	(3.6)	**558**	(4.7)
OECD average	0.00	(0.00)	-1.14	(0.00)	-0.32	(0.00)	0.30	(0.00)	1.17	(0.00)	**451**	(0.7)	483	(0.6)	506	(0.6)	**540**	(0.6)
Partners																		
Albania	-0.95	(0.04)	-2.26	(0.02)	-1.34	(0.01)	-0.64	(0.01)	0.42	(0.02)	**350**	(6.1)	373	(4.3)	391	(4.9)	**430**	(5.5)
Argentina	-0.62	(0.05)	-2.17	(0.03)	-1.02	(0.01)	-0.19	(0.01)	0.92	(0.03)	**345**	(4.9)	377	(4.6)	410	(4.5)	**468**	(6.2)
Azerbaijan	-0.64	(0.03)	-1.88	(0.01)	-1.03	(0.01)	-0.32	(0.01)	0.67	(0.02)	**338**	(5.6)	353	(3.4)	366	(3.7)	**391**	(4.7)
Brazil	-1.16	(0.03)	-2.69	(0.01)	-1.64	(0.01)	-0.76	(0.01)	0.44	(0.02)	**376**	(2.5)	401	(3.0)	413	(3.9)	**460**	(4.1)
Bulgaria	-0.11	(0.04)	-1.31	(0.03)	-0.48	(0.01)	0.20	(0.01)	1.16	(0.01)	**368**	(5.8)	418	(6.6)	442	(7.7)	**498**	(6.2)
Colombia	-1.15	(0.05)	-2.82	(0.02)	-1.60	(0.01)	-0.67	(0.01)	0.47	(0.03)	**371**	(4.7)	398	(4.4)	422	(3.9)	**462**	(4.7)
Croatia	-0.18	(0.02)	-1.28	(0.02)	-0.51	(0.01)	0.04	(0.01)	1.04	(0.02)	**440**	(3.9)	467	(3.9)	484	(4.0)	**513**	(3.9)
Dubai (UAE)	0.42	(0.01)	-0.64	(0.02)	0.31	(0.00)	0.74	(0.00)	1.29	(0.01)	**401**	(2.5)	453	(2.8)	482	(2.8)	**504**	(2.8)
Hong Kong-China	-0.80	(0.04)	-2.07	(0.01)	-1.19	(0.01)	-0.51	(0.01)	0.56	(0.03)	**509**	(3.9)	527	(2.8)	542	(2.9)	**557**	(3.4)
Indonesia	-1.55	(0.06)	-2.86	(0.01)	-2.05	(0.01)	-1.26	(0.01)	-0.04	(0.03)	**386**	(3.8)	389	(3.6)	402	(4.5)	**430**	(6.0)
Jordan	-0.57	(0.03)	-1.90	(0.02)	-0.94	(0.01)	-0.18	(0.01)	0.77	(0.02)	**375**	(3.8)	400	(3.4)	410	(4.2)	**441**	(5.2)
Kazakhstan	-0.51	(0.02)	-1.53	(0.01)	-0.83	(0.01)	-0.24	(0.01)	0.57	(0.02)	**348**	(4.0)	384	(3.1)	399	(3.6)	**432**	(5.2)
Kyrgyzstan	-0.65	(0.03)	-1.83	(0.01)	-1.01	(0.01)	-0.32	(0.01)	0.56	(0.02)	**274**	(4.1)	295	(4.0)	321	(4.2)	**369**	(6.0)
Latvia	-0.13	(0.03)	-1.24	(0.01)	-0.49	(0.01)	0.21	(0.01)	1.01	(0.02)	**456**	(4.8)	470	(3.6)	492	(3.6)	**519**	(3.6)
Liechtenstein	0.09	(0.05)	-1.11	(0.05)	-0.22	(0.02)	0.41	(0.02)	1.28	(0.06)	**463**	(7.9)	502	(7.9)	505	(9.3)	**529**	(8.2)
Lithuania	-0.05	(0.02)	-1.27	(0.02)	-0.46	(0.01)	0.33	(0.01)	1.21	(0.01)	**430**	(3.4)	455	(3.8)	477	(3.3)	**514**	(3.2)
Macao-China	-0.70	(0.01)	-1.77	(0.01)	-1.01	(0.00)	-0.48	(0.00)	0.44	(0.01)	**473**	(2.1)	485	(2.0)	491	(2.1)	**498**	(2.1)
Montenegro	-0.24	(0.02)	-1.43	(0.01)	-0.60	(0.01)	0.04	(0.01)	1.01	(0.01)	**369**	(3.1)	402	(3.2)	415	(2.9)	**447**	(2.5)
Panama	-0.81	(0.08)	-2.60	(0.04)	-1.24	(0.01)	-0.26	(0.01)	0.85	(0.05)	**336**	(7.1)	351	(6.6)	375	(6.3)	**445**	(10.9)
Peru	-1.31	(0.05)	-2.90	(0.02)	-1.77	(0.01)	-0.94	(0.01)	0.35	(0.04)	**303**	(3.3)	354	(3.1)	390	(3.7)	**434**	(7.3)
Qatar	0.51	(0.01)	-0.74	(0.01)	0.37	(0.00)	0.89	(0.00)	1.50	(0.01)	**337**	(1.8)	365	(2.3)	396	(2.7)	**394**	(2.3)
Romania	-0.34	(0.03)	-1.45	(0.04)	-0.65	(0.00)	-0.13	(0.01)	0.84	(0.02)	**381**	(5.5)	420	(4.2)	432	(4.7)	**466**	(5.3)
Russian Federation	-0.21	(0.02)	-1.20	(0.01)	-0.56	(0.00)	0.06	(0.00)	0.85	(0.01)	**424**	(3.6)	447	(3.9)	466	(3.5)	**502**	(4.9)
Serbia	0.07	(0.02)	-1.11	(0.02)	-0.32	(0.01)	0.34	(0.01)	1.37	(0.02)	**413**	(3.9)	434	(2.9)	445	(2.8)	**478**	(2.8)
Shanghai-China	-0.49	(0.04)	-1.83	(0.02)	-0.88	(0.01)	-0.11	(0.01)	0.86	(0.01)	**521**	(4.3)	546	(3.3)	564	(2.5)	**594**	(3.4)
Singapore	-0.43	(0.01)	-1.50	(0.01)	-0.65	(0.01)	-0.10	(0.01)	0.54	(0.01)	**477**	(2.4)	513	(3.2)	541	(2.4)	**575**	(3.0)
Chinese Taipei	-0.33	(0.02)	-1.40	(0.02)	-0.58	(0.00)	-0.03	(0.01)	0.71	(0.01)	**459**	(3.4)	484	(3.4)	505	(2.9)	**535**	(4.4)
Thailand	-1.31	(0.04)	-2.64	(0.01)	-1.95	(0.01)	-1.06	(0.01)	0.41	(0.03)	**399**	(3.6)	407	(2.9)	418	(2.6)	**462**	(4.6)
Trinidad and Tobago	-0.58	(0.02)	-1.77	(0.02)	-0.85	(0.01)	-0.28	(0.01)	0.59	(0.01)	**376**	(3.5)	408	(3.1)	424	(3.4)	**469**	(4.0)
Tunisia	-1.20	(0.05)	-2.62	(0.01)	-1.75	(0.01)	-0.75	(0.01)	0.54	(0.02)	**377**	(3.4)	393	(3.4)	405	(3.5)	**440**	(4.9)
Uruguay	-0.70	(0.03)	-2.16	(0.01)	-1.26	(0.01)	-0.37	(0.01)	0.99	(0.02)	**374**	(3.2)	407	(3.2)	438	(3.8)	**489**	(4.1)

Note: Values that are statistically significant are indicated in bold (see Annex A3).
StatLink ᴴᴵˢᴾ http://dx.doi.org/10.1787/888932343285

[Part 2/2]
PISA index of economic, social and cultural status and reading performance, by national quarters of this index
Table II.3.1   *Results based on students' self-reports*

	Performance on the reading scale		Change in the reading score per unit of this index		Increased likelihood of students in the bottom quarter of the ESCS scoring in the bottom quarter of the reading performance distribution		Explained variance in student performance (r-squared x 100)	
	Mean score	S.E.	Effect	S.E.	Ratio	S.E.	Percentage	S.E.
OECD								
Australia	515	(2.3)	46	(1.77)	2.1	(0.08)	12.7	(0.8)
Austria	470	(2.9)	48	(2.28)	2.4	(0.13)	16.6	(1.4)
Belgium	506	(2.3)	47	(1.48)	2.4	(0.12)	19.3	(1.0)
Canada	524	(1.5)	32	(1.44)	1.7	(0.08)	8.6	(0.7)
Chile	449	(3.1)	31	(1.51)	2.3	(0.15)	18.7	(1.6)
Czech Republic	478	(2.9)	46	(2.34)	2.0	(0.12)	12.4	(1.1)
Denmark	495	(2.1)	36	(1.42)	2.1	(0.14)	14.5	(1.0)
Estonia	501	(2.6)	29	(2.26)	1.6	(0.11)	7.6	(1.1)
Finland	536	(2.3)	31	(1.66)	1.8	(0.10)	7.8	(0.8)
France	496	(3.4)	51	(2.94)	2.4	(0.17)	16.7	(2.0)
Germany	497	(2.7)	44	(1.92)	2.6	(0.15)	17.9	(1.3)
Greece	483	(4.3)	34	(2.42)	2.2	(0.15)	12.5	(1.4)
Hungary	494	(3.2)	48	(2.17)	3.0	(0.23)	26.0	(2.2)
Iceland	500	(1.4)	27	(1.79)	1.7	(0.10)	6.2	(0.8)
Ireland	496	(3.0)	39	(2.05)	2.2	(0.16)	12.6	(1.2)
Israel	474	(3.6)	43	(2.45)	2.2	(0.13)	12.5	(1.1)
Italy	486	(1.6)	32	(1.27)	2.1	(0.08)	11.8	(0.7)
Japan	520	(3.5)	40	(2.83)	1.8	(0.10)	8.6	(1.0)
Korea	539	(3.5)	32	(2.46)	2.2	(0.16)	11.0	(1.5)
Luxembourg	472	(1.3)	40	(1.31)	2.6	(0.17)	18.0	(1.1)
Mexico	425	(2.0)	25	(0.96)	2.1	(0.10)	14.5	(1.0)
Netherlands	508	(5.1)	37	(1.90)	1.8	(0.12)	12.8	(1.2)
New Zealand	521	(2.4)	52	(1.94)	2.2	(0.12)	16.6	(1.1)
Norway	503	(2.6)	36	(2.14)	2.0	(0.11)	8.6	(1.0)
Poland	500	(2.6)	39	(1.94)	2.0	(0.12)	14.8	(1.4)
Portugal	489	(3.1)	30	(1.57)	2.0	(0.15)	16.5	(1.6)
Slovak Republic	477	(2.5)	41	(2.30)	2.1	(0.16)	14.6	(1.5)
Slovenia	483	(1.0)	39	(1.53)	2.0	(0.14)	14.3	(1.1)
Spain	481	(2.0)	29	(1.49)	2.0	(0.10)	13.6	(1.3)
Sweden	497	(2.9)	43	(2.17)	2.2	(0.13)	13.4	(1.3)
Switzerland	501	(2.4)	40	(2.09)	2.1	(0.13)	14.1	(1.4)
Turkey	464	(3.5)	29	(1.53)	2.3	(0.19)	19.0	(1.9)
United Kingdom	494	(2.3)	44	(1.86)	2.1	(0.11)	13.7	(1.0)
United States	500	(3.7)	42	(2.27)	2.2	(0.14)	16.8	(1.7)
OECD average	493	(0.5)	38	(0.34)	2.1	(0.02)	14.0	(0.2)
Partners								
Albania	385	(4.0)	31	(2.59)	1.7	(0.17)	10.7	(1.8)
Argentina	398	(4.6)	40	(2.26)	2.2	(0.18)	19.6	(2.2)
Azerbaijan	362	(3.3)	21	(2.25)	1.7	(0.15)	7.4	(1.6)
Brazil	412	(2.7)	28	(1.36)	1.7	(0.09)	13.0	(1.3)
Bulgaria	429	(6.7)	51	(2.83)	2.4	(0.22)	20.2	(2.2)
Colombia	413	(3.7)	28	(1.77)	2.1	(0.17)	16.6	(1.9)
Croatia	476	(2.9)	32	(2.04)	1.9	(0.15)	11.0	(1.3)
Dubai (UAE)	459	(1.1)	51	(1.44)	2.4	(0.13)	14.2	(0.8)
Hong Kong-China	533	(2.1)	17	(2.15)	1.7	(0.12)	4.5	(1.1)
Indonesia	402	(3.7)	17	(2.44)	1.4	(0.13)	7.8	(2.2)
Jordan	405	(3.3)	24	(2.13)	1.7	(0.12)	7.9	(1.4)
Kazakhstan	390	(3.1)	38	(2.85)	2.1	(0.14)	12.0	(1.7)
Kyrgyzstan	314	(3.2)	40	(2.86)	1.8	(0.14)	14.6	(1.8)
Latvia	484	(3.0)	29	(2.57)	1.7	(0.17)	10.3	(1.7)
Liechtenstein	499	(2.8)	26	(5.05)	2.1	(0.36)	8.4	(2.9)
Lithuania	468	(2.4)	33	(1.92)	2.0	(0.14)	13.6	(1.4)
Macao-China	487	(0.9)	12	(1.16)	1.3	(0.08)	1.8	(0.4)
Montenegro	408	(1.7)	31	(1.38)	1.9	(0.10)	10.0	(0.8)
Panama	371	(6.5)	31	(3.60)	1.7	(0.24)	18.1	(3.9)
Peru	370	(4.0)	41	(2.04)	3.0	(0.20)	27.4	(2.6)
Qatar	372	(0.8)	25	(1.18)	1.4	(0.06)	4.0	(0.4)
Romania	424	(4.1)	36	(2.81)	2.2	(0.19)	13.6	(2.1)
Russian Federation	459	(3.3)	37	(2.54)	1.9	(0.11)	11.3	(1.4)
Serbia	442	(2.4)	27	(1.59)	1.8	(0.11)	9.8	(1.0)
Shanghai-China	556	(2.4)	27	(2.09)	2.1	(0.14)	12.3	(0.8)
Singapore	526	(1.1)	47	(1.74)	2.3	(0.11)	15.3	(1.1)
Chinese Taipei	495	(2.6)	36	(2.45)	2.0	(0.12)	11.8	(1.3)
Thailand	421	(2.6)	22	(1.81)	1.5	(0.11)	13.3	(1.9)
Trinidad and Tobago	416	(1.2)	38	(1.73)	1.8	(0.14)	9.7	(0.9)
Tunisia	404	(2.9)	19	(1.79)	1.7	(0.13)	8.1	(1.5)
Uruguay	426	(2.6)	37	(1.50)	2.2	(0.14)	20.7	(1.5)

Note: Values that are statistically significant are indicated in bold (see Annex A3).
StatLink 📊 http://dx.doi.org/10.1787/888932343285

[Part 1/2]
Relationship between reading performance and socio-economic background

Table II.3.2 *Results based on students' self-reports*

	Unadjusted mean score		Mean score if the mean ESCS would be equal in all OECD countries		Strength of the relationship between student performance and the ESCS[1]		Slope of the socio-economic gradient[1,2]		Length of the projection of the gradient line					
					Percentage of explained variance in student performance		Score point difference associated with one unit increase in the ESCS		5th percentile of the ESCS		95th percentile of the ESCS		Difference between 95th and 5th percentile of the ESCS	
	Mean score	S.E.	Mean score	S.E.	performance	S.E.	in the ESCS	S.E.	Index	S.E.	Index	S.E.	Dif.	S.E.
OECD														
Australia	515	(2.3)	502	(2.0)	12.7	(0.85)	**46**	(1.8)	-0.87	(0.02)	1.51	(0.01)	2.38	(0.02)
Austria	470	(2.9)	468	(2.6)	16.6	(1.39)	**48**	(2.3)	-1.23	(0.04)	1.49	(0.04)	2.73	(0.06)
Belgium	506	(2.3)	499	(2.0)	**19.3**	(1.01)	**47**	(1.5)	-1.29	(0.03)	1.64	(0.04)	2.93	(0.06)
Canada	524	(1.5)	510	(1.4)	8.6	(0.74)	**32**	(1.4)	-0.88	(0.03)	1.76	(0.02)	2.63	(0.04)
Chile	449	(3.1)	468	(2.6)	**18.7**	(1.56)	**31**	(1.5)	-2.37	(0.04)	1.36	(0.04)	3.73	(0.05)
Czech Republic	478	(2.9)	483	(2.7)	12.4	(1.09)	**46**	(2.3)	-1.17	(0.02)	1.13	(0.02)	2.30	(0.03)
Denmark	495	(2.1)	485	(1.8)	14.5	(1.02)	**36**	(1.4)	-1.14	(0.02)	1.67	(0.02)	2.81	(0.03)
Estonia	501	(2.6)	497	(2.8)	7.6	(1.11)	**29**	(2.3)	-1.10	(0.04)	1.43	(0.03)	2.53	(0.04)
Finland	536	(2.3)	525	(2.2)	7.8	(0.82)	**31**	(1.7)	-0.91	(0.04)	1.54	(0.04)	2.45	(0.05)
France	496	(3.4)	505	(2.9)	16.7	(1.97)	**51**	(2.9)	-1.50	(0.03)	1.25	(0.06)	2.74	(0.06)
Germany	497	(2.7)	493	(2.2)	**17.9**	(1.29)	**44**	(1.9)	-1.24	(0.04)	1.70	(0.03)	2.94	(0.04)
Greece	483	(4.3)	484	(3.7)	12.5	(1.43)	34	(2.4)	-1.63	(0.04)	1.58	(0.02)	3.21	(0.04)
Hungary	494	(3.2)	504	(2.5)	**26.0**	(2.17)	**48**	(2.2)	-1.71	(0.06)	1.43	(0.03)	3.14	(0.06)
Iceland	500	(1.4)	483	(2.0)	**6.2**	(0.81)	27	(1.8)	-0.83	(0.03)	2.06	(0.02)	2.88	(0.04)
Ireland	496	(3.0)	496	(2.6)	12.6	(1.17)	39	(2.0)	-1.28	(0.03)	1.44	(0.04)	2.72	(0.04)
Israel	474	(3.6)	480	(2.8)	12.5	(1.14)	43	(2.4)	-1.53	(0.05)	1.22	(0.03)	2.75	(0.06)
Italy	486	(1.6)	490	(1.4)	**11.8**	(0.74)	32	(1.3)	-1.70	(0.04)	1.62	(0.02)	3.32	(0.04)
Japan	520	(3.5)	522	(3.0)	**8.6**	(0.96)	40	(2.8)	-1.16	(0.02)	1.16	(0.01)	2.32	(0.02)
Korea	539	(3.5)	544	(3.0)	**11.0**	(1.51)	32	(2.5)	-1.53	(0.03)	1.18	(0.03)	2.71	(0.05)
Luxembourg	472	(1.3)	466	(1.3)	**18.0**	(1.06)	40	(1.3)	-1.82	(0.04)	1.81	(0.04)	3.63	(0.05)
Mexico	425	(2.0)	456	(1.8)	14.5	(0.99)	25	(1.0)	-3.18	(0.03)	1.00	(0.06)	4.18	(0.06)
Netherlands	508	(5.1)	499	(4.6)	12.8	(1.20)	37	(1.9)	-1.12	(0.09)	1.54	(0.02)	2.66	(0.08)
New Zealand	521	(2.4)	519	(2.0)	**16.6**	(1.08)	**52**	(1.9)	-1.20	(0.02)	1.33	(0.02)	2.53	(0.03)
Norway	503	(2.6)	487	(2.4)	**8.6**	(0.96)	36	(2.1)	-0.72	(0.03)	1.64	(0.02)	2.36	(0.03)
Poland	500	(2.6)	512	(2.2)	14.8	(1.38)	39	(1.9)	-1.50	(0.03)	1.35	(0.02)	2.86	(0.03)
Portugal	489	(3.1)	499	(2.3)	16.5	(1.60)	**30**	(1.6)	-1.98	(0.03)	1.81	(0.03)	3.79	(0.04)
Slovak Republic	477	(2.5)	482	(2.1)	14.6	(1.48)	41	(2.3)	-1.24	(0.04)	1.46	(0.04)	2.70	(0.05)
Slovenia	483	(1.0)	481	(1.1)	14.3	(1.06)	39	(1.5)	-1.25	(0.02)	1.53	(0.04)	2.78	(0.03)
Spain	481	(2.0)	491	(1.8)	13.6	(1.30)	29	(1.5)	-2.04	(0.04)	1.54	(0.03)	3.58	(0.04)
Sweden	497	(2.9)	485	(2.4)	13.4	(1.33)	43	(2.2)	-1.01	(0.04)	1.55	(0.04)	2.57	(0.05)
Switzerland	501	(2.4)	498	(2.1)	14.1	(1.38)	40	(2.1)	-1.38	(0.03)	1.52	(0.03)	2.90	(0.03)
Turkey	464	(3.5)	499	(3.5)	**19.0**	(1.91)	29	(1.5)	-2.99	(0.07)	1.03	(0.07)	4.02	(0.07)
United Kingdom	494	(2.3)	488	(1.8)	13.7	(1.03)	**44**	(1.9)	-1.05	(0.04)	1.48	(0.02)	2.52	(0.04)
United States	500	(3.7)	493	(2.4)	16.8	(1.65)	42	(2.3)	-1.40	(0.08)	1.61	(0.03)	3.01	(0.08)
OECD average	493	(0.5)	494	(0.4)	14.0	(0.2)	38	(0.3)	-1.44	(0.01)	1.48	(0.01)	2.92	(0.01)
Partners														
Albania	385	(4.0)	416	(4.3)	10.7	(1.79)	**31**	(2.6)	-2.61	(0.05)	0.84	(0.05)	3.44	(0.06)
Argentina	398	(4.6)	424	(3.7)	**19.6**	(2.23)	40	(2.3)	-2.54	(0.06)	1.36	(0.05)	3.90	(0.08)
Azerbaijan	362	(3.3)	376	(3.2)	**7.4**	(1.57)	**21**	(2.3)	-2.17	(0.03)	1.01	(0.04)	3.18	(0.04)
Brazil	412	(2.7)	445	(2.9)	13.0	(1.27)	28	(1.4)	-3.05	(0.03)	0.89	(0.06)	3.94	(0.06)
Bulgaria	429	(6.7)	437	(3.6)	**20.2**	(2.19)	51	(2.8)	-1.59	(0.09)	1.49	(0.04)	3.08	(0.09)
Colombia	413	(3.7)	445	(3.3)	16.6	(1.90)	28	(1.8)	-3.21	(0.05)	0.95	(0.06)	4.15	(0.07)
Croatia	476	(2.9)	482	(2.7)	**11.0**	(1.34)	32	(2.0)	-1.61	(0.04)	1.43	(0.04)	3.04	(0.06)
Dubai (UAE)	459	(1.1)	439	(1.3)	14.2	(0.80)	51	(1.4)	-1.11	(0.04)	1.50	(0.02)	2.61	(0.04)
Hong Kong-China	533	(2.1)	548	(2.5)	**4.5**	(1.08)	17	(2.2)	-2.42	(0.04)	1.00	(0.07)	3.42	(0.08)
Indonesia	402	(3.7)	428	(5.9)	**7.8**	(2.23)	17	(2.4)	-3.11	(0.03)	0.43	(0.06)	3.55	(0.06)
Jordan	405	(3.3)	420	(3.3)	**7.9**	(1.35)	24	(2.1)	-2.23	(0.06)	1.07	(0.04)	3.30	(0.07)
Kazakhstan	390	(3.1)	410	(3.2)	12.0	(1.73)	38	(2.8)	-1.79	(0.04)	0.87	(0.05)	2.66	(0.06)
Kyrgyzstan	314	(3.2)	341	(3.6)	14.6	(1.83)	40	(2.9)	-2.13	(0.02)	0.89	(0.05)	3.02	(0.05)
Latvia	484	(3.0)	488	(2.5)	**10.3**	(1.69)	29	(2.6)	-1.47	(0.03)	1.29	(0.03)	2.75	(0.03)
Liechtenstein	499	(2.8)	497	(3.1)	8.4	(2.89)	26	(5.0)	-1.42	(0.13)	1.51	(0.06)	2.93	(0.13)
Lithuania	468	(2.4)	471	(2.2)	13.6	(1.44)	33	(1.9)	-1.52	(0.03)	1.47	(0.01)	2.99	(0.03)
Macao-China	487	(0.9)	495	(1.1)	**1.8**	(0.35)	12	(1.2)	-2.09	(0.02)	0.83	(0.04)	2.92	(0.04)
Montenegro	408	(1.7)	416	(1.4)	**10.0**	(0.84)	31	(1.4)	-1.74	(0.04)	1.35	(0.03)	3.09	(0.05)
Panama	371	(6.5)	402	(6.3)	18.1	(3.86)	31	(3.6)	-3.08	(0.10)	1.16	(0.11)	4.23	(0.14)
Peru	370	(4.0)	424	(4.4)	**27.4**	(2.62)	41	(2.0)	-3.33	(0.05)	0.85	(0.09)	4.18	(0.10)
Qatar	372	(0.8)	360	(0.9)	**4.0**	(0.36)	25	(1.2)	-1.28	(0.02)	1.73	(0.02)	3.00	(0.03)
Romania	424	(4.1)	437	(3.7)	13.6	(2.12)	36	(2.8)	-1.70	(0.08)	1.23	(0.06)	2.93	(0.09)
Russian Federation	459	(3.3)	468	(3.0)	**11.3**	(1.35)	37	(2.5)	-1.43	(0.03)	1.08	(0.03)	2.51	(0.04)
Serbia	442	(2.4)	440	(2.2)	9.8	(1.02)	27	(1.6)	-1.42	(0.04)	1.75	(0.04)	3.17	(0.05)
Shanghai-China	556	(2.4)	569	(1.9)	12.3	(1.77)	27	(2.1)	-2.16	(0.03)	1.19	(0.03)	3.35	(0.04)
Singapore	526	(1.1)	547	(1.3)	15.3	(1.11)	**47**	(1.7)	-1.82	(0.03)	0.75	(0.00)	2.57	(0.03)
Chinese Taipei	495	(2.6)	507	(2.4)	11.8	(1.34)	36	(2.4)	-1.73	(0.05)	1.02	(0.03)	2.74	(0.05)
Thailand	421	(2.6)	450	(3.4)	13.3	(1.94)	22	(1.8)	-2.84	(0.04)	0.88	(0.04)	3.72	(0.05)
Trinidad and Tobago	416	(1.2)	441	(1.7)	**9.7**	(0.86)	38	(1.7)	-2.20	(0.05)	0.92	(0.04)	3.11	(0.06)
Tunisia	404	(2.9)	426	(3.6)	**8.1**	(1.47)	19	(1.8)	-3.15	(0.06)	1.03	(0.05)	4.18	(0.06)
Uruguay	426	(2.6)	453	(2.4)	**20.7**	(1.47)	37	(1.5)	-2.49	(0.02)	1.51	(0.03)	4.00	(0.03)

Note: Values that are statistically significant are indicated in bold (see Annex A3).
1. In these columns values that are statistically significantly different from the OECD average are indicated in bold.
2. Single-level bivariate regression of reading performance on the ESCS, the slope is the regression coefficient for the ESCS.
3. Student-level regression of reading performance on the ESCS and the squared term of the ESCS, the index of curvilinearity is the regression coefficient for the squared term.
StatLink ⟐ http://dx.doi.org/10.1787/888932343285

[Part 2/2]
Relationship between reading performance and socio-economic background
Table II.3.2   *Results based on students' self-reports*

		PISA index of economic, social and cultural status (ESCS)		Variability in the ESCS		Index of curvilinearity[3]		Skewness of the distribution of the ESCS		Percentage of students with low ESCS	
		Mean index	S.E.	Standard deviation	S.E.	Score point difference associated with one unit increase in the ESCS squared	S.E.	Skewness	S.E.	Approximated by the percentage of students with a value of ESCS smaller than -1	S.E.
OECD	Australia	0.34	(0.01)	0.75	(0.01)	-2.58	(1.42)	**-0.13**	(0.03)	3.4	(0.2)
	Austria	0.06	(0.02)	0.84	(0.01)	-1.29	(1.68)	-0.06	(0.09)	8.4	(0.6)
	Belgium	0.20	(0.02)	0.93	(0.01)	1.87	(0.96)	**-0.23**	(0.05)	9.0	(0.5)
	Canada	0.50	(0.02)	0.83	(0.01)	2.79	(1.10)	**-0.30**	(0.03)	3.7	(0.3)
	Chile	-0.57	(0.04)	1.14	(0.02)	**3.53**	(0.80)	0.09	(0.04)	37.2	(1.4)
	Czech Republic	-0.09	(0.01)	0.71	(0.01)	-1.98	(2.01)	0.18	(0.04)	9.2	(0.5)
	Denmark	0.30	(0.02)	0.87	(0.01)	**-2.67**	(1.23)	-0.16	(0.04)	7.2	(0.4)
	Estonia	0.15	(0.02)	0.80	(0.01)	1.61	(1.93)	0.03	(0.04)	6.7	(0.4)
	Finland	0.37	(0.02)	0.78	(0.01)	**-3.60**	(1.41)	**-0.35**	(0.05)	3.9	(0.3)
	France	-0.13	(0.03)	0.84	(0.02)	-1.50	(1.86)	-0.14	(0.05)	13.9	(0.8)
	Germany	0.18	(0.02)	0.90	(0.01)	-2.95	(1.57)	-0.10	(0.06)	8.2	(0.5)
	Greece	-0.02	(0.02)	0.99	(0.01)	-0.29	(1.59)	-0.01	(0.05)	17.7	(1.0)
	Hungary	-0.20	(0.03)	0.97	(0.02)	**-4.71**	(1.32)	0.06	(0.05)	19.1	(1.0)
	Iceland	0.72	(0.01)	0.89	(0.01)	**-4.85**	(1.62)	**-0.31**	(0.04)	3.5	(0.3)
	Ireland	0.05	(0.03)	0.85	(0.01)	**-3.50**	(1.39)	0.03	(0.04)	10.4	(0.6)
	Israel	-0.02	(0.03)	0.89	(0.02)	2.14	(1.85)	**-0.74**	(0.07)	12.7	(0.8)
	Italy	-0.12	(0.01)	1.02	(0.01)	**-3.09**	(0.79)	0.11	(0.03)	21.4	(0.4)
	Japan	-0.01	(0.01)	0.72	(0.01)	**-4.91**	(2.15)	0.00	(0.03)	7.9	(0.4)
	Korea	-0.15	(0.03)	0.82	(0.01)	-0.06	(1.39)	-0.14	(0.04)	15.8	(0.8)
	Luxembourg	0.19	(0.01)	1.10	(0.01)	-0.13	(1.06)	**-0.37**	(0.03)	16.1	(0.6)
	Mexico	-1.22	(0.03)	1.30	(0.01)	0.23	(0.69)	0.18	(0.02)	58.2	(0.9)
	Netherlands	0.27	(0.03)	0.86	(0.02)	**4.55**	(1.65)	**-0.38**	(0.05)	6.5	(0.8)
	New Zealand	0.09	(0.02)	0.79	(0.01)	-0.15	(1.70)	**-0.13**	(0.04)	8.6	(0.5)
	Norway	0.47	(0.02)	0.74	(0.01)	**-5.03**	(1.80)	**-0.20**	(0.05)	2.4	(0.3)
	Poland	-0.28	(0.02)	0.88	(0.01)	**-3.10**	(1.49)	0.47	(0.04)	20.7	(0.8)
	Portugal	-0.32	(0.04)	1.18	(0.02)	-0.03	(0.94)	0.42	(0.04)	33.5	(1.1)
	Slovak Republic	-0.09	(0.02)	0.84	(0.01)	**-5.48**	(1.70)	0.39	(0.06)	10.4	(0.7)
	Slovenia	0.07	(0.01)	0.88	(0.01)	-0.75	(1.66)	0.13	(0.03)	10.2	(0.4)
	Spain	-0.31	(0.03)	1.09	(0.01)	-0.58	(0.90)	0.11	(0.03)	29.0	(1.0)
	Sweden	0.33	(0.02)	0.81	(0.01)	**-2.45**	(1.18)	**-0.39**	(0.10)	5.1	(0.4)
	Switzerland	0.08	(0.02)	0.88	(0.01)	-0.57	(1.29)	-0.03	(0.03)	11.1	(0.6)
	Turkey	-1.16	(0.05)	1.22	(0.02)	-0.27	(0.89)	0.31	(0.05)	58.0	(1.6)
	United Kingdom	0.20	(0.02)	0.79	(0.01)	0.84	(1.40)	-0.12	(0.05)	5.6	(0.5)
	United States	0.17	(0.04)	0.93	(0.02)	**6.61**	(1.35)	**-0.25**	(0.05)	10.4	(0.8)
	OECD average	0.00	(0.00)	0.91	(0.00)	**-0.95**	(0.25)	**-0.06**	(0.01)	14.8	(0.1)
Partners	Albania	-0.95	(0.04)	1.04	(0.02)	2.71	(1.70)	0.06	(0.04)	49.7	(1.5)
	Argentina	-0.62	(0.05)	1.19	(0.03)	**5.01**	(1.51)	-0.03	(0.05)	37.7	(1.6)
	Azerbaijan	-0.64	(0.03)	0.99	(0.02)	2.26	(1.28)	0.09	(0.04)	38.3	(1.3)
	Brazil	-1.16	(0.03)	1.21	(0.01)	**6.51**	(1.20)	0.14	(0.03)	55.7	(1.0)
	Bulgaria	-0.11	(0.04)	0.98	(0.02)	-2.79	(1.83)	-0.12	(0.07)	17.3	(1.2)
	Colombia	-1.15	(0.05)	1.27	(0.02)	3.23	(0.94)	-0.03	(0.05)	53.4	(1.8)
	Croatia	-0.18	(0.02)	0.91	(0.01)	-1.88	(1.26)	0.15	(0.04)	16.9	(0.7)
	Dubai (UAE)	0.42	(0.01)	0.79	(0.01)	-1.35	(1.62)	**-0.87**	(0.03)	5.8	(0.3)
	Hong Kong-China	-0.80	(0.04)	1.02	(0.02)	**-3.22**	(1.19)	0.16	(0.03)	44.6	(1.4)
	Indonesia	-1.55	(0.06)	1.10	(0.02)	2.74	(1.34)	0.35	(0.05)	69.5	(2.1)
	Jordan	-0.57	(0.03)	1.05	(0.02)	0.31	(1.27)	**-0.19**	(0.04)	35.8	(1.2)
	Kazakhstan	-0.51	(0.03)	0.83	(0.01)	-0.65	(1.76)	-0.05	(0.08)	30.0	(1.5)
	Kyrgyzstan	-0.65	(0.03)	0.93	(0.01)	**7.02**	(1.88)	0.05	(0.04)	37.9	(1.2)
	Latvia	-0.13	(0.03)	0.88	(0.01)	0.28	(1.92)	0.03	(0.04)	18.3	(0.9)
	Liechtenstein	0.09	(0.05)	0.94	(0.03)	-4.38	(4.29)	-0.07	(0.14)	13.4	(1.7)
	Lithuania	-0.05	(0.02)	0.97	(0.01)	0.39	(1.16)	-0.01	(0.05)	18.8	(0.8)
	Macao-China	-0.70	(0.01)	0.87	(0.01)	-0.92	(0.97)	0.27	(0.03)	38.0	(0.7)
	Montenegro	-0.24	(0.02)	0.95	(0.01)	-1.62	(1.35)	0.06	(0.03)	21.6	(0.9)
	Panama	-0.81	(0.08)	1.33	(0.04)	**8.20**	(1.28)	**-0.20**	(0.06)	43.5	(2.2)
	Peru	-1.31	(0.05)	1.25	(0.03)	0.45	(1.20)	0.11	(0.04)	61.2	(1.6)
	Qatar	0.51	(0.01)	0.91	(0.01)	-0.97	(1.04)	**-0.80**	(0.02)	7.3	(0.3)
	Romania	-0.34	(0.03)	0.92	(0.03)	-0.67	(1.12)	-0.20	(0.17)	21.1	(1.2)
	Russian Federation	-0.21	(0.02)	0.80	(0.01)	0.23	(1.83)	0.12	(0.04)	17.0	(0.9)
	Serbia	0.07	(0.02)	0.97	(0.01)	0.63	(1.11)	0.13	(0.05)	12.1	(0.6)
	Shanghai-China	-0.49	(0.04)	1.04	(0.02)	0.79	(1.32)	-0.07	(0.04)	33.1	(1.3)
	Singapore	-0.43	(0.01)	0.80	(0.01)	2.71	(1.43)	**-0.34**	(0.03)	23.7	(0.5)
	Chinese Taipei	-0.33	(0.02)	0.83	(0.01)	1.37	(1.63)	**-0.15**	(0.05)	21.1	(0.9)
	Thailand	-1.31	(0.04)	1.19	(0.02)	**4.41**	(1.28)	0.54	(0.04)	64.8	(1.4)
	Trinidad and Tobago	-0.58	(0.02)	0.93	(0.01)	**6.87**	(1.19)	**-0.17**	(0.04)	31.4	(0.7)
	Tunisia	-1.20	(0.05)	1.31	(0.02)	2.38	(0.82)	0.16	(0.04)	56.5	(1.7)
	Uruguay	-0.70	(0.03)	1.22	(0.02)	1.15	(0.97)	0.34	(0.03)	45.6	(1.0)

Note: Values that are statistically significant are indicated in bold (see Annex A3).
1. In these columns values that are statistically significantly different from the OECD average are indicated in bold.
2. Single-level bivariate regression of reading performance on the ESCS, the slope is the regression coefficient for the ESCS.
3. Student-level regression of reading performance on the ESCS and the squared term of the ESCS, the index of curvilinearity is the regression coefficient for the squared term.
StatLink ﷽ http://dx.doi.org/10.1787/888932343285

[Part 1/1]

Percentage of resilient students and disadvantaged low achievers among all students, by gender

Table II.3.3   *Results based on students' self-reports*

		Resilient and disadvantaged low achievers										
		Resilient students[1]						Disadvantaged low achievers[2]					
		All students		Girls		Boys		All students		Girls		Boys	
		%	S.E.	%	S.E.	%	S.E.	%	S.E.	%	S.E.	%	S.E.
OECD	Australia	7.7	(0.3)	9.5	(0.5)	5.8	(0.4)	4.4	(0.3)	2.9	(0.3)	6.0	(0.4)
	Austria	4.9	(0.4)	6.3	(0.5)	3.5	(0.5)	8.2	(0.6)	6.1	(0.8)	10.4	(0.7)
	Belgium	7.6	(0.3)	9.6	(0.5)	5.7	(0.4)	5.1	(0.4)	4.1	(0.5)	6.0	(0.6)
	Canada	9.8	(0.5)	11.6	(0.7)	8.0	(0.5)	2.9	(0.2)	1.8	(0.2)	3.9	(0.3)
	Chile	6.0	(0.5)	7.3	(0.8)	4.7	(0.5)	3.9	(0.5)	2.9	(0.5)	4.9	(0.7)
	Czech Republic	5.3	(0.4)	7.4	(0.6)	3.5	(0.4)	5.8	(0.5)	4.0	(0.5)	7.4	(0.7)
	Denmark	6.0	(0.5)	7.5	(0.8)	4.4	(0.5)	4.2	(0.4)	3.5	(0.4)	4.9	(0.5)
	Estonia	8.5	(0.5)	11.4	(1.0)	5.9	(0.6)	2.9	(0.4)	1.5	(0.4)	4.1	(0.7)
	Finland	11.4	(0.6)	14.4	(0.7)	8.4	(0.8)	2.2	(0.3)	1.0	(0.2)	3.5	(0.4)
	France	7.6	(0.6)	10.1	(0.9)	5.1	(0.7)	5.2	(0.5)	3.6	(0.5)	6.9	(0.8)
	Germany	5.7	(0.4)	7.2	(0.6)	4.2	(0.5)	5.1	(0.5)	3.7	(0.5)	6.5	(0.7)
	Greece	6.9	(0.5)	9.6	(0.9)	4.2	(0.5)	5.2	(0.9)	3.2	(0.6)	7.3	(1.3)
	Hungary	6.4	(0.5)	9.2	(0.9)	3.7	(0.5)	4.2	(0.7)	2.6	(0.8)	5.7	(0.8)
	Iceland	7.4	(0.5)	9.7	(0.7)	5.1	(0.6)	5.1	(0.4)	3.6	(0.5)	6.7	(0.6)
	Ireland	7.4	(0.6)	9.4	(0.8)	5.5	(0.8)	4.1	(0.4)	2.4	(0.4)	5.9	(0.7)
	Israel	6.0	(0.5)	8.4	(0.7)	3.4	(0.5)	6.9	(0.6)	5.6	(0.7)	8.3	(0.7)
	Italy	8.0	(0.3)	10.8	(0.4)	5.3	(0.3)	4.4	(0.3)	2.5	(0.3)	6.1	(0.5)
	Japan	10.5	(0.6)	12.2	(0.8)	9.0	(0.7)	3.3	(0.4)	1.9	(0.4)	4.7	(0.7)
	Korea	14.0	(0.8)	16.3	(1.3)	12.1	(0.9)	1.3	(0.4)	0.5	(0.2)	2.0	(0.6)
	Luxembourg	5.1	(0.4)	7.0	(0.6)	3.2	(0.5)	7.4	(0.4)	5.7	(0.6)	9.1	(0.6)
	Mexico	7.3	(0.4)	9.2	(0.5)	5.3	(0.4)	3.5	(0.3)	2.7	(0.3)	4.2	(0.4)
	Netherlands	8.0	(0.8)	9.2	(1.1)	6.8	(0.8)	2.8	(0.4)	2.1	(0.5)	3.5	(0.6)
	New Zealand	9.2	(0.5)	11.7	(0.7)	6.8	(0.7)	3.6	(0.4)	1.8	(0.4)	5.4	(0.6)
	Norway	6.5	(0.4)	9.3	(0.7)	3.8	(0.5)	5.1	(0.4)	3.6	(0.4)	6.6	(0.7)
	Poland	9.2	(0.5)	12.7	(0.8)	5.7	(0.6)	3.0	(0.4)	1.4	(0.3)	4.6	(0.6)
	Portugal	9.8	(0.5)	12.9	(0.8)	6.6	(0.5)	2.8	(0.3)	1.5	(0.4)	4.2	(0.5)
	Slovak Republic	5.3	(0.4)	7.0	(0.6)	3.5	(0.5)	5.6	(0.6)	3.6	(0.6)	7.7	(0.9)
	Slovenia	6.1	(0.5)	9.4	(0.8)	3.0	(0.4)	5.1	(0.3)	2.8	(0.3)	7.2	(0.5)
	Spain	9.0	(0.6)	10.5	(1.0)	7.6	(0.6)	3.3	(0.4)	2.3	(0.3)	4.3	(0.5)
	Sweden	6.4	(0.5)	8.1	(0.7)	4.6	(0.6)	5.8	(0.5)	3.4	(0.6)	8.1	(0.7)
	Switzerland	7.9	(0.5)	10.4	(0.9)	5.6	(0.4)	4.5	(0.4)	3.0	(0.4)	5.9	(0.6)
	Turkey	10.5	(0.6)	11.5	(0.8)	9.5	(0.8)	1.6	(0.3)	0.7	(0.3)	2.5	(0.5)
	United Kingdom	6.0	(0.4)	7.1	(0.6)	4.8	(0.5)	5.0	(0.4)	4.1	(0.4)	5.9	(0.6)
	United States	7.2	(0.6)	8.6	(0.9)	5.7	(0.5)	4.6	(0.4)	3.0	(0.4)	6.1	(0.6)
	OECD average	7.7	(0.3)	9.8	(0.6)	5.6	(0.3)	4.4	(0.2)	2.9	(0.2)	5.8	(0.5)
Partners	Albania	2.8	(0.4)	4.0	(0.7)	1.8	(0.6)	9.2	(0.9)	6.0	(0.9)	12.2	(1.2)
	Argentina	2.7	(0.3)	3.8	(0.5)	1.6	(0.4)	9.9	(0.9)	8.3	(0.8)	11.7	(1.1)
	Azerbaijan	1.2	(0.3)	1.4	(0.4)	1.0	(0.4)	12.4	(1.0)	11.8	(1.2)	13.1	(1.2)
	Brazil	5.5	(0.4)	7.4	(0.6)	3.4	(0.3)	4.6	(0.3)	3.9	(0.4)	5.3	(0.5)
	Bulgaria	2.3	(0.3)	3.5	(0.6)	1.3	(0.3)	11.7	(1.2)	8.2	(1.0)	15.0	(1.5)
	Colombia	5.8	(0.5)	6.6	(0.7)	4.9	(0.6)	4.5	(0.6)	4.5	(0.7)	4.4	(0.7)
	Croatia	6.7	(0.5)	9.2	(0.8)	4.4	(0.5)	4.4	(0.4)	2.4	(0.4)	6.2	(0.7)
	Dubai (UAE)	2.5	(0.3)	3.1	(0.4)	2.0	(0.3)	10.9	(0.4)	7.3	(0.5)	14.4	(0.6)
	Hong Kong-China	18.1	(0.9)	19.5	(1.3)	16.8	(1.0)	0.7	(0.2)	0.2	(0.1)	1.1	(0.3)
	Indonesia	6.0	(0.7)	8.3	(0.9)	3.7	(0.7)	2.0	(0.4)	1.3	(0.4)	2.8	(0.5)
	Jordan	3.1	(0.3)	4.9	(0.6)	1.3	(0.2)	7.4	(0.6)	4.7	(0.6)	10.0	(1.0)
	Kazakhstan	1.4	(0.3)	1.8	(0.4)	1.1	(0.3)	13.1	(1.0)	9.7	(1.1)	16.5	(1.3)
	Kyrgyzstan	0.2	(0.1)	0.3	(0.2)	0.1	(0.1)	19.7	(0.9)	17.9	(1.1)	21.6	(1.2)
	Latvia	7.7	(0.7)	10.9	(1.0)	4.5	(0.7)	2.6	(0.4)	1.4	(0.4)	3.9	(0.7)
	Liechtenstein	8.8	(1.4)	12.0	(2.7)	6.0	(1.8)	3.5	(1.1)	3.5	(1.3)	3.5	(1.8)
	Lithuania	4.9	(0.4)	7.4	(0.6)	2.5	(0.4)	4.8	(0.5)	2.6	(0.4)	7.1	(0.9)
	Macao-China	12.5	(0.5)	13.2	(0.6)	11.8	(0.7)	1.1	(0.2)	0.5	(0.2)	1.6	(0.2)
	Montenegro	2.1	(0.3)	3.0	(0.5)	1.1	(0.2)	11.0	(0.6)	8.2	(0.6)	13.7	(0.9)
	Panama	2.1	(0.5)	2.3	(0.6)	1.8	(0.8)	8.4	(1.1)	7.5	(1.1)	9.3	(1.5)
	Peru	1.2	(0.2)	1.5	(0.3)	1.0	(0.2)	11.6	(0.8)	10.7	(1.0)	12.6	(1.0)
	Qatar	0.7	(0.1)	1.0	(0.2)	0.5	(0.1)	17.0	(0.4)	15.9	(0.5)	18.0	(0.5)
	Romania	2.5	(0.4)	3.5	(0.5)	1.4	(0.4)	9.5	(1.0)	7.0	(0.9)	12.1	(1.4)
	Russian Federation	4.7	(0.5)	6.2	(0.7)	3.2	(0.4)	6.0	(0.6)	3.9	(0.6)	8.1	(1.0)
	Serbia	3.6	(0.4)	5.1	(0.7)	2.2	(0.4)	7.1	(0.6)	4.8	(0.6)	9.3	(0.8)
	Shanghai-China	18.9	(1.0)	20.6	(1.2)	17.2	(1.1)	0.3	(0.1)	0.1	(0.1)	0.5	(0.2)
	Singapore	11.9	(0.4)	12.9	(0.6)	11.0	(0.7)	2.1	(0.2)	1.1	(0.2)	3.1	(0.4)
	Chinese Taipei	9.7	(0.6)	11.9	(0.9)	7.6	(0.7)	3.0	(0.4)	1.5	(0.3)	4.4	(0.6)
	Thailand	6.7	(0.6)	8.9	(0.8)	3.8	(0.5)	1.9	(0.4)	0.9	(0.3)	3.2	(0.7)
	Trinidad and Tobago	4.7	(0.4)	6.1	(0.6)	3.2	(0.5)	8.8	(0.5)	6.6	(0.5)	11.1	(0.9)
	Tunisia	6.5	(0.5)	7.4	(0.7)	5.6	(0.6)	4.1	(0.4)	3.3	(0.5)	4.9	(0.6)
	Uruguay	4.0	(0.3)	5.3	(0.5)	2.6	(0.4)	6.9	(0.5)	5.5	(0.6)	8.5	(0.7)

1. A student is classified as resilient if he or she is in the bottom quarter of the PISA index of economic, social and cultural status (ESCS) in the country of assessment and performs in the top quarter across students from all countries after accounting for socio-economic background.
2. A student is classified as disadvantaged low achiever, if he or she is in the bottom quarter of the PISA index of economic, social and cultural status (ESCS) in the country of assessment and performs in the bottom quarter across students from all countries after accounting for socio-economic background.

StatLink ᔖᒱᔍ http://dx.doi.org/10.1787/888932343285

[Part 1/2]
Percentage of students and reading performance, by immigrant status
Table II.4.1 *Results based on students' self-reports*

	Native students				Second-generation students				First-generation students				Students with an immigrant background (first- or second-generation)			
	Percentage of students	S.E.	Mean score	S.E.	Percentage of students	S.E.	Mean score	S.E.	Percentage of students	S.E.	Mean score	S.E.	Percentage of students	S.E.	Mean score	S.E.
OECD																
Australia	80.7	(1.0)	515	(2.1)	9.9	(0.6)	541	(6.7)	9.5	(0.6)	527	(6.9)	19.3	(1.0)	534	(6.4)
Austria	84.8	(1.2)	482	(2.9)	10.5	(0.9)	428	(6.0)	4.8	(0.6)	385	(10.0)	15.2	(1.2)	414	(6.0)
Belgium	85.2	(1.1)	519	(2.2)	7.8	(0.7)	453	(6.8)	6.9	(0.7)	449	(7.8)	14.8	(1.1)	451	(6.1)
Canada	75.6	(1.3)	528	(1.5)	13.7	(0.8)	522	(3.6)	10.7	(0.7)	520	(4.6)	24.4	(1.3)	521	(3.4)
Chile	99.5	(0.1)	452	(3.0)	0.1	(0.1)	427	(46.1)	0.4	(0.1)	c	c	0.5	(0.1)	c	c
Czech Republic	97.7	(0.2)	479	(2.8)	1.4	(0.2)	448	(17.9)	0.8	(0.1)	472	(17.5)	2.3	(0.2)	457	(13.7)
Denmark	91.4	(0.4)	502	(2.2)	5.9	(0.3)	446	(4.3)	2.8	(0.2)	422	(6.2)	8.6	(0.4)	438	(3.8)
Estonia	92.0	(0.6)	505	(2.7)	7.4	(0.6)	470	(6.6)	0.6	(0.1)	470	(17.4)	8.0	(0.6)	470	(6.5)
Finland	97.4	(0.3)	538	(2.2)	1.1	(0.3)	493	(13.9)	1.4	(0.2)	449	(17.7)	2.6	(0.3)	468	(12.8)
France	86.9	(1.4)	505	(3.7)	10.0	(1.0)	450	(8.9)	3.2	(0.5)	426	(15.0)	13.1	(1.4)	444	(8.4)
Germany	82.4	(1.0)	511	(2.6)	11.7	(0.8)	457	(6.1)	5.9	(0.4)	450	(5.7)	17.6	(1.0)	455	(4.7)
Greece	91.0	(0.8)	489	(4.2)	2.9	(0.3)	456	(10.4)	6.1	(0.7)	420	(15.5)	9.0	(0.8)	432	(11.5)
Hungary	97.9	(0.3)	495	(3.1)	0.9	(0.1)	527	(12.4)	1.2	(0.2)	493	(11.6)	2.1	(0.3)	507	(8.3)
Iceland	97.6	(0.2)	504	(1.4)	0.4	(0.1)	c	c	1.9	(0.2)	418	(12.5)	2.4	(0.2)	423	(12.4)
Ireland	91.7	(0.6)	502	(3.0)	1.4	(0.2)	508	(12.8)	6.8	(0.5)	466	(7.6)	8.3	(0.6)	473	(7.1)
Israel	80.3	(1.1)	480	(3.3)	12.6	(0.7)	487	(6.5)	7.1	(0.7)	462	(9.2)	19.7	(1.1)	478	(6.4)
Italy	94.5	(0.3)	491	(1.6)	1.3	(0.1)	446	(9.4)	4.2	(0.2)	410	(4.5)	5.5	(0.3)	418	(4.2)
Japan	99.7	(0.1)	521	(3.4)	0.1	(0.0)	c	c	0.1	(0.0)	c	c	0.3	(0.1)	c	c
Korea	100.0	(0.0)	540	(3.4)	0.0	c	c	c	0.0	c	c	c	0.0	(0.0)	c	c
Luxembourg	59.8	(0.7)	495	(1.9)	24.0	(0.6)	439	(2.9)	16.1	(0.5)	448	(4.5)	40.2	(0.7)	442	(2.1)
Mexico	98.1	(0.2)	430	(1.8)	0.7	(0.1)	340	(9.9)	1.1	(0.1)	324	(9.9)	1.9	(0.2)	331	(7.9)
Netherlands	87.9	(1.4)	515	(5.2)	8.9	(1.1)	469	(8.2)	3.2	(0.5)	471	(12.5)	12.1	(1.4)	470	(7.8)
New Zealand	75.3	(1.0)	526	(2.6)	8.0	(0.6)	498	(8.3)	16.7	(0.7)	520	(4.5)	24.7	(1.0)	513	(4.7)
Norway	93.2	(0.6)	508	(2.6)	3.6	(0.4)	463	(8.0)	3.2	(0.3)	447	(7.8)	6.8	(0.6)	456	(5.9)
Poland	100.0	(0.0)	502	(2.6)	0.0	c	c	c	0.0	(0.0)	c	c	0.0	(0.0)	c	c
Portugal	94.5	(0.5)	492	(3.1)	2.7	(0.3)	476	(9.4)	2.8	(0.3)	456	(8.8)	5.5	(0.5)	466	(6.9)
Slovak Republic	99.5	(0.1)	478	(2.5)	0.3	(0.1)	528	(28.5)	0.3	(0.1)	c	c	0.5	(0.1)	c	c
Slovenia	92.2	(0.4)	488	(1.1)	6.4	(0.4)	447	(5.5)	1.4	(0.2)	414	(8.7)	7.8	(0.4)	441	(4.8)
Spain	90.5	(0.5)	488	(2.0)	1.1	(0.1)	464	(8.4)	8.4	(0.5)	428	(3.9)	9.5	(0.5)	432	(3.8)
Sweden	88.3	(1.2)	507	(2.7)	8.0	(0.8)	454	(7.5)	3.7	(0.5)	416	(11.3)	11.7	(1.2)	442	(6.9)
Switzerland	76.5	(0.9)	513	(2.2)	15.1	(0.7)	471	(4.5)	8.4	(0.5)	455	(6.7)	23.5	(0.9)	465	(4.1)
Turkey	99.5	(0.1)	466	(3.5)	0.4	(0.1)	c	c	0.1	(0.1)	c	c	0.5	(0.1)	c	c
United Kingdom	89.4	(1.0)	499	(2.2)	5.8	(0.7)	492	(8.5)	4.8	(0.4)	458	(9.5)	10.6	(1.0)	476	(7.5)
United States	80.5	(1.3)	506	(3.8)	13.0	(1.1)	483	(6.2)	6.4	(0.5)	485	(7.9)	19.5	(1.3)	484	(5.8)
OECD average	89.7	(0.1)	499	(0.5)	5.8	(0.1)	468	(2.4)	4.5	(0.1)	449	(2.0)	10.3	(0.1)	457	(1.4)
Partners																
Albania	99.4	(0.2)	389	(4.0)	0.5	(0.2)	c	c	0.1	(0.1)	c	c	0.6	(0.2)	c	c
Argentina	96.4	(0.5)	401	(4.6)	2.2	(0.3)	366	(12.6)	1.5	(0.3)	356	(26.5)	3.6	(0.5)	362	(15.2)
Azerbaijan	96.9	(0.6)	363	(3.4)	2.3	(0.5)	359	(9.6)	0.8	(0.1)	381	(12.6)	3.1	(0.6)	365	(8.8)
Brazil	99.2	(0.1)	416	(2.7)	0.5	(0.1)	321	(18.7)	0.3	(0.1)	310	(18.6)	0.8	(0.1)	317	(13.5)
Bulgaria	99.5	(0.1)	433	(6.7)	0.2	(0.1)	c	c	0.3	(0.1)	c	c	0.5	(0.1)	c	c
Colombia	99.7	(0.1)	415	(3.6)	0.3	(0.1)	c	c	0.0	(0.0)	c	c	0.3	(0.1)	313	(24.8)
Croatia	89.3	(0.6)	479	(2.9)	7.2	(0.5)	465	(5.5)	3.5	(0.3)	452	(8.4)	10.7	(0.6)	461	(5.3)
Dubai (UAE)	28.6	(0.4)	395	(2.1)	26.4	(0.6)	467	(3.2)	45.0	(0.6)	503	(2.0)	71.4	(0.4)	490	(1.4)
Hong Kong-China	60.6	(1.5)	535	(2.7)	23.9	(0.8)	543	(3.2)	15.5	(1.0)	512	(5.5)	39.4	(1.5)	531	(3.4)
Indonesia	99.7	(0.1)	403	(3.7)	0.0	c	c	c	0.3	(0.1)	c	c	0.3	(0.1)	c	c
Jordan	86.2	(0.9)	407	(3.1)	10.5	(0.7)	420	(6.5)	3.3	(0.3)	412	(8.6)	13.8	(0.9)	418	(5.7)
Kazakhstan	88.4	(1.1)	390	(3.2)	7.2	(0.8)	415	(12.1)	4.4	(0.6)	366	(8.9)	11.6	(1.1)	396	(9.7)
Kyrgyzstan	98.1	(0.3)	317	(3.1)	1.1	(0.2)	359	(19.9)	0.8	(0.2)	332	(18.7)	1.9	(0.3)	348	(14.4)
Latvia	95.5	(0.5)	485	(2.9)	4.1	(0.5)	472	(9.7)	0.4	(0.1)	c	c	4.5	(0.5)	474	(9.0)
Liechtenstein	69.7	(2.5)	510	(4.3)	13.7	(1.8)	486	(10.0)	16.7	(1.9)	474	(11.2)	30.3	(2.5)	479	(7.4)
Lithuania	98.3	(0.3)	471	(2.4)	1.6	(0.3)	447	(11.0)	0.2	(0.1)	c	c	1.7	(0.3)	448	(10.5)
Macao-China	29.6	(0.6)	482	(2.0)	54.9	(0.6)	489	(1.3)	15.5	(0.4)	491	(2.2)	70.4	(0.6)	489	(1.0)
Montenegro	93.4	(0.4)	408	(1.7)	2.5	(0.3)	433	(10.1)	4.1	(0.3)	404	(8.9)	6.6	(0.4)	415	(6.8)
Panama	96.1	(0.8)	382	(5.6)	1.4	(0.3)	398	(28.8)	2.5	(0.7)	324	(32.6)	3.9	(0.8)	350	(26.8)
Peru	99.6	(0.1)	374	(3.9)	0.3	(0.1)	c	c	0.2	(0.1)	c	c	0.4	(0.1)	c	c
Qatar	53.6	(0.4)	331	(1.3)	20.0	(0.4)	392	(2.3)	26.4	(0.4)	457	(2.1)	46.4	(0.4)	429	(1.4)
Romania	99.7	(0.1)	426	(4.0)	0.1	(0.0)	c	c	0.2	(0.1)	c	c	0.3	(0.1)	c	c
Russian Federation	87.9	(0.7)	464	(3.2)	7.2	(0.7)	435	(9.4)	4.9	(0.4)	444	(7.1)	12.1	(0.7)	439	(7.0)
Serbia	90.5	(0.6)	442	(2.4)	5.2	(0.4)	464	(6.5)	4.3	(0.4)	446	(7.8)	9.5	(0.6)	456	(4.9)
Shanghai-China	99.5	(0.1)	557	(2.3)	0.1	(0.1)	c	c	0.5	(0.1)	c	c	0.5	(0.1)	c	c
Singapore	85.6	(0.7)	526	(1.2)	4.8	(0.4)	544	(6.4)	9.6	(0.5)	521	(4.9)	14.4	(0.7)	529	(4.3)
Chinese Taipei	99.6	(0.1)	497	(2.5)	0.2	(0.1)	c	c	0.2	(0.1)	c	c	0.4	(0.1)	c	c
Thailand	100.0	(0.0)	421	(2.6)	0.0	c	c	c	0.0	c	c	c	0.0	c	c	c
Trinidad and Tobago	97.7	(0.2)	422	(1.2)	1.2	(0.2)	418	(19.7)	1.0	(0.1)	432	(18.0)	2.3	(0.2)	424	(13.3)
Tunisia	99.7	(0.1)	404	(2.9)	0.2	(0.1)	365	(30.4)	0.1	(0.1)	c	c	0.3	(0.1)	c	c
Uruguay	99.4	(0.1)	427	(2.6)	0.3	(0.1)	c	c	0.3	(0.1)	c	c	0.6	(0.1)	c	c

Note: Values that are statistically significant are indicated in bold (see Annex A3).
StatLink ⟐⟐ http://dx.doi.org/10.1787/888932343285

[Part 2/2]
Percentage of students and reading performance, by immigrant status
Table II.4.1 *Results based on students' self-reports*

	Difference in reading performance between native and second-generation students		Difference in reading performance between native and first-generation students		Difference in reading performance between second- and first-generation students		Difference in reading performance between native students and students with an immigrant background		Difference in reading performance between native students and students with an immigrant background, after accounting for socio-economic background		Pooled within-country correlations between students' socio-economic status and immigrant status		Pooled within-country correlations between schools' socio-economic status and immigrant status		Difference in the PISA index of economic, social and cultural status between native students and students with an immigrant background		Increased likelihood of first-generation students scoring in the bottom quarter of the reading performance distribution
	Score dif.	S.E.	Score dif.	S.E.	Score dif.	S.E.	Score dif.	S.E.	Score dif.	S.E.	Corr.	S.E.	Corr.	S.E.	Dif.	S.E.	Ratio	S.E.
OECD																		
Australia	-26	(7.0)	-12	(6.9)	**14**	(5.0)	**-19**	(6.5)	**-11**	(5.1)	0.01	(0.01)	0.00	(0.07)	0.01	(0.03)	**0.89**	(0.07)
Austria	54	(6.8)	97	(10.2)	43	(10.6)	67	(6.7)	37	(6.7)	-0.30	(0.02)	-0.41	(0.06)	0.73	(0.05)	2.69	(0.27)
Belgium	66	(7.1)	70	(7.4)	5	(8.0)	68	(6.0)	41	(5.3)	-0.19	(0.02)	-0.39	(0.05)	0.56	(0.06)	2.18	(0.17)
Canada	5	(3.8)	8	(4.7)	3	(4.4)	7	(3.6)	3	(3.1)	-0.02	(0.02)	0.02	(0.05)	0.08	(0.04)	1.27	(0.09)
Chile	c	c	c	c	c	c	c	c	c	c	c	c	c	c	c	c	c	c
Czech Republic	31	(17.7)	7	(16.8)	-24	(23.7)	22	(13.2)	17	(11.4)	-0.01	(0.02)	0.08	(0.10)	0.13	(0.10)	1.29	(0.42)
Denmark	56	(4.3)	79	(6.5)	24	(7.0)	63	(3.9)	36	(3.7)	-0.22	(0.02)	-0.42	(0.04)	0.75	(0.04)	2.51	(0.19)
Estonia	35	(6.5)	35	(17.1)	0	(17.1)	35	(6.3)	34	(5.8)	-0.02	(0.02)	0.01	(0.04)	0.06	(0.06)	1.49	(0.34)
Finland	45	(13.9)	89	(17.6)	44	(21.8)	70	(12.7)	60	(11.2)	-0.07	(0.03)	0.30	(0.04)	0.32	(0.12)	2.44	(0.31)
France	55	(9.5)	79	(15.3)	23	(15.9)	61	(9.0)	30	(8.4)	-0.23	(0.03)	-0.50	(0.06)	0.60	(0.05)	2.11	(0.28)
Germany	54	(6.2)	61	(6.0)	7	(7.9)	56	(4.8)	27	(4.3)	-0.27	(0.02)	-0.44	(0.04)	0.72	(0.04)	1.98	(0.16)
Greece	33	(10.3)	69	(15.2)	36	(18.0)	57	(11.1)	35	(10.9)	-0.20	(0.02)	-0.36	(0.05)	0.68	(0.06)	2.08	(0.28)
Hungary	-32	(12.4)	2	(11.7)	34	(17.5)	-12	(8.4)	-11	(7.3)	0.00	(0.02)	-0.20	(0.09)	-0.03	(0.11)	1.10	(0.31)
Iceland	c	c	86	(12.6)	c	c	81	(12.5)	61	(11.9)	-0.14	(0.02)	-0.16	(0.01)	0.81	(0.05)	2.39	(0.31)
Ireland	-6	(13.4)	36	(7.7)	42	(14.6)	29	(7.3)	33	(6.5)	0.03	(0.02)	0.04	(0.08)	-0.09	(0.06)	1.80	(0.19)
Israel	-7	(6.1)	18	(8.9)	25	(8.5)	2	(6.1)	-17	(4.7)	-0.15	(0.01)	-0.10	(0.05)	0.32	(0.06)	1.26	(0.15)
Italy	45	(9.4)	81	(4.7)	36	(10.3)	72	(4.4)	53	(4.4)	-0.14	(0.01)	-0.51	(0.02)	0.63	(0.05)	2.44	(0.14)
Japan	c	c	c	c	c	c	c	c	c	c	c	c	c	c	c	c	c	c
Korea	c	c	c	c	c	c	c	c	c	c	c	c	c	c	c	c	c	c
Luxembourg	56	(3.7)	47	(4.9)	-9	(6.0)	52	(3.0)	19	(3.1)	-0.34	(0.01)	-0.44	(0.00)	0.91	(0.03)	1.69	(0.11)
Mexico	89	(9.7)	105	(9.5)	16	(12.8)	99	(7.5)	85	(7.4)	-0.06	(0.01)	-0.28	(0.03)	0.57	(0.08)	3.15	(0.17)
Netherlands	46	(9.3)	44	(10.9)	-2	(12.3)	46	(8.0)	14	(8.0)	-0.29	(0.03)	-0.47	(0.09)	0.83	(0.07)	1.68	(0.22)
New Zealand	28	(9.0)	6	(5.0)	-22	(8.5)	13	(5.3)	14	(4.1)	0.05	(0.02)	-0.15	(0.06)	-0.03	(0.03)	1.11	(0.09)
Norway	45	(8.1)	60	(7.5)	15	(10.5)	52	(5.7)	33	(5.5)	-0.19	(0.02)	-0.12	(0.09)	0.54	(0.06)	2.11	(0.19)
Poland	c	c	c	c	c	c	c	c	c	c	c	c	c	c	c	c	c	c
Portugal	16	(9.4)	36	(8.9)	20	(11.6)	26	(7.0)	24	(6.0)	-0.01	(0.02)	-0.12	(0.05)	0.06	(0.08)	1.74	(0.21)
Slovak Republic	c	c	c	c	c	c	c	c	c	c	c	c	c	c	c	c	c	c
Slovenia	41	(5.6)	74	(8.9)	33	(10.4)	47	(4.9)	24	(4.9)	-0.18	(0.02)	-0.29	(0.01)	0.62	(0.05)	2.06	(0.29)
Spain	24	(8.3)	60	(3.8)	36	(9.0)	56	(3.6)	44	(3.4)	-0.13	(0.02)	0.02	(0.06)	0.47	(0.05)	2.17	(0.11)
Sweden	53	(7.7)	91	(11.6)	38	(12.2)	66	(7.2)	40	(6.2)	-0.23	(0.03)	-0.31	(0.08)	0.55	(0.05)	2.47	(0.25)
Switzerland	42	(3.9)	58	(6.5)	16	(7.2)	48	(3.5)	28	(3.0)	-0.24	(0.02)	-0.34	(0.06)	0.56	(0.04)	1.98	(0.12)
Turkey	c	c	c	c	c	c	c	c	c	c	c	c	c	c	c	c	c	c
United Kingdom	7	(8.6)	41	(9.7)	34	(10.7)	23	(7.6)	14	(5.4)	-0.08	(0.02)	-0.19	(0.09)	0.18	(0.09)	1.66	(0.20)
United States	22	(6.1)	21	(7.2)	-2	(7.6)	22	(5.5)	-9	(4.1)	-0.28	(0.03)	-0.49	(0.06)	0.70	(0.07)	1.30	(0.13)
OECD average	**33**	(1.7)	**52**	(1.9)	**18**	(2.4)	**43**	(1.4)	**27**	(1.3)	**-0.14**	(0.00)	**-0.22**	(0.01)	**0.44**	(0.01)	**1.89**	(0.04)
Partners																		
Albania	c	c	c	c	c	c	c	c	c	c	c	c	c	c	c	c	c	c
Argentina	35	(13.3)	46	(26.6)	10	(24.7)	40	(15.6)	16	(15.3)	-0.08	(0.02)	-0.09	(0.09)	0.58	(0.10)	1.54	(0.42)
Azerbaijan	4	(9.7)	-18	(13.0)	-22	(14.4)	-2	(9.0)	1	(8.5)	0.03	(0.02)	0.27	(0.12)	-0.08	(0.16)	0.54	(0.33)
Brazil	95	(19.0)	106	(18.8)	11	(27.2)	99	(13.8)	94	(13.3)	-0.02	(0.02)	-0.02	(0.03)	0.18	(0.24)	3.07	(0.51)
Bulgaria	c	c	c	c	c	c	c	c	c	c	c	c	c	c	c	c	c	c
Colombia	c	c	c	c	c	c	102	(24.7)	81	(24.0)	-0.03	(0.01)	0.01	(0.08)	0.77	(0.26)	c	c
Croatia	13	(5.3)	27	(8.2)	13	(8.1)	18	(5.1)	10	(4.5)	-0.10	(0.02)	-0.06	(0.07)	0.26	(0.05)	1.42	(0.23)
Dubai (UAE)	-73	(3.9)	-109	(3.0)	-36	(4.3)	-95	(2.6)	-84	(2.8)	0.20	(0.01)	0.31	(0.08)	-0.24	(0.03)	0.36	(0.04)
Hong Kong-China	-8	(3.8)	23	(6.2)	31	(5.6)	4	(4.3)	-9	(3.8)	-0.33	(0.02)	0.17	(0.14)	0.69	(0.05)	1.43	(0.13)
Indonesia	c	c	c	c	c	c	c	c	c	c	c	c	c	c	c	c	c	c
Jordan	-13	(5.8)	-5	(8.4)	8	(9.7)	-11	(5.1)	-4	(4.6)	0.11	(0.02)	0.34	(0.04)	-0.30	(0.06)	1.01	(0.16)
Kazakhstan	-25	(12.4)	24	(9.1)	49	(13.3)	-6	(10.1)	-12	(8.8)	-0.07	(0.03)	0.19	(0.07)	0.14	(0.07)	1.47	(0.19)
Kyrgyzstan	-42	(19.6)	-16	(18.7)	26	(26.6)	-31	(14.2)	-28	(12.1)	0.01	(0.03)	0.56	(0.04)	-0.06	(0.18)	0.81	(0.38)
Latvia	13	(9.2)	c	c	c	c	11	(8.4)	13	(6.9)	0.02	(0.02)	-0.14	(0.07)	-0.06	(0.10)	c	c
Liechtenstein	24	(12.0)	36	(13.5)	11	(15.2)	31	(10.3)	18	(10.9)	-0.24	(0.05)	-0.76	(0.00)	0.53	(0.10)	1.66	(0.41)
Lithuania	24	(11.4)	c	c	c	c	23	(10.8)	21	(10.9)	-0.01	(0.01)	-0.04	(0.04)	0.07	(0.12)	c	c
Macao-China	-7	(2.4)	-9	(3.0)	-2	(2.8)	-7	(2.3)	-12	(2.6)	-0.15	(0.01)	0.58	(0.00)	0.38	(0.03)	0.96	(0.07)
Montenegro	-24	(10.3)	4	(8.4)	28	(13.2)	-7	(6.5)	-2	(6.0)	0.02	(0.02)	-0.29	(0.07)	-0.14	(0.07)	0.99	(0.19)
Panama	-15	(27.4)	58	(31.4)	73	(42.5)	32	(25.4)	34	(23.0)	0.00	(0.02)	-0.19	(0.09)	-0.08	(0.18)	2.58	(0.54)
Peru	c	c	c	c	c	c	c	c	c	c	c	c	c	c	c	c	c	c
Qatar	-61	(2.7)	-125	(2.8)	-65	(3.5)	-97	(2.2)	-97	(2.2)	0.05	(0.01)	0.38	(0.00)	0.00	(0.02)	0.24	(0.02)
Romania	c	c	c	c	c	c	c	c	c	c	c	c	-0.31	(0.15)	c	c	c	c
Russian Federation	29	(9.4)	20	(6.6)	-9	(10.1)	25	(6.8)	20	(5.7)	-0.05	(0.02)	-0.27	(0.05)	0.13	(0.04)	1.27	(0.20)
Serbia	-22	(6.6)	-4	(8.0)	17	(10.1)	-14	(5.2)	-18	(5.0)	-0.04	(0.01)	-0.14	(0.07)	0.11	(0.05)	0.96	(0.17)
Shanghai-China	c	c	c	c	c	c	c	c	c	c	c	c	c	c	c	c	c	c
Singapore	-17	(6.7)	5	(5.5)	23	(7.1)	-2	(4.8)	7	(4.6)	0.10	(0.01)	-0.80	(0.01)	-0.20	(0.03)	1.13	(0.09)
Chinese Taipei	c	c	c	c	c	c	c	c	c	c	c	c	c	c	c	c	c	c
Thailand	c	c	c	c	c	c	c	c	c	c	c	c	c	c	c	c	c	c
Trinidad and Tobago	4	(19.7)	-9	(18.3)	-14	(27.1)	-2	(13.6)	7	(13.0)	0.07	(0.02)	-0.08	(0.01)	-0.38	(0.11)	1.36	(0.30)
Tunisia	c	c	c	c	c	c	c	c	c	c	c	c	c	c	c	c	c	c
Uruguay	c	c	c	c	c	c	c	c	c	c	c	c	c	c	c	c	c	c

Note: Values that are statistically significant are indicated in bold (see Annex A3).
StatLink ᵐˢ▬ http://dx.doi.org/10.1787/888932343285

Percentage of students at each proficiency level in reading, by immigrant status

Table II.4.2 *Results based on students' self-reports*

		Native students – Proficiency levels														
		Below Level 1b (less than 262.04 score points)		Level 1b (from 262.04 to less than 334.75 score points)		Level 1a (from 334.75 to less than 407.47 score points)		Level 2 (from 407.47 to less than 480.18 score points)		Level 3 (from 480.18 to less than 552.89 score points)		Level 4 (from 552.89 to less than 625.61 score points)		Level 5 (from 625.61 to less than 698.32 score points)		Level 6 (above 698.32 score points)	
		%	S.E.	%	S.E.	%	S.E.	%	S.E.	%	S.E.	%	S.E.	%	S.E.	%	S.E.
OECD	Australia	0.7	(0.1)	3.1	(0.3)	9.9	(0.4)	20.8	(0.6)	29.2	(0.7)	24.1	(0.6)	10.3	(0.5)	1.8	(0.2)
	Austria	1.3	(0.3)	6.2	(0.7)	15.5	(0.9)	24.0	(1.0)	27.8	(1.0)	19.5	(1.0)	5.3	(0.5)	0.4	(0.2)
	Belgium	0.6	(0.2)	3.2	(0.4)	9.8	(0.8)	19.2	(0.8)	27.0	(0.9)	27.6	(0.9)	11.4	(0.6)	1.2	(0.2)
	Canada	0.3	(0.1)	1.6	(0.2)	7.3	(0.4)	19.7	(0.6)	30.5	(0.6)	27.8	(0.6)	11.2	(0.5)	1.8	(0.2)
	Chile	1.1	(0.2)	6.8	(0.7)	21.6	(1.0)	33.5	(1.1)	26.1	(1.1)	9.6	(0.7)	1.3	(0.3)	0.0	(0.0)
	Czech Republic	0.7	(0.3)	5.3	(0.6)	16.5	(1.1)	27.5	(1.0)	27.4	(1.0)	17.4	(1.0)	4.7	(0.4)	0.4	(0.1)
	Denmark	0.2	(0.1)	2.4	(0.3)	10.2	(0.8)	25.2	(1.0)	34.4	(1.3)	22.4	(1.2)	4.8	(0.5)	0.3	(0.1)
	Estonia	0.1	(0.1)	2.2	(0.4)	9.9	(0.9)	25.1	(1.3)	34.1	(1.0)	22.2	(0.9)	5.8	(0.5)	0.7	(0.2)
	Finland	0.1	(0.1)	1.3	(0.2)	6.0	(0.4)	16.4	(0.6)	30.3	(0.8)	31.1	(0.8)	13.1	(0.8)	1.6	(0.3)
	France	1.8	(0.5)	4.7	(0.6)	10.3	(0.8)	20.3	(1.1)	28.2	(1.1)	24.1	(1.2)	9.3	(0.9)	1.2	(0.3)
	Germany	0.5	(0.2)	3.1	(0.4)	10.4	(0.7)	20.6	(1.0)	30.0	(1.1)	26.0	(1.1)	8.6	(0.7)	0.8	(0.2)
	Greece	1.0	(0.3)	4.8	(0.8)	13.3	(1.1)	25.3	(1.0)	30.3	(1.3)	19.3	(1.1)	5.4	(0.6)	0.7	(0.2)
	Hungary	0.4	(0.2)	4.7	(0.8)	12.2	(1.0)	23.7	(1.3)	31.2	(1.2)	21.7	(1.1)	5.8	(0.7)	0.3	(0.1)
	Iceland	0.8	(0.2)	3.8	(0.4)	11.0	(0.7)	21.9	(0.8)	31.3	(1.0)	22.4	(0.9)	7.7	(0.7)	1.0	(0.2)
	Ireland	1.3	(0.3)	3.0	(0.4)	10.4	(0.7)	23.0	(1.1)	31.9	(1.0)	23.0	(1.0)	6.7	(0.5)	0.7	(0.2)
	Israel	3.0	(0.5)	7.4	(0.7)	14.3	(0.7)	22.3	(1.1)	26.2	(1.2)	18.9	(0.8)	6.7	(0.6)	1.1	(0.2)
	Italy	1.1	(0.4)	4.6	(0.3)	13.5	(0.4)	23.9	(0.6)	29.6	(0.6)	21.1	(0.5)	5.6	(0.3)	0.5	(0.1)
	Japan	1.2	(0.4)	3.2	(0.5)	8.8	(0.7)	18.0	(0.8)	28.1	(0.9)	29.2	(1.0)	11.5	(0.7)	1.9	(0.4)
	Korea	0.1	(0.1)	0.8	(0.3)	4.6	(0.6)	15.3	(1.0)	33.0	(1.2)	33.1	(1.4)	12.0	(1.0)	1.1	(0.2)
	Luxembourg	1.2	(0.3)	4.2	(0.6)	12.0	(0.7)	23.8	(0.9)	30.5	(1.0)	21.6	(1.0)	6.3	(0.6)	0.4	(0.2)
	Mexico	2.4	(0.2)	10.5	(0.5)	25.3	(0.6)	33.8	(0.6)	22.1	(0.6)	5.5	(0.4)	0.4	(0.1)	0.0	(0.0)
	Netherlands	0.0	(0.0)	1.4	(0.3)	11.2	(1.4)	23.1	(1.5)	28.1	(1.3)	25.5	(1.7)	9.9	(1.1)	0.8	(0.3)
	New Zealand	0.8	(0.3)	2.5	(0.4)	9.2	(0.6)	18.7	(0.9)	26.8	(0.9)	25.9	(1.0)	13.1	(0.9)	2.9	(0.4)
	Norway	0.4	(0.1)	2.9	(0.4)	10.2	(0.6)	23.2	(0.8)	31.5	(0.9)	23.0	(1.2)	8.0	(0.9)	0.8	(0.2)
	Poland	0.5	(0.1)	2.9	(0.3)	10.9	(0.6)	24.5	(1.1)	31.3	(1.0)	22.6	(1.0)	6.6	(0.6)	0.7	(0.1)
	Portugal	0.5	(0.1)	3.8	(0.4)	12.4	(1.0)	25.9	(1.1)	32.2	(1.1)	20.2	(0.9)	4.8	(0.5)	0.2	(0.1)
	Slovak Republic	0.7	(0.3)	5.3	(0.6)	15.8	(0.8)	28.3	(1.0)	28.7	(1.1)	16.8	(0.8)	4.3	(0.5)	0.2	(0.1)
	Slovenia	0.6	(0.1)	4.5	(0.3)	14.4	(0.6)	25.3	(0.4)	29.8	(0.9)	20.5	(0.8)	4.7	(0.6)	0.3	(0.1)
	Spain	0.9	(0.2)	4.0	(0.3)	12.2	(0.6)	26.1	(0.9)	34.1	(1.0)	19.1	(0.8)	3.5	(0.3)	0.2	(0.1)
	Sweden	0.8	(0.2)	3.2	(0.4)	10.3	(0.7)	22.9	(1.0)	31.0	(1.0)	21.8	(0.9)	8.5	(0.6)	1.5	(0.3)
	Switzerland	0.3	(0.1)	2.6	(0.3)	9.7	(0.6)	21.3	(0.8)	31.5	(0.9)	25.3	(0.8)	8.4	(0.7)	0.8	(0.2)
	Turkey	0.7	(0.2)	5.3	(0.6)	17.8	(1.0)	32.2	(1.2)	29.5	(1.1)	12.6	(1.1)	1.9	(0.4)	0.0	(0.0)
	United Kingdom	0.6	(0.2)	3.5	(0.3)	12.6	(0.6)	24.8	(0.7)	29.3	(0.9)	20.6	(0.8)	7.5	(0.5)	1.0	(0.2)
	United States	0.4	(0.1)	3.5	(0.4)	12.1	(0.8)	23.4	(1.0)	27.9	(0.8)	22.2	(1.0)	8.9	(0.9)	1.6	(0.5)
	OECD average	0.8	(0.0)	3.9	(0.1)	12.1	(0.1)	23.6	(0.2)	29.7	(0.2)	21.8	(0.2)	7.2	(0.1)	0.9	(0.0)
Partners	Albania	10.1	(0.9)	18.5	(1.5)	27.0	(1.3)	26.2	(1.3)	14.8	(1.2)	3.2	(0.5)	0.2	(0.1)	0.0	(0.0)
	Argentina	10.1	(1.0)	15.5	(1.2)	24.9	(1.3)	25.9	(1.3)	16.3	(1.1)	6.3	(0.9)	0.9	(0.2)	0.1	(0.0)
	Azerbaijan	9.4	(1.1)	26.0	(1.2)	37.0	(1.3)	21.8	(1.2)	5.4	(0.8)	0.5	(0.2)	0.0	(0.0)	c	c
	Brazil	4.2	(0.3)	15.1	(0.6)	28.7	(0.9)	27.8	(0.8)	16.5	(0.9)	6.3	(0.6)	1.3	(0.2)	0.1	(0.1)
	Bulgaria	7.0	(1.0)	12.4	(1.3)	20.1	(1.4)	23.8	(1.1)	22.4	(1.4)	11.3	(1.2)	2.7	(0.5)	0.2	(0.1)
	Colombia	3.8	(0.7)	13.3	(1.0)	28.9	(1.2)	31.2	(1.1)	17.5	(1.0)	4.7	(0.5)	0.5	(0.2)	0.0	(0.0)
	Croatia	0.7	(0.2)	4.9	(0.5)	15.9	(1.0)	26.8	(1.1)	31.5	(1.3)	16.9	(1.1)	3.2	(0.4)	0.1	(0.1)
	Dubai (UAE)	8.2	(0.7)	17.9	(1.0)	28.3	(1.2)	27.7	(1.5)	14.3	(1.1)	3.2	(0.5)	0.3	(0.1)	0.0	(0.0)
	Hong Kong-China	0.3	(0.1)	1.3	(0.4)	6.5	(0.8)	15.6	(0.9)	30.2	(1.2)	33.5	(1.3)	11.4	(0.8)	1.2	(0.3)
	Indonesia	1.6	(0.4)	13.8	(1.3)	37.6	(1.7)	34.7	(1.4)	11.3	(1.4)	1.0	(0.3)	0.0	(0.0)	c	c
	Jordan	5.7	(0.6)	13.4	(0.8)	28.4	(1.0)	32.5	(1.0)	16.4	(1.0)	3.2	(0.4)	0.2	(0.1)	0.0	(0.0)
	Kazakhstan	7.4	(0.7)	20.3	(1.0)	31.2	(1.0)	24.4	(1.0)	12.8	(0.9)	3.5	(0.5)	0.3	(0.1)	0.0	(0.0)
	Kyrgyzstan	28.6	(1.3)	30.1	(1.0)	24.3	(1.0)	11.7	(0.9)	4.2	(0.6)	1.0	(0.3)	0.1	(0.1)	c	c
	Latvia	0.4	(0.2)	3.1	(0.6)	13.5	(1.0)	28.9	(1.4)	33.8	(1.2)	17.4	(1.0)	2.9	(0.5)	0.1	(0.1)
	Liechtenstein	0.0	c	2.5	(1.3)	10.0	(1.8)	22.0	(2.6)	31.5	(3.9)	28.0	(3.2)	5.4	(1.9)	0.6	(0.7)
	Lithuania	0.8	(0.2)	5.1	(0.6)	17.3	(0.9)	30.2	(1.1)	29.0	(1.0)	14.5	(0.9)	2.9	(0.4)	0.2	(0.1)
	Macao-China	0.4	(0.2)	3.2	(0.5)	13.4	(1.1)	31.4	(1.3)	32.7	(1.3)	16.2	(1.1)	2.7	(0.5)	0.0	(0.0)
	Montenegro	5.7	(0.6)	15.8	(0.8)	27.7	(0.8)	28.1	(0.8)	17.1	(0.9)	5.0	(0.5)	0.6	(0.2)	0.0	(0.0)
	Panama	9.8	(1.3)	21.2	(1.6)	30.7	(1.8)	22.8	(1.4)	11.3	(1.5)	3.6	(0.8)	0.6	(0.3)	0.0	(0.0)
	Peru	12.8	(0.9)	21.3	(1.0)	29.2	(1.1)	22.9	(0.9)	10.5	(0.9)	2.7	(0.5)	0.5	(0.2)	0.0	(0.0)
	Qatar	24.0	(0.6)	29.9	(0.8)	25.4	(0.8)	14.1	(0.6)	5.2	(0.4)	1.2	(0.2)	0.2	(0.1)	0.0	(0.0)
	Romania	3.8	(0.7)	12.5	(1.0)	23.8	(1.2)	31.8	(1.3)	21.2	(1.3)	6.2	(0.7)	0.7	(0.2)	0.0	(0.0)
	Russian Federation	1.2	(0.3)	6.1	(0.6)	18.3	(0.9)	31.7	(1.0)	27.8	(0.9)	11.7	(0.7)	3.0	(0.5)	0.4	(0.1)
	Serbia	1.8	(0.3)	8.7	(0.7)	22.3	(0.9)	33.5	(1.0)	25.2	(1.1)	7.7	(0.6)	0.7	(0.2)	0.0	(0.0)
	Shanghai-China	0.1	(0.1)	0.5	(0.1)	3.2	(0.5)	13.1	(0.9)	28.6	(1.2)	34.9	(1.0)	17.2	(1.0)	2.5	(0.4)
	Singapore	0.4	(0.1)	2.6	(0.3)	9.2	(0.5)	18.6	(0.5)	27.9	(0.9)	26.0	(0.8)	12.8	(0.6)	2.6	(0.4)
	Chinese Taipei	0.6	(0.2)	3.3	(0.3)	11.2	(0.6)	24.6	(0.8)	33.9	(1.1)	21.2	(1.0)	4.8	(0.8)	0.4	(0.2)
	Thailand	1.2	(0.3)	9.9	(0.8)	31.7	(1.1)	36.8	(1.1)	16.7	(0.8)	3.3	(0.5)	0.3	(0.2)	0.0	(0.0)
	Trinidad and Tobago	8.2	(0.5)	13.5	(0.6)	21.2	(0.8)	25.7	(1.0)	19.9	(0.9)	9.2	(0.5)	2.1	(0.3)	0.2	(0.1)
	Tunisia	5.4	(0.5)	15.0	(0.8)	29.6	(1.1)	31.6	(1.2)	15.1	(1.0)	3.1	(0.5)	0.2	(0.1)	0.0	(0.0)
	Uruguay	5.1	(0.5)	12.3	(0.7)	24.0	(0.7)	28.2	(0.7)	20.5	(0.8)	8.2	(0.5)	1.7	(0.3)	0.1	(0.1)

StatLink http://dx.doi.org/10.1787/888932343285

[Part 2/3]
Percentage of students at each proficiency level in reading, by immigrant status
Table II.4.2   *Results based on students' self-reports*

| | Second-generation students – Proficiency levels | | | | | | | | | | | | | | | |
| | Below Level 1b (less than 262.04 score points) | | Level 1b (from 262.04 to less than 334.75 score points) | | Level 1a (from 334.75 to less than 407.47 score points) | | Level 2 (from 407.47 to less than 480.18 score points) | | Level 3 (from 480.18 to less than 552.89 score points) | | Level 4 (from 552.89 to less than 625.61 score points) | | Level 5 (from 625.61 to less than 698.32 score points) | | Level 6 (above 698.32 score points) | |
	%	S.E.	%	S.E.	%	S.E.	%	S.E.	%	S.E.	%	S.E.	%	S.E.	%	S.E.
OECD																
Australia	0.5	(0.2)	2.4	(0.7)	8.0	(0.9)	18.6	(1.5)	27.2	(2.1)	26.8	(2.2)	13.3	(2.0)	3.2	(1.2)
Austria	2.1	(1.1)	14.6	(2.2)	26.4	(3.3)	27.4	(3.0)	20.2	(2.5)	8.3	(1.3)	0.9	(0.5)	0.0	c
Belgium	3.1	(1.3)	9.1	(1.6)	20.3	(2.5)	26.9	(2.7)	23.0	(2.3)	13.7	(2.2)	3.6	(1.2)	0.3	(0.3)
Canada	0.2	(0.2)	2.0	(0.5)	7.6	(1.1)	21.1	(1.5)	31.9	(1.9)	25.2	(1.6)	10.3	(1.1)	1.7	(0.5)
Chile	c	c	c	c	c	c	c	c	c	c	c	c	c	c	c	c
Czech Republic	5.5	(4.2)	13.4	(6.7)	15.1	(6.4)	24.2	(5.7)	19.8	(7.5)	18.0	(7.9)	3.9	(3.3)	0.0	(0.1)
Denmark	1.8	(0.6)	7.3	(1.1)	22.6	(2.2)	34.6	(2.4)	23.2	(2.5)	9.6	(1.9)	0.9	(0.4)	0.0	(0.1)
Estonia	1.5	(1.2)	4.0	(1.7)	16.5	(2.8)	31.9	(3.8)	31.5	(3.6)	12.8	(2.3)	1.6	(1.3)	0.2	(0.8)
Finland	0.0	c	3.6	(5.1)	13.9	(6.8)	30.1	(9.5)	26.7	(9.2)	17.9	(7.2)	7.0	(4.2)	0.7	(1.6)
France	3.5	(1.0)	10.6	(2.1)	21.0	(2.9)	25.3	(2.8)	22.4	(2.9)	13.3	(2.5)	3.3	(1.3)	0.5	(0.4)
Germany	2.3	(0.8)	7.6	(1.6)	19.9	(2.0)	28.9	(2.8)	24.8	(2.3)	13.9	(2.0)	2.5	(0.9)	0.2	(0.3)
Greece	2.5	(1.7)	9.2	(3.5)	19.5	(4.7)	29.7	(5.5)	21.2	(6.1)	13.9	(3.2)	3.7	(1.9)	0.3	(0.6)
Hungary	0.0	c	0.7	(1.5)	6.7	(5.4)	19.1	(8.8)	37.2	(9.0)	25.2	(7.2)	11.3	(4.7)	0.0	c
Iceland	c	c	c	c	c	c	c	c	c	c	c	c	c	c	c	c
Ireland	0.0	c	2.1	(2.7)	9.3	(6.9)	26.2	(8.3)	34.2	(7.7)	17.7	(8.5)	9.5	(5.7)	1.0	(1.6)
Israel	1.4	(0.8)	5.3	(1.3)	14.5	(1.7)	26.2	(2.3)	25.8	(1.9)	18.2	(2.4)	7.4	(1.6)	1.1	(0.5)
Italy	5.3	(2.6)	9.7	(2.8)	19.1	(3.4)	26.1	(3.7)	25.9	(3.9)	11.5	(2.7)	2.3	(1.5)	0.1	(0.3)
Japan	c	c	c	c	c	c	c	c	c	c	c	c	c	c	c	c
Korea	c	c	c	c	c	c	c	c	c	c	c	c	c	c	c	c
Luxembourg	4.6	(0.8)	11.1	(1.3)	21.6	(1.6)	26.6	(1.6)	23.9	(1.3)	10.0	(1.2)	2.1	(0.4)	0.2	(0.1)
Mexico	15.5	(4.9)	31.8	(6.2)	29.7	(6.7)	19.4	(5.5)	3.3	(2.2)	0.4	(0.4)	0.0	(0.0)	0.0	c
Netherlands	0.1	(0.2)	2.9	(0.9)	17.1	(3.3)	38.9	(3.7)	26.6	(3.3)	11.3	(2.4)	2.9	(1.2)	0.2	(0.3)
New Zealand	0.7	(0.8)	5.5	(2.1)	15.3	(2.2)	22.7	(3.3)	22.4	(2.7)	21.2	(2.8)	10.4	(2.3)	1.7	(0.9)
Norway	1.3	(1.5)	7.2	(2.7)	17.3	(4.0)	33.3	(6.0)	23.7	(3.9)	12.7	(2.9)	4.3	(1.8)	0.3	(0.5)
Poland	c	c	c	c	c	c	c	c	c	c	c	c	c	c	c	c
Portugal	0.5	(0.8)	4.2	(1.9)	13.3	(4.0)	39.3	(5.0)	25.5	(4.8)	13.1	(3.5)	3.7	(2.8)	0.5	(0.9)
Slovak Republic	c	c	c	c	c	c	c	c	c	c	c	c	c	c	c	c
Slovenia	1.3	(0.6)	9.3	(2.0)	22.2	(3.0)	31.0	(4.3)	26.0	(3.5)	8.5	(2.0)	1.3	(1.2)	0.4	(0.6)
Spain	1.7	(1.5)	5.0	(2.1)	18.9	(5.3)	34.4	(8.6)	24.9	(6.5)	12.8	(3.9)	2.1	(1.4)	0.1	(0.2)
Sweden	3.2	(1.2)	9.1	(2.4)	18.1	(2.1)	28.7	(3.0)	25.2	(2.9)	12.6	(3.1)	3.0	(1.2)	0.1	(0.2)
Switzerland	1.2	(0.5)	6.7	(1.2)	18.4	(1.8)	26.9	(1.8)	26.3	(2.0)	15.9	(1.9)	4.3	(0.9)	0.2	(0.2)
Turkey	c	c	c	c	c	c	c	c	c	c	c	c	c	c	c	c
United Kingdom	0.7	(0.7)	5.2	(1.6)	13.8	(3.0)	22.0	(3.2)	31.4	(3.2)	20.7	(3.5)	5.3	(1.9)	0.8	(0.7)
United States	0.6	(0.4)	3.7	(0.9)	15.2	(1.9)	31.8	(2.2)	26.7	(2.2)	15.0	(2.1)	5.8	(1.5)	1.3	(0.7)
OECD average	2.3	(0.3)	7.5	(0.5)	17.1	(0.7)	27.8	(0.9)	25.2	(0.9)	14.8	(0.7)	4.7	(0.4)	0.6	(0.1)
Partners																
Albania	c	c	c	c	c	c	c	c	c	c	c	c	c	c	c	c
Argentina	13.7	(4.9)	22.0	(6.8)	31.1	(6.8)	18.6	(4.8)	13.6	(5.1)	0.9	(1.3)	0.2	(0.6)	c	c
Azerbaijan	9.4	(4.0)	25.3	(5.2)	40.7	(6.1)	19.5	(5.8)	5.0	(3.8)	c	c	c	c	c	c
Brazil	21.0	(12.6)	44.8	(12.5)	22.2	(8.9)	5.8	(5.0)	6.0	(5.7)	0.2	(0.3)	0.1	(0.2)	c	c
Bulgaria	c	c	c	c	c	c	c	c	c	c	c	c	c	c	c	c
Colombia	c	c	c	c	c	c	c	c	c	c	c	c	c	c	c	c
Croatia	1.6	(0.8)	5.0	(1.7)	18.2	(3.1)	33.0	(3.1)	25.7	(3.0)	14.5	(2.3)	2.0	(1.0)	0.0	(0.2)
Dubai (UAE)	2.0	(0.5)	7.2	(1.1)	17.1	(1.4)	27.4	(1.8)	26.4	(1.5)	15.4	(1.4)	4.1	(0.8)	0.2	(0.2)
Hong Kong-China	0.1	(0.1)	1.1	(0.3)	4.9	(0.8)	14.0	(1.4)	32.0	(1.7)	33.1	(1.7)	13.3	(1.3)	1.5	(0.5)
Indonesia	c	c	c	c	c	c	c	c	c	c	c	c	c	c	c	c
Jordan	4.9	(1.6)	10.9	(2.0)	25.8	(2.5)	32.0	(2.5)	20.8	(2.4)	5.3	(1.6)	0.3	(0.3)	0.0	c
Kazakhstan	4.6	(1.9)	17.4	(3.3)	27.1	(3.6)	22.7	(2.9)	20.1	(3.3)	7.3	(2.8)	0.8	(0.9)	c	c
Kyrgyzstan	25.9	(6.6)	16.5	(7.0)	17.8	(8.7)	19.7	(6.1)	15.8	(6.2)	4.0	(3.4)	0.3	(1.0)	0.0	c
Latvia	0.2	(0.5)	4.6	(2.6)	19.2	(5.7)	27.8	(4.8)	30.7	(4.4)	14.0	(3.5)	3.4	(1.2)	c	c
Liechtenstein	c	c	2.9	(3.2)	14.7	(7.6)	29.2	(8.1)	31.7	(7.4)	20.0	(7.2)	1.5	(3.0)	0.0	c
Lithuania	0.8	(1.9)	8.6	(4.7)	23.4	(7.5)	28.5	(5.0)	29.0	(6.0)	8.8	(3.7)	0.9	(1.4)	0.0	c
Macao-China	0.2	(0.1)	2.4	(0.4)	11.1	(0.6)	30.1	(0.8)	36.3	(0.9)	17.2	(0.7)	2.8	(0.3)	0.1	(0.1)
Montenegro	2.9	(2.1)	11.2	(3.6)	26.2	(5.5)	29.5	(5.8)	20.2	(5.9)	9.5	(3.5)	0.5	(1.2)	c	c
Panama	12.0	(7.9)	24.2	(12.1)	16.4	(6.4)	20.0	(8.4)	16.3	(6.4)	10.6	(4.7)	0.6	(1.1)	c	c
Peru	c	c	c	c	c	c	c	c	c	c	c	c	c	c	c	c
Qatar	11.1	(0.8)	18.4	(1.4)	26.3	(1.3)	23.8	(1.0)	13.7	(0.9)	5.5	(0.6)	0.9	(0.3)	0.1	(0.1)
Romania	c	c	c	c	c	c	c	c	c	c	c	c	c	c	c	c
Russian Federation	3.2	(1.9)	9.7	(2.2)	23.5	(3.3)	33.2	(3.7)	21.2	(2.6)	7.8	(1.6)	1.3	(0.9)	c	c
Serbia	0.8	(0.9)	5.9	(1.7)	18.7	(3.6)	29.4	(4.5)	30.7	(4.7)	12.2	(2.7)	2.4	(1.7)	c	c
Shanghai-China	c	c	c	c	c	c	c	c	c	c	c	c	c	c	c	c
Singapore	0.2	(0.4)	2.0	(1.3)	7.4	(1.7)	15.7	(2.9)	27.3	(3.8)	24.7	(5.5)	18.7	(3.8)	4.1	(1.6)
Chinese Taipei	c	c	c	c	c	c	c	c	c	c	c	c	c	c	c	c
Thailand	c	c	c	c	c	c	c	c	c	c	c	c	c	c	c	c
Trinidad and Tobago	10.6	(7.3)	19.7	(8.8)	16.6	(7.5)	19.9	(8.1)	17.1	(8.9)	9.5	(5.9)	5.7	(4.3)	0.9	(2.0)
Tunisia	c	c	c	c	c	c	c	c	c	c	c	c	c	c	c	c
Uruguay	c	c	c	c	c	c	c	c	c	c	c	c	c	c	c	c

StatLink ⊞╦═╧ http://dx.doi.org/10.1787/888932343285

[Part 3/3]
Percentage of students at each proficiency level in reading, by immigrant status

Table II.4.2 *Results based on students' self-reports*

| | First-generation students – Proficiency levels | | | | | | | | | | | | | | | |
| | Below Level 1b (less than 262.04 score points) | | Level 1b (from 262.04 to less than 334.75 score points) | | Level 1a (from 334.75 to less than 407.47 score points) | | Level 2 (from 407.47 to less than 480.18 score points) | | Level 3 (from 480.18 to less than 552.89 score points) | | Level 4 (from 552.89 to less than 625.61 score points) | | Level 5 (from 625.61 to less than 698.32 score points) | | Level 6 (above 698.32 score points) | |
	%	S.E.	%	S.E.	%	S.E.	%	S.E.	%	S.E.	%	S.E.	%	S.E.	%	S.E.
OECD																
Australia	1.2	(0.4)	3.2	(0.6)	10.7	(1.3)	19.7	(1.6)	26.9	(1.9)	23.5	(2.3)	11.6	(1.8)	3.3	(1.2)
Austria	9.5	(2.5)	23.6	(5.3)	31.0	(5.5)	18.4	(4.8)	11.1	(2.6)	5.4	(2.2)	1.0	(0.7)	0.1	(0.3)
Belgium	2.7	(1.1)	11.1	(2.7)	22.4	(2.3)	27.0	(3.0)	20.1	(2.3)	11.8	(2.2)	4.3	(1.1)	0.6	(0.4)
Canada	0.6	(0.3)	3.0	(0.8)	9.8	(1.3)	21.0	(1.9)	25.5	(2.2)	25.3	(1.7)	12.4	(1.6)	2.3	(0.8)
Chile	c	c	c	c	c	c	c	c	c	c	c	c	c	c	c	c
Czech Republic	1.1	(2.5)	7.4	(5.8)	20.9	(7.7)	23.7	(8.1)	20.1	(6.6)	19.7	(7.8)	6.9	(4.5)	0.3	(0.8)
Denmark	2.3	(1.3)	13.2	(2.6)	27.3	(3.6)	32.5	(4.4)	18.5	(3.1)	5.4	(1.7)	0.6	(0.8)	0.1	(0.3)
Estonia	c	c	c	c	c	c	c	c	c	c	c	c	c	c	c	c
Finland	5.4	(3.4)	10.3	(5.8)	23.1	(6.0)	20.7	(5.6)	20.7	(7.6)	13.3	(6.7)	5.7	(3.9)	0.8	(1.7)
France	8.9	(3.4)	13.7	(4.8)	19.6	(4.3)	25.5	(5.3)	18.7	(4.3)	8.5	(3.2)	4.2	(2.1)	0.9	(1.0)
Germany	1.8	(1.0)	8.0	(2.0)	24.8	(2.7)	28.1	(3.1)	23.8	(3.1)	11.1	(2.7)	2.3	(1.5)	0.2	(0.3)
Greece	5.8	(3.7)	11.6	(3.7)	25.7	(4.1)	30.1	(5.2)	19.7	(3.5)	6.7	(2.6)	0.5	(0.4)	c	c
Hungary	0.0	c	0.4	(1.4)	15.0	(5.3)	27.8	(9.4)	31.9	(11.5)	22.6	(6.9)	2.3	(2.7)	c	c
Iceland	7.7	(4.4)	12.3	(4.9)	24.1	(6.8)	32.4	(7.2)	15.6	(4.6)	5.3	(3.5)	2.2	(2.8)	0.4	(1.3)
Ireland	1.6	(1.1)	8.5	(2.3)	20.7	(3.2)	24.5	(3.6)	22.9	(3.1)	17.4	(3.0)	3.8	(1.3)	0.7	(0.6)
Israel	4.1	(1.4)	9.0	(1.9)	17.0	(2.4)	23.0	(2.4)	24.9	(2.7)	17.0	(2.7)	4.3	(1.3)	0.6	(0.6)
Italy	5.2	(1.2)	15.8	(2.7)	29.5	(3.8)	26.5	(2.1)	16.2	(1.6)	6.0	(1.3)	0.8	(0.5)	0.0	(0.1)
Japan	c	c	c	c	c	c	c	c	c	c	c	c	c	c	c	c
Korea	c	c	c	c	c	c	c	c	c	c	c	c	c	c	c	c
Luxembourg	6.3	(1.2)	12.5	(1.5)	19.3	(1.8)	20.7	(1.8)	20.2	(1.6)	13.6	(1.3)	6.3	(0.9)	1.1	(0.6)
Mexico	19.8	(4.6)	36.8	(4.8)	29.1	(5.1)	9.6	(2.7)	2.8	(1.5)	1.9	(1.7)			c	c
Netherlands	0.0	c	5.0	(3.0)	23.6	(6.4)	27.4	(8.0)	24.5	(5.2)	13.8	(4.4)	5.6	(3.9)	0.1	(0.3)
New Zealand	0.9	(0.4)	3.5	(0.8)	10.9	(1.4)	20.4	(1.7)	23.9	(2.1)	22.7	(1.8)	14.3	(1.7)	3.4	(0.9)
Norway	1.5	(1.3)	9.0	(2.9)	25.4	(4.7)	27.3	(5.2)	24.5	(4.0)	9.7	(3.3)	2.4	(1.8)	0.4	(0.7)
Poland	c	c	c	c	c	c	c	c	c	c	c	c	c	c	c	c
Portugal	0.2	(0.4)	4.7	(2.3)	26.7	(4.7)	27.9	(5.2)	27.0	(5.2)	11.9	(3.3)	1.6	(1.0)	0.0	c
Slovak Republic	c	c	c	c	c	c	c	c	c	c	c	c	c	c	c	c
Slovenia	3.8	(2.1)	14.7	(4.1)	26.5	(6.7)	32.1	(8.0)	18.6	(6.8)	4.4	(2.4)	c	c	c	c
Spain	2.9	(1.1)	11.7	(1.8)	25.5	(2.4)	33.0	(2.2)	20.5	(2.4)	5.4	(1.0)	0.8	(0.5)	0.2	(0.2)
Sweden	7.8	(2.3)	13.9	(3.3)	26.0	(4.3)	25.3	(3.9)	16.5	(4.2)	7.8	(3.7)	2.4	(1.6)	0.4	(0.6)
Switzerland	2.4	(0.8)	11.1	(1.7)	20.4	(2.0)	25.7	(2.1)	21.7	(2.6)	14.0	(2.8)	4.1	(1.4)	0.7	(0.7)
Turkey	c	c	c	c	c	c	c	c	c	c	c	c	c	c	c	c
United Kingdom	2.4	(1.2)	8.2	(2.5)	18.1	(4.4)	30.1	(3.8)	25.5	(3.4)	11.2	(2.9)	3.6	(1.6)	0.9	(0.9)
United States	1.2	(0.6)	6.0	(1.5)	16.0	(2.8)	24.1	(3.5)	27.0	(4.0)	16.2	(2.8)	8.4	(2.1)	1.1	(0.9)
OECD average	4.0	(0.4)	10.7	(0.6)	21.8	(0.8)	25.3	(0.9)	21.1	(0.9)	12.3	(0.7)	4.5	(0.4)	0.8	(0.2)
Partners																
Albania	c	c	c	c	c	c	c	c	c	c	c	c	c	c	c	c
Argentina	19.9	(10.0)	18.7	(6.7)	26.8	(7.4)	20.3	(6.0)	11.6	(5.3)	2.3	(3.2)	0.4	(1.4)	c	c
Azerbaijan	c	c	c	c	c	c	c	c	c	c	c	c	c	c	c	c
Brazil	24.7	(10.5)	41.2	(14.3)	25.5	(12.9)	6.2	(8.8)	1.7	(2.8)	0.6	(1.8)	c	c	c	c
Bulgaria	c	c	c	c	c	c	c	c	c	c	c	c	c	c	c	c
Colombia	c	c	c	c	c	c	c	c	c	c	c	c	c	c	c	c
Croatia	1.7	(1.5)	7.0	(2.3)	22.8	(4.2)	32.7	(4.8)	20.9	(3.4)	12.3	(2.5)	2.7	(1.7)	c	c
Dubai (UAE)	1.1	(0.2)	4.0	(0.4)	11.1	(0.7)	22.9	(1.2)	28.6	(1.3)	22.7	(1.2)	8.5	(0.9)	1.0	(0.4)
Hong Kong-China	0.2	(0.2)	2.3	(0.7)	9.2	(1.6)	21.1	(1.8)	35.2	(2.0)	24.1	(1.9)	7.3	(1.1)	0.7	(0.4)
Indonesia	c	c	c	c	c	c	c	c	c	c	c	c	c	c	c	c
Jordan	7.1	(2.8)	12.6	(3.3)	24.7	(4.5)	33.8	(4.8)	15.2	(3.2)	6.1	(1.5)	0.6	(0.9)	0.0	c
Kazakhstan	12.5	(3.0)	26.5	(3.8)	29.7	(3.3)	21.0	(4.2)	7.1	(1.9)	2.9	(1.3)	0.4	(0.7)	c	c
Kyrgyzstan	c	c	c	c	c	c	c	c	c	c	c	c	c	c	c	c
Latvia	c	c	c	c	c	c	c	c	c	c	c	c	c	c	c	c
Liechtenstein	0.0	c	3.3	(3.1)	21.2	(6.4)	28.3	(10.7)	28.5	(9.2)	16.6	(5.2)	2.0	(2.5)	c	c
Lithuania	c	c	c	c	c	c	c	c	c	c	c	c	c	c	c	c
Macao-China	0.1	(0.1)	1.8	(0.6)	11.4	(1.1)	31.0	(1.7)	34.4	(2.0)	17.8	(1.5)	3.3	(0.8)	0.1	(0.2)
Montenegro	5.8	(3.7)	15.3	(4.6)	29.8	(4.3)	29.9	(4.8)	14.4	(4.2)	3.8	(2.1)	0.9	(0.7)	c	c
Panama	42.0	(11.2)	16.0	(5.9)	16.0	(6.1)	8.7	(4.8)	9.6	(4.8)	6.0	(3.0)	1.3	(2.1)	0.4	(1.4)
Peru	c	c	c	c	c	c	c	c	c	c	c	c	c	c	c	c
Qatar	4.4	(0.5)	9.7	(0.7)	18.2	(0.9)	24.9	(1.0)	22.6	(1.3)	14.6	(0.8)	4.8	(0.7)	0.7	(0.3)
Romania	c	c	c	c	c	c	c	c	c	c	c	c	c	c	c	c
Russian Federation	2.0	(1.0)	10.7	(2.3)	21.1	(4.2)	32.8	(5.1)	22.4	(3.7)	9.0	(2.2)	1.9	(1.0)	0.2	(0.3)
Serbia	0.5	(0.7)	8.0	(2.6)	21.2	(4.6)	35.7	(3.3)	25.9	(3.7)	8.2	(2.4)	0.3	(0.8)	0.0	c
Shanghai-China	c	c	c	c	c	c	c	c	c	c	c	c	c	c	c	c
Singapore	0.4	(0.3)	2.9	(0.8)	10.2	(1.6)	19.6	(2.4)	26.7	(2.9)	25.1	(2.7)	12.8	(2.3)	2.3	(1.1)
Chinese Taipei	c	c	c	c	c	c	c	c	c	c	c	c	c	c	c	c
Thailand	c	c	c	c	c	c	c	c	c	c	c	c	c	c	c	c
Trinidad and Tobago	12.8	(6.3)	16.3	(7.8)	12.8	(6.2)	16.8	(5.4)	14.5	(4.7)	19.9	(6.2)	6.4	(2.6)	0.5	(0.8)
Tunisia	c	c	c	c	c	c	c	c	c	c	c	c	c	c	c	c
Uruguay	c	c	c	c	c	c	c	c	c	c	c	c	c	c	c	c

StatLink ⟨⟩ http://dx.doi.org/10.1787/888932343285

[Part 1/2]
Percentage of first-generation students and reading performance, by age of arrival in the host country

Table II.4.3 *Results based on students' self-reports*

	First-generation students who arrived to the country when they were 5 years of age or younger						First-generation students who arrived to the country when they were between 6 years of age and 12 years of age						First-generation students who arrived to the country when they were older than 12 years of age					
	Percentage of students	S.E.	Performance on the reading scale Mean score	S.E.	PISA index of economic, social and cultural status (ESCS) Mean score	S.E.	Percentage of students	S.E.	Performance on the reading scale Mean score	S.E.	PISA index of economic, social and cultural status (ESCS) Mean score	S.E.	Percentage of students	S.E.	Performance on the reading scale Mean score	S.E.	PISA index of economic, social and cultural status (ESCS) Mean score	S.E.
OECD																		
Australia	35.7	(1.7)	532	(8.1)	0.45	(0.04)	39.4	(1.8)	521	(8.2)	0.46	(0.04)	24.9	(1.3)	504	(5.6)	0.39	(0.05)
Austria	31.8	(3.2)	429	(14.3)	-0.24	(0.13)	54.3	(3.8)	392	(10.9)	-0.66	(0.16)	13.9	(3.1)	386	(29.8)	-0.32	(0.33)
Belgium	40.4	(2.8)	496	(7.3)	0.11	(0.09)	43.2	(2.3)	449	(9.3)	-0.10	(0.08)	16.4	(2.9)	408	(20.8)	-0.33	(0.19)
Canada	43.4	(2.0)	518	(6.1)	0.56	(0.05)	39.0	(1.7)	529	(6.0)	0.66	(0.05)	17.6	(1.4)	480	(7.8)	0.43	(0.08)
Chile	c	c	c	c	c	c	c	c	c	c	c	c	c	c	c	c	c	c
Czech Republic	51.4	(6.5)	505	(18.6)	-0.01	(0.10)	33.9	(6.4)	c	c	c	c	14.7	(5.1)	c	c	c	c
Denmark	60.9	(2.8)	479	(8.1)	0.26	(0.07)	33.2	(2.6)	422	(8.5)	-0.29	(0.09)	5.9	(1.9)	c	c	c	c
Estonia	73.2	(7.2)	488	(12.6)	0.31	(0.13)	24.5	(6.5)	c	c	c	c	2.4	(1.5)	c	c	c	c
Finland	61.4	(5.1)	506	(14.4)	0.17	(0.11)	31.8	(4.2)	476	(17.4)	0.11	(0.22)	6.7	(2.1)	c	c	c	c
France	55.4	(4.7)	487	(12.9)	-0.18	(0.12)	35.0	(4.3)	416	(19.5)	-0.69	(0.14)	9.6	(2.5)	c	c	c	c
Germany	60.3	(2.3)	477	(7.3)	-0.13	(0.08)	35.4	(2.5)	435	(9.5)	-0.16	(0.10)	4.2	(1.1)	c	c	c	c
Greece	69.2	(4.7)	460	(8.3)	-0.48	(0.06)	25.4	(3.7)	423	(20.5)	-0.72	(0.15)	5.3	(2.3)	c	c	c	c
Hungary	40.9	(5.8)	510	(17.3)	0.01	(0.25)	39.3	(6.4)	523	(14.6)	0.11	(0.17)	19.9	(5.0)	c	c	c	c
Iceland	60.8	(3.3)	510	(9.4)	1.07	(0.09)	34.8	(3.2)	474	(11.5)	0.45	(0.12)	4.4	(1.1)	c	c	c	c
Ireland	45.0	(2.7)	507	(7.9)	0.26	(0.07)	44.4	(2.6)	486	(7.6)	0.10	(0.05)	10.5	(1.6)	453	(13.3)	0.18	(0.20)
Israel	55.4	(2.6)	497	(7.4)	-0.07	(0.07)	38.8	(2.5)	444	(12.8)	-0.54	(0.10)	5.9	(1.6)	c	c	c	c
Italy	34.2	(2.2)	456	(6.5)	-0.28	(0.07)	49.7	(2.0)	428	(5.1)	-0.67	(0.07)	16.1	(1.9)	374	(7.9)	-0.62	(0.08)
Japan	c	c	c	c	c	c	c	c	c	c	c	c	c	c	c	c	c	c
Korea	c	c	c	c	c	c	c	c	c	c	c	c	c	c	c	c	c	c
Luxembourg	51.3	(1.6)	460	(5.6)	0.01	(0.06)	35.8	(1.6)	455	(7.5)	-0.10	(0.08)	12.9	(1.1)	450	(12.7)	-0.04	(0.11)
Mexico	74.8	(2.7)	388	(5.8)	-1.24	(0.08)	18.9	(2.3)	357	(22.0)	-0.85	(0.26)	6.3	(1.2)	364	(38.5)	-0.81	(0.38)
Netherlands	59.2	(5.3)	493	(11.3)	0.00	(0.13)	37.5	(5.3)	461	(14.7)	-0.23	(0.18)	3.3	(1.8)	c	c	c	c
New Zealand	33.2	(1.9)	545	(7.2)	0.31	(0.05)	44.4	(1.9)	531	(5.4)	0.27	(0.04)	22.5	(1.7)	491	(8.0)	0.11	(0.05)
Norway	53.9	(3.4)	489	(9.0)	0.34	(0.10)	40.3	(3.0)	445	(9.7)	-0.02	(0.10)	5.8	(1.6)	c	c	c	c
Poland	c	c	c	c	c	c	c	c	c	c	c	c	c	c	c	c	c	c
Portugal	45.3	(2.8)	483	(7.1)	-0.45	(0.08)	44.3	(2.7)	472	(7.6)	-0.44	(0.07)	10.4	(1.5)	439	(12.9)	-0.87	(0.18)
Slovak Republic	c	c	c	c	c	c	c	c	c	c	c	c	c	c	c	c	c	c
Slovenia	55.8	(5.5)	445	(13.0)	-0.30	(0.14)	24.2	(4.2)	434	(15.2)	-0.47	(0.17)	20.0	(3.7)	376	(15.8)	-0.93	(0.13)
Spain	16.3	(1.0)	458	(6.1)	-0.60	(0.09)	59.8	(1.6)	439	(4.6)	-0.70	(0.05)	23.9	(1.4)	406	(7.4)	-0.73	(0.07)
Sweden	48.5	(3.5)	480	(10.5)	0.18	(0.12)	37.9	(3.1)	431	(15.2)	-0.17	(0.15)	13.7	(2.4)	384	(29.0)	-0.63	(0.32)
Switzerland	51.5	(2.8)	469	(6.6)	-0.20	(0.07)	36.5	(1.9)	453	(10.1)	-0.15	(0.10)	12.0	(2.1)	471	(19.6)	0.26	(0.19)
Turkey	c	c	c	c	c	c	c	c	c	c	c	c	c	c	c	c	c	c
United Kingdom	31.1	(2.5)	500	(12.6)	0.28	(0.10)	49.3	(3.2)	476	(8.7)	-0.06	(0.10)	19.5	(3.1)	438	(13.9)	-0.06	(0.18)
United States	45.3	(2.6)	503	(8.2)	-0.13	(0.12)	44.2	(2.8)	484	(9.1)	-0.45	(0.12)	10.5	(1.6)	473	(19.8)	-0.02	(0.25)
OECD average	49.5	(0.7)	485	(1.9)	0.00	(0.02)	38.4	(0.7)	456	(2.4)	-0.20	(0.02)	12.1	(0.4)	431	(4.7)	-0.25	(0.05)
Partners																		
Albania	c	c	c	c	c	c	c	c	c	c	c	c	c	c	c	c	c	c
Argentina	60.8	(7.7)	408	(19.7)	-0.49	(0.20)	28.6	(6.3)	c	c	c	c	10.6	(4.2)	c	c	c	c
Azerbaijan	36.2	(5.6)	c	c	c	c	48.5	(6.5)	391	(9.6)	-0.15	(0.17)	15.3	(4.2)	c	c	c	c
Brazil	61.9	(10.2)	350	(25.5)	-1.17	(0.32)	30.9	(8.5)	c	c	c	c	7.2	(5.6)	c	c	c	c
Bulgaria	c	c	c	c	c	c	c	c	c	c	c	c	c	c	c	c	c	c
Colombia	c	c	c	c	c	c	c	c	c	c	c	c	c	c	c	c	c	c
Croatia	72.0	(2.6)	465	(6.3)	-0.47	(0.07)	17.5	(2.1)	461	(10.9)	-0.17	(0.12)	10.5	(2.2)	453	(18.1)	-0.39	(0.15)
Dubai (UAE)	42.7	(1.2)	508	(3.6)	0.63	(0.02)	37.8	(1.2)	512	(3.3)	0.68	(0.02)	19.5	(0.9)	513	(5.6)	0.71	(0.03)
Hong Kong-China	45.5	(2.2)	535	(5.3)	-0.83	(0.07)	39.7	(1.7)	506	(5.7)	-1.38	(0.05)	14.8	(2.0)	487	(6.2)	-1.44	(0.07)
Indonesia	c	c	c	c	c	c	c	c	c	c	c	c	c	c	c	c	c	c
Jordan	58.0	(3.4)	428	(8.1)	-0.13	(0.09)	30.4	(3.4)	410	(13.9)	0.13	(0.14)	11.6	(1.9)	430	(20.5)	0.21	(0.15)
Kazakhstan	26.1	(3.4)	394	(15.1)	-0.40	(0.13)	50.1	(3.4)	377	(8.3)	-0.67	(0.09)	23.8	(3.6)	354	(14.0)	-1.03	(0.14)
Kyrgyzstan	75.4	(4.8)	351	(17.1)	-0.41	(0.15)	17.7	(4.0)	c	c	c	c	6.8	(2.8)	c	c	c	c
Latvia	c	c	c	c	c	c	c	c	c	c	c	c	c	c	c	c	c	c
Liechtenstein	72.4	(8.2)	c	c	c	c	27.6	(8.2)	c	c	c	c	c	c	c	c	c	c
Lithuania	c	c	c	c	c	c	c	c	c	c	c	c	c	c	c	c	c	c
Macao-China	30.6	(1.4)	490	(5.1)	-0.59	(0.06)	56.0	(1.3)	490	(2.9)	-0.88	(0.04)	13.5	(1.0)	498	(6.5)	-0.61	(0.08)
Montenegro	64.5	(2.8)	420	(7.9)	-0.16	(0.08)	28.2	(2.6)	422	(11.8)	-0.16	(0.10)	7.2	(1.3)	c	c	c	c
Panama	46.0	(6.2)	432	(25.5)	0.07	(0.27)	32.4	(4.8)	321	(46.2)	-0.54	(0.33)	21.6	(4.7)	c	c	c	c
Peru	c	c	c	c	c	c	c	c	c	c	c	c	c	c	c	c	c	c
Qatar	43.0	(1.0)	440	(3.5)	0.60	(0.02)	38.0	(1.0)	466	(3.9)	0.73	(0.02)	19.0	(0.8)	486	(5.1)	0.79	(0.03)
Romania	c	c	c	c	c	c	c	c	c	c	c	c	c	c	c	c	c	c
Russian Federation	67.9	(3.3)	455	(7.0)	-0.18	(0.06)	28.5	(3.4)	455	(10.7)	-0.38	(0.11)	3.6	(1.0)	c	c	c	c
Serbia	78.0	(3.4)	448	(7.6)	-0.07	(0.11)	16.4	(2.9)	439	(18.5)	-0.15	(0.14)	5.5	(1.8)	c	c	c	c
Shanghai-China	c	c	c	c	c	c	c	c	c	c	c	c	c	c	c	c	c	c
Singapore	42.9	(1.9)	535	(7.4)	-0.32	(0.05)	29.5	(1.6)	515	(6.6)	-0.23	(0.05)	27.7	(1.8)	513	(8.7)	-0.09	(0.05)
Chinese Taipei	c	c	c	c	c	c	c	c	c	c	c	c	c	c	c	c	c	c
Thailand	c	c	c	c	c	c	c	c	c	c	c	c	c	c	c	c	c	c
Trinidad and Tobago	64.7	(4.3)	471	(12.2)	0.31	(0.09)	24.7	(3.7)	490	(19.2)	0.09	(0.18)	10.6	(2.5)	474	(23.8)	-0.03	(0.16)
Tunisia	c	c	c	c	c	c	c	c	c	c	c	c	c	c	c	c	c	c
Uruguay	c	c	c	c	c	c	c	c	c	c	c	c	c	c	c	c	c	c

Note: Values that are statistically significant are indicated in bold (see Annex A3).
StatLink http://dx.doi.org/10.1787/888932343285

[Part 2/2]

Percentage of first-generation students and reading performance, by age of arrival in the host country

Table II.4.3 *Results based on students' self-reports*

	Difference in reading performance between first-generation students who arrived at:											
	Age 5 or younger and those who arrived at an age between 6 and 12 years		Age 5 years or younger and those who arrived at an age older than 12 years		An age between 6 and 12 and those who arrived at an age older than 12 years		Age 5 or younger and those who arrived at an age between 6 and 12 years, after accounting for ESCS		Age 5 years or younger and those who arrived at an age older than 12 years, after accounting for ESCS		An age between 6 and 12 and those who arrived at an age older than 12 years, after accounting for ESCS	
	Score dif.	S.E.	Score dif.	S.E.	Score dif.	S.E.	Score dif.	S.E.	Score dif.	S.E.	Score dif.	S.E.
Australia	11	(9.2)	**28**	(8.7)	**17**	(8.2)	9	(7.8)	**24**	(7.2)	**15**	(6.8)
Austria	38	(16.8)	44	(28.9)	6	(28.9)	19	(15.0)	39	(21.7)	20	(19.4)
Belgium	47	(11.1)	88	(21.9)	41	(19.6)	36	(9.8)	66	(14.6)	32	(12.3)
Canada	-11	(7.5)	37	(9.6)	49	(9.5)	-1	(7.3)	40	(9.7)	42	(9.5)
Chile	c	c	c	c	c	c	c	c	c	c	c	c
Czech Republic	c	c	c	c	c	c	c	c	c	c	c	c
Denmark	57	(12.3)	c	c	c	c	35	(11.7)	c	c	c	c
Estonia	c	c	c	c	c	c	c	c	c	c	c	c
Finland	30	(20.7)	c	c	c	c	29	(20.4)	c	c	c	c
France	71	(20.7)	c	c	c	c	37	(19.2)	c	c	c	c
Germany	42	(11.3)	c	c	c	c	42	(11.6)	c	c	c	c
Greece	36	(18.7)	c	c	c	c	30	(18.7)	c	c	c	c
Hungary	-12	(23.9)	c	c	c	c	-8	(20.2)	c	c	c	c
Iceland	37	(14.9)	c	c	c	c	10	(14.4)	c	c	c	c
Ireland	21	(10.0)	54	(13.7)	33	(15.7)	14	(8.6)	50	(16.4)	36	(16.4)
Israel	53	(13.9)	c	c	c	c	38	(11.9)	c	c	c	c
Italy	28	(8.0)	81	(11.0)	53	(9.7)	15	(7.2)	68	(12.2)	54	(10.2)
Japan	c	c	c	c	c	c	c	c	c	c	c	c
Korea	c	c	c	c	c	c	c	c	c	c	c	c
Luxembourg	6	(9.2)	11	(14.1)	5	(15.9)	-1	(8.1)	8	(12.1)	10	(13.0)
Mexico	31	(22.7)	24	(37.4)	-7	(40.3)	41	(20.5)	37	(28.7)	-4	(36.2)
Netherlands	32	(19.0)	c	c	c	c	27	(17.5)	c	c	c	c
New Zealand	15	(8.4)	54	(10.5)	40	(9.8)	11	(6.8)	44	(9.7)	33	(9.2)
Norway	44	(13.8)	c	c	c	c	31	(12.1)	c	c	c	c
Poland	c	c	c	c	c	c	c	c	c	c	c	c
Portugal	11	(8.7)	44	(14.4)	33	(12.8)	11	(8.1)	34	(13.5)	24	(13.0)
Slovak Republic	c	c	c	c	c	c	c	c	c	c	c	c
Slovenia	11	(19.2)	70	(21.1)	59	(21.0)	1	(19.0)	47	(21.7)	52	(21.2)
Spain	19	(6.6)	52	(9.0)	33	(8.4)	19	(6.4)	49	(8.4)	31	(7.7)
Sweden	49	(16.4)	96	(29.7)	47	(28.1)	26	(14.5)	60	(29.1)	32	(27.9)
Switzerland	16	(11.8)	-2	(20.3)	-17	(17.1)	18	(8.6)	18	(14.0)	3	(11.7)
Turkey	c	c	c	c	c	c	c	c	c	c	c	c
United Kingdom	24	(13.7)	63	(14.9)	39	(15.0)	14	(13.0)	49	(12.2)	37	(15.3)
United States	19	(9.9)	30	(18.9)	11	(19.9)	6	(9.3)	30	(14.2)	28	(14.8)
OECD average	**28**	(2.9)	**48**	(4.9)	**28**	(4.9)	**20**	(2.6)	**42**	(4.2)	**28**	(4.3)
Albania	c	c	c	c	c	c	c	c	c	c	c	c
Argentina	c	c	c	c	c	c	c	c	c	c	c	c
Azerbaijan	c	c	c	c	c	c	c	c	c	c	c	c
Brazil	c	c	c	c	c	c	c	c	c	c	c	c
Bulgaria	c	c	c	c	c	c	c	c	c	c	c	c
Colombia	c	c	c	c	c	c	c	c	c	c	c	c
Croatia	4	(12.3)	12	(19.6)	8	(17.9)	14	(11.9)	14	(18.8)	0	(16.2)
Dubai (UAE)	-4	(4.8)	-5	(7.0)	-1	(6.4)	-1	(4.4)	-1	(6.3)	0	(5.8)
Hong Kong-China	29	(6.3)	48	(7.0)	19	(6.7)	22	(6.4)	41	(7.7)	18	(6.8)
Indonesia	c	c	c	c	c	c	c	c	c	c	c	c
Jordan	19	(15.7)	-2	(21.7)	-21	(21.3)	25	(15.5)	7	(20.6)	-19	(21.7)
Kazakhstan	17	(16.8)	40	(21.3)	23	(14.0)	6	(14.2)	9	(17.3)	12	(12.8)
Kyrgyzstan	c	c	c	c	c	c	c	c	c	c	c	c
Latvia	c	c	c	c	c	c	c	c	c	c	c	c
Liechtenstein	c	c	c	c	c	c	c	c	c	c	c	c
Lithuania	c	c	c	c	c	c	c	c	c	c	c	c
Macao-China	0	(6.1)	-8	(8.6)	-7	(6.8)	-5	(6.0)	-8	(8.2)	-2	(6.8)
Montenegro	-2	(14.0)	c	c	c	c	-2	(12.6)	c	c	c	c
Panama	111	(45.0)	c	c	c	c	64	(30.0)	c	c	c	c
Peru	c	c	c	c	c	c	c	c	c	c	c	c
Qatar	-26	(5.6)	-46	(6.3)	-20	(6.2)	-20	(5.5)	-38	(6.0)	-17	(5.9)
Romania	c	c	c	c	c	c	c	c	c	c	c	c
Russian Federation	-1	(12.3)	c	c	c	c	-8	(11.8)	c	c	c	c
Serbia	10	(20.7)	c	c	c	c	4	(19.0)	c	c	c	c
Shanghai-China	c	c	c	c	c	c	c	c	c	c	c	c
Singapore	20	(10.9)	22	(10.7)	2	(11.0)	26	(10.3)	33	(10.6)	7	(10.8)
Chinese Taipei	c	c	c	c	c	c	c	c	c	c	c	c
Thailand	c	c	c	c	c	c	c	c	c	c	c	c
Trinidad and Tobago	-19	(22.2)	-3	(27.9)	16	(31.6)	-26	(20.9)	-15	(25.0)	9	(27.7)
Tunisia	c	c	c	c	c	c	c	c	c	c	c	c
Uruguay	c	c	c	c	c	c	c	c	c	c	c	c

Note: Values that are statistically significant are indicated in bold (see Annex A3).

StatLink ⟐ⁱˢᴸ http://dx.doi.org/10.1787/888932343285

[Part 1/5]
Percentage of students and reading performance, by immigrant status and language spoken at home

Table II.4.4 *Results based on students' self-reports*

	Native students speaking the language of assessment at home						Native students speaking another language at home						Second-generation students speaking the language of assessment at home					
	Percentage of students		Performance on the reading scale		PISA index of economic, social and cultural status (ESCS)		Percentage of students		Performance on the reading scale		PISA index of economic, social and cultural status (ESCS)		Percentage of students		Performance on the reading scale		PISA index of economic, social and cultural status (ESCS)	
		S.E.	Mean score	S.E.	Mean index	S.E.		S.E.	Mean score	S.E.	Mean index	S.E.		S.E.	Mean score	S.E.	Mean index	S.E.
OECD																		
Australia	76.3	(1.1)	516	(2.0)	0.35	(0.01)	0.8	(0.1)	461	(12.2)	0.12	(0.07)	36.3	(1.2)	534	(6.0)	0.37	(0.0)
Austria	86.2	(1.1)	485	(3.0)	0.18	(0.02)	1.3	(0.1)	431	(19.1)	-0.05	(0.15)	18.3	(1.8)	441	(11.6)	-0.32	(0.1)
Belgium	71.8	(1.4)	524	(2.4)	0.34	(0.02)	14.4	(0.7)	505	(5.2)	0.06	(0.03)	24.2	(1.8)	480	(8.3)	-0.04	(0.1)
Canada	73.7	(1.3)	530	(1.5)	0.53	(0.01)	2.6	(0.2)	495	(5.3)	0.45	(0.08)	36.1	(1.6)	530	(3.9)	0.43	(0.0)
Chile	99.1	(0.1)	452	(3.0)	-0.56	(0.04)	0.4	(0.1)	c	c	c	c	9.8	(4.9)	c	c	c	c
Czech Republic	97.6	(0.2)	481	(2.8)	-0.08	(0.01)	0.5	(0.1)	c	c	c	c	46.5	(5.8)	459	(17.1)	-0.38	(0.1)
Denmark	92.1	(0.4)	503	(2.2)	0.37	(0.03)	0.5	(0.1)	456	(20.7)	0.05	(0.24)	38.2	(1.8)	464	(6.3)	-0.27	(0.1)
Estonia	90.2	(0.7)	506	(2.7)	0.17	(0.02)	1.9	(0.3)	470	(9.2)	-0.03	(0.07)	82.9	(2.4)	472	(6.9)	0.13	(0.1)
Finland	95.6	(0.4)	539	(2.2)	0.37	(0.02)	1.8	(0.1)	499	(8.0)	0.60	(0.05)	15.9	(3.6)	c	c	c	c
France	85.7	(1.3)	509	(3.8)	-0.03	(0.03)	2.3	(0.4)	436	(14.9)	-0.44	(0.12)	50.9	(2.5)	470	(9.6)	-0.50	(0.1)
Germany	83.4	(1.0)	513	(2.5)	0.33	(0.02)	1.4	(0.2)	493	(13.4)	0.19	(0.10)	33.3	(2.4)	483	(8.0)	-0.28	(0.1)
Greece	90.0	(0.9)	490	(4.4)	0.05	(0.03)	1.3	(0.3)	412	(16.7)	-0.51	(0.17)	29.5	(3.2)	457	(9.9)	-0.33	(0.1)
Hungary	97.1	(0.4)	496	(3.0)	-0.18	(0.03)	0.7	(0.3)	c	c	c	c	41.0	(4.8)	527	(12.8)	0.01	(0.2)
Iceland	96.4	(0.3)	505	(1.4)	0.74	(0.01)	1.3	(0.2)	451	(16.0)	0.84	(0.10)	c	c	c	c	c	c
Ireland	89.8	(1.0)	503	(3.0)	0.04	(0.03)	2.2	(0.9)	507	(14.2)	0.15	(0.18)	16.5	(2.2)	511	(13.3)	0.09	(0.2)
Israel	77.4	(1.3)	484	(3.4)	0.04	(0.02)	4.2	(0.7)	444	(20.0)	0.04	(0.08)	50.7	(2.5)	486	(6.6)	-0.24	(0.1)
Italy	84.0	(0.4)	504	(1.4)	0.03	(0.01)	10.7	(0.4)	452	(3.7)	-0.66	(0.03)	14.2	(1.3)	471	(10.3)	-0.43	(0.1)
Japan	99.6	(0.1)	522	(3.4)	0.00	(0.01)	0.1	(0.0)	c	c	c	c	c	c	c	c	c	c
Korea	99.9	(0.0)	541	(3.4)	-0.15	(0.03)	0.1	(0.0)	c	c	c	c	c	c	c	c	c	c
Luxembourg	2.6	(0.3)	517	(11.7)	0.79	(0.10)	60.6	(0.7)	500	(2.0)	0.56	(0.02)	11.5	(0.8)	501	(6.9)	0.47	(0.1)
Mexico	96.1	(0.4)	432	(1.8)	-1.17	(0.03)	2.2	(0.2)	354	(7.4)	-2.26	(0.10)	37.7	(3.6)	347	(10.2)	-1.74	(0.1)
Netherlands	87.6	(1.4)	517	(5.2)	0.38	(0.03)	1.5	(0.5)	510	(23.1)	0.22	(0.12)	48.4	(3.1)	477	(10.6)	-0.29	(0.1)
New Zealand	72.5	(1.1)	530	(2.5)	0.10	(0.02)	2.8	(0.2)	432	(9.4)	-0.33	(0.07)	20.4	(1.5)	516	(8.9)	-0.05	(0.1)
Norway	91.2	(0.6)	509	(2.5)	0.51	(0.02)	2.0	(0.2)	466	(10.9)	0.52	(0.07)	18.1	(1.8)	484	(13.4)	0.26	(0.2)
Poland	99.4	(0.1)	503	(2.6)	-0.28	(0.02)	0.6	(0.1)	c	c	c	c	c	c	c	c	c	c
Portugal	94.2	(0.4)	493	(3.1)	-0.31	(0.04)	0.6	(0.1)	493	(14.9)	-0.07	(0.22)	47.8	(3.5)	486	(9.1)	-0.33	(0.1)
Slovak Republic	94.3	(0.8)	483	(2.6)	-0.06	(0.02)	5.2	(0.8)	413	(12.3)	-0.62	(0.12)	34.6	(10.1)	c	c	c	c
Slovenia	91.6	(0.4)	489	(1.1)	0.13	(0.01)	1.2	(0.2)	464	(14.4)	-0.04	(0.12)	40.3	(3.0)	466	(8.5)	-0.29	(0.1)
Spain	76.6	(1.0)	488	(2.0)	-0.26	(0.04)	13.9	(0.9)	489	(4.1)	-0.27	(0.07)	6.0	(0.3)	466	(11.9)	-0.48	(0.2)
Sweden	88.5	(1.1)	509	(2.7)	0.40	(0.02)	1.2	(0.2)	454	(19.4)	0.18	(0.10)	28.4	(2.4)	473	(10.2)	0.09	(0.1)
Switzerland	75.6	(0.9)	516	(2.1)	0.22	(0.02)	3.1	(0.3)	490	(7.9)	0.17	(0.06)	28.9	(2.3)	498	(5.6)	-0.17	(0.1)
Turkey	95.8	(0.6)	468	(3.6)	-1.12	(0.05)	3.7	(0.5)	409	(11.1)	-2.15	(0.12)	c	c	c	c	c	c
United Kingdom	88.3	(1.0)	501	(2.3)	0.23	(0.03)	1.3	(0.2)	433	(11.5)	0.05	(0.11)	38.3	(3.4)	504	(8.9)	0.26	(0.1)
United States	79.3	(1.4)	507	(3.7)	0.33	(0.04)	1.4	(0.2)	453	(14.5)	-0.27	(0.14)	31.2	(1.8)	496	(8.1)	-0.02	(0.1)
OECD average	85.9	(0.1)	502	(0.6)	0.07	(0.01)	4.4	(0.1)	460	(2.5)	-0.13	(0.02)	32.3	(0.6)	481	(1.9)	-0.16	(0.0)
Partners																		
Albania	98.4	(0.3)	389	(4.0)	-0.95	(0.04)	1.0	(0.2)	367	(19.9)	-0.99	(0.31)	c	c	c	c	c	c
Argentina	95.9	(0.5)	404	(4.6)	-0.60	(0.05)	0.7	(0.1)	c	c	c	c	53.5	(5.7)	376	(13.1)	-1.27	(0.1)
Azerbaijan	90.0	(1.2)	361	(3.4)	-0.67	(0.03)	6.9	(1.0)	385	(10.7)	-0.21	(0.16)	64.2	(6.6)	359	(10.3)	-0.67	(0.2)
Brazil	98.6	(0.2)	416	(2.7)	-1.15	(0.03)	0.6	(0.1)	362	(12.4)	-0.76	(0.16)	64.6	(7.9)	322	(18.9)	-1.27	(0.3)
Bulgaria	89.0	(1.8)	446	(6.5)	-0.01	(0.04)	10.5	(1.7)	343	(10.0)	-0.91	(0.08)	c	c	c	c	c	c
Colombia	99.3	(0.1)	416	(3.6)	-1.15	(0.05)	0.4	(0.1)	371	(25.8)	-0.33	(0.22)	c	c	c	c	c	c
Croatia	88.0	(0.8)	479	(2.9)	-0.15	(0.04)	1.3	(0.3)	470	(21.5)	-0.25	(0.19)	65.8	(2.2)	466	(5.4)	-0.32	(0.1)
Dubai (UAE)	16.1	(0.4)	386	(2.9)	0.02	(0.03)	9.4	(0.4)	415	(4.4)	0.75	(0.03)	17.1	(0.7)	480	(5.0)	0.31	(0.0)
Hong Kong-China	57.8	(1.6)	540	(2.8)	-0.56	(0.03)	2.8	(0.8)	466	(8.8)	0.18	(0.24)	57.8	(1.6)	546	(3.2)	-1.13	(0.0)
Indonesia	35.5	(2.1)	409	(6.4)	-1.00	(0.09)	64.3	(2.1)	400	(3.6)	-1.85	(0.05)	c	c	c	c	c	c
Jordan	84.0	(1.2)	408	(3.1)	-0.62	(0.03)	2.2	(0.3)	388	(12.9)	-0.25	(0.14)	72.4	(1.7)	423	(6.6)	-0.38	(0.1)
Kazakhstan	79.4	(1.3)	388	(3.2)	-0.51	(0.03)	9.0	(0.7)	405	(8.3)	-0.31	(0.07)	57.1	(3.9)	418	(12.9)	-0.54	(0.1)
Kyrgyzstan	79.6	(1.6)	308	(3.2)	-0.76	(0.02)	18.6	(1.6)	359	(6.6)	-0.19	(0.04)	51.6	(5.7)	373	(24.1)	-0.53	(0.2)
Latvia	87.1	(1.3)	488	(3.0)	-0.12	(0.03)	8.6	(1.2)	472	(9.2)	-0.32	(0.07)	75.1	(4.9)	484	(9.6)	0.00	(0.1)
Liechtenstein	69.5	(3.0)	513	(4.5)	0.24	(0.05)	0.7	(0.5)	c	c	c	c	27.1	(4.4)	c	c	c	c
Lithuania	94.7	(0.8)	473	(2.5)	-0.03	(0.02)	3.6	(0.7)	433	(7.5)	-0.29	(0.07)	56.7	(7.8)	435	(13.3)	-0.20	(0.2)
Macao-China	24.0	(0.6)	492	(2.3)	-0.57	(0.03)	5.5	(0.2)	450	(3.5)	0.13	(0.04)	71.9	(0.7)	494	(1.3)	-0.89	(0.0)
Montenegro	92.4	(0.4)	411	(1.7)	-0.24	(0.02)	1.0	(0.2)	362	(14.5)	-0.66	(0.14)	35.7	(3.0)	439	(10.0)	0.15	(0.1)
Panama	92.4	(1.4)	385	(5.5)	-0.79	(0.08)	3.9	(0.9)	317	(20.3)	-1.22	(0.34)	20.7	(5.3)	413	(35.5)	-0.30	(0.2)
Peru	94.7	(0.8)	381	(4.0)	-1.24	(0.05)	4.9	(0.8)	272	(7.6)	-2.45	(0.09)	c	c	c	c	c	c
Qatar	34.2	(0.4)	336	(1.6)	0.32	(0.02)	19.4	(0.3)	326	(2.3)	0.80	(0.02)	28.1	(0.7)	394	(2.7)	0.25	(0.0)
Romania	96.6	(0.6)	428	(4.0)	-0.34	(0.03)	3.1	(0.6)	361	(13.1)	-0.89	(0.34)	c	c	c	c	c	c
Russian Federation	80.9	(1.4)	468	(3.3)	-0.16	(0.03)	7.0	(1.1)	421	(9.1)	-0.57	(0.09)	49.0	(4.3)	446	(6.0)	-0.29	(0.1)
Serbia	89.0	(0.6)	443	(2.4)	0.09	(0.02)	1.6	(0.3)	406	(12.4)	-0.56	(0.15)	53.5	(2.7)	466	(6.9)	0.10	(0.1)
Shanghai-China	98.1	(0.3)	558	(2.3)	-0.47	(0.03)	1.3	(0.2)	493	(12.1)	-1.40	(0.15)	c	c	c	c	c	c
Singapore	37.8	(0.8)	561	(2.0)	-0.03	(0.01)	48.0	(1.0)	503	(1.9)	-0.79	(0.02)	9.7	(1.1)	591	(13.4)	0.23	(0.1)
Chinese Taipei	77.9	(1.2)	510	(2.6)	-0.19	(0.02)	21.7	(1.2)	472	(4.1)	-0.71	(0.04)	c	c	c	c	c	c
Thailand	51.4	(1.7)	431	(3.3)	-0.86	(0.05)	48.6	(1.7)	413	(3.5)	-1.78	(0.04)	c	c	c	c	c	c
Trinidad and Tobago	95.4	(0.3)	425	(1.3)	-0.57	(0.02)	2.3	(0.2)	351	(14.6)	-0.73	(0.10)	49.9	(5.4)	418	(19.8)	-0.45	(0.1)
Tunisia	99.6	(0.1)	404	(2.9)	-1.20	(0.05)	0.1	(0.0)	c	c	c	c	52.2	(12.8)	c	c	c	c
Uruguay	97.3	(0.2)	430	(2.5)	-0.68	(0.03)	2.2	(0.4)	383	(9.0)	-1.28	(0.11)	c	c	c	c	c	c

Notes: Values that are statistically significant are indicated in bold (see Annex A3). The percentages of immigrant and native students speaking the language of assessment at home and not speaking the language of assessment at home is calculated over the total student population. The percentages of first- and second-generation students speaking the language of assessment at home and not speaking the language of assessment at home is calculated over the total immigrant student population.

StatLink ᴍᴤᴘ http://dx.doi.org/10.1787/888932343285

[Part 2/5]
Percentage of students and reading performance, by immigrant status and language spoken at home

Table II.4.4 *Results based on students' self-reports*

	Second-generation students speaking another language at home						First-generation students speaking the language of assessment at home						First-generation students speaking another language at home					
	Percentage of students		Performance on the reading scale		PISA index of economic, social and cultural status (ESCS)		Percentage of students		Performance on the reading scale		PISA index of economic, social and cultural status (ESCS)		Percentage of students		Performance on the reading scale		PISA index of economic, social and cultural status (ESCS)	
		S.E.	Mean score	S.E.	Mean index	S.E.		S.E.	Mean score	S.E.	Mean index	S.E.		S.E.	Mean score	S.E.	Mean index	S.E.
OECD																		
Australia	15.6	(1.0)	527	(9.2)	0.07	(0.1)	27.6	(1.3)	530	(4.8)	0.51	(0.0)	20.6	(1.4)	505	(11.8)	0.29	(0.1)
Austria	50.6	(3.0)	428	(7.3)	-0.62	(0.0)	7.9	(1.7)	416	(28.5)	-0.08	(0.2)	23.3	(2.0)	387	(11.0)	-0.85	(0.2)
Belgium	27.4	(2.1)	442	(10.7)	-0.45	(0.1)	24.8	(3.4)	463	(12.9)	-0.03	(0.1)	23.5	(1.8)	435	(10.5)	-0.36	(0.1)
Canada	19.9	(1.0)	517	(5.7)	0.22	(0.1)	15.0	(0.8)	535	(6.3)	0.72	(0.1)	29.0	(1.5)	516	(5.5)	0.51	(0.0)
Chile	3.4	(3.1)	c	c	c	c	c	c	c	c	c	c	c	c	c	c	c	c
Czech Republic	14.5	(4.3)	c	c	c	c	7.5	(2.6)	c	c	c	c	31.4	(4.1)	485	(21.5)	-0.02	(0.2)
Denmark	30.8	(1.7)	440	(5.6)	-0.52	(0.1)	9.8	(1.4)	442	(10.5)	-0.18	(0.1)	21.2	(2.0)	420	(8.3)	-0.42	(0.1)
Estonia	9.7	(2.0)	454	(14.5)	-0.12	(0.1)	6.3	(1.1)	c	c	c	c	1.1	(0.5)	c	c	c	c
Finland	28.4	(4.4)	476	(16.7)	0.21	(0.2)	10.2	(2.6)	c	c	c	c	45.5	(5.0)	446	(19.7)	-0.18	(0.2)
France	25.4	(2.4)	433	(13.3)	-0.92	(0.1)	9.3	(1.4)	451	(21.3)	-0.43	(0.2)	14.4	(2.1)	431	(18.6)	-0.87	(0.2)
Germany	33.1	(2.0)	448	(8.3)	-0.56	(0.1)	8.7	(1.2)	480	(11.2)	-0.27	(0.1)	25.0	(1.8)	450	(8.1)	-0.24	(0.1)
Greece	3.5	(1.2)	c	c	c	c	31.0	(2.4)	441	(16.6)	-0.75	(0.1)	35.9	(3.8)	404	(20.3)	-0.82	(0.1)
Hungary	1.7	(1.1)	c	c	c	c	52.4	(5.2)	494	(11.6)	-0.32	(0.1)	4.9	(2.6)	c	c	c	c
Iceland	c	c	c	c	c	c	14.6	(4.0)	c	c	c	c	69.4	(5.1)	425	(14.6)	-0.27	(0.1)
Ireland	1.7	(0.8)	c	c	c	c	38.2	(3.2)	494	(9.5)	0.32	(0.1)	43.6	(3.9)	444	(11.4)	-0.01	(0.1)
Israel	14.2	(1.3)	523	(9.1)	-0.04	(0.2)	9.5	(0.9)	464	(12.6)	-0.55	(0.1)	25.6	(2.3)	476	(8.9)	-0.36	(0.1)
Italy	8.9	(1.1)	443	(12.0)	-0.67	(0.2)	18.5	(1.5)	431	(9.9)	-0.47	(0.1)	58.5	(2.1)	410	(4.9)	-0.83	(0.0)
Japan	c	c	c	c	c	c	c	c	c	c	c	c	c	c	c	c	c	c
Korea	c	c	c	c	c	c	c	c	c	c	c	c	c	c	c	c	c	c
Luxembourg	47.7	(1.3)	439	(3.5)	-0.64	(0.0)	11.8	(0.7)	540	(8.3)	0.82	(0.1)	29.0	(1.2)	433	(6.0)	-0.56	(0.1)
Mexico	2.9	(1.2)	c	c	c	c	44.1	(3.6)	350	(8.8)	-1.68	(0.1)	15.2	(2.8)	284	(14.9)	-2.34	(0.2)
Netherlands	23.1	(2.1)	463	(10.8)	-0.74	(0.1)	8.9	(1.4)	483	(20.8)	-0.20	(0.2)	19.5	(2.1)	471	(15.1)	-0.52	(0.2)
New Zealand	12.1	(1.3)	469	(13.3)	-0.31	(0.1)	32.2	(1.6)	553	(5.9)	0.41	(0.0)	35.3	(1.4)	491	(6.0)	0.06	(0.0)
Norway	35.0	(3.5)	453	(9.4)	-0.02	(0.1)	5.0	(1.4)	c	c	c	c	41.9	(3.2)	440	(7.8)	-0.21	(0.1)
Poland	c	c	c	c	c	c	c	c	c	c	c	c	c	c	c	c	c	c
Portugal	2.9	(1.1)	c	c	c	c	33.1	(3.4)	463	(11.5)	-0.32	(0.1)	16.2	(2.5)	455	(10.5)	-0.27	(0.1)
Slovak Republic	13.2	(8.4)	c	c	c	c	c	c	c	c	c	c	c	c	c	c	c	c
Slovenia	41.9	(2.9)	439	(6.7)	-0.58	(0.1)	4.3	(1.2)	c	c	c	c	13.5	(2.0)	412	(11.3)	-0.81	(0.1)
Spain	5.1	(0.9)	458	(14.1)	-0.53	(0.2)	51.8	(2.8)	436	(4.5)	-0.76	(0.1)	37.0	(2.6)	414	(6.1)	-0.79	(0.1)
Sweden	39.1	(2.6)	445	(8.2)	-0.16	(0.1)	5.6	(1.2)	c	c	c	c	26.9	(2.1)	415	(13.2)	-0.35	(0.1)
Switzerland	34.6	(1.7)	465	(5.2)	-0.55	(0.0)	14.1	(2.0)	507	(10.9)	0.34	(0.1)	22.3	(1.4)	436	(6.0)	-0.59	(0.1)
Turkey	c	c	c	c	c	c	c	c	c	c	c	c	c	c	c	c	c	c
United Kingdom	17.3	(2.2)	471	(10.1)	-0.11	(0.2)	14.4	(1.8)	470	(11.8)	0.10	(0.1)	30.0	(2.5)	457	(10.3)	-0.16	(0.1)
United States	35.5	(1.7)	473	(7.2)	-0.70	(0.1)	9.0	(1.2)	513	(12.8)	0.02	(0.1)	24.3	(1.9)	476	(8.4)	-0.55	(0.1)
OECD average	20.7	(0.5)	462	(2.2)	-0.37	(0.0)	18.8	(0.4)	474	(2.9)	-0.13	(0.0)	28.0	(0.5)	439	(2.4)	-0.44	(0.0)
Partners																		
Albania	c	c	c	c	c	c	c	c	c	c	c	c	c	c	c	c	c	c
Argentina	6.9	(3.3)	c	c	c	c	29.4	(4.4)	377	(26.7)	-1.05	(0.1)	10.2	(2.8)	c	c	c	c
Azerbaijan	10.9	(4.2)	c	c	c	c	18.7	(3.6)	c	c	c	c	6.1	(2.8)	c	c	c	c
Brazil	0.1	(0.1)	c	c	c	c	31.1	(7.9)	305	(20.9)	-1.69	(0.4)	4.2	(3.1)	c	c	c	c
Bulgaria	c	c	c	c	c	c	c	c	c	c	c	c	c	c	c	c	c	c
Colombia	c	c	c	c	c	c	c	c	c	c	c	c	c	c	c	c	c	c
Croatia	1.4	(0.5)	c	c	c	c	31.1	(2.0)	454	(8.5)	-0.59	(0.1)	1.6	(0.5)	c	c	c	c
Dubai (UAE)	19.3	(0.7)	463	(3.8)	0.32	(0.0)	27.5	(0.8)	528	(3.4)	0.74	(0.0)	36.1	(0.8)	488	(3.0)	0.51	(0.0)
Hong Kong-China	3.0	(0.5)	497	(14.8)	-0.58	(0.2)	30.9	(1.4)	520	(4.9)	-1.35	(0.0)	8.3	(1.0)	484	(12.3)	-1.49	(0.1)
Indonesia	c	c	c	c	c	c	c	c	c	c	c	c	c	c	c	c	c	c
Jordan	3.8	(0.7)	389	(19.2)	-0.30	(0.2)	21.4	(1.6)	420	(9.2)	-0.15	(0.1)	2.4	(0.4)	c	c	c	c
Kazakhstan	5.2	(1.6)	381	(18.4)	-0.74	(0.3)	33.2	(3.9)	360	(9.4)	-0.80	(0.1)	4.4	(1.0)	411	(18.5)	-0.48	(0.1)
Kyrgyzstan	8.2	(4.3)	c	c	c	c	29.9	(5.5)	c	c	c	c	10.3	(4.6)	c	c	c	c
Latvia	15.8	(4.4)	c	c	c	c	c	c	c	c	c	c	c	c	c	c	c	c
Liechtenstein	18.9	(4.0)	c	c	c	c	25.6	(4.6)	c	c	c	c	28.4	(4.5)	c	c	c	c
Lithuania	34.0	(8.0)	c	c	c	c	c	c	c	c	c	c	c	c	c	c	c	c
Macao-China	6.1	(0.3)	451	(4.5)	-0.23	(0.1)	20.2	(0.6)	496	(2.5)	-0.82	(0.0)	1.8	(0.2)	447	(8.7)	-0.25	(0.1)
Montenegro	2.7	(1.4)	c	c	c	c	54.3	(3.6)	415	(7.7)	-0.16	(0.1)	7.3	(2.8)	c	c	c	c
Panama	11.1	(3.3)	412	(34.6)	-0.48	(0.2)	36.5	(5.1)	371	(42.6)	-0.47	(0.3)	31.7	(5.8)	c	c	c	c
Peru	c	c	c	c	c	c	c	c	c	c	c	c	c	c	c	c	c	c
Qatar	14.8	(0.6)	390	(5.4)	0.39	(0.0)	30.1	(0.7)	449	(3.0)	0.66	(0.0)	27.0	(0.6)	470	(3.7)	0.66	(0.0)
Romania	c	c	c	c	c	c	c	c	c	c	c	c	c	c	c	c	c	c
Russian Federation	10.4	(5.0)	389	(26.1)	-0.57	(0.1)	31.6	(3.2)	459	(7.7)	-0.23	(0.1)	8.9	(1.5)	392	(14.4)	-0.57	(0.1)
Serbia	1.1	(0.5)	c	c	c	c	43.8	(2.8)	446	(7.2)	-0.19	(0.1)	1.6	(0.6)	c	c	c	c
Shanghai-China	c	c	c	c	c	c	c	c	c	c	c	c	c	c	c	c	c	c
Singapore	23.7	(1.5)	526	(7.5)	-0.67	(0.1)	11.4	(1.1)	559	(9.4)	0.11	(0.1)	55.2	(1.9)	516	(5.4)	-0.24	(0.0)
Chinese Taipei	c	c	c	c	c	c	c	c	c	c	c	c	c	c	c	c	c	c
Thailand	c	c	c	c	c	c	c	c	c	c	c	c	c	c	c	c	c	c
Trinidad and Tobago	4.6	(2.1)	c	c	c	c	28.7	(4.5)	423	(26.4)	-0.03	(0.2)	16.8	(3.8)	c	c	c	c
Tunisia	c	c	c	c	c	c	c	c	c	c	c	c	c	c	c	c	c	c
Uruguay	c	c	c	c	c	c	c	c	c	c	c	c	c	c	c	c	c	c

Notes: Values that are statistically significant are indicated in bold (see Annex A3). The percentages of immigrant and native students speaking the language of assessment at home and not speaking the language of assessment at home is calculated over the total student population. The percentages of first- and second-generation students speaking the language of assessment at home and not speaking the language of assessment at home is calculated over the total immigrant student population.
StatLink ⟐ http://dx.doi.org/10.1787/888932343285

[Part 3/5]
Percentage of students and reading performance, by immigrant status and language spoken at home

Table II.4.4   *Results based on students' self-reports*

| | Students with an immigrant background (first- and second-generation) speaking the language of assessment at home | | | | | | Students with an immigrant background (first- and second-generation) speaking another language at home | | | | | | Increased likelihood of immigrant students speaking another language at home of scoring in the bottom quarter of the reading performance distribution | |
| | Percentage of students | | Performance on the reading scale | | PISA index of economic, social and cultural status (ESCS) | | Percentage of students | | Performance on the reading scale | | PISA index of economic, social and cultural status (ESCS) | | | |
		S.E.	Mean score	S.E.	Mean index	S.E.		S.E.	Mean score	S.E.	Mean index	S.E.	Ratio	S.E.
OECD														
Australia	14.7	(0.6)	532	(4.5)	0.43	(0.03)	8.3	(0.7)	515	(9.7)	0.19	(0.04)	**1.13**	(0.10)
Austria	3.3	(0.5)	433	(14.0)	-0.25	(0.08)	9.2	(0.8)	415	(6.8)	-0.69	(0.06)	**2.19**	(0.22)
Belgium	6.8	(0.7)	471	(8.5)	-0.04	(0.08)	7.0	(0.7)	439	(8.8)	-0.41	(0.07)	**2.31**	(0.17)
Canada	12.1	(0.8)	532	(3.8)	0.52	(0.04)	11.6	(0.8)	517	(4.8)	0.39	(0.05)	**1.29**	(0.10)
Chile	c	c	c	c	c	c	c	c	c	c	c	c	c	c
Czech Republic	1.0	(0.2)	463	(14.9)	-0.39	(0.10)	0.9	(0.1)	491	(18.1)	0.05	(0.15)	0.98	(0.39)
Denmark	3.6	(0.2)	460	(5.7)	-0.25	(0.06)	3.9	(0.2)	432	(5.3)	-0.48	(0.06)	**2.47**	(0.16)
Estonia	7.1	(0.6)	473	(6.7)	0.13	(0.07)	0.9	(0.2)	451	(13.2)	-0.01	(0.10)	**1.94**	(0.42)
Finland	0.7	(0.1)	500	(18.0)	0.31	(0.18)	1.9	(0.3)	457	(14.1)	-0.03	(0.14)	**2.34**	(0.27)
France	7.2	(0.8)	467	(9.1)	-0.49	(0.07)	4.7	(0.6)	432	(10.8)	-0.90	(0.09)	**2.25**	(0.25)
Germany	6.4	(0.5)	482	(7.0)	-0.28	(0.05)	8.9	(0.7)	449	(6.6)	-0.42	(0.06)	**2.12**	(0.20)
Greece	5.3	(0.5)	449	(9.4)	-0.55	(0.07)	3.5	(0.5)	410	(19.5)	-0.78	(0.11)	**2.19**	(0.35)
Hungary	2.0	(0.2)	509	(8.2)	-0.17	(0.10)	0.1	(0.1)	c	c	c	c	c	c
Iceland	0.5	(0.1)	c	c	c	c	1.8	(0.2)	426	(14.8)	-0.17	(0.11)	**2.25**	(0.34)
Ireland	4.4	(0.4)	500	(8.5)	0.25	(0.08)	3.6	(0.4)	445	(11.2)	0.00	(0.11)	**2.23**	(0.26)
Israel	11.1	(0.6)	482	(6.4)	-0.29	(0.06)	7.3	(0.8)	493	(8.1)	-0.24	(0.08)	0.86	(0.13)
Italy	1.7	(0.1)	448	(8.1)	-0.46	(0.07)	3.6	(0.2)	414	(4.5)	-0.81	(0.04)	**2.64**	(0.15)
Japan	c	c	c	c	c	c	c	c	c	c	c	c	c	c
Korea	c	c	c	c	c	c	c	c	c	c	c	c	c	c
Luxembourg	8.6	(0.4)	521	(5.1)	0.64	(0.05)	28.2	(0.6)	437	(3.1)	-0.61	(0.03)	**2.58**	(0.22)
Mexico	1.5	(0.1)	349	(6.9)	-1.70	(0.10)	0.3	(0.1)	278	(13.9)	-2.24	(0.16)	**3.73**	(0.28)
Netherlands	6.3	(0.9)	478	(10.8)	-0.28	(0.08)	4.7	(0.6)	467	(10.0)	-0.64	(0.10)	**1.89**	(0.22)
New Zealand	13.0	(0.6)	538	(5.2)	0.23	(0.04)	11.7	(0.6)	486	(6.4)	-0.03	(0.03)	**1.72**	(0.14)
Norway	1.6	(0.2)	489	(12.6)	0.25	(0.14)	5.3	(0.5)	446	(6.5)	-0.12	(0.06)	**2.19**	(0.17)
Poland	c	c	c	c	c	c	c	c	c	c	c	c	c	c
Portugal	4.2	(0.4)	476	(7.6)	-0.33	(0.08)	1.0	(0.2)	448	(10.5)	-0.42	(0.16)	**1.90**	(0.39)
Slovak Republic	c	c	c	c	c	c	c	c	c	c	c	c	c	c
Slovenia	3.2	(0.3)	462	(8.0)	-0.27	(0.07)	4.0	(0.3)	433	(5.6)	-0.63	(0.05)	**1.86**	(0.22)
Spain	5.5	(0.4)	439	(4.5)	-0.73	(0.06)	4.0	(0.4)	419	(6.0)	-0.75	(0.08)	**2.30**	(0.18)
Sweden	3.5	(0.3)	469	(9.2)	0.07	(0.08)	6.8	(0.8)	433	(7.8)	-0.24	(0.06)	**2.28**	(0.20)
Switzerland	9.2	(0.7)	501	(5.1)	0.00	(0.12)	12.2	(0.6)	454	(4.4)	-0.57	(0.04)	**2.26**	(0.14)
Turkey	c	c	c	c	c	c	c	c	c	c	c	c	c	c
United Kingdom	5.5	(0.7)	495	(7.6)	0.22	(0.08)	4.9	(0.5)	462	(8.3)	-0.14	(0.11)	**1.66**	(0.22)
United States	7.8	(0.6)	500	(7.8)	-0.01	(0.09)	11.5	(0.9)	475	(6.2)	-0.64	(0.08)	**1.41**	(0.13)
OECD average	5.6	(0.1)	478	(1.7)	-0.13	(0.02)	6.1	(0.1)	445	(1.9)	-0.42	(0.02)	**2.04**	(0.05)
Partners														
Albania	c	c	c	c	c	c	c	c	c	c	c	c	c	c
Argentina	2.8	(0.4)	376	(14.9)	-1.19	(0.07)	0.6	(0.2)	c	c	c	c	c	c
Azerbaijan	2.6	(0.5)	364	(9.1)	-0.55	(0.19)	0.5	(0.2)	c	c	c	c	c	c
Brazil	0.8	(0.1)	317	(14.4)	-1.41	(0.24)	0.0	(0.0)	c	c	c	c	c	c
Bulgaria	c	c	c	c	c	c	c	c	c	c	c	c	c	c
Colombia	0.3	(0.1)	309	(25.9)	-1.96	(0.27)	c	c	c	c	c	c	c	c
Croatia	10.4	(0.6)	462	(5.3)	-0.41	(0.05)	0.3	(0.1)	c	c	c	c	c	c
Dubai (UAE)	33.3	(0.7)	510	(2.3)	0.57	(0.02)	41.3	(0.6)	479	(2.2)	0.44	(0.01)	**0.60**	(0.05)
Hong Kong-China	35.0	(1.2)	537	(2.9)	-1.21	(0.03)	4.5	(0.6)	488	(11.5)	-1.24	(0.11)	**1.91**	(0.26)
Indonesia	c	c	c	c	c	c	c	c	c	c	c	c	c	c
Jordan	12.9	(0.9)	422	(6.2)	-0.33	(0.07)	0.9	(0.1)	380	(15.1)	-0.12	(0.15)	**1.68**	(0.43)
Kazakhstan	10.5	(1.1)	397	(10.3)	-0.64	(0.07)	1.1	(0.2)	395	(13.8)	-0.62	(0.17)	0.84	(0.27)
Kyrgyzstan	1.5	(0.3)	360	(18.2)	-0.63	(0.19)	0.3	(0.1)	c	c	c	c	c	c
Latvia	3.5	(0.4)	486	(9.0)	0.04	(0.11)	0.8	(0.2)	442	(20.3)	-0.45	(0.24)	**2.15**	(0.60)
Liechtenstein	15.7	(2.1)	505	(10.9)	0.18	(0.14)	14.1	(2.1)	456	(11.8)	-0.82	(0.13)	**2.28**	(0.60)
Lithuania	1.1	(0.2)	438	(13.4)	-0.19	(0.19)	0.7	(0.2)	c	c	c	c	c	c
Macao-China	64.9	(0.6)	494	(1.0)	-0.87	(0.01)	5.6	(0.2)	450	(4.2)	-0.23	(0.05)	**1.91**	(0.17)
Montenegro	5.9	(0.4)	425	(6.2)	-0.04	(0.07)	0.7	(0.2)	c	c	c	c	c	c
Panama	2.1	(0.4)	386	(30.6)	-0.41	(0.19)	1.6	(0.4)	307	(28.7)	-1.16	(0.23)	**2.66**	(0.49)
Peru	c	c	c	c	c	c	c	c	c	c	c	c	c	c
Qatar	27.0	(0.4)	423	(2.0)	0.46	(0.02)	19.4	(0.4)	442	(3.0)	0.56	(0.02)	**0.47**	(0.03)
Romania	c	c	c	c	c	c	c	c	c	c	c	c	c	c
Russian Federation	9.8	(0.6)	451	(5.1)	-0.26	(0.04)	2.3	(0.8)	390	(15.9)	-0.57	(0.09)	**2.34**	(0.41)
Serbia	9.2	(0.6)	457	(4.8)	-0.03	(0.05)	0.3	(0.1)	c	c	c	c	c	c
Shanghai-China	c	c	c	c	c	c	c	c	c	c	c	c	c	c
Singapore	3.0	(0.3)	574	(7.6)	0.16	(0.05)	11.3	(0.5)	519	(4.9)	-0.37	(0.03)	**1.22**	(0.10)
Chinese Taipei	c	c	c	c	c	c	c	c	c	c	c	c	c	c
Thailand	c	c	c	c	c	c	c	c	c	c	c	c	c	c
Trinidad and Tobago	1.8	(0.2)	420	(16.8)	-0.31	(0.12)	0.5	(0.1)	436	(34.1)	0.14	(0.21)	**1.64**	(0.54)
Tunisia	c	c	c	c	c	c	c	c	c	c	c	c	c	c
Uruguay	c	c	c	c	c	c	c	c	c	c	c	c	c	c

Notes: Values that are statistically significant are indicated in bold (see Annex A3). The percentages of immigrant and native students speaking the language of assessment at home and not speaking the language of assessment at home is calculated over the total student population. The percentages of first- and second-generation students speaking the language of assessment at home and not speaking the language of assessment at home is calculated over the total immigrant student population.

StatLink 🔗 http://dx.doi.org/10.1787/888932343285

[Part 4/5]

Percentage of students and reading performance, by immigrant status and language spoken at home

Table II.4.4   *Results based on students' self-reports*

	Pooled within-country correlations between school immigrant status and language spoken at home		Difference in reading performance between:							
			Native students and students with an immigrant background who speak a language at home that is different from the language of assessment		Native students and students with an immigrant background who speak a language at home that is different from the language of assessment, after accounting for ESCS		Native students speaking the language of assessment at home and native students speaking another language		Native students speaking the language of assessment at home and native students speaking another language, after accounting for ESCS	
	Correlation	S.E.	Dif.	S.E.	Dif.	S.E.	Dif.	S.E.	Dif.	S.E.
OECD										
Australia	0.87	(0.02)	1	(9.6)	-8	(8.5)	55	(12.2)	45	(12.2)
Austria	0.90	(0.02)	69	(7.5)	31	(7.3)	54	(18.9)	38	(15.6)
Belgium	0.39	(0.07)	82	(8.7)	48	(7.6)	19	(5.5)	7	(5.0)
Canada	0.73	(0.02)	12	(5.1)	7	(4.6)	35	(5.3)	33	(4.8)
Chile	0.04	(0.05)	c	c	c	c	c	c	c	c
Czech Republic	0.55	(0.07)	-10	(17.6)	-4	(15.4)	c	c	c	c
Denmark	0.88	(0.01)	70	(5.4)	39	(4.9)	47	(20.5)	36	(19.9)
Estonia	0.08	(0.07)	55	(13.5)	50	(13.3)	36	(9.5)	31	(9.5)
Finland	0.43	(0.05)	81	(13.9)	69	(12.6)	40	(8.0)	47	(7.8)
France	0.73	(0.07)	75	(11.3)	29	(12.4)	73	(15.4)	55	(12.5)
Germany	0.83	(0.02)	64	(6.7)	33	(6.7)	21	(13.3)	16	(12.6)
Greece	0.73	(0.10)	79	(19.3)	50	(20.6)	78	(17.4)	60	(15.4)
Hungary	0.04	(0.10)	c	c	c	c	c	c	c	c
Iceland	0.83	(0.01)	78	(14.9)	56	(15.2)	54	(16.1)	57	(15.8)
Ireland	0.27	(0.13)	57	(11.2)	56	(10.8)	-5	(14.1)	0	(12.0)
Israel	0.54	(0.12)	-11	(8.2)	-30	(7.4)	40	(20.3)	37	(17.3)
Italy	0.41	(0.05)	85	(4.9)	62	(4.8)	53	(3.8)	34	(3.4)
Japan	0.27	(0.10)	c	c	c	c	c	c	c	c
Korea	-0.01	(0.01)	c	c	c	c	c	c	c	c
Luxembourg	-0.55	(0.00)	63	(4.0)	26	(4.6)	17	(11.6)	9	(12.0)
Mexico	0.49	(0.06)	152	(13.5)	128	(12.0)	79	(7.6)	54	(7.4)
Netherlands	0.72	(0.10)	50	(8.8)	12	(9.3)	6	(23.7)	1	(22.0)
New Zealand	0.84	(0.02)	40	(7.1)	34	(5.9)	98	(9.4)	76	(9.8)
Norway	0.89	(0.03)	62	(6.7)	40	(6.4)	44	(10.0)	44	(9.0)
Poland	-0.03	(0.01)	c	c	c	c	c	c	c	c
Portugal	0.49	(0.11)	45	(10.8)	41	(9.8)	-1	(14.6)	6	(13.3)
Slovak Republic	0.04	(0.04)	c	c	c	c	71	(12.3)	49	(9.5)
Slovenia	0.78	(0.03)	56	(5.8)	27	(6.2)	24	(14.7)	18	(14.4)
Spain	0.11	(0.05)	69	(5.8)	55	(5.7)	0	(4.0)	0	(4.6)
Sweden	0.92	(0.02)	75	(8.1)	46	(7.2)	55	(19.1)	43	(16.9)
Switzerland	0.66	(0.05)	62	(4.1)	34	(4.2)	26	(7.7)	25	(6.6)
Turkey	0.08	(0.11)	c	c	c	c	59	(12.1)	29	(12.1)
United Kingdom	0.75	(0.06)	37	(8.5)	20	(6.2)	68	(11.5)	62	(11.1)
United States	0.93	(0.02)	32	(6.5)	-10	(5.0)	55	(14.5)	26	(12.9)
OECD average	0.49	(0.01)	57	(1.9)	35	(1.8)	43	(2.6)	33	(2.4)
Partners										
Albania	0.11	(0.13)	c	c	c	c	22	(19.9)	22	(15.2)
Argentina	0.34	(0.10)	c	c	c	c	c	c	c	c
Azerbaijan	0.12	(0.09)	c	c	c	c	-24	(11.0)	-15	(8.5)
Brazil	0.04	(0.05)	c	c	c	c	54	(12.4)	65	(12.7)
Bulgaria	0.00	(0.05)	c	c	c	c	103	(10.5)	61	(10.4)
Colombia	0.01	(0.05)	c	c	c	c	45	(25.8)	67	(23.7)
Croatia	0.05	(0.05)	c	c	c	c	9	(21.6)	6	(17.4)
Dubai (UAE)	0.39	(0.00)	-83	(3.3)	-76	(3.2)	-29	(5.5)	-9	(5.8)
Hong Kong-China	0.11	(0.12)	49	(11.7)	35	(11.1)	73	(9.2)	90	(8.2)
Indonesia	-0.01	(0.04)	c	c	c	c	9	(6.4)	-6	(4.7)
Jordan	0.10	(0.08)	28	(15.5)	40	(16.2)	20	(12.7)	25	(14.3)
Kazakhstan	0.00	(0.05)	-4	(14.1)	-9	(13.1)	-17	(8.0)	-9	(6.7)
Kyrgyzstan	0.15	(0.07)	c	c	c	c	-52	(6.5)	-30	(5.4)
Latvia	0.08	(0.08)	45	(19.5)	36	(18.5)	16	(9.6)	8	(8.1)
Liechtenstein	0.56	(0.01)	57	(13.7)	34	(14.7)	c	c	c	c
Lithuania	0.36	(0.10)	c	c	c	c	41	(7.9)	32	(7.2)
Macao-China	-0.52	(0.00)	34	(4.6)	36	(4.5)	42	(4.3)	56	(4.5)
Montenegro	0.27	(0.16)	c	c	c	c	48	(14.6)	36	(15.5)
Panama	0.65	(0.07)	75	(28.2)	64	(25.3)	68	(21.1)	56	(12.7)
Peru	0.06	(0.08)	c	c	c	c	109	(8.3)	61	(8.7)
Qatar	0.13	(0.00)	-109	(3.7)	-108	(3.6)	10	(2.8)	17	(2.7)
Romania	0.06	(0.10)	c	c	c	c	67	(13.2)	48	(10.9)
Russian Federation	0.04	(0.16)	74	(15.6)	58	(14.1)	47	(9.6)	31	(7.6)
Serbia	0.12	(0.10)	c	c	c	c	37	(12.3)	20	(12.1)
Shanghai-China	0.40	(0.10)	c	c	c	c	65	(12.1)	41	(10.4)
Singapore	-0.08	(0.04)	10	(5.4)	14	(5.2)	58	(3.0)	28	(3.4)
Chinese Taipei	-0.09	(0.06)	c	c	c	c	38	(4.5)	22	(4.3)
Thailand	c	c	c	c	c	c	18	(4.4)	-2	(3.6)
Trinidad and Tobago	0.42	(0.01)	-12	(34.1)	16	(35.0)	74	(14.9)	70	(15.0)
Tunisia	0.55	(0.17)	c	c	c	c	c	c	c	c
Uruguay	0.06	(0.05)	c	c	c	c	47	(9.0)	25	(8.4)

Notes: Values that are statistically significant are indicated in bold (see Annex A3). The percentages of immigrant and native students speaking the language of assessment at home and not speaking the language of assessment at home is calculated over the total student population. The percentages of first- and second-generation students speaking the language of assessment at home and not speaking the language of assessment at home is calculated over the total immigrant student population.

StatLink ⟐⟐⟐ http://dx.doi.org/10.1787/888932343285

[Part 5/5]
Percentage of students and reading performance, by immigrant status and language spoken at home

Table II.4.4 *Results based on students' self-reports*

| | Difference in reading performance between: | | | | | | | |
| | Students with an immigrant background speaking the language of assessment at home and immigrant students speaking another language | | Students with an immigrant background speaking the language of assessment at home and students with an immigrant background speaking another language, after accounting for ESCS | | Native students speaking another language at home and students with an immigrant background speaking another language at home | | Native students speaking another language at home and students with an immigrant background speaking another language at home, after accounting for ESCS | |
	Dif.	S.E.	Dif.	S.E.	Dif.	S.E.	Dif.	S.E.
Australia	18	(7.0)	6	(6.8)	-54	(16.8)	-53	(16.1)
Austria	18	(14.1)	3	(12.8)	16	(20.1)	-3	(17.5)
Belgium	32	(9.6)	19	(9.2)	66	(9.3)	46	(8.4)
Canada	15	(5.0)	11	(4.8)	-22	(7.3)	-25	(6.5)
Chile	c	c	c	c	c	c	c	c
Czech Republic	-28	(22.9)	-6	(21.2)	c	c	c	c
Denmark	27	(7.2)	20	(6.7)	24	(20.9)	7	(20.4)
Estonia	23	(14.4)	20	(14.5)	19	(15.6)	19	(15.6)
Finland	42	(19.7)	30	(19.2)	42	(17.5)	20	(16.8)
France	35	(10.4)	17	(11.0)	3	(17.4)	-17	(16.6)
Germany	34	(8.8)	28	(8.7)	44	(14.1)	24	(14.3)
Greece	39	(16.0)	31	(16.0)	2	(24.7)	-6	(23.6)
Hungary	c	c	c	c	c	c	c	c
Iceland	c	c	c	c	25	(21.9)	-3	(28.3)
Ireland	54	(14.1)	46	(14.1)	62	(16.9)	56	(16.3)
Israel	-10	(8.2)	-12	(7.9)	-49	(18.6)	-61	(16.3)
Italy	34	(9.7)	24	(8.5)	38	(5.9)	34	(5.7)
Japan	c	c	c	c	c	c	c	c
Korea	c	c	c	c	c	c	c	c
Luxembourg	84	(6.1)	43	(6.6)	62	(3.9)	26	(4.6)
Mexico	71	(15.5)	62	(14.0)	76	(14.3)	76	(13.1)
Netherlands	11	(11.6)	4	(11.0)	44	(23.5)	20	(23.8)
New Zealand	53	(7.3)	39	(7.0)	-54	(11.6)	-37	(11.9)
Norway	43	(14.2)	29	(12.2)	20	(12.7)	-8	(11.8)
Poland	c	c	c	c	c	c	c	c
Portugal	28	(10.6)	25	(10.7)	45	(17.9)	32	(17.7)
Slovak Republic	c	c	c	c	c	c	c	c
Slovenia	29	(9.9)	24	(10.5)	32	(15.7)	17	(16.0)
Spain	20	(7.2)	19	(7.5)	69	(6.8)	61	(6.4)
Sweden	36	(10.1)	20	(9.6)	21	(20.1)	2	(17.4)
Switzerland	47	(6.0)	29	(7.6)	37	(9.4)	13	(9.2)
Turkey	c	c	c	c	c	c	c	c
United Kingdom	32	(8.4)	19	(8.3)	-30	(12.4)	-39	(11.7)
United States	26	(8.1)	5	(7.0)	-22	(14.9)	-31	(14.1)
OECD average	31	(2.3)	22	(2.2)	20	(3.1)	7	(3.1)
Albania	c	c	c	c	c	c	c	c
Argentina	c	c	c	c	c	c	c	c
Azerbaijan	c	c	c	c	c	c	c	c
Brazil	c	c	c	c	c	c	c	c
Bulgaria	c	c	c	c	c	c	c	c
Colombia	c	c	c	c	c	c	c	c
Croatia	c	c	c	c	c	c	c	c
Dubai (UAE)	30	(3.3)	23	(3.3)	-64	(4.9)	-78	(4.8)
Hong Kong-China	49	(11.4)	50	(10.9)	-21	(11.5)	-52	(14.0)
Indonesia	c	c	c	c	c	c	c	c
Jordan	42	(16.9)	48	(17.6)	9	(20.5)	12	(20.7)
Kazakhstan	2	(14.5)	3	(12.9)	11	(14.0)	-3	(13.5)
Kyrgyzstan	c	c	c	c	c	c	c	c
Latvia	44	(21.3)	26	(19.1)	30	(19.0)	30	(18.7)
Liechtenstein	49	(17.0)	43	(20.5)	c	c	c	c
Lithuania	c	c	c	c	c	c	c	c
Macao-China	44	(4.2)	55	(4.1)	0	(6.0)	-5	(6.1)
Montenegro	c	c	c	c	c	c	c	c
Panama	79	(25.0)	33	(21.9)	10	(29.6)	11	(25.5)
Peru	c	c	c	c	c	c	c	c
Qatar	-19	(3.9)	-14	(3.6)	-115	(4.5)	-127	(4.1)
Romania	c	c	c	c	c	c	c	c
Russian Federation	60	(16.7)	54	(16.9)	30	(18.4)	30	(17.1)
Serbia	c	c	c	c	c	c	c	c
Shanghai-China	c	c	c	c	c	c	c	c
Singapore	55	(9.1)	36	(9.0)	-16	(5.7)	0	(5.7)
Chinese Taipei	c	c	c	c	c	c	c	c
Thailand	c	c	c	c	c	c	c	c
Trinidad and Tobago	-16	(41.7)	11	(39.2)	-85	(35.9)	-74	(39.9)
Tunisia	c	c	c	c	c	c	c	c
Uruguay	c	c	c	c	c	c	c	c

Notes: Values that are statistically significant are indicated in bold (see Annex A3). The percentages of immigrant and native students speaking the language of assessment at home and not speaking the language of assessment at home is calculated over the total student population. The percentages of first- and second-generation students speaking the language of assessment at home and not speaking the language of assessment at home is calculated over the total immigrant student population.
StatLink http://dx.doi.org/10.1787/888932343285

[Part 1/1]

Performance of students with an immigrant background in the host country, by country of origin

Table II.4.5   *Results based on students' self-reports*

Host country	Country of origin	Performance in reading		Performance in reading after accounting for socio-economic background within each immigrant group		Performance in reading after accounting for socio-economic background of the host country	
		Mean score	S.E.	Mean score	S.E.	Mean score	S.E.
Australia	China	566	(17.1)	561	(14.9)	563	(14.8)
	Korea	529	(18.8)	528	(16.5)	524	(16.4)
	Philippines	513	(8.5)	518	(7.5)	524	(7.4)
	South Africa	531	(8.5)	520	(8.8)	510	(8.2)
	United Kingdom	528	(3.4)	532	(3.2)	522	(3.2)
	United States	550	(10.8)	546	(11.1)	548	(11.0)
Austria	Former Yugoslavia	418	(7.3)	423	(7.0)	444	(6.9)
	Germany	483	(10.5)	482	(9.3)	473	(9.1)
	Poland	489	(20.4)	491	(20.5)	496	(21.1)
	Turkey	375	(6.4)	379	(6.3)	422	(6.7)
Belgium	France	479	(15.2)	495	(11.8)	488	(12.1)
	Germany	487	(10.4)	491	(9.6)	489	(9.5)
	Turkey	413	(10.2)	413	(10.4)	457	(10.9)
	African countries	469	(6.9)	480	(5.6)	486	(5.6)
Czech Republic	Russian Federation	461	(13.7)	463	(15.0)	462	(16.1)
Denmark	Former Yugoslavia	454	(9.5)	453	(9.1)	475	(9.2)
	Pakistan	430	(9.3)	437	(11.5)	463	(12.1)
	Turkey	416	(5.9)	417	(5.7)	455	(5.9)
Finland	Russian Federation	505	(13.4)	494	(14.1)	507	(13.7)
	Sweden	505	(8.1)	511	(7.6)	509	(7.7)
Germany	Former Yugoslavia	448	(13.9)	446	(12.6)	466	(11.7)
	Italy	465	(13.8)	470	(13.2)	480	(13.1)
	Poland	481	(7.7)	481	(7.6)	489	(7.8)
	Russian Federation	483	(6.3)	487	(6.2)	500	(6.3)
	Turkey	426	(6.5)	424	(6.5)	462	(6.7)
Greece	Albania	439	(11.9)	440	(11.9)	464	(11.7)
	Russian Federation	431	(17.0)	442	(14.9)	444	(14.6)
Ireland	United Kingdom	504	(4.7)	524	(4.2)	501	(4.1)
Israel	France	498	(9.0)	497	(9.6)	481	(9.5)
	Russian Federation	504	(6.2)	505	(5.8)	505	(5.9)
	United States	539	(11.5)	532	(10.6)	520	(10.7)
Luxembourg	Former Yugoslavia	412	(7.3)	413	(7.1)	433	(7.2)
	France	499	(4.9)	492	(4.6)	487	(4.6)
	Germany	500	(6.6)	484	(6.4)	483	(6.3)
	Italy	443	(7.1)	440	(7.1)	443	(7.0)
	Portugal	413	(3.1)	427	(4.0)	451	(4.2)
	United Kingdom	545	(13.7)	516	(14.4)	503	(13.5)
Mexico	United States	415	(7.6)	434	(8.6)	401	(7.9)
Netherlands	Germany	529	(16.6)	528	(14.3)	529	(14.4)
	Turkey	446	(11.1)	448	(10.2)	484	(11.2)
New Zealand	China	564	(10.5)	572	(10.1)	563	(9.5)
	Korea	508	(11.1)	510	(11.2)	494	(11.4)
	South Africa	545	(10.5)	555	(9.0)	527	(9.1)
	United Kingdom	559	(4.4)	566	(4.1)	542	(4.0)
Norway	Sweden	492	(12.6)	485	(10.8)	490	(11.3)
Portugal	Brazil	499	(7.1)	486	(8.0)	488	(6.6)
	African countries	496	(5.5)	498	(4.0)	485	(4.2)
Switzerland	Albania	384	(14.1)	382	(13.7)	413	(13.7)
	Austria	506	(10.8)	510	(10.1)	505	(9.9)
	Former Yugoslavia	450	(4.9)	454	(4.6)	471	(4.7)
	France	538	(8.4)	530	(6.2)	521	(6.1)
	Germany	538	(6.4)	528	(6.2)	522	(6.1)
	Italy	476	(5.8)	477	(5.5)	480	(5.3)
	Portugal	482	(9.7)	492	(10.1)	517	(10.0)
Switzerland	Turkey	425	(9.8)	424	(9.6)	455	(10.2)
Turkey	Germany	478	(16.5)	508	(12.4)	458	(13.1)
United Kingdom	Pakistan	507	(16.7)	500	(16.3)	509	(16.3)
	African countries	487	(15.3)	480	(14.0)	483	(13.7)
Argentina	Brazil	349	(31.6)	356	(33.0)	349	(32.7)
Croatia	Italy	471	(18.0)	469	(19.9)	460	(22.9)
Liechtenstein	Austria	519	(11.4)	513	(10.3)	511	(10.3)
Macao-China	Philippines	444	(12.6)	444	(12.0)	433	(12.4)
	Portugal	486	(11.5)	463	(11.6)	472	(11.4)
Montenegro	Albania	373	(14.3)	376	(13.1)	392	(13.1)
Uruguay	Brazil	413	(12.9)	425	(13.5)	417	(13.0)

StatLink http://dx.doi.org/10.1787/888932343285

PISA 2009 RESULTS: OVERCOMING SOCIAL BACKGROUND – VOLUME II

[Part 1/2]
Characteristics of schools attended by students with and without an immigrant background
(Scores standardised within each country sample)

Table II.4.6 *Results based on students' self-reports and school principals' reports*

					Positive mean index indicates more favourable characteristics												
	Percentage of students in schools that have more than 25% students with an immigrant background		Percentage of students in schools that have more than 50% students with an immigrant background		School average PISA index of economic, social and cultural status						Index of quality of educational resources					
					Native students		Immigrant students		Difference (N-I)		Native students		Immigrant students		Difference (N-I)	
	%	S.E.	%	S.E.	Mean index	S.E.	Mean index	S.E.	Dif.	S.E.	Mean index	S.E.	Mean index	S.E.	Dif.	S.E.
Australia	38.2	(2.7)	11.2	(2.0)	-0.02	(0.03)	0.11	(0.08)	-0.13	(0.07)	-0.01	(0.06)	0.05	(0.08)	-0.06	(0.08)
Austria	20.7	(2.9)	7.0	(1.6)	0.10	(0.04)	-0.52	(0.11)	**0.62**	(0.11)	0.03	(0.07)	-0.16	(0.10)	0.19	(0.10)
Belgium	18.5	(2.3)	8.2	(1.9)	0.10	(0.03)	-0.46	(0.11)	**0.56**	(0.11)	0.05	(0.06)	-0.24	(0.11)	**0.29**	(0.09)
Canada	36.7	(2.1)	19.2	(2.2)	-0.02	(0.03)	0.11	(0.09)	-0.13	(0.08)	-0.02	(0.04)	0.07	(0.08)	-0.10	(0.07)
Chile	0.0	(0.0)	0.0	c	0.01	(0.04)	c	c	c	c	0.01	(0.07)	c	c	c	c
Czech Republic	0.4	(0.2)	0.0	c	0.00	(0.04)	0.03	(0.14)	-0.03	(0.13)	0.00	(0.07)	0.16	(0.12)	-0.16	(0.10)
Denmark	7.2	(0.7)	2.6	(0.3)	0.06	(0.06)	-0.62	(0.07)	**0.68**	(0.07)	0.00	(0.08)	0.03	(0.06)	-0.04	(0.07)
Estonia	12.4	(1.5)	1.8	(1.0)	0.01	(0.05)	-0.15	(0.09)	0.16	(0.08)	0.00	(0.07)	0.01	(0.10)	-0.02	(0.11)
Finland	0.0	(0.0)	0.0	c	-0.01	(0.07)	0.18	(0.14)	-0.19	(0.11)	-0.01	(0.07)	0.31	(0.20)	-0.32	(0.16)
France	16.6	(3.0)	5.3	(1.9)	0.09	(0.06)	-0.52	(0.12)	**0.61**	(0.12)	w	w	w	w	w	w
Germany	27.2	(2.8)	5.5	(1.4)	0.12	(0.05)	-0.47	(0.07)	**0.59**	(0.07)	0.03	(0.08)	-0.17	(0.08)	**0.20**	(0.07)
Greece	7.9	(1.3)	3.8	(1.1)	0.06	(0.06)	-0.61	(0.10)	**0.67**	(0.11)	0.02	(0.08)	-0.19	(0.17)	0.21	(0.16)
Hungary	0.0	c	0.0	c	0.00	(0.04)	0.26	(0.13)	**-0.26**	(0.13)	0.00	(0.08)	0.09	(0.15)	-0.09	(0.12)
Iceland	0.6	(0.0)	0.0	c	0.02	(0.01)	-0.38	(0.12)	**0.40**	(0.12)	0.00	(0.01)	-0.19	(0.09)	**0.19**	(0.09)
Ireland	4.7	(1.7)	0.0	c	0.02	(0.06)	-0.02	(0.10)	0.03	(0.09)	0.00	(0.09)	-0.05	(0.12)	0.05	(0.08)
Israel	32.5	(3.4)	7.0	(2.0)	0.07	(0.06)	-0.18	(0.09)	**0.25**	(0.08)	-0.01	(0.08)	0.09	(0.08)	-0.10	(0.08)
Italy	3.0	(0.5)	0.9	(0.2)	0.03	(0.02)	-0.49	(0.09)	**0.52**	(0.09)	0.00	(0.03)	-0.02	(0.06)	0.02	(0.05)
Japan	0.0	c	0.0	c	0.00	(0.04)	c	c	c	c	0.00	(0.08)	c	c	c	c
Korea	0.0	c	0.0	c	0.00	(0.07)	c	c	c	c	0.00	(0.09)	c	c	c	c
Luxembourg	72.4	(0.1)	23.9	(0.1)	0.11	(0.01)	-0.15	(0.02)	**0.26**	(0.03)	0.05	(0.01)	-0.07	(0.01)	**0.12**	(0.02)
Mexico	0.6	(0.2)	0.2	(0.1)	0.03	(0.03)	-0.48	(0.08)	**0.51**	(0.07)	0.02	(0.03)	-0.40	(0.08)	**0.42**	(0.08)
Netherlands	12.2	(2.3)	4.7	(1.7)	0.13	(0.05)	-0.89	(0.21)	**1.02**	(0.19)	0.00	(0.09)	-0.02	(0.17)	0.02	(0.18)
New Zealand	37.6	(3.0)	13.8	(1.8)	0.00	(0.04)	0.04	(0.07)	-0.04	(0.08)	-0.03	(0.06)	0.11	(0.07)	**-0.14**	(0.06)
Norway	3.0	(1.0)	1.0	(0.7)	0.02	(0.07)	-0.18	(0.16)	0.19	(0.13)	-0.02	(0.07)	0.27	(0.12)	**-0.29**	(0.10)
Poland	0.0	c	0.0	c	0.00	(0.05)	c	c	c	c	0.00	(0.07)	c	c	c	c
Portugal	2.1	(0.9)	0.7	(0.4)	0.00	(0.06)	0.01	(0.09)	-0.01	(0.09)	0.00	(0.08)	-0.08	(0.08)	0.08	(0.09)
Slovak Republic	0.0	c	0.0	c	0.00	(0.05)	c	c	c	c	0.00	(0.08)	c	c	c	c
Slovenia	7.5	(0.3)	0.4	(0.2)	0.04	(0.01)	-0.45	(0.04)	**0.49**	(0.05)	0.00	(0.01)	0.02	(0.06)	-0.01	(0.06)
Spain	10.5	(1.5)	0.6	(0.3)	0.03	(0.03)	-0.24	(0.06)	**0.27**	(0.05)	0.01	(0.06)	-0.06	(0.07)	0.07	(0.06)
Sweden	12.4	(2.7)	3.1	(1.4)	0.06	(0.06)	-0.40	(0.16)	**0.46**	(0.15)	0.02	(0.07)	-0.15	(0.17)	0.18	(0.17)
Switzerland	40.1	(3.5)	8.7	(1.6)	0.06	(0.06)	-0.17	(0.08)	**0.23**	(0.07)	0.02	(0.08)	-0.08	(0.09)	**0.11**	(0.05)
Turkey	0.0	c	0.0	c	0.01	(0.06)	c	c	c	c	0.00	(0.08)	c	c	c	c
United Kingdom	12.6	(2.0)	5.5	(1.4)	0.05	(0.04)	-0.27	(0.09)	0.31	(0.19)	0.02	(0.07)	-0.16	(0.10)	0.18	(0.10)
United States	30.7	(3.1)	12.7	(2.2)	0.13	(0.07)	-0.50	(0.12)	**0.63**	(0.11)	0.01	(0.06)	-0.04	(0.13)	0.05	(0.12)
OECD average	13.8	(0.4)	4.3	(0.3)	0.04	(0.01)	-0.26	(0.02)	**0.31**	(0.02)	0.01	(0.01)	-0.03	(0.02)	**0.04**	(0.02)
Albania	0.3	(0.3)	0.0	c	0.01	(0.06)	c	c	c	c	0.01	(0.08)	c	c	c	c
Argentina	1.5	(0.9)	0.3	(0.3)	0.01	(0.07)	-0.36	(0.11)	**0.37**	(0.11)	0.01	(0.08)	-0.13	(0.13)	0.14	(0.11)
Azerbaijan	2.0	(1.0)	0.4	(0.4)	0.00	(0.06)	0.14	(0.29)	-0.14	(0.30)	-0.01	(0.09)	0.12	(0.25)	-0.12	(0.22)
Brazil	0.0	(0.0)	0.0	(0.0)	0.02	(0.04)	-0.31	(0.10)	**0.33**	(0.10)	0.01	(0.04)	-0.19	(0.14)	0.21	(0.13)
Bulgaria	0.0	c	0.0	c	0.02	(0.07)	c	c	c	c	0.00	(0.09)	c	c	c	c
Colombia	0.0	c	0.0	c	0.01	(0.06)	-0.24	(0.18)	0.25	(0.18)	0.00	(0.07)	-0.07	(0.18)	0.07	(0.20)
Croatia	8.1	(2.0)	0.0	c	0.01	(0.05)	-0.04	(0.08)	0.05	(0.06)	0.00	(0.08)	-0.03	(0.11)	0.03	(0.07)
Dubai (UAE)	81.7	(0.1)	68.3	(0.2)	-0.39	(0.02)	0.17	(0.01)	**-0.57**	(0.02)	-0.39	(0.02)	0.16	(0.01)	**-0.56**	(0.02)
Hong Kong-China	81.2	(3.0)	26.0	(3.7)	0.19	(0.08)	-0.29	(0.05)	**0.49**	(0.07)	0.04	(0.09)	-0.06	(0.09)	0.11	(0.06)
Indonesia	0.0	c	0.0	c	0.00	(0.08)	c	c	c	c	0.00	(0.09)	c	c	c	c
Jordan	19.9	(2.7)	1.1	(1.1)	-0.05	(0.05)	0.38	(0.10)	**-0.44**	(0.08)	0.00	(0.07)	0.03	(0.13)	-0.03	(0.11)
Kazakhstan	12.7	(2.4)	5.4	(1.3)	0.01	(0.07)	-0.08	(0.13)	0.09	(0.12)	0.01	(0.07)	-0.10	(0.12)	0.12	(0.11)
Kyrgyzstan	0.4	(0.4)	0.4	(0.4)	0.00	(0.05)	0.33	(0.30)	-0.33	(0.29)	0.00	(0.08)	0.12	(0.30)	-0.12	(0.29)
Latvia	3.7	(1.1)	0.0	c	0.00	(0.06)	0.04	(0.15)	-0.04	(0.14)	0.00	(0.07)	0.02	(0.09)	-0.02	(0.09)
Liechtenstein	59.4	(0.5)	2.5	(0.2)	0.06	(0.03)	-0.18	(0.07)	**0.24**	(0.10)	-0.05	(0.03)	0.17	(0.07)	**-0.23**	(0.10)
Lithuania	0.6	(0.6)	0.0	c	0.01	(0.04)	-0.10	(0.11)	0.11	(0.10)	0.00	(0.07)	0.31	(0.20)	-0.32	(0.19)
Macao-China	100.0	(0.0)	85.2	(0.1)	0.39	(0.02)	-0.16	(0.01)	**0.55**	(0.03)	0.08	(0.02)	-0.03	(0.01)	**0.12**	(0.03)
Montenegro	4.3	(0.3)	0.3	(0.3)	-0.01	(0.03)	0.29	(0.09)	**-0.31**	(0.07)	0.00	(0.01)	-0.08	(0.06)	0.08	(0.06)
Panama	3.5	(1.6)	1.0	(0.3)	0.02	(0.09)	0.24	(0.25)	-0.22	(0.26)	0.02	(0.10)	0.28	(0.29)	-0.26	(0.28)
Peru	0.0	c	0.0	c	0.02	(0.05)	c	c	c	c	0.01	(0.06)	c	c	c	c
Qatar	68.0	(0.1)	40.5	(0.1)	-0.07	(0.02)	0.10	(0.01)	**-0.17**	(0.01)	0.02	(0.01)	-0.03	(0.01)	**0.05**	(0.02)
Romania	0.0	c	0.0	c	-0.01	(0.06)	c	c	c	c	0.00	(0.07)	c	c	c	c
Russian Federation	8.1	(2.4)	1.5	(1.3)	0.02	(0.05)	-0.11	(0.10)	0.13	(0.10)	-0.01	(0.08)	0.06	(0.10)	-0.07	(0.06)
Serbia	6.3	(2.0)	0.0	c	-0.01	(0.04)	0.11	(0.08)	-0.12	(0.07)	-0.01	(0.08)	0.02	(0.12)	-0.03	(0.09)
Shanghai-China	0.0	c	0.0	c	0.01	(0.06)	c	c	c	c	0.00	(0.08)	c	c	c	c
Singapore	10.0	(0.3)	0.3	(0.2)	-0.03	(0.01)	0.20	(0.04)	**-0.23**	(0.04)	0.01	(0.04)	0.01	(0.04)	-0.01	(0.04)
Chinese Taipei	0.0	c	0.0	c	0.01	(0.06)	c	c	c	c	0.00	(0.07)	c	c	c	c
Thailand	0.0	c	0.0	c	0.00	(0.05)	c	c	c	c	0.00	(0.07)	c	c	c	c
Trinidad and Tobago	0.7	(0.0)	0.3	(0.0)	0.01	(0.01)	0.49	(0.12)	**-0.49**	(0.12)	0.01	(0.01)	0.07	(0.13)	-0.06	(0.13)
Tunisia	0.0	c	0.0	c	0.00	(0.07)	c	c	c	c	0.00	(0.09)	c	c	c	c
Uruguay	0.0	c	0.0	c	0.01	(0.03)	c	c	c	c	0.00	(0.06)	c	c	c	c

Note: Values that are statistically significant are indicated in bold (see Annex A3).
StatLink ⟶ http://dx.doi.org/10.1787/888932343285

[Part 2/2]

Characteristics of schools attended by students with and without an immigrant background
(Scores standardised within each country sample)

Table II.4.6   *Results based on students' self-reports and school principals' reports*

	Negative mean index indicates more favourable characteristics											
	Student/teacher ratio						Index of teacher shortage					
	Native students		Immigrant students		Difference (N-I)		Native students		Immigrant students		Difference (N-I)	
	Mean index	S.E.	Mean index	S.E.	Dif.	S.E.	Mean index	S.E.	Mean index	S.E.	Dif.	S.E.
Australia	-0.01	(0.05)	0.03	(0.10)	-0.04	(0.08)	0.03	(0.06)	-0.12	(0.08)	**0.15**	(0.07)
Austria	0.03	(0.06)	-0.15	(0.08)	**0.18**	(0.08)	-0.01	(0.08)	0.07	(0.11)	-0.08	(0.10)
Belgium	0.03	(0.04)	-0.11	(0.11)	0.14	(0.10)	-0.04	(0.06)	0.20	(0.08)	**-0.24**	(0.08)
Canada	0.01	(0.04)	-0.03	(0.07)	0.04	(0.06)	0.05	(0.03)	-0.18	(0.06)	**0.22**	(0.06)
Chile	0.01	(0.09)	c	c	c	c	0.00	(0.09)	c	c	c	c
Czech Republic	0.00	(0.06)	0.28	(0.19)	-0.28	(0.17)	0.00	(0.06)	0.08	(0.11)	-0.08	(0.10)
Denmark	0.02	(0.06)	-0.19	(0.06)	**0.20**	(0.07)	-0.01	(0.07)	0.10	(0.07)	-0.11	(0.06)
Estonia	0.01	(0.07)	-0.08	(0.14)	0.09	(0.12)	0.01	(0.07)	-0.09	(0.10)	0.09	(0.09)
Finland	0.00	(0.08)	0.11	(0.14)	-0.11	(0.10)	0.00	(0.07)	-0.08	(0.15)	0.08	(0.14)
France	w	w	w	w	w	w	w	w	w	w	w	w
Germany	0.00	(0.06)	-0.01	(0.09)	0.01	(0.07)	-0.03	(0.07)	0.15	(0.09)	**-0.18**	(0.06)
Greece	0.01	(0.08)	-0.11	(0.10)	0.12	(0.10)	0.00	(0.08)	0.02	(0.10)	-0.03	(0.10)
Hungary	0.00	(0.09)	-0.17	(0.11)	0.17	(0.10)	0.00	(0.09)	-0.12	(0.12)	0.12	(0.10)
Iceland	0.01	(0.01)	-0.39	(0.10)	**0.40**	(0.11)	-0.01	(0.01)	0.29	(0.10)	**-0.30**	(0.10)
Ireland	0.03	(0.08)	-0.14	(0.11)	**0.17**	(0.08)	0.00	(0.09)	0.08	(0.12)	-0.08	(0.08)
Israel	0.06	(0.08)	-0.29	(0.08)	**0.35**	(0.09)	0.01	(0.08)	-0.02	(0.10)	0.03	(0.08)
Italy	0.01	(0.03)	-0.09	(0.07)	0.10	(0.06)	0.00	(0.04)	-0.05	(0.08)	0.06	(0.07)
Japan	0.00	(0.06)	c	c	c	c	0.00	(0.07)	c	c	c	c
Korea	0.00	(0.06)	c	c	c	c	0.00	(0.10)	c	c	c	c
Luxembourg	0.00	(0.01)	0.00	(0.02)	0.00	(0.03)	0.03	(0.01)	-0.05	(0.02)	**0.08**	(0.03)
Mexico	0.00	(0.03)	-0.06	(0.04)	0.06	(0.05)	0.00	(0.03)	0.02	(0.09)	-0.02	(0.08)
Netherlands	0.03	(0.10)	-0.19	(0.10)	**0.22**	(0.11)	0.04	(0.08)	-0.23	(0.15)	0.28	(0.16)
New Zealand	-0.04	(0.06)	0.16	(0.07)	**-0.20**	(0.07)	0.00	(0.07)	-0.01	(0.07)	0.00	(0.07)
Norway	-0.01	(0.07)	0.13	(0.13)	-0.14	(0.09)	0.00	(0.08)	-0.09	(0.20)	0.10	(0.18)
Poland	0.00	(0.07)	c	c	c	c	0.00	(0.08)	c	c	c	c
Portugal	0.02	(0.08)	-0.25	(0.09)	**0.27**	(0.11)	0.00	(0.07)	0.05	(0.14)	-0.06	(0.12)
Slovak Republic	0.00	(0.08)	c	c	c	c	0.00	(0.07)	c	c	c	c
Slovenia	-0.01	(0.01)	0.12	(0.06)	**-0.13**	(0.06)	0.00	(0.01)	0.03	(0.05)	-0.04	(0.05)
Spain	0.03	(0.04)	-0.23	(0.04)	**0.26**	(0.05)	0.00	(0.04)	-0.02	(0.06)	0.02	(0.05)
Sweden	0.02	(0.07)	-0.11	(0.12)	0.13	(0.10)	-0.01	(0.08)	0.08	(0.12)	-0.09	(0.11)
Switzerland	0.01	(0.08)	-0.04	(0.09)	0.05	(0.04)	0.00	(0.06)	-0.01	(0.07)	0.01	(0.05)
Turkey	-0.01	(0.06)	c	c	c	c	0.00	(0.09)	c	c	c	c
United Kingdom	0.04	(0.06)	-0.35	(0.14)	**0.39**	(0.13)	-0.03	(0.06)	0.24	(0.13)	**-0.27**	(0.14)
United States	-0.07	(0.07)	0.29	(0.15)	**-0.36**	(0.13)	-0.04	(0.08)	0.14	(0.11)	-0.17	(0.11)
OECD average	0.01	(0.01)	-0.07	(0.02)	**0.08**	(0.02)	0.00	(0.01)	0.02	(0.02)	-0.02	(0.02)
Albania	0.00	(0.07)	c	c	c	c	0.00	(0.06)	c	c	c	c
Argentina	0.00	(0.07)	0.00	(0.15)	0.00	(0.10)	0.00	(0.07)	-0.11	(0.12)	0.11	(0.12)
Azerbaijan	-0.01	(0.08)	0.24	(0.17)	-0.25	(0.15)	-0.01	(0.10)	0.14	(0.24)	-0.15	(0.23)
Brazil	-0.01	(0.05)	0.07	(0.22)	-0.08	(0.20)	-0.01	(0.05)	0.31	(0.18)	-0.33	(0.17)
Bulgaria	0.01	(0.10)	c	c	c	c	0.00	(0.10)	c	c	c	c
Colombia	-0.01	(0.08)	0.39	(0.28)	-0.40	(0.27)	0.00	(0.09)	0.51	(0.23)	**-0.51**	(0.22)
Croatia	0.01	(0.08)	-0.03	(0.09)	0.04	(0.07)	-0.01	(0.07)	0.10	(0.12)	-0.12	(0.09)
Dubai (UAE)	-0.39	(0.01)	0.15	(0.01)	**-0.54**	(0.02)	0.36	(0.02)	-0.13	(0.01)	**0.49**	(0.02)
Hong Kong-China	-0.04	(0.06)	0.07	(0.07)	-0.11	(0.06)	-0.03	(0.09)	0.04	(0.09)	-0.06	(0.05)
Indonesia	0.00	(0.08)	c	c	c	c	0.00	(0.08)	c	c	c	c
Jordan	-0.07	(0.07)	0.40	(0.13)	**-0.47**	(0.09)	-0.01	(0.08)	0.05	(0.12)	-0.06	(0.09)
Kazakhstan	-0.01	(0.06)	0.07	(0.13)	-0.09	(0.13)	-0.02	(0.08)	0.13	(0.15)	-0.15	(0.14)
Kyrgyzstan	-0.01	(0.06)	0.52	(0.16)	**-0.53**	(0.15)	0.00	(0.09)	0.14	(0.13)	-0.14	(0.13)
Latvia	-0.01	(0.07)	0.18	(0.15)	-0.19	(0.14)	0.00	(0.08)	0.13	(0.19)	-0.13	(0.17)
Liechtenstein	-0.01	(0.04)	0.02	(0.08)	-0.03	(0.12)	0.05	(0.04)	-0.11	(0.08)	0.17	(0.12)
Lithuania	0.00	(0.06)	-0.20	(0.15)	0.20	(0.14)	0.00	(0.08)	-0.19	(0.16)	0.19	(0.15)
Macao-China	-0.02	(0.02)	0.01	(0.01)	-0.04	(0.03)	0.06	(0.02)	-0.03	(0.01)	**0.09**	(0.03)
Montenegro	-0.02	(0.02)	0.37	(0.05)	**-0.38**	(0.06)	-0.01	(0.02)	0.09	(0.08)	-0.10	(0.08)
Panama	0.01	(0.07)	0.11	(0.17)	-0.10	(0.14)	0.03	(0.10)	0.12	(0.17)	-0.10	(0.19)
Peru	0.01	(0.07)	c	c	c	c	-0.01	(0.07)	c	c	c	c
Qatar	-0.28	(0.01)	0.33	(0.01)	**-0.61**	(0.02)	0.14	(0.01)	-0.15	(0.01)	**0.29**	(0.02)
Romania	0.00	(0.06)	c	c	c	c	0.01	(0.08)	c	c	c	c
Russian Federation	0.01	(0.06)	-0.09	(0.09)	0.10	(0.06)	0.00	(0.08)	-0.03	(0.12)	0.03	(0.08)
Serbia	0.01	(0.06)	-0.01	(0.04)	0.02	(0.07)	0.00	(0.08)	0.00	(0.10)	-0.01	(0.07)
Shanghai-China	0.00	(0.06)	c	c	c	c	0.00	(0.08)	c	c	c	c
Singapore	0.02	(0.02)	-0.15	(0.04)	**0.17**	(0.04)	0.02	(0.01)	-0.08	(0.05)	0.10	(0.06)
Chinese Taipei	0.00	(0.06)	c	c	c	c	0.00	(0.08)	c	c	c	c
Thailand	0.00	(0.05)	c	c	c	c	0.00	(0.08)	c	c	c	c
Trinidad and Tobago	0.02	(0.01)	-0.39	(0.09)	**0.42**	(0.09)	-0.01	(0.01)	-0.10	(0.10)	0.10	(0.10)
Tunisia	0.00	(0.08)	c	c	c	c	0.00	(0.08)	c	c	c	c
Uruguay	0.00	(0.06)	c	c	c	c	0.00	(0.05)	c	c	c	c

Note: Values that are statistically significant are indicated in bold (see Annex A3).
StatLink ᵐˢᵖ http://dx.doi.org/10.1787/888932343285

[Part 1/1]
Between- and within-school variance in reading performance
Table II.5.1 *Results based on students' self-reports*

	Total variance in student performance[2]	Variance in student performance between schools	Variance in student performance within schools	Total variance in student performance expressed as a percentage of the average variance in student performance across OECD countries[3]	Variance in student performance between schools[4]	Variance in student performance within schools	Variance explained by the PISA index of economic, social and cultural status of students — Between-school	Within-school	Variance explained by the PISA index of economic, social and cultural status of students and schools — Between-school	Within-school	Variance explained by students' study programmes — Between-school	Within-school	Variance explained by students' study programmes and the PISA index of economic, social and cultural status of students and schools — Between-school	Within-school	Index of academic inclusion[5] (Proportion of variance in student performance within schools)
OECD															
Australia	9 783	2 692	7 631	112.9	31.1	88.1	13.5	5.4	21.0	5.3	3.6	2.4	20.9	8.2	73.9
Austria	10 028	5 588	4 454	115.8	64.5	51.4	2.5	1.3	32.8	1.2	51.1	0.4	53.6	1.6	44.4
Belgium	10 360	5 343	4 833	119.6	61.7	55.8	-3.2	1.9	40.4	1.9	49.6	13.6	54.1	14.4	47.5
Canada	8 163	1 877	6 780	94.2	21.7	78.3	6.2	3.6	9.6	3.4	2.1	3.0	10.0	6.1	78.3
Chile	6 833	4 893	4 005	78.9	56.5	46.2	13.8	0.5	38.9	0.5	30.8	1.2	47.8	1.8	45.0
Czech Republic	8 516	4 249	4 428	98.3	49.0	51.1	3.4	0.9	32.6	0.7	38.7	0.0	41.3	1.0	51.0
Denmark	6 987	1 134	6 012	80.6	13.1	69.4	6.5	6.5	9.0	6.7	2.1	0.3	9.4	6.9	84.1
Estonia	6 933	1 557	5 595	80.0	18.0	64.6	4.3	1.7	8.2	1.5	1.7	1.1	8.1	2.6	78.2
Finland	7 467	665	6 993	86.2	7.7	80.7	1.7	5.4	1.8	5.5	0.0	0.0	1.8	5.5	91.3
France	w	w	w	w	w	w	w	w	w	w	w	w	w	w	w
Germany	8 978	5 890	3 890	103.6	68.0	44.9	4.4	0.2	45.7	0.1	55.5	1.8	57.0	1.8	39.8
Greece	9 054	4 745	5 558	104.5	54.8	64.2	9.9	1.8	21.8	1.7	35.7	-0.4	39.5	1.4	53.9
Hungary	8 133	5 846	2 923	93.9	67.5	33.7	8.6	0.3	43.9	0.2	47.5	-0.1	54.9	0.1	33.3
Iceland	9 211	1 348	8 186	106.3	15.6	94.5	3.4	5.5	3.7	5.5	5.0	0.2	7.3	5.6	85.9
Ireland	9 053	2 805	6 966	104.5	32.4	80.4	13.5	4.1	18.9	4.2	3.1	4.7	19.2	9.0	71.3
Israel	12 438	6 250	6 615	143.6	72.1	76.4	8.3	4.4	30.9	4.5	5.5	1.5	40.7	5.8	51.4
Italy	9 193	6 695	4 085	106.1	77.3	47.2	5.9	0.4	33.7	0.3	45.3	0.2	47.3	0.6	37.9
Japan	10 072	5 087	5 386	116.3	58.7	62.2	-4.2	0.7	30.5	0.7	-5.1	-0.4	33.9	0.6	51.4
Korea	6 271	2 741	5 283	72.4	31.6	61.0	7.9	2.2	16.8	2.2	12.4	-0.1	24.2	2.2	65.8
Luxembourg	10 759	5 335	6 906	124.2	61.6	79.7	33.3	4.2	50.5	4.1	56.8	24.8	57.7	25.9	56.4
Mexico	7 158	3 583	3 869	82.6	41.4	44.7	4.3	-0.1	15.2	0.0	14.1	-0.2	20.6	-0.1	51.9
Netherlands	7 857	5 107	2 795	90.7	59.0	32.3	3.2	0.7	26.7	0.7	51.1	5.1	51.6	5.6	35.4
New Zealand	10 575	2 622	8 228	122.1	30.3	95.0	15.1	9.2	21.8	9.3	0.8	1.7	21.8	10.9	75.8
Norway	8 310	874	7 598	95.9	10.1	87.7	2.0	5.3	2.7	5.4	0.5	0.4	2.9	5.6	89.7
Poland	7 950	1 585	6 869	91.8	18.3	79.3	10.0	7.7	12.0	7.9	3.3	0.3	12.3	8.0	81.2
Portugal	7 534	2 565	5 191	87.0	29.6	59.9	9.6	3.6	17.4	3.5	20.1	14.5	23.3	15.8	66.9
Slovak Republic	8 135	2 989	4 565	93.9	34.5	52.7	7.3	1.9	19.4	1.8	19.6	1.0	26.7	2.8	60.4
Slovenia	8 260	4 142	3 102	95.3	47.8	35.8	1.1	0.7	20.0	0.6	38.2	0.0	38.5	0.5	42.8
Spain	7 658	1 690	6 048	88.4	19.5	69.8	7.0	5.0	9.5	5.0	0.0	0.0	9.5	5.0	78.2
Sweden	9 729	1 877	8 290	112.3	21.7	95.7	10.0	10.7	14.7	10.7	3.0	0.2	15.1	10.8	81.5
Switzerland	8 735	2 740	5 652	100.8	31.6	65.2	7.1	3.1	15.4	3.0	9.6	0.2	19.3	3.3	67.4
Turkey	6 714	6 536	3 245	77.5	75.4	37.5	13.8	0.8	51.7	0.8	64.4	1.3	67.4	2.2	33.2
United Kingdom	9 096	2 775	6 684	105.0	32.0	77.2	15.0	4.6	24.7	4.6	2.7	-0.3	25.9	4.8	70.7
United States	9 330	3 638	6 476	107.7	42.0	74.8	17.4	2.9	31.8	2.8	9.8	3.8	33.7	6.4	64.0
OECD average	8 718	3 616	5 591	100.6	41.7	64.5	8.5	3.2	23.8	3.2	21.2	2.6	30.7	5.5	61.4
Partners															
Albania	9 969	3 127	7 105	115.1	36.1	82.0	11.1	2.4	19.5	2.3	3.5	0.1	20.7	2.6	69.4
Argentina	11 714	8 456	5 523	135.2	97.6	63.7	16.1	0.7	57.7	0.6	29.0	4.3	70.3	4.5	39.5
Azerbaijan	5 702	2 490	3 459	65.8	28.7	39.9	1.8	0.5	3.8	0.5	1.0	0.6	4.8	1.0	58.2
Brazil	8 838	4 417	4 702	102.0	51.0	54.3	3.8	-0.2	27.6	-0.1	21.6	3.3	37.5	3.5	51.6
Bulgaria	12 823	6 418	6 439	148.0	74.1	74.3	2.2	2.5	48.3	2.3	26.3	2.0	50.5	4.2	50.1
Colombia	7 495	3 162	4 813	86.5	36.5	55.6	12.6	0.5	28.0	0.6	8.5	9.0	28.7	9.4	60.4
Croatia	7 669	4 045	4 473	88.5	46.7	51.6	6.4	0.6	23.1	0.7	37.6	10.2	37.9	10.4	52.5
Dubai (UAE)	11 390	5 732	5 439	131.5	66.2	62.8	2.3	2.4	22.8	2.5	5.5	3.6	26.3	5.3	48.7
Hong Kong-China	7 058	3 143	4 360	81.5	36.3	50.3	1.8	0.2	7.0	0.2	4.1	3.4	9.3	3.5	58.1
Indonesia	4 418	1 749	2 298	51.0	20.2	26.5	1.2	0.0	4.2	0.0	5.1	0.0	6.6	0.0	56.8
Jordan	8 243	3 312	5 461	95.2	38.2	63.0	6.9	4.2	8.1	4.2	0.0	0.0	8.1	4.2	62.2
Kazakhstan	8 285	2 887	5 078	95.6	33.3	58.6	6.4	2.1	12.5	2.1	-0.6	1.0	11.3	3.1	63.8
Kyrgyzstan	9 752	3 266	5 901	112.6	37.7	68.1	9.1	2.4	19.3	2.4	3.9	0.8	21.0	3.2	64.4
Latvia	6 394	1 391	5 200	73.8	16.1	60.0	5.3	2.4	8.1	2.2	2.1	0.8	9.3	3.4	78.9
Liechtenstein	6 896	2 944	3 453	79.6	34.0	39.9	4.4	0.8	23.2	0.8	7.5	1.0	23.6	1.7	54.0
Lithuania	7 472	1 864	5 190	86.3	21.5	59.9	5.4	2.4	10.4	2.4	7.5	0.0	11.7	2.4	73.6
Macao-China	5 799	2 882	4 179	66.9	33.3	48.2	8.3	0.2	11.7	0.2	15.0	6.3	15.9	6.5	59.2
Montenegro	8 634	3 150	5 587	99.7	36.4	64.5	8.5	1.3	25.6	1.3	23.6	7.3	26.8	8.0	63.9
Panama	9 860	5 942	4 213	113.8	68.6	48.6	2.0	0.5	33.4	0.5	14.0	1.7	42.6	2.0	41.5
Peru	9 670	5 886	4 623	111.6	67.9	53.4	13.9	0.6	49.5	0.7	18.9	5.2	54.7	5.6	44.0
Qatar	13 313	6 676	5 891	153.7	77.1	68.0	0.3	1.0	13.1	1.1	33.5	2.5	35.9	3.1	46.9
Romania	8 105	4 057	3 832	93.6	46.8	44.2	7.4	1.0	17.5	1.1	14.2	0.1	25.4	1.2	48.6
Russian Federation	8 050	1 965	5 826	92.9	22.7	67.3	6.1	2.3	9.4	2.3	2.5	3.9	8.9	5.5	74.8
Serbia	7 018	3 909	4 123	81.0	45.1	47.6	4.8	0.6	22.8	0.4	25.7	4.0	29.1	4.2	51.3
Shanghai-China	6 427	2 551	4 095	74.2	29.4	47.3	4.8	0.0	20.3	0.0	11.5	0.1	23.7	0.4	61.6
Singapore	9 499	3 387	6 195	109.6	39.1	71.5	11.2	4.6	23.6	4.6	3.0	2.1	24.6	7.1	64.7
Chinese Taipei	7 446	2 772	5 808	85.9	32.0	67.0	9.7	3.8	16.3	3.8	11.7	-0.1	19.3	4.2	67.7
Thailand	5 164	1 231	3 052	59.6	14.2	35.2	1.2	0.1	3.3	0.1	3.2	0.9	5.0	1.1	71.3
Trinidad and Tobago	12 755	8 320	5 148	147.2	96.0	59.4	0.4	1.3	56.3	1.3	36.4	6.9	71.4	7.6	38.2
Tunisia	7 253	3 034	4 291	83.7	35.0	49.5	-1.2	-0.1	6.5	-0.1	27.9	2.2	30.1	2.3	58.6
Uruguay	9 859	4 807	5 835	113.8	55.5	67.3	21.1	2.2	41.5	2.2	39.3	8.0	48.2	9.6	54.8

1. The variance components were estimated for all students in participating countries with data on socio-economic background and study programmes.
2. The total variance in student performance is calculated from the square of the standard deviation for the students used in the analysis. The statistical variance in student performance and not the standard deviation is used for this comparison to allow for the decomposition.
3. The sum of the between- and within-school variance components, as an estimate from a sample, does not necessarily add up to the total.
4. In some countries, sub-units within schools were sampled instead of schools and this may affect the estimation of the between-school variance components (see Annex A2).
5. The index of academic inclusion is calculated as 100*(1-rho), where rho stands for the intra-class correlation of performance, i.e. the variance in student performance between schools, divided by the sum of the variance in student performance between schools and the variance in student performance within schools.

StatLink ⟐ http://dx.doi.org/10.1787/888932343285

[Part 1/2]

Decomposition of the gradient of the PISA index of economic, social and cultural status (ESCS) into between- and within-school components[1]

Table II.5.2   *Results based on students' self-reports*

	Overall effect of ESCS[2]		Within-school effects of ESCS[3]			Student variability in the distribution of ESCS					
	Score point difference associated with one unit increase in the ESCS	S.E.	Student-level score point difference associated with one unit increase in the student-level ESCS	S.E.	Explained within-school variance	25th percentile of the student distribution of ESCS	S.E.	75th percentile of the student distribution of ESCS	S.E.	Interquartile range of the distribution of the student-level ESCS	S.E.
OECD											
Australia	46	(1.8)	30	(1.9)	6.1	-0.19	(0.01)	0.90	(0.02)	1.09	(0.01)
Austria	48	(2.3)	10	(2.0)	2.3	-0.49	(0.02)	0.58	(0.02)	1.08	(0.02)
Belgium	47	(1.5)	13	(1.4)	3.4	-0.46	(0.02)	0.92	(0.03)	1.38	(0.03)
Canada	32	(1.4)	21	(1.4)	4.3	-0.05	(0.02)	1.12	(0.01)	1.17	(0.02)
Chile	31	(1.5)	8	(1.8)	1.1	-1.38	(0.04)	0.26	(0.05)	1.64	(0.04)
Czech Republic	46	(2.3)	14	(2.0)	1.4	-0.58	(0.02)	0.38	(0.02)	0.96	(0.02)
Denmark	36	(1.4)	28	(1.7)	9.7	-0.31	(0.02)	0.94	(0.02)	1.25	(0.02)
Estonia	29	(2.3)	16	(2.1)	2.3	-0.46	(0.02)	0.76	(0.03)	1.22	(0.03)
Finland	31	(1.7)	28	(2.0)	6.8	-0.16	(0.02)	0.98	(0.02)	1.14	(0.02)
France	w	w	w	w	w	w	w	w	w	w	w
Germany	44	(1.9)	10	(1.6)	0.1	-0.41	(0.02)	0.79	(0.03)	1.20	(0.02)
Greece	34	(2.4)	14	(1.8)	2.6	-0.73	(0.03)	0.74	(0.05)	1.48	(0.03)
Hungary	48	(2.2)	7	(1.7)	0.5	-0.85	(0.02)	0.49	(0.04)	1.34	(0.04)
Iceland	27	(1.8)	24	(1.8)	5.8	0.09	(0.02)	1.40	(0.02)	1.31	(0.03)
Ireland	39	(2.0)	27	(2.2)	5.2	-0.55	(0.02)	0.66	(0.04)	1.21	(0.03)
Israel	43	(2.4)	18	(2.3)	5.8	-0.56	(0.03)	0.63	(0.03)	1.19	(0.03)
Italy	32	(1.3)	5	(0.8)	0.7	-0.86	(0.01)	0.55	(0.02)	1.41	(0.01)
Japan	40	(2.8)	5	(2.7)	1.1	-0.55	(0.02)	0.53	(0.02)	1.08	(0.02)
Korea	32	(2.5)	20	(2.9)	3.6	-0.72	(0.03)	0.44	(0.03)	1.16	(0.02)
Luxembourg	40	(1.3)	21	(3.0)	5.2	-0.52	(0.02)	1.01	(0.02)	1.53	(0.02)
Mexico	25	(1.0)	3	(0.9)	0.0	-2.23	(0.02)	-0.23	(0.05)	2.00	(0.04)
Netherlands	37	(1.9)	5	(1.5)	2.2	-0.31	(0.03)	0.93	(0.03)	1.24	(0.03)
New Zealand	52	(1.9)	36	(2.9)	9.7	-0.44	(0.01)	0.65	(0.03)	1.09	(0.02)
Norway	36	(2.1)	28	(2.8)	6.1	-0.03	(0.02)	1.00	(0.02)	1.02	(0.02)
Poland	39	(1.9)	31	(2.2)	9.9	-0.90	(0.01)	0.22	(0.05)	1.12	(0.05)
Portugal	30	(1.6)	17	(1.3)	5.9	-1.24	(0.03)	0.45	(0.08)	1.69	(0.06)
Slovak Republic	41	(2.3)	17	(2.1)	3.4	-0.67	(0.02)	0.38	(0.05)	1.05	(0.04)
Slovenia	39	(1.5)	2	(1.1)	1.7	-0.59	(0.01)	0.77	(0.03)	1.36	(0.03)
Spain	29	(1.5)	21	(1.0)	7.2	-1.14	(0.03)	0.50	(0.05)	1.64	(0.04)
Sweden	43	(2.2)	34	(2.2)	11.1	-0.21	(0.03)	0.93	(0.02)	1.14	(0.03)
Switzerland	40	(2.1)	20	(1.6)	4.6	-0.53	(0.03)	0.71	(0.04)	1.24	(0.03)
Turkey	29	(1.5)	8	(1.5)	2.2	-2.09	(0.04)	-0.31	(0.06)	1.78	(0.04)
United Kingdom	44	(1.9)	27	(2.0)	6.0	-0.35	(0.02)	0.76	(0.02)	1.11	(0.02)
United States	42	(2.3)	23	(2.9)	3.8	-0.45	(0.05)	0.86	(0.05)	1.31	(0.04)
OECD average	38	(0.3)	18	(0.3)	4.3	-0.64	(0.00)	0.65	(0.01)	1.29	(0.01)
Partners											
Albania	31	(2.6)	13	(2.6)	2.8	-1.68	(0.04)	-0.24	(0.05)	1.45	(0.04)
Argentina	40	(2.3)	9	(1.7)	0.9	-1.50	(0.06)	0.25	(0.07)	1.74	(0.05)
Azerbaijan	21	(2.3)	8	(1.7)	1.3	-1.39	(0.03)	0.09	(0.05)	1.48	(0.05)
Brazil	28	(1.4)	3	(1.2)	-0.2	-2.10	(0.04)	-0.30	(0.04)	1.80	(0.03)
Bulgaria	51	(2.8)	11	(2.3)	3.1	-0.77	(0.04)	0.61	(0.06)	1.38	(0.04)
Colombia	28	(1.8)	9	(1.5)	1.1	-2.11	(0.07)	-0.20	(0.05)	1.91	(0.06)
Croatia	32	(2.0)	10	(2.0)	1.3	-0.78	(0.02)	0.40	(0.04)	1.18	(0.03)
Dubai (UAE)	51	(1.4)	19	(2.0)	4.0	0.06	(0.01)	0.95	(0.01)	0.89	(0.01)
Hong Kong-China	17	(2.2)	3	(1.5)	0.4	-1.51	(0.03)	-0.12	(0.05)	1.39	(0.03)
Indonesia	17	(2.4)	1	(1.1)	0.1	-2.39	(0.06)	-0.77	(0.08)	1.62	(0.06)
Jordan	24	(2.1)	18	(1.7)	6.7	-1.29	(0.03)	0.25	(0.05)	1.54	(0.04)
Kazakhstan	38	(2.8)	19	(2.4)	3.6	-1.11	(0.03)	0.09	(0.04)	1.20	(0.03)
Kyrgyzstan	40	(2.9)	16	(1.8)	3.5	-1.33	(0.03)	0.06	(0.05)	1.39	(0.03)
Latvia	29	(2.6)	19	(2.6)	3.6	-0.83	(0.02)	0.56	(0.04)	1.38	(0.03)
Liechtenstein	26	(5.0)	3	(2.9)	2.1	-0.57	(0.09)	0.81	(0.09)	1.38	(0.13)
Lithuania	33	(1.9)	16	(1.8)	4.0	-0.82	(0.04)	0.76	(0.02)	1.58	(0.03)
Macao-China	12	(1.2)	6	(2.0)	0.3	-1.29	(0.01)	-0.14	(0.01)	1.15	(0.01)
Montenegro	31	(1.4)	11	(1.6)	2.0	-0.91	(0.02)	0.43	(0.03)	1.34	(0.03)
Panama	31	(3.6)	3	(2.5)	1.0	-1.81	(0.11)	0.26	(0.13)	2.07	(0.11)
Peru	41	(2.0)	8	(1.6)	1.2	-2.21	(0.06)	-0.44	(0.07)	1.77	(0.07)
Qatar	25	(1.2)	7	(1.5)	1.6	0.01	(0.01)	1.12	(0.00)	1.11	(0.01)
Romania	36	(2.8)	10	(2.0)	2.5	-0.91	(0.03)	0.21	(0.05)	1.12	(0.04)
Russian Federation	37	(2.5)	21	(2.2)	3.3	-0.83	(0.02)	0.42	(0.04)	1.25	(0.02)
Serbia	27	(1.6)	6	(1.9)	0.8	-0.61	(0.02)	0.74	(0.03)	1.35	(0.03)
Shanghai-China	27	(2.1)	4	(1.6)	0.1	-1.27	(0.05)	0.35	(0.05)	1.61	(0.05)
Singapore	47	(1.7)	26	(2.0)	6.4	-0.97	(0.02)	0.16	(0.01)	1.12	(0.02)
Chinese Taipei	36	(2.4)	21	(2.1)	5.6	-0.89	(0.03)	0.23	(0.02)	1.12	(0.03)
Thailand	22	(1.8)	2	(1.6)	0.2	-2.29	(0.02)	-0.44	(0.07)	1.85	(0.06)
Trinidad and Tobago	38	(1.7)	2	(1.6)	2.2	-1.17	(0.02)	0.05	(0.02)	1.21	(0.02)
Tunisia	19	(1.8)	2	(1.6)	-0.2	-2.26	(0.05)	-0.24	(0.05)	2.01	(0.04)
Uruguay	37	(1.5)	15	(1.5)	3.3	-1.64	(0.02)	0.20	(0.06)	1.84	(0.05)

1. In some countries, sub-units within schools were sampled instead of schools as administrative units and this may affect the estimation of school-level effects (see Annex A2).
2. Single-level bivariate regression of reading performance on the ESCS, the slope is the regression coefficient for the ESCS.
3. Two-level regression of reading performance on student ESCS and school mean ESCS: within-school slope for ESCS and explained variance at the student level by the model.
4. Two-level regression of reading performance on student ESCS and school mean ESCS: between-school slope for ESCS and explained variance at the school level by the model.
5. Distribution of the school mean ESCS, percentiles calculated at student-level.
6. The index of social inclusion is calculated as 100*(1-rho), where rho stands for the intra-class correlation of socio-economic background, i.e. the variance in the PISA index of social, economic and cultural status of students between schools, divided by the sum of the variance in students' socio-economic background between schools and the variance in students' socio-economic background within schools.

StatLink ⟐⟐⟐ http://dx.doi.org/10.1787/888932343285

[Part 2/2]
Decomposition of the gradient of the PISA index of economic, social and cultural status (ESCS) into between- and within-school components[1]

Table II.5.2   *Results based on students' self-reports*

	Between-school effects of ESCS[4]			School variability in the distribution of ESCS[5]						Index of social inclusion[6]
	School-level score point difference associated with one unit increase in the school mean ESCS	S.E.	Explained between-school variance	25th percentile of the school mean distribution of ESCS	S.E.	75th percentile of the school mean distribution of ESCS	S.E.	Interquartile range of the distribution of the school mean ESCS	S.E.	Proportion of ESCS variance within schools
Australia	66	(6.2)	67.6	0.04	(0.03)	0.58	(0.02)	0.55	(0.03)	76.4
Austria	80	(13.2)	50.9	-0.22	(0.03)	0.38	(0.04)	0.61	(0.05)	69.2
Belgium	111	(6.1)	65.5	-0.19	(0.02)	0.63	(0.04)	0.82	(0.04)	69.8
Canada	32	(6.7)	44.2	0.26	(0.01)	0.76	(0.02)	0.50	(0.02)	82.4
Chile	50	(4.3)	69.0	-1.10	(0.04)	-0.04	(0.06)	1.06	(0.07)	48.6
Czech Republic	123	(7.7)	66.5	-0.33	(0.02)	0.12	(0.06)	0.45	(0.07)	75.1
Denmark	42	(5.9)	69.1	0.02	(0.04)	0.57	(0.03)	0.55	(0.04)	83.6
Estonia	41	(12.5)	45.6	-0.11	(0.02)	0.38	(0.04)	0.50	(0.04)	81.5
Finland	19	(10.3)	23.2	0.15	(0.01)	0.58	(0.05)	0.43	(0.05)	89.2
France	w	w	w	w	w	w	w	w	w	w
Germany	122	(8.4)	67.2	-0.16	(0.04)	0.55	(0.05)	0.71	(0.06)	76.0
Greece	44	(10.7)	39.8	-0.34	(0.05)	0.31	(0.08)	0.66	(0.08)	68.0
Hungary	76	(7.3)	65.0	-0.62	(0.04)	0.23	(0.02)	0.85	(0.05)	54.2
Iceland	11	(11.3)	23.6	0.47	(0.00)	1.03	(0.00)	0.55	(0.00)	82.8
Ireland	53	(7.7)	58.5	-0.25	(0.05)	0.25	(0.04)	0.50	(0.06)	76.7
Israel	102	(14.1)	42.9	-0.35	(0.06)	0.33	(0.03)	0.68	(0.06)	76.7
Italy	67	(11.1)	43.5	-0.56	(0.02)	0.30	(0.02)	0.85	(0.03)	73.9
Japan	137	(15.5)	51.9	-0.30	(0.02)	0.28	(0.04)	0.58	(0.05)	78.2
Korea	62	(8.7)	53.2	-0.49	(0.06)	0.09	(0.04)	0.58	(0.06)	74.1
Luxembourg	65	(9.6)	82.0	-0.18	(0.00)	0.64	(0.00)	0.82	(0.00)	73.3
Mexico	30	(3.3)	36.7	-1.83	(0.04)	-0.68	(0.04)	1.15	(0.05)	56.2
Netherlands	93	(16.2)	45.2	0.04	(0.05)	0.54	(0.02)	0.50	(0.05)	76.2
New Zealand	61	(9.3)	72.1	-0.19	(0.04)	0.37	(0.02)	0.56	(0.04)	78.9
Norway	31	(14.7)	26.6	0.31	(0.03)	0.62	(0.03)	0.31	(0.04)	91.2
Poland	29	(5.7)	65.4	-0.61	(0.05)	-0.07	(0.03)	0.54	(0.05)	73.3
Portugal	40	(5.7)	58.9	-0.81	(0.05)	-0.01	(0.05)	0.80	(0.06)	73.2
Slovak Republic	72	(12.0)	56.2	-0.40	(0.03)	0.18	(0.04)	0.58	(0.05)	76.6
Slovenia	77	(11.3)	41.8	-0.29	(0.00)	0.41	(0.00)	0.70	(0.00)	75.0
Spain	25	(3.9)	48.4	-0.76	(0.03)	0.02	(0.04)	0.78	(0.04)	77.1
Sweden	52	(10.1)	67.9	0.10	(0.04)	0.52	(0.02)	0.42	(0.04)	85.7
Switzerland	66	(11.6)	48.6	-0.21	(0.02)	0.37	(0.06)	0.58	(0.05)	85.4
Turkey	60	(7.4)	68.5	-1.65	(0.09)	-0.71	(0.07)	0.94	(0.10)	63.5
United Kingdom	69	(7.0)	77.1	-0.07	(0.03)	0.45	(0.03)	0.53	(0.04)	81.6
United States	63	(12.1)	75.7	-0.23	(0.04)	0.51	(0.06)	0.73	(0.05)	70.7
OECD average	63	(1.7)	55.1	-0.33	(0.01)	0.31	(0.01)	0.65	(0.01)	74.8
Albania	39	(7.4)	54.0	-1.34	(0.07)	-0.59	(0.07)	0.75	(0.09)	67.7
Argentina	69	(5.5)	59.1	-1.18	(0.05)	-0.04	(0.05)	1.14	(0.07)	59.8
Azerbaijan	25	(7.5)	13.2	-1.08	(0.04)	-0.20	(0.05)	0.88	(0.07)	72.0
Brazil	53	(3.8)	54.2	-1.70	(0.06)	-0.82	(0.05)	0.88	(0.07)	64.7
Bulgaria	81	(7.7)	65.2	-0.46	(0.11)	0.26	(0.08)	0.72	(0.12)	57.9
Colombia	41	(3.7)	76.7	-1.76	(0.06)	-0.63	(0.08)	1.14	(0.10)	60.2
Croatia	69	(14.4)	49.4	-0.50	(0.03)	0.06	(0.03)	0.57	(0.04)	77.2
Dubai (UAE)	80	(9.2)	34.5	0.05	(0.00)	0.81	(0.00)	0.77	(0.00)	62.4
Hong Kong-China	33	(15.0)	19.4	-1.20	(0.02)	-0.55	(0.06)	0.65	(0.05)	69.9
Indonesia	25	(5.2)	20.8	-2.12	(0.07)	-1.06	(0.23)	1.06	(0.23)	61.3
Jordan	18	(11.2)	21.2	-0.93	(0.02)	-0.34	(0.07)	0.59	(0.07)	76.4
Kazakhstan	50	(7.8)	37.4	-0.79	(0.03)	-0.25	(0.05)	0.55	(0.05)	71.7
Kyrgyzstan	62	(8.6)	51.2	-1.02	(0.02)	-0.37	(0.02)	0.65	(0.03)	72.0
Latvia	30	(8.5)	50.6	-0.47	(0.03)	0.15	(0.04)	0.61	(0.04)	75.4
Liechtenstein	121	(22.0)	68.3	-0.20	(0.00)	0.65	(0.00)	0.84	(0.00)	88.2
Lithuania	43	(6.7)	48.2	-0.38	(0.02)	0.29	(0.03)	0.67	(0.04)	73.7
Macao-China	19	(10.3)	35.3	-0.99	(0.00)	-0.46	(0.00)	0.53	(0.00)	65.2
Montenegro	67	(14.8)	70.4	-0.58	(0.01)	0.14	(0.00)	0.72	(0.01)	77.2
Panama	57	(10.5)	48.7	-1.41	(0.13)	-0.17	(0.17)	1.23	(0.18)	57.7
Peru	59	(4.0)	72.9	-1.96	(0.06)	-0.79	(0.07)	1.17	(0.09)	50.7
Qatar	80	(11.0)	17.0	0.21	(0.00)	0.86	(0.00)	0.65	(0.00)	70.6
Romania	40	(10.0)	37.4	-0.66	(0.03)	-0.02	(0.07)	0.64	(0.07)	65.3
Russian Federation	38	(7.6)	41.5	-0.52	(0.02)	0.05	(0.03)	0.57	(0.03)	71.5
Serbia	53	(21.2)	50.5	-0.28	(0.02)	0.31	(0.06)	0.58	(0.06)	76.6
Shanghai-China	58	(5.1)	69.0	-0.95	(0.07)	-0.05	(0.06)	0.90	(0.09)	66.3
Singapore	86	(12.8)	60.3	-0.68	(0.00)	-0.23	(0.01)	0.46	(0.01)	81.7
Chinese Taipei	52	(21.6)	50.8	-0.63	(0.05)	-0.07	(0.04)	0.55	(0.06)	80.1
Thailand	18	(7.3)	23.3	-1.97	(0.05)	-0.75	(0.09)	1.23	(0.11)	48.9
Trinidad and Tobago	145	(9.6)	58.7	-0.94	(0.00)	-0.28	(0.00)	0.66	(0.01)	77.3
Tunisia	26	(7.6)	18.7	-1.71	(0.09)	-0.75	(0.08)	0.96	(0.10)	67.2
Uruguay	48	(4.8)	74.7	-1.29	(0.04)	-0.36	(0.03)	0.93	(0.05)	59.8

1. In some countries, sub-units within schools were sampled instead of schools as administrative units and this may affect the estimation of school-level effects (see Annex A2).
2. Single-level bivariate regression of reading performance on the ESCS, the slope is the regression coefficient for the ESCS.
3. Two-level regression of reading performance on student ESCS and school mean ESCS: within-school slope for ESCS and explained variance at the student level by the model.
4. Two-level regression of reading performance on student ESCS and school mean ESCS: between-school slope for ESCS and explained variance at the school level by the model.
5. Distribution of the school mean ESCS, percentiles calculated at student-level.
6. The index of social inclusion is calculated as 100*(1-rho), where rho stands for the intra-class correlation of socio-economic background, i.e. the variance in the PISA index of social, economic and cultural status of students between schools, divided by the sum of the variance in students' socio-economic background between schools and the variance in students' socio-economic background within schools.

StatLink ⟐⟐⟐⟐ http://dx.doi.org/10.1787/888932343285

[Part 1/1]

Parents' educational support at home at the beginning of primary school and student performance, before and after accounting for socio-economic background

Table II.5.3 *Results based on reports from students' parents*

Score point difference between students whose parents often (weekly or daily) undertook the following activities with them when they attended the first year of primary education and students whose parents did not

		Read books				Tell stories				Sing songs				Play with alphabet toys				Talk about things parents had done			
		Before accounting for ESCS[1]		After accounting for ESCS		Before accounting for ESCS		After accounting for ESCS		Before accounting for ESCS		After accounting for ESCS		Before accounting for ESCS		After accounting for ESCS		Before accounting for ESCS		After accounting for ESCS	
		Score dif.	S.E.	Score dif.	S.E.	Score dif.	S.E.	Score dif.	S.E.	Score dif.	S.E.	Score dif.	S.E.	Score dif.	S.E.	Score dif.	S.E.	Score dif.	S.E.	Score dif.	S.E.
OECD	Chile	18	(2.5)	12	(2.4)	28	(3.1)	15	(2.9)	25	(3.8)	12	(3.4)	19	(3.1)	9	(3.1)	22	(3.1)	11	(3.0)
	Denmark	30	(5.4)	17	(5.6)	1	(3.6)	-1	(3.5)	14	(3.6)	8	(3.6)	-10	(3.2)	-9	(3.2)	48	(8.2)	32	(9.7)
	Germany	51	(5.2)	29	(4.8)	7	(4.1)	-1	(3.8)	20	(4.0)	10	(3.4)	-11	(3.8)	-8	(3.4)	46	(6.9)	22	(6.4)
	Hungary	33	(5.5)	19	(4.8)	29	(5.1)	10	(3.6)	10	(3.4)	2	(2.9)	-2	(3.7)	-5	(2.6)	15	(4.6)	-3	(4.2)
	Italy	21	(1.9)	11	(1.8)	29	(2.1)	17	(1.9)	16	(1.8)	9	(1.7)	6	(2.0)	1	(1.9)	45	(4.0)	32	(3.8)
	Korea	25	(3.6)	13	(3.3)	13	(3.2)	4	(3.0)	11	(2.5)	4	(2.3)	2	(2.6)	-2	(2.5)	9	(2.7)	3	(2.6)
	New Zealand	63	(8.7)	44	(8.4)	22	(5.2)	12	(4.6)	20	(4.6)	11	(4.6)	9	(4.5)	4	(4.2)	44	(8.1)	28	(7.2)
	Portugal	23	(3.4)	6	(3.0)	28	(3.4)	10	(3.1)	22	(3.2)	9	(2.9)	17	(3.2)	3	(2.8)	16	(4.2)	1	(4.0)
Partners	Croatia	9	(3.5)	2	(3.2)	12	(3.3)	3	(3.1)	5	(3.2)	0	(3.0)	-7	(3.5)	-10	(3.3)	9	(4.0)	2	(4.0)
	Hong Kong-China	11	(3.1)	1	(3.0)	14	(3.3)	3	(3.1)	7	(2.6)	-1	(2.4)	6	(2.8)	-1	(2.6)	9	(2.6)	3	(2.6)
	Lithuania	4	(3.7)	0	(3.5)	6	(3.3)	-2	(3.5)	0	(2.8)	-2	(2.5)	-12	(3.6)	-10	(3.1)	13	(4.4)	5	(4.0)
	Macao-China	5	(2.0)	2	(2.0)	9	(2.3)	5	(2.4)	5	(2.0)	2	(2.2)	3	(2.1)	-1	(2.2)	9	(2.3)	6	(2.3)
	Panama	22	(8.7)	12	(8.0)	33	(7.6)	20	(7.1)	18	(6.9)	2	(5.5)	34	(8.1)	16	(6.4)	58	(10.2)	35	(8.3)
	Qatar	36	(2.9)	27	(2.9)	49	(2.8)	37	(2.9)	45	(2.7)	36	(2.7)	35	(3.1)	25	(3.1)	30	(3.7)	21	(3.7)

Score point difference between students whose parents often (weekly or daily) undertook the following activities with them when they attended the first year of primary education and students whose parents did not

		Talk about what parents had read				Play word games				Write letters or words				Read aloud signs and labels			
		Before accounting for ESCS		After accounting for ESCS		Before accounting for ESCS		After accounting for ESCS		Before accounting for ESCS		After accounting for ESCS		Before accounting for ESCS		After accounting for ESCS	
		Score dif.	S.E.	Score dif.	S.E.	Score dif.	S.E.	Score dif.	S.E.	Score dif.	S.E.	Score dif.	S.E.	Score dif.	S.E.	Score dif.	S.E.
OECD	Chile	16	(2.4)	4	(2.3)	14	(2.6)	5	(2.4)	19	(3.4)	11	(3.2)	22	(2.7)	13	(2.6)
	Denmark	11	(4.5)	7	(4.5)	10	(3.5)	6	(3.3)	5	(4.0)	1	(3.7)	9	(4.1)	3	(3.8)
	Germany	17	(3.8)	6	(3.2)	7	(3.7)	-1	(3.5)	3	(6.6)	-3	(5.4)	22	(4.3)	10	(4.1)
	Hungary	18	(4.2)	8	(3.7)	8	(3.7)	3	(2.8)	-2	(5.7)	-1	(4.9)	11	(4.5)	2	(3.2)
	Italy	20	(1.8)	11	(1.7)	20	(2.1)	12	(1.9)	23	(2.2)	14	(2.0)	22	(2.1)	14	(1.9)
	Korea	12	(2.7)	4	(2.6)	10	(2.8)	3	(2.6)	15	(3.3)	7	(3.0)	8	(2.7)	1	(2.5)
	New Zealand	22	(4.1)	16	(3.8)	22	(4.1)	12	(3.7)	37	(6.1)	23	(5.8)	39	(4.5)	22	(4.1)
	Portugal	16	(2.9)	4	(2.7)	15	(2.6)	3	(2.5)	19	(3.4)	6	(3.2)	14	(3.5)	3	(3.2)
Partners	Croatia	5	(3.5)	-1	(3.3)	10	(3.1)	1	(2.9)	-7	(6.5)	-10	(5.6)	6	(3.8)	-1	(3.3)
	Hong Kong-China	-1	(3.5)	-6	(3.5)	3	(3.0)	-5	(2.8)	13	(2.8)	5	(2.6)	8	(2.9)	0	(2.9)
	Lithuania	3	(3.2)	1	(3.0)	-2	(3.0)	-3	(2.7)	-12	(4.9)	-11	(4.1)	-1	(3.6)	-5	(3.3)
	Macao-China	2	(2.7)	-1	(2.7)	3	(2.6)	0	(2.7)	6	(2.5)	2	(2.6)	0	(2.0)	-3	(2.1)
	Panama	29	(9.7)	16	(8.5)	14	(6.3)	7	(6.4)	13	(9.2)	7	(8.8)	21	(7.4)	11	(6.7)
	Qatar	21	(3.2)	14	(3.1)	24	(3.3)	16	(3.2)	42	(3.5)	32	(3.6)	37	(3.4)	26	(3.5)

Note: Values that are statistically significant are indicated in bold (see Annex A3).
1. ESCS: PISA index of economic, social and cultural status.
StatLink ᅤᅳᅵ아 http://dx.doi.org/10.1787/888932343285

[Part 1/1]

Parents' educational support at home at age 15 and student performance, before and after accounting for socio-economic background

Table II.5.4 *Results based on reports from students' parents*

		Score point difference between students whose parents often (weekly or daily) do the following things with them and students whose parents do not														
		Discuss political or social issues				Discuss books, films or television programmes				Discuss how well their child is doing at school				Eat (the main meal) with their child around the table			
		Before accounting for ESCS[1]		After accounting for ESCS		Before accounting for ESCS		After accounting for ESCS		Before accounting for ESCS		After accounting for ESCS		Before accounting for ESCS		After accounting for ESCS	
		Score dif.	S.E.	Score dif.	S.E.	Score dif.	S.E.	Score dif.	S.E.	Score dif.	S.E.	Score dif.	S.E.	Score dif.	S.E.	Score dif.	S.E.
OECD	Chile	**38**	(2.3)	**21**	(2.0)	**23**	(3.1)	**15**	(2.6)	**20**	(4.6)	6	(5.0)	10	(5.2)	-2	(4.6)
	Denmark	**26**	(4.1)	**15**	(3.9)	**22**	(3.9)	**15**	(3.9)	3	(6.4)	1	(6.5)	2	(9.1)	-14	(8.8)
	Germany	**31**	(3.5)	**13**	(3.1)	**17**	(3.9)	**8**	(3.4)	-4	(5.6)	-5	(5.1)	**36**	(10.4)	**18**	(9.2)
	Hungary	**21**	(4.1)	6	(3.4)	7	(5.7)	6	(4.5)	-1	(11.6)	-5	(9.9)	-2	(6.7)	-6	(5.8)
	Italy	**42**	(2.1)	**27**	(2.0)	**27**	(2.5)	**20**	(2.4)	**29**	(4.8)	**16**	(4.6)	**30**	(6.9)	**21**	(6.1)
	Korea	**22**	(3.6)	**15**	(3.2)	**9**	(2.5)	**6**	(2.4)	**17**	(3.0)	**9**	(2.6)	**27**	(7.4)	**19**	(6.5)
	New Zealand	**32**	(3.9)	**17**	(3.2)	**27**	(5.0)	**16**	(4.1)	2	(5.3)	-2	(5.0)	1	(4.9)	-6	(4.4)
	Portugal	**37**	(3.5)	**17**	(2.9)	**27**	(3.6)	**13**	(3.3)	-2	(5.9)	-11	(5.5)	**38**	(11.1)	**26**	(10.1)
Partners	Croatia	**26**	(2.9)	**15**	(2.7)	**18**	(3.5)	**10**	(3.3)	9	(7.9)	3	(7.6)	**-23**	(6.0)	**-18**	(5.9)
	Hong Kong-China	**15**	(3.1)	**9**	(2.9)	**10**	(2.9)	**6**	(2.8)	**14**	(3.3)	**5**	(2.9)	**27**	(7.1)	**21**	(7.1)
	Lithuania	**22**	(2.6)	**12**	(2.4)	4	(3.3)	0	(3.1)	**26**	(8.4)	9	(7.9)	5	(7.1)	-4	(6.1)
	Macao-China	**14**	(2.1)	**11**	(2.0)	**9**	(2.0)	**6**	(2.1)	3	(2.5)	-1	(2.5)	**28**	(3.9)	**26**	(4.0)
	Panama	**38**	(6.8)	**18**	(4.7)	**23**	(10.4)	5	(8.1)	**26**	(10.3)	14	(8.9)	7	(7.6)	7	(7.9)
	Qatar	**32**	(3.1)	**24**	(3.1)	**29**	(3.6)	**23**	(3.4)	**37**	(3.9)	**26**	(3.9)	**53**	(5.4)	**43**	(4.9)

		Score point difference between students whose parents often (weekly or daily) do the following things with them and students whose parents do not														
		Spend time just talking to their child				Go to a bookstore or library with their child				Talk with their child about what he/she is reading on his/her own				Help their child with his/her homework			
		Before accounting for ESCS		After accounting for ESCS		Before accounting for ESCS		After accounting for ESCS		Before accounting for ESCS		After accounting for ESCS		Before accounting for ESCS		After accounting for ESCS	
		Score dif.	S.E.	Score dif.	S.E.	Score dif.	S.E.	Score dif.	S.E.	Score dif.	S.E.	Score dif.	S.E.	Score dif.	S.E.	Score dif.	S.E.
OECD	Chile	**11**	(3.6)	-1	(3.1)	-4	(5.5)	-4	(4.7)	4	(2.9)	4	(2.5)	**-17**	(2.8)	**-18**	(2.4)
	Denmark	18	(12.7)	3	(12.6)	-3	(9.0)	1	(8.4)	6	(3.2)	4	(3.0)	**-13**	(2.9)	**-15**	(2.7)
	Germany	**61**	(15.4)	28	(15.7)	1	(6.8)	5	(6.1)	**13**	(3.6)	7	(2.9)	**-48**	(4.3)	**-42**	(3.5)
	Hungary	**24**	(8.4)	9	(7.4)	-4	(7.7)	-4	(5.7)	-2	(4.0)	-1	(2.9)	**-45**	(3.8)	**-37**	(2.8)
	Italy	**16**	(4.0)	7	(3.6)	3	(2.9)	-1	(2.6)	**18**	(1.9)	**10**	(1.7)	**-29**	(1.9)	**-38**	(1.8)
	Korea	**24**	(4.6)	**16**	(4.2)	**17**	(5.9)	**10**	(5.1)	**16**	(3.6)	**8**	(3.2)	-7	(4.8)	**-11**	(4.5)
	New Zealand	**24**	(9.7)	7	(9.1)	8	(5.2)	**11**	(4.8)	**8**	(3.6)	4	(3.0)	**-15**	(4.0)	**-18**	(3.5)
	Portugal	**14**	(5.7)	5	(5.7)	0	(3.7)	-6	(3.6)	**7**	(3.2)	1	(3.0)	**-28**	(2.9)	**-31**	(2.6)
Partners	Croatia	2	(6.2)	-5	(6.1)	-1	(6.2)	-5	(5.9)	-5	(2.7)	**-8**	(2.7)	**-42**	(3.4)	**-40**	(3.0)
	Hong Kong-China	**24**	(4.5)	**16**	(4.2)	7	(4.4)	3	(4.4)	2	(2.9)	-3	(2.8)	**-14**	(3.0)	**-19**	(2.9)
	Lithuania	**19**	(5.3)	**10**	(4.5)	-3	(4.3)	-4	(4.0)	5	(2.8)	2	(2.5)	**-33**	(3.1)	**-29**	(2.8)
	Macao-China	**8**	(2.4)	4	(2.4)	0	(3.8)	-4	(3.8)	-5	(2.2)	-7	(2.2)	**-14**	(2.3)	**-16**	(2.3)
	Panama	**27**	(9.1)	12	(7.2)	**-25**	(6.6)	**-17**	(7.3)	**-14**	(6.6)	-6	(5.6)	**-30**	(9.1)	**-25**	(8.0)
	Qatar	**37**	(4.7)	**25**	(4.4)	**-31**	(3.3)	**-30**	(3.1)	4	(3.5)	2	(3.4)	**-17**	(2.8)	**-20**	(2.8)

Note: Values that are statistically significant are indicated in bold (see Annex A3).
1. ESCS: PISA index of economic, social and cultural status.
StatLink ᵃᵈˢ᷈ᴸ http://dx.doi.org/10.1787/888932343285

[Part 1/2]

Pre-primary school attendance, performance in reading and students' socio-economic background

Table II.5.5 *Results based on students' self-reports*

	Percentage of students with:						Average performance in reading of students with:						Students' PISA index of economic, social and cultural status with:					
	No pre-primary school attendance		Pre-primary school attendance for one year or less		Pre-primary school attendance for more than one year		No pre-primary school attendance		Pre-primary school attendance for one year or less		Pre-primary school attendance for more than one year		No pre-primary school attendance		Pre-primary school attendance for one year or less		Pre-primary school attendance for more than one year	
	%	S.E.	%	S.E.	%	S.E.	Mean score	S.E.	Mean score	S.E.	Mean score	S.E.	Mean index	S.E.	Mean index	S.E.	Mean index	S.E.
OECD																		
Australia	4.4	(0.3)	45.3	(0.6)	50.3	(0.7)	465	(5.4)	512	(2.5)	525	(2.7)	0.05	(0.04)	0.25	(0.02)	0.46	(0.01)
Austria	2.3	(0.3)	12.5	(0.7)	85.2	(0.7)	438	(10.7)	447	(5.2)	480	(3.0)	-0.30	(0.13)	-0.17	(0.03)	0.14	(0.02)
Belgium	2.5	(0.3)	3.8	(0.3)	93.6	(0.4)	417	(8.8)	435	(6.6)	520	(2.1)	-0.34	(0.10)	-0.02	(0.06)	0.26	(0.02)
Canada	9.5	(0.3)	42.3	(0.7)	48.2	(0.7)	491	(3.8)	520	(1.6)	539	(2.0)	0.20	(0.03)	0.43	(0.02)	0.64	(0.02)
Chile	15.0	(0.8)	52.8	(0.8)	32.2	(0.9)	419	(3.8)	452	(3.4)	465	(3.7)	-1.19	(0.06)	-0.59	(0.04)	-0.22	(0.04)
Czech Republic	3.9	(0.3)	9.5	(0.5)	86.6	(0.6)	452	(9.0)	481	(5.1)	484	(2.8)	-0.22	(0.06)	-0.16	(0.03)	-0.05	(0.01)
Denmark	2.2	(0.2)	28.1	(0.8)	69.8	(0.8)	421	(7.4)	479	(2.9)	505	(2.2)	-0.31	(0.07)	0.18	(0.03)	0.36	(0.02)
Estonia	10.3	(0.6)	10.0	(0.5)	79.7	(0.7)	498	(3.9)	489	(5.3)	504	(2.8)	-0.06	(0.04)	-0.07	(0.05)	0.21	(0.02)
Finland	5.0	(0.3)	28.9	(0.9)	66.1	(1.0)	525	(8.8)	524	(2.7)	543	(2.4)	0.07	(0.06)	0.19	(0.03)	0.47	(0.02)
France	1.7	(0.2)	5.2	(0.4)	93.1	(0.4)	395	(18.2)	446	(9.3)	503	(3.4)	-0.78	(0.19)	-0.42	(0.06)	-0.10	(0.03)
Germany	4.9	(0.4)	10.4	(0.6)	84.7	(0.8)	452	(7.5)	463	(5.5)	513	(2.7)	-0.22	(0.08)	-0.10	(0.05)	0.27	(0.02)
Greece	5.4	(0.4)	28.5	(1.0)	66.1	(1.1)	424	(10.3)	472	(5.0)	493	(4.4)	-0.62	(0.06)	-0.09	(0.04)	0.06	(0.04)
Hungary	1.4	(0.2)	4.1	(0.4)	94.5	(0.5)	452	(17.3)	461	(12.0)	498	(3.0)	-0.35	(0.16)	-0.44	(0.13)	-0.18	(0.03)
Iceland	3.0	(0.3)	3.6	(0.3)	93.4	(0.4)	460	(11.4)	480	(9.6)	504	(1.5)	0.13	(0.10)	0.41	(0.09)	0.75	(0.01)
Ireland	17.4	(0.7)	41.5	(1.0)	41.2	(1.1)	475	(4.1)	506	(3.6)	500	(3.7)	-0.22	(0.04)	0.02	(0.03)	0.19	(0.03)
Israel	5.5	(0.4)	20.1	(0.8)	74.5	(0.9)	374	(8.4)	444	(4.9)	497	(3.3)	-0.69	(0.07)	-0.14	(0.04)	0.07	(0.03)
Italy	5.2	(0.2)	8.7	(0.3)	86.1	(0.4)	416	(5.4)	460	(3.6)	494	(1.6)	-0.50	(0.05)	-0.19	(0.04)	-0.09	(0.01)
Japan	0.9	(0.1)	2.2	(0.2)	96.9	(0.3)	483	(15.6)	467	(10.9)	522	(3.3)	-0.23	(0.10)	-0.31	(0.08)	0.00	(0.01)
Korea	5.9	(0.5)	15.9	(0.7)	78.1	(1.0)	526	(7.7)	532	(5.5)	542	(3.4)	-0.55	(0.06)	-0.27	(0.04)	-0.10	(0.03)
Luxembourg	4.5	(0.3)	10.4	(0.5)	85.0	(0.5)	415	(7.7)	446	(4.8)	479	(1.4)	-0.43	(0.07)	-0.03	(0.06)	0.25	(0.01)
Mexico	10.3	(0.4)	19.5	(0.4)	70.2	(0.5)	378	(3.6)	424	(2.5)	434	(1.9)	-1.88	(0.04)	-1.45	(0.03)	-1.05	(0.03)
Netherlands	3.5	(0.6)	1.9	(0.4)	94.6	(0.6)	487	(16.8)	511	(13.0)	513	(5.2)	0.00	(0.18)	0.26	(0.10)	0.31	(0.03)
New Zealand	9.3	(0.5)	21.9	(0.7)	68.8	(0.8)	472	(6.1)	517	(4.5)	532	(2.2)	-0.24	(0.05)	0.00	(0.03)	0.16	(0.02)
Norway	9.3	(0.5)	6.4	(0.4)	84.3	(0.7)	477	(5.2)	489	(5.8)	508	(2.7)	0.16	(0.04)	0.26	(0.04)	0.52	(0.02)
Poland	2.3	(0.3)	47.8	(1.4)	49.9	(1.5)	463	(10.6)	489	(3.1)	514	(3.0)	-0.52	(0.12)	-0.59	(0.02)	0.03	(0.03)
Portugal	19.1	(0.9)	20.7	(0.8)	60.2	(1.1)	467	(4.7)	478	(4.1)	502	(3.1)	-0.81	(0.04)	-0.54	(0.04)	-0.08	(0.04)
Slovak Republic	5.0	(0.4)	12.2	(0.7)	82.8	(0.9)	423	(9.9)	475	(4.6)	483	(2.4)	-0.56	(0.07)	-0.20	(0.04)	-0.04	(0.02)
Slovenia	17.3	(0.7)	14.3	(0.6)	68.4	(0.8)	469	(3.7)	466	(4.6)	494	(1.3)	-0.30	(0.04)	-0.06	(0.04)	0.21	(0.02)
Spain	4.6	(0.3)	8.5	(0.5)	86.8	(0.5)	435	(5.7)	452	(4.0)	489	(2.0)	-0.74	(0.05)	-0.54	(0.07)	-0.26	(0.03)
Sweden	9.8	(0.4)	24.1	(0.9)	66.1	(1.0)	451	(6.3)	495	(4.0)	509	(2.9)	0.02	(0.05)	0.27	(0.04)	0.40	(0.02)
Switzerland	2.3	(0.3)	26.5	(1.8)	71.3	(1.8)	421	(9.1)	502	(5.0)	504	(2.7)	-0.47	(0.08)	0.02	(0.03)	0.12	(0.03)
Turkey	71.6	(1.3)	20.2	(0.9)	8.2	(0.7)	452	(3.1)	496	(5.5)	510	(7.3)	-1.53	(0.03)	-0.37	(0.06)	0.21	(0.08)
United Kingdom	5.8	(0.5)	28.2	(0.7)	66.0	(0.8)	430	(7.3)	487	(2.9)	507	(2.3)	-0.14	(0.06)	0.12	(0.03)	0.27	(0.03)
United States	1.8	(0.4)	27.7	(0.9)	70.6	(1.0)	459	(16.8)	492	(3.1)	505	(3.9)	-0.33	(0.16)	-0.11	(0.03)	0.30	(0.04)
OECD average	8.3	(0.1)	19.5	(0.1)	72.2	(0.1)	449	(1.6)	479	(1.0)	503	(0.5)	-0.41	(0.01)	-0.13	(0.01)	0.13	(0.01)
Partners																		
Albania	24.5	(1.3)	22.7	(1.0)	52.7	(1.3)	371	(5.4)	385	(5.7)	404	(4.6)	-1.27	(0.06)	-0.95	(0.07)	-0.78	(0.04)
Argentina	4.7	(0.6)	29.1	(1.4)	66.2	(1.4)	331	(12.5)	379	(4.6)	416	(5.4)	-1.33	(0.10)	-1.00	(0.05)	-0.39	(0.06)
Azerbaijan	68.7	(1.5)	14.6	(0.9)	16.7	(1.0)	356	(3.6)	371	(5.6)	384	(5.3)	-0.80	(0.03)	-0.35	(0.06)	-0.20	(0.05)
Brazil	21.3	(0.7)	33.4	(0.8)	45.3	(1.1)	379	(2.9)	414	(3.6)	439	(3.2)	-1.68	(0.03)	-1.24	(0.04)	-0.84	(0.04)
Bulgaria	11.4	(0.6)	14.8	(0.5)	73.8	(1.0)	399	(8.9)	412	(7.8)	441	(7.0)	-0.40	(0.08)	-0.16	(0.05)	-0.05	(0.04)
Colombia	18.5	(1.2)	53.3	(1.3)	28.2	(1.2)	380	(5.1)	419	(3.5)	429	(5.0)	-1.92	(0.06)	-1.09	(0.03)	-0.74	(0.06)
Croatia	26.8	(1.2)	21.2	(0.7)	52.1	(1.1)	461	(4.9)	465	(3.6)	490	(3.5)	-0.63	(0.03)	-0.38	(0.04)	0.14	(0.03)
Dubai (UAE)	12.9	(0.4)	27.8	(0.7)	59.2	(0.7)	404	(3.9)	460	(3.1)	478	(1.7)	-0.01	(0.03)	0.45	(0.02)	0.52	(0.01)
Hong Kong-China	2.8	(0.4)	4.9	(0.3)	92.3	(0.5)	462	(13.3)	486	(7.0)	538	(2.1)	-1.66	(0.08)	-1.23	(0.10)	-0.75	(0.04)
Indonesia	46.0	(2.1)	29.9	(1.4)	24.1	(1.5)	382	(3.4)	416	(4.8)	422	(5.8)	-1.95	(0.05)	-1.25	(0.07)	-1.14	(0.07)
Jordan	28.0	(1.2)	45.3	(1.0)	26.7	(0.9)	389	(3.9)	415	(3.4)	426	(4.8)	-0.96	(0.04)	-0.52	(0.04)	-0.19	(0.05)
Kazakhstan	58.1	(1.5)	14.9	(0.7)	27.0	(1.3)	375	(2.9)	400	(5.1)	420	(5.2)	-0.75	(0.03)	-0.28	(0.04)	-0.11	(0.04)
Kyrgyzstan	62.7	(1.6)	17.8	(1.2)	19.5	(1.0)	299	(3.2)	326	(4.7)	371	(5.7)	-0.86	(0.03)	-0.48	(0.05)	-0.10	(0.05)
Latvia	21.5	(1.2)	12.8	(0.7)	65.7	(1.3)	475	(3.7)	480	(4.7)	489	(3.2)	-0.39	(0.04)	-0.31	(0.05)	0.00	(0.03)
Liechtenstein	1.2	(0.6)	6.1	(1.4)	92.7	(1.5)	423	(41.6)	479	(19.5)	502	(3.1)	-0.84	(0.51)	0.09	(0.20)	0.10	(0.05)
Lithuania	37.6	(1.0)	11.8	(0.5)	50.6	(0.9)	452	(3.0)	467	(5.3)	483	(2.7)	-0.40	(0.03)	-0.01	(0.05)	0.22	(0.03)
Macao-China	3.2	(0.2)	9.9	(0.4)	86.9	(0.4)	426	(6.0)	464	(3.5)	492	(1.1)	-0.61	(0.07)	-0.73	(0.04)	-0.70	(0.01)
Montenegro	35.8	(0.6)	22.3	(0.8)	41.9	(0.8)	394	(2.3)	412	(4.3)	424	(2.4)	-0.64	(0.04)	-0.21	(0.03)	0.11	(0.02)
Panama	22.0	(1.4)	45.3	(1.6)	32.7	(1.4)	345	(5.9)	385	(6.4)	402	(9.1)	-1.51	(0.09)	-0.75	(0.08)	-0.35	(0.12)
Peru	15.1	(0.7)	26.3	(0.8)	58.6	(1.1)	337	(5.3)	368	(4.1)	392	(4.6)	-1.89	(0.07)	-1.39	(0.05)	-1.07	(0.06)
Qatar	38.3	(0.5)	38.7	(0.5)	23.0	(0.4)	342	(1.5)	382	(1.7)	422	(2.5)	0.08	(0.02)	0.74	(0.02)	0.82	(0.02)
Romania	4.8	(0.4)	7.6	(0.4)	87.6	(0.9)	384	(10.7)	403	(8.9)	429	(4.0)	-0.85	(0.17)	-0.52	(0.07)	-0.30	(0.03)
Russian Federation	21.4	(1.1)	11.2	(0.6)	67.4	(1.3)	439	(4.2)	451	(5.2)	468	(3.6)	-0.50	(0.04)	-0.27	(0.03)	-0.11	(0.04)
Serbia	13.0	(0.7)	50.1	(0.9)	36.9	(0.9)	426	(6.1)	442	(2.6)	450	(3.1)	-0.25	(0.06)	0.03	(0.02)	0.26	(0.03)
Shanghai-China	2.5	(0.5)	10.7	(0.7)	86.8	(1.0)	495	(14.1)	524	(5.8)	561	(2.1)	-1.37	(0.17)	-1.01	(0.07)	-0.40	(0.03)
Singapore	2.3	(0.2)	6.6	(0.4)	91.1	(0.4)	438	(10.0)	487	(7.1)	532	(1.3)	-0.76	(0.06)	-0.54	(0.05)	-0.41	(0.01)
Chinese Taipei	1.6	(0.2)	13.7	(0.5)	84.7	(0.5)	458	(11.2)	483	(4.4)	498	(2.6)	-0.56	(0.13)	-0.49	(0.04)	-0.30	(0.02)
Thailand	2.1	(0.2)	9.2	(0.5)	88.7	(0.6)	384	(6.5)	387	(4.1)	427	(2.6)	-1.64	(0.14)	-1.71	(0.06)	-1.26	(0.04)
Trinidad and Tobago	9.6	(0.5)	28.8	(0.7)	61.6	(0.8)	372	(5.5)	422	(3.3)	428	(1.9)	-1.08	(0.04)	-0.56	(0.03)	-0.50	(0.02)
Tunisia	48.1	(2.0)	31.3	(1.4)	20.6	(1.0)	389	(3.5)	415	(3.7)	430	(4.6)	-1.76	(0.06)	-0.76	(0.05)	-0.55	(0.06)
Uruguay	12.8	(0.7)	15.9	(0.6)	71.3	(0.8)	368	(5.3)	405	(4.1)	444	(2.6)	-1.33	(0.05)	-1.13	(0.04)	-0.47	(0.03)

Note: Values that are statistically significant are indicated in bold (see Annex A3).

StatLink http://dx.doi.org/10.1787/888932343285

[Part 2/2]
Pre-primary school attendance, performance in reading and students' socio-economic background
Table II.5.5 *Results based on students' self-reports*

| | | Difference in student performance in reading between students who report having attended pre-primary school (ISCED 0) for one year or less and those without pre-primary school attendance | | | | Difference in student performance in reading between students who report having attended pre-primary school (ISCED 0) for more than one year and those without pre-primary school attendance | | | | Increased likelihood of students who did not attend pre-primary school scoring in the bottom quarter of the national reading performance distribution | |
| | | Before accounting for the socio-economic background of students | | After accounting for the socio-economic background of students | | Before accounting for the socio-economic background of students | | After accounting for the socio-economic background of students | | | |
		Score dif.	S.E.	Score dif.	S.E.	Score dif.	S.E.	Score dif.	S.E.	Ratio	S.E.
OECD	Australia	47	(5.2)	36	(4.9)	60	(5.4)	39	(4.6)	1.82	(0.11)
	Austria	9	(11.0)	2	(10.6)	42	(10.6)	21	(10.3)	1.78	(0.24)
	Belgium	18	(10.7)	7	(11.5)	103	(8.6)	76	(8.2)	2.91	(0.22)
	Canada	29	(4.1)	23	(3.9)	48	(4.0)	33	(4.1)	1.65	(0.12)
	Chile	34	(3.8)	18	(3.2)	47	(3.8)	14	(3.5)	1.74	(0.11)
	Czech Republic	29	(9.6)	27	(8.9)	32	(8.6)	25	(7.9)	1.69	(0.20)
	Denmark	58	(7.7)	38	(7.8)	84	(7.6)	58	(7.8)	2.60	(0.25)
	Estonia	-9	(6.3)	-9	(6.5)	5	(4.1)	-2	(4.1)	1.05	(0.12)
	Finland	-1	(8.7)	-5	(8.1)	18	(8.6)	5	(7.9)	1.19	(0.17)
	France	51	(18.0)	27	(15.0)	108	(18.1)	65	(13.0)	2.69	(0.35)
	Germany	11	(8.7)	6	(8.7)	61	(7.0)	40	(7.4)	2.01	(0.19)
	Greece	48	(9.8)	31	(9.6)	69	(9.1)	49	(8.6)	2.19	(0.20)
	Hungary	9	(20.0)	13	(19.1)	45	(16.8)	36	(16.7)	1.64	(0.35)
	Iceland	20	(14.3)	13	(13.3)	44	(11.6)	28	(11.5)	1.44	(0.24)
	Ireland	31	(4.8)	21	(4.7)	24	(4.7)	8	(4.5)	1.47	(0.11)
	Israel	70	(7.4)	52	(7.3)	123	(8.7)	91	(8.5)	3.05	(0.19)
	Italy	44	(6.1)	34	(5.5)	79	(5.5)	65	(5.2)	2.32	(0.11)
	Japan	-16	(16.6)	-20	(16.4)	39	(14.8)	24	(12.8)	1.41	(0.27)
	Korea	6	(6.4)	-4	(6.4)	16	(7.1)	2	(6.8)	1.22	(0.17)
	Luxembourg	31	(9.3)	11	(8.8)	64	(7.9)	36	(8.0)	2.13	(0.17)
	Mexico	46	(3.8)	39	(3.7)	56	(3.3)	36	(3.2)	2.06	(0.10)
	Netherlands	25	(18.1)	14	(15.2)	26	(15.9)	8	(9.2)	1.64	(0.33)
	New Zealand	45	(6.8)	32	(6.4)	60	(6.3)	39	(5.8)	1.91	(0.13)
	Norway	11	(6.4)	8	(6.5)	31	(5.2)	18	(5.0)	1.41	(0.12)
	Poland	26	(10.7)	30	(10.1)	51	(10.8)	30	(10.6)	1.61	(0.24)
	Portugal	11	(5.1)	4	(5.1)	35	(4.6)	15	(4.2)	1.47	(0.12)
	Slovak Republic	52	(10.3)	34	(8.9)	60	(9.6)	38	(8.2)	2.06	(0.20)
	Slovenia	-3	(5.9)	-12	(5.4)	26	(4.2)	7	(3.9)	1.43	(0.10)
	Spain	17	(6.6)	11	(6.4)	53	(5.4)	39	(5.7)	1.93	(0.13)
	Sweden	44	(6.5)	30	(6.0)	58	(6.6)	38	(6.0)	1.90	(0.14)
	Switzerland	81	(9.8)	62	(8.2)	84	(10.0)	59	(8.5)	2.58	(0.24)
	Turkey	44	(4.8)	13	(3.9)	58	(7.1)	11	(5.9)	2.06	(0.22)
	United Kingdom	56	(7.3)	45	(6.6)	76	(7.9)	57	(6.2)	2.15	(0.18)
	United States	33	(16.0)	18	(12.7)	46	(15.0)	12	(12.0)	1.64	(0.25)
	OECD average	30	(1.72)	19	(1.58)	54	(1.58)	33	(1.40)	1.88	(0.03)
Partners	Albania	14	(6.5)	4	(6.0)	32	(5.8)	18	(5.0)	1.43	(0.12)
	Argentina	48	(12.8)	39	(11.8)	84	(12.8)	46	(11.1)	2.04	(0.24)
	Azerbaijan	15	(5.6)	6	(5.3)	28	(5.6)	16	(5.2)	1.48	(0.19)
	Brazil	35	(4.0)	28	(4.2)	60	(3.6)	38	(3.5)	1.87	(0.11)
	Bulgaria	13	(8.3)	-4	(7.4)	42	(8.0)	19	(5.8)	1.56	(0.17)
	Colombia	39	(4.1)	21	(4.2)	49	(5.3)	15	(4.4)	1.75	(0.13)
	Croatia	4	(5.6)	-4	(5.1)	29	(5.5)	5	(5.3)	1.35	(0.12)
	Dubai (UAE)	56	(5.0)	35	(4.9)	74	(4.6)	51	(4.7)	2.22	(0.12)
	Hong Kong-China	24	(14.9)	18	(14.7)	76	(13.5)	62	(13.7)	2.22	(0.27)
	Indonesia	34	(4.8)	27	(4.5)	40	(6.2)	30	(5.6)	1.98	(0.23)
	Jordan	26	(3.6)	16	(3.2)	38	(5.3)	20	(4.8)	1.55	(0.11)
	Kazakhstan	26	(5.0)	10	(4.2)	46	(5.6)	25	(4.6)	1.54	(0.13)
	Kyrgyzstan	27	(4.6)	16	(4.2)	72	(6.3)	47	(5.0)	1.77	(0.17)
	Latvia	5	(5.1)	3	(4.8)	14	(3.7)	2	(3.6)	1.38	(0.10)
	Liechtenstein	56	(47.1)	40	(55.3)	79	(41.2)	56	(49.9)	2.29	(1.21)
	Lithuania	15	(5.6)	2	(5.2)	31	(3.4)	11	(3.2)	1.55	(0.11)
	Macao-China	37	(6.8)	37	(6.6)	65	(6.1)	66	(5.9)	2.38	(0.19)
	Montenegro	18	(4.5)	6	(5.2)	30	(3.7)	9	(4.1)	1.38	(0.11)
	Panama	41	(6.3)	23	(5.5)	57	(7.8)	25	(6.5)	1.72	(0.19)
	Peru	31	(5.5)	13	(4.9)	55	(5.6)	23	(4.6)	1.84	(0.15)
	Qatar	40	(2.6)	30	(2.7)	80	(3.1)	70	(3.4)	1.51	(0.06)
	Romania	18	(11.1)	8	(8.8)	45	(10.5)	25	(8.7)	1.67	(0.25)
	Russian Federation	11	(5.1)	3	(5.3)	29	(4.2)	15	(3.8)	1.48	(0.13)
	Serbia	16	(5.9)	10	(5.2)	24	(6.2)	10	(5.6)	1.40	(0.13)
	Shanghai-China	29	(12.3)	20	(10.1)	66	(14.1)	42	(11.0)	2.42	(0.33)
	Singapore	49	(12.2)	38	(11.5)	94	(10.2)	78	(9.9)	2.46	(0.24)
	Chinese Taipei	26	(10.9)	23	(9.8)	41	(11.3)	32	(10.1)	1.79	(0.25)
	Thailand	3	(7.4)	5	(7.2)	43	(6.9)	35	(6.6)	1.93	(0.26)
	Trinidad and Tobago	50	(6.8)	31	(6.5)	55	(5.9)	34	(5.8)	1.93	(0.17)
	Tunisia	26	(4.6)	10	(4.3)	41	(5.4)	23	(5.1)	1.66	(0.14)
	Uruguay	36	(5.0)	31	(5.2)	76	(5.0)	46	(4.9)	2.13	(0.13)

Note: Values that are statistically significant are indicated in bold (see Annex A3).
StatLink ⎙⎗┛ http://dx.doi.org/10.1787/888932343285

[Part 1/1]

Relationship between pre-primary school attendance and performance, by quality of pre-primary school education

Table II.5.6

	Regression coefficients							
	Attendance*quality indicator		Attendance		Socio-economic background of students		Socio-economic background of schools	
	Coef.	S.E.	Coef.	S.E.	Coef.	S.E.	Coef.	S.E.
Percentage of students attended pre-primary school	**4.73**	(0.62)	**-27.13**	(5.52)	**17.82**	(0.26)	**59.04**	(0.98)
Average duration of pre-primary schools	**9.93**	(1.53)	**-9.13**	(3.56)	**17.81**	(0.27)	**59.34**	(1.01)
Average pupils-to-teacher ratio in pre-primary schools	**-1.13**	(0.19)	**29.98**	(3.09)	**17.27**	(0.29)	**58.48**	(1.01)
Public expenditure on pre-primary school per student (ppp)	**1.27**	(0.56)	**7.91**	(2.97)	**17.76**	(0.28)	**59.87**	(1.09)

Notes: Values that are statistically significant are indicated in bold (see Annex A3).
The model is run only for the OECD countries where the data are available.
This is a regression model with country fixed effects and interactions between individual pre-primary school attendance and one of the system-level quality indicators.
Variables included in the model are: escs, xescs, attendance, attendance*quality indicator, country fixed effect.
  escs= PISA index of economic, social and cultural status (student-level variable)
  xescs=school average of escs (school-level variable)
  immig: 0=native student, 1=student with an immigrant background (student-level variable)
  attendance: 0=not attended pre-primary school, 1=attended pre-primary school (student-level variable)
Quality indicators are:
  Percentage of students attended pre-primary school (system-level variable)
  Average duration of pre-primary school (system-level variable)
  Pupils-to-teacher ratio in pre-primary schools (system-level variable)
  Public expenditure on pre-primary school per student (ppp) (system-level variable)

StatLink 🔗 http://dx.doi.org/10.1787/888932343285

[Part 1/1]

Relationship between performance, pre-primary school attendance and socio-economic background[1]

Table II.5.7

		Difference in performance for students who attended a pre-primary school		Difference in performance for students with higher socio-economic background[2]		Additional difference in performance for students with higher socio-economic background[2] who attended pre-primary school	
		Change in score	S.E.	Change in score	S.E.	Change in score	S.E.
OECD	Australia	30	(4.8)	32	(4.7)	-2	(5.2)
	Austria	6	(9.3)	19	(8.6)	-9	(9.2)
	Belgium	45	(8.2)	13	(7.5)	0	(7.7)
	Canada	21	(3.8)	12	(4.0)	7	(3.8)
	Chile	9	(3.9)	12	(3.0)	-2	(2.9)
	Czech Republic	21	(6.1)	17	(8.9)	-2	(9.1)
	Denmark	32	(10.1)	24	(8.5)	3	(8.8)
	Estonia	-10	(4.1)	18	(4.4)	-2	(4.8)
	Finland	1	(7.3)	33	(7.2)	-5	(7.6)
	France	w	w	w	w	w	w
	Germany	22	(6.1)	1	(8.0)	11	(8.4)
	Greece	26	(7.4)	3	(7.7)	13	(7.7)
	Hungary	11	(10.7)	7	(9.0)	3	(8.8)
	Iceland	14	(12.8)	23	(11.9)	6	(11.7)
	Ireland	10	(4.3)	23	(4.6)	8	(5.5)
	Israel	60	(8.9)	15	(7.9)	9	(8.1)
	Italy	34	(3.9)	-5	(6.1)	11	(6.3)
	Japan	-2	(10.6)	27	(18.4)	-24	(18.6)
	Korea	-9	(6.8)	17	(7.5)	-5	(7.4)
	Luxembourg	5	(7.8)	18	(5.8)	-2	(5.9)
	Mexico	33	(3.8)	5	(2.4)	5	(1.9)
	Netherlands	0	(8.2)	5	(6.6)	0	(6.8)
	New Zealand	25	(4.9)	34	(6.1)	3	(6.6)
	Norway	9	(5.2)	13	(5.4)	23	(6.2)
	Poland	23	(10.7)	31	(8.9)	2	(8.9)
	Portugal	9	(4.4)	14	(2.6)	4	(3.0)
	Slovak Republic	12	(7.1)	25	(5.9)	-10	(6.3)
	Slovenia	-1	(3.3)	5	(3.2)	0	(3.3)
	Spain	25	(7.4)	16	(6.2)	3	(6.1)
	Sweden	22	(4.7)	31	(5.1)	0	(5.2)
	Switzerland	36	(8.8)	24	(6.6)	-7	(7.0)
	Turkey	1	(3.5)	10	(2.7)	0	(2.6)
	United Kingdom	36	(5.8)	26	(6.7)	0	(6.5)
	United States	3	(11.0)	50	(9.2)	-24	(9.4)
	OECD average	17	(1.3)	18	(1.3)	1	(1.3)
Partners	Albania	-4	(5.7)	26	(4.8)	-5	(4.3)
	Argentina	27	(11.0)	15	(7.4)	0	(6.7)
	Azerbaijan	1	(4.2)	15	(3.1)	-5	(4.9)
	Brazil	33	(5.7)	7	(2.9)	6	(2.4)
	Bulgaria	0	(6.9)	13	(4.5)	3	(4.6)
	Colombia	21	(6.2)	6	(4.1)	5	(3.1)
	Croatia	-3	(3.5)	12	(2.5)	-1	(3.2)
	Dubai (UAE)	20	(4.6)	14	(5.2)	6	(4.9)
	Hong Kong-China	35	(13.8)	1	(7.5)	-1	(7.6)
	Indonesia	24	(4.9)	4	(3.1)	4	(2.5)
	Jordan	17	(3.6)	16	(3.2)	4	(3.0)
	Kazakhstan	8	(3.6)	14	(2.6)	5	(3.4)
	Kyrgyzstan	14	(3.9)	18	(3.1)	7	(4.1)
	Latvia	-5	(3.6)	23	(4.0)	-5	(4.1)
	Liechtenstein	47	(17.2)	-73	(17.6)	74	(19.8)
	Lithuania	-1	(3.1)	23	(2.3)	-6	(2.6)
	Macao-China	41	(6.4)	8	(6.2)	1	(6.1)
	Montenegro	-3	(3.3)	12	(2.9)	0	(3.5)
	Panama	15	(7.0)	2	(5.0)	8	(4.3)
	Peru	14	(7.2)	8	(4.8)	4	(3.4)
	Qatar	1	(2.6)	0	(1.7)	19	(2.5)
	Romania	27	(10.5)	-4	(6.7)	19	(7.7)
	Russian Federation	8	(4.1)	17	(3.8)	6	(3.8)
	Serbia	5	(3.9)	7	(3.2)	2	(3.6)
	Shanghai-China	24	(10.7)	4	(5.9)	1	(5.8)
	Singapore	47	(11.7)	26	(10.6)	-10	(10.7)
	Chinese Taipei	9	(10.6)	28	(13.2)	-13	(13.2)
	Thailand	40	(11.6)	5	(6.7)	10	(6.2)
	Trinidad and Tobago	8	(7.7)	7	(5.8)	-3	(5.8)
	Tunisia	0	(4.5)	7	(2.8)	3	(2.4)
	Uruguay	45	(6.2)	3	(3.8)	13	(3.5)

Note: Values that are statistically significant are indicated in bold (see Annex A3).
1. Reading performance is regressed on the following variables: student attended pre-primary school; student's socio-economic background; (student attended pre-primary school)*(student's socio-economic background); a square of student's socio-economic background; school's socio-economic background; gender; student with an immigrant background; school in rural area; school in a city; school size; a square of school size; and private school.
2. Students with higher socio-economic background correspond to students with a one unit higher PISA index of economic, social and cultural status than the OECD average.

StatLink ᵐˢᵖ http://dx.doi.org/10.1787/888932343285

[Part 1/1]

Table II.5.8 Relationship between performance, pre-primary school attendance and immigrant status[1]

| | | Difference in performance for students who attended a pre-primary school | | Difference in performance for students with an immigrant background | | Additional difference in performance for students with an immigrant background who attended a pre-primary school | |
		Change in score	S.E.	Change in score	S.E.	Change in score	S.E.
OECD	Australia	27	(4.7)	4	(9.0)	6	(10.1)
	Austria	7	(10.9)	-22	(22.1)	2	(21.2)
	Belgium	60	(12.6)	11	(18.5)	-30	(19.1)
	Canada	16	(3.5)	-23	(7.3)	27	(7.9)
	Chile	c	c	c	c	c	c
	Czech Republic	21	(6.1)	-9	(33.1)	7	(32.9)
	Denmark	29	(13.1)	-24	(14.9)	5	(15.2)
	Estonia	-10	(4.2)	-24	(16.3)	-4	(16.5)
	Finland	-4	(7.1)	-96	(27.5)	76	(27.3)
	France	w	w	w	w	w	w
	Germany	20	(8.0)	-8	(15.6)	1	(14.8)
	Greece	24	(8.4)	3	(23.9)	-18	(22.1)
	Hungary	9	(9.3)	-11	(25.5)	11	(26.4)
	Iceland	15	(12.7)	-39	(26.9)	7	(29.2)
	Ireland	4	(4.4)	-57	(15.7)	57	(16.0)
	Israel	56	(8.5)	29	(20.3)	-10	(19.4)
	Italy	31	(4.5)	-20	(8.7)	-9	(9.9)
	Japan	c	c	c	c	c	c
	Korea	c	c	c	c	c	c
	Luxembourg	4	(28.1)	-24	(28.8)	1	(29.2)
	Mexico	25	(2.9)	-55	(10.6)	-19	(12.7)
	Netherlands	-8	(8.7)	-2	(19.8)	18	(19.0)
	New Zealand	17	(7.6)	-6	(11.4)	15	(11.8)
	Norway	10	(5.1)	-30	(13.2)	26	(13.6)
	Poland	c	c	c	c	c	c
	Portugal	7	(3.5)	-23	(7.6)	1	(8.4)
	Slovak Republic	c	c	c	c	c	c
	Slovenia	-1	(3.3)	-13	(10.1)	2	(9.8)
	Spain	24	(6.2)	-37	(9.0)	-7	(9.0)
	Sweden	19	(5.3)	-29	(15.1)	15	(15.0)
	Switzerland	36	(14.9)	-17	(16.7)	4	(18.0)
	Turkey	c	c	c	c	c	c
	United Kingdom	43	(6.4)	31	(14.3)	-25	(14.5)
	United States	-3	(13.5)	-26	(22.1)	37	(21.2)
	OECD average	18	(1.9)	-19	(3.6)	7	(3.6)
Partners	Albania	c	c	c	c	c	c
	Argentina	29	(8.7)	7	(36.4)	-13	(32.9)
	Azerbaijan	3	(4.8)	-1	(11.6)	-7	(14.4)
	Brazil	23	(3.2)	-93	(17.7)	4	(22.3)
	Bulgaria	c	c	c	c	c	c
	Colombia	13	(3.6)	-25	(25.9)	-71	(29.0)
	Croatia	-2	(3.6)	-2	(7.0)	-8	(7.9)
	Dubai (UAE)	11	(8.1)	54	(9.3)	14	(9.8)
	Hong Kong-China	50	(17.8)	32	(19.9)	-19	(19.7)
	Indonesia	c	c	c	c	c	c
	Jordan	15	(2.7)	5	(8.1)	-6	(9.2)
	Kazakhstan	5	(3.5)	5	(6.9)	12	(7.3)
	Kyrgyzstan	10	(3.4)	41	(17.0)	-27	(25.0)
	Latvia	-3	(3.9)	-5	(17.2)	-7	(17.6)
	Liechtenstein	6	(47.9)	0	(10.2)	0	(0.0)
	Lithuania	0	(3.1)	-32	(15.5)	34	(20.0)
	Macao-China	41	(8.0)	15	(9.5)	-2	(9.7)
	Montenegro	-3	(3.5)	-1	(8.0)	-5	(10.8)
	Panama	4	(5.1)	-36	(17.8)	22	(22.3)
	Peru	c	c	c	c	c	c
	Qatar	1	(2.7)	40	(2.9)	20	(4.0)
	Romania	c	c	c	c	c	c
	Russian Federation	6	(3.9)	-14	(8.7)	4	(9.4)
	Serbia	5	(3.9)	13	(8.9)	-4	(9.4)
	Shanghai-China	c	c	c	c	c	c
	Singapore	53	(11.2)	-5	(17.1)	5	(17.4)
	Chinese Taipei	c	c	c	c	c	c
	Thailand	c	c	c	c	c	c
	Trinidad and Tobago	11	(5.8)	-11	(46.5)	0	(46.0)
	Tunisia	c	c	c	c	c	c
	Uruguay	c	c	c	c	c	c

Note: Values that are statistically significant are indicated in bold (see Annex A3).
1. Reading performance is regressed on the following variables: student attended pre-primary school; student with an immigrant background; (student attended pre-primary school)*(student with an immigrant background); student's socio-economic background; a square of student's socio-economic background; school's socio-economic background; gender; school in rural area; school in a city; school size; a square of school size; and private school.

StatLink ⟨⟩ http://dx.doi.org/10.1787/888932343285

[Part 1/1]

Relationship between pre-primary school attendance and performance, by immigrant status and quality of pre-primary school education

Table II.5.9

Quality indicators	Regression coefficients											
	Attendance* immigrant* quality indicator		Attendance* immigrant		Immigrant		Attendance		Socio-economic background of students		Socio-economic background of schools	
	Coef.	S.E.	Coef.	S.E.	Coef.	S.E.	Coef.	S.E.	Coef.	S.E.	Coef.	S.E.
Percentage of students attended pre-primary school	1.67	(2.28)	7.51	(21.37)	-31.06	(3.03)	8.94	(0.94)	17.70	(0.26)	58.88	(0.99)
Average duration of pre-primary schools	-14.83	(2.00)	55.63	(5.00)	-31.76	(3.02)	7.82	(0.99)	17.71	(0.27)	59.25	(1.00)
Average pupils-to-teacher ratio in pre-primary schools	-0.44	(0.32)	26.97	(5.21)	-34.65	(3.44)	8.74	(1.09)	17.25	(0.29)	58.39	(1.02)
Public expenditure on pre-primary school per student (ppp)	2.81	(0.78)	6.62	(5.48)	-28.82	(3.18)	10.91	(1.03)	17.78	(0.28)	60.05	(1.09)

Notes: Values that are statistically significant are indicated in bold (see Annex A3).
The model is run only for the OECD countries where the data are available.
This is a regression model with country fixed effects and interactions between individual pre-primary school attendance, individual immigrant status and one of the system-level quality indicators.
Variables included in the model are: escs, xescs, immig, attendance, attendance*immig, attendance*immig*quality indicator, country fixed effect
  escs= PISA index of economic, social and cultural status (student-level variable)
  xescs=school average of escs (school-level variable)
  immig: 0=native student, 1=student with an immigrant background (student-level variable)
  attendance: 0=not attended pre-primary school, 1=attended pre-primary school (student-level variable)
Quality indicators are:
  Percentage of students attended pre-primary school (system-level variable)
  Average duration of pre-primary school (system-level variable)
  Pupils-to-teacher ratio in pre-primary schools (system-level variable)
  Public expenditure on pre-primary school per student (ppp) (system-level variable)

StatLink 📊 http://dx.doi.org/10.1787/888932343285

[Part 1/2]

Residuals in performance for the bottom and top quarters of the PISA index of economic, social and cultural status (ESCS), by schools' socio-economic background[1]

Table II.5.10 *Results based on students' self-reports*

	Schools with disadvantaged socio-economic intake					Schools with average or mixture of socio-economic intake				
	Percentage of students	Students in the bottom quarter of ESCS		Students in the top quarter of ESCS		Percentage of students	Students in the bottom quarter of ESCS		Students in the top quarter of ESCS	
		Percentage of students	Difference between observed and predicted reading performance	Percentage of students	Difference between observed and predicted reading performance		Percentage of students	Difference between observed and predicted reading performance	Percentage of students	Difference between observed and predicted reading performance
	S.E.	S.E.	Score dif. / S.E.	S.E.	Score dif. / S.E.	S.E.	S.E.	Score dif. / S.E.	S.E.	Score dif. / S.E.

OECD

Country	% (S.E.)	% bottom (S.E.)	Score dif. (S.E.)	% top (S.E.)	Score dif. (S.E.)	% (S.E.)	% bottom (S.E.)	Score dif. (S.E.)	% top (S.E.)	Score dif. (S.E.)
Australia	33.0 (2.1)	57.8 (2.7)	-15 (3.7)	10.6 (1.0)	-32 (7.1)	38.3 (2.4)	34.5 (2.6)	11 (3.8)	33.9 (2.6)	-19 (3.8)
Austria	29.7 (2.5)	54.6 (3.4)	-35 (4.8)	6.8 (1.1)	-77 (9.7)	42.6 (3.5)	37.2 (3.6)	28 (7.2)	37.8 (4.0)	-24 (6.3)
Belgium	32.1 (2.5)	58.7 (3.2)	-26 (4.9)	8.1 (1.1)	-80 (8.1)	36.3 (3.1)	33.8 (3.3)	27 (5.2)	27.5 (2.8)	-22 (5.4)
Canada	19.0 (1.7)	37.3 (2.8)	-9 (4.2)	5.3 (0.8)	-38 (5.4)	59.6 (2.1)	56.4 (2.8)	9 (2.6)	54.4 (2.6)	-4 (3.0)
Chile	45.5 (3.1)	80.8 (3.1)	-1 (4.1)	10.1 (1.4)	-46 (7.8)	21.5 (3.0)	15.4 (2.9)	17 (6.6)	14.0 (2.2)	-41 (7.2)
Czech Republic	22.0 (3.0)	41.4 (4.4)	-28 (5.7)	6.9 (1.3)	-73 (9.4)	56.3 (3.8)	54.0 (4.5)	10 (4.4)	48.1 (3.8)	-31 (5.5)
Denmark	18.6 (2.3)	35.9 (3.6)	-13 (4.2)	5.6 (0.9)	-7 (8.8)	60.1 (3.3)	58.5 (3.8)	5 (3.8)	53.4 (4.3)	-6 (3.1)
Estonia	20.1 (2.7)	37.0 (4.4)	-6 (7.2)	7.2 (1.1)	-25 (12.1)	54.9 (3.2)	55.4 (4.4)	5 (4.3)	48.4 (3.5)	-11 (4.5)
Finland	15.9 (2.2)	26.1 (3.5)	1 (7.2)	6.0 (1.1)	17 (12.1)	62.5 (3.8)	65.0 (4.0)	0 (3.8)	54.0 (4.7)	-5 (3.8)
France	29.7 (2.7)	56.8 (3.7)	-39 (7.4)	6.4 (1.2)	-108 (16.4)	44.2 (4.0)	37.1 (3.8)	43 (7.8)	37.9 (4.7)	-15 (8.7)
Germany	24.9 (2.4)	49.6 (3.5)	-42 (5.2)	4.8 (0.9)	-113 (12.3)	48.0 (3.1)	43.8 (3.4)	17 (5.4)	40.4 (3.8)	-34 (5.5)
Greece	24.6 (3.0)	49.8 (4.2)	-37 (10.9)	5.3 (1.1)	-78 (21.2)	48.9 (3.8)	43.0 (4.1)	24 (5.7)	41.1 (3.9)	2 (4.7)
Hungary	33.0 (2.2)	68.8 (3.3)	-23 (5.7)	5.9 (1.1)	-73 (13.7)	32.7 (3.7)	24.8 (3.3)	27 (8.1)	24.8 (3.2)	-39 (6.6)
Iceland	20.4 (0.2)	39.1 (1.4)	-3 (5.4)	7.2 (0.7)	-10 (11.8)	47.3 (0.2)	48.2 (1.5)	-1 (3.8)	40.4 (1.4)	-12 (4.5)
Ireland	24.6 (3.3)	45.6 (4.9)	-20 (7.5)	6.1 (1.2)	-21 (14.1)	55.3 (3.9)	50.6 (4.8)	12 (4.5)	50.0 (4.6)	-4 (4.4)
Israel	27.0 (3.4)	52.1 (4.9)	-11 (8.9)	7.9 (1.4)	-88 (19.0)	39.4 (3.7)	39.9 (4.8)	-8 (7.2)	31.8 (3.7)	-40 (8.4)
Italy	32.2 (1.3)	59.3 (1.8)	-33 (4.4)	8.8 (0.6)	-85 (5.1)	37.4 (1.7)	33.0 (1.9)	32 (4.1)	31.0 (1.6)	-29 (4.0)
Japan	30.1 (2.4)	56.6 (3.4)	-33 (7.4)	11.2 (1.3)	-96 (9.7)	39.2 (3.2)	35.6 (3.3)	28 (7.1)	34.2 (3.3)	-23 (6.7)
Korea	29.4 (3.1)	57.9 (3.7)	-23 (7.2)	8.4 (1.9)	-60 (12.6)	45.8 (3.9)	35.8 (3.7)	25 (4.4)	42.1 (4.9)	-5 (4.2)
Luxembourg	46.0 (0.2)	73.9 (1.2)	-17 (3.0)	19.1 (1.1)	-70 (7.6)	22.2 (0.1)	17.7 (1.0)	17 (6.3)	20.2 (1.0)	-14 (5.6)
Mexico	33.3 (1.6)	68.8 (1.7)	-11 (3.7)	6.0 (0.6)	-52 (4.9)	37.8 (1.8)	27.6 (1.7)	20 (4.0)	30.0 (2.1)	-25 (3.1)
Netherlands	21.5 (3.3)	40.9 (4.9)	-20 (5.8)	4.8 (1.0)	-94 (10.5)	54.7 (3.5)	51.9 (4.6)	13 (9.7)	47.4 (3.9)	-23 (10.7)
New Zealand	24.1 (2.5)	45.1 (3.9)	-13 (6.5)	6.2 (1.1)	-31 (15.1)	49.8 (2.9)	48.5 (3.8)	14 (4.5)	44.1 (2.9)	-6 (4.9)
Norway	12.4 (2.4)	22.3 (3.9)	0 (7.5)	3.9 (0.8)	-24 (11.8)	71.6 (3.7)	72.6 (4.0)	-4 (3.4)	65.5 (4.7)	-7 (4.6)
Poland	30.0 (3.2)	50.8 (4.5)	-8 (4.5)	9.1 (1.5)	-8 (8.2)	50.7 (4.0)	44.4 (4.5)	5 (5.4)	47.0 (4.6)	-4 (4.5)
Portugal	32.2 (3.1)	56.4 (3.8)	-17 (6.0)	7.6 (1.1)	-56 (7.3)	44.6 (3.3)	38.2 (3.7)	21 (4.4)	40.2 (3.5)	-10 (3.6)
Slovak Republic	25.3 (2.8)	45.8 (4.3)	-26 (7.1)	7.7 (1.3)	-74 (8.3)	51.2 (3.9)	48.1 (4.3)	5 (5.4)	44.8 (4.5)	-35 (5.3)
Slovenia	29.6 (0.4)	54.4 (1.3)	-25 (2.7)	6.8 (0.6)	-92 (7.8)	42.0 (0.4)	38.5 (1.3)	23 (3.5)	35.8 (1.3)	-31 (4.4)
Spain	31.9 (2.8)	57.1 (3.7)	-7 (4.4)	9.9 (1.6)	-15 (5.5)	43.7 (2.6)	38.5 (3.5)	11 (4.1)	34.6 (2.4)	-10 (3.6)
Sweden	19.8 (2.7)	34.1 (4.4)	-9 (7.7)	6.4 (1.2)	-18 (13.6)	60.7 (3.5)	60.4 (4.5)	-2 (4.5)	55.6 (4.1)	-13 (4.8)
Switzerland	26.0 (3.1)	49.4 (4.0)	-17 (7.9)	9.3 (1.5)	-42 (6.8)	48.4 (3.2)	48.3 (3.8)	2 (4.2)	39.0 (3.4)	-25 (4.9)
Turkey	35.1 (3.5)	63.6 (4.1)	-14 (4.8)	8.9 (1.5)	-47 (5.4)	34.2 (3.3)	29.0 (3.7)	10 (5.7)	27.4 (3.3)	-28 (5.5)
United Kingdom	26.5 (2.6)	48.3 (3.6)	-16 (5.0)	7.7 (1.1)	-61 (11.0)	50.2 (3.4)	45.4 (3.6)	10 (3.8)	44.2 (3.7)	-12 (4.1)
United States	32.2 (3.5)	60.6 (4.0)	-6 (4.9)	9.1 (1.6)	-43 (7.9)	38.0 (3.5)	32.9 (3.8)	13 (5.3)	29.7 (3.8)	2 (5.1)
OECD average	27.6 (0.4)	50.9 (0.6)	-18 (1.0)	7.7 (0.2)	-54 (1.9)	46.2 (0.5)	42.5 (0.6)	14 (0.9)	39.7 (0.6)	-18 (0.9)

Partners

Country	% (S.E.)	% bottom (S.E.)	Score dif. (S.E.)	% top (S.E.)	Score dif. (S.E.)	% (S.E.)	% bottom (S.E.)	Score dif. (S.E.)	% top (S.E.)	Score dif. (S.E.)
Albania	26.4 (2.6)	55.2 (3.7)	-5 (9.2)	5.6 (1.1)	-79 (15.8)	45.5 (3.6)	40.3 (3.8)	14 (5.9)	38.1 (4.0)	-31 (6.2)
Argentina	33.1 (3.5)	62.1 (4.4)	-8 (6.8)	5.6 (1.2)	-85 (21.2)	36.1 (3.5)	34.2 (4.0)	25 (8.6)	24.1 (3.5)	-44 (10.8)
Azerbaijan	32.1 (3.3)	61.4 (4.4)	-3 (8.3)	9.3 (1.6)	-30 (10.9)	36.3 (4.1)	31.4 (4.2)	6 (5.9)	31.3 (4.1)	-23 (4.8)
Brazil	33.4 (2.7)	65.1 (2.8)	-2 (3.4)	9.6 (1.2)	-66 (7.7)	41.7 (2.6)	31.7 (2.6)	20 (4.6)	33.9 (2.3)	-40 (4.8)
Bulgaria	27.4 (3.6)	58.2 (5.2)	-26 (5.0)	5.4 (1.0)	-120 (14.0)	41.4 (3.9)	35.3 (4.8)	21 (10.5)	33.5 (4.1)	-41 (7.0)
Colombia	37.3 (3.6)	70.5 (5.4)	-3 (5.7)	11.4 (2.0)	-50 (9.6)	31.1 (3.8)	26.7 (4.2)	18 (5.5)	21.3 (3.0)	-31 (5.4)
Croatia	30.5 (3.2)	52.0 (4.2)	-24 (5.2)	10.1 (1.6)	-50 (11.2)	45.8 (4.0)	42.7 (4.2)	17 (5.5)	40.8 (4.4)	-28 (6.3)
Dubai (UAE)	31.0 (0.1)	66.2 (1.3)	-18 (2.4)	9.7 (0.8)	-73 (8.6)	26.2 (0.2)	22.3 (1.1)	21 (5.5)	16.4 (1.0)	-31 (7.2)
Hong Kong-China	41.1 (3.5)	64.6 (4.0)	-16 (5.6)	12.0 (1.8)	-43 (8.0)	37.0 (3.7)	32.1 (3.9)	14 (7.3)	31.4 (4.2)	-8 (7.3)
Indonesia	38.9 (3.8)	69.8 (4.0)	0 (4.7)	9.3 (1.6)	-36 (8.7)	34.2 (3.8)	25.9 (3.8)	17 (6.9)	24.9 (4.0)	-28 (6.7)
Jordan	28.8 (3.3)	50.0 (4.3)	4 (5.8)	9.6 (1.4)	-5 (9.7)	48.4 (3.5)	46.6 (4.2)	-6 (5.7)	40.8 (3.5)	-8 (4.8)
Kazakhstan	23.7 (3.0)	49.6 (4.3)	-11 (6.4)	6.9 (1.3)	-54 (9.8)	49.9 (3.3)	44.8 (4.0)	1 (5.1)	41.3 (3.7)	-20 (5.3)
Kyrgyzstan	29.4 (3.0)	55.4 (4.3)	0 (6.2)	11.0 (1.6)	-53 (7.7)	44.6 (3.6)	39.4 (4.2)	9 (5.8)	36.6 (3.1)	-37 (6.5)
Latvia	24.6 (3.4)	47.4 (4.9)	-3 (8.3)	5.9 (1.3)	-19 (10.0)	49.5 (4.1)	45.8 (4.8)	5 (5.1)	44.0 (4.6)	-13 (4.6)
Liechtenstein	27.1 (0.5)	40.9 (3.6)	-23 (12.0)	9.7 (2.8)	-46 (25.3)	46.9 (0.6)	51.7 (3.8)	-5 (9.7)	38.6 (4.9)	-51 (11.8)
Lithuania	24.3 (2.4)	45.7 (3.6)	-19 (5.0)	5.7 (0.9)	-38 (11.4)	49.5 (3.3)	48.3 (3.7)	15 (4.0)	42.6 (3.7)	-20 (5.0)
Macao-China	60.1 (0.0)	81.3 (0.9)	-6 (4.0)	32.3 (1.0)	-13 (4.1)	13.5 (0.0)	11.0 (0.7)	16 (4.9)	12.1 (0.7)	-10 (5.9)
Montenegro	37.3 (1.1)	63.4 (2.0)	-21 (3.1)	16.7 (1.0)	-52 (6.7)	24.4 (0.5)	21.3 (1.5)	-1 (5.5)	21.6 (1.1)	-38 (6.6)
Panama	38.0 (4.6)	70.5 (5.4)	17 (10.1)	7.6 (2.2)	-42 (16.0)	33.2 (4.7)	27.7 (5.3)	8 (5.7)	19.0 (4.6)	-53 (13.7)
Peru	38.7 (2.6)	78.5 (2.5)	-10 (4.0)	8.8 (1.3)	-92 (8.6)	26.7 (2.9)	18.3 (2.4)	19 (7.3)	19.1 (3.0)	-45 (5.8)
Qatar	30.4 (0.1)	59.7 (0.7)	0 (2.2)	10.7 (0.5)	-35 (6.4)	29.6 (0.2)	27.4 (0.8)	-20 (4.2)	22.3 (0.8)	-55 (5.4)
Romania	28.0 (3.0)	53.2 (4.1)	-31 (8.3)	7.4 (1.3)	-78 (13.4)	41.3 (3.9)	37.3 (4.0)	21 (6.0)	32.1 (4.3)	-25 (6.6)
Russian Federation	27.0 (2.9)	50.5 (4.0)	-2 (5.5)	7.5 (1.3)	-29 (17.1)	45.9 (3.6)	42.7 (4.0)	0 (4.4)	37.2 (3.5)	-26 (4.9)
Serbia	33.3 (3.5)	52.9 (4.4)	-20 (5.0)	12.7 (1.9)	-62 (8.6)	43.7 (3.5)	41.0 (4.1)	20 (5.4)	38.0 (3.8)	-18 (6.4)
Shanghai-China	35.8 (3.1)	68.8 (3.8)	-15 (5.3)	8.3 (1.3)	-57 (9.1)	30.5 (3.7)	25.0 (3.8)	31 (6.6)	24.9 (3.9)	-19 (6.2)
Singapore	23.7 (0.3)	38.7 (1.1)	-16 (3.5)	9.5 (0.7)	-55 (9.1)	54.6 (0.7)	56.8 (1.1)	5 (3.0)	45.7 (1.3)	-22 (3.7)
Chinese Taipei	28.2 (3.0)	50.9 (4.3)	-16 (5.1)	10.4 (1.8)	-56 (9.1)	45.0 (3.9)	40.3 (4.4)	15 (4.7)	40.9 (4.2)	-13 (4.5)
Thailand	43.0 (2.8)	77.0 (3.1)	2 (4.3)	6.6 (1.1)	-51 (10.5)	23.7 (3.0)	17.7 (3.0)	10 (6.7)	17.4 (2.7)	-43 (7.1)
Trinidad and Tobago	29.2 (0.3)	50.7 (1.4)	-38 (4.6)	9.3 (1.0)	-123 (12.7)	44.1 (0.4)	43.0 (1.3)	30 (4.8)	34.8 (1.3)	-50 (4.9)
Tunisia	31.2 (3.2)	62.2 (4.1)	-6 (5.3)	7.6 (1.4)	-56 (12.2)	39.7 (3.8)	31.6 (3.9)	14 (5.2)	34.7 (4.3)	-12 (6.9)
Uruguay	37.7 (2.2)	65.8 (2.8)	-15 (4.1)	8.8 (1.1)	-66 (9.7)	37.0 (2.4)	30.7 (2.8)	25 (5.0)	31.1 (2.4)	-19 (5.7)

Note: Values that are statistically significant are indicated in bold (see Annex A3).
1. Schools with an average or mixture of socio-economic intake are not statistically significantly different from the country average. Schools with an advantaged (disadvantaged) socio-economic intake are above (below) the country average.
StatLink ᴬᴵˢᴸ http://dx.doi.org/10.1787/888932343285

[Part 2/2]
Residuals in performance for the bottom and top quarters of the PISA index of economic, social and cultural status (ESCS), by schools' socio-economic background[1]

Table II.5.10   *Results based on students' self-reports*

			Schools with advantaged of socio-economic intake							
			Students in the bottom quarter of ESCS				Students in the top quarter of ESCS			
					Difference between observed and predicted reading performance				Difference between observed and predicted reading performance	
	Percentage of students	S.E.	Percentage of students	S.E.	Score dif.	S.E.	Percentage of students	S.E.	Score dif.	S.E.
Australia	28.7	(1.8)	7.7	(0.9)	**49**	(8.4)	55.5	(2.5)	**19**	(4.6)
Austria	27.7	(2.8)	8.2	(1.1)	**97**	(9.9)	55.4	(4.0)	**29**	(6.4)
Belgium	31.7	(1.8)	7.5	(0.9)	**88**	(7.0)	64.4	(2.6)	**25**	(3.3)
Canada	21.4	(1.6)	6.2	(0.8)	**27**	(7.7)	40.3	(2.7)	**18**	(3.8)
Chile	32.9	(2.5)	3.7	(0.8)	**58**	(13.0)	76.0	(2.5)	**18**	(3.3)
Czech Republic	21.7	(2.1)	4.6	(0.8)	**92**	(14.5)	45.1	(3.4)	**44**	(6.1)
Denmark	21.4	(2.7)	5.6	(1.1)	**20**	(10.2)	41.1	(4.4)	7	(4.6)
Estonia	24.9	(2.4)	7.6	(1.2)	**35**	(7.7)	44.5	(3.5)	**23**	(6.7)
Finland	21.6	(3.2)	8.8	(1.7)	-10	(9.5)	40.0	(4.8)	1	(3.8)
France	26.2	(3.1)	6.2	(1.2)	**79**	(11.4)	55.7	(4.8)	**24**	(6.0)
Germany	27.1	(2.4)	6.6	(1.0)	**103**	(9.7)	54.8	(3.9)	**29**	(3.7)
Greece	26.5	(3.3)	7.2	(1.3)	**49**	(6.1)	53.6	(4.0)	8	(4.9)
Hungary	34.3	(2.8)	6.4	(1.0)	**104**	(7.7)	69.3	(3.1)	**16**	(3.6)
Iceland	32.3	(0.2)	12.8	(1.1)	10	(8.8)	52.4	(1.5)	9	(3.6)
Ireland	20.1	(2.5)	3.8	(0.6)	**31**	(17.5)	43.8	(4.6)	3	(5.5)
Israel	33.6	(2.8)	8.0	(1.2)	**49**	(10.7)	60.2	(3.5)	**38**	(4.7)
Italy	30.4	(1.2)	7.8	(0.6)	**78**	(3.8)	60.2	(1.7)	**21**	(2.6)
Japan	30.7	(2.5)	7.8	(1.2)	**84**	(8.0)	54.6	(3.2)	**30**	(5.1)
Korea	24.8	(3.6)	6.3	(1.3)	**40**	(10.5)	49.5	(5.3)	**14**	(6.7)
Luxembourg	31.8	(0.1)	8.3	(0.8)	**78**	(8.3)	60.7	(1.3)	**26**	(2.9)
Mexico	28.9	(1.5)	3.6	(0.3)	**54**	(5.6)	64.0	(2.2)	**17**	(3.0)
Netherlands	23.7	(2.5)	7.2	(1.3)	**95**	(7.9)	47.7	(3.9)	**43**	(5.1)
New Zealand	26.0	(1.9)	6.5	(1.0)	**51**	(10.3)	49.6	(2.9)	**15**	(4.5)
Norway	16.1	(2.9)	5.1	(1.1)	5	(9.0)	30.7	(4.6)	12	(6.2)
Poland	19.3	(2.7)	4.8	(0.9)	24	(14.3)	44.0	(4.6)	6	(6.2)
Portugal	23.2	(2.6)	5.5	(1.2)	**58**	(12.1)	52.2	(3.7)	**12**	(4.6)
Slovak Republic	23.5	(2.7)	6.1	(1.3)	**91**	(12.0)	47.5	(4.4)	**36**	(5.1)
Slovenia	28.4	(0.3)	7.1	(1.0)	**105**	(7.2)	57.4	(1.2)	**34**	(2.8)
Spain	24.4	(1.8)	4.4	(0.6)	**27**	(8.3)	55.5	(2.8)	**10**	(4.7)
Sweden	19.6	(2.6)	5.5	(1.3)	**34**	(9.8)	37.9	(4.1)	**22**	(6.7)
Switzerland	25.6	(2.7)	8.0	(1.3)	**81**	(11.3)	51.6	(3.7)	**33**	(5.4)
Turkey	30.6	(3.1)	7.4	(1.3)	**86**	(8.9)	63.6	(3.5)	**20**	(5.7)
United Kingdom	23.3	(2.3)	6.4	(0.9)	**38**	(9.0)	48.1	(3.7)	**25**	(4.3)
United States	29.9	(3.6)	6.4	(1.4)	**28**	(11.1)	61.2	(4.5)	**20**	(6.0)
OECD average	26.2	(0.4)	6.6	(0.2)	**57**	(1.7)	52.6	(0.6)	**21**	(0.8)
Albania	28.1	(3.3)	4.5	(1.0)	**50**	(13.2)	56.3	(4.2)	**30**	(6.1)
Argentina	30.8	(3.3)	3.7	(0.9)	**97**	(10.2)	70.2	(3.8)	**33**	(4.8)
Azerbaijan	31.6	(3.2)	7.2	(1.4)	**27**	(7.8)	59.3	(4.2)	**19**	(5.9)
Brazil	24.9	(2.1)	3.2	(0.6)	**46**	(13.3)	56.5	(2.5)	**40**	(5.4)
Bulgaria	31.2	(3.4)	6.5	(1.3)	**97**	(12.6)	61.2	(4.4)	**35**	(7.3)
Colombia	31.6	(3.3)	2.8	(0.6)	**64**	(12.6)	67.3	(3.5)	**23**	(5.0)
Croatia	23.7	(3.0)	5.2	(1.2)	**79**	(10.2)	49.2	(4.5)	**30**	(5.5)
Dubai (UAE)	42.8	(0.1)	11.6	(0.9)	**27**	(8.3)	73.9	(1.2)	**17**	(3.0)
Hong Kong-China	21.9	(2.9)	3.2	(0.8)	**93**	(13.1)	56.6	(4.7)	13	(6.5)
Indonesia	26.9	(3.8)	4.3	(1.1)	**41**	(15.0)	65.8	(4.7)	**20**	(6.9)
Jordan	22.8	(2.5)	3.5	(0.8)	**32**	(11.5)	49.5	(3.6)	13	(8.9)
Kazakhstan	26.4	(3.0)	5.6	(1.2)	**36**	(10.1)	51.8	(3.9)	**24**	(8.2)
Kyrgyzstan	25.9	(2.2)	5.2	(1.0)	**52**	(11.7)	52.4	(3.0)	**47**	(7.7)
Latvia	25.8	(3.2)	6.8	(1.3)	**43**	(9.6)	50.1	(4.7)	**17**	(4.8)
Liechtenstein	25.9	(0.4)	7.4	(3.0)	**83**	(17.9)	51.6	(4.9)	**45**	(9.4)
Lithuania	26.3	(2.5)	6.0	(1.1)	**55**	(9.3)	51.7	(3.6)	**28**	(4.8)
Macao-China	26.4	(0.0)	7.7	(0.8)	12	(7.3)	55.6	(1.0)	5	(2.5)
Montenegro	38.4	(0.7)	15.2	(1.0)	**65**	(6.7)	61.6	(1.0)	**28**	(3.0)
Panama	28.8	(4.2)	1.8	(0.8)	33	(23.3)	73.4	(5.4)	**41**	(11.9)
Peru	34.7	(2.9)	3.2	(0.7)	**62**	(16.7)	72.1	(3.4)	**17**	(6.5)
Qatar	39.9	(0.2)	12.9	(0.7)	6	(6.6)	67.0	(0.8)	**18**	(2.8)
Romania	30.7	(3.6)	9.5	(1.6)	**52**	(12.2)	60.5	(4.6)	**21**	(6.9)
Russian Federation	27.1	(2.7)	6.8	(1.2)	**37**	(9.4)	55.3	(3.4)	**25**	(7.0)
Serbia	23.0	(2.5)	6.2	(1.3)	**72**	(9.6)	49.2	(4.3)	**32**	(4.2)
Shanghai-China	33.7	(3.1)	6.2	(1.0)	**59**	(7.1)	66.8	(4.0)	**17**	(4.2)
Singapore	21.7	(0.5)	4.5	(0.6)	**98**	(13.1)	44.9	(1.2)	**41**	(3.7)
Chinese Taipei	26.9	(2.8)	8.7	(1.5)	**43**	(11.0)	48.7	(4.0)	**28**	(7.0)
Thailand	33.3	(2.6)	5.3	(1.0)	**48**	(12.3)	76.1	(2.9)	**18**	(5.3)
Trinidad and Tobago	26.6	(0.2)	6.4	(0.6)	**123**	(11.3)	55.9	(1.4)	**62**	(3.1)
Tunisia	29.1	(3.6)	6.2	(1.6)	**46**	(13.8)	57.7	(4.5)	**22**	(6.8)
Uruguay	25.3	(1.4)	3.4	(0.7)	**68**	(9.5)	60.1	(2.3)	**20**	(4.4)

OECD (upper group) · *Partners* (lower group)

Note: Values that are statistically significant are indicated in bold (see Annex A3).
1. Schools with an average or mixture of socio-economic intake are not statistically significantly different from the country average. Schools with an advantaged (disadvantaged) socio-economic intake are above (below) the country average.
StatLink ᴍᴤᴘ http://dx.doi.org/10.1787/888932343285

ANNEX B2
RESULTS FOR REGIONS WITHIN COUNTRIES

[Part 1/1]
Performance by proficiency level in reading and socio-economic background

Table S.II.a *Results based on students' self-reports*

	Percentage of students who are								Average index of socio-economic background							
	Top performers (Levels 5 or 6) in reading		Strong performers (Level 4) in reading		Moderate performers (Levels 2 or 3) in reading		Lowest performers (below Level 2) in reading		Top performers (Levels 5 or 6) in reading		Strong performers (Level 4) in reading		Moderate performers (Levels 2 or 3) in reading		Lowest performers (below Level 2) in reading	
	%	S.E.	%	S.E.	%	S.E.	%	S.E.	Mean index	S.E.	Mean index	S.E.	Mean index	S.E.	Mean index	S.E.
Adjudicated																
Belgium (Flemish Community)	12.6	(0.9)	27.1	(1.0)	47.3	(1.3)	13.0	(0.8)	0.79	(0.0)	0.50	(0.0)	0.03	(0.0)	-0.38	(0.0)
Spain (Andalusia)	1.7	(0.6)	12.2	(1.4)	60.5	(1.9)	25.6	(2.4)	0.32	(0.3)	0.11	(0.1)	-0.50	(0.1)	-1.13	(0.1)
Spain (Aragon)	4.8	(0.8)	21.3	(1.3)	58.7	(1.9)	15.1	(1.6)	0.49	(0.1)	0.13	(0.1)	-0.26	(0.1)	-0.75	(0.1)
Spain (Asturias)	5.7	(1.0)	21.3	(1.9)	55.3	(1.8)	17.7	(1.4)	0.49	(0.2)	0.21	(0.1)	-0.28	(0.1)	-0.78	(0.1)
Spain (Balearic Islands)	1.8	(0.7)	13.3	(1.9)	57.7	(1.9)	27.2	(2.5)	0.45	(0.3)	0.28	(0.2)	-0.22	(0.1)	-0.74	(0.1)
Spain (Basque Country)	4.5	(0.5)	20.5	(0.8)	60.0	(1.2)	14.9	(1.2)	0.48	(0.1)	0.22	(0.1)	-0.12	(0.0)	-0.51	(0.1)
Spain (Canary Islands)	1.8	(0.5)	10.9	(0.9)	55.0	(2.0)	32.3	(2.2)	0.23	(0.3)	-0.08	(0.1)	-0.56	(0.0)	-0.97	(0.1)
Spain (Cantabria)	4.7	(0.8)	19.2	(1.8)	58.2	(1.5)	17.8	(1.4)	0.36	(0.1)	0.23	(0.1)	-0.22	(0.1)	-0.71	(0.1)
Spain (Castile and Leon)	6.2	(1.1)	22.8	(1.7)	58.1	(1.8)	12.9	(1.7)	0.50	(0.1)	0.21	(0.1)	-0.30	(0.1)	-0.75	(0.1)
Spain (Catalonia)	3.8	(0.7)	23.0	(2.0)	59.9	(2.0)	13.4	(1.8)	0.24	(0.2)	0.10	(0.1)	-0.29	(0.1)	-0.89	(0.1)
Spain (Ceuta and Melilla)	1.3	(0.4)	7.9	(0.8)	43.6	(1.4)	47.2	(1.3)	c	c	0.47	(0.1)	-0.26	(0.0)	-1.03	(0.0)
Spain (Galicia)	3.5	(0.8)	19.6	(1.4)	58.6	(1.5)	18.3	(1.6)	0.25	(0.2)	-0.02	(0.1)	-0.44	(0.1)	-0.74	(0.1)
Spain (La Rioja)	6.1	(0.9)	23.7	(1.4)	53.4	(1.8)	16.9	(1.2)	0.49	(0.1)	0.13	(0.1)	-0.37	(0.0)	-0.83	(0.1)
Spain (Madrid)	6.0	(1.2)	23.4	(1.7)	57.9	(1.8)	12.7	(1.5)	0.72	(0.2)	0.37	(0.2)	-0.19	(0.1)	-0.71	(0.1)
Spain (Murcia)	2.5	(0.5)	15.9	(1.6)	62.9	(1.9)	18.6	(2.1)	0.44	(0.2)	0.21	(0.2)	-0.46	(0.1)	-1.00	(0.1)
Spain (Navarre)	5.0	(1.0)	22.1	(1.5)	58.4	(1.7)	14.6	(1.2)	0.52	(0.2)	0.32	(0.1)	-0.30	(0.0)	-0.70	(0.1)
United Kingdom (Scotland)	9.3	(0.9)	20.7	(1.1)	54.4	(1.3)	15.6	(1.0)	0.76	(0.1)	0.50	(0.0)	0.10	(0.0)	-0.25	(0.1)
Non-adjudicated																
Belgium (French Community)	9.8	(0.9)	23.0	(1.1)	45.3	(1.6)	21.9	(1.5)	0.92	(0.06)	0.64	(0.05)	0.12	(0.04)	-0.46	(0.05)
Belgium (German-Speaking Community)	6.5	(1.0)	23.7	(1.7)	52.9	(2.0)	16.9	(1.2)	0.68	(0.11)	0.44	(0.08)	0.19	(0.04)	-0.11	(0.07)
Finland (Finnish Speaking)	14.9	(0.8)	31.1	(0.9)	46.3	(1.2)	7.7	(0.6)	0.69	(0.03)	0.48	(0.03)	0.24	(0.03)	-0.07	(0.06)
Finland (Swedish Speaking)	8.4	(0.9)	25.7	(1.6)	54.0	(1.6)	12.0	(1.0)	1.05	(0.08)	0.80	(0.06)	0.48	(0.04)	0.19	(0.06)
Italy (Provincia Abruzzo)	3.5	(0.8)	19.2	(1.7)	56.4	(2.1)	20.9	(1.8)	0.65	(0.17)	0.36	(0.07)	-0.04	(0.05)	-0.49	(0.08)
Italy (Provincia Autonoma di Bolzano)	5.8	(0.6)	20.3	(1.3)	56.4	(1.6)	17.5	(1.3)	0.34	(0.10)	0.02	(0.04)	-0.26	(0.03)	-0.53	(0.08)
Italy (Provincia Basilicata)	3.2	(0.5)	15.6	(1.3)	57.2	(2.3)	24.1	(2.3)	0.38	(0.21)	0.14	(0.08)	-0.27	(0.03)	-0.65	(0.06)
Italy (Provincia Calabria)	1.5	(0.4)	11.1	(1.4)	54.6	(2.5)	32.9	(2.4)	c	c	0.32	(0.12)	-0.13	(0.07)	-0.69	(0.05)
Italy (Provincia Campania)	1.9	(0.5)	11.8	(1.9)	55.0	(2.6)	31.4	(2.7)	c	c	0.18	(0.13)	-0.26	(0.07)	-0.68	(0.06)
Italy (Provincia Emilia Romagna)	9.0	(1.0)	25.6	(2.0)	48.0	(2.3)	17.4	(1.7)	0.85	(0.11)	0.52	(0.08)	-0.08	(0.05)	-0.64	(0.10)
Italy (Provincia Friuli Venezia Giulia)	10.0	(1.3)	26.4	(1.9)	50.2	(2.2)	13.3	(1.7)	0.49	(0.09)	0.16	(0.06)	-0.13	(0.05)	-0.55	(0.07)
Italy (Provincia Lazio)	4.6	(1.0)	19.3	(1.2)	54.3	(1.9)	21.8	(1.7)	0.57	(0.13)	0.50	(0.10)	0.16	(0.06)	-0.29	(0.08)
Italy (Provincia Liguria)	6.2	(1.0)	20.8	(2.0)	54.7	(3.2)	18.3	(3.9)	0.46	(0.13)	0.27	(0.09)	0.03	(0.04)	-0.47	(0.10)
Italy (Provincia Lombardia)	10.9	(1.7)	28.1	(2.0)	49.4	(2.2)	11.6	(1.5)	0.45	(0.07)	0.26	(0.07)	-0.13	(0.04)	-0.82	(0.11)
Italy (Provincia Marche)	7.4	(1.1)	23.4	(1.8)	51.9	(2.6)	17.3	(3.3)	0.36	(0.10)	0.15	(0.06)	-0.16	(0.05)	-0.52	(0.06)
Italy (Provincia Molise)	2.0	(0.7)	15.3	(1.3)	60.0	(1.9)	22.8	(1.4)	c	c	0.45	(0.12)	-0.12	(0.05)	-0.59	(0.07)
Italy (Provincia Piemonte)	7.5	(1.2)	22.5	(1.7)	51.4	(2.0)	18.6	(2.4)	0.60	(0.10)	0.25	(0.06)	-0.25	(0.05)	-0.61	(0.13)
Italy (Provincia Puglia)	4.1	(0.9)	20.5	(1.7)	57.9	(2.3)	17.5	(1.7)	0.06	(0.14)	-0.06	(0.09)	-0.46	(0.06)	-0.81	(0.07)
Italy (Provincia Sardegna)	3.3	(0.7)	16.4	(1.4)	55.9	(1.8)	24.5	(1.8)	0.62	(0.13)	0.22	(0.11)	-0.29	(0.06)	-0.57	(0.06)
Italy (Provincia Sicilia)	2.7	(0.7)	13.4	(1.6)	52.5	(3.3)	31.4	(3.7)	0.80	(0.24)	0.39	(0.11)	-0.20	(0.08)	-0.67	(0.09)
Italy (Provincia Toscana)	6.4	(0.8)	23.6	(1.4)	50.9	(2.1)	19.1	(2.0)	0.50	(0.13)	0.31	(0.07)	0.02	(0.04)	-0.32	(0.06)
Italy (Provincia Trento)	9.5	(1.3)	24.7	(1.7)	51.6	(1.8)	14.3	(1.3)	0.44	(0.10)	0.10	(0.06)	-0.23	(0.04)	-0.52	(0.09)
Italy (Provincia Umbria)	6.9	(1.0)	22.1	(1.6)	51.1	(2.2)	19.9	(2.2)	0.69	(0.09)	0.44	(0.06)	0.03	(0.04)	-0.38	(0.06)
Italy (Provincia Valle d'Aosta)	9.3	(0.9)	25.9	(1.8)	53.5	(2.0)	11.3	(0.9)	0.35	(0.11)	0.10	(0.07)	-0.21	(0.05)	-0.56	(0.10)
Italy (Provincia Veneto)	7.5	(1.1)	24.3	(1.8)	53.7	(2.6)	14.5	(2.2)	0.48	(0.16)	0.18	(0.09)	-0.14	(0.06)	-0.48	(0.09)
United Kingdom (England)	8.2	(0.6)	20.3	(0.9)	54.1	(0.9)	17.4	(0.9)	0.74	(0.05)	0.53	(0.03)	0.14	(0.03)	-0.20	(0.04)
United Kingdom (Northern Ireland)	9.5	(0.7)	21.9	(1.2)	52.1	(1.8)	16.6	(1.7)	0.64	(0.07)	0.39	(0.05)	0.06	(0.03)	-0.36	(0.04)
United Kingdom (Wales)	5.1	(0.6)	16.1	(1.0)	56.5	(1.2)	22.3	(1.3)	0.65	(0.09)	0.46	(0.06)	0.15	(0.03)	-0.15	(0.03)

Note: See Table II.2.1 for national data.
StatLink http://dx.doi.org/10.1787/888932343304

[Part 1/2]
Schools' average socio-economic background and resources
Table S.II.b   *Results based on students' self-reports and school principals' reports*

	Simple correlation between the schools' socio-economic background and:									
	Index of teacher shortage		Percentage of full-time teachers		Percentage of certified teachers among all full-time teachers		Percentage of teachers with university-level degree (ISCED 5A) among all full-time teachers		Index of school responsibility in resource allocation	
	Correlation	S.E.	Correlation	S.E.	Correlation	S.E.	Correlation	S.E.	Correlation	S.E.
Adjudicated										
Belgium (Flemish Community)	-0.09	(0.08)	**-0.17**	(0.07)	**0.15**	(0.07)	**0.57**	(0.04)	0.01	(0.10)
Spain (Andalusia)	0.07	(0.12)	-0.31	(0.20)	c	c	c	c	**0.65**	(0.10)
Spain (Aragon)	0.23	(0.14)	**-0.30**	(0.10)	c	c	c	c	**0.59**	(0.08)
Spain (Asturias)	-0.05	(0.12)	0.06	(0.10)	c	c	c	c	**0.61**	(0.09)
Spain (Balearic Islands)	-0.07	(0.16)	**-0.38**	(0.15)	c	c	c	c	**0.50**	(0.15)
Spain (Basque Country)	0.09	(0.07)	-0.09	(0.09)	c	c	c	c	**0.30**	(0.08)
Spain (Canary Islands)	-0.21	(0.12)	**-0.51**	(0.13)	c	c	c	c	**0.56**	(0.12)
Spain (Cantabria)	0.02	(0.11)	**-0.48**	(0.13)	c	c	c	c	**0.52**	(0.10)
Spain (Castile and Leon)	0.10	(0.17)	-0.19	(0.17)	c	c	c	c	**0.44**	(0.08)
Spain (Catalonia)	-0.11	(0.22)	**-0.31**	(0.15)	c	c	c	c	**0.39**	(0.11)
Spain (Ceuta and Melilla)	**-0.15**	(0.01)	**-0.20**	(0.01)	c	c	c	c	**0.63**	(0.01)
Spain (Galicia)	0.12	(0.14)	**-0.29**	(0.14)	c	c	c	c	**0.27**	(0.13)
Spain (La Rioja)	**0.08**	(0.01)	**-0.07**	(0.01)	c	c	c	c	**0.38**	(0.01)
Spain (Madrid)	-0.13	(0.11)	-0.08	(0.13)	c	c	c	c	**0.41**	(0.15)
Spain (Murcia)	0.16	(0.18)	-0.03	(0.17)	c	c	c	c	**0.34**	(0.16)
Spain (Navarre)	0.06	(0.11)	**-0.35**	(0.05)	c	c	c	c	**0.61**	(0.06)
United Kingdom (Scotland)	-0.14	(0.09)	-0.08	(0.11)	-0.26	(0.15)	-0.02	(0.16)	**0.53**	(0.09)
Non-adjudicated										
Belgium (French Community)	**-0.30**	(0.09)	**-0.20**	(0.10)	0.03	(0.14)	**0.60**	(0.14)	-0.03	(0.10)
Belgium (German-Speaking Community)	**-0.46**	(0.01)	**0.12**	(0.01)	**0.53**	(0.00)	**0.81**	(0.00)	**-0.15**	(0.01)
Finland (Finnish Speaking)	0.00	(0.08)	**0.21**	(0.06)	0.03	(0.10)	0.03	(0.10)	**0.25**	(0.12)
Finland (Swedish Speaking)	**-0.21**	(0.01)	**-0.20**	(0.01)	**-0.06**	(0.01)	**-0.06**	(0.01)	**0.17**	(0.01)
Italy (Provincia Abruzzo)	-0.10	(0.13)	-0.08	(0.14)	0.11	(0.07)	-0.02	(0.21)	**0.32**	(0.15)
Italy (Provincia Autonoma di Bolzano)	**-0.16**	(0.03)	**0.07**	(0.01)	**0.41**	(0.01)	**0.29**	(0.01)	**0.22**	(0.01)
Italy (Provincia Basilicata)	-0.14	(0.12)	**0.35**	(0.10)	**0.37**	(0.08)	**0.38**	(0.06)	0.00	(0.08)
Italy (Provincia Calabria)	0.08	(0.14)	-0.02	(0.15)	0.08	(0.26)	**0.54**	(0.07)	0.00	(0.05)
Italy (Provincia Campania)	**0.27**	(0.13)	-0.16	(0.19)	-0.12	(0.21)	-0.04	(0.15)	**0.27**	(0.12)
Italy (Provincia Emilia Romagna)	-0.14	(0.14)	**-0.29**	(0.15)	**0.23**	(0.08)	**0.35**	(0.14)	**-0.17**	(0.06)
Italy (Provincia Friuli Venezia Giulia)	0.01	(0.14)	**0.43**	(0.11)	**0.36**	(0.05)	-0.09	(0.09)	-0.09	(0.14)
Italy (Provincia Lazio)	0.15	(0.13)	0.08	(0.19)	0.27	(0.18)	0.14	(0.14)	-0.03	(0.16)
Italy (Provincia Liguria)	0.05	(0.13)	-0.08	(0.17)	**0.57**	(0.08)	-0.16	(0.14)	0.07	(0.12)
Italy (Provincia Lombardia)	0.01	(0.11)	-0.12	(0.12)	**0.38**	(0.08)	0.20	(0.12)	0.02	(0.09)
Italy (Provincia Marche)	-0.10	(0.17)	-0.04	(0.16)	**0.29**	(0.11)	-0.08	(0.20)	0.03	(0.19)
Italy (Provincia Molise)	**-0.24**	(0.01)	-0.04	(0.05)	**0.14**	(0.01)	**0.08**	(0.02)	0.01	(0.04)
Italy (Provincia Piemonte)	0.15	(0.12)	0.21	(0.16)	0.18	(0.13)	0.19	(0.16)	0.04	(0.11)
Italy (Provincia Puglia)	0.01	(0.13)	0.23	(0.15)	0.28	(0.17)	**0.28**	(0.09)	-0.17	(0.13)
Italy (Provincia Sardegna)	**-0.24**	(0.16)	**-0.29**	(0.20)	**0.29**	(0.08)	**-0.30**	(0.22)	**0.35**	(0.12)
Italy (Provincia Sicilia)	-0.12	(0.16)	0.18	(0.09)	0.12	(0.10)	0.06	(0.14)	**0.38**	(0.15)
Italy (Provincia Toscana)	0.01	(0.15)	**-0.25**	(0.10)	0.14	(0.18)	0.07	(0.19)	**0.19**	(0.06)
Italy (Provincia Trento)	**0.24**	(0.09)	**-0.13**	(0.04)	**0.46**	(0.09)	**0.58**	(0.03)	0.03	(0.02)
Italy (Provincia Umbria)	-0.04	(0.11)	-0.03	(0.11)	0.28	(0.18)	-0.01	(0.16)	-0.18	(0.10)
Italy (Provincia Valle d'Aosta)	**-0.35**	(0.01)	**0.25**	(0.01)	**0.52**	(0.01)	**0.60**	(0.01)	**-0.17**	(0.01)
Italy (Provincia Veneto)	-0.01	(0.16)	0.07	(0.17)	0.31	(0.19)	0.21	(0.16)	0.03	(0.23)
United Kingdom (England)	**-0.16**	(0.07)	**-0.39**	(0.07)	0.07	(0.09)	-0.18	(0.12)	**0.14**	(0.07)
United Kingdom (Northern Ireland)	-0.12	(0.09)	-0.04	(0.12)	**0.20**	(0.08)	c	c	0.04	(0.14)
United Kingdom (Wales)	-0.15	(0.09)	**-0.26**	(0.08)	0.04	(0.06)	**0.17**	(0.07)	0.12	(0.12)

Notes: Values that are statistically significant are indicated in bold (see Annex A3). See Table II.2.2 for national data.
StatLink ⌐ℸ⅃⌐ http://dx.doi.org/10.1787/888932343304

[Part 2/2]
Schools' average socio-economic background and resources
Table S.II.b *Results based on students' self-reports and school principals' reports*

	Simple correlation between the schools' socio-economic background and:									
	Index of school curriculum responsibility		Index of quality of school's educational resources		Computer/student ratio		Student/teacher ratio		School size	
	Correlation	S.E.	Correlation	S.E.	Correlation	S.E.	Correlation	S.E.	Correlation	S.E.
Adjudicated										
Belgium (Flemish Community)	-0.05	(0.08)	0.03	(0.08)	**-0.25**	(0.06)	**0.68**	(0.04)	**0.31**	(0.08)
Spain (Andalusia)	**0.34**	(0.12)	0.04	(0.10)	**-0.15**	(0.07)	**0.56**	(0.11)	**0.49**	(0.11)
Spain (Aragon)	**0.26**	(0.09)	0.17	(0.15)	0.20	(0.11)	**0.63**	(0.07)	0.33	(0.20)
Spain (Asturias)	**0.40**	(0.11)	**0.27**	(0.14)	**-0.33**	(0.12)	**0.67**	(0.06)	**0.64**	(0.05)
Spain (Balearic Islands)	0.05	(0.13)	0.05	(0.14)	**-0.23**	(0.09)	0.34	(0.19)	0.27	(0.15)
Spain (Basque Country)	**0.22**	(0.08)	0.06	(0.08)	**-0.16**	(0.05)	**0.49**	(0.05)	**0.50**	(0.06)
Spain (Canary Islands)	0.26	(0.22)	-0.07	(0.22)	**-0.18**	(0.08)	0.34	(0.22)	-0.01	(0.18)
Spain (Cantabria)	-0.15	(0.13)	-0.20	(0.15)	**-0.36**	(0.14)	**0.57**	(0.09)	0.30	(0.16)
Spain (Castile and Leon)	0.09	(0.12)	-0.19	(0.13)	-0.29	(0.16)	**0.59**	(0.09)	**0.61**	(0.09)
Spain (Catalonia)	-0.09	(0.16)	0.00	(0.10)	-0.19	(0.14)	0.29	(0.11)	0.19	(0.17)
Spain (Ceuta and Melilla)	**0.13**	(0.02)	**-0.30**	(0.01)	**-0.16**	(0.01)	**0.67**	(0.00)	**0.16**	(0.01)
Spain (Galicia)	0.07	(0.14)	**-0.20**	(0.10)	**-0.51**	(0.10)	**0.51**	(0.11)	**0.60**	(0.11)
Spain (La Rioja)	**0.20**	(0.01)	**-0.09**	(0.01)	**-0.19**	(0.01)	**0.55**	(0.00)	**0.57**	(0.01)
Spain (Madrid)	0.27	(0.16)	**0.45**	(0.13)	-0.13	(0.11)	0.38	(0.14)	**0.64**	(0.10)
Spain (Murcia)	0.20	(0.26)	-0.08	(0.19)	-0.15	(0.13)	**0.47**	(0.13)	**0.45**	(0.11)
Spain (Navarre)	0.16	(0.09)	**0.16**	(0.08)	0.32	(0.12)	**0.66**	(0.04)	**0.61**	(0.07)
United Kingdom (Scotland)	0.16	(0.11)	-0.11	(0.10)	0.12	(0.13)	0.03	(0.10)	0.16	(0.11)
Non-adjudicated										
Belgium (French Community)	**0.25**	(0.08)	0.00	(0.09)	**-0.33**	(0.08)	**0.73**	(0.06)	**0.40**	(0.09)
Belgium (German-Speaking Community)	0.02	(0.00)	**0.20**	(0.00)	**-0.36**	(0.01)	**0.72**	(0.00)	**0.46**	(0.00)
Finland (Finnish Speaking)	0.04	(0.10)	0.14	(0.09)	-0.02	(0.10)	0.13	(0.08)	**0.36**	(0.07)
Finland (Swedish Speaking)	**-0.18**	(0.01)	**0.06**	(0.01)	**0.18**	(0.01)	0.00	(0.00)	**0.13**	(0.01)
Italy (Provincia Abruzzo)	-0.23	(0.12)	**0.31**	(0.10)	**-0.35**	(0.13)	**0.75**	(0.08)	**0.28**	(0.08)
Italy (Provincia Autonoma di Bolzano)	0.04	(0.03)	**0.25**	(0.01)	0.00	(0.01)	-0.05	(0.01)	**-0.32**	(0.01)
Italy (Provincia Basilicata)	-0.15	(0.12)	**0.40**	(0.07)	**-0.19**	(0.08)	**0.69**	(0.04)	**0.31**	(0.07)
Italy (Provincia Calabria)	0.01	(0.15)	-0.08	(0.10)	-0.15	(0.13)	**0.79**	(0.04)	**0.49**	(0.09)
Italy (Provincia Campania)	-0.11	(0.14)	0.05	(0.08)	-0.18	(0.14)	**0.60**	(0.07)	0.16	(0.12)
Italy (Provincia Emilia Romagna)	0.17	(0.14)	0.11	(0.13)	**-0.32**	(0.12)	**0.49**	(0.12)	**0.40**	(0.14)
Italy (Provincia Friuli Venezia Giulia)	0.02	(0.08)	0.03	(0.14)	**-0.35**	(0.10)	**0.52**	(0.05)	**0.17**	(0.04)
Italy (Provincia Lazio)	0.14	(0.13)	0.12	(0.14)	-0.18	(0.24)	**0.58**	(0.06)	0.14	(0.11)
Italy (Provincia Liguria)	0.15	(0.12)	-0.08	(0.12)	**-0.36**	(0.10)	**0.65**	(0.06)	**0.50**	(0.09)
Italy (Provincia Lombardia)	0.15	(0.15)	0.16	(0.12)	**-0.31**	(0.09)	0.24	(0.16)	0.17	(0.10)
Italy (Provincia Marche)	0.17	(0.17)	0.05	(0.14)	**-0.28**	(0.08)	**0.74**	(0.06)	**0.41**	(0.08)
Italy (Provincia Molise)	**0.18**	(0.03)	**0.50**	(0.03)	**-0.46**	(0.03)	**0.81**	(0.01)	**0.30**	(0.01)
Italy (Provincia Piemonte)	0.19	(0.13)	**0.26**	(0.12)	**-0.47**	(0.08)	0.44	(0.14)	0.23	(0.13)
Italy (Provincia Puglia)	-0.04	(0.16)	0.10	(0.16)	**-0.38**	(0.12)	**0.70**	(0.06)	**0.41**	(0.11)
Italy (Provincia Sardegna)	0.17	(0.14)	0.17	(0.11)	**-0.40**	(0.09)	**0.57**	(0.10)	0.18	(0.13)
Italy (Provincia Sicilia)	0.07	(0.11)	0.25	(0.16)	-0.03	(0.13)	**0.60**	(0.08)	**0.28**	(0.12)
Italy (Provincia Toscana)	0.08	(0.12)	0.17	(0.17)	0.02	(0.16)	**0.43**	(0.16)	0.10	(0.07)
Italy (Provincia Trento)	**0.12**	(0.04)	**0.21**	(0.09)	**-0.11**	(0.03)	**0.59**	(0.04)	**0.39**	(0.03)
Italy (Provincia Umbria)	0.11	(0.10)	**-0.20**	(0.09)	**-0.41**	(0.09)	**0.76**	(0.03)	**0.50**	(0.07)
Italy (Provincia Valle d'Aosta)	**-0.07**	(0.01)	**-0.07**	(0.01)	**-0.61**	(0.00)	**0.33**	(0.01)	**0.14**	(0.01)
Italy (Provincia Veneto)	0.11	(0.12)	0.09	(0.11)	**-0.33**	(0.09)	**0.44**	(0.15)	0.25	(0.09)
United Kingdom (England)	0.10	(0.06)	0.01	(0.07)	0.00	(0.10)	-0.13	(0.07)	0.11	(0.08)
United Kingdom (Northern Ireland)	-0.08	(0.11)	0.03	(0.12)	-0.10	(0.10)	0.21	(0.11)	**0.39**	(0.08)
United Kingdom (Wales)	-0.02	(0.09)	-0.05	(0.08)	0.00	(0.10)	-0.08	(0.12)	**0.29**	(0.08)

Note: Values that are statistically significant are indicated in bold (see Annex A3). See Table II.2.2 for national data.
StatLink http://dx.doi.org/10.1787/888932343304

[Part 1/3]

Reading performance and socio-economic background, by school location

Table S.II.c   *Results based on students' self-reports and school principals' reports*

	Percentage of students					Average performance in reading				
	Students attending schools located in a village, hamlet or rural area (fewer than 3 000 people)	Students attending schools located in a small town (3 000 to about 15 000 people)	Students attending schools located in a town (15 000 to about 100 000 people)	Students attending schools located in a city (100 000 to about 1 000 000 people)	Students attending schools located in a large city (with over 1 000 000 people)	Students attending schools located in a village, hamlet or rural area (fewer than 3 000 people)	Students attending schools located in a small town (3 000 to about 15 000 people)	Students attending schools located in a town (15 000 to about 100 000 people)	Students attending schools located in a city (100 000 to about 1 000 000 people)	Students attending schools located in a large city (with over 1 000 000 people)
	% S.E.	% S.E.	% S.E.	% S.E.	% S.E.	Mean score S.E.	Mean score S.E.	Mean score S.E.	Mean score S.E.	Mean score S.E.
Adjudicated										
Belgium (Flemish Community)	1.7 (0.9)	32.2 (3.6)	52.8 (4.2)	11.4 (2.3)	1.9 (1.2)	c c	533 (7.1)	515 (5.8)	503 (16.1)	c c
Spain (Andalusia)	6.0 (3.2)	23.8 (4.9)	33.0 (6.0)	37.2 (6.5)	0.0 c	c c	447 (11.6)	463 (8.5)	469 (9.4)	c c
Spain (Aragon)	8.8 (2.9)	20.9 (4.7)	17.7 (4.7)	52.5 (3.6)	0.0 c	479 (8.8)	462 (11.7)	507 (8.4)	508 (4.1)	c c
Spain (Asturias)	10.0 (4.2)	27.4 (5.2)	18.9 (4.7)	43.8 (2.7)	0.0 c	490 (28.6)	470 (5.7)	479 (12.9)	508 (8.3)	c c
Spain (Balearic Islands)	2.1 (2.1)	24.7 (6.3)	36.5 (6.7)	36.7 (4.6)	0.0 c	c c	458 (8.0)	443 (8.9)	473 (11.9)	c c
Spain (Basque Country)	1.9 (1.0)	24.1 (2.8)	36.5 (2.9)	36.8 (3.0)	0.7 (0.7)	c c	490 (4.6)	487 (4.5)	506 (5.8)	c c
Spain (Canary Islands)	8.1 (3.9)	34.7 (7.1)	37.2 (6.3)	20.0 (5.0)	0.0 c	c c	429 (8.1)	453 (10.3)	481 (13.1)	c c
Spain (Cantabria)	13.1 (4.3)	33.8 (5.1)	23.1 (4.4)	30.0 (3.1)	0.0 c	486 (13.8)	479 (6.5)	479 (13.3)	505 (7.1)	c c
Spain (Castile and Leon)	14.8 (5.2)	13.5 (4.3)	30.6 (6.0)	39.0 (5.2)	2.1 (2.1)	454 (11.0)	497 (8.9)	506 (6.3)	519 (6.7)	c c
Spain (Catalonia)	0.0 c	15.3 (6.2)	41.6 (7.3)	22.4 (5.7)	20.6 (3.3)	c c	510 (17.8)	495 (8.6)	498 (13.7)	508 (8.8)
Spain (Ceuta and Melilla)	0.0 c	0.0 c	100.0 (0.0)	0.0 c	0.0 c	c c	c c	412 (2.5)	c c	c c
Spain (Galicia)	7.6 (3.4)	44.5 (5.3)	27.1 (6.4)	20.8 (4.7)	0.0 c	457 (14.7)	477 (5.9)	499 (8.3)	504 (8.9)	c c
Spain (La Rioja)	3.4 (0.2)	31.4 (0.4)	19.7 (0.4)	45.5 (0.4)	0.0 c	c c	478 (4.5)	491 (5.9)	516 (3.5)	c c
Spain (Madrid)	1.9 (1.8)	11.3 (5.0)	24.3 (5.4)	14.4 (2.4)	48.1 (3.7)	c c	462 (17.5)	489 (8.8)	512 (7.4)	518 (6.3)
Spain (Murcia)	4.3 (3.1)	28.2 (5.4)	39.5 (5.2)	28.0 (5.0)	0.0 c	c c	463 (7.5)	484 (7.2)	493 (12.3)	c c
Spain (Navarre)	7.3 (2.0)	27.6 (2.5)	22.8 (3.9)	42.3 (4.1)	0.0 c	454 (8.4)	486 (5.6)	492 (9.1)	515 (5.4)	c c
United Kingdom (Scotland)	5.3 (2.3)	31.8 (4.3)	36.7 (4.1)	26.2 (3.8)	0.0 c	499 (10.3)	507 (7.2)	494 (3.6)	499 (7.9)	c c
Non-adjudicated										
Belgium (French Community)	5.7 (2.5)	10.6 (2.8)	47.9 (5.4)	14.9 (3.7)	20.9 (3.9)	514 (41.2)	482 (16.0)	490 (9.2)	491 (17.6)	487 (18.6)
Belgium (German-Speaking Community)	0.0 c	49.9 (0.2)	50.1 (0.2)	0.0 c	0.0 c	c c	501 (4.2)	c c	c c	c c
Finland (Finnish Speaking)	10.6 (2.0)	26.0 (3.1)	37.2 (4.1)	26.1 (3.3)	0.0 c	529 (7.8)	534 (4.7)	538 (3.5)	544 (5.5)	c c
Finland (Swedish Speaking)	19.4 (0.2)	35.8 (0.4)	23.6 (0.3)	21.3 (0.3)	0.0 c	495 (5.1)	503 (4.9)	519 (4.8)	532 (5.2)	c c
Italy (Provincia Abruzzo)	1.6 (1.6)	13.4 (5.5)	62.6 (5.2)	22.4 (4.0)	0.0 c	c c	458 (40.4)	489 (9.5)	480 (10.9)	c c
Italy (Provincia Autonoma di Bolzano)	1.8 (0.1)	27.7 (0.6)	57.4 (0.9)	13.1 (0.3)	0.0 c	c c	486 (2.9)	495 (5.6)	483 (5.2)	c c
Italy (Provincia Basilicata)	3.4 (2.0)	47.2 (6.0)	49.3 (5.5)	0.0 c	0.0 c	c c	464 (10.0)	484 (5.1)	c c	c c
Italy (Provincia Calabria)	0.0 c	44.8 (5.7)	45.6 (6.4)	9.5 (3.0)	0.0 c	c c	435 (8.2)	455 (10.5)	473 (22.2)	c c
Italy (Provincia Campania)	0.6 (0.6)	12.0 (4.9)	54.2 (7.0)	18.6 (4.4)	14.6 (4.7)	c c	455 (23.5)	447 (10.0)	465 (14.1)	444 (34.4)
Italy (Provincia Emilia Romagna)	0.0 c	13.3 (4.8)	33.0 (5.9)	53.7 (6.9)	0.0 c	c c	456 (25.0)	512 (11.6)	508 (10.6)	c c
Italy (Provincia Friuli Venezia Giulia)	0.3 (0.0)	27.4 (5.6)	56.7 (5.3)	15.6 (4.1)	0.0 c	c c	481 (16.0)	535 (7.5)	531 (8.9)	c c
Italy (Provincia Lazio)	0.0 c	5.7 (3.5)	46.4 (8.6)	3.5 (3.3)	44.3 (7.3)	c c	c c	474 (11.4)	c c	497 (10.3)
Italy (Provincia Liguria)	0.0 c	8.3 (4.6)	62.6 (5.6)	29.1 (3.9)	0.0 c	c c	c c	502 (13.2)	478 (12.9)	c c
Italy (Provincia Lombardia)	1.7 (1.6)	19.0 (5.1)	49.0 (6.5)	14.2 (4.6)	16.1 (5.1)	c c	528 (22.7)	517 (8.7)	525 (15.7)	536 (24.0)
Italy (Provincia Marche)	0.9 (0.6)	18.2 (6.0)	74.5 (6.7)	6.5 (3.8)	0.0 c	c c	503 (18.0)	501 (12.5)	c c	c c
Italy (Provincia Molise)	1.7 (0.1)	19.2 (1.1)	79.0 (1.1)	0.0 c	0.0 c	c c	458 (8.5)	474 (3.3)	c c	c c
Italy (Provincia Piemonte)	1.4 (1.5)	15.8 (4.3)	54.2 (8.2)	26.5 (7.5)	2.1 (2.1)	c c	477 (16.2)	508 (11.3)	501 (27.2)	c c
Italy (Provincia Puglia)	0.0 c	12.7 (5.4)	68.1 (6.4)	19.3 (5.6)	0.0 c	c c	473 (38.9)	489 (8.4)	502 (14.7)	c c
Italy (Provincia Sardegna)	1.8 (1.4)	27.6 (7.2)	30.8 (7.3)	39.7 (6.2)	0.0 c	c c	445 (21.2)	463 (13.3)	492 (10.5)	c c
Italy (Provincia Sicilia)	0.0 c	16.4 (4.0)	50.7 (5.9)	30.8 (5.5)	2.1 (2.1)	c c	442 (17.8)	447 (11.0)	472 (17.8)	c c
Italy (Provincia Toscana)	3.8 (2.3)	13.5 (5.5)	52.2 (7.3)	30.5 (6.0)	0.0 c	c c	510 (17.1)	494 (11.6)	489 (19.2)	c c
Italy (Provincia Trento)	4.3 (1.9)	31.1 (4.4)	29.9 (3.4)	34.7 (3.8)	0.0 c	c c	489 (10.9)	506 (7.8)	526 (12.9)	c c
Italy (Provincia Umbria)	0.0 c	13.9 (4.7)	55.1 (5.8)	31.0 (5.0)	0.0 c	c c	466 (22.5)	483 (9.9)	523 (11.4)	c c
Italy (Provincia Valle d'Aosta)	18.2 (0.4)	16.5 (0.4)	65.3 (0.4)	0.0 c	0.0 c	472 (5.2)	526 (6.3)	524 (2.7)	c c	c c
Italy (Provincia Veneto)	6.4 (3.7)	5.6 (3.0)	47.2 (6.8)	40.8 (8.2)	0.0 c	c c	c c	521 (10.3)	508 (14.0)	c c
United Kingdom (England)	6.6 (2.3)	21.2 (3.2)	39.3 (4.6)	20.2 (3.4)	12.6 (2.4)	516 (14.7)	505 (5.7)	496 (6.0)	490 (10.8)	485 (11.0)
United Kingdom (Northern Ireland)	6.6 (4.0)	27.2 (4.4)	33.7 (4.4)	31.4 (3.7)	1.1 (1.1)	461 (17.2)	510 (9.7)	519 (8.9)	484 (13.5)	c c
United Kingdom (Wales)	10.7 (2.6)	36.9 (4.0)	32.7 (3.9)	18.0 (2.9)	1.6 (1.1)	486 (10.2)	475 (4.8)	471 (6.3)	488 (10.5)	c c

Note: Values that are statistically significant are indicated in bold (see Annex A3). See Table II.2.6 for national data.
StatLink 🔍 http://dx.doi.org/10.1787/888932343304

[Part 2/3]
Reading performance and socio-economic background, by school location

Table S.II.c *Results based on students' self-reports and school principals' reports*

	PISA index of economic, social and cultural status (ESCS)					Average performance in reading after accounting for ESCS				
	Students attending schools located in a village, hamlet or rural area (fewer than 3 000 people)	Students attending schools located in a small town (3 000 to about 15 000 people)	Students attending schools located in a town (15 000 to about 100 000 people)	Students attending schools located in a city (100 000 to about 1 000 000 people)	Students attending schools located in a large city (with over 1 000 000 people)	Students attending schools located in a village, hamlet or rural area (fewer than 3 000 people)	Students attending schools located in a small town (3 000 to about 15 000 people)	Students attending schools located in a town (15 000 to about 100 000 people)	Students attending schools located in a city (100 000 to about 1 000 000 people)	Students attending schools located in a large city (with over 1 000 000 people)
	Mean index S.E.	Mean index S.E.	Mean index S.E.	Mean index S.E.	Mean index S.E.	Mean score S.E.	Mean score S.E.	Mean score S.E.	Mean score S.E.	Mean score S.E.
Adjudicated										
Belgium (Flemish Community)	c c	0.27 (0.06)	0.16 (0.04)	0.16 (0.14)	c c	c c	531 (5.4)	518 (4.4)	507 (11.1)	c c
Spain (Andalusia)	c c	-0.94 (0.08)	-0.57 (0.12)	-0.28 (0.16)	c c	c c	460 (10.9)	464 (8.2)	460 (7.1)	c c
Spain (Aragon)	-0.61 (0.14)	-0.49 (0.10)	-0.18 (0.19)	-0.05 (0.10)	c c	488 (9.0)	469 (10.9)	506 (5.0)	504 (2.8)	c c
Spain (Asturias)	-0.24 (0.35)	-0.59 (0.07)	-0.30 (0.12)	0.04 (0.09)	c c	492 (19.8)	482 (6.5)	485 (11.2)	500 (7.5)	c c
Spain (Balearic Islands)	c c	-0.47 (0.06)	-0.51 (0.06)	0.06 (0.15)	c c	c c	463 (7.1)	449 (8.6)	465 (9.4)	c c
Spain (Basque Country)	c c	-0.13 (0.06)	-0.19 (0.05)	0.06 (0.06)	c c	c c	491 (4.3)	491 (4.2)	503 (5.4)	c c
Spain (Canary Islands)	c c	-0.79 (0.10)	-0.59 (0.13)	-0.35 (0.18)	c c	c c	434 (6.8)	453 (9.2)	478 (10.8)	c c
Spain (Cantabria)	-0.26 (0.26)	-0.35 (0.08)	-0.21 (0.17)	0.03 (0.15)	c c	488 (11.0)	484 (6.8)	480 (11.1)	499 (6.0)	c c
Spain (Castile and Leon)	-0.71 (0.12)	-0.24 (0.15)	-0.17 (0.11)	-0.03 (0.13)	c c	467 (10.4)	500 (8.4)	507 (5.8)	516 (4.6)	c c
Spain (Catalonia)	c c	0.00 (0.22)	-0.30 (0.15)	-0.42 (0.15)	-0.14 (0.16)	c c	504 (14.0)	497 (7.2)	501 (13.3)	505 (7.0)
Spain (Ceuta and Melilla)	c c	c c	-0.55 (0.03)	c c	c c	c c	c c	414 (2.3)	c c	c c
Spain (Galicia)	-0.87 (0.13)	-0.59 (0.07)	-0.18 (0.14)	0.01 (0.11)	c c	463 (13.8)	480 (5.9)	497 (6.8)	498 (8.9)	c c
Spain (La Rioja)	c c	-0.56 (0.04)	-0.49 (0.07)	0.04 (0.04)	c c	c c	487 (4.4)	499 (6.0)	507 (3.6)	c c
Spain (Madrid)	c c	-0.29 (0.16)	-0.14 (0.21)	-0.27 (0.12)	0.07 (0.20)	c c	472 (13.3)	491 (4.9)	519 (6.2)	515 (5.3)
Spain (Murcia)	c c	-0.76 (0.10)	-0.48 (0.14)	0.05 (0.17)	c c	c c	472 (7.1)	486 (5.5)	484 (8.4)	c c
Spain (Navarre)	-0.62 (0.07)	-0.47 (0.05)	-0.22 (0.06)	0.10 (0.07)	c c	467 (7.8)	495 (5.8)	493 (8.9)	507 (4.3)	c c
United Kingdom (Scotland)	0.12 (0.06)	0.30 (0.05)	0.16 (0.04)	0.11 (0.09)	c c	502 (9.6)	505 (5.8)	496 (2.8)	504 (5.2)	c c
Non-adjudicated										
Belgium (French Community)	0.47 (0.26)	0.14 (0.11)	0.15 (0.07)	0.12 (0.13)	0.30 (0.17)	503 (25.8)	488 (11.2)	496 (5.8)	496 (12.9)	489 (9.6)
Belgium (German-Speaking Community)	c c	0.16 (0.03)	c c	c c	c c	c c	503 (4.2)	c c	c c	c c
Finland (Finnish Speaking)	0.10 (0.04)	0.25 (0.03)	0.36 (0.03)	0.56 (0.05)	c c	537 (8.3)	538 (4.7)	539 (3.0)	537 (4.6)	c c
Finland (Swedish Speaking)	0.30 (0.06)	0.49 (0.03)	0.58 (0.04)	0.94 (0.04)	c c	504 (5.1)	507 (4.7)	519 (4.8)	520 (5.7)	c c
Italy (Provincia Abruzzo)	c c	-0.09 (0.33)	-0.03 (0.07)	0.12 (0.14)	c c	c c	460 (34.2)	489 (8.3)	477 (9.2)	c c
Italy (Provincia Autonoma di Bolzano)	c c	-0.35 (0.03)	-0.18 (0.03)	-0.06 (0.05)	c c	c c	491 (3.2)	495 (5.6)	479 (5.2)	c c
Italy (Provincia Basilicata)	c c	-0.33 (0.06)	-0.23 (0.05)	c c	c c	c c	465 (8.6)	483 (4.6)	c c	c c
Italy (Provincia Calabria)	c c	-0.47 (0.11)	-0.16 (0.08)	0.28 (0.22)	c c	c c	441 (6.6)	453 (9.2)	459 (18.6)	c c
Italy (Provincia Campania)	c c	-0.47 (0.26)	-0.31 (0.08)	-0.21 (0.13)	-0.46 (0.27)	c c	459 (18.8)	447 (8.8)	461 (12.4)	448 (29.9)
Italy (Provincia Emilia Romagna)	c c	-0.45 (0.20)	0.04 (0.10)	0.20 (0.10)	c c	c c	481 (17.4)	513 (8.3)	503 (8.1)	c c
Italy (Provincia Friuli Venezia Giulia)	c c	-0.38 (0.07)	0.12 (0.04)	0.07 (0.09)	c c	c c	485 (16.0)	532 (8.0)	529 (8.0)	c c
Italy (Provincia Lazio)	c c	c c	-0.01 (0.09)	c c	0.39 (0.07)	c c	c c	478 (10.3)	c c	491 (9.2)
Italy (Provincia Liguria)	c c	c c	0.00 (0.07)	0.03 (0.13)	c c	c c	c c	502 (12.1)	478 (10.4)	c c
Italy (Provincia Lombardia)	c c	-0.16 (0.14)	-0.09 (0.06)	0.05 (0.10)	0.30 (0.22)	c c	532 (19.0)	519 (7.0)	523 (14.5)	525 (19.4)
Italy (Provincia Marche)	c c	-0.13 (0.19)	-0.11 (0.05)	c c	c c	c c	504 (14.1)	502 (11.1)	c c	c c
Italy (Provincia Molise)	c c	-0.26 (0.07)	-0.08 (0.04)	c c	c c	c c	462 (7.4)	473 (3.1)	c c	c c
Italy (Provincia Piemonte)	c c	-0.60 (0.17)	-0.08 (0.06)	0.06 (0.20)	c c	c c	493 (13.4)	506 (9.7)	496 (20.9)	c c
Italy (Provincia Puglia)	c c	-0.23 (0.28)	-0.49 (0.06)	-0.28 (0.17)	c c	c c	470 (32.9)	491 (7.6)	499 (12.6)	c c
Italy (Provincia Sardegna)	c c	-0.44 (0.11)	-0.34 (0.08)	-0.01 (0.13)	c c	c c	451 (18.9)	465 (12.5)	487 (8.7)	c c
Italy (Provincia Sicilia)	c c	-0.58 (0.09)	-0.26 (0.07)	-0.01 (0.18)	c c	c c	454 (17.0)	447 (10.3)	465 (16.1)	c c
Italy (Provincia Toscana)	c c	0.01 (0.09)	0.01 (0.07)	0.24 (0.10)	c c	c c	511 (15.8)	497 (18.0)	486 (17.5)	c c
Italy (Provincia Trento)	c c	-0.32 (0.05)	0.01 (0.07)	-0.06 (0.08)	c c	c c	496 (10.5)	502 (6.6)	525 (11.0)	c c
Italy (Provincia Umbria)	c c	-0.01 (0.14)	-0.02 (0.06)	0.30 (0.10)	c c	c c	469 (19.2)	488 (8.3)	515 (9.5)	c c
Italy (Provincia Valle d'Aosta)	-0.40 (0.06)	-0.26 (0.07)	0.01 (0.04)	c c	c c	478 (5.5)	529 (6.3)	522 (3.0)	c c	c c
Italy (Provincia Veneto)	c c	c c	-0.11 (0.06)	0.13 (0.11)	c c	c c	c c	522 (9.3)	504 (11.8)	c c
United Kingdom (England)	0.37 (0.11)	0.25 (0.05)	0.21 (0.04)	0.20 (0.08)	0.14 (0.11)	511 (11.3)	506 (4.2)	497 (4.7)	493 (7.9)	490 (8.3)
United Kingdom (Northern Ireland)	0.02 (0.03)	0.16 (0.05)	0.21 (0.06)	0.02 (0.06)	c c	464 (16.7)	510 (8.3)	518 (7.3)	491 (12.0)	c c
United Kingdom (Wales)	0.20 (0.06)	0.13 (0.04)	0.11 (0.04)	0.34 (0.09)	c c	489 (8.4)	477 (4.0)	474 (5.5)	485 (8.9)	c c

Notes: Values that are statistically significant are indicated in bold (see Annex A3). See Table II.2.6 for national data.
StatLink ᴍᴏᴩ⤷ http://dx.doi.org/10.1787/888932343304

[Part 3/3]
Reading performance and socio-economic background, by school location
Table S.II.c *Results based on students' self-reports and school principals' reports*

	Difference in the reading score											
	BEFORE accounting for the PISA index of economic, social and cultural status of students (ESCS)						AFTER accounting for the PISA index of economic, social and cultural status of students (ESCS)					
	Students in small town schools versus rural schools		Students in town schools versus rural schools		Students in city or large city schools versus in rural schools		Students in small town schools versus rural schools		Students in town schools versus rural schools		Students in city or large city schools versus in rural schools	
	Score dif.	S.E.	Score dif.	S.E.	Score dif.	S.E.	Score dif.	S.E.	Score dif.	S.E.	Score dif.	S.E.
Adjudicated												
Belgium (Flemish Community)	c	c	c	c	c	c	c	c	c	c	-8	(10.8)
Spain (Andalusia)	c	c	c	c	c	c	c	c	c	c	c	(11.9)
Spain (Aragon)	-17	(14.4)	**28**	(12.1)	**29**	(10.0)	**-19**	(14.0)	18	(10.8)	12	c
Spain (Asturias)	-20	(30.4)	-10	(34.3)	18	(29.9)	-11	(22.8)	-7	(25.0)	-23	c
Spain (Balearic Islands)	c	c	c	c	c	c	c	c	c	c	c	c
Spain (Basque Country)	c	c	c	c	c	c	**-35**	(17.2)	**-35**	(16.7)	c	c
Spain (Canary Islands)	c	c	c	c	c	c	c	c	c	c	c	c
Spain (Cantabria)	-7	(15.2)	-7	(19.5)	19	(15.5)	-4	(14.2)	-8	(15.0)	c	c
Spain (Castile and Leon)	**43**	(13.2)	**52**	(14.1)	**67**	(13.1)	**36**	(13.4)	**41**	(13.4)	**49**	(11.5)
Spain (Catalonia)	c	c	c	c	c	c	c	c	c	c	c	(12.7)
Spain (Ceuta and Melilla)	c	c	c	c	c	c	c	c	c	c	0	c
Spain (Galicia)	20	(14.8)	**43**	(17.1)	47	(17.5)	16	(13.1)	29	(14.7)	14	c
Spain (La Rioja)	c	c	c	c	c	c	c	c	c	c	19	(10.2)
Spain (Madrid)	c	c	c	c	c	c	c	c	c	c	c	(9.5)
Spain (Murcia)	c	c	c	c	c	c	c	c	c	c	c	(15.7)
Spain (Navarre)	**31**	(9.9)	**37**	(12.4)	**60**	(10.0)	**29**	(9.5)	**29**	(11.8)	**83**	(17.0)
United Kingdom (Scotland)	8	(11.8)	-5	(10.7)	0	(12.8)	2	(10.9)	-6	(9.9)	2	(17.8)
Non-adjudicated												
Belgium (French Community)	-32	(44.4)	-24	(44.4)	-26	(43.8)	-13	(30.5)	-6	(27.5)	c	(8.4)
Belgium (German-Speaking Community)	c	c	c	c	c	c	c	c	c	c	8	c
Finland (Finnish Speaking)	6	(9.1)	10	(8.5)	15	(9.6)	1	(9.6)	2	(8.9)	c	c
Finland (Swedish Speaking)	9	(6.8)	**24**	(7.3)	**37**	(7.4)	3	(6.7)	14	(7.3)	c	c
Italy (Provincia Abruzzo)	c	c	c	c	c	c	c	c	c	c	c	c
Italy (Provincia Autonoma di Bolzano)	c	c	c	c	c	c	c	c	c	c	c	c
Italy (Provincia Basilicata)	c	c	c	c	c	c	c	c	c	c	c	c
Italy (Provincia Calabria)	c	c	c	c	c	c	c	c	c	c	c	(16.1)
Italy (Provincia Campania)	c	c	c	c	c	c	c	c	c	c	c	c
Italy (Provincia Emilia Romagna)	c	c	c	c	c	c	c	c	c	c	c	c
Italy (Provincia Friuli Venezia Giulia)	c	c	c	c	c	c	c	c	c	c	c	(20.8)
Italy (Provincia Lazio)	c	c	c	c	c	c	c	c	c	c	c	c
Italy (Provincia Liguria)	c	c	c	c	c	c	c	c	c	c	17	c
Italy (Provincia Lombardia)	c	c	c	c	c	c	**90**	(21.4)	**82**	(10.6)	c	c
Italy (Provincia Marche)	c	c	c	c	c	c	c	c	c	c	30	c
Italy (Provincia Molise)	c	c	c	c	c	c	c	c	c	c	c	c
Italy (Provincia Piemonte)	c	c	c	c	c	c	c	c	c	c	c	(9.3)
Italy (Provincia Puglia)	c	c	c	c	c	c	c	c	c	c	c	c
Italy (Provincia Sardegna)	c	c	c	c	c	c	c	c	c	c	38	c
Italy (Provincia Sicilia)	c	c	c	c	c	c	c	c	c	c	30	c
Italy (Provincia Toscana)	c	c	c	c	c	c	c	c	c	c	c	(27.4)
Italy (Provincia Trento)	c	c	c	c	c	c	-10	(17.2)	-3	(14.0)	c	(19.9)
Italy (Provincia Umbria)	c	c	c	c	c	c	c	c	c	c	-18	c
Italy (Provincia Valle d'Aosta)	**55**	(7.5)	**53**	(6.0)	c	c	**53**	(7.5)	**43**	(6.6)	c	c
Italy (Provincia Veneto)	c	c	c	c	c	c	c	c	c	c	c	(11.7)
United Kingdom (England)	-11	(15.4)	-20	(17.5)	-28	(16.2)	-5	(11.2)	-13	(13.0)	c	c
United Kingdom (Northern Ireland)	**50**	(18.6)	**59**	(20.6)	28	(21.5)	**44**	(17.6)	**51**	(19.0)	-11	c
United Kingdom (Wales)	-10	(11.4)	-14	(11.7)	-2	(14.2)	-11	(8.8)	-14	(9.2)	c	c

Notes: Values that are statistically significant are indicated in bold (see Annex A3). See Table II.2.6 for national data.
StatLink http://dx.doi.org/10.1787/888932343304

[Part 1/2]
PISA index of economic, social and cultural status and reading performance, by quarters of this index

Table S.II.d *Results based on students' self-reports*

	PISA index of economic, social and cultural status										Performance on the reading scale, by quarters of this index							
	All students		Bottom quarter		Second quarter		Third quarter		Top quarter		Bottom quarter		Second quarter		Third quarter		Top quarter	
	Mean index	S.E.	Mean index	S.E.	Mean index	S.E.	Mean index	S.E.	Mean index	S.E.	Mean score	S.E.	Mean score	S.E.	Mean score	S.E.	Mean score	S.E.
Adjudicated																		
Belgium (Flemish Community)	0.20	(0.02)	-0.96	(0.02)	-0.14	(0.01)	0.53	(0.01)	1.36	(0.01)	472	(3.4)	503	(3.2)	532	(3.3)	572	(3.7)
Spain (Andalusia)	-0.57	(0.08)	-1.91	(0.02)	-1.07	(0.01)	-0.27	(0.01)	0.95	(0.03)	420	(9.0)	447	(5.6)	471	(5.8)	508	(5.6)
Spain (Aragon)	-0.22	(0.06)	-1.51	(0.03)	-0.61	(0.01)	0.11	(0.01)	1.14	(0.04)	465	(6.2)	483	(5.1)	501	(4.6)	533	(4.3)
Spain (Asturias)	-0.22	(0.05)	-1.51	(0.02)	-0.64	(0.01)	0.10	(0.01)	1.15	(0.03)	448	(6.0)	474	(4.2)	504	(5.9)	540	(7.1)
Spain (Balearic Islands)	-0.28	(0.06)	-1.62	(0.02)	-0.69	(0.01)	0.05	(0.01)	1.13	(0.03)	419	(6.6)	451	(7.7)	470	(5.7)	495	(5.4)
Spain (Basque Country)	-0.08	(0.03)	-1.33	(0.02)	-0.41	(0.01)	0.29	(0.01)	1.14	(0.01)	464	(4.3)	487	(3.6)	504	(3.5)	525	(3.6)
Spain (Canary Islands)	-0.62	(0.05)	-1.90	(0.02)	-1.04	(0.01)	-0.33	(0.01)	0.77	(0.04)	419	(6.4)	430	(6.7)	464	(4.9)	487	(6.6)
Spain (Cantabria)	-0.19	(0.06)	-1.50	(0.03)	-0.58	(0.01)	0.11	(0.02)	1.20	(0.02)	447	(5.8)	483	(5.5)	493	(6.1)	530	(4.8)
Spain (Castile and Leon)	-0.19	(0.07)	-1.49	(0.02)	-0.58	(0.01)	0.14	(0.01)	1.18	(0.02)	466	(5.7)	492	(5.7)	515	(6.4)	542	(4.4)
Spain (Catalonia)	-0.26	(0.08)	-1.57	(0.03)	-0.64	(0.02)	0.10	(0.01)	1.07	(0.03)	466	(7.2)	484	(6.6)	511	(6.9)	533	(4.9)
Spain (Ceuta and Melilla)	-0.55	(0.03)	-2.15	(0.03)	-0.99	(0.02)	-0.08	(0.01)	0.99	(0.03)	360	(4.7)	387	(4.9)	436	(5.7)	472	(5.2)
Spain (Galicia)	-0.39	(0.06)	-1.68	(0.02)	-0.76	(0.01)	-0.08	(0.01)	0.97	(0.03)	455	(4.5)	480	(5.2)	494	(5.9)	515	(7.3)
Spain (La Rioja)	-0.28	(0.08)	-1.53	(0.03)	-0.68	(0.01)	0.02	(0.01)	1.08	(0.02)	457	(5.7)	486	(5.4)	505	(5.8)	547	(4.8)
Spain (Madrid)	-0.07	(0.11)	-1.42	(0.03)	-0.48	(0.01)	0.28	(0.02)	1.34	(0.03)	465	(6.3)	491	(4.9)	510	(5.1)	552	(7.4)
Spain (Murcia)	-0.43	(0.09)	-1.80	(0.03)	-0.90	(0.01)	-0.12	(0.02)	1.10	(0.05)	445	(5.5)	470	(5.2)	488	(5.8)	521	(6.8)
Spain (Navarre)	-0.18	(0.04)	-1.46	(0.02)	-0.58	(0.01)	0.15	(0.01)	1.16	(0.03)	464	(4.7)	476	(5.7)	511	(5.4)	539	(5.8)
United Kingdom (Scotland)	0.19	(0.03)	-0.84	(0.01)	-0.11	(0.01)	0.46	(0.01)	1.24	(0.02)	458	(3.9)	487	(3.7)	513	(3.9)	549	(4.4)
Non-adjudicated																		
Belgium (French Community)	0.19	(0.04)	-1.05	(0.03)	-0.13	(0.01)	0.55	(0.01)	1.40	(0.02)	427	(6.0)	471	(5.1)	516	(4.3)	563	(4.4)
Belgium (German-Speaking Community)	0.23	(0.03)	-0.83	(0.03)	-0.08	(0.01)	0.50	(0.01)	1.32	(0.03)	470	(5.7)	489	(5.7)	498	(6.5)	538	(6.7)
Finland (Finnish Speaking)	0.36	(0.02)	-0.65	(0.01)	0.10	(0.00)	0.67	(0.00)	1.30	(0.01)	505	(3.4)	530	(2.9)	550	(3.1)	567	(2.9)
Finland (Swedish Speaking)	0.57	(0.02)	-0.45	(0.02)	0.32	(0.01)	0.91	(0.01)	1.52	(0.02)	478	(5.3)	492	(5.1)	526	(5.0)	553	(4.7)
Italy (Provincia Abruzzo)	-0.03	(0.04)	-1.24	(0.04)	-0.37	(0.01)	0.23	(0.01)	1.24	(0.02)	437	(9.5)	473	(6.2)	491	(6.3)	519	(5.7)
Italy (Provincia Autonoma di Bolzano)	-0.22	(0.02)	-1.28	(0.03)	-0.52	(0.01)	0.00	(0.01)	0.93	(0.02)	455	(5.1)	491	(6.0)	499	(5.9)	519	(5.1)
Italy (Provincia Basilicata)	-0.28	(0.03)	-1.43	(0.02)	-0.63	(0.01)	-0.05	(0.01)	0.99	(0.03)	444	(7.4)	458	(5.9)	483	(5.9)	507	(4.4)
Italy (Provincia Calabria)	-0.25	(0.06)	-1.60	(0.02)	-0.67	(0.01)	0.04	(0.01)	1.21	(0.03)	412	(6.0)	434	(6.0)	455	(8.4)	492	(5.7)
Italy (Provincia Campania)	-0.33	(0.06)	-1.61	(0.03)	-0.74	(0.01)	0.00	(0.01)	1.05	(0.03)	417	(8.7)	436	(7.2)	463	(8.3)	491	(7.7)
Italy (Provincia Emilia Romagna)	0.06	(0.04)	-1.27	(0.02)	-0.28	(0.01)	0.37	(0.01)	1.42	(0.03)	440	(8.3)	493	(4.3)	519	(5.2)	561	(5.8)
Italy (Provincia Friuli Venezia Giulia)	-0.05	(0.04)	-1.20	(0.02)	-0.33	(0.01)	0.19	(0.01)	1.15	(0.02)	473	(6.8)	502	(7.6)	529	(6.0)	548	(6.6)
Italy (Provincia Lazio)	0.14	(0.05)	-1.12	(0.03)	-0.16	(0.01)	0.45	(0.01)	1.40	(0.02)	434	(6.3)	487	(5.4)	487	(6.1)	516	(7.1)
Italy (Provincia Liguria)	0.02	(0.05)	-1.18	(0.03)	-0.29	(0.01)	0.28	(0.01)	1.25	(0.03)	452	(15.8)	491	(11.6)	497	(8.9)	525	(7.1)
Italy (Provincia Lombardia)	-0.03	(0.04)	-1.31	(0.04)	-0.34	(0.01)	0.28	(0.01)	1.23	(0.03)	474	(8.5)	515	(6.2)	539	(5.9)	559	(5.9)
Italy (Provincia Marche)	-0.11	(0.03)	-1.29	(0.02)	-0.42	(0.01)	0.16	(0.01)	1.11	(0.03)	466	(9.5)	486	(11.9)	512	(5.3)	531	(5.6)
Italy (Provincia Molise)	-0.12	(0.03)	-1.37	(0.02)	-0.48	(0.01)	0.13	(0.01)	1.24	(0.04)	426	(5.7)	474	(4.3)	474	(5.2)	509	(5.6)
Italy (Provincia Piemonte)	-0.14	(0.04)	-1.38	(0.04)	-0.49	(0.01)	0.14	(0.01)	1.17	(0.03)	457	(4.9)	484	(7.2)	503	(11.2)	544	(8.1)
Italy (Provincia Puglia)	-0.42	(0.05)	-1.63	(0.02)	-0.80	(0.01)	-0.12	(0.01)	0.87	(0.04)	463	(6.6)	477	(7.1)	501	(7.4)	517	(4.9)
Italy (Provincia Sardegna)	-0.25	(0.05)	-1.55	(0.02)	-0.66	(0.01)	0.04	(0.01)	1.19	(0.03)	445	(6.6)	460	(4.6)	462	(7.0)	510	(6.5)
Italy (Provincia Sicilia)	-0.24	(0.07)	-1.58	(0.02)	-0.71	(0.02)	0.06	(0.01)	1.27	(0.04)	401	(15.7)	442	(8.5)	470	(7.8)	501	(10.2)
Italy (Provincia Toscana)	0.06	(0.04)	-1.13	(0.03)	-0.25	(0.01)	0.35	(0.01)	1.26	(0.03)	453	(6.7)	493	(7.9)	510	(5.4)	521	(5.5)
Italy (Provincia Trento)	-0.13	(0.03)	-1.22	(0.03)	-0.42	(0.01)	0.08	(0.01)	1.05	(0.02)	474	(5.3)	499	(5.4)	513	(4.7)	549	(5.9)
Italy (Provincia Umbria)	0.08	(0.03)	-1.13	(0.03)	-0.23	(0.01)	0.33	(0.01)	1.36	(0.03)	445	(7.0)	486	(8.1)	502	(5.8)	534	(6.3)
Italy (Provincia Valle d'Aosta)	-0.12	(0.03)	-1.29	(0.03)	-0.42	(0.01)	0.15	(0.01)	1.09	(0.03)	480	(6.6)	507	(5.8)	523	(5.1)	547	(5.0)
Italy (Provincia Veneto)	-0.06	(0.05)	-1.25	(0.02)	-0.40	(0.01)	0.20	(0.01)	1.19	(0.03)	475	(9.1)	496	(7.5)	515	(5.2)	538	(7.9)
United Kingdom (England)	0.21	(0.02)	-0.79	(0.02)	-0.05	(0.01)	0.48	(0.01)	1.21	(0.01)	451	(3.4)	483	(3.7)	510	(3.4)	544	(3.8)
United Kingdom (Northern Ireland)	0.12	(0.02)	-0.87	(0.02)	-0.17	(0.01)	0.38	(0.01)	1.13	(0.01)	452	(7.3)	486	(4.3)	520	(5.2)	548	(5.2)
United Kingdom (Wales)	0.16	(0.03)	-0.78	(0.01)	-0.11	(0.01)	0.39	(0.01)	1.13	(0.02)	443	(4.2)	466	(4.5)	483	(4.3)	520	(5.1)

Notes: Values that are statistically significant are indicated in bold (see Annex A3). See Table II.3.1 for national data.
StatLink http://dx.doi.org/10.1787/888932343304

[Part 2/2]
**PISA index of economic, social and cultural status and reading performance,
by quarters of this index**

Table S.II.d   *Results based on students' self-reports*

	Change in the reading score per unit of this index		Increased likelihood of students in the bottom quarter of the PISA index of social, economic and cultural status, scoring in the bottom quarter of the reading performance distribution		Explained variance in student performance (r-squared x 100)	
	Effect	S.E.	Ratio	S.E.	Percentage	S.E.
Adjudicated						
Belgium (Flemish Community)	41.5	(2.0)	2.20	(0.12)	16.5	(1.3)
Spain (Andalusia)	30.2	(2.7)	2.26	(0.22)	14.5	(2.3)
Spain (Aragon)	26.3	(2.0)	1.82	(0.22)	10.0	(1.5)
Spain (Asturias)	34.4	(2.6)	2.23	(0.24)	14.7	(2.5)
Spain (Balearic Islands)	27.1	(2.7)	2.13	(0.21)	10.2	(1.6)
Spain (Basque Country)	24.4	(1.8)	1.85	(0.15)	8.0	(1.1)
Spain (Canary Islands)	26.6	(2.9)	1.76	(0.23)	9.2	(2.0)
Spain (Cantabria)	28.1	(2.4)	2.10	(0.26)	11.0	(1.9)
Spain (Castile and Leon)	28.9	(2.3)	1.95	(0.24)	12.5	(2.0)
Spain (Catalonia)	26.6	(3.0)	1.89	(0.24)	11.1	(2.3)
Spain (Ceuta and Melilla)	37.2	(2.0)	2.07	(0.21)	19.1	(1.9)
Spain (Galicia)	22.7	(2.5)	1.75	(0.20)	7.1	(1.7)
Spain (La Rioja)	34.8	(2.5)	1.84	(0.22)	14.9	(1.9)
Spain (Madrid)	30.6	(3.1)	2.11	(0.33)	15.5	(3.4)
Spain (Murcia)	27.3	(2.5)	2.11	(0.30)	14.9	(3.0)
Spain (Navarre)	30.2	(2.5)	1.83	(0.19)	13.7	(2.3)
United Kingdom (Scotland)	43.6	(2.3)	2.04	(0.13)	14.4	(1.5)
Non-adjudicated						
Belgium (French Community)	53.7	(2.8)	2.80	(0.21)	23.4	(2.0)
Belgium (German-Speaking Community)	29.9	(3.5)	1.73	(0.23)	7.7	(1.8)
Finland (Finnish Speaking)	31.5	(1.8)	1.85	(0.11)	8.1	(0.9)
Finland (Swedish Speaking)	35.6	(2.9)	1.81	(0.19)	10.4	(1.7)
Italy (Provincia Abruzzo)	33.8	(4.7)	2.02	(0.24)	12.8	(2.9)
Italy (Provincia Autonoma di Bolzano)	27.4	(3.6)	1.93	(0.22)	6.6	(1.8)
Italy (Provincia Basilicata)	27.6	(3.0)	1.64	(0.16)	9.3	(1.8)
Italy (Provincia Calabria)	28.4	(2.3)	1.75	(0.21)	12.0	(1.7)
Italy (Provincia Campania)	27.3	(4.3)	1.80	(0.19)	9.3	(2.3)
Italy (Provincia Emilia Romagna)	44.3	(3.3)	2.73	(0.29)	21.9	(3.0)
Italy (Provincia Friuli Venezia Giulia)	33.6	(4.2)	1.94	(0.23)	11.0	(2.2)
Italy (Provincia Lazio)	29.6	(3.7)	2.38	(0.30)	10.0	(2.5)
Italy (Provincia Liguria)	28.6	(6.7)	1.98	(0.23)	8.2	(3.0)
Italy (Provincia Lombardia)	33.9	(3.3)	2.44	(0.23)	14.1	(2.5)
Italy (Provincia Marche)	28.3	(3.8)	1.66	(0.21)	8.1	(1.5)
Italy (Provincia Molise)	30.1	(2.4)	2.30	(0.27)	13.0	(1.9)
Italy (Provincia Piemonte)	35.1	(3.2)	1.98	(0.36)	13.5	(3.1)
Italy (Provincia Puglia)	24.2	(2.8)	1.64	(0.18)	7.6	(1.7)
Italy (Provincia Sardegna)	24.5	(3.3)	1.44	(0.19)	8.1	(2.1)
Italy (Provincia Sicilia)	34.7	(5.6)	1.98	(0.36)	14.6	(3.7)
Italy (Provincia Toscana)	27.6	(3.6)	1.94	(0.17)	7.4	(1.9)
Italy (Provincia Trento)	34.2	(3.9)	1.90	(0.15)	10.8	(2.4)
Italy (Provincia Umbria)	35.4	(3.0)	2.03	(0.27)	12.5	(2.1)
Italy (Provincia Valle d'Aosta)	27.1	(3.3)	1.83	(0.22)	8.4	(1.9)
Italy (Provincia Veneto)	27.2	(4.8)	1.63	(0.17)	8.2	(2.5)
United Kingdom (England)	44.4	(2.2)	2.13	(0.13)	13.8	(1.2)
United Kingdom (Northern Ireland)	48.0	(3.5)	2.32	(0.24)	15.2	(2.0)
United Kingdom (Wales)	39.0	(2.7)	1.86	(0.16)	10.2	(1.4)

Notes: Values that are statistically significant are indicated in bold (see Annex A3). See Table II.3.1 for national data.
StatLink http://dx.doi.org/10.1787/888932343304

[Part 1/2]
Relationship between reading performance and socio-economic background
Table S.II.e   *Results based on students' self-reports*

| | Unadjusted mean score | | Mean score if the mean ESCS would be equal in all OECD countries | | Strength of the relationship between student performance and the ESCS | | Slope of the socio-economic gradient[1] | | Length of the projection of the gradient line | | | | | |
| | | | | | | | | | 5th percentile of the ESCS | | 95th percentile of the ESCS | | Difference between 95th and 5th percentile of the ESCS | |
	Mean score	S.E.	Mean score	S.E.	Percentage of explained variance in student performance	S.E.	Score point difference associated with one unit on the ESCS	S.E.	Index	S.E.	Index	S.E.	Dif.	S.E.
Adjudicated														
Belgium (Flemish Community)	519	(2.3)	511	(2.0)	16.5	(1.31)	41	(2.0)	-1.21	(0.05)	1.61	(0.02)	2.82	(0.05)
Spain (Andalusia)	461	(5.5)	479	(4.3)	14.5	(2.33)	30	(2.7)	-2.18	(0.04)	1.39	(0.10)	3.58	(0.09)
Spain (Aragon)	495	(4.1)	501	(3.4)	10.0	(1.47)	26	(2.0)	-1.86	(0.09)	1.52	(0.10)	3.38	(0.13)
Spain (Asturias)	490	(4.8)	499	(4.3)	14.7	(2.48)	34	(2.6)	-1.81	(0.06)	1.51	(0.11)	3.32	(0.11)
Spain (Balearic Islands)	457	(5.6)	466	(4.3)	10.2	(1.62)	27	(2.7)	-2.04	(0.04)	1.55	(0.09)	3.59	(0.08)
Spain (Basque Country)	494	(2.9)	497	(2.6)	8.0	(1.14)	24	(1.8)	-1.71	(0.04)	1.41	(0.04)	3.12	(0.05)
Spain (Canary Islands)	448	(4.3)	467	(4.3)	9.2	(1.96)	27	(2.9)	-2.17	(0.08)	1.15	(0.11)	3.32	(0.13)
Spain (Cantabria)	488	(4.1)	494	(3.8)	11.0	(1.86)	28	(2.4)	-1.83	(0.04)	1.53	(0.04)	3.36	(0.04)
Spain (Castile and Leon)	503	(4.9)	509	(3.8)	12.5	(2.04)	29	(2.3)	-1.84	(0.07)	1.53	(0.05)	3.37	(0.06)
Spain (Catalonia)	498	(5.2)	505	(4.3)	11.1	(2.31)	27	(3.0)	-1.92	(0.10)	1.44	(0.09)	3.36	(0.10)
Spain (Ceuta and Melilla)	412	(2.5)	434	(2.8)	19.1	(1.86)	37	(2.0)	-2.52	(0.09)	1.40	(0.07)	3.92	(0.12)
Spain (Galicia)	486	(4.4)	495	(4.2)	7.1	(1.67)	23	(2.5)	-1.99	(0.03)	1.34	(0.07)	3.33	(0.07)
Spain (La Rioja)	498	(2.4)	508	(2.4)	14.9	(1.89)	35	(2.5)	-1.83	(0.08)	1.46	(0.04)	3.29	(0.09)
Spain (Madrid)	503	(4.4)	507	(3.0)	15.5	(3.43)	31	(3.1)	-1.77	(0.11)	1.64	(0.10)	3.41	(0.10)
Spain (Murcia)	480	(5.1)	493	(3.8)	14.9	(3.03)	27	(2.5)	-2.09	(0.08)	1.55	(0.09)	3.64	(0.11)
Spain (Navarre)	497	(3.1)	503	(3.1)	13.7	(2.29)	30	(2.5)	-1.85	(0.06)	1.47	(0.06)	3.32	(0.07)
United Kingdom (Scotland)	500	(3.2)	494	(2.6)	14.4	(1.50)	44	(2.3)	-1.08	(0.03)	1.53	(0.06)	2.61	(0.06)
Non-adjudicated														
Belgium (French Community)	490	(4.2)	484	(3.2)	23.4	(2.03)	54	(2.8)	-1.38	(0.07)	1.69	(0.04)	3.07	(0.08)
Belgium (German-Speaking Community)	499	(2.8)	492	(3.0)	7.7	(1.76)	30	(3.5)	-1.09	(0.04)	1.58	(0.05)	2.67	(0.05)
Finland (Finnish Speaking)	538	(2.4)	527	(2.3)	8.1	(0.87)	31	(1.8)	-0.91	(0.03)	1.50	(0.05)	2.41	(0.05)
Finland (Swedish Speaking)	511	(2.6)	492	(3.4)	10.4	(1.69)	36	(2.9)	-0.76	(0.06)	1.74	(0.04)	2.51	(0.07)
Italy (Provincia Abruzzo)	480	(4.8)	481	(4.1)	12.8	(2.93)	34	(4.7)	-1.58	(0.06)	1.61	(0.07)	3.19	(0.08)
Italy (Provincia Autonoma di Bolzano)	490	(3.2)	497	(3.5)	6.6	(1.82)	27	(3.6)	-1.58	(0.06)	1.28	(0.04)	2.85	(0.07)
Italy (Provincia Basilicata)	473	(4.5)	481	(3.8)	9.3	(1.77)	28	(3.0)	-1.73	(0.05)	1.54	(0.09)	3.27	(0.12)
Italy (Provincia Calabria)	448	(5.2)	455	(4.6)	12.0	(1.68)	28	(2.3)	-1.87	(0.05)	1.73	(0.14)	3.59	(0.14)
Italy (Provincia Campania)	451	(6.6)	460	(5.7)	9.3	(2.33)	27	(4.3)	-1.83	(0.03)	1.47	(0.07)	3.29	(0.07)
Italy (Provincia Emilia Romagna)	502	(4.0)	501	(3.6)	21.9	(3.02)	44	(3.3)	-1.58	(0.05)	1.84	(0.11)	3.43	(0.11)
Italy (Provincia Friuli Venezia Giulia)	513	(4.7)	515	(4.1)	11.0	(2.23)	34	(4.2)	-1.52	(0.04)	1.57	(0.08)	3.09	(0.08)
Italy (Provincia Lazio)	481	(3.9)	477	(3.6)	10.0	(2.47)	30	(3.7)	-1.54	(0.09)	1.75	(0.07)	3.29	(0.11)
Italy (Provincia Liguria)	491	(9.3)	491	(8.6)	8.2	(3.00)	29	(6.7)	-1.58	(0.10)	1.62	(0.08)	3.19	(0.11)
Italy (Provincia Lombardia)	522	(5.5)	523	(4.8)	14.1	(2.48)	34	(3.3)	-1.60	(0.03)	1.60	(0.05)	3.20	(0.06)
Italy (Provincia Marche)	499	(7.3)	502	(6.3)	8.1	(1.46)	28	(3.8)	-1.55	(0.04)	1.50	(0.05)	3.05	(0.07)
Italy (Provincia Molise)	471	(2.8)	474	(2.8)	13.0	(1.93)	30	(2.4)	-1.69	(0.05)	1.70	(0.07)	3.39	(0.08)
Italy (Provincia Piemonte)	496	(5.9)	502	(5.7)	13.5	(3.09)	35	(3.2)	-1.69	(0.06)	1.58	(0.06)	3.27	(0.08)
Italy (Provincia Puglia)	489	(5.0)	500	(4.4)	7.6	(1.72)	24	(2.8)	-1.87	(0.05)	1.39	(0.09)	3.26	(0.10)
Italy (Provincia Sardegna)	469	(4.3)	475	(3.5)	8.1	(2.11)	25	(3.3)	-1.83	(0.02)	1.79	(0.05)	3.61	(0.05)
Italy (Provincia Sicilia)	453	(8.3)	462	(6.8)	14.6	(3.66)	35	(5.6)	-1.83	(0.08)	1.73	(0.08)	3.55	(0.11)
Italy (Provincia Toscana)	493	(4.5)	493	(4.1)	7.4	(1.91)	28	(3.6)	-1.48	(0.05)	1.68	(0.09)	3.15	(0.10)
Italy (Provincia Trento)	508	(2.7)	513	(2.5)	10.8	(2.36)	34	(3.9)	-1.55	(0.04)	1.47	(0.02)	3.02	(0.05)
Italy (Provincia Umbria)	490	(5.3)	489	(4.6)	12.5	(2.12)	35	(3.0)	-1.54	(0.08)	1.75	(0.06)	3.29	(0.09)
Italy (Provincia Valle d'Aosta)	514	(2.2)	518	(2.2)	8.4	(1.89)	27	(3.3)	-1.64	(0.03)	1.46	(0.06)	3.10	(0.07)
Italy (Provincia Veneto)	505	(5.2)	507	(4.5)	8.2	(2.48)	27	(4.8)	-1.52	(0.03)	1.61	(0.07)	3.13	(0.07)
United Kingdom (England)	495	(2.8)	488	(2.2)	13.8	(1.23)	44	(2.2)	-1.04	(0.04)	1.48	(0.02)	2.52	(0.05)
United Kingdom (Northern Ireland)	499	(4.1)	496	(3.8)	15.2	(1.98)	48	(3.5)	-1.11	(0.03)	1.38	(0.05)	2.49	(0.06)
United Kingdom (Wales)	476	(3.4)	472	(2.9)	10.2	(1.40)	39	(2.7)	-1.02	(0.04)	1.44	(0.05)	2.46	(0.06)

Notes: Values that are statistically significant are indicated in bold (see Annex A3). See Table II.3.2 for national data.
1. Single-level bivariate regression of reading performance on the ESCS, the slope is the regression coefficient for the ESCS.
2. Student-level regression of reading performance on the ESCS and the squared term of the ESCS, the index of curvilinearity is the regression coefficient for the squared term.
StatLink ⟶ http://dx.doi.org/10.1787/888932343304

[Part 2/2]
Relationship between reading performance and socio-economic background
Table S.II.e *Results based on students' self-reports*

	PISA index of economic, social and cultural status (ESCS)		Variability in the ESCS		Index of curvilinearity[2]		Skewness in the distribution of ESCS		Percentage of students with low ESCS	
	Mean index	S.E.	Standard deviation	S.E.	Score point difference associated with one unit increase in the ESCS squared	S.E.	Skewness	S.E.	Approximated by the percentage of students with a value of ESCS smaller than -1	S.E.
Adjudicated										
Belgium (Flemish Community)	0.20	(0.02)	0.91	(0.01)	2.52	(1.29)	**-0.19**	(0.05)	7.7	(0.5)
Spain (Andalusia)	-0.57	(0.08)	1.11	(0.03)	-1.51	(1.90)	**0.34**	(0.08)	40.0	(2.7)
Spain (Aragon)	-0.22	(0.06)	1.02	(0.03)	-0.43	(1.92)	0.06	(0.07)	24.2	(1.7)
Spain (Asturias)	-0.22	(0.05)	1.03	(0.03)	-0.31	(1.62)	0.12	(0.06)	24.2	(1.3)
Spain (Balearic Islands)	-0.28	(0.06)	1.07	(0.02)	-2.90	(1.57)	0.09	(0.06)	26.8	(2.0)
Spain (Basque Country)	-0.08	(0.03)	0.97	(0.01)	-0.60	(1.49)	**-0.18**	(0.05)	17.1	(0.9)
Spain (Canary Islands)	-0.62	(0.05)	1.03	(0.03)	0.23	(1.98)	**0.29**	(0.04)	39.2	(2.1)
Spain (Cantabria)	-0.19	(0.06)	1.04	(0.02)	-3.67	(2.05)	0.10	(0.06)	22.5	(1.9)
Spain (Castile and Leon)	-0.19	(0.07)	1.03	(0.02)	-1.72	(2.21)	0.05	(0.07)	23.0	(2.3)
Spain (Catalonia)	-0.26	(0.08)	1.03	(0.03)	-0.93	(2.11)	0.00	(0.07)	25.4	(2.6)
Spain (Ceuta and Melilla)	-0.55	(0.03)	1.22	(0.02)	0.00	(1.53)	-0.05	(0.05)	36.9	(1.3)
Spain (Galicia)	-0.39	(0.06)	1.02	(0.02)	-1.36	(2.33)	0.13	(0.06)	29.1	(2.1)
Spain (La Rioja)	-0.28	(0.02)	1.01	(0.02)	-1.20	(2.70)	0.09	(0.06)	25.4	(1.2)
Spain (Madrid)	-0.07	(0.11)	1.07	(0.03)	0.64	(2.39)	0.02	(0.09)	19.9	(2.3)
Spain (Murcia)	-0.43	(0.09)	1.12	(0.03)	-1.50	(1.56)	**0.23**	(0.06)	33.5	(2.8)
Spain (Navarre)	-0.18	(0.04)	1.02	(0.02)	-0.05	(1.60)	0.02	(0.06)	21.3	(1.4)
United Kingdom (Scotland)	0.19	(0.03)	0.81	(0.01)	2.05	(2.24)	0.06	(0.04)	6.3	(0.6)
Non-adjudicated										
Belgium (French Community)	0.19	(0.04)	0.96	(0.02)	2.30	(1.48)	**-0.27**	(0.08)	10.5	(0.9)
Belgium (German-Speaking Community)	0.23	(0.03)	0.83	(0.02)	**5.99**	(2.88)	0.06	(0.07)	6.7	(0.9)
Finland (Finnish Speaking)	0.36	(0.02)	0.77	(0.01)	**-3.93**	(1.53)	**-0.36**	(0.05)	4.0	(0.4)
Finland (Swedish Speaking)	0.57	(0.02)	0.78	(0.02)	3.78	(2.87)	**-0.22**	(0.08)	2.2	(0.5)
Italy (Provincia Abruzzo)	-0.03	(0.04)	0.96	(0.02)	-5.47	(5.69)	**0.17**	(0.07)	16.6	(1.6)
Italy (Provincia Autonoma di Bolzano)	-0.22	(0.02)	0.86	(0.01)	**-8.19**	(2.71)	**0.20**	(0.06)	17.2	(1.0)
Italy (Provincia Basilicata)	-0.28	(0.03)	0.95	(0.02)	-0.72	(2.37)	**0.37**	(0.05)	23.4	(1.5)
Italy (Provincia Calabria)	-0.25	(0.06)	1.09	(0.02)	-0.12	(1.85)	**0.32**	(0.05)	28.7	(2.1)
Italy (Provincia Campania)	-0.33	(0.06)	1.04	(0.03)	2.29	(2.33)	**0.20**	(0.07)	29.6	(1.8)
Italy (Provincia Emilia Romagna)	0.06	(0.04)	1.04	(0.03)	**-3.60**	(1.50)	0.04	(0.05)	17.0	(1.5)
Italy (Provincia Friuli Venezia Giulia)	-0.05	(0.04)	0.91	(0.01)	-4.66	(2.60)	**0.14**	(0.05)	15.9	(0.9)
Italy (Provincia Lazio)	0.14	(0.05)	0.97	(0.02)	**-5.85**	(1.83)	-0.04	(0.06)	12.9	(1.4)
Italy (Provincia Liguria)	0.02	(0.05)	0.95	(0.02)	**-4.43**	(2.15)	0.04	(0.06)	14.0	(1.5)
Italy (Provincia Lombardia)	-0.03	(0.03)	0.99	(0.03)	**-4.70**	(1.54)	-0.16	(0.14)	18.7	(0.9)
Italy (Provincia Marche)	-0.11	(0.03)	0.93	(0.02)	-2.33	(2.33)	**0.19**	(0.05)	19.9	(0.9)
Italy (Provincia Molise)	-0.12	(0.03)	1.01	(0.02)	-4.10	(2.41)	**0.29**	(0.06)	21.3	(1.4)
Italy (Provincia Piemonte)	-0.14	(0.04)	0.99	(0.03)	-1.98	(3.03)	**0.11**	(0.06)	20.3	(1.4)
Italy (Provincia Puglia)	-0.42	(0.05)	0.98	(0.02)	0.96	(1.88)	**0.34**	(0.05)	30.9	(2.0)
Italy (Provincia Sardegna)	-0.25	(0.05)	1.07	(0.02)	3.43	(1.89)	**0.34**	(0.06)	27.1	(1.9)
Italy (Provincia Sicilia)	-0.24	(0.07)	1.10	(0.03)	-4.02	(3.81)	**0.33**	(0.07)	28.4	(2.1)
Italy (Provincia Toscana)	0.06	(0.04)	0.93	(0.02)	**-6.26**	(2.16)	0.00	(0.08)	13.1	(0.8)
Italy (Provincia Trento)	-0.13	(0.03)	0.89	(0.02)	-1.25	(2.62)	0.09	(0.07)	14.8	(1.3)
Italy (Provincia Umbria)	0.08	(0.03)	0.97	(0.02)	-2.89	(2.39)	**0.13**	(0.05)	13.4	(0.9)
Italy (Provincia Valle d'Aosta)	-0.12	(0.03)	0.92	(0.02)	0.58	(2.80)	0.08	(0.07)	18.1	(1.2)
Italy (Provincia Veneto)	-0.06	(0.05)	0.95	(0.02)	-0.52	(2.32)	**0.18**	(0.05)	17.5	(1.2)
United Kingdom (England)	0.21	(0.02)	0.79	(0.01)	0.71	(1.64)	**-0.15**	(0.05)	5.5	(0.6)
United Kingdom (Northern Ireland)	0.12	(0.02)	0.78	(0.01)	-1.55	(3.10)	0.04	(0.05)	6.9	(0.7)
United Kingdom (Wales)	0.16	(0.03)	0.75	(0.01)	1.68	(1.88)	0.11	(0.06)	5.3	(0.5)

Notes: Values that are statistically significant are indicated in bold (see Annex A3). See Table II.3.2 for national data.
1. Single-level bivariate regression of reading performance on the ESCS, the slope is the regression coefficient for the ESCS.
2. Student-level regression of reading performance on the ESCS and the squared term of the ESCS, the index of curvilinearity is the regression coefficient for the squared term.
StatLink http://dx.doi.org/10.1787/888932343304

[Part 1/2]
Percentage of students and reading performance, by immigrant status
Table S.II.f   *Results based on students' self-reports*

	Native students						Second-generation students					
	Percentage of students	S.E.	Performance on the reading scale		% scoring below Level 2		Percentage of students	S.E.	Performance on the reading scale		% scoring below Level 2	
			Mean score	S.E.	%	S.E.			Mean score	S.E.	%	S.E.
Adjudicated												
Belgium (Flemish Community)	91.0	(1.0)	526	(2.7)	11.2	(1.0)	4.5	(0.6)	450	(7.8)	32.2	(4.5)
Spain (Andalusia)	94.2	(0.7)	465	(5.5)	24.2	(2.4)	0.6	(0.2)	c	c	c	c
Spain (Aragon)	87.8	(1.1)	504	(4.1)	12.3	(1.5)	0.7	(0.2)	c	c	c	c
Spain (Asturias)	94.8	(0.9)	495	(4.9)	16.5	(1.4)	0.6	(0.2)	c	c	c	c
Spain (Balearic Islands)	84.7	(1.9)	466	(5.3)	23.7	(2.5)	2.3	(0.5)	467	(19.8)	c	c
Spain (Basque Country)	95.3	(0.5)	499	(2.8)	13.3	(1.1)	0.4	(0.1)	c	c	c	c
Spain (Canary Islands)	88.3	(1.5)	451	(4.9)	31.8	(2.5)	2.1	(0.4)	c	c	c	c
Spain (Cantabria)	92.9	(1.0)	492	(4.0)	16.3	(1.2)	0.6	(0.2)	c	c	c	c
Spain (Castile and Leon)	94.7	(0.8)	508	(4.7)	11.5	(1.6)	0.4	(0.2)	c	c	c	c
Spain (Catalonia)	88.8	(1.3)	508	(5.0)	9.9	(1.5)	1.7	(0.4)	c	c	c	c
Spain (Ceuta and Melilla)	89.3	(0.8)	420	(2.7)	44.9	(1.4)	7.0	(0.7)	386	(10.3)	59.3	(5.9)
Spain (Galicia)	95.8	(0.5)	489	(4.2)	17.3	(1.5)	0.9	(0.2)	c	c	c	c
Spain (La Rioja)	86.9	(1.0)	511	(2.6)	12.3	(1.0)	1.1	(0.3)	c	c	c	c
Spain (Madrid)	83.7	(1.7)	514	(4.9)	10.5	(1.5)	1.8	(0.4)	c	c	c	c
Spain (Murcia)	87.5	(1.4)	489	(4.8)	15.4	(2.1)	1.0	(0.3)	c	c	c	c
Spain (Navarre)	87.3	(1.0)	505	(3.3)	12.9	(1.2)	0.7	(0.2)	c	c	c	c
United Kingdom (Scotland)	96.0	(0.5)	503	(3.0)	14.9	(1.0)	1.4	(0.3)	529	(17.2)	7.3	(5.9)
Non-adjudicated												
Belgium (French Community)	77.9	(2.2)	508	(3.8)	17.2	(1.3)	12.3	(1.2)	456	(10.4)	32.6	(3.7)
Belgium (German-Speaking Community)	79.0	(1.4)	504	(3.4)	14.8	(1.5)	1.5	(0.4)	c	c	c	c
Finland (Finnish Speaking)	97.3	(0.4)	540	(2.4)	7.2	(0.5)	1.2	(0.2)	494	(14.0)	17.5	(6.0)
Finland (Swedish Speaking)	98.8	(0.3)	512	(2.6)	12.0	(1.0)	0.6	(0.2)	c	c	c	c
Italy (Provincia Abruzzo)	95.2	(0.5)	485	(4.6)	19.1	(1.8)	0.8	(0.2)	c	c	c	c
Italy (Provincia Autonoma di Bolzano)	94.0	(0.8)	497	(2.5)	15.5	(1.3)	0.6	(0.2)	c	c	c	c
Italy (Provincia Basilicata)	99.5	(0.2)	473	(4.6)	24.0	(2.3)	0.4	(0.2)	c	c	c	c
Italy (Provincia Calabria)	98.3	(0.4)	450	(5.0)	32.4	(2.3)	0.3	(0.1)	c	c	c	c
Italy (Provincia Campania)	98.7	(0.4)	453	(6.6)	30.8	(2.7)	0.5	(0.2)	c	c	c	c
Italy (Provincia Emilia Romagna)	89.9	(0.9)	516	(3.8)	13.4	(1.8)	3.0	(0.5)	440	(19.2)	37.6	(11.1)
Italy (Provincia Friuli Venezia Giulia)	90.7	(1.0)	520	(4.5)	11.4	(1.4)	2.3	(0.4)	491	(25.9)	19.4	(9.5)
Italy (Provincia Lazio)	93.2	(1.2)	486	(3.9)	19.6	(1.6)	2.1	(0.4)	461	(17.0)	c	c
Italy (Provincia Liguria)	92.3	(1.1)	498	(8.4)	15.6	(3.5)	1.6	(0.4)	c	c	c	c
Italy (Provincia Lombardia)	91.7	(1.3)	530	(4.9)	8.4	(1.2)	1.7	(0.4)	480	(21.1)	c	c
Italy (Provincia Marche)	92.0	(0.9)	505	(7.5)	15.2	(3.7)	1.8	(0.3)	c	c	c	c
Italy (Provincia Molise)	98.0	(0.5)	473	(2.8)	21.8	(1.5)	0.4	(0.2)	c	c	c	c
Italy (Provincia Piemonte)	89.3	(1.4)	506	(5.3)	15.4	(2.2)	1.6	(0.3)	c	c	c	c
Italy (Provincia Puglia)	98.7	(0.2)	491	(5.0)	17.1	(1.7)	0.5	(0.1)	c	c	c	c
Italy (Provincia Sardegna)	98.4	(0.4)	471	(4.0)	23.7	(1.7)	0.5	(0.2)	c	c	c	c
Italy (Provincia Sicilia)	99.2	(0.5)	456	(8.2)	30.6	(3.7)	0.6	(0.2)	c	c	c	c
Italy (Provincia Toscana)	92.1	(1.3)	499	(4.0)	17.0	(1.6)	1.4	(0.3)	c	c	c	c
Italy (Provincia Trento)	91.4	(0.9)	516	(2.2)	12.0	(1.0)	1.5	(0.4)	c	c	c	c
Italy (Provincia Umbria)	90.6	(1.5)	500	(4.6)	16.9	(1.9)	1.2	(0.3)	c	c	c	c
Italy (Provincia Valle d'Aosta)	94.7	(0.7)	519	(2.2)	9.8	(1.0)	0.7	(0.3)	c	c	c	c
Italy (Provincia Veneto)	92.6	(1.0)	512	(4.8)	12.0	(2.0)	2.0	(0.5)	c	c	c	c
United Kingdom (England)	88.0	(1.2)	500	(2.7)	16.6	(0.9)	6.7	(0.9)	491	(8.7)	19.9	(3.6)
United Kingdom (Northern Ireland)	96.8	(0.5)	502	(3.5)	16.3	(1.5)	0.9	(0.2)	c	c	c	c
United Kingdom (Wales)	96.7	(0.6)	479	(3.3)	21.9	(1.2)	1.3	(0.3)	471	(22.6)	28.1	(9.7)

Note: See Tables II.4.1 and II.4.2 for national data.
StatLink ᴍᴤᴘ http://dx.doi.org/10.1787/888932343304

[Part 2/2]
Percentage of students and reading performance, by immigrant status

Table S.II.f *Results based on students' self-reports*

| | First-generation students | | | | | | Students with an immigrant background (first- or second-generation) | | | | | |
| | Percentage of students | S.E. | Performance on the reading scale | | % scoring below Level 2 | | Percentage of students | S.E. | Performance on the reading scale | | % scoring below Level 2 | |
			Mean score	S.E.	%	S.E.			Mean score	S.E.	%	S.E.
Adjudicated												
Belgium (Flemish Community)	4.6	(0.7)	463	(7.8)	28.5	(3.7)	9.0	(1.0)	457	(6.1)	30.3	(3.2)
Spain (Andalusia)	5.2	(0.6)	406	(13.9)	48.4	(7.7)	5.8	(0.7)	412	(14.3)	46.0	(8.0)
Spain (Aragon)	11.5	(1.1)	435	(7.4)	35.1	(4.4)	12.2	(1.1)	439	(7.6)	33.8	(4.5)
Spain (Asturias)	4.6	(0.7)	424	(7.2)	42.8	(6.3)	5.2	(0.9)	433	(9.0)	39.6	(6.7)
Spain (Balearic Islands)	13.0	(1.7)	423	(13.1)	43.6	(5.9)	15.3	(1.9)	430	(11.4)	41.5	(4.7)
Spain (Basque Country)	4.4	(0.5)	427	(7.8)	41.6	(4.8)	4.7	(0.5)	428	(6.9)	41.1	(4.5)
Spain (Canary Islands)	9.6	(1.6)	433	(12.0)	38.0	(4.9)	11.7	(1.5)	437	(9.2)	37.4	(4.0)
Spain (Cantabria)	6.6	(0.9)	443	(10.5)	33.5	(6.2)	7.1	(1.0)	444	(10.8)	33.4	(6.5)
Spain (Castile and Leon)	4.9	(0.9)	421	(13.5)	37.2	(7.4)	5.3	(0.8)	427	(13.0)	35.5	(7.0)
Spain (Catalonia)	9.5	(1.2)	417	(9.2)	44.3	(6.2)	11.2	(1.3)	425	(9.4)	40.7	(5.7)
Spain (Ceuta and Melilla)	3.6	(0.4)	349	(19.8)	72.3	(7.1)	10.7	(0.8)	374	(10.2)	63.7	(4.8)
Spain (Galicia)	3.3	(0.4)	436	(9.8)	28.4	(8.7)	4.2	(0.5)	442	(8.8)	27.0	(7.0)
Spain (La Rioja)	12.0	(1.0)	422	(9.9)	47.0	(6.1)	13.1	(1.0)	427	(9.4)	44.7	(5.8)
Spain (Madrid)	14.6	(1.6)	453	(7.1)	25.2	(4.2)	16.3	(1.7)	456	(6.7)	23.9	(3.8)
Spain (Murcia)	11.5	(1.3)	424	(7.7)	42.0	(5.6)	12.5	(1.4)	426	(7.7)	42.2	(5.6)
Spain (Navarre)	12.0	(1.0)	447	(6.6)	27.7	(3.9)	12.7	(1.0)	451	(6.5)	26.5	(3.8)
United Kingdom (Scotland)	2.6	(0.3)	463	(16.6)	34.1	(7.6)	4.0	(0.5)	486	(13.2)	24.9	(5.9)
Non-adjudicated												
Belgium (French Community)	9.8	(1.3)	438	(12.2)	41.3	(5.6)	22.1	(2.2)	448	(9.7)	36.5	(3.9)
Belgium (German-Speaking Community)	19.4	(1.4)	483	(6.0)	22.6	(3.1)	21.0	(1.4)	482	(5.8)	22.8	(3.0)
Finland (Finnish Speaking)	1.5	(0.3)	449	(18.1)	38.9	(8.1)	2.7	(0.4)	469	(13.0)	29.4	(5.8)
Finland (Swedish Speaking)	0.7	(0.2)	c	c	c	c	1.2	(0.3)	c	c	c	c
Italy (Provincia Abruzzo)	4.0	(0.5)	354	(35.7)	67.1	(6.5)	4.8	(0.5)	375	(30.9)	58.0	(5.9)
Italy (Provincia Autonoma di Bolzano)	5.4	(0.8)	397	(29.0)	50.3	(11.8)	6.0	(0.8)	400	(26.7)	49.6	(10.7)
Italy (Provincia Basilicata)	0.1	(0.1)	c	c	c	c	0.5	(0.2)	c	c	c	c
Italy (Provincia Calabria)	1.4	(0.3)	c	c	c	c	1.7	(0.4)	c	c	c	c
Italy (Provincia Campania)	0.8	(0.3)	c	c	c	c	1.3	(0.4)	c	c	c	c
Italy (Provincia Emilia Romagna)	7.0	(0.7)	381	(14.2)	55.7	(5.2)	10.1	(0.9)	399	(10.7)	50.3	(4.7)
Italy (Provincia Friuli Venezia Giulia)	7.0	(1.0)	431	(17.4)	37.9	(7.8)	9.3	(1.0)	445	(15.3)	33.4	(6.6)
Italy (Provincia Lazio)	4.6	(1.2)	407	(16.6)	56.5	(11.7)	6.8	(1.2)	424	(14.4)	46.9	(9.2)
Italy (Provincia Liguria)	6.2	(0.8)	401	(17.4)	52.6	(9.0)	7.7	(1.1)	414	(17.6)	48.5	(8.7)
Italy (Provincia Lombardia)	6.6	(1.2)	414	(8.9)	52.5	(5.5)	8.3	(1.3)	428	(9.6)	46.9	(5.2)
Italy (Provincia Marche)	6.3	(0.8)	441	(11.3)	36.6	(8.8)	8.0	(0.9)	436	(10.9)	39.5	(7.8)
Italy (Provincia Molise)	1.6	(0.4)	c	c	c	c	2.0	(0.5)	c	c	c	c
Italy (Provincia Piemonte)	9.1	(1.4)	415	(10.5)	47.7	(6.9)	10.7	(1.4)	420	(11.9)	44.8	(6.8)
Italy (Provincia Puglia)	0.8	(0.2)	c	c	c	c	1.3	(0.2)	c	c	c	c
Italy (Provincia Sardegna)	1.0	(0.4)	c	c	c	c	1.6	(0.4)	c	c	c	c
Italy (Provincia Sicilia)	0.2	(0.1)	c	c	c	c	0.8	(0.3)	c	c	c	c
Italy (Provincia Toscana)	6.5	(1.3)	429	(18.1)	43.9	(11.8)	7.9	(1.3)	437	(16.5)	41.9	(10.3)
Italy (Provincia Trento)	7.1	(0.8)	423	(10.8)	44.3	(5.7)	8.6	(0.9)	430	(10.3)	40.2	(5.7)
Italy (Provincia Umbria)	8.2	(1.4)	416	(12.2)	47.8	(6.0)	9.4	(1.5)	420	(11.9)	46.0	(5.5)
Italy (Provincia Valle d'Aosta)	4.6	(0.7)	428	(14.6)	39.5	(10.4)	5.3	(0.7)	439	(14.6)	36.3	(9.2)
Italy (Provincia Veneto)	5.4	(0.9)	432	(17.1)	42.7	(8.7)	7.4	(1.0)	426	(15.1)	43.4	(7.5)
United Kingdom (England)	5.3	(0.5)	457	(10.3)	28.3	(5.4)	12.0	(1.2)	476	(7.9)	23.6	(3.1)
United Kingdom (Northern Ireland)	2.3	(0.5)	468	(21.3)	32.5	(7.7)	3.2	(0.5)	485	(18.2)	27.3	(6.7)
United Kingdom (Wales)	2.0	(0.4)	458	(13.5)	35.7	(5.9)	3.3	(0.6)	463	(14.0)	32.7	(5.4)

Note: See Tables II.4.1 and II.4.2 for national data.
StatLink ᐧᔆᒪᐧ http://dx.doi.org/10.1787/888932343304

[Part 1/1]

Performance differences between students with and without an immigrant background, by immigrant status

Table S.II.g   *Results based on students' self-reports*

	Difference in the reading score							
	BEFORE accounting for the economic, social and cultural status of students (ESCS)				**AFTER accounting for the economic, social and cultural status of students (ESCS)**			
	Native students versus students with an immigrant background		Native students versus students with an immigrant background who speak a language at home that is different from the language of assessment		Native students versus students with an immigrant background		Native students versus students with an immigrant background who speak a language at home that is different from the language of assessment	
	Score dif.	S.E.	Score dif.	S.E.	Score dif.	S.E.	Score dif.	S.E.
Adjudicated								
Belgium (Flemish Community)	-70	(6.8)	-73	(9.2)	-44	(6.5)	-40	(8.9)
Spain (Andalusia)	-53	(14.6)	c	c	-44	(12.0)	c	c
Spain (Aragon)	-65	(7.0)	-80	(8.5)	-50	(7.7)	-61	(8.6)
Spain (Asturias)	-63	(10.1)	c	c	-44	(10.8)	c	c
Spain (Balearic Islands)	-36	(11.0)	-36	(10.3)	-25	(9.8)	-25	(9.7)
Spain (Basque Country)	-71	(6.4)	-73	(10.4)	-56	(5.6)	-58	(9.6)
Spain (Canary Islands)	-15	(10.7)	c	c	-15	(10.4)	c	c
Spain (Cantabria)	-49	(10.4)	c	c	-35	(9.1)	c	c
Spain (Castile and Leon)	-81	(12.4)	c	c	-66	(11.9)	c	c
Spain (Catalonia)	-82	(9.3)	-75	(9.7)	-65	(8.8)	-56	(10.2)
Spain (Ceuta and Melilla)	-46	(10.8)	-68	(16.4)	-18	(10.2)	-43	(17.1)
Spain (Galicia)	-47	(8.0)	-49	(9.6)	-45	(7.3)	-46	(8.7)
Spain (La Rioja)	-84	(9.9)	-96	(18.1)	-64	(8.8)	-73	(16.0)
Spain (Madrid)	-59	(8.8)	-65	(12.6)	-36	(8.0)	-39	(12.0)
Spain (Murcia)	-63	(8.4)	-69	(16.9)	-46	(7.2)	-59	(15.1)
Spain (Navarre)	-54	(6.8)	-66	(16.9)	-32	(7.5)	-42	(17.5)
United Kingdom (Scotland)	-18	(12.8)	-25	(20.3)	-10	(12.0)	-18	(18.9)
Non-adjudicated								
Belgium (French Community)	-60	(9.9)	-75	(12.2)	-29	(7.7)	-37	(10.4)
Belgium (German-Speaking Community)	-22	(7.0)	-58	(1 2.4)	-24	(7.0)	-57	(11.8)
Finland (Finnish Speaking)	-71	(12.8)	-82	(14.1)	-61	(11.3)	-69	(12.8)
Finland (Swedish Speaking)	c	c	c	c	c	c	c	c
Italy (Provincia Abruzzo)	-110	(30.6)	c	c	-84	(22.4)	c	c
Italy (Provincia Autonoma di Bolzano)	-97	(27.0)	-94	(23.0)	-87	(26.3)	-83	(21.7)
Italy (Provincia Basilicata)	c	c	c	c	c	c	c	c
Italy (Provincia Calabria)	c	c	c	c	c	c	c	c
Italy (Provincia Campania)	c	c	c	c	c	c	c	c
Italy (Provincia Emilia Romagna)	-117	(9.3)	-120	(14.0)	-83	(8.0)	-81	(11.4)
Italy (Provincia Friuli Venezia Giulia)	-74	(15.1)	-96	(19.3)	-59	(13.5)	-78	(17.5)
Italy (Provincia Lazio)	-62	(14.9)	-68	(13.7)	-48	(15.2)	-52	(13.2)
Italy (Provincia Liguria)	-84	(14.2)	-87	(18.8)	-66	(12.6)	-70	(16.4)
Italy (Provincia Lombardia)	-102	(9.1)	-108	(12.3)	-74	(9.4)	-82	(12.9)
Italy (Provincia Marche)	-69	(10.2)	-78	(11.5)	-49	(10.6)	-56	(11.6)
Italy (Provincia Molise)	c	c	c	c	c	c	c	c
Italy (Provincia Piemonte)	-86	(11.0)	-87	(10.8)	-63	(11.6)	-59	(10.4)
Italy (Provincia Puglia)	c	c	c	c	c	c	c	c
Italy (Provincia Sardegna)	c	c	c	c	c	c	c	c
Italy (Provincia Sicilia)	c	c	c	c	c	c	c	c
Italy (Provincia Toscana)	-63	(16.2)	-53	(19.4)	-41	(15.2)	-34	(19.8)
Italy (Provincia Trento)	-87	(10.2)	-97	(12.4)	-71	(9.4)	-76	(12.6)
Italy (Provincia Umbria)	-79	(11.4)	-85	(18.2)	-56	(10.2)	-55	(19.5)
Italy (Provincia Valle d'Aosta)	-80	(15.1)	c	c	-69	(14.8)	c	c
Italy (Provincia Veneto)	-86	(14.7)	-89	(16.6)	-72	(14.8)	-75	(18.1)
United Kingdom (England)	-24	(8.1)	-38	(9.2)	-15	(5.7)	-20	(6.7)
United Kingdom (Northern Ireland)	-17	(17.1)	-32	(21.8)	-12	(16.4)	-25	(21.7)
United Kingdom (Wales)	-16	(13.6)	-38	(19.1)	-10	(12.0)	-31	(18.3)

Notes: Values that are statistically significant are indicated in bold (see Annex A3). See Tables II.4.1 and II.4.4 for national data.
StatLink ⫸ http://dx.doi.org/10.1787/888932343304

[Part 1/2]

Characteristics of schools attended by students with and without an immigrant background
(Scores standardised within each country sample)

Table S.II.h   *Results based on students' self-reports and school principals' reports*

	Percentage of students in schools that have more than 25% students with an immigrant background		Percentage of students in schools that have more than 50% students with an immigrant background		Positive mean index indicates more favourable characteristics											
					School average PISA index of economic, social and cultural status						Index of quality of educational resources					
					Native students		Immigrant students		Difference (N-I)		Native students		Immigrant students		Difference (N-I)	
	%	S.E.	%	S.E.	Mean index	S.E.	Mean index	S.E.	Dif.	S.E.	Mean index	S.E.	Mean index	S.E.	Dif.	S.E
Adjudicated																
Belgium (Flemish Community)	14.6	(2.8)	7.6	(2.1)	0.05	(0.03)	-0.62	(0.08)	**0.67**	(0.09)	-0.02	(0.09)	-0.19	(0.12)	0.17	(0.12)
Spain (Andalusia)	5.9	(3.3)	0.0	c	-0.03	(0.07)	-0.22	(0.14)	0.19	(0.14)	-0.02	(0.14)	0.18	(0.12)	-0.20	(0.12)
Spain (Aragon)	7.7	(3.7)	0.0	c	0.04	(0.06)	-0.63	(0.08)	**0.66**	(0.09)	0.03	(0.15)	0.03	(0.17)	0.01	(0.12)
Spain (Asturias)	3.7	(2.6)	0.0	c	0.03	(0.06)	-0.53	(0.09)	**0.56**	(0.11)	0.01	(0.14)	-0.26	(0.17)	0.28	(0.17)
Spain (Balearic Islands)	26.9	(6.2)	3.8	(2.7)	0.06	(0.07)	-0.34	(0.10)	**0.40**	(0.13)	0.03	(0.14)	0.00	(0.18)	0.02	(0.11)
Spain (Basque Country)	4.5	(1.6)	2.3	(1.1)	0.03	(0.03)	-0.69	(0.08)	**0.73**	(0.08)	-0.04	(0.07)	0.21	(0.22)	-0.26	(0.21)
Spain (Canary Islands)	20.0	(5.7)	0.0	c	-0.03	(0.05)	0.00	(0.09)	-0.03	(0.11)	0.07	(0.15)	-0.29	(0.18)	0.36	(0.19)
Spain (Cantabria)	3.9	(2.7)	0.0	c	0.03	(0.06)	-0.48	(0.10)	**0.51**	(0.10)	0.04	(0.12)	-0.08	(0.18)	0.12	(0.17)
Spain (Castile and Leon)	0.0	c	0.0	c	0.01	(0.07)	-0.55	(0.13)	**0.56**	(0.13)	0.03	(0.15)	-0.04	(0.22)	0.06	(0.16)
Spain (Catalonia)	12.0	(4.6)	0.0	c	0.05	(0.08)	-0.65	(0.09)	**0.70**	(0.10)	0.02	(0.16)	-0.07	(0.17)	0.09	(0.12)
Spain (Ceuta and Melilla)	4.8	(4.6)	0.0	c	0.06	(0.03)	-0.57	(0.07)	**0.63**	(0.08)	-0.06	(0.01)	0.10	(0.09)	-0.16	(0.10)
Spain (Galicia)	0.0	c	0.0	c	-0.02	(0.06)	0.02	(0.14)	-0.04	(0.14)	-0.01	(0.13)	0.06	(0.19)	-0.07	(0.12)
Spain (La Rioja)	13.0	(5.0)	6.5	(3.6)	0.07	(0.03)	-0.62	(0.08)	**0.68**	(0.09)	0.03	(0.02)	0.23	(0.09)	-0.19	(0.10)
Spain (Madrid)	25.5	(6.1)	3.9	(2.7)	0.16	(0.11)	-0.64	(0.07)	**0.80**	(0.09)	0.03	(0.13)	-0.16	(0.15)	0.19	(0.12)
Spain (Murcia)	13.7	(4.8)	0.0	c	0.06	(0.08)	-0.58	(0.10)	**0.64**	(0.11)	0.04	(0.16)	-0.09	(0.19)	0.13	(0.11)
Spain (Navarre)	14.3	(5.0)	2.0	(2.0)	0.13	(0.04)	-0.67	(0.08)	**0.80**	(0.08)	0.00	(0.10)	-0.11	(0.11)	0.11	(0.10)
United Kingdom (Scotland)	1.0	(1.0)	0.0	c	0.02	(0.03)	-0.21	(0.12)	0.22	(0.12)	-0.01	(0.10)	-0.20	(0.18)	0.20	(0.15)
Non-adjudicated																
Belgium (French Community)	32.7	(4.5)	12.7	(3.2)	0.13	(0.03)	-0.46	(0.09)	**0.59**	(0.09)	-0.01	(0.10)	-0.04	(0.15)	0.04	(0.11)
Belgium (German-Speaking Community)	20.0	(12.6)	0.0	c	-0.03	(0.04)	0.08	(0.07)	-0.10	(0.08)	0.05	(0.02)	-0.15	(0.06)	**0.20**	(0.08)
Finland (Finnish Speaking)	0.0	(0.0)	0.0	c	0.00	(0.03)	-0.40	(0.16)	**0.41**	(0.16)	0.01	(0.09)	0.32	(0.21)	-0.31	(0.17)
Finland (Swedish Speaking)	0.0	c	0.0	c	0.00	(0.03)	c	c	c	c	-0.09	(0.01)	c	c	c	c
Italy (Provincia Abruzzo)	3.8	(2.7)	3.8	(2.7)	0.03	(0.04)	-0.90	(0.28)	**0.93**	(0.28)	0.09	(0.15)	-0.37	(0.17)	**0.45**	(0.21)
Italy (Provincia Autonoma di Bolzano)	9.3	(3.1)	2.3	(1.6)	-0.01	(0.02)	-0.52	(0.09)	**0.51**	(0.10)	-0.10	(0.01)	0.16	(0.14)	-0.27	(0.14)
Italy (Provincia Basilicata)	0.0	c	0.0	c	-0.01	(0.04)	c	c	c	c	0.04	(0.07)	c	c	c	c
Italy (Provincia Calabria)	1.9	(1.9)	0.0	c	-0.01	(0.05)	c	c	c	c	-0.02	(0.12)	c	c	c	c
Italy (Provincia Campania)	1.9	(1.9)	1.9	(1.9)	0.00	(0.06)	c	c	c	c	-0.01	(0.13)	c	c	c	c
Italy (Provincia Emilia Romagna)	13.7	(4.8)	2.0	(1.9)	0.09	(0.05)	-0.70	(0.08)	**0.79**	(0.09)	0.00	(0.13)	-0.06	(0.20)	0.06	(0.16)
Italy (Provincia Friuli Venezia Giulia)	10.3	(4.0)	0.0	c	0.03	(0.04)	-0.54	(0.08)	**0.57**	(0.08)	0.07	(0.14)	0.20	(0.26)	-0.13	(0.16)
Italy (Provincia Lazio)	1.9	(1.9)	1.9	(1.9)	0.05	(0.06)	-0.50	(0.09)	**0.55**	(0.11)	-0.04	(0.11)	-0.21	(0.15)	0.17	(0.14)
Italy (Provincia Liguria)	7.8	(3.8)	0.0	c	0.01	(0.05)	-0.76	(0.12)	**0.77**	(0.11)	-0.03	(0.15)	0.04	(0.17)	-0.07	(0.09)
Italy (Provincia Lombardia)	15.1	(4.9)	1.9	(1.9)	0.04	(0.03)	-0.99	(0.14)	**1.03**	(0.15)	0.05	(0.14)	-0.13	(0.18)	0.18	(0.13)
Italy (Provincia Marche)	3.9	(2.7)	2.0	(1.9)	0.05	(0.04)	-0.81	(0.05)	**0.86**	(0.06)	-0.08	(0.16)	0.20	(0.20)	-0.28	(0.20)
Italy (Provincia Molise)	0.0	c	0.0	c	0.06	(0.03)	c	c	c	c	0.19	(0.03)	c	c	c	c
Italy (Provincia Piemonte)	7.7	(3.7)	5.8	(3.2)	-0.04	(0.04)	-0.69	(0.12)	**0.65**	(0.12)	-0.10	(0.13)	-0.59	(0.16)	**0.49**	(0.13)
Italy (Provincia Puglia)	0.0	c	0.0	c	0.00	(0.05)	c	c	c	c	0.01	(0.15)	c	c	c	c
Italy (Provincia Sardegna)	0.0	c	0.0	c	-0.01	(0.05)	c	c	c	c	-0.02	(0.15)	c	c	c	c
Italy (Provincia Sicilia)	0.0	c	0.0	c	-0.04	(0.06)	c	c	c	c	0.00	(0.13)	c	c	c	c
Italy (Provincia Toscana)	1.9	(1.9)	1.9	(1.9)	0.05	(0.04)	-0.77	(0.07)	**0.82**	(0.07)	0.01	(0.14)	-0.16	(0.16)	0.17	(0.13)
Italy (Provincia Trento)	5.9	(3.3)	0.0	c	0.06	(0.03)	-0.54	(0.11)	**0.60**	(0.11)	0.08	(0.08)	-0.32	(0.16)	**0.40**	(0.12)
Italy (Provincia Umbria)	14.5	(4.8)	1.8	(1.8)	0.12	(0.03)	-0.66	(0.12)	**0.79**	(0.13)	-0.06	(0.14)	0.09	(0.18)	-0.15	(0.14)
Italy (Provincia Valle d'Aosta)	4.2	(4.1)	0.0	c	0.03	(0.03)	-0.49	(0.09)	**0.52**	(0.11)	0.00	(0.01)	-0.28	(0.14)	0.29	(0.15)
Italy (Provincia Veneto)	5.7	(3.2)	3.8	(2.6)	0.00	(0.05)	-0.60	(0.07)	**0.60**	(0.08)	0.02	(0.13)	-0.02	(0.13)	0.04	(0.12)
United Kingdom (England)	14.5	(2.7)	6.1	(1.9)	0.01	(0.03)	-0.23	(0.13)	0.24	(0.13)	0.03	(0.09)	-0.18	(0.11)	0.21	(0.12)
United Kingdom (Northern Ireland)	0.0	c	0.0	c	0.00	(0.03)	-0.18	(0.14)	0.18	(0.14)	-0.02	(0.12)	0.21	(0.20)	-0.23	(0.18)
United Kingdom (Wales)	1.5	(1.1)	0.8	(0.8)	0.02	(0.04)	-0.22	(0.17)	0.24	(0.17)	-0.02	(0.07)	-0.23	(0.16)	0.21	(0.15)

Notes: Values that are statistically significant are indicated in bold (see Annex A3). See Table II.4.6 for national data.
StatLink http://dx.doi.org/10.1787/888932343304

[Part 2/2]

Characteristics of schools attended by students with and without an immigrant background
(Scores standardised within each country sample)

Table S.II.h   *Results based on students' self-reports and school principals' reports*

	Student/teacher ratio						Index of teacher shortage					
Negative mean index indicates more favourable characteristics												
	Native students		Immigrant students		Difference (N-I)		Native students		Immigrant students		Difference (N-I)	
	Mean index	S.E.	Mean index	S.E.	Dif.	S.E	Mean index	S.E.	Mean index	S.E.	Dif.	S.E.
Adjudicated												
Belgium (Flemish Community)	0.02	(0.06)	-0.38	(0.10)	**0.39**	(0.09)	-0.01	(0.07)	0.07	(0.16)	-0.08	(0.15)
Spain (Andalusia)	-0.05	(0.08)	-0.13	(0.12)	0.07	(0.12)	-0.02	(0.14)	-0.10	(0.13)	0.08	(0.11)
Spain (Aragon)	-0.03	(0.07)	-0.24	(0.10)	**0.21**	(0.08)	-0.02	(0.14)	-0.04	(0.15)	0.02	(0.11)
Spain (Asturias)	0.02	(0.07)	-0.24	(0.11)	0.25	(0.13)	-0.01	(0.13)	0.08	(0.23)	-0.08	(0.17)
Spain (Balearic Islands)	0.12	(0.14)	-0.43	(0.15)	**0.55**	(0.12)	0.03	(0.13)	0.03	(0.20)	0.00	(0.13)
Spain (Basque Country)	0.04	(0.05)	-0.38	(0.11)	**0.42**	(0.12)	0.04	(0.08)	-0.20	(0.09)	**0.24**	(0.10)
Spain (Canary Islands)	0.01	(0.14)	-0.24	(0.11)	0.25	(0.16)	0.02	(0.11)	0.02	(0.17)	0.00	(0.12)
Spain (Cantabria)	-0.05	(0.07)	-0.10	(0.13)	0.05	(0.12)	0.00	(0.15)	0.02	(0.25)	-0.02	(0.16)
Spain (Castile and Leon)	0.01	(0.10)	0.01	(0.20)	0.00	(0.16)	0.02	(0.18)	0.13	(0.22)	-0.11	(0.17)
Spain (Catalonia)	0.01	(0.14)	-0.36	(0.10)	**0.37**	(0.13)	0.03	(0.11)	-0.07	(0.15)	0.10	(0.12)
Spain (Ceuta and Melilla)	0.02	(0.01)	-0.26	(0.06)	**0.29**	(0.07)	0.01	(0.01)	-0.03	(0.07)	0.04	(0.08)
Spain (Galicia)	-0.01	(0.06)	-0.07	(0.11)	0.05	(0.08)	-0.01	(0.14)	-0.03	(0.18)	0.02	(0.12)
Spain (La Rioja)	-0.06	(0.01)	-0.23	(0.07)	**0.17**	(0.08)	-0.06	(0.01)	0.04	(0.07)	-0.11	(0.08)
Spain (Madrid)	0.13	(0.11)	-0.12	(0.14)	0.25	(0.14)	0.03	(0.13)	0.10	(0.18)	-0.07	(0.14)
Spain (Murcia)	0.03	(0.12)	-0.24	(0.16)	0.27	(0.14)	0.00	(0.17)	0.04	(0.24)	-0.04	(0.17)
Spain (Navarre)	0.13	(0.06)	-0.33	(0.08)	**0.47**	(0.09)	-0.07	(0.13)	-0.34	(0.10)	**0.27**	(0.12)
United Kingdom (Scotland)	0.05	(0.09)	-0.06	(0.24)	0.11	(0.22)	-0.02	(0.09)	-0.06	(0.16)	0.04	(0.13)
Non-adjudicated												
Belgium (French Community)	0.10	(0.07)	-0.18	(0.16)	**0.29**	(0.14)	-0.01	(0.10)	0.08	(0.10)	-0.09	(0.10)
Belgium (German-Speaking Community)	0.00	(0.02)	-0.06	(0.06)	0.05	(0.08)	-0.08	(0.02)	0.34	(0.07)	**-0.42**	(0.08)
Finland (Finnish Speaking)	0.01	(0.08)	0.10	(0.14)	-0.09	(0.11)	0.01	(0.08)	-0.02	(0.16)	0.03	(0.15)
Finland (Swedish Speaking)	0.20	(0.01)	c	c	c	c	0.01	(0.01)	c	c	c	c
Italy (Provincia Abruzzo)	0.03	(0.11)	-0.57	(0.11)	**0.60**	(0.12)	-0.02	(0.11)	0.26	(0.44)	-0.28	(0.43)
Italy (Provincia Autonoma di Bolzano)	0.34	(0.01)	0.03	(0.10)	**0.31**	(0.10)	0.19	(0.02)	-0.20	(0.14)	**0.39**	(0.13)
Italy (Provincia Basilicata)	-0.05	(0.06)	c	c	c	c	-0.01	(0.11)	c	c	c	c
Italy (Provincia Calabria)	-0.02	(0.08)	c	c	c	c	0.01	(0.13)	c	c	c	c
Italy (Provincia Campania)	0.02	(0.12)	c	c	c	c	-0.01	(0.14)	c	c	c	c
Italy (Provincia Emilia Romagna)	0.04	(0.11)	-0.43	(0.09)	**0.47**	(0.11)	-0.05	(0.16)	0.07	(0.17)	-0.12	(0.13)
Italy (Provincia Friuli Venezia Giulia)	-0.02	(0.08)	-0.13	(0.10)	0.11	(0.11)	0.11	(0.13)	0.04	(0.20)	0.07	(0.12)
Italy (Provincia Lazio)	-0.03	(0.11)	-0.29	(0.14)	0.26	(0.15)	0.04	(0.16)	-0.30	(0.18)	**0.34**	(0.17)
Italy (Provincia Liguria)	-0.09	(0.08)	-0.35	(0.13)	0.26	(0.14)	-0.01	(0.15)	0.04	(0.17)	-0.05	(0.12)
Italy (Provincia Lombardia)	-0.09	(0.10)	0.00	(0.29)	-0.09	(0.25)	-0.08	(0.12)	-0.12	(0.24)	0.04	(0.19)
Italy (Provincia Marche)	0.02	(0.09)	-0.41	(0.09)	**0.43**	(0.11)	0.01	(0.15)	0.00	(0.20)	0.01	(0.15)
Italy (Provincia Molise)	0.22	(0.02)	c	c	c	c	-0.07	(0.02)	c	c	c	c
Italy (Provincia Piemonte)	-0.07	(0.13)	-0.12	(0.16)	0.05	(0.11)	-0.05	(0.15)	-0.12	(0.30)	0.07	(0.26)
Italy (Provincia Puglia)	0.02	(0.10)	c	c	c	c	-0.02	(0.15)	c	c	c	c
Italy (Provincia Sardegna)	-0.07	(0.12)	c	c	c	c	-0.01	(0.14)	c	c	c	c
Italy (Provincia Sicilia)	-0.06	(0.12)	c	c	c	c	-0.04	(0.15)	c	c	c	c
Italy (Provincia Toscana)	-0.02	(0.14)	-0.23	(0.12)	0.20	(0.13)	-0.02	(0.14)	-0.08	(0.34)	0.06	(0.32)
Italy (Provincia Trento)	0.03	(0.04)	-0.18	(0.09)	**0.21**	(0.09)	-0.05	(0.08)	-0.10	(0.20)	0.05	(0.15)
Italy (Provincia Umbria)	0.11	(0.08)	-0.20	(0.14)	**0.31**	(0.12)	-0.07	(0.14)	-0.20	(0.22)	0.12	(0.19)
Italy (Provincia Valle d'Aosta)	-0.01	(0.01)	0.12	(0.14)	-0.13	(0.14)	-0.01	(0.01)	0.31	(0.12)	**-0.31**	(0.13)
Italy (Provincia Veneto)	-0.09	(0.10)	-0.06	(0.18)	-0.03	(0.14)	0.01	(0.14)	-0.16	(0.21)	0.17	(0.18)
United Kingdom (England)	0.04	(0.08)	-0.43	(0.16)	**0.47**	(0.14)	-0.02	(0.08)	0.22	(0.14)	-0.24	(0.15)
United Kingdom (Northern Ireland)	0.00	(0.13)	-0.06	(0.31)	0.06	(0.24)	0.01	(0.11)	-0.15	(0.14)	0.16	(0.14)
United Kingdom (Wales)	0.02	(0.08)	-0.04	(0.19)	0.06	(0.18)	0.04	(0.10)	-0.12	(0.22)	0.16	(0.20)

Notes: Values that are statistically significant are indicated in bold (see Annex A3). See Table II.4.6 for national data.
StatLink ᵐˢᵖ http://dx.doi.org/10.1787/888932343304

[Part 1/1]
Between- and within-school variance in reading performance
Table S.II.i   *Results based on students' self-reports*

	Total variance in student performance[2]	Variance in student performance between schools	Variance in student performance within schools	Total variance in student performance expressed as a percentage of the average variance in student performance across OECD countries[3]	Variance in student performance between schools[4]	Variance in student performance within schools	Variance explained by the PISA index of economic, social and cultural status of students		Variance explained by the PISA index of economic, social and cultural status of students and schools		Variance explained by students' study programmes		Variance explained by students' study programmes and the PISA index of economic, social and cultural status of students and schools		Index of academic inclusion[5]
							Between-school	Within-school	Between-school	Within-school	Between-school	Within-school	Between-school	Within-school	Proportion of variance in student performance within schools
Adjudicated															
Belgium (Flemish Community)	8 801	5 499	4 282	101.6	63.5	49.4	7.0	1.2	43.9	1.2	52.1	12.2	54.5	12.4	48.7
Spain (Andalusia)	7 932	1 439	6 552	91.6	16.6	75.6	5.8	8.4	6.8	8.4	0.0	0.0	6.8	8.4	82.6
Spain (Aragon)	7 221	759	6 413	83.4	8.8	74.0	4.8	4.2	5.8	4.3	0.0	0.0	5.8	4.3	88.8
Spain (Asturias)	8 756	1 327	7 463	101.1	15.3	86.1	5.0	8.4	6.0	8.3	0.0	0.0	6.0	8.3	85.2
Spain (Balearic Islands)	8 426	1 250	7 125	97.3	14.4	82.2	5.0	5.5	7.7	5.6	0.0	0.0	7.7	5.6	84.6
Spain (Basque Country)	7 000	2 134	5 327	80.8	24.6	61.5	6.6	1.7	11.6	1.7	0.0	0.0	11.6	1.7	76.1
Spain (Canary Islands)	8 417	2 109	6 620	97.2	24.3	76.4	7.5	3.9	10.2	4.0	0.0	0.0	10.2	4.0	78.6
Spain (Cantabria)	7 782	954	6 686	89.8	11.0	77.2	3.4	6.2	3.4	6.2	0.0	0.0	3.4	6.2	85.9
Spain (Castile and Leon)	7 169	1 359	6 073	82.8	15.7	70.1	6.1	5.3	8.4	5.4	0.0	0.0	8.4	5.4	84.7
Spain (Catalonia)	6 771	1 207	5 589	78.2	13.9	64.5	4.9	4.5	6.1	4.5	0.0	0.0	6.1	4.5	82.5
Spain (Ceuta and Melilla)	10 871	5 373	7 065	125.5	62.0	81.6	31.8	5.4	51.8	5.4	0.0	0.0	51.8	5.4	65.0
Spain (Galicia)	7 643	988	6 682	88.2	11.4	77.1	3.3	1.9	6.2	2.0	0.0	0.0	6.2	2.0	87.4
Spain (La Rioja)	8 331	1 650	7 182	96.2	19.0	82.9	8.0	8.7	11.5	8.7	0.0	0.0	11.5	8.7	86.2
Spain (Madrid)	7 142	1 828	5 615	82.4	21.1	64.8	9.4	4.8	14.0	5.0	0.0	0.0	14.0	5.0	78.6
Spain (Murcia)	6 450	1 125	5 201	74.5	13.0	60.0	4.5	5.5	4.8	5.4	0.0	0.0	4.8	5.4	80.6
Spain (Navarre)	7 019	1 158	5 850	81.0	13.4	67.5	5.1	5.6	6.7	5.6	0.0	0.0	6.7	5.6	83.3
United Kingdom (Scotland)	8 872	1 611	7 668	102.4	18.6	88.5	11.1	6.9	15.6	6.8	0.5	3.7	15.8	10.0	86.4
Non-adjudicated															
Belgium (French Community)	11 905	6 123	5 672	137.4	70.7	65.5	1.1	2.9	53.2	2.9	54.7	15.4	64.6	17.0	47.6
Belgium (German-Speaking Community)	8 062	3 746	5 008	93.1	43.2	57.8	0.4	0.4	35.2	0.3	38.5	13.7	39.2	13.8	62.1
Finland (Finnish Speaking)	7 420	621	6 983	85.7	7.2	80.6	1.9	5.3	2.2	5.4	0.0	0.0	2.2	5.4	94.1
Finland (Swedish Speaking)	7 526	497	7 133	86.9	5.7	82.3	3.1	7.1	3.1	7.1	0.0	0.0	3.1	7.1	94.8
Italy (Provincia Abruzzo)	8 267	3 565	4 000	95.4	41.2	46.2	4.5	0.0	21.6	0.0	33.7	0.1	33.9	0.3	48.4
Italy (Provincia Autonoma of Bolzano)	8 558	5 608	4 534	98.8	64.7	52.3	0.2	0.2	15.5	0.2	52.7	2.1	52.7	2.3	53.0
Italy (Provincia Basilicata)	7 396	3 683	3 849	85.4	42.5	44.4	1.1	0.3	32.8	0.1	33.7	0.0	36.9	0.2	52.1
Italy (Provincia Calabria)	8 015	4 641	3 926	92.5	53.6	45.3	2.2	0.3	26.8	0.2	39.4	0.0	43.5	0.0	49.0
Italy (Provincia Campania)	8 625	3 330	4 370	99.6	38.4	50.4	4.6	0.0	12.4	0.0	27.1	3.0	27.3	3.1	50.7
Italy (Provincia Emilia Romagna)	9 821	5 609	4 862	113.4	64.7	56.1	6.9	2.0	48.9	1.9	55.9	0.0	57.8	1.9	49.5
Italy (Provincia Friuli Venezia Giulia)	8 508	5 292	3 956	98.2	61.1	45.7	4.4	0.3	41.3	0.4	60.9	40.9	61.1	40.6	46.5
Italy (Provincia Lazio)	8 334	4 727	3 952	96.2	54.6	45.6	3.6	0.2	16.7	0.4	29.6	0.0	29.7	0.0	47.4
Italy (Provincia Liguria)	8 896	4 438	4 512	102.7	51.2	52.1	1.8	0.4	18.6	0.3	29.4	2.8	29.6	2.8	50.7
Italy (Provincia Lombardia)	8 034	5 757	3 835	92.7	66.5	44.3	7.8	0.2	42.2	0.3	50.1	0.9	51.0	0.9	47.7
Italy (Provincia Marche)	8 538	4 273	3 821	98.6	49.3	44.1	0.9	0.2	20.5	0.2	26.3	0.0	26.3	0.0	44.8
Italy (Provincia Molise)	7 120	3 656	4 049	82.2	42.2	46.7	3.7	0.3	25.8	0.4	22.2	0.2	27.5	0.4	56.9
Italy (Provincia Piemonte)	8 965	4 520	4 373	103.5	52.2	50.5	0.0	0.6	15.0	0.7	30.4	0.0	30.9	0.0	48.8
Italy (Provincia Puglia)	7 433	3 787	3 580	85.8	43.7	41.3	0.0	0.1	15.8	0.1	24.2	0.0	25.1	0.1	48.2
Italy (Provincia Sardegna)	8 728	4 148	4 481	100.7	47.9	51.7	0.9	0.0	27.9	0.0	42.7	0.0	43.2	0.0	51.3
Italy (Provincia Sicilia)	10 092	4 332	3 623	116.5	50.0	41.8	0.0	0.4	7.2	0.3	19.0	0.3	20.9	0.3	35.9
Italy (Provincia Toscana)	9 137	4 579	4 307	105.5	52.9	49.7	1.0	0.7	9.3	0.8	42.3	0.0	42.4	0.0	47.1
Italy (Provincia Trento)	8 671	6 817	4 086	100.1	78.7	47.2	5.0	0.2	64.7	0.5	68.2	0.0	72.9	0.2	47.1
Italy (Provincia Umbria)	9 735	4 896	4 568	112.4	56.5	52.7	1.3	2.4	25.3	2.4	26.5	1.9	30.0	4.4	46.9
Italy (Provincia Valle d'Aosta)	7 425	4 547	3 924	85.7	52.5	45.3	0.0	0.2	28.8	0.1	39.9	0.0	42.3	0.1	52.9
Italy (Provincia Veneto)	8 076	3 801	3 922	93.2	43.9	45.3	0.0	0.1	18.6	0.0	21.3	0.0	24.3	0.0	48.6
United Kingdom (England)	9 106	2 785	6 633	105.1	32.2	76.6	15.2	4.6	25.4	4.7	0.0	0.0	25.4	4.7	72.8
United Kingdom (Northern Ireland)	9 378	4 701	4 970	108.3	54.3	57.4	5.2	2.0	36.4	1.8	0.0	0.0	36.4	1.8	53.0
United Kingdom (Wales)	8 686	1 262	7 600	100.3	14.6	87.7	6.0	8.2	8.0	8.3	0.0	0.0	8.0	8.3	87.5

Note: See Table II.5.1 for national data.
1. The variance components were estimated for all students in participating countries with data on socio-economic background and study programmes.
2. The total variance in student performance is calculated from the square of the standard deviation for the students used in the analysis. The statistical variance in student performance and not the standard deviation is used for this comparison to allow for the decomposition.
3. The sum of the between- and within-school variance components, as an estimate from a sample, does not necessarily add up to the total.
4. In some countries, sub-units within schools were sampled instead of schools and this may affect the estimation of the between-school variance components (see Annex A2).
5. The index of academic inclusion is calculated as 100* (1- rho), where rho stands for the intra-class correlation of performance, *i.e.* the variance in student performance beteen schools, divided by the sum of the variance in student performance between schools and the variance in student performance within schools.

StatLink http://dx.doi.org/10.1787/888932343304

Annex C

THE DEVELOPMENT AND IMPLEMENTATION OF PISA –
A COLLABORATIVE EFFORT

INTRODUCTION

PISA is a collaborative effort, bringing together scientific expertise from the participating countries, steered jointly by their governments on the basis of shared, policy-driven interests.

A PISA Governing Board on which each country is represented determines, in the context of OECD objectives, the policy priorities for PISA and oversees adherence to these priorities during the implementation of the programme. This includes the setting of priorities for the development of indicators, for the establishment of the assessment instruments and for the reporting of the results.

Experts from participating countries also serve on working groups that are charged with linking policy objectives with the best internationally available technical expertise. By participating in these expert groups, countries ensure that the instruments are internationally valid and take into account the cultural and educational contexts in OECD Member countries, the assessment materials have strong measurement properties, and the instruments place an emphasis on authenticity and educational validity.

Through National Project Managers, participating countries implement PISA at the national level subject to the agreed administration procedures. National Project Managers play a vital role in ensuring that the implementation of the survey is of high quality, and verify and evaluate the survey results, analyses, reports and publications.

The design and implementation of the surveys, within the framework established by the PISA Governing Board, is the responsibility of external contractors. For PISA 2009, the questionnaire development was carried out by a consortium led by Cito International in partnership with the University of Twente. The development and implementation of the cognitive assessment and of the international options was carried out by a consortium led by the Australian Council for Educational Research (ACER). Other partners in this consortium include cApStAn Linguistic Quality Control in Belgium, the *Deutsches Institut für Internationale Pädagogische Forschung* (DIPF) in Germany, the National Institute for Educational Policy Research in Japan (NIER), the *Unité d'analyse des systèmes et des pratiques d'enseignement* (aSPe) in Belgium and WESTAT in the United States.

The OECD Secretariat has overall managerial responsibility for the programme, monitors its implementation on a day-to-day basis, acts as the secretariat for the PISA Governing Board, builds consensus among countries and serves as the interlocutor between the PISA Governing Board and the international consortium charged with the implementation of the activities. The OECD Secretariat also produces the indicators and analyses and prepares the international reports and publications in co-operation with the PISA consortium and in close consultation with Member countries both at the policy level (PISA Governing Board) and at the level of implementation (National Project Managers).

The following lists the members of the various PISA bodies and the individual experts and consultants who have contributed to PISA.

Members of the PISA Governing Board

Chair: Lorna Bertrand

OECD countries

Australia: Tony Zanderigo

Austria: Mark Német

Belgium: Christiane Blondin, Isabelle Erauw and Micheline Scheys

Canada: Pierre Brochu, Patrick Bussière and Tomasz Gluszynski

Chile: Leonor Cariola

Czech Republic: Jana Strakova

Denmark: Tine Bak

Estonia: Maie Kitsing

Finland: Jari Rajanen

France: Bruno Trosseille

Germany: Annemarie Klemm, Maximilian Müller-Härlin and Elfriede Ohrnberger

Greece: Panagiotis Kazantzis (1/7/05 – 31/03/10) Vassilia Hatzinikita (from 31/03/10)

Hungary: Benő Csapó

Iceland: Júlíus K. Björnsson

Ireland: Jude Cosgrove

Israel: Michal Beller

Italy: Piero Cipollone

Japan: Ryo Watanabe

Korea: Whan Sik Kim

Luxembourg: Michel Lanners

Mexico: Francisco Ciscomani

Netherlands: Paul van Oijen

New Zealand: Lynne Whitney

Norway: Anne-Berit Kavli

Poland: Stanislaw Drzazdzewski

Portugal: Carlos Pinto Ferreira

Slovak Republic: Julius Hauser, Romana Kanovska and Paulina Korsnakova

Slovenia: Andreja Barle Lakota

Spain: Carme Amorós Basté and Enrique Roca Cobo

Sweden: Anita Wester

Switzerland: Ariane Baechler Söderström and Heinz Rhyn

Turkey: Meral Alkan

United Kingdom: Lorna Bertrand and Mal Cooke

United States: Daniel McGrath and Eugene Owen

Observers

Albania: Ndricim Mehmeti

Argentina: Liliana Pascual

Azerbaijan: Talib Sharifov

Brazil: Joaquim José Soares Neto

Bulgaria: Neda Kristanova

Colombia: Margarita Peña

Croatia: Michelle Braš-Roth

Dubai (United Arab Emirates): Mariam Al Ali

Hong Kong-China: Esther Sui-chu Ho

Indonesia: Mansyur Ramli

Jordan: Khattab Mohammad Abulibdeh

Kazakhstan: Yermekov Nurmukhammed Turlynovich

Kyrgyz Republic: Inna Valkova

Latvia: Andris Kangro

Liechtenstein: Christian Nidegger

Lithuania: Rita Dukynaitė

Macao-China: Kwok-cheung Cheung

Montenegro: Zeljko Jacimovic

Panama: Arturo Rivera

Peru: Liliana Miranda Molina

Qatar: Adel Sayed

Romania: Roxana Mihail

Russian Federation: Galina Kovalyova

Serbia: Dragica Pavlovic Babic

Shanghai-China: Minxuan Zhang

Singapore: Low Khah Gek

Chinese Taipei: Chih-Wei Hue and Fou-Lai Lin

Thailand: Precharn Dechsri

Trinidad and Tobago: Harrilal Seecharan

Tunisia: Kameleddine Gaha

Uruguay: Andrés Peri

PISA 2009 National Project Managers

Albania: Alfonso Harizaj

Argentina: Antonio Gutiérrez

Australia: Sue Thomson

Austria: Ursula Schwantner

Azerbaijan: Emin Meherremov

Belgium: Ariane Baye and Inge De Meyer

Brazil: Sheyla Carvalho Lira

Bulgaria: Svetla Petrova

Canada: Pierre Brochu and Tamara Knighton

Chile: Ema Lagos

Chinese Taipei: Pi-Hsia Hung

Colombia: Francisco Ernesto Reyes

Croatia: Michelle Braš Roth

Czech Republic: Jana Paleckova

Denmark: Niels Egelund

Dubai (United Arab Emirates): Mariam Al Ali

Estonia: Gunda Tire

Finland: Jouni Välijärvi

France: Sylvie Fumel

Germany: Nina Jude and Eckhard Klieme

Greece: Panagiotis Kazantzis (from 1/7/05 to 18/11/08) Chryssa Sofianopoulou (from 18/11/08)

Hong Kong-China: Esther Sui-chu Ho

Hungary: Ildikó Balázsi

Iceland: Almar Midvik Halldorsson

Indonesia: Burhanuddin Tola

Ireland: Rachel Perkins

Israel: Inbal Ron Kaplan and Joel Rapp

Italy: Laura Palmerio

Japan: Ryo Watanabe

Jordan: Khattab Mohammad Abulibdeh

Kazakhstan: Damitov Bazar Kabdoshevich

Korea: Kyung-Hee Kim

Kyrgyz Republic: Inna Valkova

Latvia: Andris Kangro

Liechtenstein: Christian Nidegger

Lithuania: Jolita Dudaitė

Luxembourg: Bettina Boehm

Macao-China: Kwok-cheung Cheung

Mexico: María-Antonieta Díaz-Gutiérrez

Montenegro: Verica Ivanovic

Netherlands: Erna Gille

New Zealand: Maree Telford

Norway: Marit Kjaernsli

Panama: Zoila Castillo

Peru: Liliana Miranda Molina

Poland: Michal Federowicz

Portugal: Anabela Serrão

Qatar: Asaad Tounakti

Romania: Silviu Cristian Mirescu

Russian Federation: Galina Kovalyova

Serbia: Dragica Pavlovic Babic

Shanghai-China: Jing Lu and MinXuan Zhang

Singapore: Chia Siang Hwa and Poon Chew Leng

Slovak Republic: Paulina Korsnakova

Slovenia: Mojca Straus

Spain: Lis Cercadillo

Sweden: Karl-Göran Karlsson

Switzerland: Christian Nidegger

Thailand: Sunee Klainin

Trinidad and Tobago: Harrilal Seecharan

Tunisia: Kameleddine Gaha

Turkey: Müfide Çaliskan

United Kingdom: Jenny Bradshaw and Mal Cooke

United States: Dana Kelly and Holly Xie

Uruguay: María Sánchez

OECD Secretariat

Andreas Schleicher (Overall co-ordination of PISA and partner country/economy relations)

Marilyn Achiron (Editorial support)

Marika Boiron (Editorial support)

Simone Bloem (Analytic services)

Francesca Borgonovi (Analytic services)

Niccolina Clements (Editorial support)

Michael Davidson (Project management and analytic services)

Juliet Evans (Administration and partner country/economy relations)

Miyako Ikeda (Analytic services)

Maciej Jakubowski (Analytic services)

Guillermo Montt (Analytic services)

Diana Morales (Administrative support)

Soojin Park (Analytic services)

Mebrak Tareke (Editorial support)

Sophie Vayssettes (Analytic services)

Elisabeth Villoutreix (Editorial support)

Karin Zimmer (Project management)

Pablo Zoido (Analytic services)

PISA Expert Groups for PISA 2009

Reading Expert Group

Irwin Kirsch (Education Testing Service, New Jersey, USA)

Sachiko Adachi (Nigata University, Japan)

Charles Alderson (Lancaster University, UK)

John de Jong (Language Testing Services, Netherlands)

John Guthrie (University of Maryland, USA)

Dominique Lafontaine (University of Liège, Belgium)

Minwoo Nam (Korea Institute of Curriculum and Evaluation)

Jean-François Rouet (University of Poitiers, France)

Wolfgang Schnotz (University of Koblenz-Landau, Germany)

Eduardo Vidal-Abarca (University of Valencia, Spain

Mathematics Expert Group

Jan de Lange (Chair) (Utrecht University, Netherlands)

Werner Blum (University of Kassel, Germany)

John Dossey (Illinois State University, USA)

Zbigniew Marciniak (University of Warsaw, Poland)

Mogens Niss (University of Roskilde, Denmark)

Yoshinori Shimizu (University of Tsukuba, Japan)

Science Expert Group

Rodger Bybee (Chair) (BSCS, Colorado Springs, USA)

Peter Fensham (Queensland University of Technology, Australia)

Svein Lie (University of Oslo, Norway)

Yasushi Ogura (National Institute for Educational Policy Research, Japan)

Manfred Prenzel (University of Kiel, Germany)

Andrée Tiberghien (University of Lyon, France)

Questionnaire Expert Group

Jaap Scheerens (Chair) (University of Twente, Netherlands

Pascal Bressoux (Pierre Mendès University, France)

Yin Cheong Cheng (Hong Kong Institute of Education, Hong Kong-China)

David Kaplan (University of Wisconsin – Madison, USA)

Eckhard Klieme (DIPF, Germany)

Henry Levin (Columbia University, USA)

Pirjo Linnakylä (University of Jyväskylä, Finland)

Ludger Wößmann (University of Munich, Germany)

PISA Technical Advisory Group

Keith Rust (Chair) (Westat, USA)

Ray Adams (ACER)

John de Jong (Language Testing Services, Netherlands)

Cees Glas (University of Twente, Netherlands)

Aletta Grisay (Consultant, Saint-Maurice, France)

David Kaplan (University of Wisconsin – Madison, USA)

Christian Monseur (University of Liège, Belgium)

Sophia Rabe-Hesketh (University of California – Berkeley, USA)

Thierry Rocher (Ministry of Education, France)

Norman Verhelst (CITO, Netherlands)

Kentaro Yamamoto (ETS, New Jersey, USA)

Rebecca Zwick (University of California – Santa Barbara, USA)

PISA 2009 Consortium for questionnaire development

Cito International

Johanna Kordes

Hans Kuhlemeier

Astrid Mols

Henk Moelands

José Noijons

University of Twente

Cees Glas

Khurrem Jehangir

Jaap Scheerens

PISA 2009 Consortium for the development and implementation of the cognitive assessment and international options

Australian Council for Educational Research

Ray Adams (Director of the PISA 2009 Consortium)

Susan Bates (Project administration)

Alla Berezner (Data management and analysis)

Yan Bibby (Data processing and analysis)

Esther Brakey (Administrative support)

Wei Buttress (Project administration and quality monitoring)

Renee Chow (Data processing and analysis)

Judith Cosgrove (Data processing and analysis and national centre support)

John Cresswell (Reporting and dissemination)

Alex Daraganov (Data processing and analysis)

Daniel Duckworth (Reading instruments and test development)

Kate Fitzgerald (Data processing and sampling)

Daniel Fullarton (IT services)

Eveline Gebhardt (Data processing and analysis)

Mee-Young Handayani (Data processing and analysis)

Elizabeth Hersbach (Quality assurance)

Sam Haldane (IT services and computer-based assessment)

Karin Hohlfield (Reading instruments and test development)

Jennifer Hong (Data processing and sampling)

Tony Huang (Project administration and IT services)

Madelaine Imber (Reading instruments and administrative support)

Nora Kovarcikova (Survey operations)

Winson Lam (IT services)

Tom Lumley (Print and electronic reading instruments and test development)

Greg Macaskill (Data management and processing and sampling)

Ron Martin (Science instruments and test development)

Barry McCrae (Electronic Reading Assessment manager, science instruments and test development)

Juliette Mendelovits (Print and electronic reading instruments and test development)

Martin Murphy (Field operations and sampling)

Thoa Nguyen (Data processing and analysis)

Penny Pearson (Administrative support)

Anna Plotka (Graphic design)

Alla Routitsky (Data management and processing)

Wolfram Schulz (Management and data analysis)

Dara Searle (Print and electronic reading instruments and test development)

Naoko Tabata (Survey operations)

Ross Turner (Management, mathematics instruments and test development)

Daniel Urbach (Data processing and analysis)

Eva Van de gaer (Data analysis)

Charlotte Waters (Project administration, data processing and analysis)

Maurice Walker (Electronic Reading Assessment and sampling)

Wahyu Wardono (Project administration and IT services)

Louise Wenn (Data processing and analysis)

Yan Wiwecka (IT services)

Westat

Eugene Brown (Weighting)

Fran Cohen (Weighting)

Susan Fuss (Sampling and weighting)

Amita Gopinath (Weighting)

Sheila Krawchuk (Sampling, weighting and quality monitoring)

Thanh Le (Sampling, weighting, and quality monitoring)

Jane Li (Sampling and weighting)

John Lopdell (Sampling and weighting)

Shawn Lu (Weighting)

Keith Rust (Director of the PISA Consortium for sampling and weighting)

William Wall (Weighting)

Erin Wilson (Sampling and weighting)

Marianne Winglee (Weighting)

Sergey Yagodin (Weighting)

The National Institute for Educational Research in Japan

Hidefumi Arimoto (Reading instruments and test development)

Hisashi Kawai (Reading instruments and test development)

cApStAn Linguistic Quality Control

Steve Dept (Translation and verification operations)

Andrea Ferrari (Translation and verification methodology)

Laura Wäyrynen (Verification management)

Unité d'analyse des systèmes et des pratiques d'enseignement (aSPe)

Ariane Baye (Print reading and electronic reading instruments and test development)

Casto Grana-Monteirin (Translation and verification)

Dominique Lafontaine (Member of the Reading Expert Group)

Christian Monseur (Data analysis and member of the TAG)

Anne Matoul (Translation and verification)

Patricia Schillings (Print reading and electronic reading instruments and test development)

Deutsches Institut für Internationale Pädagogische Forschung (DIPF)

Cordula Artelt (University of Bamberg) (Reading instruments and framework development)

Michel Dorochevsky (Softcon) (Software Development)

Frank Goldhammer (Electronic reading instruments and test development)

Dieter Heyer (Softcon) (Software Development)

Nina Jude (Electronic reading instruments and test development)

Eckhard Klieme (Project Co-Director at DIPF)

Holger Martin (Softcon) (Software Development)

Johannes Naumann (Electronic reading instruments and test development)

Jean-Paul Reeff (International Consultant)

Heiko Roelke (Project Co-Director at DIPF)

Wolfgang Schneider (University of Würzburg) (Reading instruments and framework development)

Petra Stanat (Humboldt University, Berlin) (Reading instruments and test development)

Britta Upsing (Electronic reading instruments and test development)

Other experts

Tobias Dörfler, (University of Bamberg) (Reading instrument development)

Tove Stjern Frønes (ILS, University of Oslo) (Reading instrument development)

Béatrice Halleux (Consultant, HallStat SPRL) (Translation/ verification referee and French source development)

Øystein Jetne (ILS, University of Oslo) (Print reading and electronic reading instruments and test development)

Kees Lagerwaard (Institute for Educational Measurement of Netherlands) (Math instrument development)

Pirjo Linnakylä (University of Jyväskylä) (Reading instrument development)

Anne-Laure Monnier (Consultant, France) (French source development)

Jan Mejding (Danish Schoool of Education, University of Aarhus) (Print reading and electronic reading development)

Eva Kristin Narvhus (ILS, University of Oslo) (Print reading and electronic reading instruments, test instruments and test development)

Rolf V. Olsen (ILS, University of Oslo) (Science instrument development)

Robert Laurie (New Brunswick Department of Education, Canada) (Science instrument development)

Astrid Roe (ILS, University of Oslo) (Print reading and electronic reading instruments and test development)

Hanako Senuma (University of Tamagawa, Japan) (Math instrument development)

Other contributors to this publication

Fung-Kwan Tam (Layout)

ORGANISATION FOR ECONOMIC CO-OPERATION AND DEVELOPMENT

The OECD is a unique forum where governments work together to address the economic, social and environmental challenges of globalisation. The OECD is also at the forefront of efforts to understand and to help governments respond to new developments and concerns, such as corporate governance, the information economy and the challenges of an ageing population. The Organisation provides a setting where governments can compare policy experiences, seek answers to common problems, identify good practice and work to co-ordinate domestic and international policies.

The OECD member countries are: Australia, Austria, Belgium, Canada, Chile, the Czech Republic, Denmark, Finland, France, Germany, Greece, Hungary, Iceland, Ireland, Israel, Italy, Japan, Korea, Luxembourg, Mexico, the Netherlands, New Zealand, Norway, Poland, Portugal, the Slovak Republic, Slovenia, Spain, Sweden, Switzerland, Turkey, the United Kingdom and the United States. The European Commission takes part in the work of the OECD.

OECD Publishing disseminates widely the results of the Organisation's statistics gathering and research on economic, social and environmental issues, as well as the conventions, guidelines and standards agreed by its members.

OECD PUBLISHING, 2, rue André-Pascal, 75775 PARIS CEDEX 16
(98 2010 08 1 P) ISBN 978-92-64-09146-7 – No. 57727 2010